W9-ATL-513

◆ ◆ ◆

ACHIEVING QUALITY THROUGH CONTINUAL IMPROVEMENT

◆ ◆ ◆

ACHIEVING QUALITY THROUGH CONTINUAL IMPROVEMENT

CLAUDE W. BURRILL
JOHANNES LEDOLTER

WILEY

John Wiley & Sons, Inc.

New York ◆ Chichester ◆ Weinheim ◆ Brisbane ◆ Singapore ◆ Toronto

ACQUISITIONS EDITOR   Beth L. Golub
MARKETING MANAGER   Carlise Paulson
PRODUCTION EDITOR   Jeanine Furino
DESIGNER   Kevin Murphy
ILLUSTRATION EDITOR   Anna Melhorn

This book was set in ITC Garamond Light by Matrix Publishing Services and printed and bound by Malloy Lithograph. The cover was printed by Lehigh Press.

This book is printed on acid-free paper.

Library of Congress Cataloging-in-Publication Data
Burrill, Claude W.
    Achieving quality through continual improvement / Claude W.
Burrill.
    p. cm.
    Includes index.
    ISBN 0-471-09220-7 (cloth : alk. paper)
    1. Total quality management. 2. ISO 9000 Series Standards.
    3. Quality assurance. I. Ledolter, Johannes. II. Title.
    HD62.15.B866   1998
658.5′62—dc21
                                            98-15989
                                          CIP

ISBN 0-471-09220-7

Printed in the United States of America

10 9 8 7 6 5 4 3 2 1

Authors

Claude W. Burrill is a consultant on quality and project management. He is an Adjunct Professor in the School of Business at the University of Iowa. He received a Ph.D. in Mathematics from the University of Iowa in 1952, and an honorary doctorate from William Patterson College of New Jersey in 1979. His experience includes a year as a Fulbright Scholar at the University of Manchester, UK, ten years as a member of the New York University Graduate Center at Bell Labs, and ten years as a member of the IBM Systems Research Institute. He has held visiting faculty appointments at Columbia University, Dartmouth College, and the National University of Singapore, and he has lectured and consulted internationally. He has authored or coauthored eight books on a variety of topics, including mathematics, probability, computer modeling, quality, and project management. He and Professor Ledolter are coauthors of the book *Statistical Quality Control: Strategies and Tools for Continual Improvement*, published by Wiley in 1999.

Johannes Ledolter is a Professor at the University of Iowa in the Department of Statistics and Actuarial Science and the Department of Management Sciences, and a Professor of the Wirtschaftsuniversität Vienna, Austria. He received a Ph.D. in Statistics from the University of Wisconsin-Madison in 1975. Professor Ledolter held visiting positions at the University of Wisconsin, Princeton University, and Yale University. His area of research centers around time series analysis and forecasting, statistical methods for quality improvement, and applications of statistics in business and engineering. He has coauthored the books *Statistical Methods for Forecasting*, published by Wiley in 1983, *Applied Statistics for Engineers and Physical Scientists*, published by Macmillan (Prentice-Hall) in 1992, and *Statistical Quality Control: Strategies and Tools for Continual Improvement*, published by Wiley in 1999. Professor Ledolter is a Fellow of the American Statistical Association, and an Elected Member of the International Statistical Institute.

Preface

This is a book on how to achieve quality. The quality of goods, services and information products depends on the underlying processes that are needed for their creation; these processes must be designed, constructed, documented, stabilized, and continually improved. And they must be operated properly by well trained, highly motivated people.

Courses on Quality are generally taught in two different ways: "technique-oriented" courses that emphasize statistical tools, and "management-oriented" courses that stress the managerial aspects of quality. This book is intended as a main text for a managerial-oriented course on quality. Undergraduate business and MBA students comprise our primary audience for this book. However, this text is also useful for a technique-oriented course because it serves as a reference on the business-side of quality.*

The coverage of this text is comprehensive; it discusses all aspects of quality: quality of goods, services, and information products, as well as the processes that are necessary to achieve quality. The discussion is based on a Total Quality Management (TQM) methodology and on the ISO 9000 guidelines, an internationally acknowledged quality standard. The presentation is self-contained; apart from common sense, no prior background in business and statistics is needed.

Many illustrative examples and illustrations are included in this book, and many useful exercises are listed at the end of each chapter. The exercises can be assigned to check the readers' understanding of the material. In several of the exercises, we ask students to read and comment on current papers in the quality literature; most of these readings are taken from *Quality Progress*, a publication of the American Society for Quality.

The book is organized into six parts and 24 chapters. You should be able to cover all chapters in a one-semester, or one-quarter course. Several case studies are given in the Appendix. You may want to discuss these cases during class or use them as additional readings.

We acknowledge the contributions of all those people from whom we learned. Learning is incremental, and we could not have written this book without utilizing the information provided by those who came before us. We would like to thank the following reviewers for their many constructive comments during the de-

---

*For a text that focuses on problem-solving and statistical tools for achieving quality, we refer you to our other book: *Statistical Quality Control: Strategies and Tools for Continual Improvement*, Wiley 1999.

velopment of this book: Nael A. Aly, California State University, Stanislaus; George F. Heiurich, Raytheon Aircraft; Steven Hillmer, University of Kansas; Glenn Milligan, Ohio State University; Willard Price, University of the Pacific; William Turnquist, Central Washington University; William Winchell, Ferris State University. We credit Richard Stump, a quality consultant, for many fruitful discussions. We thank the various professional societies, companies, and publishers who have given permission to reproduce their materials in our text; permission credit is acknowledged at the appropriate places in the book. We also express our thanks and appreciation to our editor at Wiley, Beth Lang Golub, and her efficient staff. Finally, we thank our families for their understanding. Writing a book is a time-consuming process; by giving that precious time, our families made this book happen.

We hope that you will find our book useful. If you have any comments or suggestions that could help us improve this book, please write to us. You can reach us through our publisher, John Wiley & Sons, or through the Department of Statistics and Actuarial Science at the University of Iowa, Iowa City, Iowa 52242. Our e-mail address is ledolter@stat.uiowa.edu.

Contents

PART I

◆ ◆ ◆

Introduction

The first part of this book, Chapters 1 through 6, provides a general introduction to the subject of quality. It lays the groundwork for the remaining chapters, which include a detailed discussion of how to attain and improve quality.

The discussion of the history of the quality movement in Chapter 2 helps put quality into perspective. The view of quality has evolved over time. The focus has shifted from an inspection approach designed to screen out unacceptable products to a strategy that emphasizes the continual improvement of products and processes.

Chapter 3 discusses the cost of quality, which consists of the costs of prevention, appraisal, and failure. The aim of management is to reduce the total cost of quality. In order to have a significant impact on total cost, the cost of failure must be reduced. A common strategy for achieving this reduction is to spend more on prevention; it is always cheaper to do a job right the first time than to do it over. Quality improvement brings many benefits: quality improvement cuts costs; the resulting lower costs allow lower prices; lower prices increase market share, which results in benefits of scale and further cost reductions. Moreover, quality improvements in the design of products increase the demand.

People are an integral part of quality: customers, who should be delighted when using the product; managers, who have responsibility for quality; workers, who build and check products; suppliers, who provide subcomponents; and society, which is impacted by the products. Chapter 4 explores the various relationships between people and quality.

Quality is an attribute of a product, and to understand quality one needs to understand how products come into existence; this is one of the messages of Chapter 5. A product is the output of a process, which is a logically related collection of operations that work together to produce a given result. If you want to improve the quality of a product, you must improve the processes that are used to produce it. This means all processes related to the product: production processes, management processes, training processes, and so on. We distinguish among several categories of products: goods (such as nuts and bolts), services (such as banking, health care, and education), and information products (such as plans, designs, and bills); each category raises different quality issues.

Chapter 6 explores the meaning of quality. Various definitions of quality are reviewed, including those by quality experts such as Deming, Juran, Feigenbaum, Crosby, and Ishikawa, as well as the quality definition of ISO, the International Standards Organization. According to our own working definition, quality means meeting the requirements and standards established for a product. Quality simply means producing what you are supposed to produce. It applies not only to consumer products, but also to all products of all processes.

Chapter 1

Introduction to Quality

American business has made progress toward quality over the past several years. But I don't believe we can truly make quality a way of life for every American until we make quality a part of every student's education.

—Edwin Artzt, Chairman of the Board and Chief Executive, Procter & Gamble Co. [1]

◆ 1.1 Introduction

This book is about quality. It is about the quality of goods that people make (cars, refrigerators, books, . . .), the services they provide (delivery of health care, instruction, financial services . . .), and the information they generate (reports, forecasts, bills, . . .). And it is about the processes involved in producing such products. In this work we discuss what people mean by quality, how quality can be measured, and how quality can be improved.

Our views on quality can be summarized in the following seven premises:

---

[1] Edwin Artzt, "Developing the Next Generation of Quality Leaders," *Quality Progress*, October 1992, p. 25.

1. **Quality is a profitable investment.**
   Commitment to quality pays substantial dividends and may mean the survival of an organization.

2. **The first step toward quality is understanding and a long-term commitment.**
   A basic understanding of fundamental quality concepts and a belief in the importance of quality are prerequisites to any successful quality improvement program.

3. **Top management support is essential to quality improvement.**
   Without top management support, efforts toward quality improvement will be sporadic, frustrating, and unrewarding. With top management understanding and support, improvements can be far reaching.

4. **For the most part, achievement of quality simply requires good business practice and common sense.**
   Quality requires performing all business functions well; very little can be classified as a *special* quality function.

5. **The procedural side of quality calls for a focus on the processes for conducting business.**
   While quality is a characteristic of a product, the way to attain quality products is to improve the processes that are used to make them. The monitoring and improvement of processes play an important role in any quality improvement strategy.

6. **The human side of quality calls for active employee participation.**
   To tap the full creative talents of the organization, management must enable all workers to be involved actively in the planning, operation, and control of their work processes.

7. **Everyone gains from quality.**
   Customers gain from quality by getting products that meet their requirements; workers and managers gain satisfaction from a job well done; stockholders gain from improved company performance; and society gains from having more reliable products and less waste of resources.

◆ 1.2 Meaning of Quality

Quality means different things to different people; a producer may have a different view than a consumer, a boss may have a different view than a worker, and society as a whole may view quality differently than individual citizens.

Here are some general observations:

◆ Sometimes the term *quality* is used in referring to the attributes or characteristics of a product. Of a car a person might ask, "What are its qualities?"

◆ But to some people, *quality* is a term used to describe only superior products: one talks about a quality car but seldom refers to quality hog-slaughtering.

◆ The term *quality* sometimes is used to distinguish "grades" of products: Is this a low-quality car or a high-quality car?

◆ One might also regard a *quality* product as one that appears and performs exactly as it should—it meets the requirements established for it. If you produced a report that meets the requirements of an assignment, wouldn't you feel that you had done a quality job?

These introductory remarks show that "quality" is not a simple concept. We will explore its meaning in Chapter 6. Until that point, you can think of a quality product as one that appears and performs as it should—that is, it meets the requirements established for it.

◆ 1.3 Quality and Customers

Peter Drucker[2] writes that the purpose of a business is to create a customer—that is, to provide some product or service that a customer wants. No matter what the business may be, customers want quality, and to satisfy this want, organizations must provide *customer-driven quality*. But what does quality mean to a customer? This is a nontrivial question, one we will address at various points in this book. At a minimum, however, it is safe to assume a customer wants a product to appear and function "as advertised." Customers expect to get what they pay for.

Customers have a general understanding that the true cost of a product is not just the price paid to the seller; it also includes the time, effort, and expense of acquiring the product, keeping it in good working order, and disposing of the product at the end of its useful life. In many cases, these "added costs" greatly exceed the price paid to the seller. The purchase of a $20 hammer by an organization requires authorization, filling out a purchase order, recording receipt of the shipment, and writing a check for the purchase. When all the costs are added up, the hammer could easily cost the organization $50 and perhaps as much as $100. If that hammer is defective, the customer is out the entire cost of procurement, not just the $20. From the customer's view, it makes good economic sense to look for quality products.

Today manufacturers are aware of the consumer's interest in quality products; that's obvious from the number of advertisements extolling the quality of their products. The next time you pick up a magazine, notice the number of firms suggesting that quality is their chief concern. Judging from some of their products, however, one is entitled to a certain amount of skepticism about many of these claims. But whether or not producers really are dedicated to quality, their ads show that producers *believe* customers want quality.

---

[2]*Management: Tasks, Responsibilities, Practices* (New York: Harper & Row, 1973), p. 61.

And this belief is supported by evidence. For example, *Datamation* polled more than 300 information systems (IS) managers to learn what criteria they use in choosing a computer vendor. The quality/reliability of the product was the top criterion, rating 9.6 on a scale of 1 to 10. By comparison, product performance rated only 9.2 and price/performance only 8.1.[3]

◆ 1.4 Quality and Competitive Advantage

Organizations don't embark on a quality improvement effort simply to be nice. They do it for economic reasons, and they do it to achieve organizational goals. These are examples of the impact quality can have:

◆ *Better price.* A critical relationship exists between the customers' perception of product quality and the price the product can command in the marketplace. The better customers judge the quality of a product relative to its competitors, the more they will pay for it.

◆ *Lower production cost.* Higher perceived quality need not result in higher production costs. In fact, it should cost *less* to produce a quality product. This statement is a bedrock Japanese concept, but it jars the intuition of many business executives until they realize that, in fact, it is always cheaper to do a job right the first time than to do it over.

◆ *Faster response.* The way to attain quality is to improve production processes. A company with quality processes for handling orders, producing products, and delivering them can provide fast response to customer requests.

◆ *Reduced inventory.* When the production line runs smoothly with predictable results, inventory levels can be reduced. For companies engaged in mass-produced products, this translates into a lower cost of production.

◆ *Improved competitive position in the marketplace.* A customer who is satisfied with quality will tell 8 people about it; a dissatisfied customer will tell 22.[4] By properly exploiting the customer's preference for quality products, a firm can increase sales, forestall competition, and end up dominating the market.

In the 1980s, however, many quality improvement efforts in the United States were half-hearted or, at least, not serious enough to impress customers. In a 1981 study[5], half the executives of major U.S. appliance manufacturers reported that the relia-

---

[3]*Datamation*, June 15, 1994, p. 39.

[4]A. V. Feigenbaum, "Quality: The Strategic Business Imperative," *Quality Progress*, Vol. 19, February 1986, p. 27.

[5]Hirotaka Takeuchi and John A. Quelch, "Quality Is More Than Making a Good Product," *Harvard Business Review* (July–August 1983): pp. 139–145.

bility of their products had improved recently, but only 21 percent of U.S. consumers agreed. This difference between producer and consumer perceptions most likely stemmed from a difference in their frames of reference. U.S. producers measured quality of their products against what they were producing a few years previously, and they saw improvement. Consumers measured U.S. products against competing products in the marketplace, and they saw a decline.

In today's fiercely competitive environment, quality is more than an optional extra. It is a competitive tool, one that can be used to differentiate one company from another. In industries where this tool is being employed, those that ignore quality very likely will be passed by. "We're convinced that excellence in quality is the road to competitive advantage and outstanding financial performance."[6]

◆ 1.5 Quality and Management

Many quality programs are established almost as a "flavor of the month" activity. A catchy slogan is devised ("We think quality is neat!"), a quality organization is established and told to work miracles, and teams of quality emissaries are sent to the far reaches of the corporate empire. These "corporate sea gulls" descend on the local units, eat their food, squawk a lot, crap all over the place, and fly out.[7] And the positive impact on quality is all generated by the company's publicity department.

Unless quality is firmly embraced as a basic belief of the organization, directed by aggressive but realistic quality goals, and actively pursued, quality will not happen. Just talking about quality might make top management feel good, but it will accomplish very little. To achieve quality leadership, an organization must change what it believes, what it rewards, and much of what it does. The effort is more like the American Revolution than the changing of the Guard at Buckingham Palace.

The basic aim of the organization must be to build the right product, to build it right the first time, and to build it at a cost that is competitive. Among the changes this goal will require in a typical organization are these:

- ◆ *Change in focus.* Ask someone, "What does your company do?" The reply is likely to be: "We build cars." Or "We are in the fast-food business." The emphasis generally is on the product, not the customer—on what the company provides, not on what the customer wants. But if quality is to be serious business, an organization must shift its focus to the customer. The attitude must be, "We provide value to our customers."

- ◆ *Change in approach to workers.* Many managers still fail to emphasize employee participation and development. The quality movement could be the

---

[6]Douglas D. Danforth, Chairman of the Westinghouse Electric Corporation, "A Common Commitment to Total Quality," *Quality Progress,* April 1986, p. 16.

[7]We owe this description of "corporate sea gull" behavior to a training film produced by Philip Crosby.

catalyst that makes workers partners with managers in serving the customer.

♦ *Change in view of the product.* In the period after World War II when consumer products were scarce, customers were happy to get *any* product—a car loaded with flaws was better than no car. Today, customers are more demanding. Not only do they require quality goods, but they also demand quality services and quality information.

♦ *Change in extent.* Because customers are more demanding, producers must expand the compass of their quality efforts. Originally, quality efforts were focused mainly on the production line. Later the focus extended back toward design and forward toward marketing and customer service. Today, it is recognized that every business function impacts every other, and all must produce quality products if the customer is to be satisfied.

To make these changes in the organization, management must also change. It must change its approach to quality from the old-style emphasis on inspection, test, and rework to an emphasis on continual process improvement. It must be more consistent, basing its actions on facts, not the latest management fad. It must learn to reward efforts to improve quality, and not to fight fires. And it must change its time horizon. Quality takes time; it does not happen overnight. It requires an investment of resources today for results in the future. Quality is a journey, not a destination.

♦ 1.6 Quality and Workers

Quality is important to the consumer and the company, but what about workers? What's in it for them?

A worker is entitled to receive personal satisfaction and reward from the efforts put forth for a firm. Monetary benefits such as salary and vacation time certainly influence the workers' attitude both on and off the job. So do praise, positive feedback, and the pride that comes from producing quality products. Job satisfaction and perceived reward are greater when quality products are being produced.

Among the specific benefits derived from producing quality products are:

♦ *Satisfaction from doing a job well.* Everyone likes to have a reputation for excellence.

♦ *Pride in being a member of a winning team.* An organization with a reputation for quality products is viewed positively by the community. People associated with the organization enjoy being part of a winning team.

♦ *Fewer false starts and fewer wasted efforts.* When defects are discovered, work has to be redone—not just the defective work, but also some good work that depends crucially on the defective work. If the electrical wiring of a building is defective, it may be necessary to open the walls to correct the problem, thereby destroying the quality work of the plasterer. It is frustrating to do a good job, produce a quality product, and then see it tossed out because of a defect created elsewhere in the process.

◆ *Better control of one's time.* Fewer defects bring less unplanned rework, and this means better control over time. An organization that produces quality products makes fewer disruptive demands on the worker's time, resulting in less unscheduled overtime and fewer canceled vacations.

A worker's attitude toward his or her job might be intangible, but it can be inferred from certain tangible measures. Consider the example of a plant that Toyota took over from General Motors.[8] While General Motors ran the plant, the absentee rate was around 20 percent, and there were about 5000 labor grievances outstanding at any time (amounting to about one per worker). After Toyota took charge, the absentee rate dropped to under 2 percent, and grievances dropped to nearly zero. A "them versus us" attitude was replaced by one of cooperation. Clearly, worker satisfaction improved.

Quality also has an impact on the direct monetary benefits given to workers. In the short run, the impact of quality might not be too apparent because wage rates for all firms are based on market supply and demand factors. But in the long run, wages must be tied to productivity, and this is where quality enters the picture. A firm producing quality products usually has a low cost of production and a high level of productivity. It can afford to pay its workers a reasonable wage. A competing firm with a high defect rate will have higher costs of production and lower productivity. Such a firm can stay in business only by matching its low productivity with low wages.

One of the greatest benefits workers gain from quality is the job security that comes from their firm's ability to compete. For years, job security didn't mean much to Americans because work was plentiful and wage gains could be secured through collective bargaining. It has now become apparent to most labor leaders that unions can fight management but not the market. To preserve our high standard of living, increasingly it is necessary for American labor and management to cooperate and improve the quality of American products.

◆ 1.7 Quality and Production Processes

Every enterprise, small or large, public or private, accomplishes its work through various production processes. These processes differ from enterprise to enterprise; generally, they are interconnected and are related to the organizational structure of the enterprise. If the organization is to produce products that meet customers' requirements, then all of the production processes must mesh properly and must produce quality products.

---

[8] This story is discussed further in Section 2.6.

For example, the garment industry is comprised of hundreds of enterprises, some very large and many of them small "mom and pop" establishments. Regardless of its size, a manufacturer needs processes to assess the marketplace, design garments that have customer appeal, purchase necessary materials and supplies, manufacture quality garments, and deliver them to customers. They also must have personnel processes to hire, train, and reward workers; accounting processes to handle financial transactions; and management processes to direct operations. If a garment manufacturer is to deliver quality products, then every production process of the organization must produce quality output:

- Market research must assess market demand correctly.
- Design must create garments that have customer appeal.
- Sales must obtain orders.
- Personnel must provide workers with the appropriate skills and training.
- Manufacturing must build quality garments.
- Quality control must ensure that defective products are discovered and segregated to prevent their shipment.
- Packaging, warehousing, and shipping must ensure that garments reach customers on time and in good condition.
- Accounting must record the transaction correctly.
- Management must direct operations and provide suitable rewards for all concerned.

The customers for the manufacturer are retail establishments. If the manufacturer's marketing system, production system, delivery system, accounting system, personnel system, or any other support system fails to function properly, then customers will not be satisfied. To have a reputation for quality, every production process of the organization must produce quality products.

◆ 1.8 Quality and Products

Quality is an attribute of a product. A *product* is something that is produced; it is something that is created, performed, constructed, or in some way brought into existence. Products can be classified into three types. *Goods* are physical objects, often described as wares or merchandise. The goods that come readily to mind are manufactured products, such as cars, television sets, clothing, and computers. *Services* are actions that give benefit to someone. Examples are serving a meal, providing transportation, and giving a lecture. *Information* can be described as knowledge, news, advice, or intelligence. Examples of information products are books, plans, reports, and income tax returns.

Some products are a combination of these three basic product types. For ex-

DISPLAY 1.1 ◆ Division of the U.S. Economy by Industries

	Share of Employment, 1993 (percent)	Growth in Employment 1989–1993 (percent)
Goods	14.7	−6.5
Information	15.3	3.2
Services	70.0	5.2

Source: Business Week, November 7, 1994, p. 116.

ample, when you buy a car (a good), you also are provided certain sales and de-livery services as well as information about how to maintain the car. When you have a meal in a restaurant (a service), you are provided with food (a good) from a menu (information) and are given a check (information) indicating the cost. When classifying any product as a good, service, or information, we are looking at the major aspect of the product, recognizing that aspects of other product types might be involved, too.

Originally, quality efforts were focused on goods, but the importance of infor-mation and service industries in today's economy can be seen from Display 1.1.

Goods

The goods that most people think of are products they buy or otherwise obtain from others; we will call these *final* products. Not quite so obvious is the fact that these final products are themselves constructed of products, which we call *sub-products*. Other names for subproducts are *parts*, *subassemblies*, and *components*. For example, some of the subproducts used to produce a car are steering wheels, brakes, and seats.

Another type of product is a *support* product that, while not part of a product, is necessary for its production. The production of a building might require a scaf-fold, which is a support product. The production of most products requires plans, reports, and other documents to support production.

Whether a product is classified as a final product, a subproduct, or a support product is a matter of convenience, and it depends on one's point of view. A rail-ing on a building scaffold is a final product to the carpenter who builds it, a sub-product to the person responsible for constructing the scaffold, and part of a support product to the person constructing the building.

Service

Service is an important part of advanced societies. In the United States, almost three-fourths of the nonfarm labor force is employed in service industries, and over two-thirds of the nation's gross domestic product (GDP) is derived from service.[9] Some examples of services are:

- Education
- Health care
- Public administration
- Law enforcement
- Mail/package delivery
- Leisure and entertainment
- Hospitality and hotel industry
- Financial services
- Insurance

Firms in the service industry vary from large international corporations to small shops. Service generally is people-intensive, and high personnel turnover is common in some industries. General quality principles apply throughout the industry but because the industry is so nonhomogeneous, these principles take different forms with different emphasis among the different service sections. The quality literature reflects this diversity, and there is extensive material on each of the major service sections mentioned here.

As Display 1.1 shows, the bulk of the recent growth in U.S. employment has been in service industries. Service is also an important function in nonservice industries. For example, it is estimated that up to 90 percent of all employees working in the manufacturing section perform administrative and service functions.[10] In addition, much of management's time is spent in providing services. Examples include counseling workers, building teams, and speaking at the Rotary Club.

Several problems are involved in measuring the quality of service products. One is that it is difficult to define the requirements for service. What is friendly service? What is an excellent lecture, one that delivers content or one that is entertaining? Another problem is high variability in measuring service. Have you ever had exactly the same service on two occasions and been satisfied one time but dissatisfied the other? Possibly because the first time you had just gotten a raise, and the second an unwelcome letter from the IRS. Another problem is that people do not agree on what is good service. Have you and a friend ever disagreed about the quality of the service the two of you had just received jointly? Service products also present a technical problem that does not apply to goods: you cannot provide a service, check it for quality, and then deliver it to the customer. The prod-

---

[9]William J. Stanton, Michael J. Etzel, and Bruce J. Walker: *Marketing*, (New York: McGraw Hill, 1991), p. 488.

[10]René Quevedo, "Quality, Waste, and Value in White-Collar Environments," *Quality Progress*, January 1991, p. 33.

uct and the action of creating it are intertwined. For service, "the process is the product."

Because judging the quality of a service is more difficult than judging the quality of a good, attempts sometimes are made to "convert" a service product into a good. Cleaning a hotel room is a case in point. This is a service, but the objective of the activity is fairly clear: a clean room. Although it is somewhat vague to specify the quality of "cleaning," it is possible to stipulate exactly what constitutes a "clean room." Having done so, you have a choice of viewing the product as the cleaning of a hotel room—a service—or a clean room—a good.

Information

When asked for examples of products, most people will mention manufactured products—items produced by blue-collar workers in a factory. Some will mention service, thinking of people who work for banks, hotels, or airlines. Only a few, however, think of information as a product.

As Display 1.2 shows, about 60 percent of U.S. employment is in managerial and professional specialties or in technical, sales, and administrative support positions—white-collar jobs. White-collar workers spend their time in offices, on the sales floor, and behind the cashier's window. Some of them are busy making coffee, taking the paper jam out of the copier, or cleaning the conference room. But most spend a significant part of their working time filling out reports, talking on the telephone, dealing with documents, examining shipping orders, and other activities that involve information in one form or another. Most white-collar workers can be described as *information workers*. Blue-collar workers, on the other hand, spend most of their time handling "real" products, such as nuts and bolts, parts, lumber, and steel. But blue-collar workers also spend time handling shop orders, bills of materials, shipping documents, and production control systems—information work. Taking all these factors together, a picture emerges of the United States as truly an information society.

To comprehend the importance of information products in an industrial society,

DISPLAY 1.2 ◆ Employed Persons in the United States in 1993 (in thousands)

Managerial and professional specialty	32,280
Technical, sales, and administrative support	36,814
Service occupations	16,522
Precision production, craft, and repair	13,326
Operators, fabricators, and laborers	17,038
Farming, forestry, and fishing	3,326
Total	119,306

Source: Bureau of Labor Statistics, United States Department of Labor.

let us consider four somewhat overlapping classes of information: information produced by information industries, required business information, computer-generated information, and quality system information.

Information Industries

Many industries that might be classified as manufacturing or service organizations are, in fact, in the information business. Some, such as publishing, finance, and research organizations, are heavily involved in generating information. Others, such as telephone, radio, and television, are involved with the distribution of information. Still others, such as research and legal services, require information as a vital input and produce information as an important output.

Business Information

Every organization needs information to conduct its business. Typical information used or processed by most businesses includes:

- Policies and directives
- Orders for products and records of payments
- Plans and reports on production
- Product requirements documentation and product standards
- Product designs
- Product installation and operating instructions
- Work schedules
- Operating data
- Records relating to personnel, inventories, finance, and so on

Computerized Information

Today a large and growing amount of business information is processed by computers using programs generated by the Information Systems (IS) Department.

James E. Olson, President of AT&T, stated that while a decade ago plant managers at AT&T controlled 90% of the output, today they control only 15%. Most products come from other plants or outside suppliers. As a result, factories are becoming big information centers. Plants have large computer systems monitoring the factory in real time, tracking all processes and all products that enter and leave the factory.[11]

IS departments produce a variety of information products, including requirements documents, design documents, computer programs, test cases, and operat-

---

[11]James E. Olson, "The State of Quality in the U.S. Today," *Quality Progress,* July 1985, p. 32.

ing instructions. The computer programs produced by IS are, in turn, used to produce the information needed by sales, manufacturing, accounting, management, and other units that carry out the firm's business. Because firms are vitally dependent on the information provided by their computer information systems, it is critical that a firm's software be defect-free. Demands for quality software are great today, and they are increasing very rapidly.

In the next decade, quality demands [placed on computer software] will increase by not just 2 or 3 or even 10 times, but by closer to factors of 100 or even 1000.

—Watts S. Humphrey[12]

Quality Systems Information

The quality system of an organization (which we will discuss in Chapter 13) is itself an information product. It consists of the descriptions of the processes, procedures, and instructions required to produce products, as well as the records to show proper operation of the system. If these information products are defective, then the organization's primary products are likely to be defective, too.

Product Quality

Goods have been the major focus and major beneficiary of modern quality movement. The great improvement in the quality of goods since the 1950s has been due largely to worldwide competition, which awakened consumers to the possibility of better quality and made them more demanding. Today it is not sufficient simply to supply a good that "works"; it must also satisfy customer wants.

The quality of business information has improved but at a slower rate than that of goods. For computerized information processes, a large variation exists between the best and the worst. The majority of firms still do not have time to do things right but find time to do them over. Most firms focus on building products and give little effort to improving the building process. Change is driven by the desire to have new technology, not improved processes.

Service providers were the last to embrace the quality movement. In the last decade, considerable progress has been made, especially in areas that experience strong competition, such as financial services and the hospitality industry. Where there is less competition, however, there has been less improvement; most federal agencies are an example. On October 20, 1995, the U.S. Postal Service took out a third of a page ad to announce: "Skeptics notwithstanding, First-Class Mail is on time 87% of the time."

---

[12] Watts S. Humphrey, *Managing the Software Process* (Reading, Mass.: Addison-Wesley Publishing Co., 1990), p. 390.

◆ 1.9 Improving Quality

Quality Control

One way to ensure that customers receive quality products is through *quality control*. By that we mean the inspection of products prior to shipment to customers. One approach is to inspect every product and to rework or discard defective items prior to shipping. If such *100 percent inspection* is not feasible, *sample inspection* plans can be used to check only certain parts of the shipments. Emphasis on quality control was the old approach to quality assurance, and much of the earlier literature on quality dealt with various sampling schemes for inspecting products prior to shipment.

Reliance on quality control can provide the customer with quality products but at a high price because the price must reflect the cost of discarding or reworking defective items. A producer who relies on inspection to weed out faulty products generally will have a hard time competing with another supplier who can do the job right the first time.

Another disadvantage in relying on inspection is that inspection often comes *too late*. Assume, for example, that you are a steel producer shipping steel billets to a rolling mill and that you inspect the billets before shipping from inventory. If you do find unacceptable products, it is usually very difficult to link products to the conditions that existed at the time of production. You probably don't recall what went wrong in your meltshop at the time the billet was produced, so you don't know what corrective action to take. Moreover, if much time has passed since the first occurrence of a problem, you may have produced many unacceptable products before discovering that a problem exists. Not recognizing defects and their causes immediately can result in considerable waste.

We don't mean to imply, however, that all inspections are useless. Inspection, for example, can play an important role in evaluating the suitability of the logistics system that transported materials or components to your company. Components may leave the supplier perfectly conforming, but things could go wrong on the road. Inspection can be a valuable tool in such situations.

Moving from Control to Prevention

The new approach to quality is to improve production processes so as to prevent defects. The key to staying competitive is to *do it right the first time, on time, every time*. If the underlying production processes can be improved so that there is very little chance of failing to meet the specifications, then you can save the cost of (1) inspection and (2) scrap and rework. Consequently, items can be produced more cheaply and the firm can stay competitive.

Much better than relying on control is to monitor processes on an ongoing basis. This approach allows you to recognize at once when something has gone wrong and to take immediate corrective action to fix the problem.

◆ 1.10 Quality and Cultural Patterns

People's attitudes toward quality differ from country to country, being shaped by a country's unique culture, history, and experiences. Germans think of quality as meeting standards; the French relate it to luxury; the Japanese relate quality to perfection; and Americans' idea of quality is that "it works."

G. Clotaire Rapaille, a French-born psychologist and international marketing researcher, has studied *quality archetypes* in various countries. Archetypes are the underlying structures and patterns of a given culture; they represent the means by which that culture pre-organizes the way people in it function for their own survival. Archetypes exist in the mind below the level of consciousness; they represent the cultural cognitive structure that is available to individuals in a particular culture.

Some Characteristics of Americans

Rapaille undertook studies of how Americans unconsciously react to quality and quality improvement. We have summarized several of his findings.[13]

In general, Americans are forward looking, optimistic, interested in their potential, rather than their present situation. Not doing things right generates feelings of anger and guilt, which suggests readiness for quality improvement. On the other hand, Americans learn by trial and error, from mistakes and experiencing failure; they believe that doing things "right the first time" deprives them of an important step in their learning process. Moreover, each American believes he or she is unique; regimenting everyone to follow exactly the same procedure impinges on their uniqueness and individuality.

Americans are in a perpetual search for new identities. Once they attain one identity or goal, they search for a new one. To motivate a person to improve, that person must be given a new potential identity to strive for.

Americans have a bias for action. Their response to a challenge is to act—shoot first and ask questions later. They like to watch a football player dodge through the opposition, run down the field, and make a 70-yard touchdown. They want to see the same kind of action in a program to improve quality—a big push, a special effort to accomplish the job, then off to another challenge. This has more appeal than the thought that continual improvement goes on forever.

American Views on Quality

Americans accept imperfection. "Nobody's perfect," "to err is human." As long as it works, why complain? "If it ain't broke, don't fix it." Americans are particularly

---

[13]Karen Bemowski, "Quality, American Style," *Quality Progress*, February 1993, p. 65.

tolerant of bad service because most of them have never experienced truly excellent service.

Quality has a negative connotation for Americans. They react negatively because usually they hear about quality when something is wrong. "Quality control" sounds restrictive to Americans, and "total quality control" sounds totally restrictive. And if everything were perfect, where would be the challenge?

Americans admit they are part of the quality problem, judging that about a third of the quality problems are due to their negative attitude, apathy, poor workmanship, or lack of effort. Another 20 percent of the problems are judged to stem from lack of tools and training.

American Views on Quality Improvement

Americans must experience a certain amount of frustration, anxiety, or discomfort before starting a quality improvement effort; if we are comfortable, we have no incentive to change. When we do decide to make a change, we prefer to improve by deconstruction (taking apart the old) and start from scratch rather than building on or repairing what already exists. Gradual step-by-step improvement does not excite us.

Americans think that change generally is for the better. They view change positively if they control it, negatively if it is forced upon them. Nine out of ten believe they can make a difference in improving quality.

A vision or impossible dream is a key motivator for Americans to support quality improvement. Becoming "the best" motivates us, but producing the best products does not. A crisis or challenge excites us—the bigger, the better. But playing catch-up does not. Breakthroughs are viewed positively, but improving in incremental steps does not interest us. Few believe that our mistakes have helped to make us better persons.

The reward we receive for our improvement efforts should be immediate and forward looking. Timing is essential—a six-month-old reward does not have much effect.

Given these views, management has a real challenge in rallying support for a quality program.

◆ 1.11 Quality in the United States Today

At the beginning of this decade, American firms were talking a good quality game, but their results were mixed. For example, a 1990 survey of American workers showed that 25 percent were "naysayers" about quality and 36 percent were not involved in their organization's quality improvement effort.[14] Only 29 percent of the respondents reported satisfaction with the results of quality efforts, and only

---

[14]1990 ASQC/Gallup Survey, *The Improvement Potential of American Workers*.

DISPLAY 1.3 ◆ Perceptions of Quality by U.S. and Asian Workers in 1995

Perception	Mean United States	Mean Asia
Quality is a problem in my company.	2.91	2.98
Top management is strongly committed to quality.	3.98	3.89
Middle management is strongly committed to quality.	3.90	3.82
We set the level of quality required on materials and services provided by suppliers.	3.61	3.60
My company warrants our products from failure due to workmanship or material quality.	4.04	3.71
We believe our product quality is essential to our sales.	4.44	4.31

1 = strongly disagree, 5 = strongly agree

Source: Burhan F. Yavas, "Quality Management Practices Worldwide: Convergence or Divergence," *Quality Progress*, October 1995, p. 57.

14 percent reported that workers were fully empowered to make quality improvements. A 1992 survey also showed limited efforts to improve quality:[15]

◆ Twenty-nine percent of American companies reported that senior management evaluated the consequences of their company's quality performance less than once a year.

◆ Only 22 percent of U.S. companies and 14 percent of Canadian businesses regularly translated customer expectations into the design of new products or services—while 40 percent of German businesses and 58 percent of Japanese businesses were doing so.

◆ Use of technology in meeting customer expectations was of prime concern to only 22 percent of American companies.

◆ Eighty-eight percent of American companies did not use process improvement on a regular basis.

◆ Senior management of 20 percent of U.S. businesses did not conduct a regular review of quality performance versus only 2 percent in Japan.

However, the situation is changing for the better. Based on a 1994 Price Waterhouse study, 70 percent of the organizations surveyed believed that their quality initiatives were successful. Moreover, organizations that had actively implemented quality initiatives for more than two years were more likely to have "very successful" initiatives than those that had programs for less than two years.[16]

The results of a study of U.S. and Asian firms in the electronics industry conducted in 1995 are shown in Display 1.3. In the electronics industry at least, it is

---

[15]"Study Finds Limited Evidence of Corporate Commitment to Quality," *On Q*, August/September 1992.

[16]"Reports of the Demise of Quality are Exaggerated," *Quality Progress*, News Department, January 1994, p. 22.

clear that the United States no longer lags behind its Asian competitors.[17]

◆ 1.12 The Outlook for Quality

There has been a dramatic change from the post–World War II seller's market to today's buyer's market—customers now demand quality products at a reasonable price delivered when promised. Producers of goods tend to recognize this change and are attempting to improve quality, but the picture is mixed for service and information providers. Many of them are still in the learning stage.

We have no crystal ball, but some reasonable conjectures about the future of quality can be made:

- ◆ The explosion of interest in quality will continue.
- ◆ Quality will be a global concern, thanks in no small way to the ISO initiative. (We will discuss the International Standards Organization (ISO) guidelines in Chapter 13.)
- ◆ Interest in quality will expand from goods to information, service, and the nonprofit sector.
- ◆ Customers' demand for quality products will continue to grow.
- ◆ To provide quality products, workers will be further empowered with knowledge, skills, and responsibility.
- ◆ Quality will be an integral part of a manager's job.

◆ Exercises and Additional Readings

1. From newspapers, journals, television, and other sources, collect articles that contain information relating to quality: quality concepts, quality initiatives, quality problems, and so forth. Save these articles as a source of information that can be used to illustrate the various quality concepts discussed in later chapters of this book.

2. List several products that you regard to be quality products. For each, describe what there is about them that leads you to your opinion.

3. State what quality means to *you*. Does your definition cover a quality car, a quality college education, a quality haircut?

---

[17]B. F. Yavas, "A Comparison of the Quality Perceptions of U.S. and Asian Firms in the Electronic Industry," *Management Science International Review* 35, No. 2 (1995): excerpted from *Quality Progress*, October 1995, p. 57.

4. (a) Ask 10 individuals who have *not* studied about quality this question: "In which of these two groupings would you place the concept of quality?"

   Grouping 1: Life, growth, breakthrough, . . .

   Grouping 2: Rigidity, conformity, status quo, . . .

   Summarize your results.

   (b) A survey found that "quality has a strong negative connotation" for most Americans—most place quality in the second grouping. Did your group do the same?

5. A small airline offers inexpensive, no-frills service between Westchester Airport (north of New York City) and Chicago Midway Airport. Neither airport is convenient for making connections to other major airlines. Do you consider this to be a quality service? Discuss.

6. During the week, you eat at a fast-food outlet that provides good food and service at a reasonable price. On Saturday night, you dine on ris de veau and a fine bottle of wine at an expensive French restaurant, which is noted for its service. Comment on the quality of your two eating establishments.

7. Many products actually are a combination of goods, services, and information. What are some of the goods, services, and information you receive when you buy (a) a meal in a restaurant, (b) a packaged vacation, (c) a college education?

8. In an educational institution, what are some of the work products of (a) an instructor, (b) a student, and (c) an administrator?

9. Consider some job that you have performed in the past. What were your work products? Who were your customers? Were your customers satisfied with the quality of your products? How do you know? What could you have done to improve the quality of your products?

10. Discuss why prizes such as the "worker of the month" may not always be such a good idea for rewarding quality performance. If you really want to single out an individual for outstanding performance, how do you think it should be done?

11. A *purchaser* is a person or an organization who buys a product. A *customer* is a person or an organizational function that uses a product. Of course, the purchaser and the customer might be the same, but in a large organization they typically are not. Discuss the quality-related problems that can arise in an organization when the customer (user of a product) is not the purchaser (buyer of the product).

12. The *producer* of a product might be viewed as an organization that builds a product or the actual individuals who do so. Discuss the quality-related problems that result from the different motivations and views of these producers.

13. What are the major production processes within a university? How does each process impact the quality of learning?

14. What are the major processes within a restaurant? How does each process impact the quality of dining?

15. Making a sales call is a service. If you were a manager of sales, what would you state as the objective of this activity? (Consider such factors as the reputation of the firm, the probability of making a sale to a specific customer, etc.)

16. Read Christopher W. L. Hart and Paul E. Morrison, "Students Aren't Learning Quality Principles in Business Schools," *Quality Progress*, January 1992, p. 25. Summarize the major points of the article.

17. In *Software Quality Metrics* (1979), Barry Boehm gives an example of an Air Force software system that costs $75 per instruction to develop and $4000 per instruction to maintain. (Maintenance includes correcting errors, rectifying omissions, and making modifications, changes, and improvements.) What are some reasons why software revision is so costly?

18. Read J. M. Juran, "Strategies for World-Class Quality," *Quality Progress*, March 1991, p. 81. Summarize the eight lessons learned from the experiences of Baldrige Award winners and others with successful quality initiatives. (The Baldrige Award program is discussed in Chapter 24.)

19. Read John Ryan, "Different Lands, Different Views," *Quality Progress*, November 1991, pp. 25–29 concerning consumers' views of quality. Summarize the "made in my own country" factor in assessing quality.

20. Ask five people to define quality. What insights can you obtain from these five answers?

21. "Quality brings lower cost and higher demand." Give examples where this statement is (a) true; (b) false.

22. Why is it important that managers learn and know about quality?

23. List some application areas for sample inspection plans. What are some of the advantages of these plans? What are the disadvantages?

History of the Quality Movement

There are lessons to be learned from the experiences of the successful companies. The common success factors are:

> *Focusing on customer needs*
> *Upper managers in charge of quality*
> *Training the entire hierarchy to manage for quality*
> *Employee involvement*

—Joseph M. Juran[1]

Understanding what quality is and how it can be achieved has evolved over time. Knowledge of these historical trends provides the needed background for the detailed discussion of quality in subsequent chapters.

---

[1]Joseph M. Juran, "World War II and the Quality Movement," *Quality Progress*, December 1991, p. 24.

◆ 2.1 In the Beginning

Centuries ago, products were produced by individual workers, who monitored the quality of their products because they knew their livelihood depended on their reputation. Later, as commerce grew, production shifted to multiworker shops dominated by a master craftsman who supervised the work of several apprentices. The master trained the apprentices, saw that they knew how to do their work properly, and examined the finished products to see that they were satisfactory. Quality was important to the master since he was also the owner of the shop and his income was at stake. The commercial advantage of producing quality products was understood even by some in high government positions. For example, Jean-Baptiste Colbert, the great minister of Louis XIV, wrote in 1664, "If our factories could, through care, impose the superior quality of our products, foreigners would see the advantage of purchasing French goods and money would flow to our kingdom."[2]

As work expanded, the task of controlling quality was delegated to an inspector; this task eventually expanded to a full-time effort. With the coming of the Industrial Age, this *inspection-oriented quality control* concept was adopted by emerging factories. As factory size increased, foremen were appointed with responsibility for production; quality control was accomplished by full-time inspectors, who reported to the foremen. This organizational structure, however, caused problems because the first priority of foremen was to increase production, and frequently this goal was achieved at the expense of quality. During World War I, the quality of military products fell so low that many companies relocated inspectors into a newly created inspection department reporting directly to the factory manager. This organizational structure became the norm until after World War II; in some companies it is still the practice today.

Modern Quality Management

Bell Telephone Laboratories was the birthplace of modern quality management. From the work of Walter A. Shewhart in the 1920s grew a *process-oriented quality control* concept that replaced the traditional approach. Early in their careers, quality pioneers Joseph M. Juran and W. Edwards Deming both worked for Bell—Juran at Bell Labs and Deming at Western Electric, a Bell company that was closely associated with the Labs. And after World War II, it was Bell people who carried modern quality concepts to Japan. Although Bell Labs is best known as the birthplace of the transistor, history may show modern quality management to be a more important contribution to humankind. Indeed, Lord Cherwell (Winston Churchill's science adviser) once stated that Bell Labs' most important contribution to the British effort in World War II was the concept of quality control and quality assurance.[3]

---

[2]*Quality Progress*, June 1983, p. 31.

[3]*Quality Progress*, July 1985, p. 35.

The techniques employed in quality control were statistical, which consisted basically of sampling methods and control charts. As a result, quality control naturally evolved as the domain of technical specialists; it is noteworthy that the five quality leaders we discuss in Section 2.9 all had engineering or science backgrounds. As an academic subject, quality control fell under the industrial engineering curriculum; in many colleges and universities it remains there today.

To accommodate the new quality concepts, organizations established quality control departments that reported directly to the factory manager or vice president for manufacturing. These departments absorbed the traditional inspection departments, and from them they inherited the role of inspector—the policeman who catches you if you don't do your job properly. Some departments continue to play this role today.

Upper and middle managers had little involvement with early quality efforts, for it was considered an operational activity. The prevailing attitude among upper managers remained that quality control costs money but is necessary to ensure that production lives up to acceptable quality levels (AQLs).

The advent of statistical quality control shifted attention from the product to the production process, but the shift was gradual. The major focus prior to World War II remained on product quality, not process improvement. Emphasis was on appraisal and rejection or repair of those products that failed to meet requirements. There was much discussion on evolving ways to prevent defects, and some efforts were made in quality planning; but these efforts had little impact.

Britain, the birthplace of modern statistics, took an active interest in statistical quality control prior to World War II and also made advances in establishing industrial standards, adopting British Standards 600 in 1935. In Britain, also, quality control evolved as a separate department, and quality control activities were grafted onto the production process as a means of meeting AQLs.

◆ 2.2 World War II

World War II witnessed a large expansion of quality control activities, both in the United States and Britain. The need to increase factory production dramatically while using many people new to the workforce brought unprecedented demands on industry. Quality control techniques were used widely to help meet production quotas and generally were recognized as making an important contribution to the war effort. As one Japanese put it, "One might even speculate that the Second World War was won by quality control and by the utilization of modern statistics. Certain statistical methods researched and utilized by the allied powers were so effective that they were classified as military secrets until the surrender of Nazi Germany."[4]

---

[4]Kaoru Ishikawa, *What Is Total Quality Control?*, translated by David J. Lu (Englewood Cliffs, N.J.: Prentice-Hall, 1985), p. 14.

During World War II quality control techniques were widely disseminated through courses conducted by the War Production Board (WPB). "Right the first time" was the challenge; control charts and sampling were the techniques taught to bring production within AQLs. The WPB did its job well; altogether American production was very satisfactory in terms of quantity, quality, and cost.

◆ 2.3 The Postwar Period

At the close of World War II, America had the only major production facility in the world. Britain, Germany, France, Russia, Japan—all were bombed out. The "tigers" of Asia—Korea, Taiwan, Hong Kong, and Singapore—were barely cubs. Australia, South America, the Middle East, and India accounted for a relatively small portion of world production. At the same time, demand was enormous; replacing destroyed factories and satisfying years of pent-up civilian demand placed a high premium on everything being produced. Manufacturers could sell whatever they produced at a handsome profit. Who needed quality?

The period immediately after the war marked the high point of quality control for the next three decades. A number of factors—lack of wartime urgency, ability in the immediate postwar period to sell virtually anything produced, increased prosperity, demographic and social changes—combined to lessen Americans' concerns for quality products. Management abandoned the concepts learned in the wartime quality control courses; many felt that these were a wartime excess and that a return to civilian common sense was required.

During the war, many new people had entered the quality profession, and in 1946 a group of quality professionals banded together to establish the *American Society for Quality Control* (ASQC). An amalgamation of earlier quality associations, it has grown to become the dominant American organization for quality professionals. Traditionally, ASQC was concerned primarily with manufacturing; in recent years, its interest has broadened to include services and information. To reflect this broadened interest and to deemphasize control as a means of achieving quality, in 1997 the name of the organization was changed to the *American Society for Quality* (ASQ).

One phenomenon of the immediate postwar years was the rise of complex systems—complex military, aerospace, and computer systems. These systems were plagued with problems. In 1950, only one-third of the U.S. Navy's electronic devices worked properly, and it was estimated that every vacuum tube used by the military had to be backed by nine in the supply chain. To deal with such unacceptable failure rates, a new discipline called reliability engineering emerged. Drawing heavily from probability and statistics, design reviews, environmental testing, analysis of reliability data, and other techniques, practitioners of this discipline attempted to minimize field failures. Sometimes reliability engineers were placed in a separate department, but more often they were merged into the quality department, thereby giving a boost to that department's declining stature. This also reemphasized the statistical nature of quality control at a time when many professionals were attempting to draw attention to the importance of management.

Despite receiving less attention, the quality movement did make progress in the postwar period. The focus of quality gradually moved from product control to process improvement, from inspection to prevention. The view of quality as an added cost gradually changed to a recognition that it brings cost reduction and improved productivity. These changes, all of which started before the war, slowly gained momentum in the postwar period. Two major changes, however, that followed the war were a better understanding of the role of management in quality improvement and the understanding that quality applied everywhere, not just to the production line. Juran deserves credit for initiating the first of these changes.

It is important that top management be quality-minded. In the absence of sincere manifestation of interest at the top, little will happen below.

—Joseph M. Juran[5]

Generally accepted today by quality professionals, this statement was revolutionary when Juran wrote it in 1945. To promote an understanding of this concept, Juran widely proclaimed the fact that of all the inhibitors to quality, at most 20 percent are under the control of workers. Eighty percent require changing the process, which management controls; thus, 80 percent of quality inhibitors are the responsibility of management. This fact was contrary to the prevailing conventional wisdom that workers are the cause of quality problems.

W. Edwards Deming, who earlier had been instrumental in promoting statistical quality control, added his voice through the years to Juran's call for management involvement. It would be gratifying to state that droves of managers heard and responded to these messages, but that was not to happen until the late 1970s.

◆ 2.4 The 1960s

The prosperity of the 1950s spilled over into the early 1960s. Together with the postwar baby boom that started in the late 1940s, this prosperity led to an affluent, youth-oriented society. Consumers, particularly the young whose discretionary income was great, were content with cheap, shoddy merchandise as long as it had appeal. Few cared if a product didn't last; this was a throwaway society looking for fads and fashions, not durability and value.

As manufacturers responded to the throwaway attitude, quality levels declined. This brought a backlash of product safety legislation, liability suits, and a rise of consumerism, raising the price industry was forced to pay for lax quality levels.

The major economic event during the 1960s, however, happened gradually, and so it did not make the headlines. Slowly and steadily, the war-torn areas of the world restored their productive capacity. As this happened, the economic picture slowly changed from a seller's to a buyer's market. Instead of reacting to the sit-

---

[5]*Quality Progress*, September 1986, p. 54.

uation by using quality as a competitive tool, the United States' top managers ignored quality in the belief that good salesmanship was all that was required.

A positive development that did emerge during the 1960s was the second major change in the direction of the quality effort. This was a shift of focus from the factory floor to the entire production process; this change was promoted by Armand V. Feigenbaum in his 1961 book, *Total Quality Control: Engineering and Management.* As described by Feigenbaum, total quality control (TQC) is "an effective system for integrating the quality development, quality maintenance, and quality improvement efforts of the various groups in an organization so as to enable production and service at the most economical levels which allows for full customer satisfaction."[6]

Although Feigenbaum spoke of total quality control, his primary interest clearly lay in manufactured products. But his book broadened the horizon of the quality movement to the entire production process: marketing, engineering, purchasing, and manufacturing. However, concern did not yet extend to the information and services areas.

Feigenbaum proposed extending the quality effort to all functional areas; he did not propose extending it to a concern for all employees. In fact, according to Kaoru Ishikawa, Japan's leading exponent of quality, "Fearing that quality which is everybody's job in a business can become nobody's job, Feigenbaum suggested that TQC be buttressed and serviced by a well organized management function whose only area of specialization is product quality and whose only area of operation is in the quality control jobs."[7]

◆ 2.5 The 1970s

The 1970s were a troubled time for the United States. The Watergate scandals, opposition to the Vietnam War and final defeat in Indochina, the rise of OPEC (Organization of Petroleum Exporting Countries) and the oil crises, a growing suspicion of nuclear power—all of these problems sapped the nation's energy. The economic boom of the 1960s faltered, and a severe recession followed the huge oil price hikes early in the decade. With all these problems, quality received very little attention as an issue.

Although Japan had been eroding American markets for years, its success went unnoticed until suddenly people realized that Detroit was under siege. It was one thing to lose the shipping, camera, television, and other markets, but the car industry represented such a large part of the gross national product that it captured attention.

America's immediate reaction was to make excuses: Japan depends on cheap

---

[6]*Total Quality Control: Engineering and Management* (New York: McGraw-Hill, 1961), p. 6.

[7]*What Is Total Quality Control?*, p. 90.

labor; Japanese workers are exploited; there is something in their culture; American workers are lazy, they don't care; . . . These excuses were made to explain how the United States, which had won the war with Japan, was in danger of losing the peace. What was to become known as "The (first) Motorola Story"[8] punctured most of those excuses:

> *Motorola, at one time the first name in television sets, encountered serious production problems and in the mid-70s sold their television plant to a Japanese company. Bringing in only a handful of top managers, the Japanese proceeded to redesign the television set, revamp the production process, and retrain the workers. Prior to coming under Japanese management, the plant produced between 150 and 180 defects for every 100 sets shipped. After three years of Japanese management, the defect rate was 3 or 4 per 100 sets. A comparable factory in Japan at that time would produce about 0.5 defects per 100 sets.*[9]

The Motorola story had a sobering effect on American manufacturers. Juran, who told the story, went on to say that he had other, unpublished data showing that this example was not extreme but, rather, typical of American versus Japanese defect rates. A similar story was heard about Whirlpool Corporation's Warwick factory in Arkansas, which was taken over by Sanyo. Failure rates of close to 10 percent were brought to below 2 percent under Japanese management.[10] With this evidence, it was hard to deny that the problem was American management, not American workers or some special aspect of Japanese culture. Still, little change took place. No one wanted to accept the fact that American management had to change, but no one had a good alternative, so they just worried.

◆ 2.6 The 1980s

The dawn of the 1980s brought the promise of salvation to dispel the worries of the late 1970s, for it was then that the United States discovered quality circles and Phil Crosby.

Quality circles first appeared in Japan in 1962, and Juran had described their benefits to America as early as 1967.[11] In 1973, Lockheed Aircraft sent a team of observers to Japan to learn the essence of quality circles and bring the concept

---

[8]The Second Motorola Story is the amazing success the company enjoyed once it committed itself to quality.

[9]Joseph M. Juran, "Japanese and Western Quality—A Contrast in Methods and Results," *Management Review* (November 1978), p. 27.

[10]This story is discussed in Section 4.6.

[11]An extensive discussion of quality circles appeared in Joseph M. Juran, "The QC Circle Phenomenon," *Industrial Quality Control*, January 1967, p. 329. This article also contains Juran's prophetic statement that Japan would attain world quality leadership.

back to America. But America was not ready for the message until the 1980s. Faced with a recession and mounting Japanese competition, it jumped on a quality circle bandwagon to "harness workers' brainpower" so as to improve productivity and quality. Interest grew overnight, and growth was explosive. By the end of 1984, it was estimated that as many as 1 million workers in as many as 8000 locations were involved in quality circles.[12] Then the movement fizzled as rapidly as it grew: it was estimated that by 1987 as many as half the circles had been disbanded.[13]

Some reasons behind the failure of the quality circle movement were as follows.[14]

- Many upper managers still believed that poor workers were the cause of their quality problems; they installed circles as a quick fix to that problem.

- Circles were installed without proper preparation. Untrained managers were unsure how to handle circles.

- Some circles were directed by facilitators or outside consultants, thereby bypassing the normal supervisory structure.

- Circles were not installed as part of a comprehensive quality improvement effort. They were seen as an isolated action that would work miracles.

In commenting on the rise and fall of quality circles, Juran observed that it would take at least a decade for organizations to learn how to manage for quality. As they learned, he expected renewed interest in employee involvement. Thus he predicted a revival of quality circles before the end of the century.[15]

Philip Crosby was to have a somewhat more dramatic impact on the United States. In early 1980 his book, *Quality Is Free*, was very favorably reviewed by *Business Week*. Response was immediate; overnight the book was sold out, and the publisher had to rush through additional printings. Americans were eager to learn about quality, and Crosby's style of instruction was to their liking. Thousands learned the absolutes of quality from his book; thousands more attended the Quality College that Crosby established in Florida to deliver his message. This was the first sensible mass reaction to the quality problem facing America, the first major step taken by many organizations to face the Japanese threat.

But news on the quality front still was not good. As Juran observed,[16] the U.S. quality crises deepened in the 1980s. Management still had not gotten the mes-

---

[12]Donald D. White and David A. Bednar, "Locating Problems with Quality Circles," *National Productivity Review* (Winter 1984–85), p. 45.

[13]H. James Harrington and Wayne S. Rieker, "Quality Control Circles," *Journal for Quality and Participation* (March 1988), p. 18.

[14]Joseph M. Juran, "QC Circles in the West," *Quality Progress*, September 1987, p. 60.

[15]White and Bedner, "Locating Problems with Quality Circles," p. 45.

[16]Joseph M. Juran, "World War II and the Quality Movement," *Quality Progress*, December 1991, p. 24.

sage. For example, in discussing problems with defense contractors in 1985, Defense Secretary Casper Weinberger stated: "We now have a system where major weapons go through regularly scheduled meetings. There are only two items on [a meeting's] agenda: 'Are you on time and are you within budget?' "[17]

In 1985, the Japanese view of quality assurance became widely known in the United States with the publication of Ishikawa's *What Is Total Quality Control?*[18] When it appeared, this book was truly earth-shaking and exhilarating to American quality professionals. Ishikawa stated that Japanese efforts to involve all employees in studying and promoting quality began in 1949. In a 1968 national symposium, Japanese-style total quality management activities were reinforced using the term *company-wide quality control*. However, it was not until the publication of Ishikawa's book that Americans began to understand that quality depends on the proper functioning of all aspects of an organization—all the people, processes, technology, information, and management.

Problems in the Automobile Industry

In 1986, the well-publicized "NUMMI story" proved that U.S. firms still had much to learn from the Japanese.

> *General Motors had an auto-assembly plant in Fremont, CA, which they closed in 1982. Later they turned it over to Toyota Motor Corporation as part of a joint venture called New United Motor Manufacturing, Inc. (NUMMI). By 1986, Toyota had reopened the plant and hired back most of the former United Auto Worker members who still wanted to work. Soon NUMMI was producing cars of nearly the same quality as those Toyota made in Japan. With half the workers employed by General Motors, Toyota was turning out approximately the same number of cars. Their drastic cut in the cost of production was the result of better production and management systems, driven by the goal of producing quality products.[19]*

It is amazing that in spite of their dramatic loss of market share, American car manufacturers displayed a lack of concern about quality right through the 1980s! For example, in 1989 the Cadillac Division of General Motors introduced the Allente. Maryann Keller, who did a study of GM, reported that the car was riddled with defects: the car leaked in the rain; squeaks and rattles abounded; windshield glass had ripples in it; automatic door locks tended to break, sometimes locking people inside the car; and the list goes on. All these faults in a car that was top of the

---

[17]*Business Week*, May 27, 1985, p. 144.

[18]The Japanese quality movement is discussed in Section 2.10

[19]*Business Week*, July 14, 1986, p. 47.

line for GM and cost almost two and a half years pay for the average American at that time. Maryann Keller then reported the most amazing part of the story:

> *The most remarkable aspect of the entire Allante fiasco was that the problems customers were finding with their new cars weren't news to Cadillac. They had all been duly noted at the Milford proving ground long before the car hit the market.*

And she continued:

> *The Allante fiasco is perhaps the most searing example of the cynical attitude General Motors has traditionally had toward its customers. Let it go to market, they figured. We'll fix the problems later—if the customers even notice them.[20]*

Problems in the Semiconductor Industry

Another typical example of the quality problem in America was the disturbing story about the quality of semiconductors reported by David A. Garvin of the Harvard Business School:

> *In 1980, Hewlett Packard tested 16K RAM chips from three U.S. and three Japanese semiconductor manufacturers. At incoming inspection, the Japanese chips had a failure rate of zero; the American chip failed at a rate of between 11 and 19 per 1,000. After 1,000 hours of use, the Japanese failure rate was between 1 and 2 per 1,000; the American rate was up to 27 per 1,000.[21]*

American manufacturers reacted to this news impulsively. Some claimed that Japan sent only its best chips to America; others disputed the data. But most got the message: the semiconductor industry was under attack.

Garvin also published a disturbing report on a study he had conducted on failure rates among producers of various other products:[22]

- ◆ Failure rates of products from the highest quality producers were between 500 and 1000 times less than those of products from the lowest.

- ◆ Japanese companies were far superior to their U.S. counterparts, their average assembly-line defect rate was almost 70 times lower, and their average first-year service call rate nearly 17 times better.

- ◆ The poorest Japanese company typically had a failure rate less than half that of the best U.S. manufacturer.

---

[20]Maryann Keller, *Rude Awakening* (New York: Harper Perennial, 1989), pp. 216-217.

[21]David A. Garvin, "Competing on the Eight Dimensions of Quality," *Harvard Business Review* (November–December 1987), p. 103. His framework first appeared in a preliminary form in an article in the *Sloan Management Review* (Fall 1984).

[22]David A. Garvin, "Quality on the Line," *Harvard Business Review* (September–October 1983), p. 65.

Garvin went on to compare Japanese and U.S. companies on various dimensions: programs, policies, and attitudes; information systems related to quality matters; product design; production and workforce policies; and vendor management. He concluded that on all counts, American industry was behind Japan. However, he ended his gloomy report with favorable news: When Hewlett-Packard repeated its semiconductor study two years after the original 1980 study reported earlier, it found that the U.S. companies had virtually closed the gap. This showed that the quality war was not lost, but winning it was going to be a tough battle.

The Malcolm Baldrige National Quality Award (MBNQA)

A major quality event of the decade was the establishment in 1987 of the Malcolm Baldrige National Quality Award (MBNQA). Regulations establish three categories for the award: companies or subsidiaries; small businesses; and service companies. Up to two awards can be made in each category per year. Responsibility for administering the award now falls on the National Institute of Standards and Technology, which relies on a board of examiners in reaching its decision.

The MBNQA has been controversial from the beginning. In contrast with the Deming Prize,[23] it is competitive in nature, which implies winners and losers. In addition, winners must share their experience with others; doing so can be a heavy financial burden, especially for small organizations. Applications for the award have declined in recent years. In spite of these problems, Juran best summed up the overall value of the award:

> *For the first time since the quality crisis descended on us, I have become optimistic. I now feel that we have a fighting chance to make enormous strides during the 1990s, and once again to make "Made in USA" the symbol of World Class Quality.*[24]

A more detailed discussion of the Malcolm Baldrige National Quality Improvement Award will be given in Section 24.2.

◆ 2.7 Total Quality Management

Few management methodologies have created as much overall excitement in recent years as has **total quality management (TQM).** Mysterious to many even after several years of a growing executive awareness that quality is a powerful competitive force, TQM has had a controversial existence. It has been praised by those who have successfully interwoven TQM concepts into their organizational

---

[23]The Deming Prize is discussed in Sections 2.10 and 24.2.

[24]J.M. Juran, "Made in USA: A Break in the Clouds," Juran Institute, 1990.

culture and panned by those who had problems in doing so. In spite of this controversy, a wide variety of U.S. organizations in all sectors have begun to study and apply TQM concepts.

Origins of TQM

For his article "Competing on the Eight Dimensions of Quality," David Garvin researched to discover the beginnings of TQM, but he came up empty![25] He concluded that no single book or article marks the inception of strategic quality management but that the line of demarcation was in the early 1980s. Some beginnings of TQM may be found in Feigenbaum's *Total Quality Control*. His definition of total quality control augured well for TQM methodology to come later.

It was the Japanese who developed Feigenbaum's original concept once they became aware of it. Their concept of total quality control (or TQC, the term used in Japan for what in the United States is called TQM) described quality in wider terms, encompassing a larger number of company functions than the more narrowly focused ones beginning in the United States. While the Japanese were perfecting their special brand of TQC throughout the 1970s, quality professionals such as Juran, Feigenbaum, Deming, and Crosby were criss-crossing the United States preaching the grass-roots quality concepts found in the then current TQM systems.

By the early 1980s, however, people in the United States were still not seeing TQM defined in terms and concepts that are used today. While Japan's success and their company-wide quality control were in the news, the person in the United States who did most to nurture the seeds of TQM thought was Myron Tribus, then director of the Center for Advanced Engineering Study (CAES) at MIT.

A Definition of Total Quality Management?

As the concept of TQM gained acceptance, many organizations attempted to define exactly what they were implementing. In 1990, SEMATECH (semiconductor manufacturing technology), a consortium dedicated to keeping the U.S. semiconductor industry viable and competitive in the global marketplace, published this definition:

> *Total Quality Management is a [holistic] business management methodology that aligns the activities of all employees in an organization with the common focus of customer satisfaction [to be achieved] through continuous improvement in the quality of all activities [processes], goods and services.*[26]

The SEMATECH definition of TQM stands up to most challenges by those who try to provide a lengthier explanation of TQM. It has the key ingredients of TQM,

---

[25]D. Garvin, *Harvard Business Review* (November–December 1987): p. 101.

[26]SEMATECH, 1990.

precisely worded to give the full meaning without losing any of the essential concepts as TQM is now practiced in the United States.

We have added the word "holistic" to the original definition to emphasize the fact that successful TQM systems include *all* functions in the company, not just the quality department as was true for many companies not long ago. A case in point is provided by Motorola. In applying for the Malcolm Baldrige Award, each functional area, including the legal function, was required by Motorola to prepare an internal application addressing the Award criteria, doing so just as if each was a separate company. This may have given rise to the first published account of a legal staff expounding on such concepts as a basic quality philosophy and six-sigma quality.[27]

TQM is a *management methodology*, a way to run the business, not a fad or some gimmick to spur productivity momentarily or to improve some special factor. In embracing TQM, management must substantially change the culture of the business so that TQM principles can take hold. Once TQM is focused on the strategic aims for business success, the direction will be visible and known to all employees. Then each group can align its plans and activities with those of top management.

Early TQM Success Stories

Several U.S. companies stand out for their early efforts to establish TQM. A few examples are these:

- *Nashua Corporation.* It owes much of its success to W. Edwards Deming whom it hired as a consultant for statistical process control and team-based problem solving.

- *Xerox Corporation.* After being nearly destroyed by its Japanese competitors in the copier business, the Xerox Corporation adopted the management style introduced by its own Japanese division, Fuji Xerox.

- *Motorola Incorporated.* On losing its major position in the market for television sets to a Japanese competitor, it regrouped and became a leader again.

- *Intel.* Intel was one of a small group of Fortune 500 companies to make the team concept an integral part of the work environment.

- *Dayton-Hudson Corporation.* This diversified retailing company published statements of cultural and operational philosophy far ahead of its competitors as it moved to establish a "Theory Z" company (whose objective is to develop the organization's ability to coordinate people, not technology, in order to achieve productivity). This transformation required the creation of new structures, new incentives, and a new philosophy of management.

---

[27]*Chicago Tribune*, December 12, 1992, Business page 1. Motorola's Six Sigma concept will be explained in Section 20.8.

- ◆ *Corning Inc.* (formerly Corning Glass Works). A company that had become "stodgy" as described by stock analysts, Corning took a new tack based on the leadership and quality initiatives taken by CEO Jamie Houghton, a member of the founding family. The implementation of TQM and the techniques learned in that process served Corning very well as it expanded its product lines. For example, Corning added Revere Ware to its product offerings using the same channels of distribution as for its glassware.

- ◆ *Hewlett-Packard.* Hewlett-Packard was an early adopter of the Japanese-style management based on quality principles—so early that it used the Japanese term *TQC.* A significant factor in its early involvement was its joint venture with Yokogawa Hewlett-Packard, owned by H-P and Yokogawa Electric Works.

◆ 2.8 The 1990s

By the beginning of the 1990s, a small number of American organizations had raised their quality to world-class levels. Some, but not all, were Baldrige Award winners. Those organizations that were successful displayed characteristics that can be described as a total quality management (TQM) approach to quality:

- ◆ Upper management commitment and involvement
- ◆ Linkage of quality efforts to clear strategic goals
- ◆ Demand of a financial payback from their quality efforts
- ◆ A focus on customer requirements
- ◆ Employee involvement
- ◆ Training at all levels
- ◆ Continual quality improvement
- ◆ Customization of the quality program to fit the organization

Clear signs were emerging that quality efforts were beneficial to organizations:

- ◆ *Fortune* studied several current applications of TQM in its article "TQM, More Than a Dying Fad?"[28] *Fortune's* conclusion was that, while the TQM movement has critics, the principles of TQM can deliver big payoffs when properly applied.

- ◆ The U.S. General Accounting Office conducted a study of 20 companies with highly rated TQM systems, as judged by their scores on the Baldrige Award Criteria. These companies had positive results in 59 out of 65 mea-

---

[28]*Fortune*, October 18, 1993.

sures of success used by the General Accounting Office (GAO). This study showed a positive trend for the participating companies.[29]

- ◆ A MAPI study[30] of 131 companies found that the application of TQM resulted in an improvement in the overall quality of their goods and services.

But the picture was not entirely rosy in the early 1990s:

- ◆ In January of 1990, nine hours of chaos gripped AT&T and its telephone customers as a giant switch in lower Manhattan malfunctioned and sent out trouble messages to other switches across the country. The software bug that caused the problem had eluded three layers of testing and had lain dormant for over a month until a juxtaposition of conditions caused it to be virulent.[31]

- ◆ Near the end of 1990, a flaw was discovered in the mirror of the $1.5 billion Hubble Space Telescope, which had been launched the previous April. Not as horrible as the 1986 *Challenger* disaster, still the flaw confirmed that serious quality control problems continued to plague the National Space and Aeronautics Agency (NASA).[32]

- ◆ The United States was not alone in having problems: In 1990, Source Perrier, one of the bluest chips on the French stock exchange, had to recall all stocks of Perrier from around the world following reports of benzene contamination of their bottled sparkling water.[33]

- ◆ In June 1990, graduates of the U.S. Naval Academy were issued diplomas that were signed by the academy's top officers and bore the inscription: "The Seal of the Navel Academy is hereunto affixed." And good for a belly laugh.[34]

World Trade

A phenomenon of our times is the large and growing importance of world trade; see Display 2.1.[35] This trend has been accelerated by the unification of Europe into the European Union and by the rapid growth of some of the less developed countries of Latin America, South America, and Asia. For example, China is now the third largest world economy behind the United States and Japan.

---

[29]U.S. General Accounting Office Report, "U.S. Companies Improve Performance Through Quality Efforts," May 1991.

[30]Manufacturers' Alliance for Productivity and Innovation, "Survey on Quality—Using the Malcolm Baldrige Award Criteria to Determine the State of the Art."

[31]*Business Week*, January 29, 1990, p. 39.

[32]*New York Times*, November 28, 1990, p. B7.

[33]*International Herald Tribune*, February 15, 1990, p. 1.

[34]*The Sunday Times*, June 3, 1990, p. 7.

[35]Further discussion of world trade and its impact on quality is found in Section 4.8.

DISPLAY 2.1 ◆ U.S. Exports,
   1950–1990, Selected Years

Year	U.S. Exports and Reexports Excluding Military Grant Aid (Billions U.S. $)
1950	10
1960	20
1970	43
1980	221
1990	394

Source: World Almanac, 1995, p. 202.

To deal confidently with any supplier, a customer needs assurance that quality products will be supplied. This assurance is particularly important when customer and supplier are in separate countries, entailing separate legal systems and grievance procedures. Thus, the growth in world trade has been an important stimulus for developing effective ways for customers to feel confident about the quality of the goods supplied to them, especially when the supplier is not just around the corner where his operations can be easily checked out.

One approach to gaining quality assurance is to inspect all incoming products, but this is expensive and seldom practical. A better approach is to have confidence in the quality systems of the various suppliers. Two methods can be used to gain this assurance. One is for the customer to review each supplier's system. But this method is costly and time-consuming for both the customer (who has many suppliers) and the supplier (who has many customers, each of whom might want to evaluate his quality system). It is practical only for an important customer (e.g., the Defense Department or a major car company) who can dictate quality conditions that all suppliers must follow.

An alternative, more practical method for gaining confidence is to insist that the supplier meet some standard that is acceptable to the customer. An example of this method is provided by the Underwriters Laboratories (UL) of the United States. For more than 70 years, the UL has conducted evaluations of manufacturers' quality systems. A purchaser of an electrical product need not check the suppliers' quality system; all that need be checked is that the product carries the Underwriter label. This label is an assurance that the producer's system meets all applicable government requirements and the standards established by the UL.

The International Standards Organization: ISO 9000

The main quality story of the 1990s is the growing worldwide acceptance of *ISO 9000*, an internationally acknowledged quality management standard. A more detailed discussion of ISO 9000 appears in Chapter 13; here we give only a brief account of the need for such a standard and its genesis.

The countries of Europe formed the European Community primarily to develop a common market. As part of this bold effort, they enacted various treaties to abolish the trade barriers among the member states and replaced them with a unified method for regulating trade. The new trade regulations are very complex. Products are classified as either regulated or nonregulated. Regulated products are those that have important implications for health, safety, or the environment; we will not discuss such products here.

For nonregulated products, the multitude of technical barriers was replaced with a principle of registration. *Registration* is a process whereby a third party gives written assurance that a firm's product, process, or service conforms to specific requirements, and then registers it in an appropriately available list, which any prospective customer can examine. ISO 9000 provides such specific requirements; the assurance is based on the results of an audit of the firm's quality system. (Quality system audits are described in Section 13.11.)

The ISO 9000 Series of standards was developed by the International Standards Organization (ISO) in 1987 in order to provide quality assurance requirements and guidelines for suppliers. These standards are for the processes the supplier uses to produce products, not standards for products. The aim of the series is to satisfy customers' confidence in the quality systems of their suppliers. This confidence should, in turn, give customers confidence in the quality of the supplier's products.[36]

ISO 9000 is a series of management system standards; the series refers to policies, procedures, controls, and other components of a management system. It is important to distinguish the ISO 9000 series from product technical requirements, such as standards for product performance, product testing, impact on the environment, occupational health and safety, and so on.

ISO 9000 registration is not mandated by the EC for nonregulated products. However, market forces are driving a move to registration; most European customers are requiring that a supplier be registered as in compliance with ISO 9000 before they will do business with them, whether or not the product is regulated. Moreover, individual countries often attach legal requirements to the ISO standards.

The ISO 9000 series consists of three conformance standards:

ISO 9001: Quality systems—Model for quality assurance in design/development, production, installation, and servicing

ISO 9002: Quality systems—Model for quality assurance in production, installation, and servicing.

ISO 9003: Quality systems—Model for quality assurance in final inspection and test.

ISO 9001 is the most comprehensive of the three standards. It is used when the supplier must ensure conformance to specified needs throughout the production

---

[36]For a brief history of ISO 9000, see J. M. Juran, "World War II and the Quality Movement," *Quality Progress*, December 1991, p. 19.

cycle. ISO 9002 addresses production, installation, and servicing, but it omits the design function. ISO 9003 is the least comprehensive standard; it addresses only final inspection and testing.

Registration is against one of these three standards. Through the years, however, other standards have been provided for specialized operations. For example, ISO 14000 on Standards for Environmental Management was added in 1996. The ISO 9000 series has been adopted by more than 50 countries, including the United States and all of our major trading partners.

These are some of the reasons U.S. companies give for becoming ISO 9000 certified:[37]

◆ Customers demand it

◆ Customers will treat ISO 9000-registered suppliers preferentially

◆ Competitors are achieving registration

◆ Good approach to improve quality

◆ Customers demand quality; this is good way to show commitment

◆ U.S. is doing it as European divisions are certified

◆ Industry is moving that way

◆ ISO 9000 registration is one of the keys to process improvement

The Future

Of course, statements about the future direction of quality are only speculation. Here is one view:

◆ ISO registration will proceed rapidly throughout the world. A major benefit of this trend will be finally to convince managers of the benefits to be gained from pursuing quality.

◆ Having stabilized their processes as part of obtaining ISO registration, more organizations will begin to practice continual process improvement.

◆ Employee empowerment and other "human factor" concepts will make progress.

◆ Competition on the quality front will intensify; those who don't improve product quality will not survive.

What do you think will happen?

---

[37]This list is from *Quality Progress*, May 1994, p. 29, except the last item, which is from *Quality Progress*, March 1994, p. 23.

◆ 2.9 Five American Quality Leaders

There were giants in the earth in those days.

—Genesis vi. 4

Walter A. Shewhart

On May 16, 1924, Walter A. Shewhart submitted a memorandum to his superiors at Bell Telephone Laboratories in which he described the concept of a control chart. That document marks the beginning of modern quality management, making it one of the few disciplines that can mark its exact birth. With this document, Shewhart permanently altered the course of industrial history.

Shewhart received B.A. and M.A. degrees from the University of Illinois and a Ph.D. in physics from the University of California at Berkeley in 1917. He then taught briefly at Illinois and California before joining Western Electric in 1918 as an engineer. Later, his unit became part of Bell Telephone Laboratories, where he served as a member of the technical staff until his retirement in 1956.

In 1931, Shewhart published *Economic Control of Quality of Manufactured Product*, which explored all aspects of control charts—theory, philosophy, applications, and economics. As the first publication in a new discipline, the book was remarkably complete in its coverage, bringing the disciplines of statistics, engineering, and economics together to bear on the subject.

During his career, Shewhart lectured widely on quality control both here and abroad. He was a member of the visiting committee at Harvard's Department of Social Relations, an honorary professor at Rutgers, a member of the advisory committee of the Princeton Mathematics Department, and was active in many professional societies. Among the groups he served as a consultant were the War Department, the United Nations, and the government of India.

Shewhart's invention of the control chart,[38] a simple but highly effective tool, represented one initial step toward, in his own words, "the formulation of a scientific basis for securing economic control." That invention made him known as the father of statistical quality control, and it marks him as the founder of modern quality management.

W. Edwards Deming

The best known American proponent of quality is W. Edwards Deming. In Japan, his name is a household word because its highest quality award, the Deming Prize, established in 1951, is named in his honor to recognize his contribution to their quality efforts. In the United States, however, Deming did not become well known

---

[38]For a discussion of control charts, see Chapter 20.

to the public until his provocative NBC News White Paper telecast in 1980, "If Japan Can, Why Can't We?"

Born in Sioux City, Iowa, at the turn of the century, Deming moved with his family at an early age, eventually settling in Cody, Wyoming. He obtained degrees from the University of Wyoming and University of Colorado, and taught at various universities before receiving a Ph.D. in Physics from Yale University in 1927. That year he joined the U.S. Department of Agriculture and moved from there to the Bureau of the Census in 1939. In 1946, he became a professor of statistics in the Graduate School of Business Administration at New York University and began a consulting practice, which he maintained until his death in 1993.

While at the Department of Agriculture, Deming became acquainted with Walter Shewhart and later brought Shewhart's principles into use on clerical operations for the 1940 census. During World War II, Deming was a consultant to the Secretary of War. In that capacity he taught Shewhart's methods to a number of individuals who later formed the core of the statistical quality control movement in the United States.

In 1946, the War Department sent Deming to Japan to study agricultural production, and he returned in 1948 to conduct more of these studies. His major influence on Japan, however, came in 1950, when he taught statistical methods to important people from Japanese industry. In the following years, Deming returned to Japan several times as teacher and consultant to Japanese industry; Japan's success with quality improvement owes much to these efforts. In recognition of this, Japan named its highest quality award the Deming Application Prize.

Deming's best-known contribution to the field of quality are his 14 points for management, which are discussed in Section 22.2. His views and advice on quality are expressed in his book *Out of the Crisis*, which was published in 1986. Deming was a consultant to scores of companies and governmental agencies. He also played important roles in several professional societies.

Deming has been described as a curmudgeon; as the high prophet of quality control; as an imperious old man; as the founder of the third wave of the Industrial Revolution; and as a national folk hero of the Japanese. His lecture style was often blunt and brusque, and he could be impatient with management. But in spite of his confrontational style, Deming had a reputation for being a kind, thoughtful person who always had time to help anyone with a desire to learn. Through his teaching and consulting he did as much as anyone to further the cause of quality.

Joseph M. Juran

Joseph M. Juran is a quality professional's professional. His writings are thoughtful, scholarly, and precise, and they are a rich source of ideas distilled from years of experience. His greatest contribution to quality is the observation that quality depends primarily on management.

Juran was born in Rumania in 1904 and immigrated to the United States as a youth. On receiving a B.S. in Electrical Engineering from Minnesota in 1924, he joined Bell Telephone Laboratories as an engineer, remaining with them until 1941.

During that period, he obtained a J.D. from Loyola, making him one of the few, if not the only, lawyer among the leading quality pioneers. Shortly after joining the labs, he was one of three men assigned to a new department to carry out what today would be known as statistical quality control. This and a later assignment in management laid a foundation for his life-long interest in the role of management relative to quality.

Juran held a series of government jobs during World War II; then in 1945 he joined New York University (NYU) as chairman of what later became the Department of Industrial Engineering. This assignment allowed him the opportunity to write and edit the first edition of the well-known *Quality Control Handbook*. Among other topics, that first edition provided an economic basis for quality by discussing the cost of quality—prevention, appraisal, and failure. First published in 1951, the handbook grew from 15 to more than 50 chapters and has been translated into many languages.

Juran left NYU in 1951 to devote full time to consulting, writing, and teaching. Some years later he formed the Juran Institute to consolidate these efforts.

An invitation to lecture in Japan in 1954 (described further in the next section) helped to redirect the Japanese quality efforts. Soon Juran started reporting to America about developments in Japan; typical was the following comment that appeared in *Industrial Quality Control* in January 1967: "The Japanese are headed for world quality leadership, and will attain it in the next two decades because no one else is moving there at the same pace." In fact, they didn't take quite that long.

Aside from his emphasis on top-management involvement, some of Juran's contributions to quality are the Pareto principle, the cost of quality, project-by-project approach to quality improvement, management breakthrough, the quality trilogy, and his emphasis on the importance of widespread education on quality. On the latter point, he wrote in the February 1979 issue of *Quality:* "The central ingredient of the Japanese revolution has been a massive training program. . . . Planning for training should receive one of the highest priorities in any program." Juran has now retired from active public life.

Armand V. Feigenbaum

The name Armand V. Feigenbaum and the term *total quality control* are virtually synonymous. His concept of extending quality control beyond the production line was a major contribution to the field.

Feigenbaum was born in 1920. In 1942, he received a B.S. from Union College and joined General Electric, with whom he stayed until 1956. After various assignments, he served for 10 years as manager of worldwide manufacturing operations and quality control for GE. In 1958, he became president and chief executive officer of General Systems Company, an engineering firm that designs and installs systems.

In 1951, Feigenbaum received a Ph.D. degree from MIT. That same year his concept of extending quality control beyond the production line was published in the book *Quality Control: Principles, Practice, and Administration*, later published under the better-known title *Total Quality Control*. TQC called for "interfunctional teams" from marketing, design, manufacturing, inspection, and shipping; these teams were to share responsibility for the quality of all phases of design and manufacturing. In addition to TQC, Feigenbaum is known for quality cost management. Many of his ideas support those developed earlier by Juran.

Philip B. Crosby

Philip B. Crosby was a conspicuous leader of the 1980 resurgence of interest in quality. His book, *Quality Is Free*, had instant appeal with businesspeople, making his name known overnight.

For 14 years, Crosby was corporate vice president and director of quality for the ITT Corporation. During that period, he created the Zero Defects and Buck a Day (BAD) schemes for promoting quality. After the instant success of *Quality Is Free*, Crosby left ITT to form his own company, Phil Crosby Associates. The Crosby Colleges conducted by that organization taught his concepts of quality to thousands.

Among Crosby's better known quality concepts are the quality management maturity grid, his absolutes of quality management, and his quality improvement program. He is also a promoter of the cost of quality, as developed by Juran and Feigenbaum.

Active as a lecturer, writer, and star in his own videos on quality, Crosby continues to be one of the chief promoters of quality concepts in America.

◆ 2.10 Quality in Japan

A Brief History

Today Japan is a leader in quality, but it was not always so. Before World War II, Japan competed on price, not quality; Japanese goods had a reputation for being cheap and shoddy. This fact alone should have dispelled the notion commonly held by Westerners in much of the postwar period that Japanese quality comes from something inherent in their culture.

Taking a lead from American practice at the time, prewar quality control in Japan was primarily inspection-oriented. Quality control was exercised by units, called the inspection or quality control department, that were independent of production.

Motivating Factors

After the war, several factors converged to make Japan receptive to quality improvement. A major factor was the economic situation. World War II had left Japan devastated with factories destroyed and people near starvation. It was clear to many leaders that the standard of living could not be raised if Japan were to adhere to its prewar practice of competing on the basis of cheap labor. An attempt had to be made to produce more advanced products, and this would require more attention to quality.

A second factor making Japan receptive to quality was a change in management structure. Immediately after the war, many of Japan's top executives were dismissed because of their actual or presumed association with the wartime regime. Replacements were chosen from the ranks of operating managers, people with wide experience in business who had started at a low level and had worked their way up. This change in management was to have a tremendous effect because, not only were able people appointed, but also the action introduced the prospect of promotion as an incentive to able junior managers. It gave Japan an organization closer to the traditional American model, where top executives generally rise from the operating ranks, in contrast to a traditional European model, where promotion more often depended on class and education. Searching for guidance, the new top executives in Japan were receptive to new ideas, including the idea that quality might answer Japan's economic problems.[39]

A third factor was dissatisfaction with the inspection-oriented attempt to achieve quality that was practiced before and during the war. Quality professionals were beginning to recognize the limitations in this approach, some of which have been listed by Ishikawa:

- Inspectors are unnecessary personnel who reduce company productivity.
- Inspection places quality responsibility on the inspector, not the producer.
- Feedback on quality from the inspection department to manufacturing takes too much time.
- Inspectors cannot keep pace when production speeds.
- Statistical sampling is unsatisfactory when dealing with defective parts per million.
- For complex products, quality cannot be assured through inspection alone.
- Reliance on inspection does not guarantee quality because not all defects will be found. Where defects are found and corrected, the resulting product is more likely to be unsatisfactory than one that was initially defect free.[40]

Beginning of Statistical Quality Control

The push for Japan to adopt new quality concepts came from the U.S. occupation forces, which faced a major obstacle: failure of the domestic telephone service. The office of the Supreme Commander for the Allied Powers (SCAP) depended on that system for its own internal communication. Moreover, SCAP was concerned that poor communications might cause misunderstandings, which might lead to civil unrest. Although deemed essential, the phone system was in fact hindered by unreliable equipment and war damage. So in May 1946 the American authorities

---

[39]Kenneth Hopper, "Quality, Japan and the US: The First Chapter," *Quality Progress*, September 1985, p 34.

[40]Ishikawa, *What Is Total Quality Control?*, p. 76.

ordered the Japanese to learn modern quality control techniques and fix the problem.[41] And they did; that was the start of Japan's quality movement.

The first effort to instruct the Japanese in quality principles was a course offered by the Civil Communications Section (CCS) of the occupation forces. This course, known simply as CCS, was prepared and taught by Charles Protzman, a senior manufacturing executive from Western Electric, and Homer Sarasohn, a development engineer who had fought in the Pacific War. The course also had the support of their supervisor, Frank Polkinghorn, from Bell Labs. Little known in the West, CCS was conducted twice between late 1948 and early 1950. Participants later became top executives of Japanese communications equipment manufacturers, companies such as Fujitsu, Furukawa, Hitachi, Matsushita, Mitsubishi Electric, Nippon Electric, Sanyo, Sharp, Sumitomo Electric, and Toshiba (or their predecessor companies). In addition to extensive discussion of quality control, important management concepts were covered. For example, Sarasohn taught participants that "the primary objective of the company is to put the quality of the product ahead of any other consideration. A profit or a loss notwithstanding, the emphasis will always be on quality." He also quoted Andrew Carnegie: "The surest foundation of a business concern is quality. And after quality—a long time after—comes cost."

Although it was offered only twice, the CCS course played an important role in starting Japanese industry on its new path. Perhaps the best documented evidence of CCS's impact appeared in the fifteenth anniversary edition of *Quality Control* published in 1965 by the Union of Japanese Scientists and Engineers (JUSE). The publication honored five Japanese quality pioneers. All five cited CCS as an early source of their quality knowledge; three of the five attended the first CCS class.[42]

Visit by W. Edwards Deming

Credit for introducing quality to Japan generally falls to W. Edwards Deming who in 1950, at the invitation of the JUSE, gave an eight-day seminar on statistical quality control for managers and engineers. He followed this with a one-day seminar for company presidents and top managers. Deming's lectures came after the CCS courses, but the force of his reputation and personality, and the reinforcement of this visit to Japan with several others, combined to give his lectures more weight. His 1950 lectures often are described as the seed from which the Japanese quality movement grew.

Deming's JUSE lectures covered three main points:

◆ How to use the "plan, do, check, act" (PDCA) cycle.

◆ The importance of having a feel for dispersion in statistics.

◆ Process control through the use of control charts and how to use them.

---

[41]Ibid., p. 15.

[42]Hopper, "Quality, Japan and the US," p. 34.

The Deming Prize

The first major award for quality anywhere was the Deming Prize, established in 1951 and named after Deming in recognition of his assistance in putting the Japanese economy back on its feet after World War II. The money needed to establish the first awards was donated by Deming from the royalties on his statistics book used in training Japanese scientists and engineers. The Prize is noncompetitive; to win, a participating company must meet established measures of capability in a variety of quality functions as assessed by a team of quality consultants.

Visit by Joseph M. Juran

The early Japanese efforts in quality overemphasized the importance of statistical methods, such as statistical quality control. Some of the problems caused by this emphasis are listed by Ishikawa:[43]

- Workers found statistical methods difficult.

- Standards required to apply the concepts were not always available.

- There was a dearth of data.

- Even when available, data were seldom useful.

- Workers feared that measuring devices used to collect data were put there to monitor their work.

- Quality control remained the preserve of engineers and workers; top and middle management showed little interest.

Japan's early overemphasis on statistical methods was tempered by the 1954 visit of Joseph M. Juran, who conducted seminars for top and middle management in which he emphasized the roles they had to play. Made at the invitation of JUSE, Juran's visit marked a transition in the Japanese quality from a focus on technology and the factory floor to a focus on management and all areas of the organization.

Education and Training

From the beginning of their quality movement, the Japanese emphasized training everyone in the organization on the principles of quality. Innumerable seminars and conferences introduced the concept to top and middle managers and informed them of the part they must play. But there were too many foremen and group leaders to be trained in this way; other methods had to be devised. One method was a weekly radio program on QC, which was started in 1956 and continued until 1962. In 1957, a correspondence course on quality was offered through the Japan Shortwave Broadcasting Corporation. In 1960, a weekly TV series on quality was started, and the Japanese government declared November as National Quality Month.

---

[43]Ishikawa, *What Is Total Quality Control?*, p. 18.

The journal *Gemba-to-QC* or *Quality Control for the Foreman* was started in 1962. It was in the first issue of this journal that quality circles were advocated under the name of QC circles. Although people in the United States think of QC circles as being aimed primarily at improving work processes, this is not the Japanese view. Circles are organized for the purpose of study; people study to avoid making recurring mistakes. Quality circles are the primary vehicle for teaching quality concepts to workers.

Japanese education and training are not only extensive, but also in depth. The basic quality course designed by JUSE, a model for courses throughout industry, extends over a six-month period. Each month, students receive one week of classroom training; the rest of the month they practice on the job what they have learned in the classroom. Thus, the JUSE course is a combination of study and practice.

It should be noted that education on quality starts from a very firm base. Education has been compulsory in Japan since the Meiji Restoration in 1868; after World War II it was extended to nine years. Students are given strong family support, and over 90 percent complete high school. Literacy in Japan is among the highest in the world. Extensive education and training on quality, therefore, are being supplied to perhaps the best educated labor force in the world.

Summary of Japanese Quality History

History shows that the Japanese quality movement has passed through three stages. Successively, emphasis has been on product control, process improvement, and product improvement.

Following the Western lead, Japan emphasized product control before World War II. The aim was to inspect products and catch defects before they were shipped. The product control approach to quality was abandoned in about 1949 and replaced with an emphasis on process improvement. First, they got their processes under control; this was accomplished by employing statistical quality control techniques to stabilize processes and remove assignable causes of variation. Later, they attempted to remove all causes of defects.

Japan gradually moved to a third stage in which the emphasis is on product improvement, on *what* is being produced defect free. During the 1970s, the Japanese came to understand that their quality emphasis did not reach back to the stage where new products were developed—it did not emphasize sufficiently the purpose of the production process. They gradually adopted a total quality control (TQC) approach, extending quality concepts to every process and every job. In particular, they concentrated heavily on the task of determining what customers wanted and the design process. The aim now is to produce products that the customers truly want.

In short, the Japanese approach has been crawl, walk, run. They are ahead in the race and running hard. Can they be caught?

Kaoru Ishikawa

American businesspeople are familiar with the names of several Japanese leaders who have led their companies to excellence. Not too many, however, know the name Kaoru Ishikawa, Japan's foremost authority on quality. It can be argued that he did more than anyone else to create the quality revolution that has brought Japan its great competitive advantage. Professor, consultant, and author, he helped many companies, Japanese and foreign, to achieve excellence.

Born in 1915, the son of a prominent industrialist, Ishikawa graduated from Tokyo University in 1939 with a degree in applied chemistry. He spent the next eight years in the nonacademic world, first as a naval technical officer during the war and later with an industrial firm. In 1947, he returned to the University of Tokyo as a professor of engineering, where his experiments soon required him to gain an understanding of statistics and statistical quality control. This marked the beginning of his life-long involvement with the field of quality. Later, Ishikawa became president of Musashi Institute of Technology in Tokyo, a post he held until his death in 1989.

Even a partial list of Ishikawa's activities reveals that his life is inseparable from the history of the Japanese quality movement. He was active in Japanese and international standardization activities. He was named chief executive director of QC Circle Headquarters of JUSE and served on various committees to organize meetings and conferences on quality. He was a member of the editorial board of *Quality Control for the Foreman* and editor of two widely used books on quality circles provided by JUSE. He was a member of the committee for the Deming Prize and therefore was involved in auditing companies seeking that coveted prize.

Beginning in 1961, Ishikawa took the position that "quality control cannot be implemented by merely following national or international standards. These standards may be taken into consideration, but . . . quality control must have the higher goals of meeting the requirements of consumers and creating quality which satisfies them."[44] In recent years, many U.S. producers have taken a similar position; they understand that the key to quality is determining what the customer *really* wants and then providing it.

Ishikawa's best known technical contribution is the Ishikawa *cause-and-effect* or *fishbone diagram*. (We discuss this tool in Section 21.7.) This powerful tool can easily be used by nonspecialists to analyze and solve quality problems. His most important contribution, however, was the key role he played in the development of TQC, the specifically Japanese quality strategy described earlier.

Japan's Contributions

As with all foreign imports, Japan has evolved its own unique interpretation of quality-related matters. Japan made four major innovations.

First, Japan's executives realized before any others that quality can be used as a *competitive strategy*. They were the first to understand fully that quality drives down cost and pulls up demand; that cost and demand advantages can be used to reduce price, which further expands demand and brings economies of scale;

---

[44]Ibid., p.8.

and that repetitive cycles of price and cost reduction can drive competitors from the field.

Second, Japan understood before any others that quality is not the domain of technical experts but is the *job of everyone*. In the West, phrases such as "Quality is everybody's job" have been used for years, but most managers took them as slogans, not serious principles. Japan was the first to put this concept into practice. Through quality circles, consensus management, and the general Japanese attitude toward group participation, quality was transformed from the concern of a few professionals to the concern of all. Japan was the first to exploit the creative genius of workers in a quest for quality.

Japan's third contribution to the quality effort, and a more recent innovation, was a *deeper understanding of quality*. This understanding arose by examining quality more intently from the customers' view. Westerners tended to focus on producing a defect-free product; the Japanese, understanding well how to do that, went beyond it and focused on the true nature of customer requirements themselves. Realizing that quality means more to a customer than a defect-free product, they sought to understand just what it is the customer wants. It is easy for a Westerner to claim, "But we have always done that, too." To this we reply that the idea may not be new in the West, but making the idea a practical reality has yet to happen in many American companies.

Japan's fourth contribution was to broaden the quality movement to all parts of the organization—*company-wide quality control*. This is a natural extension of moves in the West toward total quality control. Again it is something that some Westerners might not acknowledge as being different from directions here, but it is.

◆ Exercises and Additional Readings

1. Read J. M. Juran, "The Upcoming Century of Quality," *Quality Progress*, August 1994, p. 29. Summarize Juran's prognosis for the future of quality.

2. Write a brief report on the early history of the quality movement. Use as reference Brad Stratton, "Not the Best Years of Their Lives," *Quality Progress*, May 1996, pp. 24–30.

3. Read and write a brief report of Michael G. Freeman, "Don't Throw Scientific Management Out with the Bathwater," *Quality Progress*, April 1996, pp. 61–64.

4. (Case study) For some major company, examine its annual reports for 1975, 1985, and 1995. Prepare a brief report on how the company's emphasis and approach to quality have changed over the period.

5. Read J. M. Juran, "World War II and the Quality Movement," *Quality Progress*, December 1991, pp. 19–24.

   (a) Summarize the three waves of statistical quality control (SQC) discussed by Juran.

(b) Summarize the impact that the postwar Air Force review of quality assurance had on the approach to quality assurance.

(c) Summarize Juran's prognosis for the 1990s and beyond.

6. Read Suzanne Axland, "Forecasting the Future of Quality," *Quality Progress*, February 1993, p. 21. Summarize the view of the future of quality as described by (a) Crosby, (b) Feigenbaum, and (c) Juran.

7. Read David Garvin, "Competing on the Eight Dimensions of Quality," *Harvard Business Review* (November–December, 1987): p. 101.

(a) Describe briefly Garvin's eight dimensions of quality.

(b) Summarize Garvin's view on the origin of strategic quality management.

8. Read J. M. Juran, "Managing for Quality," *Journal for Quality and Participation*, Vol. 11, No. 1 (March 1988), pp. 8–12. What, according to Juran, were the key factors in Japan's success in achieving quality?

9. Read Joseph M. Juran, "The Upcoming Century of Quality," *Quality Progress*, August 1994, p. 29. Summarize the changes Juran says must be made by a company to attain world-class quality.

10. Read "U.S. Firms See Striking Paybacks from ISO 9000 Registration," *Quality Progress*, January 1994, p. 26. Compare this report with the view expressed by Juran in the article cited in Exercise 1.

11. Read Behnam Nakhai and Joao S. Neves, "The Deming, Baldrige, and European Quality Awards," *Quality Progress*, April 1994, p. 33. Summarize the similarities and differences among the three awards discussed in the article.

12. Read Stanley A. Marash and Donald W. Marquardt, "Quality, Standards, and Free Trade," *Quality Progress*, May 1994, p. 27. List some of the reasons for U.S. producers to comply with the ISO 9000 standards.

13. From your collection of articles on quality (Exercise 1, Chapter 1), give some examples of the impact of TQM on organizations. What lesson can you learn from these articles?

14. Read and discuss Robert Burney, "TQM in a Surgery Center," *Quality Progress*, January 1994, p. 97.

15. Read Herbert W. Hoover, Jr., "What Went Wrong in U.S. Business's Attempt to Rescue Its Competitiveness?," *Quality Progress*, July 1995, p. 83. (a) Describe briefly the failure of the fluid-handling equipment manufacturer's TQM effort. (b) Summarize the author's observations concerning what it takes for a TQM effort to be successful.

16. Read George P. Bohan "Focus the Strategy to Achieve Results," *Quality Progress*, July 1995, p. 89. (a) What two things must a leader do to make a commitment to TQM successful? (b) Summarize the author's comments on each of these actions. (c) Discuss briefly the three goals the author says will serve the purposes of most organizations.

17. Read "The State of Quality in the U.S. Today: The Quality Guidance System," *Quality Progress*, October 1986, p. 35. Summarize the efforts made to establish TQM in the early 1980s by the five companies featured in the article.

18. Read and summarize John A. Goodman, Gary F. Bargatee, and Cynthia Grimm, "The Key Problem with TQM," *Quality Progress*, January 1994, p. 45.

19. Read one of the many books on W. Edwards Deming, such as:

    (a) H. R. Neave, *The Deming Dimension* (Knoxville, Tenn.: SPC Press, 1990).

    (b) F. Voehl et al., *Deming: The Way We Knew Him* (Delray Beach, Fla: St. Lucie Press, 1995).

    (c) M. Walton: *The Deming Management Method* (New York: Dodd, Mead & Co., 1986).

    Describe the main message that the book conveys about Deming's contributions to quality.

20. Read and summarize Robert J. Masters, "Overcoming the Barriers to TQM's Success," *Quality Progress*, May 1996, p. 53.

21. Read Part I of Chapter II in Kaoru Ishikawa, *What Is Total Quality Control?* Summarize Ishikawa's account of the history of quality activities in Japan.

22. Review and summarize the contributions of the five quality leaders in Section 2.9.

23. What were some of the innovations that Japanese quality experts developed to foster quality?

24. In this chapter we mentioned the Malcolm Baldrige Quality Award, the Deming Prize, and the system of ISO 9000 registration. Discuss their common features and objectives; discuss their differences.

25. Use the internet to obtain additional information on the quality leaders whom we discussed in Sections 2.9 and 2.10. For example, use any internet browser to search for "W. Edwards Deming." You will find many websites with information on Deming. Refine your search by looking for his biography or the Deming Prize. Do the same for the other quality leaders. Summarize the information that you find through your web searches, pointing to information that goes beyond the material provided in this text.

26. Use the internet to obtain information on the International Standards Organization and the ISO 9000 standards. Summarize the information that you obtained. In carrying out your search, you will notice the many consulting firms that advertise services that lead to ISO certification.

27. Consult the website of the American Society for Quality (ASQ). Describe its focus and summarize its services. The website for ASQ is www.asq.org. Look for information on the Baldrige Quality Award.

The Value of Implementing Quality

We've saved several billion dollars over the last year because of our focus on quality improvement. . . . So to me, there is no doubt about the fact that it has enhanced our bottom line.

—Gary L. Tooker, Vice Chairman and Chief Executive, Motorola[1]

◆ 3.1 The Cost of Quality

In the early days of the quality movement, there were no special techniques to help a manager make a rational economic evaluation of a quality improvement effort. Then in the 1950s, J. M. Juran called attention to the "gold in the mine" of costs associated with quality. Soon after that, General Electric developed the concept known today as the *cost of quality*. A. V. Feigenbaum did much to promote this concept, and the idea boomed in the 1960s when the Department of Defense required an evaluation of the cost of quality for defense contracts. The next major boost for the concept came in the 1980s when Phil Crosby adopted it as a central component of his quality improvement program. The cost of quality concept has lost some of its popularity in recent years, but nothing more comprehensive has evolved to replace it.

---

[1]Karen Bemowski, "Motorola's Fountain of Youth," *Quality Progress*, October 1995, p. 31.

An organization must pay to achieve quality, but it also pays for lack of quality. The concern of management should be the total amount spent in the quality area: the cost of achieving quality and the penalty for failing to do so. This total amount is called the *cost of quality* (COQ).

Three Cost Categories

Quality costs can be classified into the three categories shown in Display 3.1. First, there are *prevention* costs—money required to prevent errors and to do the job right the first time. This category includes money spent to establish methods and

---

DISPLAY 3.1 ◆ Components of the Cost of Quality

Some Typical Prevention Components
- Selling top management
- Plans for quality improvement
- Installation of standards, methods, and procedures
- Installation of tools
- Quality training and education
- Quality awareness and motivation
- Preventive maintenance
- Other quality improvement projects
- Report of quality status
- Quality assurance consultation
- Quality assessments
- Evaluation of vendors and subcontractors

Some Typical Appraisal Components
- Walkthroughs and inspections
- Preparation for reviews
- Quality reviews
- Preparation for product testing
- Product testing
- Quality audits

Some Typical Failure Components
- Cost of recalling faulty products
- Repair and rework
- Staff turnover caused by quality problems
- Lost production due to quality problems
- Cost of projects canceled because of quality problems
- Assets lost because of quality problems
- Benefits lost because of quality problems
- Legal liability from poor quality

---

procedures, train workers, and plan for quality. All prevention money is spent before the product is built.

Second, there are *appraisal* costs—money spent to review completed products against requirements. Appraisal includes the costs of inspections, testing, and reviews. Appraisal money is spent after the product is built but before it is shipped to the customer.

Third, there are *failure* costs—all the costs associated with defective products. Some failure costs arise from scrapping products or repairing them to make them meet requirements. Others are costs generated by failures, such as the cost of operating faulty products, damage caused by using them, and costs incurred because an acceptable product was not available.

These three categories—prevention, appraisal, and failure—cover all expenses involved in achieving quality, as well as the penalty paid for failing to do so. Therefore, the sum of these costs is the total cost of quality; that is:

Cost of quality = Cost of Prevention + Cost of Appraisal + Cost of Failure

Failure Costs

Failure costs usually are the largest component of the cost of quality. Some of these costs are dramatic, as the following examples illustrate.

- In 1981, Eastern Air Lines lost as much as $20,000 a minute as a result of its failure to make ticket bookings whenever its computer reservation system broke down.

- Merrill Lynch could drop $50,000 in just one wheat futures order during a two-minute computer outage.

- In 1981, Rockwell International Corporation spent $100,000 a year to lease duplicate communications lines. This investment was judged worthwhile if the main line failed only once a year.[2]

These are examples of costly failures, but in all cases the probability of failure is relatively low. The major elements of failure cost are the expenses that go on day after day because of ordinary (that is, nondramatic) quality problems. Some failure costs are *internal*; that is, they are costs associated with defects found before a product is transferred to a customer. Examples of internal failures are rework, scrap, large work-in-process inventories, excessive material handling, warranty and service costs, and the clerical and management effort required to correct mistakes. Other failure costs are *external*; that is, they are costs associated with defects found after a product is shipped. Among external failure costs are warranty and service costs, the cost of investigating and adjusting defective products, and allowances for substandard products. Individually, these failures are insignificant; collectively, they represent a huge waste of money and effort.

---

[2]*Business Week*, September 7, 1981, pp. 70–74.

One very important failure cost is largely ignored in the quality literature because it is so difficult to measure: business that is lost because potential customers are "turned off" by a firm's reputation for poor quality, or by its poor reputation for handling failures that do occur.

Failure costs frequently go unnoticed because conventional accounting and reporting systems do not highlight them. Many failure costs are hidden because they are built into standard costs, overhead, or burden rates. Some are treated as part of production cost; an example is the time workers sit idle because the "computer is down." Some failure costs are overlooked because they are charged to someone else's budget. For example, the cost borne by the sales department in correcting a billing error might well be overlooked when computing the cost of quality for the billing department. Failure costs, which can cripple an organization's ability to compete, must be ferreted out and highlighted.

Reducing the Cost of Quality

The aim of management is to minimize the cost of quality. It makes no difference if this is done by reducing all three components or by increasing some and decreasing others enough to lower the total cost. To have a significant impact on the total cost, the cost of failure must be reduced, and the usual strategy for achieving this objective is to spend more on prevention. *It is always cheaper to do a job right the first time than to do it over.* Money spent on prevention is more than recouped by decreasing the costs of appraisal and failure; see Display 3.2.

In the manufacturing area, it is not uncommon for a quality improvement effort to cut the cost of quality in half. Remember that this savings is net because the cost of quality includes the added prevention costs that make this savings possible. It could take several years to achieve such a reduction, but after that the savings go on forever—a permanent reduction in manufacturing cost.

> **Example.**   In a two-year period the Willimantic Division of Rogers Corporation reduced its cost of quality from 18.9 percent of total manufacturing cost to 10.9 percent.[3]

Problems with the Cost of Quality

The cost of quality is a useful tool for gaining management attention and commitment to a quality improvement effort, but it is less useful as a tool for guiding that effort. The COQ is expressed in dollars, which is the natural language of an organization's upper levels. But at lower levels, the natural language involves products, and quality is measured by defect rates, not dollars. The number of "bugs" per thousand lines of code is more meaningful to a software department than is their cost of quality. Process improvement is guided more by defect information

---

[3]*Productivity Digest*, November 1987, p. 11.

DISPLAY 3.2 ◆ The Cost of Quality

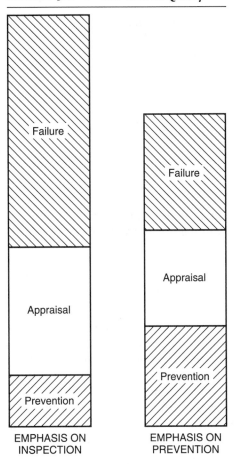

than by a department's COQ. The COQ is to an organization as the starter is to a car: it can get things going, but another device is needed to power it.

Another problem with the COQ is that many companies are very poor at estimating this quantity. In a 1987 survey, top executives were asked to estimate their cost of quality. The results, shown in Display 3.3, are discouraging. Only 4 percent estimated that their cost of quality exceeded 20 percent, which quality experts regarded as the correct range for the average U.S. business at that time. The average of all COQ estimates was approximately 6 percent; this figure is slightly below the figure quality experts regarded as the average cost of quality for Japanese companies. Commenting on these results, David Kearns, chairman of Xerox Corporation, stated: "The survey shows that many people still do not understand the connection between cost and quality. Seventy percent of the respondents ei-

DISPLAY 3.3 ◆ Cost of Quality Estimates[a]

Cost of Quality	Percent Responding
Don't know	27
0–4%	44
5–9%	19
10–19%	6
20+%	4

[a]John Ryan, "Quality and the Competitive Advantage: 1987 Gallup Survey," *Quality Progress*, December 1987, p. 12.

ther did not know or thought their quality costs were less than five percent. You will not change the culture with that kind of data or those kinds of perceptions."[4]

◆ 3.2 Quality and Productivity

The *productivity* of a process is the ratio of the value added by the process to the value of the labor and capital consumed. For a given output, productivity goes up as the cost of labor and capital goes down. Thus, productivity improvement and cost reduction are two sides of the same coin. Having discussed the impact of quality on cost, logically there is no need to discuss quality and productivity. Nonetheless, we will review the latter connection because much of the quality literature is couched in terms of productivity gain, not cost reduction.

Let's recognize, first of all, that improved quality generally will add to costs *if* the emphasis is on finding defects and correcting them. But no fully developed quality program takes that approach. The best way to improve quality is to prevent the errors from happening; with this approach, improving quality generally leads to higher productivity. The Japanese have known this for years. By employing this approach, they "have been able to upgrade quality phenomenally. Over a period of time, this has resulted in a substantial increase in productivity which has in turn made it possible to effect a cost down (reduce costs), which then has led to an increase in sales and in profit."[5]

Example. In an effort to become more competitive, an AT&T factory in Shreveport installed a quality system integrated from the ground up and affecting each and every process. It reports that the "result today is a factory

[4]John Ryan, "1987 ASQC/Gallup Survey," *Quality Progress*, December 1987, p. 12.
[5]Kaoru Ishikawa, *What Is Total Quality Control?* (Englewood Cliffs, N.J.: Prentice-Hall, 1985), p. 167.

in which labor productivity has as much as doubled on some product lines, workmanship has improved, and product costs have been slashed."[6]

Quality brings productivity, but what about the other way around? Does the improvement of productivity bring with it an improvement in quality? It need not because, as Professor Martin K. Starr of Columbia University has observed, "Productivity is measured with no reference to customer satisfaction as a result of product quality."[7]

Productivity and Employees

An important issue surrounding quality and productivity is the human issue—the reaction of people to these concepts. When managers say "productivity," workers hear "work harder." They tend to resist productivity improvement programs (in a subtle way, of course) and view them negatively because they expect the organization's gains to be at their personal expense. Perhaps organizational fat needs to be trimmed, but no individual likes to be put on a diet.

Quality, on the other hand, is popular. People like the idea of producing error-free products and being proud of their output; they like the idea of less rework and seeing less of their hard work scrapped because of faulty requirements. An organization that is solidly behind quality usually has the support of the troops.

◆ 3.3 Quality and the Customer

Life-Cycle Costs

Frank M. Gryna has pointed out that the true cost of a product to a customer is not just the purchase price; it is the *life-cycle cost* of a product. He defines this to be the total cost to the customer of purchasing, using, and maintaining the product over its life less any residual value. For a hamburger, the life-cycle cost is more or less the purchase price—not counting possible waste disposal problems and the cost of repairing plugged arteries. But for an automobile, it is the purchase price, operating costs, maintenance costs, storage costs, and disposal costs less any resale value. The life-cycle cost of a product can be many times its purchase price; for example, Gryna estimates that this ratio is 4.8 for a home freezer and 1.9 for a gas range or a television set.[8]

Life-cycle cost is a logical, fundamentally sound concept, and many consumers

---

[6]*Management Review*, January 1988, p. 35.

[7]*The Quality Review*, Fall 1987, p. 6.

[8]J. M. Juran and Frank M. Gryna, *Quality Planning and Analysis*, 3rd ed. (New York: McGraw-Hill, 1993), p. 90.

use some variation of the concept to evaluate products. *Consumer Reports* and other publications thrive by providing information on performance characteristics, operating costs, resale values, and other data that can be used to estimate life-cycle costs for a wide variety of products—cars, household appliances, tools, and so on. The popularity of such publications shows that many buyers attempt to behave rationally.

On the other hand, Gryna himself points out that acceptance of the life-cycle cost concept has been slow to develop. He suggests that this is due in part to the difficulty of estimating future costs, and in part to cultural resistance: The skills, habits, and practices of purchasing managers, product designers, and marketing people have all been built around the concept of original purchase pricing. Moreover, many government contracts and company purchasing policies give heavy weight to price in making purchase decisions. An attempt to swim against the prevailing tide by emphasizing life-cycle cost is not likely to be a successful marketing tactic.

Price and Perceived Quality

Customers base purchasing decisions largely on two factors: price and perceived quality. As we just remarked, "price" generally means purchase price, although the life-cycle cost might be a more appropriate measure. *Perceived quality* is the customer's judgment or perception of the quality of a product relative to that of competing products. This perception is based on whatever product and service factors the customer considers to be important: function, design, convenience, service, and so on. Perceived quality is the customer's view of product quality in contrast to the traditional producer's "conformance to requirements" view of quality.

To learn how perceived quality and price interrelate in a customer's purchasing decision, the Strategic Planning Institute of Cambridge, Massachusetts, conducted a very large research project on marketing: Profit Impact of Market Strategy (PIMS). Their findings are based on the analysis of their PIMS database, which contains information on the marketing experiences, good and bad, of over 2500 diverse product and service businesses operated in North America, Europe, and Australia. These findings do much to clarify the relationship between quality and price.[9]

The interaction of customers and suppliers in the marketplace tends to align products along a "price/performance curve," as shown in Display 3.4. All points on the price/performance curve offer the same value to a customer; by moving up the curve, a customer is achieving greater perceived quality for a greater price but at no sacrifice of value. The highest point P on the curve is the premium position; the lowest point E is the economy position. All points above the price/performance curve provide the customer with less value; those below provide more. As the dis-

---

[9]Phillip Thompson, Glenn DeSouze and Bradley Gale, "The Strategic Management of Service Quality," *Quality Progress,* June 1985, p. 21.

DISPLAY 3.4 ◆ Price/Performance Curve

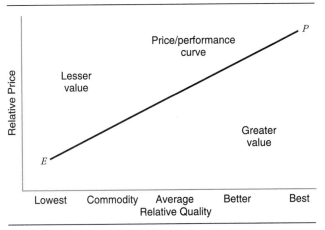

Note: The price/performance curve need not be linear

play shows, products perceived by customers to have higher quality can command a higher price.[10]

◆ 3.4 The Japanese Quality Strategy

Emphasis on quality can bring a decrease in cost and greater customer satisfaction, a powerful marketing combination. First to recognize this fact were the Japanese who devised an effective strategy to use quality for market domination; it is this strategy that has powered their economic triumph. Our discussion of the Japanese strategy is keyed to Display 3.5.[11]

Impact 1. Quality Improvement Cuts Costs

The first principle in the Japanese strategy is to embrace quality and strive to produce error-free products. This strategic principle is based on an understanding that quality improvement results in a lower cost of production. The Japanese know that quality improvement takes time, but they are prepared to make the necessary investment to achieve long-term benefits.

---

[10]Bradley T. Gale and Richard Klavans, "Formulating a Quality Improvement Strategy," *Journal of Business Strategy* (Winter 1995): pp. 21–32.

[11]Our discussion of the Japanese quality strategy is gleaned from James C. Abegglen and George Stalk, Jr., *Kaisha, the Japanese Corporation* (New York: Basic Books, 1985).

DISPLAY 3.5 ◆ Impacts of the
Japanese Quality Strategy

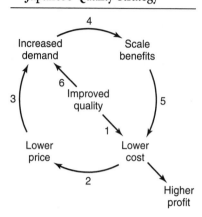

Impact 2. Lower Costs Allow Lower Prices

Who should get the benefit of the cost savings brought by improved quality? The producer through higher profits, or the customer through lower prices? Or should the benefits be shared?

The second principle in the Japanese strategy is to pass a significant portion of the savings from quality improvement to the customer in the form of price reductions or improved products at a constant price. The Japanese believe that "If a company pursues the goal of attaining a short-term profit, it will lose competitiveness in the international market, and it will lose profit in the long-run."[12]

Impact 3. Lower Price Brings Increased Market Share

Lower price and better quality generate increased demand. This increase is not just the traditional increased volume that would result from price competition—an effect that economists describe as "moving down the demand curve." Lower price *and* better quality generate a perception of value that results in an actual "shift in the demand curve," as is depicted in Display 3.6.

Increased demand translates into increased market share, a primary goal of the Japanese. They understand that increased market share forestalls competition and in the long run can lead to market dominance.

Impact 4. Increased Market Share Brings Benefits of Scale

Increased market share brings many benefits. One is the economy of scale brought about by the increased levels of production. As volume increases, production capacity can be more fully utilized and fixed costs of production can be spread over a larger base; these and other economies mean that the average cost of production decreases as the scale is magnified.

---

[12]Ishikawa, *What Is Total Quality Control?*, p. 104.

DISPLAY 3.6 ◆ Demand Shift Induced
by an Improvement in Quality

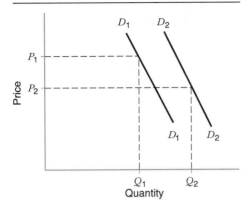

Another cost benefit of increased production is known as the *learning curve* effect. As a company gains experience, people learn how to produce a product more efficiently. Since learning depends on experience, which is a function of how many items have been produced to date, it is clear that the larger the total production, the sooner learning takes place. In short, increased volume speeds learning, thereby speeding cost reduction.

Impact 5. Scale Benefits Generate Further Cost Reductions

Increased market share brings lower production costs to augment the savings produced by quality improvement. In turn, these lower costs allow still lower prices, and the cycle continues to the joy of customers, the profit of the producer, and the consternation of competitors. Toyota and other Japanese manufacturers have mastered this competitive tactic.

Impact 6. Quality of Design Increases Demand

Originally, the Japanese strategy consisted of the two principles we described above: striving to produce error-free products and passing much of the cost savings on to customers. Gradually, a third strategic principle evolved: striving to design products that meet true customer requirements. Before anyone else, the Japanese came to realize that producing error-free products was not enough. To attract customers, it is also necessary to study their true requirements carefully and to design products that gain enthusiastic acceptance.

As Ishikawa observed, "American consumers bought Japanese-made compacts irrespective of price because of their reliability and fuel efficiency."[13]

---

[13]Ishikawa, *What Is Total Quality Control?*, p. 105.

◆ 3.5 Quality as an Investment

Cost of quality can be described within an accounting framework—it focuses on costs. The Japanese strategy adopts a marketing view—it focuses heavily on the customer reaction to quality. Either of these views can be used to justify a quality improvement program, and both present compelling reasons to embrace quality improvement. But neither view is likely to provide sufficient justification for the typical American organization to undertake a serious quality improvement effort.

Most American organizations have a standard process for reviewing and approving any request for funds, including funds for a quality improvement program. A major step in the typical fund-allocation process is a review by the financial department. To gain the approval of finance, a request for funds (for quality improvement, a new plant, or whatever) must meet the financial department's stringent investment requirements; in general this means the proposed investment must provide an adequate return with a manageable level of risk. To gain approval for an improvement effort, quality must be viewed as an investment.

Quality Investment Costs

The investment required by a quality effort is not small. Simply sending all employees—managers and workers—to a short course on the principles of quality consumes many man-hours. Equally large blocks of time can be consumed in devising ways to improve processes. Management time is required, too; Juran estimates that a quality improvement effort will add 10 percent to management's workload.[14]

Establishing a quality function in an organization requires an expenditure, but not a large one. Costs of installing quality include:

◆ Selling the organization on the importance and value of quality.

◆ Training each employee in the organization on quality fundamentals and providing special training to many.

◆ Stabilizing processes to make their performance consistent.

◆ Improving processes to make certain that products meet requirements consistently.

Quality Investment Benefits

When asked to describe the benefits of quality, people list many factors: better products, faster delivery time, improved quality of work life, improved employee satisfaction and morale, improved productivity, decreased inventory, reduced ab-

---

[14]Joseph M. Juran, "Catching Up: How Is the West Doing?" *Quality Progress*, November 1985, p. 21.

senteeism, reduced legal exposure from defective products, improved corporate image, improved status within the investment community, and so on. This is not an exhaustive list of benefits, nor does it precisely reflect the words used by various organizations, but it does reflect the tone of their remarks. The following example is typical of what people actually say.

> **Example.** According to Raymond L. Larkin, executive vice president, quality improvement at American Express produced benefits that "far surpassed our original objectives."[15] Specifically, quality improvement
>
> ◆ Sharpened the company's focus on the customer
>
> ◆ Improved productivity
>
> ◆ Contributed millions in increased profits
>
> ◆ Improved employee morale and pride in the company, their work, and themselves
>
> ◆ Provided a tremendous training experience, encompassing all functions and all products
>
> ◆ Improved the company's competitive edge

Quality Investment Evaluation

The rewards of quality are difficult to quantify, which is one reason they tend to be ignored. Incidentally, in Japan little effort is spent in attempting to justify quality; the Japanese are convinced that quality is the correct strategy, so why bother trying to prove the obvious? Certainly, their commercial success vindicates their faith in quality. Justification based on faith, however, is not likely to find much support in an American boardroom.

Managers who claim to base all management decisions on "hard facts" find it difficult to deal with the reality that many benefits of quality are hard to quantify. It might be fairly easy to estimate the reduction in production costs, but this benefit is only the tip of the iceberg—the part one measures because it is visible. How much is bad quality costing in loss of business? How many accounts have gone to competitors who offer faster service? less paperwork? correct bills? less required maintenance? a friendlier interface? How much will a quality effort reduce exposure to product liability claims?

One cannot expect to achieve "accounting-like" accuracy in assessing an investment in quality. Both risks and rewards depend heavily on the actions and reactions of people, making their analysis less predictable than that of, say, analyzing a buy-rent situation. One must take a broad view; doing so is more likely to lead to a correct decision than an attempt to narrow one's vision to aspects that can more readily be quantified.

---

[15]*Productivity Digest*, February 1988, p. 15.

◆ 3.6 Quality and Time

Time and Quality Improvement

Quality is an investment—you invest today and reap the benefits in the future. But how long does it take? How long before a quality improvement effort pays off?

A single improvement requires selecting a problem to tackle, determining the cause of the problem, devising a system change to remove the cause, gaining approval to make the change, installing it, and verifying that the change is effective. All of this could take anywhere from several days to several months. But after that the benefits start to accrue; just how large the benefits are depends on how frequent and devastating the error was. If the problem is well selected, the payoff should be very high—a relatively quick, profitable investment.

But this is only one incremental step on the quest for quality, one of many that must be made to have a significant effect on the overall operations of the enterprise. That's the nature of a quality improvement program. It is not a big, spectacular event, but just a large collection of little efforts. Quality improvement is like an army of ants devouring an elephant—one hardly notices the efforts of a single ant, but in time all that is left of the elephant are the bones.

Quality improvement takes time. Consider the Japanese experience. It started in 1945 when the American occupational forces told the Japanese to fix up their telephone service. Twenty years later they had established a quality leadership position in several industries. Thirty years later, their reputation for quality was well known to many American business leaders, whose markets had been taken over by Japanese firms. Forty years later, their reputation for quality was well known even to the American in the street.

The step-by-step nature of quality improvement doesn't fit well with the American temperament. Americans like spectacular events. They have little patience for plodding step after step toward a distant goal, and they are not excited to learn that quality improvement is like that. But it's a fact. To improve quality, top managers must understand the step-by-step nature of quality improvement and prepare the organization to live with this reality.

Top managers must take a long-term view of quality, not deviating from this direction because of momentary changes in the business cycle or corporate profits. If a quality improvement is interrupted, it's very difficult to go back and pick up the momentum. Often, restarting is worse than starting from scratch because one needs to overcome disappointment and disbelief generated by the interruption. Once started, a program should be continued at a constant pace. In the Japanese view, a quality improvement program is forever, and this is the only attitude to take.

Production Time and Quality

Not content with their commanding competitive advantage in being able to produce quality products, Japanese manufacturers have added another competitive strength—the ability to respond more quickly to the marketplace than their competitors.[16]

◆ Matsushita cut the time to build a washing machine from 360 hours to 2 hours.

◆ Toyota helped a supplier reduce the time to produce a component from 15 days to 1.

◆ Japanese producers can develop a plastic injection mold in one-third the time (and at one-third the cost) of U.S. competitors.

◆ Japan can develop a new automobile in half the time (and with half the people) required by U.S. and German competitors.

These reduced times allow companies to respond more quickly to customer demand, run a more flexible production line, and increase product innovation—usually cutting production costs in the bargain. Time reductions often are accomplished by speeding physical processes, but much of the improvement comes from speeding the information processes, which are a significant element of sales, order entry, design, production, and most other organizational efforts.

Not all success stories are Japanese. Atlas Door, an American company, produces industrial doors, a product with such variety that most manufacturing is done to order. As part of a concentrated effort to reduce the time to fill an order, Atlas streamlined and automated its order entry process. With the old system, it took more than a week to respond to a request for price and delivery date. With the new system, 95 percent of incoming orders can be priced and scheduled while the caller is still on the phone. This and similar time savings on the production floor means faster delivery of products; in turn, this advantage brings Atlas lower costs and allows them to command higher prices than competitors. It also has propelled Atlas to be the leading door supplier to 80 percent of their distributors.

A Singapore example of using information technology to speed processing is the Portnet system developed by the Port of Singapore Authority. Designed to handle the port entry documentation, the system greatly reduces the time and aggravation faced by a cargo owner in moving incoming cargo from the Port.

Before Portnet, a cargo owner checked the newspaper for ship arrival and then spent hours getting the necessary documents for cargo removal. These documents were then taken to the office of the shipping agent for endorsement. Next, the endorsed documents were lodged with the Port for physical pickup, which was usually delayed at the gate by customs which had to make a physical inspection of the cargo.

With Portnet, an electronic record of the shipment is created before the ship arrives. A cargo owner can check for his shipment availability by phone, create the

---

[16]The reference for this subsection is Claude W. Burrill, "IT and Time," *Information Technology*, Vol. 3, No. 2 (March 1990).

port entry document in his office, and send it electronically to the Port. Alerted by a phone call from the owner, the shipping agent can then endorse the document electronically. There is no need for the owner to leave his office except for physical pickup; even this is speeded up because the customs officer can inspect the electronic file. Any questionable cargo can be removed under customs seal and inspected later at the owner's premises, thereby cutting gate delays.

Benefits of Accelerating Processes

The goal of reducing processing time meshes well with the goal of improving product quality because both are achieved through process improvement. Both require analyzing the process and making changes—in one case to cut time, in the other to cut errors. It is well established that cutting errors will cut costs, and many examples show that cutting processing time also can cut costs. Thus, intelligent process improvements can lead to improved competitiveness in three dimensions: quality, time, and cost.

◆ 3.7 Quality Improvement Examples

We conclude this chapter with several examples that illustrate the benefits of quality.

Example 1.   Yokogawa-Hewlett-Packard (YHP), the Japanese subsidiary of Hewlett-Packard, won the Deming Prize in 1982. During the five years of preparation, it cut its manufacturing costs by 42 percent and its inventory by 64 percent. Failure rates went down 60 percent, the R&D cycle time was cut by more than a third, productivity doubled, and profits and market share improved by about a factor of three.

Spurred by YHP's example, in 1979 the parent company launched a decade-long effort to cut defects by 90 percent. Halfway into that effort, John A. Young, president and CEO of HP, cited a specific example of the improvement that effort produced. "In the U.S., we have improved the quality of our order processing. We now do a much better job of entering, filling, and billing orders. So now our customers pay us more promptly, and that shows in accounts receivable."

In 1978, accounts were outstanding for an average of 62 days; by 1985, this had been cut to an average of 54 days. That improvement alone benefited HP by more than $100 million.[17]

---

[17]John A. Young, "Teamwork is More Easily Praised than Practiced," *Quality Progress,* August 1985, p. 31.

Example 2. Texas Instruments Defense Systems & Electronic Group (TI-DSEG) is the nation's eighth largest defense electronics contractor. It started a quality improvement effort in 1983 with four pilot teams. Today there are more than 1900 teams consisting of employees from all units and levels. Because of team efforts, the number of customer-conducted quality audits has decreased by 72 percent since 1987, and the number of formal complaints has decreased by 62 percent since 1988. In a customer survey, TI-DSEG topped its main competitors in all 11 customer satisfaction categories, including cost-effective pricing, technology deployment, and product support. In addition, revenues per worker increased from about $80,000 in 1987 to more than $125,000 in 1991.[18]

Example 3. IBM Federal Systems Company in Houston derives 98 percent of its revenue from providing complex information processing systems for NASA. IBM's version of total quality management includes a goal of 6-sigma quality, or 3.4 defects per million units. The quality of the software it provides to NASA has improved steadily, dropping from a defect rate of two errors per thousand lines of code in 1983 to almost no errors today. In February 1993 it stated, "The last two systems delivered to NASA contained no errors at all."[19]

Example 4. The George Washington University Medical Center (GWUMC) in Washington, D.C., began its quality improvement initiative in the spring of 1989. Among its accomplishments thus far are a reduction in the accounts receivable turnaround by 20 days, a $75,000 annual saving in linen expenditures, and a dramatic improvement in patient perceptions of care and attention. Written complaints to the hospital decreased steadily, and waiting time in pre-admissions surgical-screening services decreased from several hours to an average of 50 minutes.[20]

Example 5. The Research and Engineering Department at Lockheed Fort Worth Company identified the root causes of problems and applied corrective action to prevent their reoccurrence. As a result, the in-process rejection rate fell from 35 percent in July 1990 to 3 percent in July 1991. Final product rejections decreased from 3.5 percent in July 1990 to 0 percent in July 1991. Scrap and rework costs were reduced from $14,000 per month in May 1990 to $800 per month in August 1991.[21]

---

[18]Karen Bemowski, "Ceremony Honors the 1992 Baldrige Award Recipients," *Quality Progress*, February 1993, p. 29.

[19]Suzanne Axland, "NASA's Low Award Recognizes High Quality," *Quality Progress*, February 1993, p. 34.

[20]Roger L. Chaufournier and Christine St. Andre, "Total Quality Management in an Academic Health Center," *Quality Progress*, April 1993, p. 65.

[21]James L. Boteler, "Using Prevention Techniques," *Quality Progress*, July 1993, p. 107.

Example 6. North American Life, a Canadian company, began an improvement effort several years ago. Virtually everyone participated in quality improvement teams, which examined the way processes worked, challenged the status quo, and found ways to make the processes work more effectively. These teams saved the company millions of dollars and improved its ability to respond to customers' needs in a more effective and timely manner. The company has now decided to include several higher-purpose objectives in its list of business objectives. These objectives aim to improve Canada and society as a whole.[22]

Example 7. George Westinghouse Vocational and Technical High School is the largest vocational and technical high school in New York City. The school had most of the problems of an inner-city school: a high dropout rate, an aging faculty, students entering with poor reading and math skills, unmotivated students, and students with low self-esteem and a history of failure. In 1988, the school decided to use TQM techniques to help them respond to these educational challenges. As a result, class cutting was reduced by 39.9 percent in a six-week period. A group of 151 students who had failed every class was identified at the beginning of 1991; six months later, only 11 of that group were failing. As a result of promoting quality concepts, students have become more involved in after-school activities; membership in the PTA grew from 12 to 211 members; requests for admission to Westinghouse have increased, with more than 10 applicants for each seat; and several New York colleges have agreed to run a coordinated program with Westinghouse. Probably the greatest success is that Ricoh Corporation signed a partnership agreement with the school, and in September 1993 Westinghouse students began learning to repair Ricoh copy machines.[23]

Example 8. Every employee at Ames Rubber Corporation, a 1993 Baldrige Award winner, is involved in the company's quality efforts. Over the past five years, employee ideas have saved the company more than $3 million; in 1993, the savings averaged more than $2700 per employee.[24]

Example 9. University Microfilms, Inc. of Ann Arbor, Michigan, has a 75-employee division that puts dissertations on microfilm. This division started a quality improvement effort in 1988. By 1992, production had increased 168 percent, shipping errors had decreased 41 percent, cycle time had decreased 77 percent—and workers were 25 percent more productive.[25]

---

[22]William E. Bradford, "Quality: Canadian's Shared Mission," *Quality Progress*, October 1993, p. 27.

[23]Franklin P. Schargel, "Total Quality in Education," *Quality Progress*, October 1993, p. 68.

[24]Karen Bemowski, "The Quality Forum IX: Breaking with Tradition," *Quality Progress*, December 1993, p. 45.

[25]Bruce M. Sheridan, "Changing Service Quality in America," *Ibid.*, p. 99.

◆ Exercises and Additional Readings

1. From your collection of articles on quality (see Exercise 1, Chapter 1), give some examples of the value of implementing quality. What lesson can you learn from these articles?

2. Lee Iacocca, CEO of the Chrysler Corporation, in his autobiography states: "Quality and productivity are two sides of the same coin. Everything you do for quality improves your productivity." Do you agree with this statement? Can you give examples where (a) quality improves at the expense of productivity, and (b) vice versa?

3. Quality can differentiate a company from its competitors; reinforce dealer loyalty; and generate sales leads. List other benefits of quality not described in this chapter.

4. Read "Advertising Quality" in *Quality Progress*, June 1986, p. 57, and summarize the link between advertising and the perception of quality.

5. Read the section on Life-cycle Costs in J. M. Juran and Frank M. Gryna, Jr., *Quality Planning and Analysis*, 3rd ed. (New York: McGraw-Hill Book Co., 1993), pp. 89–90. Discuss how product quality impacts life-cycle costs and purchasing decisions.

6. Read *Datamation*, June 1, 1986, p. 123, which describes an incorrect credit report issued by Dun and Bradstreet. What was the cost of this quality problem? What important principle regarding faulty data did the Supreme Court ruling imply?

7. Read and summarize the account in *New Scientist*, May 19, 1988, p. 39, of the Sylvia Robins suit against Unisys and Rockwell concerning a quality problem. This story is about software quality and "whistle blowing"; it triggered a subsequent congressional investigation.

8. Read the report in *Quality Progress*, March 1994, pp. 16–18, of a two-year study of 100 contractors. Summarize the impact that the failure to adhere to quality standards had on contractors' profit margins.

9. Read Karen Bemowski, "Ceremony Honors the 1992 Baldrige Award Winners," *Quality Progress*, February 1993, p. 27. Summarize the benefits gained from the quality efforts at the five companies described in the article.

10. Read Ellen Chesney, Joan Dickenson, Anita Lawrence, and Cathy Talmanis, "Improving Health Care on a Tight Budget," *Quality Progress*, April 1993, pp. 25–28. Describe the benefits that resulted from Burnaby Hospital's six-step quality improvement initiative.

11. Read Dwight Kirscht and Jennifer M. Tunnel, "Boise Cascade Stakes a Claim on Quality," *Quality Progress*, November 1993, p. 91. This paper describes the Boise Cascade Timber and Wood Products Division system for scheduling trucks. Describe the benefits of the improvement program that the company conducted.

12. Read Michael E. Berkin, "Dun and Bradstreet Conducts Operation Clean Slate," *Quality Progress*, November 1993, p. 105. Describe the benefits that accrued from a quality improvement effort at Dun & Bradstreet Information Services.

13. Read Frank S. Leonard and W. Earl Sasser, "The Incline of Quality," *Harvard Business Review* (September/October 1982): 163–171. (a) What were the seven major areas of concern about quality within Polaroid? (b) Discuss briefly Polaroid's response to these problems. From this article, give examples showing that quality improvement led to increased productivity.

14. Read John Ryan, "The Productivity/Quality Connection—Plugging in at Westinghouse Electric," *Quality Progress*, December 1983, p. 26. How does Westinghouse's Conditions of Excellence for Quality enhance both quality and productivity?

15. By writing *Quality Is Free*, Phil Crosby did as much as anyone to alert the United States to the importance of quality. However, some people, including these authors, believe that the title of his book is misleading. Is quality really free? Give reasons for your answer.

16. There are always risks associated with management actions, including a quality improvement program. Discuss possible risks and address ways of reducing these risks.

17. Obtain the annual reports of several manufacturing companies that are listed on the stock exchange. You can get this information from a local stockbroker. Discuss the companies' emphasis on quality.

18. Review the main components of the Japanese quality strategy.

19. Interview managers at several local companies (production as well as service companies). Review their quality strategies and ask them to assess the value of quality as an investment and the time it takes to realize the benefits.

20. Using examples, discuss the three components of the cost of quality. Which costs are usually the most difficult to obtain?

21. Give several examples of products and their associated life-cycle costs.

22. One of your major competitors just invested in some equipment that will improve the quality of a product he offers to customers. You are now faced with making a similar investment so that you can match his quality level. Discuss how your investment might lead to (a) lower reported earnings; (b) higher reported earnings.

23. Use an internet browser to search for information on the cost of quality. Summarize your findings and review how they relate to the discussion in this chapter.

People and Quality

In my experience, people can face almost any problem except the problems of people.
—W. Edwards Deming[1]

Fundamentally, quality improvement involves two sets of issues: technical issues and people issues. The bulk of the literature on quality deals with technical elements; but, as the above comment by Deming indicates, the difficult problems are those that deal with people. This chapter introduces the various quality stakeholders and describes briefly their roles and concerns. In later chapters, we will discuss ideas and techniques on how to work with people so as to improve quality.

◆ 4.1 Customers and Quality

Marketing people have a saying: "It all starts with a sale." "It" certainly can refer to quality. If there were no customers for a product—if nobody were to buy, use, or in some way be influenced by a product—would it really matter if the product functioned properly, appeared as it should, or offered the designated service?

---

[1]W. Edwards Deming, *Out of the Crisis* (Cambridge, Mass.: Massachusetts Institute of Technology, Center for Advanced Engineering Study, 1986), p. 85.

Who Is the Customer?

A *customer* is a person who receives or uses a product. The customer might also be called a *patient* if the provider were a doctor or dentist, a *client* if the provider were a lawyer or architect, a *passenger* if the provider were an airline, or a *patron* if the provider were an artist. Nonetheless, *customer* would more or less do for all.

There are three sets of customers for most products, and it is important that all three be considered in any discussion of quality.

One is the set of *external customers*. This set consists of people outside the producing organization who typically pay for the products they receive. Examples of external customers are those who buy cars from a car dealer or from a used car lot, those who buy meals in restaurants, and the patrons who attend concerts.

Generally, there are many external customers for a product. For example, consider this book you are reading. You certainly are a customer for the book. If the book is being used for a class, other external customers include the professor who teaches the class, the bookstore that bought the book from the publisher, and the parents who paid for the book.

A second set of customers comprises the *internal customers*. These are people within the producing organization who are supplied products that they use in performing their job. Shipping is the customer of production, which is the customer of sales. And most parts of an organization are customers of the Information Systems Department, which builds and operates their information systems.

Use of the word "customer" in this context is somewhat unnatural; most people apply it to the final purchaser of a product—the retail customer. Some might prefer the word "user" for the next person or process, but the use of "customer" is fairly well embedded in the quality literature. The important point here is not the term but the concept: We are talking about *all* products, not just final assemblies, and we are talking about *all* the people who use these products.

A third set of customers for a product is *society*. It consists of all people who are not internal or external customers but are nevertheless impacted by it. This group includes a neighbor who might be annoyed by the noise of your lawn mower, the public that might be injured by your car, and the community that is impacted by environmental damage, health hazards, and other community problems caused by the products you use.

For years, producers paid little attention to the wider concerns of society. This situation has changed dramatically in recent years. Many producers now openly recognize that society at large must be considered as a customer for their products. And, of course, many laws and regulations have been enacted to prevent damage to society that is caused by inappropriate products. This topic will be discussed further in Section 4.8.

Serving Customers

An organization must establish policies, methods, procedures, and instructions for serving its various customers. But quality actions cannot be reduced to a set of rules, particularly for service products. Rules and formal instructions help by establishing procedures for meeting customer requirements, but delivering quality products also requires a proper attitude. A good summary is the golden rule: "Do unto others as you would have them do unto you." Such an attitude will help to provide good products in situations that could never be anticipated in a book of rules.

The following story illustrates how important it is to understand the concept of quality, as contrasted with simply following a checklist of quality actions.

> *I read (a story) in the* New York Times *Op Ed page a while back. Judging from her name and parts of the story, the author was American, the wife of a Japanese businessman working in the States. The story concerned a problem with a purchase—a VCR, as I recall—they made at a leading Japanese department store while in Japan on a visit. The clerk, new to the job, inadvertently sold them a display machine that was only a shell; it had no internal mechanism. Only when they got to their in-laws and tried to demonstrate it did the couple discover that the machine did not work. By then, the department store was closed, so all they (the Japanese husband, in particular) could do was fume until morning.*
>
> *Meanwhile, the store had discovered the error and started a frantic search for the couple. They had a name from the credit card receipt, so [they] called all the major hotels within fifty miles of Tokyo. But, of course, to no avail since the couple was staying with their in-laws. The store then waited for American Express to open in New York (which was in the middle of the night in Japan). From them they obtained the number of the couple's New York apartment, and eventually contacted someone there who supplied the couple's Tokyo address. Early the day after the error had been committed, it was rectified with profuse apology and a small gift to help right the wrong that had been inflicted.[2]*

Obviously, quality had become a way of life for the Japanese store. The store had no specific procedure for dealing with this particular unusual problem; its action had to be based on principle, not procedure. Its response to the problem indicates a deep-seated belief in providing quality service and a high standard for that service.

◆ 4.2 Managers and Quality

The responsibility of managers is to set objectives for the organization, establish a structure whereby objectives can be achieved, plan for production, authorize performance of the required tasks, lead the efforts, and check the results.

---

[2]Claude W. Burrill, "Quality, Value, and Profit," *International Journal of Value-Based Management*, Vol. 1, No. 1 (1988), p. 65.

Quality is an important part of this responsibility, and every management action has some bearing on quality. To carry out their quality responsibility, managers must understand the meaning of quality, the benefits of quality, their role in achieving quality, and what they must do to carry out that role. They must then make a commitment to quality and back that commitment with actions.

Part of managers' responsibility is to make certain everyone in the organization understands the commitment to quality and has proper training in quality concepts. Managers also must monitor the quality system to see that it is operating properly and that it is being improved continually.

The single most important factor in the success of a quality program is top management's attitude and support. Having a positive attitude often requires a change in management perception and practice—a change from an old concept that quality is achieved by controlling employees and checking products to a new concept that quality involves empowerment and process improvement. And this change is not easily made by many top managers.

Basic Beliefs

The quality of an organization's products depends fundamentally on its basic beliefs. If the organization does not have a fundamental belief in striving for quality in everything it does, it will likely not achieve a reputation for quality. Top management must believe in quality and must clearly articulate this basic belief to all concerned individuals.

Simply stating a belief in quality will not make it happen, however. Quality requires the combined effort of everyone in the organization; it can be achieved only if all employees strive in that direction. But employees who are badly treated, distrusted, tightly controlled, and have no job security are unlikely to identify with the organization or be greatly concerned with its goals. For employees to "sign on" to the quality policy, they must have a feeling that their well-being is tied to that of the organization.

Achieving quality requires not only a basic belief in quality, but also a basic belief in people. If people are treated with humanity and respect, if the organization has concern for their happiness and well-being, then people will take pride in their work and work products. With proper procedures, training, and guidance, they will produce quality products.

Frequently, companies that embark on a quality program express their commitment with a phrase indicating that the customer comes first. One who took a different tack is Hal F. Rosenbluth, chief executive officer of Rosenbluth, Inc., a worldwide travel agency headquartered in Philadelphia.

> *Our secret is controversial. It centers around our basic belief that companies must put their people—not their customers first.*
>
> *You might wonder how our clients feel about this. For our people, the clients are priority number one. Our company has built a solid reputation in the field of customer service (in fact, our client retention rate is 96 percent), but we have actually done it by focusing inside, on our own people.*

> *Companies have profound and far-reaching effects on the lives of the peo-*
> *ple who work for them, so it becomes the obligation of companies to make the*
> *effects positive. All too often companies bring stress, fear, and frustration to*
> *their people—feelings they bring home with them each night. This creates prob-*
> *lems at home which people bring back to work in the morning. The cycle is*
> *both terrible and typical, but not what most companies would want as their*
> *legacy. It's certainly not what our company wants; especially when there are*
> *so many things we can all do to enrich the lives of our people.[3]*

Rosenbluth Travel practices what it preaches, and the results are startling. In addition to happy, loyal employees, it showed "7,500% growth in revenue over the
past fifteen years (from $20 million to $1.5 billion), while maintaining profitability
above industry standards."[4] Rosenbluth's approach to quality may seem unusual to
you but not to Ishikawa. He states that "In management, the first concern of the
company is the happiness of people who are connected with it. . . . Consumers
come next."[5]

Direction

One specific task of management is to set a direction for the organization. This involves establishing the purpose, mission, policies, strategy, priorities, and goals. All
of these have a strong impact on the quality of the products the organization provides its customers. Management might express a basic belief in quality, but the
test of its commitment is how well this belief is supported by the direction the organization takes. And what the formal documents say is not nearly as important
as what takes place in practice.

Making a sincere commitment to quality has a tremendous impact on an organization. Ishikawa describes this impact as "a thought revolution in management."[6]
A sincere commitment to quality requires a complete rethinking of the organization's statements of direction, and any change in direction will reverberate throughout the organization.

Processes and Structure

To make an organization's beliefs and intentions effective, they must be backed
by appropriate processes and an effective organizational structure. Included in the
organizational structure should be an effective Quality Assurance (QA) group whose
mission is to support management's efforts to achieve quality.

---

[3]Hal F. Rosenbluth and Diane McFerrin Peters, *The Customer Comes Second* (New York: William Morrow,
1992), p. 9.

[4]Ibid., p. 9.

[5]Kaoru Ishikawa, *What Is Total Quality Control?*, translated by David J. Lu (Englewood Cliffs, N.J.: Prentice
Hall, 1985), p. 97.

[6]Ibid., p. 44.

Plans

Management also must establish targets for the organization, build plans for achieving these targets, and allocate resources for the effort. The importance of quality to the organization is revealed by examining the results of this planning effort: Is there a comprehensive plan for quality? Does it provide for quality improvement? Was the plan for quality developed by line management? Does it mesh with plans for products, personnel, plant, and other major aspects of the organization? Is the quality function properly staffed and funded?

Education and Training

To achieve quality, proper education and training of all employees is vital. "Quality starts with education and ends with education."[7]

Everyone in an organization needs clear instruction for doing their job and training in how to do it. In particular, they need training in concepts of quality, and the use of tools and techniques for doing quality work, for checking that their work products are correct, and for making improvement in their work processes. They also need guidance in performing their work and feedback on how well they are doing.

Practice

What an organization says it does and what it actually does do not always agree. Theory is interesting, but practice is what counts.

- ◆ Do people really believe management is committed to quality? Is the company leader a champion and spokesperson for quality?
- ◆ Is the Quality Plan realistic, and sufficiently ambitious? Is it enabled with sufficient resources? management attention?
- ◆ Do managers at all levels understand and communicate the quality message? Do they have responsibility for educating and nurturing subordinates?
- ◆ Is there an adversarial relationship between management and labor? Are workers afraid to tell management the truth?
- ◆ Is the reward system supportive of the quality objectives? Do rewards go to those who "put out fires" rather than those who prevent them?

---

[7]Ibid., p. 13.

◆ 4.3 Quality Assurance[8]

In a very small organization, the top manager is responsible for everything from the quality function to cleaning the toilets. But in an organization with several levels of management, any serious attempt to produce quality products requires a special group of quality professionals to aid in that effort. This *Quality Assurance* (QA) group serves as a focal point for quality matters.

Quality Assurance must report directly to the CEO; this gives it the independence needed to be effective. It should be staffed with competent, knowledgeable professionals who understand both the technical and human aspects of quality. Members of this group should be viewed as consultants, advisers, and trainers who are there to help everyone in the organization produce quality products. Among the duties of QA are:

- ◆ To assist top management in formulating and implementing a quality program.
- ◆ To provide education and assistance in the organization's efforts to install a quality system.
- ◆ To serve as an interface to external organizations on matters concerning quality.

The selection, training, and importance given to quality professionals have a considerable impact on the quality program. The impact is twofold: Better quality professionals will give better advice, and better treatment of quality professionals will elevate them in the eyes of all employees, thereby giving them more clout. The attention given to a quality program in an organization is directly proportional to the respect people have for the vice president of quality.

Several questions can be asked about the quality function of an organization:

- ◆ Is quality the job of the quality professionals, or is it everybody's job?
- ◆ Are the quality professionals policemen or advisers?
- ◆ If you are a misfit on the job, are you likely to be made a quality professional?
- ◆ Are you afraid the actions of the quality professionals will prevent you from getting a raise?
- ◆ How is quality control integrated with cost control and control of delivery date?
- ◆ Does the quality movement concentrate on the factory floor, or does it also encompass the office? information systems? management? marketing? suppliers? other areas?

---

[8]Quality Assurance is discussed further in Chapter 15.

◆ 4.4 Workers and Quality

Three basic actions of workers have a direct impact on the quality of their products. Their first impact is in producing the product. Do they "build quality in"? That is, do they produce products that meet their established requirements? Their second impact on quality is in performing quality control. Do they adequately check the products they produce? Their third impact is on the processes they use to produce products. Do they continually attempt to improve their work processes—the methods, procedures, and techniques they use in producing their products?

Workers are heavily dependent on the organization to provide suitable facilities and resources to perform these quality-related tasks. In outline, this is what they need:

◆ An environment that fosters work—workers require respect from management, a cheerful workplace, and appropriate intrinsic and extrinsic rewards.

◆ Proper and stable work processes—workers require an effective process for producing the output required of them.

◆ Properly defined work requirements—workers must understand what they are to produce and their responsibility for producing it.

◆ Effective plans and controls—there must be an appropriate plan to guide their efforts and appropriate checks to verify the quality of their output.

◆ Adequate resources—workers need proper education and training to perform the tasks expected of them, appropriate time to do the work, and the tools and materials needed to do the job.

What workers also need is management's meaningful consideration of their ideas and suggestions about all the items just listed. It is a mistake for management to build the work environment, work processes, work requirements, the planning and control system, and then to allocate resources without input from the people who do the work. The people who do the work know more about it than management does; their suggestions often will lead to better products and reduced costs. But a larger reason for listening to the workers is to gain their commitment to the production effort. It is much easier to "buy into" a production system you helped to shape than one that is imposed on you without regard for your views.

Workers need a well-defined job with the elements just listed, but this alone does not satisfy their wants. Workers are no different than managers. They want security, not the fear of losing their job or the onus of being blamed for defects that are the result of a faulty process. They want work satisfaction and pride in what they are doing. They want a reasonable reward for what they have done—not only a reasonable financial reward, but also reasonable recognition that they can display to their friends and family. And they want a career; in their later years they would like to look back on what they have done with satisfaction.

How well management promotes quality by providing a proper workplace and satisfying the wants of their workers can be ascertained by asking questions such as these:

- Do people take pride in their work?

- Can people make full use of their abilities?

- Do people feel they need to hide defective workmanship to avoid getting a "black mark"? Do they omit tests or falsify test results out of fear?

- Do people feel secure in their jobs? Do they view new technology as a threat?

- Is turnover excessively high? Do people leave as soon as they can find another job?

- Are people proud to tell others for whom they work? Do they encourage their friends to join the organization?

Teamwork

Teamwork is required in all organizations; it is essential for production and for quality improvement. In many organizations it flourishes; these are organizations where management trusts workers, empowers them to use their brains, not just their brawn, and values their experience and ideas. As with many factors affecting quality, effective teamwork depends on the basic beliefs of management.

How well management is promoting teamwork in the organization can be ascertained by asking questions such as the following.

- Do teams help to combine the efforts of all employees in achieving quality?

- Does the reward system stifle teamwork?

- Are teams empowered to make decisions concerning their work processes, or must mangement approve every action?

- Is management more concerned with the number of improvement teams in the organization than their accomplishments? Are the accomplishments akin to rearranging the deck chairs on the Titanic?

- Are improvement teams properly formed, properly trained, and properly empowered to be effective?

- Are employees enthusiastic about participating in improvement teams?

- Is there competition or cooperation among departments and divisions?

- Do quality improvement efforts extend across departmental lines?

◆ 4.5 The Work Environment

The Workplace

The formal basic beliefs of management are stated in a document, but the actual basic beliefs are revealed by what is practiced in the workplace. Basic beliefs are reflected in the organizational structure, distribution of power, and matters that receive the most management attention. Moreover, the actual basic beliefs are most clearly seen in emergency situations.

An example of poor work environment facing many Americans in the 1980s is illustrated by an incident that occurred on the General Motors assembly line at that time.

There were other things that gnawed at us. For instance, I remember one night they stuck this old woman down on the Rivet Line. It was ridiculous, just another example of GM's total aimless approach in evaluating the capabilities and limitations of a given worker. The Rivet Line was simply no place for such an old gal. The (rivet) guns were heavy and very temperamental. The sensible thing to do would have been to place the old woman up in Trim or the Final Line.

On her second day down on the chain-hitch job, the old woman walloped her head on a rivet gun, knocking herself senseless and straight to the floor. She lay there sprawled beneath the crawl of the carriages like a rag doll. Immediately one of the guys ran over and pushed the stop button and shut down the line.

Uh-oh. The red alert. If for whatever reason you wanted to mobilize a frantic bunch of white-collar power thugs in the direction of your area, nothing worked as well as pushing that sacred stop button. They'd come swoopin' outta the rafters like hawks on a bunny. Within thirty seconds, every tie within a 300-yard radius was on the scene—demanding answers, squawkin' into walkie-talkies, huffin' and puffin' like the universe had flipped over on their windpipes.

What a pathetic display of compassion this turned out to be. While this little old woman lay crumpled beneath the crawling frame carriers, all these nervous pricks wanted to know was WHO IN THE HELL TURNED THIS LINE OFF?[9]

Quality Programs

Quality in an organization starts with a management commitment. Making a commitment is easy; making the commitment a reality is not. Unfortunately, many organizations make a sincere commitment to quality, start an improvement effort that turns out to be ineffective, and end up setting back true quality improvement by several years.

It requires an effective quality program to gain the commitment of all the employees, teach them fundamental ideas and techniques, and make organizational changes needed to install quality improvements. However, some programs have more of a circus atmosphere than the appearance of a serious, dedicated management effort. They attract attention but have no substance. Employees usually see these crude efforts for what they are—a management gimmick. An example is a device GM used in the 1980s to interest employees in quality improvement.

[9]Ben Hamper, *Rivethead* (New York: Warner Books, 1991), p. 110.

The GM Truck & Bus plan began fiddling with various Quality-minded plots as a means to enthuse the work force. . . . The management at the Truck Plant decided what the Quality concept really needed was a mascot. Conceived in a moment of sheer visionary enlightenment, the plan was to dress up the mascot as a large cat. Fittingly, this rat-in-cat's clothing was to be called Quality Cat. Somewhere along the line, an even more brilliant mind upstairs decided Quality Cat was sort of a dull title. Therefore, a contest was organized in an attempt to give the Quality Cat a more vital name.

. . . The eventual winner of the contest was a worker who stumbled upon the inspired moniker Howie Makem. Sadly, my intriguing entry, Wando Kwit, finished way the hell down the list somewhere right between Roger's Pussy and Tuna Meowt.[10]

Opinions about Howie varied. Here are a few:

Do they really think I'll perform a better job with a huge cat lurchin' over me? If they really want to charge up all these boneheads, why not bring in some Playboy Bunnies? I'm thirty years old, not thirteen.

Christ, what's next? They'll probably bring in Fred Rogers to pass out balloons and lollipops.

I don't find anything the least bit humorous about having some suck-ass in a cat's costume roamin' through my place of work. What they are tellin' us is that we are so retarded growth-wise that all we can relate to are characters along the lines of Saturday morning cartoon figures. Bring out Bozo! Hail Huckleberry Hound.

My fondest wish is that Howie gets his tail snagged in the chin gear and is mercilessly ground into Kibbles & Bits.[11]

Howie Makem might have relieved some of the tedium of the production line, but do you think he showed that GM had much respect for their employees? Did Howie suggest a serious commitment by GM to quality?

Quality and Office Politics

Quality improvement efforts are also subject to office politics. As an example, the quality professionals of one large blue-chip company planned a large educational effort to introduce quality concepts to the various levels of management. Unfortunately for them, the financial people also were planning a similar educational effort to introduce a new system for making financial decisions. Management wasn't ready to give up time for two courses, so the word came down that the

---

[10]Ibid., p. 112.

[11]Ibid., pp. 113, 114.

two courses should be combined into one. Finance, the older, more entrenched group, volunteered to add quality modules to their course. This offer was accepted, so the financial people gave management their introduction to quality. You can guess the results. Perhaps it is a coincidence, but half-a dozen years later the blue-chip company had lost much of its luster in the marketplace.

Office politics is a strong influence on the direction an organization takes. Entrenched groups rightly recognize that the quality movement might gain political clout at their expense. No matter how compelling the case for quality, a quality improvement effort will not succeed unless it is backed by a force that is persuasive and knows how to deal with organizational politics.

◆ 4.6 Suppliers and Quality

A *supplier* is a person who provides a product to a customer. A supplier might be called a *producer, builder, provider, vendor,* or a multitude of other terms. Just as there are internal and external customers, so there are internal and external suppliers.

Internal Suppliers

An *internal supplier* is any person or group in the organization that supplies a product to an internal customer. Engineering Design is a supplier to Production, who is a supplier to Sales.

It's hard to think of anyone in a large organization who is not an internal supplier, but it is very easy to find people who have never thought of themselves in this light. In many organizations, people view themselves simply as employees—they just do what they are told. They view their internal customers as fellow workers who, like them, are trying to make a living. If there are problems, it's because management doesn't run things properly. Not everyone has this attitude, but it is far from uncommon. Is this attitude the fault of the workers or the fault of management?

One large change wrought by the modern quality movement is a greater focus on internal customer/supplier relationships. With empowerment and proper training, people soon learn to identify all of their internal customers, determine their requirements, devise ways to meet these requirements, and obtain from their own suppliers the required inputs. This effort is necessary for an organization to function smoothly. Conceptually, it is a simple task; in practice, it can take much time and effort to put an effective system in place, and constant maintenance to keep it running properly.

Another common problem in organizations is that, by inhibiting communication, the chain of command in an organization can adversely impact quality. To illustrate this, assume that a college instructor needs a change in lighting in the classroom for a certain course she is teaching. She approaches the custodian, who says he can make the change but not without proper authorization. Typically, the custodian reports through a chain of command that leads to the administrative vice president, and the instructor's chain leads to the academic vice president. The two chains of command merge in the office of the president, but nobody thinks the president should be bothered with such a trivial problem as altering lighting in a certain classroom. So who should make the decision? The course might well be over before such a weighty matter is decided.

External Suppliers

An *external supplier* (also referred to as a *subcontractor* or as a *vendor*) is anyone outside the organization that supplies products to it. This could be a physical product, such as raw materials, parts, components, and subassemblies; or a service product, such as cafeteria services, cleaning, information processing, and accounting; or an information product such as newspapers and tax regulations. On average, American manufacturers purchase about 50 percent of their production cost from external suppliers.[12]

Traditionally, organizations have dealt with their external suppliers at arms length. Contracts were negotiated by the purchasing department with the assistance of the legal department to verify that contracts were binding on the external supplier and that terms were as favorable as possible to the purchasing organization. At times, the finance department reviewed contracts so that it could keep an eye on costs. The customer–supplier relationship was not regarded as a long-term involvement; commitment was only for the period specified in the contract. The traditional relationship definitely could not be called a partnership.

In most organizations, standard practice was to source products from several external suppliers. This encouraged competition on price and prevented the organization from being held hostage to a strike or a disaster that might befall a single source. Products received from external suppliers were inspected by the receiving department; sometimes inspection was by sampling, sometimes 100 percent.

Traditionally, product quality was never as important as price in a purchasing decision and generally not as important as on-time delivery. Sometimes an external supplier's suggestions about product requirements were considered, but generally product requirements were fixed before a proposal was put out for bid. It was not common practice for an external supplier to talk directly to the real customers and learn what they wanted; discussion was with the purchasing department, and requirements were fixed in the request for price quotation.

---

[12]Kaoru Ishikawa, *What is Total Quality Control?*, translated by David J. Lu (Englewood Cliffs, N.J.: Prentice-Hall, 1985), p. 152.

Partnerships

The traditional method of dealing with external suppliers is still widely practiced in the United States. However, many organizations that are striving for quality have replaced this hands-off approach with one of a *partnership*. These organizations recognize that the quality of their products depends largely on the quality of the products they receive from their external suppliers. And they have learned they are more likely to receive quality products if the customer-supplier relationship is based on cooperation and trust.

Customers want quality products at a fair price. External suppliers want a profitable, continuing business opportunity. By having a cooperative instead of an adversarial relationship, both parties can gain what they desire.

To build partnerships, customers and external suppliers work together closely and reveal information that traditionally was considered confidential. For example, in addition to the traditional product requirements, the customer might reveal how the product is used. External suppliers are prepared to show customers their processes as well as their products. The two work together to improve the design of the supplier's products.

Often the new customer–supplier partnership causes a change in the supplier's delivery of the product. Packaging might be changed to make it more convenient for the customer; or small quantity, just-in-time shipments might be made to reduce the customer's need for inventory storage space. This new partnership also allows for a change in the way customers determine the quality of incoming supplies. Instead of inspecting products, customers can inspect the external supplier's quality system. This examination covers all policies and processes that affect quality: the external supplier's quality policy, process for designing, building, and inspecting the product, the employee training process, and so on. If the quality system is satisfactory, the customer can be reasonably confident that the external supplier's products will meet requirements consistently.

Because this new approach of customers toward external suppliers builds lasting relationships, it is essential to select external suppliers carefully, know them well, and develop understanding and trust. All of this takes time and effort, but the rewards are better products and a more dependable supply. For the supplier, the reward is a satisfied customer and the prospect of repeat business: a win-win relationship.

The Japanese were first to develop this new approach to the customer–supplier relationship. More recently, this approach has been widely adopted as the basis for the European ISO 9000 quality initiative. But the basic idea of developing strong ties between the two is not new.

> *In the days of main-frame computing, IBM built its business very largely on the practice of being a dependable supplier that went beyond the contract terms to help customers. For example, every Data Processing (DP) Manager knew that in the event of a disaster, say a fire or a flood, they could depend on IBM to send needed equipment and an army of support personnel to get the "shop" running again; and the close relationship between IBM and its customers fa-*

cilitated such assistance. What most DP managers were buying from IBM in that period was security and assurance of support, not just equipment. One factor that contributed to IBM's decline in recent years is that the risk of a disaster is not as great in the era of smaller computers and distributed computing, so a close customer-supplier relationship is less important to the DP Manager.

Here is another example of the benefits that can accrue to a external supplier from building a close relationship.

In the early 1980's, Sanyo Manufacturing Corporation (a Japanese company) purchased from Warwick Electronics Corp. a facility in Forrest City, Ark. that manufactured television sets. This facility relied on an outside vendor to supply the cardboard boxes in which the television sets were shipped. At first, Sanyo was not pleased:

"The Japanese managers were shocked by the quality of those cardboard boxes. There were imperfections in the cardboard, the letters printed on them were often uneven, and the color (all the printing is done in 'Sanyo blue') wasn't uniform."

To correct the situation, the Japanese managers went to their supplier and told him they wanted perfect boxes. The supplier told them it could not be done; or, if done, it would cost a fortune. The managers then told the supplier to supply perfect boxes or they would get a different supplier. With this pistol to his head, the supplier agreed to try.

"So I [the supervisor of incoming inspection at the Warwick plant] worked with them for over a year, and by the end of that time they were producing boxes that met our specifications. Recently Sharp and Toshiba [two major Japanese companies] set up plants in Memphis and Lebanon, Tennessee, respectively, and this company went to them and said, "We can make perfect boxes. Sanyo buys all their boxes from us. Why don't you?" They got the business and now they're telling me, "Thanks for showing us that we can make boxes to Japanese standards."[13]

◆ 4.7 Stockholders and Quality

For many organizations, another important group involved with the company are the public stockholders. Stockholders have two basic requirements:

◆ High return on their investment in the form of dividends and stock appreciation

◆ Low risk and no unpleasant surprises

---

[13]Harvard Business School Case 9-682-045 (1981, Rev. 8/86), "Sanyo Manufacturing Corporation—Forest City, Arkansas," p. 5.

A properly executed quality program can help to achieve both of these objectives.

An emphasis on quality can bring a decrease in cost and increase in market share. Ceteris paribus, these improvements will result in higher earnings per share. Stock appreciation should follow.

A quality program will have little impact on risks that arise from outside the producing organization, such as war, riots, acts of God, and a sudden shift in consumer taste. But it can help to lessen the risks that arise from internal actions, such as unscheduled downtime that impacts delivery to customers, faulty products that result in canceled orders, or incidents of poor service that damage the organization's reputation. A reduction in these risks should cause earnings to be more regular and more predictable. And this stability should be reflected in a more predictable market performance.

It should be noted, however, that the benefits of a quality program generally do not show up immediately. In fact, the start of a crusade for quality might be marked by a decrease in profit, not an increase. This is because an effort to improve quality can require a large investment in education and process improvement. As with most investments, a quality effort requires an expenditure of resource today for a return tomorrow—decreased financial performance today for improved performance tomorrow. Unlike many investments, however, the return builds over time instead of diminishing.

Komatsu, the Japanese heavy equipment manufacturer, acknowledges the importance of quality to organizational performance by having a board member who is in charge of quality assurance.[14]

◆ 4.8 Society and Quality

Society as a Customer

The customers for a car include the person who buys it and the mechanic who services it, but what about the society that is impacted by it? Society, too, is a customer. Society "uses" the car and has something to say about its characteristics.

Society is a potential customer for every product, and the needs of society must be considered when building the product. For information products, one of those needs is to respect the privacy of individuals. Another is to ensure that personal data are accurate and are given reasonable protection against unwarranted disclosure. Still another is to ensure that information systems faults do not jeopardize the life or property of individuals, as could happen, for instance, with a faulty air traffic control system or a faulty system for controlling a nuclear power plant.

The failure to regard society as a customer can lead to dire consequences for the producer. People might not patronize an organization that offers offending products. If damage is suffered as a result of a product, the courts might be used

---

[14]Masaaki Imai, *Kaizen* (New York: Random House Business Division, 1986), p. 140.

to gain redress. If there is widespread concern, society might enact laws to give their demands clout. Consequences such as these can be minimized by viewing society as a customer and considering the needs of society along with those of other customers.

Impact of Quality on Society

We start by describing a quality problem that had a temporary effect on a large sector of society. It reads like a movie script, but it really happened.

> *In November 1965, the largest power failure in history blacked out large parts of Northeastern U.S. and parts of Ontario and Quebec. Starting somewhere near Niagara, it moved eastward darkening New York state, then hit Massachusetts, Connecticut, Vermont, New Hampshire, and Maine.*
>
> *New York City lost electricity about 5:30 pm, right at the peak of evening rush hour and at a time when the Winter sky was darkening. The city was chaotic. Thousands were trapped in building elevators; some 800,000 were stranded in the subway. Incoming flights to La Guardia were diverted to other cities and all outgoing flights were canceled. The East and West Side Highways leading out of Manhattan were blocked with massive traffic jams. Cab drivers demanded exorbitant fares, but could hardly move on the crowded streets.*
>
> *How did New Yorkers react? There was some looting and minor vandalism, but people reacted amazingly well! Drivers used extreme caution and courtesy. A few amateurs helped to direct traffic. Restaurants served cold food and warm beer by candle light. Tenants in high rise apartment buildings discovered the seemingly endless flights of stairs leading to their apartments. People actually talked to strangers and people they had been meeting day after day for years, but had never acknowledged.*
>
> *Power was restored in Manhattan at 4:00 am the next morning. But the blackout did have a lasting effect: Nine months after the event, all New York City maternity hospitals were filled to capacity. Of course, there had been no T.V.*

In some ways, the behavior of New Yorkers during the blackout was similar to that of the Cockneys during the World War II blitz of London. Is there something about a crisis that builds teamwork? Can something be learned from these two examples of behavior to aid in quality improvement?

Some quality problems have a widespread, long-lasting impact on society:

- For years, a significant sector of society has been harmed by tobacco products.

- Defective cars kill or maim thousands of innocent victims each year.

- In 1978, Love Canal became the nation's first officially proclaimed environmental disaster. Ten years later, more than 900 locations had been identified as toxic waste sites. Only about 2 percent of these had been cleaned up or contained.

◆ Oil spills have caused tremendous damage to the environment and local economies. Torey Canyon (1967), Amoco Cadiz (1978), Monogahella (1988), Exxon Valdez (1989), the 1994 pipeline rupture in Siberia—no doubt this list of horrors will be extended.

Major disasters affecting environmental quality capture the headlines. But another massive disaster that gets much less attention is the economic impact on the United States that originates from our lack of concern about quality. The Japanese dedication to quality since World War II has steadily improved their standard of living and their trade position vis-à-vis the United States. Scores of American jobs have been "shipped to Japan" because the Japanese succeeded in using quality as a competitive advantage to capture market share from us. America's loss of market share and jobs was felt first by the camera, television, and other electronic industries. Eventually, it spread to the automotive industry, which was the industrial heart of America at that time. The steady erosion of America's portion in the worldwide automotive sales can be seen in Display 4.1.

The arrogance of the U.S. automotive industry toward Japanese competition in the post–World War II period was startling. When Japan first made inroads in California, Detroit was not disturbed. Their attitude was that it would take years for the Japanese to develop the vast service network provided by major U.S. automakers. Without a service network, they reasoned, it would be impossible for Japan to penetrate into the Heartland. But the Japanese were clever; instead of playing by Detroit's rules and building a large service network, they brought in cars that didn't need much service! Detroit had never considered this quality tactic.

It is amazing that in spite of their dramatic loss of market share, American car manufacturers displayed a lack of concern about quality right through the 1980s!

DISPLAY 4.1 ◆ Percentage of Worldwide Automobile Demand Captured by the United States and Japan[a]

Year	United States	Japan
1950	75.7	0.3
1960	47.9	2.9
1970	28.2	18.0
1980	20.8	28.7
1990	20.3	28.0

[a] *World Almanac and Book of Facts,* 1995, p. 208.

Recall our discussion in Section 2.6 of General Motors' fiasco with its Allente automobile.

Display 4.2 contains statistics concerning U.S. foreign trade in the years 1970 and 1990. Several interesting points emerge. First, foreign trade grew dramatically in the 20-year period from 1970 to 1990. Second, the United States went from a trade surplus in 1970 to a massive trade deficit by 1990. Third, the total trade deficit in that year, which was approximately $100,000 million, is mostly due to the trade deficit in the manufacturing sector of the economy.

Not all of our trade deficit in manufacturing can be traced to quality problems. But certainly the inability of manufacturers to produce goods that meet customers' requirements is a major factor in the tremendous change in our trade picture. And it has had a big impact on the standard of living of American workers.

Yet another interesting observation can be made from Display 4.2. In 1990, the United States had a huge trade deficit in the manufacturing sector, but that was partially offset by a trade surplus in the agricultural sector. In other words, on a net basis the United States is an exporter of raw materials and an importer of finished products. Some people regard this as a characteristic of a Third World economy.

Impact of Society on Quality

Not only does quality impact society, but society also has an impact on quality. In some ways, society impacts quality negatively:

◆ In the post–World War II period, demand for consumer goods was so strong that people would accept any product regardless of shoddy workmanship and minor defects. If customers don't demand quality, there is little incentive for a producer to provide it.

DISPLAY 4.2 ◆ U.S. Exports and Imports for selected years and commodities (in millions of dollars)[a]

	Exports	Imports
Year 1970		
Total trade	$ 42,593	$ 39,963
Manufacturing	32,132	30,335
Agriculture	4,841	5,539
Year 1990		
Total trade	$394,045	$495,042
Manufacturing	298,687	388,806
Agriculture	38,716	22,378

[a]U.S. Department of Commerce.

◆ Labor-management relations in many industries are based on a confrontational model. Management and labor focus on how the pie will be divided,
   and the customer and quality are neglected in the process.

◆ Governments do not correctly cost many of the services they provide. Often
   taxes, permits, and fees do not take into account the true cost to society of
   handling pollution, waste disposal, and public health problems.

In other ways, society has a positive impact on quality:

◆ Various government standards help to assert society's requirements for safety,
   health, and a certain uniformity of products.

◆ Laws concerning the disposal of waste, protection of natural habitats, and
   rules concerning endangered species help to assert society's concern about
   the environment and wildlife.

◆ The international ISO 9000 initiative has a positive influence worldwide by
   focusing management attention on quality and the need for a documented
   quality system.

◆ National initiatives, such as the Deming Prize in Japan and the Baldrige
   Award in the United States, give publicity to the quality issue and encourage organizations to make quality improvements.

Education is a societal issue that has both negative and positive impacts on quality. Some people think that much of education in America is in decline; that bodes
ill for our ability to turn out workers who will be able to meet the quality challenges facing the country. But there is also good news on the education front. A
growing number of colleges and universities, even secondary schools, are placing
a greater emphasis on the subject of quality. Most large firms have at least some
level of quality education for their employees.

The world is moving toward a more integrated world economy, and quality is
a necessity to remain competitive in that new economic order. To maintain full
employment and have a high standard of living, a country must learn to play the
quality game.

◆ 4.9 Quality and You

The industrial world is learning rapidly about the need and benefit of committing
to quality; this understanding is creating opportunities for people who understand
quality concepts and how to apply them. A few readers of this book will build careers as quality professionals: quality assurance personnel, quality assurance managers, quality auditors, and quality consultants. But the large and growing need is
for managers in all areas who understand quality concepts and how to achieve
quality in the workplace.

Every manager should understand

- What quality is and is not
- Why quality is vital to an organization
- The human side of quality
- How quality can be improved
- How to manage an improvement effort
- How to produce quality products themselves
- How to manage others so they will produce quality products

This knowledge can be learned, and you are well along in the learning process. Having the skill to apply this knowledge is largely a matter of practice. And the best time to start practicing is now—making certain that all of your work products are quality products.

◆ Exercises and Additional Readings

1. What are some names used for customers other than those given in Section 4.1?

2. Every process has *primary* and *secondary* customers—those that benefit directly from the process and those that benefit further down the line. Who are some of the primary and secondary customers for an airline reservation system?

3. As a student, you are a customer of your educational institution and the institution is your supplier. (a) List any requirements you have that your supplier is not meeting. (b) What can be done to improve the situation?

4. Some college instructors assign students to teams and ask them to develop a team solution to an assignment. (a) What are the benefits of such an assignment? (b) What are the problems? (c) What can be done to improve the quality of the learning experience?

5. Discuss how teams in industry differ from teams formed in a college class for the purpose of accomplishing a specific assignment. How might product quality be impacted by these differences?

6. Read John D.W. Beck and Neil M. Yeager, "How to Prevent Teams from Failing," *Quality Progress*, March 1996, p. 27. What is your opinion of this article?

7. Read and summarize Steven Crom and Herbert France, "Teamwork Brings Breakthrough Improvements in Quality and Climate," *Quality Progress*, March 1996, p. 39.

8. Read and summarize David E. Balch and Robert Blanck, "Measuring the Quality of Work Life," *Quality Progress*, November 1989, p. 44.

9. Read and summarize Stanley M. Moss, "Appraise Your Performance Appraisal Process," *Quality Progress*, November 1989, p. 58. What is its impact on quality?

10. What steps are involved in building and testing a computer program? What are some of the intermediate products that are built at these various steps? How might the products differ between (a) a product built by one person for his or her own use and (b) a product built by a team for the registrar of a university?

11. Read George Eckes, "Practical Alternatives to Performance Appraisals," *Quality Progress*, November 1994, p. 57. What are your views of the three appraisal processes discussed in the article: (a) traditional employee appraisals, (b) customer-supplied appraisals, and (c) process appraisals? Discuss each from its impact on the employee and on product quality.

12. Willard Zangwill in his paper "Ten Mistakes CEOs Make About Quality," *Quality Progress*, June 1994, p. 43, lists 10 major mistakes by top managers that prevent their organizations from developing excellent quality programs.

    Failing to lead.
    Thinking that planning devolves from financial or marketing goals.
    Believing that being close to the customer and planning for customer satisfaction is sufficient.
    Believing that quality means inspection.
    Believing that quality improvement is too expensive.
    Managing by intuition and not by fact.
    Using misguided incentives and developing a distorted culture.
    Changing targets each year.
    Failing to follow the best practice.
    Believing Baldrige Award examiners are stupid.

    Elaborate on each of the 10 mistakes.

13. Give additional examples of how the quality of products and services (or the lack thereof) impacts society.

14. Discuss how the work (study) environment at your university affects the quality of your work. List ways of improving the environment.

15. Talk to janitors at your university. Ask them about how they view quality. Ask them whether management shares their views of quality.

16. Discuss the student–professor relationship in terms of customer and supplier. Compare this with a diner–restaurant relationship.

17. Interview someone in the Quality Assurance organization of a local company. Summarize their duties and their satisfaction with their job.

18. Talk to workers at these companies and assess their views on quality. Are workers convinced that quality (or the lack of quality) has an impact on their wages and job security?

19. Talk to managers at these companies and assess the companies' relationships with external suppliers. How close are they to true partnerships?

20. Determine if your educational institution has a Quality Assurance organization. What functional areas does it serve? How is quality assured in other areas?

21. What is the definition of Quality Assurance given in Sections 24.1 and 24.2 of J. M. Juran and Frank M. Gryna, *Quality Planning and Analysis*, 3rd ed. (New York: McGraw-Hill, 1993)? Compare that with the definition given in this chapter.

22. Read and summarize Koji Kobayashi, "Quality Management at the NEC Corporation," *Quality Progress*, April 1986, p. 18. What does this article say about leadership?

23. Think of a university as the provider of instruction. Describe its various customers.

Chapter 5

Products, Processes, and Quality

◆ 5.1 Custom Products and Consumer Products

Quality is an attribute of a product. To enhance our understanding of quality, therefore, we need a better understanding of products and how they come into existence.

In Chapter 1, we categorized products as goods, services, and information. Products can also be distinguished by the class of customers for whom they are designed. This classification is useful because the classes are handled differently when it comes to determining product requirements and possibly in examining the product to determine that it is satisfactory.

A *custom product* is one that is produced for specific customers who can specify the requirements for the product; it is "custom-made." Examples are a house constructed for a specific family and an atomic submarine built for the U.S. Navy.

At the other extreme, a *consumer product* or *commodity* is one for which there is a large class of customers no one of whom is dominant enough to dictate product requirements. Examples are cars, TV programs, airline seats, and other products available in the open market. A software product produced by an organization for its own accounting department is a custom product, but a software accounting package produced for sale to the general public is a consumer product.

Clearly, many products fall between these two extremes; they are designed for several customers, all of whom can be identified. Examples are a defense system that is sold to the Army and the Navy and a production scheduling system to be used by all the plants of a company. If one understands how to handle both custom and consumer products, then it is possible to make sensible adjustments for products that lie between these extremes.

Consumer products themselves are of two types. One type we will refer to as a *standard catalog product*. This product is sold "as is"; the supplier will not change the product to meet a requirement of a specific customer. Most products we buy in a supermarket or bookstore are of this type. Another type of consumer product is one available in *standard variations*. An example is a restaurant meal; you vary the meal by your choice of items from the menu. Another example is a car; you can have it in black or red, with a standard or deluxe radio, and so on.

From a customer's point of view, products available in standard variations offer more choice. From our point of view, offering standard variations adds some complexity to the supplier's processes.

◆ 5.2 Processes

Our concern in this book is with the quality of products. But every product is produced by some process, and the quality of a product depends *greatly* on the process used to produce it. This means that an extremely important class of custom products are the processes used by an organization to produce their products and conduct their business. To understand how to achieve quality, therefore, it is necessary to have a solid understanding of *process concepts*.

A *process* is a logically related collection of actions or operations that work together to produce a given result—it transforms *inputs* into *outputs*, or products. The actions or operations might be performed by people, by machines, or by a combination of these. For the process to be effective, appropriate ingredients and a conducive atmosphere are required.

Sometimes a process is referred to as a *function* because in mathematical terminology a function is a transformation or mapping of inputs into outputs. Other terms that are used for a process are a *work effort* or a *work activity*.

Because a process is viewed in terms of its inputs and outputs only, these items in effect *define* the process. At this level of description, one is concerned only with *what* work does, not *how* inputs are converted into outputs. A process view of work is similar to that taken by engineers who sometimes look on a process as a "black box" that accepts certain inputs and produces certain outputs. The advantage of this view is that it enables one to concentrate on the objective—what is to be done—before jumping into the details of how, when, where, and by whom.

DISPLAY 5.1 ◆ Examples of Work Processes

Input	Process	Output
Paint, paintbrush, ladder, paint	Paint house	Painted house, empty cans
Concert hall, piano, audience	Give piano recital	Satisfied audience
Plans, land, materials, building permit	Build structure	Structure

An example of a process is an automobile assembly line. The products (completed cars) are assembled from parts by means of a process involving men and machines (including robots); the nature of the process requires continual monitoring to ensure that it functions smoothly. Other examples are given in Display 5.1.

Knowledge of Process Concepts

A general lack of knowledge about process concepts is a primary reason for poor quality products. Consider the information systems area. Most organizations have an IS Department consisting of a group of professionals who build, maintain, and operate their computerized processes. In most organizations, the IS people are among those most familiar with the concept of a process. Most IS people have received formal training in process-related concepts; a large number have studied processes as part of a requirement for a college degree. Their job calls on them to build processes, repair processes, and enhance processes. One would expect, therefore, that the processes in the IS Department would be as well understood, as well managed, and as effective as any in the organization. It may come as a surprise, therefore, to learn that *over half of the projects to build complex information systems are canceled*.[1] Thrown away. Down the drain. What this shocking fact tells us is that people with formal training in building processes are unable to establish effective processes for their own business. If people whose very job is to build processes do not have effective development processes, then what about those without such a background and perspective? The discussion in this chapter should help you understand process concepts.

◆ 5.3 Input-Process-Output Diagram: A Simple Tool for Describing Processes

For a complex work activity with many inputs and outputs, the simple format of Display 5.1 may not be suitable for describing the work process. It might be better to depict the process by means of an *input-process-output diagram*. An exam-

---

[1]"Software's Chronic Crises," *Scientific American*, September 1994, pp. 86–95. A "complex information system" is one with over 10,000 function points.

DISPLAY 5.2 ◆ Example of an Input-Process-Output Diagram

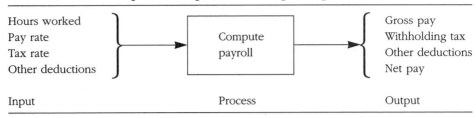

Hours worked		Compute		Gross pay
Pay rate		payroll		Withholding tax
Tax rate				Other deductions
Other deductions				Net pay
Input		Process		Output

ple is given in Display 5.2; this shows an input-process-output diagram for the function "compute payroll."

The convenience of input-process-output diagrams becomes apparent when we are dealing with several related processes. For example, to accomplish the process "Cook Dinner," one may require that this be preceded by the process "Obtain Supplies." If the input to "Cook Dinner" lists the item "fish," but this item is not in the output of "Obtain Supplies," then there is a problem with the design.

We think of a process as converting inputs into outputs; but often an input-process-output diagram is constructed in the opposite order. One starts with the required outputs, which are determined by the customers. Then one determines a set of inputs that are needed to produce the required outputs.

Considerable latitude is taken in documenting the inputs and outputs of a process. What tends to be listed in an input-process-output diagram are those items that require attention; those that don't require attention usually are omitted. For example, to operate an assembly plant successfully there must be a conducive environment—the right amount of heat, sufficient electricity, a supportive administrative staff, cafeteria facilities for the workers, and so on. But to list all of these as inputs in a diagram would serve no purpose if that diagram is to be used for planning work schedules of the production workers. For this purpose it is more helpful to omit these items and simply note that appropriate infrastructure and support must be provided.

To strike a balance between specifying too little and too much detail, the guiding principle in creating an input-process-output diagram should be that it is to serve as a tool for helping to solve a problem, not for creating one.

◆ 5.4 Work Systems

A process is an operation—a transformation or a function. A related *system* is a method for accomplishing that transformation; it is an assemblage of components that interact in an orderly way to achieve some goal or produce some product. A process has to do with *what* is accomplished, and a system with *how* it is accomplished.

Example. You produce a product in Bird in the Hand, Pennsylvania for a customer located in What Cheer, Iowa. You need a system to accomplish the process of transporting the product from Bird in the Hand to What Cheer. The system you employ might involve the Post Office, United Parcel, the Internet, or a carrier pigeon.

Example. The distinction between process and system is reflected in mathematical notation. The notation $y = f(x)$ indicates that x is transformed by some process into y. One system for accomplishing this is $y = 2x + 3$; another is $y = 10 + \sin x$.

A system facilitates a process.[2] For example, an accounting system is an appropriate, orderly arrangement of computer hardware, software, procedures, and other elements that provides a method for accomplishing the accounting function. An office system might consist of equipment and people working together to process specified information.

A system to accomplish work can be very simple; an example would be a system for obtaining coffee for a small meeting (unless, of course, it needs the approval of administration, finance, and personnel). But many work systems are very complex and require considerable effort to build, maintain, and operate. Some examples of complex systems are:

◆   The system for handling patients in the emergency ward of a hospital

◆   A system for refining petroleum

And a contender for the title of "World's Most Complex System" is the United States government.

The key elements of any system are equipment, materials, information, and techniques. A system can be manual, mechanized, automated (computerized), or a combination of these. A system might be subdivided into disjoint subsystems that are distributed over several departments or functional units. Mechanized systems tend to be concentrated on the factory floor. Most of the automated systems are the responsibility of the IS Department. However, a growing portion of automated information processing takes place on mini- and microcomputers distributed throughout the organization; responsibility for these systems is often as diffuse as the equipment itself.

It is possible to establish many different systems to accomplish the work of a process. For example, consider the process: Feed Family, with the output being a family having had a satisfactory meal. One system for accomplishing this process could involve the purchase of food and its preparation. Another system could involve the use of a fast-food outlet.

Technology influences the choice of a system. For example, the accounting process could be accomplished with a system based on use of a quill pen or one based on use of a computer.

---

[2]Robert W. Anthony, *Planning and Control Systems: A Framework for Analysis* (Cambridge, Mass.: Graduate School of Business, Harvard University, 1965) p. 5.

Improvement and Innovation

A major technique for improving quality is to make beneficial changes in the systems used to produce products. At times the change is an incremental *improvement* in an existing system; at other times the change is an *innovation*, meaning that the existing system is replaced with another, better system. For instance, *reengineering* is a popular technique for replacing an existing system for accomplishing work with a more effective system. (Reengineering is discussed in Section 11.12.)

Process versus System

A major reason for distinguishing a process from a system is to emphasize the difference between the function required and the means of accomplishing the function. This distinction is very useful when designing a system: It forces one to answer the question, "What function is required?" before getting involved with the question, "How should the required function be accomplished?"

The computer industry, which is relatively new, clearly distinguishes between "process" and "system." For example, reference is made to an accounting *system* to accomplish the accounting function (or process). However, the engineering community, which has dominated the modern quality movement, often does not make a clear distinction between process and system.

In practice, the terms *process* and *system* often are confused and used interchangeably. For example, people might speak of building a manufacturing process when it is more accurate to say they are building a manufacturing system. Quality professionals speak about process improvement when they really are referring to improvement of the system that facilitates the process.

Careless use of the words "process" and "system" usually causes no problems because the two notions are so closely related, and context usually makes it clear which notion is intended. *Therefore, we shall follow common practice and use the terms* process *and* system *somewhat interchangeably; we will make a clear distinction between these two concepts only when doing so is necessary to avoid confusion.*

◆ 5.5 Flowchart: A Useful Tool for Describing Systems

A *flowchart* is a useful tool for mapping the time sequence of events in a process. A flowchart shows the chronological steps that an operation follows; it displays the order in which work steps are performed and the logic that governs the order of executing the various steps. Flowcharts can be used both to design and to document a process. Various symbols are used to denote the elements in a flowchart. Boxes or rectangles are used to represent tasks or work activities in the process, and diamonds are used to show points in the process where decisions need to be taken. An example of a decision point represented by a diamond is the decision "if it is under 100 pounds, do this; otherwise, do that." Arrows show the chronological flow of the process; an arrow from step A to step B indicates that A must be completed before B can be started. Other constructs may be used to represent inputs and outputs, documents, special operations, and flow conditions.

Flowcharts are useful in many ways. They provide a visual display of processes; they document current knowledge about processes, and they identify problem areas and complexity; their use stimulates ideas for process improvement and identifies data-gathering areas; and they are important for communication and training about processes.

A flowchart can provide a very general picture of the process, outlining the general process flow; or it can be very specific, showing every individual step within

DISPLAY 5.3 ◆ Flowchart: Procedure for
Assigning a Qualified Operator to a Task

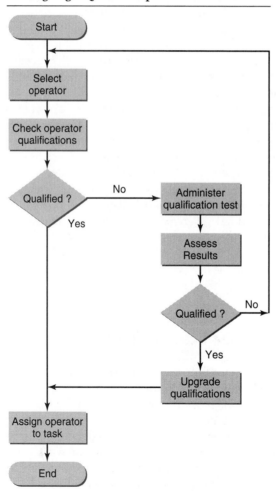

an operation. How much detail is provided depends on the particular objective. Sometimes it is enough just to understand the basic outline of the process. At other times, it is important to understand the process in detail before one can identify problem areas.

A flowchart helps us to visualize the sequence of events. For example, the flowchart in Display 5.3 helps us to understand the procedure for assigning a qualified operator to a certain task. Further discussion of flowcharts is presented in Section 17.3.

◆ 5.6 The System Life Cycle

A system passes through major *stages* that are part of a *life cycle*, as depicted in Display 5.4. The first major stage for a system is the *proposal stage*. This involves identifying all customers to be served by the system and determining the requirements of those customers. Ideas for proposed systems are documented and evaluated. From this comes a proposal for a system to serve the customers, which is evaluated by management.

The second stage in a system life cycle is the *building stage*. The major task in this stage is the design and construction of the proposed system. Management's task is to plan and control the work effort. The building stage terminates when the developed, tested, and approved system has been installed and is operational.

The third stage of a system is the *operation stage*. Whereas the first two stages involve cost, the third stage enables the organization to benefit by using the system to do productive work. The focus during this stage is on using the system to produce products. The main task relating to the system is maintenance (repair and enhancement). The main management task is the continual evaluation of the system during operations to determine if the system meets specified requirements and to decide when there is a need for major revision, replacement, or withdrawal of the system.

The system enters its fourth and final stage, the *replacement stage*, when it is decided that a major change is required. If withdrawal is in order, the major task is to shut down the system. If major revision or replacement is in order, the replacement system is constructed (starting its life cycle); when it is ready, a major task of the replacement stage is the migration from the old to the new system.

DISPLAY 5.4 ◆ Stages in the System Life Cycle

Stages:	I Propose	II Build	III Operate	IV Replace
Management Tasks	Authorize system	Monitor construction	Evaluate system	Authorize replacement
Work Tasks	Determine requirements	Construct system	Operate and maintain system	Migrate to new system

The set of four stages for a system is called the *system life cycle* to acknowledge that the "cradle to grave" process is repeated through a succession of systems.

The System Life Cycle and Quality

The quality issues relating to a system differ as one progresses through the system life cycle.

The proposal stage of a system's life cycle establishes the mold for the system's quality. Are all potential users of the system identified? Are all requirements of all customers established? Are conflicting requirements resolved satisfactorily? Is the basic system design concept reasonable? Is the quality of system inputs, system operation, and system outputs a dominant consideration? Is the need to facilitate quality improvement being considered?

The task relating to quality in the building stage is to ensure that the system meets all requirements. Quality control is a dominant issue: Do all supplies and construction materials meet requirements? Do the various work products meet requirements? Are all standards being met?

During the operation stage, the quality issue is: Does the system provide users the products they require? Is the quality of process inputs properly monitored? Are system operators properly trained? Are operating instructions correct? Are system outputs properly monitored for quality? Is the system being measured to discover potential problems and to provide input for process improvement? Is the output stable over time?

During the replacement phase, the major quality issues are: Have we learned anything from this system that can help us to improve the quality of the new system? What's the best way to make certain these lessons are not forgotten?

◆ 5.7 Production Processes

It requires a process to clean your room and a process to clean a manufacturing plant. Clearly, these tasks differ in magnitude, but there is another important difference: the second task is performed in an organizational setting. To perform the task, supplies must be furnished by the supply department, the training department will instruct you in how to do the job, management must authorize and schedule the activity, the union must be satisfied that you are not being exploited, the payroll department will pay you for the effort, and so on. You get the picture. Accomplishing even a simple task within an organizational setting can be a complex undertaking.

When it is necessary to distinguish them from other processes, a process for accomplishing work within an organizational structure will be referred to as a *production process*. Such a process consists of all entities required to produce a class of products. Examples of a production process are an order entry process, a product requirements determination process, a manufacturing process, a training process, and a marketing process.

Unfortunately, the term *production process* can suggest that the term should be applied only to "major" processes, but this is not our intent. For example, the process of filling an order from stock is a production process. It might take only 10 minutes to fill the order, but it still requires a procedure, certain training, authorization, and reporting.

Any work effort accomplished within an organization can be viewed as operating a production process. Two major issues that distinguish a production process from, say, brushing you teeth are the need for management and control, and the need to interface properly with other production processes of the organization. *Quality improvement in an organization is largely a matter of improving production processes and their interfaces.*

Organization and Production Processes

The production processes of an organization are managed through its organizational structure. This structure provides a framework for managing people and their work efforts. The organizational structure provides answers to the questions of why, who, and when work is accomplished. The production processes answer questions of what, where, and how work is accomplished.

Usually, the organizational structure of a firm is aligned with the central components of its major production processes: marketing, manufacturing, shipping, accounting, and so on. But there are other major production processes that cut across organizational lines; an example is the payroll system.

A significant management challenge is to identify, define, organize, operate, and manage the network of production processes required to provide quality products on-time and at an acceptable cost. Management must have assurance that

- Processes are defined effectively.
- Processes are created, deployed, and implemented properly.
- Processes are operated properly.
- Processes are monitored to assure that they are providing expected results in an effective manner.

◆ 5.8 Process Documentation

Procedures

Typically, processes cross organizational lines. For example, the process "Deliver Instruction" within a university involves the academic department that provides the instruction and the administration that provides the classroom and equipment. For effective delivery, certain academic tasks and administrative tasks must be performed. This means that the total work effort must be coordinated effectively.

To manage and accomplish the required work of a process, the total work effort is divided into appropriate work efforts called *procedures*. Each procedure is identified and defined so that its work activity is accomplished by people residing within one department of the organization. In other words, the work of the process is subdivided into a collection of disjoint activities, each of which is accomplished by a single department. This division facilitates the management of work: making work assignments to accomplish the tasks, monitoring and controlling the work, and appraising work products and work performance.

A procedure is a specified way to perform an activity so as to comply with standards. It details the way the principles and practices established by the organization are to be performed, and it fixes the organizational responsibility for performance. A procedure provides workers with a step-by-step guide for performing tasks. It may also instruct on the tools, machines, and techniques to be used; and it might reference standards to be met. Together standards and procedures help to make work tasks and work products more uniform.

An example of a procedure is the statement in Display 5.5 describing how to

---

DISPLAY 5.5 ◆ Procedure for a Peer Review

General

A peer review is a structured review of a product conducted in a penalty-free environment for the purpose of detecting errors in the product. The review is conducted by a monitor; comments are recorded by a secretary.

Procedure

Arrange review

1. Management schedules review.
2. Management appoints review team, monitor, and secretary.
3. Monitor distributes review agenda, product to be reviewed, and the product requirements (at least two working days in advance).
4. Prior to review, reviewers independently examine product for conformance to requirements.

Conduct review

5. Monitor describes the purpose of a peer review and presents overview of the product.
6. Reviewers present major concerns.
7. Reviewee (the author of the product) walks through product element by element, asking reviewers to state their concerns and observations.
8. Secretary records issues raised by reviewers (there is no discussion of issues).

Wrap-up review

9. Monitor distributes list of issues.
10. Reviewee resolves issues.
11. Monitor distributes resolutions to all review members. (There is no report to management except that the review has been conducted.)

conduct a peer review of a work product. (A detailed discussion of peer reviews is given in Section 12.15.)

Work Instructions

To perform the tasks associated with a procedure, it is necessary to have *work instructions* (or, simply, *instructions*). Work instructions are detailed requirements for a particular task. They might be known as operating instructions, service instructions, review or inspection instructions, and so on. Work instructions must be traceable back to and in accordance with the requirements of some departmental procedure.

Work instructions tell how to perform a task. They should not be confused with work assignments, which are part of the work management process. An example of a work instruction arising in the context of a peer review is given in Display 5.6.

Records

The various documents just discussed define the quality system. But it is also necessary to demonstrate to customers, auditors, or examiners that the quality system is being operated properly. To do so, it is necessary to record the systems operation.

Records are a means of documenting the results of actions taken in operating

---

DISPLAY 5.6 ◆ Instruction for Conducting a Peer Review

Process: Peer Review
Instruction: Recording Concerns

1. During a review, any member of the review team can raise an issue concerning the product.
2. Using a flip chart or Story Board, the secretary of the review team will document the issue in a statement and display the statement on a screen so that all reviewers can view it.
3. The person who raised the issue will review the statement for clarity and accuracy, taking into account any comments or queries by other review members. After making necessary modifications and being satisfied with the statement, the reviewer will approve it. (*Note:* No attempt is made in the review to deal with the issue during the review meeting.)
4. After all concerns about the product have been raised and recorded, the monitor may elect to have the list of concerns reviewed to determine if there are duplicate concerns or concerns that might best be combined. This review of the list will be conducted by the secretary, who will propose suitable changes. Any change to a concern in the list must be approved by the person who initially raised the concern.
5. The list of concerns will be complete at the end of the meeting, and the secretary will distribute it to members of the review team and the reviewees within two working days of the review.

---

the quality system. Examples of quality records are operations logs, test data, test reports, calibration data, inspection reports, and review reports. Quality records must be maintained to demonstrate conformance to the requirements of the quality system.

◆ 5.9 The System Development Process

After this discussion of product and process, we face an interesting paradox: Whether something is called a product or a process depends on one's point of view! Let's look at an example.

An automotive production line is used to produce cars. Most of us—certainly the people operating the line—regard the cars as the product and the line as the process used to produce the product. But let's step back and look at the line from the viewpoint of the industrial engineers whose job it was to design the line. To them it is a product—a product of their process for designing and building production facilities.

A similar example can be found in the information systems area. To the operators who use it, an information system is part of the process used to produce information. But to the system development group, the information system is a product; it was a product of their product development system or project process. But one doesn't have to stop the example at this point. What about the project process; where did that come from? Obviously, the project process itself was the output of another activity, which might be referred to as the process of building a project methodology.

These examples illustrate that a process is something that must be built just as surely as a car must be. Perhaps this point is obvious to you, but unfortunately it is often overlooked. When people are assigned a job that involves operating a process (in fact, every job amounts to that!), they usually accept the process as a given—somewhat like the building they work in and the hours they work. Unfortunately, their managers do this too. As a result, often no one thinks about the process itself and how it can be improved.

Designing and building a process is not a simple task. It involves decomposing the process into subprocesses, finding a way to accomplish each subprocess, and sequencing these efforts so that the outputs of one subprocess are available when required as inputs to another. It also requires managing the total development effort to ensure that quality is achieved, resources are properly deployed, and schedules are maintained.

We will use the term *system development process* for a process used to develop a production system. The activity of developing a specific production system is a *system development project.*

The distinction we are making between the system development process and other processes might seem pedantic and akin to splitting hairs. But it is a very useful distinction and is, in fact, commonly recognized by the terms used in describing system work. For example, we talk about *building* an automobile production line and *operating* an automobile production line. And everyone understands that "building the line" refers to work involved with the system development process, whereas operating refers to work involved with building cars. The logical problem one has, of course, is that you operate the system development process to build a system.

Some differences between building a system and operating a system are these:

◆ Constructing a system is a single-time effort; operating a system usually is a repetitive effort.

◆ Constructing a system is a complex activity requiring highly trained personnel with specialized knowledge and can require considerable time and resource. Operating the system usually does not require as much time, expense, or training.

Some impacts on quality from building and operating a system are as follows.

◆ An error in constructing a system can impact all products produced by the system; an error in operating a system is more localized.

◆ Quality problems in operating a system often can be corrected through changes in personnel systems for selecting, training, supervising, and rewarding operators. Quality problems in building a system require analyzing the problems, discovering their root cause, and modifying the system.

◆ It is not uncommon to find a system that was not carefully planned and constructed—it just grew. Perhaps it was designed by the first person assigned the task and has been followed ever since without critical examination.

◆ 5.10 Projects and Project Management

At times it is useful to classify processes by how frequently they are performed. Some processes, such as the one used to put a man on the moon, are designed to be exercised only once. Others, such as an automobile production line, are used more or less continuously and produce a large number of virtually identical products.

A *project* is a single-time effort needed to produce a product that can be viewed as unique. Examples are a project to determine requirements for a new process; a project to design the process; a project to build and install a process and verify that it is effective; and a project to make improvements in an existing process. Other examples of projects are writing a term paper, obtaining a college degree, constructing an office building, installing an operating procedure, and reengineering a process.

Projects can be contrasted with *continuing efforts*. The latter are ongoing, repetitive tasks that are best viewed as operating an existing process or executing a procedure. Good examples are the task of filling an order for a standard consumer product and working on a production line. A process that is to be performed repetitively might be called a *production line*; performing it is *operating* the line.

The classification of a particular effort as a project or continuing effort is somewhat arbitrary and a matter of convenience. Is teaching a class a project or a continuing effort? If you are doing it once, you will probably treat it as a project. If you present the same material year after year, you might be treating it as a continuing effort.

Projects are a mechanism for creating, changing, and building. They are a basic mechanism for innovation and renewal—a mechanism for creating new production processes or making basic process improvements. *Project-by-project improvement* is a basic, highly successful strategy for improving quality.

For a project to be successful, it is necessary to have a clear objective, appropriate resources (including qualified personnel), and a well-defined *project methodology* (project process). The methodology comprises a formal collection of explicit or referenced principles, policies, methods, procedures, instructions, standards, and definitions detailing how a project is to be accomplished and specifying how a project should interface with related processes.[3] A typical project methodology specifies how the project work should be subdivided into phases and standard tasks, procedures for accomplishing the work, policies and procedures related to the management of the work, and standards for work and work products. As with any process, some person should be appointed as the *methodology manager* with responsibility to ensure that the project methodology is evaluated regularly, improved, and replaced with a better methodology if warranted.

Project Management

A *project manager* is in charge of a specific operation of a project process. To be effective, a project manager must have knowledge of projects and project management, but a full discussion of these topics is beyond the scope of this book. Project management should be a standard offering in business schools, but it is not. However, a number of excellent books have been written on the subject.

◆ 5.11 Process Variability

Benjamin Franklin observed that in this world nothing is certain but death and taxes. Most things in life are random or probabilistic, not predictable or deterministic. In some significant way, every process exhibits randomness, even the process of dying: We know we will die, but we don't know just when.

---

[3]Claude W. Burrill and Leon W. Ellsworth, *Modern Project Management*, (Tenafly, NJ: Burrill-Ellsworth Associates, 1983), p. 10.

The time it takes to cash a check at a bank will vary from one cashing to the next. The number of defects produced by a TV production line will vary from set to set. The thickness of paper produced by a paper machine will vary along the length of the reel. The grade a student receives will vary from test to test. All these examples illustrate the variation in the output of a process from product to product.

Sources of Process Variability

Sometimes it is possible to identify the reason for variation. For example, if you cash a check each day at your bank, you probably will find it takes much longer than usual just before or after a bank holiday. And most likely it will take longer on any day a local company distributes its paychecks. These are *assignable causes* of variation; the change in typical behavior of the process can be ascribed or assigned to these causes. Aside from identifiable, assignable variation, however, there is variation whose cause cannot readily be identified. This general, *nonassignable*, or *common-cause variation*, or *noise* is generally viewed as part of the process.

Any part of a process can be a source of variation. Consider, for example, the time it takes you to write a term paper. What might cause you to miss your deadline?

> *Well, you might not have received the assignment—you missed a class, the instructor did not hand it out when promised, you were to get it from a friend who forgot about it. Then you started working on the assignment—you found the references you needed were not in the library; an unexpected quiz in another course needed your attention; and the computer acted up and garbled your file. All of this made you ill, affecting your ability to work. Then a sudden panic took hold when you realized you were late. So you dashed off something (not a quality product) to meet your schedule! And you promised to do things differently next time (improve your process).*

Sources of variability in a manufacturing process include materials, skills, tools, procedures, conditions in the plant, supervision—every part of the process.

Understanding Variation and Its Cause

Variability is a fact of life. It cannot be eliminated, but it can be understood, managed, and kept within acceptable limits.

Processes generally exhibit much more variation than people realize. By nature and training we tend to think in a deterministic way, even though the world around us is probabilistic; therefore, we overlook the randomness we experience. A 20-minute commute to the job each morning can easily vary from 15 minutes to 30 minutes depending on traffic conditions; with a heavy snow, it can be much worse. But we still describe it as a 20-minute commute. For a complex manufacturing process, the reject rate might vary on a day-to-day basis from 1 to 5 percent; but the average defect rate usually gets the most attention. The time it takes to produce a module of computer code can vary from two to five days depending on the number of interruptions, the ambiguities in the requirements, the availability of equipment, and so on. But interruptions, ambiguities, and delays are all part of the software development process; they contribute to the time it takes to produce a product and to the number of its defects. Variation should be expected, but usually it comes as a surprise and disappointment. An important task in improving the quality of a process is to measure process variation, understand it and find its sources, and reduce it to acceptable levels.

Understanding Variation: Deming's Red Bead Experiment

W. Edwards Deming used the following simple experiment to teach effectively about variation. Six people take part in an experiment, which consists of taking samples from a jar of 4000 beads. Twenty percent of the beads in the jar are red, and 80 percent are white. Each person stirs the jar of beads, draws blindfolded a sample of 50 beads, counts the number of red beads in the sample, and returns the beads to the jar. The objective is to produce white beads because the customer will not accept red beads.

The experiment is carried out, and, for our particular illustration, it is found that six selected participants "produced" the following numbers (and percentages) of red beads:

	Number of Reds	Percentage of Reds
Jon	4	8
Bob	9	18
Jane	10	20
Tim	8	16
Elvira	15	30
Bruce	5	10

In this particular experiment, the physical circumstances for the six people are as much alike as possible. Nevertheless, people vary in their "performance." The performances of the six employees all come from the same process. They all draw from the same jar, and the process defect rate is represented by the 20 percent red beads in the jar of 4000. The process is *stable* because the conditions (that is, the number of red beads in the jar) do not change over time and from one participant to the next.[4] The individual results have nothing to do with working hard or being lazy; they are determined by the process and the luck of the draw. With 50 draws

---

[4]We will say more about stability of processes in Chapter 20 when we discuss statistical process control and control charts.

from such a jar, one can expect $(50)(0.2) = 10$ red beads, on average. Furthermore, calculations with the binomial distribution show that for samples of size 50, more than 99 percent of the samples will have between 2 and 18 red beads. (For a discussion of the binomial distribution, we refer you to Chapter 8 of our book, *Statistical Quality Control: Strategies and Tools for Continual Improvement*, John Wiley, 1999.)

The fluctuations in the results of the six participants are due to chance factors. While it is true that Jon and Bruce recorded the fewest defects this time around, there is no resaon to believe that their future performance will be better than that of Jane and Elvira. It also would be a waste of time trying to find out why Elvira has produced 15 red beads and why Jon has only 4. Reading too much into random fluctuations from a stable process and assigning "cause" to and acting on such random fluctuations would only make things worse. Instead of reacting to the random variations from a stable process, management should make changes and improve the process. That is, it should reduce the number of red beads produced by the system.

Under some traditional management models, Jon would be recognized as "Employee of the Month," while Elvira would be demoted. However, management action that rewards Jon and punishes Elvira on the basis of such data is clearly wrong. Basic knowledge about the process and its associated variability shows that it was "pure luck" that Jon ended up with the smallest number of red beads. The next time around, the situation could be completely different. This experiment illustrates that it is all too easy to blame workers for faults that belong to the system. Deming's message is that people should not be punished or rewarded for performance over which they have no control.

The Danger of Tampering: Deming's Funnel Experiment

> *If anyone adjusts a stable process to try to compensate for a result that is undesirable, or for a result that is extra good, the output that follows will be worse than if he had left the process alone.*
>
> —W. Edwards Deming[5]

Process variation is a fact of life: Even if a process is stable over time, the individual outcomes from it will vary. Observed variations from a stable system contain no useful information on how to improve the system. They are the result of the many common, and unassignable, causes of variation that affect the system. Nevertheless, people are always tempted to make changes on the basis of such random variations. For example, they make adjustments because of a complaint from a single customer, because of a single defective item, or because of one or two particularly good results. Deming calls the making of such ad-hoc

---

[5]*Out of the Crisis* (Cambridge, Mass.: Massachusetts Institute of Technology, Center for Advanced Engineering Study, 1986), p. 327.

changes to an already stable process "tampering" or "overadjustment." One can show, through the simple *funnel experiment* described in the next paragraph, that tampering with a stable system will make things worse and will increase the variability in the outcomes. Tampering with a stable process, though understandable because everyone wants to do their best, should be resisted. Improvements of a stable process can come only from fundamental changes to the system.

The purpose of Deming's funnel experiment is to demonstrate the very large losses that result from overadjustment. The experiment proceeds as follows. Designate a point on the table as the target. Take a funnel and construct a holder for the funnel that suspends the funnel several feet above the table with the tip of the funnel directly over the target. Take a marble or a rubber ball, drop it through the funnel, and mark the spot on the table where it comes to rest. Repeat the experiment several times, always leaving the funnel fixed and aimed at the target. The results of this experiment represent the outcomes of a stable system. You will observe variability among the rest locations; many random causes, such as slight changes in the air circulation at the time of the drop and unevenness in the way the marble leaves the holder, contribute to the variability. Display 5.6 shows the variation graphically; rest locations are represented by solid circles.

Next, let us consider the consequences of tampering with this stable system. Tampering strategies adjust the position of the funnel after each drop, according to one of several rules. For the following discussion, assume that the target is at the point with zero coordinates and that the marble comes to rest at location z.

Strategy 1 moves the funnel into the opposite direction, by -z from its *previous* position. More specifically, if the marble lands one unit to the left and two units above the target, then the next drop is made after moving the holder of the funnel one unit to the right and two units below the previous funnel position. We say that the adjustment involves memory inasmuch as the current position of the funnel depends on its previous position.

The results of strategy 1 are given as the open circles in Display 5.6. The results vary around the target. The system is still stable, but the variability of the deviations from the target has increased.

Strategy 2 moves the holder of the funnel from the original funnel position directly over the target by the amount -z. With this particular adjustment, no memory is involved. For example, if the marble lands one unit to the left and two units above the target, then the position of the holder for the next drop is set at $+1$ and -2 as measured from the initial funnel position.

The results of strategy 2 are given by the "×" symbols in Display 5.7. Under this tampering strategy the system "explodes." The impact positions move further and further away from the target, alternating from one side to the other.

Strategy 3 sets the funnel right over the spot where the last marble came to rest. It "follows" the marble; if the last marble is one unit to the left and two units above the target, then the funnel position of the next drop is set at -1 and $+2$. Strategy 3 imitates an operator who tries to achieve uniformity by attempting to make every piece like the last one. This strategy also leads to a system that explodes. The impact positions move further and further away from the target, but now in only one direction from the target. (Note that the impact positions for this third strategy are not shown in Display 5.7.)

DISPLAY 5.7 ◆ Results of the Funnel Experiment

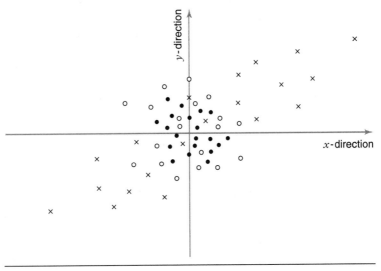

●No tampering; ○ Strategy 1; × Strategy 2.

This experiment illustrates that variability is increased if one tampers with a stable system where deviations from the target are purely random and cannot be assigned a cause. Of course, adjustment is called for if one can confirm a reason for the deviation.

◆ 5.12 Improving Quality

It is not uncommon to find processes in organizations that are not performing satisfactorily and are in need of improvement. Some processes were not designed in a conscious way—they just grew. Others were designed but were not carefully managed and modified to adjust for changes in the product line. Still others were designed across organizational lines but with poor interdepartmental interfaces. Some processes were not built as designed or have been inappropriately modified. Others were built without considering the requirements of all concerned groups. "Peripheral" processes such as recruitment, training, and quality control often are neglected because they were not the "real" concern of the organization. As a result, many operators are not properly trained, and quality concepts are not properly deployed.

If a process is not producing satisfactory results, then there is something wrong with the process, the inputs to the process, the operation of the process, the management of the production effort, or the management of the process. Ways to enhance process performance might be to improve the process for inspecting incoming supplies; the processes for selecting and training operators; or the management of the process and its operation. With a little thought, you can no doubt think of other possibilities.

Notice that each of the ways we have suggested for improving the final product amounts to the improvement of some process! In fact, *if you want to improve the quality of your products, then you must improve the processes used to produce them.* This means the production, management, and training processes—all processes related to your product. To get a better product, you must have a better process; it's as simple as that.

What all this implies is that opportunities abound for improving quality and productivity.

◆ 5.13 Summary

In this and earlier chapters, we have introduced many important concepts. Let us summarize them:

- A *product* is a good, a service, or information.

- A product is the output of a *process*, which is a logically related collection of actions or operations that work together to produce a given result. Other terms for a process are a *work effort*, a collection of *work activities*, or a *function*.

- A process requires certain *inputs*, which are then transformed by the process into *outputs*.

- A *system* is an assemblage of objects that interact in an orderly way to achieve some goal or produce some product. A system is the means by which a process is accomplished.

- A process is defined by *procedures* and *instructions*; the results of operating a process are documented in *records*.

- Every process must be constructed; the task of constructing a process is an example of a *project*. Operating a process is a *continuing effort*.

- Project-by-project improvement is a basic strategy for improving quality.

- Every process exhibits *variability*, which may be due to *assignable causes* or *noise*.

- Tampering with a stable system will increase process variability.

◆ Exercises and Additional Readings

1. List inputs and outputs to the process: Brew Coffee.
2. The ISO definition of a process is any transformation that adds value. Critique this definition.
3. Ishikawa describes a process as a collection of cause factors. Comment on this description.

4. Construct an input-process-output diagram for the process "Compute income taxes."

5. What processes are involved in a department store serving its customers?

6. (a) What products are produced by you as a student?

    (b) Who are the customers for your products? your suppliers?

    (c) What are the major processes you operate to meet the requirements of your customers?

    (d) What are the major sources of variation in the products and processes listed in (a) and (c)?

7. In driving a specific car, what are some sources of variation for the number of miles one gets from a gallon of gas?

8. What are some of the sources of variation for the grade you get in a course?

9. Does it take a production process to build a production process (as defined in 5.6)? Discuss.

10. What are some of the sources of variation in the time it will take a dentist to clean someone's teeth?

11. Find examples of quality problems (a) due to a fault in a system; (b) due to improper operation of a system.

12. A defective car is produced on an automobile assembly line. What are some possible causes of the problem?

13. List some of the components of a production process for producing (a) a hamburger, (b) a house, (c) a term paper.

14. Look up articles in *Quality Progress* that discuss products, processes, and their relationship to quality. Summarize the key points that are made in these papers.

15. Read the original description of the "red bead experiment" in W. Edwards Deming, *Out of the Crisis*, (Cambridge, Mass.: MIT Center for Advanced Engineering Study, 1982), pp. 110–112. Discuss its implications for managers.

16. Read J. M. Juran, "How the West Is Doing," *Quality Progress*, November 1985, pp. 18–22. Summarize Juran's comments on project-by-project improvement.

17. Read and summarize the project-by-project approach to quality improvement described in Chapter 3 of J. M. Juran and Frank M. Gryna, *Quality Planning and Analysis*, 3rd ed. (New York: McGraw-Hill, 1993).

18. (Group project) Construct a funnel and carry out the funnel experiment described in Section 5.11.

19. This exercise is adapted from H.V. Roberts and B.F. Sergesketter: *Quality Is Personal* (New York: Free Press, 1993), p. 147.

   During World War II, Roberts had an opportunity to zero in his M1 rifle (that is, set the sights correctly) by unlimited use of a rifle range for a whole afternoon. He reasoned that he would fire from the prone position (which is very steady), check the deviation of the resulting shot from the bull's-eye, and adjust the sights to compensate for the error. He thought that one or two shots would suffice to get the right setting of the sights. After a whole afternoon of firing (and checking and resetting), he found to his chagrin that he was no closer to being zeroed in than he had been at the start.

Explain. Relate this to our discussion of tampering. Can you think of a better approach for setting the sights? In particular, discuss the following statement.

What Roberts should have done was to fire, say, ten or twenty rounds without touching the sights, make the statistical analysis of the average horizontal and vertical deviations from the bull's-eye, and adjust the sights accordingly.

20. Give additional examples of situations in business where you suspect tampering.

21. It is stated that "*every* product is the result of operating a process."

   (a) What process is involved in constructing a new computer program?

   (b) What process is involved in constructing the process you described as the answer to part (a) of this question?

22. Read and discuss Gipsie B. Ranney, "The Implications of Variation," *Quality Progress*, December 1990, pp. 71–77. Summarize the effects of variation.

23. Read Thomas J. Boardman and Eileen C. Boardman, "Don't Touch That Funnel!" *Quality Progress*, December 1990, pp. 65–69. Relate the results of their experiments to our discussion of tampering in Section 5.11.

24. Discuss why it is so important to document processes.

25. Construct a flowchart of (a) the registration process at your university; (b) the patient admission procedure in the emergency room at your local hospital; (c) the application process for a job; and (d) the college admission process.

26. Read and summarize John T. Burr, "The Tools of Quality Part 1: Going with the Flow(chart)," *Quality Progress*, June 1990, p. 64.

27. Use the internet browser and search for selected key words, such as Juran/Gryna's system life cycle, Deming's red bead and funnel experiments, and flowcharts. Summarize your findings.

Exploring the Meaning of Quality

In business, there is only one definition of quality—the customer's definition.

—President George Bush[1]

In this chapter we will examine some popular views of quality and learn how these views support or hinder a formal definition. Then we examine the definitions of quality given by several well-known quality professionals and the International Standards Organization (ISO).

---

[1]Brad Stratton, "Xerox and Milliken Receive Malcolm Baldrige Quality Award," *Quality Progress*, December 1989, p. 17.

◆ 6.1 Popular Views of Quality

One popular view is that quality is an intangible attribute, similar to truth, beauty, and goodness. It can be discussed and judged, but it cannot be weighed or measured. When Shakespeare wrote "the quality of mercy is not strained," he referred to the essence of mercy, an attribute as elusive as the beauty of a rose or the goodness of a saint.[2] His was similar to the popular view that quality cannot be described precisely and completely, the view that people perceive it in different ways. These different interpretations prevent people from really understanding one another when they discuss quality; therefore, in such a view, quality can never be managed and controlled in the same way that one can control time and cost.

Another popular view is that quality refers to the ideal or almost ideal. Quality standards are absolute, and part of being an educated and cultured individual is to understand the standards for high performance in one's field of expertise. With this view one *knows* that a quality car gives superior performance, is dependable, and has trend-setting style; a car that is a reliable workhorse might be practical, but it doesn't deserve a quality label. In this view, most products are not quality products and, furthermore, were never intended to be; they were designed to be practical and functional, not special. Moreover, quality just costs too much for most people to afford, even if they could recognize and appreciate it.

Closely related to the notion that quality means perfection is the idea that it is a positive trait. A quality product has a touch of class. "The quality" was a Victorian phrase for the upper class of society. Quality is associated with paintings, artistic performances, jewelry, fine clothes, and other expensive items. One usually does not speak of quality garbage collection or quality pool hustling. In fact, those activities are hardly acknowledged by people who think quality means perfection.

In everyday speech, or what we will refer to as the *literary* use of the term, "quality" is a vague, fuzzy notion. It is highly subject to opinion; people differ in assessments of what is a quality product and what is not. A literary use of the word "quality" is fine if the aim is to convey emotions or a sense of aesthetics. But it is inadequate as the basis of a calculated attempt to produce satisfactory products. What is needed is a *technical* definition of quality—a precise definition that can be used to guide the production of products that people value.

◆ 6.2 A Consumer's View of Quality

In an attempt to understand quality, we might ask typical consumers for their definitions. We are likely to hear, "I can't define 'quality,' but I know it when I see it!" That view is fairly prevalent because most people do not spend a great deal of time thinking about what they regard as a philosophical question. To most peo-

---

[2]*The Merchant of Venice*

ple, quality is an elusive, vague concept that they cannot pin down; but they make judgments about quality all the time.

Consumers don't need to define quality; all they need to do is to judge each specific product. Quality, however perceived, is one dimension that weighs in a purchase decision. And it is clear that people differ in their judgments about the quality of products just as they differ in their judgments about the beauty of people or the taste of cheese. This diversity of views compounds a producer's problem in attempting to deliver appropriate products and makes it imperative that he understand what quality is all about, in particular, how it is defined.

◆ 6.3 Attributes of a Definition

To help managers and workers produce quality products, a practical down-to-earth definition is required. Such a definition must have several attributes. First, a workable definition must be *precise*. It need not require that quality be counted or measured or otherwise quantified, but it must be sufficiently precise for a group of informed people to be in general agreement about their quality assessments.

A second attribute of a workable definition is that is must be *flexible*. It cannot allude to fixed or absolute standards but must recognize different grades of requirements for products. A workable definition must allow for judging the quality of a Chevrolet as well as a Cadillac.

A third attribute is that it should be *universally applicable*. It must apply to all products and must apply over time. This requires that a definition cannot be self-contained but must reference standards or measures established for the purpose of judging quality.

A fourth attribute is that it must *conflict as little as possible with general views of quality*. Of course, it is not possible to avoid all conflict—popular views are themselves contradictory. But a formal definition should promote the same general goal of better products as do most of the popular views.

A final attribute of a workable definition is that it be *operational*. It should be understandable, easy to use, and one that people can do business with.

In the next few sections we review various definitions of quality, including those by quality experts such as Deming, Juran, Feigenbaum, Crosby, and Ishikawa, as well as the quality definition of ISO, the International Standards Organization.

◆ 6.4 Deming's Definition of Quality

What is quality? W. Edwards Deming approaches this question as follows:

What is quality? What would someone mean by the quality of a shoe? Let us suppose that it is a man's shoe that he is asking about. Does he mean by good quality that it wears a long time? Or that it takes a shine well? That it feels comfortable? That it is waterproof? That the price is right in consideration of whatever he considers quality? Put another way, what quality-characteristics are important to the customer?[3]

No answers are supplied to these questions; instead, further questions are raised. But rather than pursue this question–question game, we might learn something of Deming's views by examining some of his comments about quality.

◆ Quality can be defined only in terms of the agent. Who is the judge of quality? In the mind of the production worker, he produces quality if he can take pride in his work. . . . Quality to the plant manager means to get the numbers out and to meet specifications.[4]

◆ The consumer is the most important part of the production line. Quality should be aimed at the needs of the consumer, present and future.[5]

◆ The quality of any product or service has many scales. A product may get a high mark, in the judgment of the consumer, on one scale, and a low mark on another. This paper that I am writing on has a number of qualities. [Deming then lists four qualities, the first being] "It is a sulfate paper, 16 pounds."[6]

Deming also states that "the problems inherent in attempts to define the quality of a product, almost any product, were stated by the master, Walter A. Shewhart." He then quotes the following passage from Shewhart's book:

The difficulty in defining quality is to translate future needs of the user into measurable characteristics, so that a product can be designed and turned out to give satisfaction at a price that the user will pay.[7]

Discussion

Deming's definition of quality certainly does not meet the needs of a serious student who is struggling to understand the basic concepts of quality; such a person would require that the definition be explicit and understandable. Nonetheless, we can derive several important facts from his definition and comments:

---

[3]W. Edwards Deming, *Out of the Crisis* (Cambridge, Mass.: MIT Center for Advanced Engineering Study, 1986), p. 169.

[4]Ibid., p. 168.

[5]Ibid., p. 174.

[6]Ibid., p. 169.

[7]Walter A. Shewhart, *Economic Control of Quality of Manufactured Product* (New York: Van Nostrand, 1931), Chapter 4.

- Quality concepts apply to products and to services.

- Quality has many "scales" (Deming) or "characteristics" (Shewhart); an example might be that a shoe is waterproof.

- Quality should be aimed at the needs of the customer.

- Quality means meeting the product quality characteristics that are important to the customer.

Combining these facts, we would conclude that customers for a product should establish what they want (the required "quality characteristics"); then a quality product is one that satisfies those requirements (has those characteristics). Thus, Deming seems to say that quality means "meeting product requirements" or "conformance to requirements."

There are some troublesome inconsistencies in Deming's comments. On the one hand, we are told that quality "should be aimed at the needs of the consumer." On the other hand, he suggests that quality can be defined one way by a production worker and another way by a plant manager. Deming raises the fundamental question, "Who is the judge of quality?" but he does not answer it. Also, Deming discusses products and services but does not focus on information as a product to which quality concepts apply.

◆ 6.5 Juran's Definition of Quality

J. M. Juran defines quality as follows:

> *An essential requirement of . . . products is that they meet the needs of those members of society who will actually use them. This concept of* fitness for use *is universal. . . . The popular term for fitness for use is* quality, *and our basic definition becomes* quality means fitness for use.[8]

A very precise writer, Juran adds further comments to amplify and help explain this definition. A study of his comments reveals his logical view of the fundamental issues:

- Products consist of good and services.

- An essential requirement of products is that they meet the needs of those . . . who will actually use them.

- "Fitness for use" applies to a variety of users [—the manufacturer who enhances the product, the merchant who buys the enhanced product, the purchaser, and the maintenance shop].

---

[8]J. M. Juran and Frank M. Gryna, Jr., *Quality Planning and Analysis*, 2nd ed. (New York: McGraw-Hill, 1980), p. 1.

- ◆ A product has many elements of fitness for use, called "quality characteristics"; these are the fundamental building blocks out of which quality is constructed. Quality characteristics are the means by which "fitness for use" is translated into the language of the technologist.

- ◆ Quality characteristics can be grouped into various species, such as structural (e.g., length), sensory (e.g., taste), time-oriented (e.g., reliability), commercial (e.g., warranty), and ethical (e.g., courtesy).

- ◆ Quality characteristics can be classified into categories known as "parameters." Two major parameters are quality of design and quality of conformance. A good deal of confusion arises when the word "quality" is used without making clear whether the speaker is referring to quality of design or quality of conformance.

- ◆ Quality of conformance is the extent to which goods and services conform to the intent of the design.[9]

Discussion

An examination of Juran's definition and comments reveals the following:

- ◆ Juran's definition of quality has a clear customer orientation; quality is to be judged by the user's reaction to the product. And he makes it clear that "user" refers to anyone who uses a product, not just the primary customer.

- ◆ Products to Juran clearly include both goods and services, and he points out clearly that quality concepts apply to both. To him a "good" refers to a physical product or ware, and a "service" to an action or labor.

- ◆ "Fitness for use" appears to mean that products "meet the needs of those who will actually use them." Thus, "fitness for use" is a question of whether products measure up to the user's standards and requirements.

- ◆ "Fitness for use" is explained in terms of "quality characteristics," which are characteristics of the product.

1993 Modifications

The 1980 edition of *Quality Planning and Analysis*, from which the foregoing material was taken, was updated in 1993. One change is in the definition of quality: "Quality is customer satisfaction. 'Fitness for use' is an alternative short definition."[10] Although "customer satisfaction" might be viewed as a somewhat more stringent requirement than "fitness for use," essentially there is no basic change in recognizing that the user or customer still is the judge of quality. Another change is in

---

[9]Ibid., pp. 1, 2.

[10]J. M. Juran and Frank M. Gryna, Jr., *Quality Planning and Analysis*, 3rd ed. (New York: McGraw-Hill, 1993), p. 3.

the definition of a product: "A 'product' is the output of any process. Three categories of products can be identified: goods, software, and service."[11]

The definition and listing of categories broaden the meaning of "product" to include software—an important category of products to which quality concepts must be applied. However, still excluded are other important information products, such as requirement documents, designs, quality audit reports, and term papers.

A third change of note is the explicit recognition that there are external and internal customers for products.[12] External customers are "ultimate users and all intermediate processors, as well as merchants . . . and government regulatory bodies." Thus it has been made clear that "customer" should not be interpreted narrowly; the definition leaves room to include the notion that "the next person on the line is your customer."

◆ 6.6 Feigenbaum's Definition of Quality

A. V. Feigenbaum defines quality as follows:

Product and service quality can be defined as: The total composite product and service characteristics of marketing, engineering, manufacturing, and maintenance through which the product and service in use will meet the expectations of the customer.

Several comments by Feigenbaum amplify this definition:

- ◆ Quality is a customer determination, not an engineer's determination, not a marketing determination or a general management determination. It is based upon the customer's actual experience with the product or service, measured against his or her *requirements*—stated or unstated, conscious or merely sensed, technically operational or entirely subjective—and always representing a moving target in a competitive market.

- ◆ Reliability, serviceability, and maintainability . . . are "characteristics" which make up the composite of product and service quality.

- ◆ It is the "total customer-satisfaction"-oriented concept of "quality" that must be controlled.

- ◆ In the phrase "quality control," the word "quality" does not have the popular meaning of "best" in any abstract sense. To industry, it means "best for satisfying certain customer conditions," whether the product is tangible . . . or intangible. Important among these customer conditions are (1) the actual end use and (2) the selling price of the product or service.[13]

---

[11]Ibid.

[12]Ibid.

[13]A. V. Feigenbaum, *Total Quality Control*, 3rd ed. (New York: McGraw-Hill, 1983), pp. 7, 9.

Discussion

An examination of Feigenbaum's definition and his amplifying remarks lead to several conclusions:

- ◆ Feigenbaum distinguishes services from products (thereby differing from Juran's terminology) but recognizes that quality concepts apply to both.

- ◆ Feigenbaum emphasizes that quality requires the attention of many areas—marketing, engineering, manufacturing, and maintenance.

- ◆ Feigenbaum's definition of quality is definitely customer oriented. Quality means meeting the "expectations" of the customer. It also means being best for certain "customer conditions," the important ones being (1) the actual use and (2) the selling price of the product.

- ◆ We are told categorically that "quality is a customer determination" measured against the customer's requirements—"stated or unstated, conscious or merely sensed, technically operational or entirely subjective." It is not clear how this can be implemented operationally; how can one know customers' unstated, subjective requirements?

- ◆ Although Feigenbaum titled his book *Total Quality Control* and he includes services in his definition, it is clear that his focus is overwhelmingly on manufactured products.

Feigenbaum's comments are somewhat confusing and too engineering-oriented to have wide appeal. Indeed, the definition itself is ambiguous and open to different interpretations. To prove that, ask several people to read the definition and explain what it means; very likely you will find doubt and differences of interpretation.

◆ 6.7 Crosby's Definition of Quality

Philip Crosby is absolutely clear about his definition of quality:

Quality is conformance to requirements.[14]

With such an unambiguous definition, little supporting comment is necessary. But a few of Crosby's remarks will amplify and motivate the definition:

- ◆ The first struggle . . . is to overcome the "conventional wisdom" regarding quality. . . . It says that quality means goodness, that it is unmeasurable; that

---

[14]Philip B. Crosby, *Quality Is Free* (New York: McGraw-Hill, 1979), p. 9.

error is inevitable; and that people just don't give a damn about doing good work.[15]

◆ Quality has much in common with sex. Everyone is for it. (Under certain conditions, of course.) Everyone feels they understand it. (Even though they wouldn't want to explain it.) Everyone thinks execution is only a matter of following natural inclinations. (After all, we do get along somehow.)[16]

◆ [This is an abridged passage in which Crosby is speaking through a fictional quality manager who was attempting to define "quality":]

We looked at some of the modern definitions. "Fitness for use" has a nice ring, and in fact has a lot of meaning, particularly when you are talking about the design concept of a product. But that isn't what we are doing. We had to come up with something we could use in practical terms that everyone could understand and that we could use to do the job. We kicked around ideas about defect prevention and taking measurement and corrective action and all that stuff. Finally we reached a combined conclusion. Instead of thinking of quality in terms of goodness or desirability we are looking at it as a means of meeting requirements. It's conformance or noncomformance and that is it.[17]

Discussion

The scenario just quoted makes it clear that Crosby's focus is mainly on the build effort, not the design effort. In Juran's phrase, Crosby seems more oriented toward quality of conformance than quality of design. One might fault Crosby on this score; but, in fact, he does openly what many quality professionals in America do in practice: focus on building products (services as well as goods).

◆ 6.8 Ishikawa's Definition of Quality

Ishikawa does not present a simple definition of quality in the English-language reference source we are using. Nonetheless, it is instructive to examine Ishikawa's views on three interrelated concepts: quality, true quality characteristics, and quality control.

On *quality*, Ishikawa makes the following observations:

◆ Narrowly interpreted, quality means quality of product. Broadly interpreted, quality means quality of work, quality of service, quality of information,

---

[15]Ibid., p. 8.

[16]Ibid., p. 15.

[17]Ibid., p. 44.

quality of process, quality of division, quality of people, including workers, engineers, managers, and executives, quality of system, quality of company, quality of objectives, etc. To control quality in its every manifestation is our basic approach.[18]

◆ One must always strive to supply a product with just quality, just price, and just amount.[19]

◆ I want to emphasize that the term quality means quality, and that the term extends to the quality of work in offices, in the service-related industries and in the financial sector.[20]

From these comments it is clear that quality is a property of a product; it is separate from the cost of the product and the quantity produced but related to these considerations.

In describing quality, Ishikawa goes on to introduce the concept of *true quality characteristics*:

◆ Of course, the product sold must not be flawed or defective, but this alone is not sufficient. It is necessary to insure quality of design, making certain that the product is fully functional in the way the consumer expects. In other words, the product must have true quality characteristics.[21]

◆ True quality characteristics are very difficult to measure. . . . As for automobiles, how can one measure the characteristic of being "easy driving"?[22]

◆ Conditions to achieve true quality . . . we shall call "substitute quality characteristics."[23]

◆ The procedure to obtain substitute quality characteristics is as follows. First one must determine the true quality characteristics of a given product and then deal with the questions of how to measure such characteristics and how to determine the product's quality standards. Once they become discernible, substitute quality characteristics which are likely to have a bearing on true quality characteristics will be chosen. Next comes the task of determining the relationship between true and substitute quality characteristics through quality analysis and through statistics. Only then can one know how much use of substitute quality characteristics can be made to satisfy true quality characteristics.[24]

---

[18]Kaoru Ishikawa, *What Is Total Quality Control? The Japanese Way*, translated by David J. Lu (Englewood Cliffs, N.J.: Prentice-Hall, 1985), p. 45.

[19]Ibid.

[20]Ibid., p. 92.

[21]Ibid., p. 76.

[22]Ibid., p. 50.

[23]Ibid., p. 47.

[24]Ibid.

Discussion

Since Ishikawa does not follow the "definition, theorem, proof" style of exposition usual in the West, it is difficult to present his ideas with a few isolated quotes. One can, however, glean the following from the preceding comments:

◆ At one point Ishikawa writes, "the term quality means quality." In other words, everyone knows what quality is; all that is needed is a mechanism for achieving it. But at another point he states that the aim is to provide quality that can "satisfy the requirements of consumers."

◆ Ishikawa's view is that quality is definitely customer-oriented. A quality product must have "true quality characteristics," which must be expressed in customers' terms.

◆ To provide quality products, it is necessary to determine appropriate substitute characteristics and make certain the product possesses them. This determination must be made before the product can be built; therefore, Ishikawa is indirectly saying that true quality depends heavily on the product's design, not just its manufacture.

◆ Quality concepts apply to everything: goods, services, and information, and also to people, plans, systems, and so on.

◆ Quality of products is related to all other aspects: price, delivery date, volume of production. More generally, Ishikawa sees quality as a basic theme running through the entire organization.

Ishikawa's comments on quality are stimulating because they are refreshingly different from the traditional Western views. Essentially, Ishikawa is concerned less with what quality is (basically, meeting customer requirements) than with how quality can be achieved. He raises questions about the meaning of "true" and "substitute" quality characteristics, as well as about the role of quality and quality control in the scope and practice of management.

◆ 6.9 ISO Definition of Quality

ISO International Standard 8402 contains the following definition:

> Quality *is the totality of features and characteristics of a product or service that bear on its ability to satisfy stated or implied needs.*

To amplify the definition, the standard adds three notes to discuss various situations.

◆ The first discussion note states that needs are specified in contractual situations, but they must be identified and defined in other situations.

- The second discussion note states that needs may change with time; therefore, it is necessary to revisit product specifications periodically.
- The third discussion note states that needs may relate to many different aspects, including needs of usability, reliability, maintainability, and safety.

How does the ISO definition of quality, together with the clarifying discussion notes, relate to the definitions we have discussed previously? ISO states that quality is a characteristic or feature of a product, which reminds one of a similar statement by Feigenbaum. These characteristics and features should satisfy certain needs, much as Juran, Deming, and Ishikawa state. In contractual situations, the needs will be stated as requirements, and these must be met, as Crosby holds.

One aspect of the ISO definition that is not stressed by the quality gurus we have discussed is that requirements may change over time. On the other hand, the ISO definition talks about satisfying needs but fails to say whose needs are to be considered. This is much the same as Crosby's succinct definition which fails to state whose requirements must be conformed to. But it is unlike Ishikawa, who makes it clear that a broad interpretation of "quality" covers everyone who deals in any way with the product.

◆ 6.10 Comments on the Definitions

The definitions we have examined are somewhat contradictory, perhaps leaving you puzzled and confused as to what quality is. You will be further confused after reading several other definitions quoted in the Exercises at the end of this chapter. At this stage you may well be wondering, "How have people been able to do *anything* to improve quality when the experts cannot agree on a definition?" The answer, of course, is that people traditionally have been concerned largely with one application: making certain that products produced on a manufacturing line satisfy the requirements and standards established for them. Today, however, it is recognized that this is insufficient; quality concepts must be applied to a broader range of products and across the entire product cycle, not just to the build phase. To accommodate this wider purview, attempts are being made to strengthen the foundations of quality. Fundamental questions are being asked for the first time, and the present confusion is part of the process of reaching a consensus on the answers.

Although examination of all these definitions and comments reveals some confusion, conflict, and ambiguity, it also reveals some points of general agreement, notably:

- Quality is an attribute of a product.
- Products consist of goods and services, and the definition of quality should encompass both. In spite of its pervasive nature, information is slighted as a product in most of the writings we have reviewed.

- Products have requirements; "scales," "characteristics," "conditions," and "standards," and similar terms may have slightly different connotations, but they all say what the product should be like—what is required.

- Requirements are specific to a particular product; no general list of requirements (e.g., "reliability," "serviceability," etc.) can be constructed that will apply to all products. Attempts to build such a list would only narrow the applicability of the concepts.

- The customer's view of quality is paramount; any useful definition of quality must take this into account. At the same time, a definition must allow the builder of the product to judge quality when the product is produced.

From all these definitions and observations, what do you conclude? Wouldn't you agree that all of the definitions we have discussed are aiming at essentially the same concept? That is, basically a product should satisfy, even delight a customer, and if it surprises a customer, it should be a pleasant surprise. And doesn't this general concept agree fairly well with your own notion of a quality product?

◆ 6.11 A Working Definition of Quality

Having explored the pros and cons of various definitions, we adopt the following working definition. We say that *quality* means meeting the product requirements and standards established for a product. For simplicity, we generally abbreviate this statement as:

Quality means "meets requirements."

Quality simply means producing what you were supposed to produce. And it applies to the product of *any* process, including the requirements, design, build, and test processes. This definition is simple, precise, and unambiguous—it's a definition that can be applied to any product.

Several implications follow directly from this definition of quality:

- *Quality is binary.* Either a product meets requirements or it does not; quality is a "yes-no" or binary decision. Either the product passes or it fails; there is no "gentleman's C."

- *Quality focuses on requirements.* Since the whole point is to meet requirements, it follows that these requirements must be well defined. The task of stating requirements often is very difficult; traditionally, it has been a major reason for poor quality. The definition of quality places a heavy burden exactly where it should fall—on the specification of product requirements.

- *Requirements must be in writing.* Because everything depends on requirements, they must be clearly understood; the best way to ensure this understanding is to put the requirements in writing.

◆   *Requirements must be verifiable.* Since *meeting* requirements is the test of
     quality, there must be some test to assess whether or not requirements have
     been met.

Quality means "meets requirements" is a practical, straightforward, useful definition. But if you need a formal definition that can be defended easily, use the ISO
definition. It is reasonable and the closest we have to an internationally recognized
definition of quality.

◆ 6.12 Tenets of Quality

To this point, we have looked narrowly at the meaning of quality—that is, at its
definition. But what does it mean to an organization that is embarking on a quality improvement effort? What does it require?

An organization that makes a commitment to quality should understand the following fundamental facts; we call them the *tenets of quality.*

1. *Quality is directed at customer satisfaction.*
   The aim of quality is to give customers the product they want. The challenge
   is to understand true customer needs and to translate these into products that
   will satisfy those needs.

   *The consumer is the most important part of the production line. Quality
   should be aimed at the needs of the consumer, present and future.*[25]

2. *Quality means "meets requirements."*
   Quality is simply delivering what was promised. It's arriving on schedule;
   tasting as it should; being the right color; and weighing the right amount;
   performing as it should. A quality product is one that meets its requirements.

3. *Quality applies to every product.*
   Quality applies to all physical products, all information products, and all service products. It applies to products that are supplied to the producing organization, products that are produced and consumed within it, and products
   that are supplied to outside customers.

   Because it applies to all products, effective quality improvement must be
   organizationwide. It cannot be achieved by an isolated functional department;
   it requires a systems approach that links all departments.

4. *Quality is a profitable investment.*
   Quality is an investment—you invest today and reap the benefits in the future.
   Moreover, quality is a *very* profitable investment, as we discussed in Chapter 3.

---

[25]Deming, *Out of the Crisis*, p. 5.

Long-term profitability belongs to the companies with the lowest operating costs and the ingrained reputation for quality.

—Feigenbaum[26]

5. *Quality requires changing an organization's culture.*
Quality must be part of the organization's basic belief system. This means changing the organization's culture to make quality a principle in all operations.

6. *Quality requires top management leadership.*
If top management is not solidly behind a quality effort, forget it—it won't happen. Quality improvement requires top management's time and effort; it cannot be delegated. Because quality improvement means reshaping the corporate culture, everyone in the organization needs constant reassurance that management is 100 percent behind the effort.

Unless the person in charge, the one who has the full power, that is, the president or the chairman, takes the initiative and assumes leadership in implementing quality control, the program cannot succeed.

—Ishikawa[27]

I would like to reiterate the absolute necessity for top-level belief in and commitment to quality. . . . If top management does not passionately believe in and actively demonstrate its belief in quality, then you can be certain the program will fail.

—Raymon L. Larkin, Executive Vice President, American Express[28]

7. *Quality is everybody's job.*
To satisfy customers, it is necessary to produce quality products in all operations: requirements, design, advertising, marketing, manufacturing, servicing, billing, personnel, finance—every functional area. This means that quality is everybody's job. Each individual is responsible for the quality of his or her work products. Management must encourage teams and local units to innovate and find ways to improve quality and productivity. And quality professionals must provide the required education, training, and assistance in these quality-related efforts.

8. *Quality equates to "good business practice."*
To produce quality products consistently, the organization must do a good job of development, manufacturing, sales, and service. And to do these jobs prop-

---

[26]Armand V. Feigenbaum, "Quality: The Strategic Business Imperative," *Quality Progress*, February 1986, p. 29.

[27]Ishikawa, *What Is Total Quality Control?*, p. 122.

[28]*Productivity Digest* (Singapore), February 1988, p. 15.

erly, there must be good support from accounting, personnel, building maintenance, information systems, and so on. This means that quality is *not* an issue separate from the general business practice. What it takes to produce quality products, therefore, can be described simply as good business practice.

> *The wealth of a nation depends on its people, management, and government, more than on its natural resources. The problem is where to find good management. It would be a mistake to export American management to a friendly country.*[29] *[This was written in 1986; since then, much has changed.]*

9. *Quality requires a focus on people.*
   Business is accomplished through people operating systems. But it is also people who build the systems and maintain them. So ultimately quality depends entirely on people. To achieve quality, an organization must convince its people to make a commitment to quality. Doing things right is a matter of having proper systems, procedures, instructions, raw materials, equipment, and training. But it is also a matter of attitude. Most people want to achieve—to be members of a winning team. It takes a constant focus on people and their requirements to draw out this behavior—to build a culture of achievement.

10. *Quality is achieved through process improvement.*
    All work in an organization is accomplished through processes. Therefore, the way to improve quality is to improve all of the organization's processes—the production, personnel, management, and marketing processes, and so on. Processes should be documented to stabilize them, measured to learn their behavior, and improved to make them more effective. To accomplish these ends, a structure for managing change must be in place. One role for the Quality Assurance function is to serve as a catalyst in the improvement effort.

11. *Quality improvement is forever.*
    Top managers must understand that quality improvement takes time. They must be prepared to take a long-term view of quality, not deviating from their direction because of momentary changes in the business cycle or corporate profits. If a quality improvement is interrupted for whatever reason, it's very difficult to go back and pick up the momentum. Often restarting is worse than starting from scratch because both disappointment and disbelief must be overcome. Once started, a program should be continued at a constant pace. In the Japanese view, a quality improvement program is forever; this is the only attitude to take.

12. *Quality must be a fundamental long-term goal of the organization.*
    Quality must be a fundamental goal. It should be viewed as a strategy to increase sales, reduce costs, and help to secure jobs for employees.

---

[29]Deming, *Out of the Crisis*, p. 6.

If a company follows the principle of "quality first," its profits will increase in the long-run. If a company pursues the goal of attaining a short-term profit, it will lose competitiveness in the international market, and will lose profit in the long run.

—Ishikawa[30]

The secret of Japan's success is an unrelenting, some might say fanatical, adherence to what amounts to a de facto national policy. That policy is quality first.

—Dana M. Cound[31]

◆ Exercises and Additional Readings

1. Apply the criteria of Section 6.3 to the definitions given in Sections 6.4 through 6.9.

2. Comment on how you as a producer can implement the ISO definition of quality.

3. Comment on the following definitions of quality:

(a) "Quality is neither mind nor matter, but a third entity independent of the two . . . even though Quality cannot be defined, you know what it is." (R. M. Pirsig, *Zen and the Art of Motorcycle Maintenance* [New York: Morrow, 1974], pp. 185, 213)

(b) "Quality consists of the capacity to satisfy wants." (C. D. Edwards, "The Meaning of Quality," *Quality Progress*, October 1968, p. 37)

(c) "Quality is the degree of excellence at an acceptable price and the control of variability at an acceptable cost." (R. A. Broh, *Managing Quality for Higher Profits* [New York: McGraw-Hill, 1982], p. 3)

(d) "In the final analysis of the marketplace, the quality of a product depends on how well it fits patterns of consumer preferences." (A. A. Kuehn and R. L. Day, "Strategy of Product Quality," *Harvard Business Review* [November–December 1962], p. 101)

(e) "Quality is achieving or reaching for the highest standard as against being satisfied with the sloppy or fraudulent." (B. W. Tuchman, "The Decline of Quality," *New York Times Magazine*, November 2, 1980, p. 38)

(f) "Quality is the degree to which a specific product satisfies the wants of a specific consumer." (H. L. Gilmore, "Product Conformance Cost," *Quality Progress*, June 1974, p. 16)

---

[30]Ibid., p. 104.

[31]Dana M. Cound, "A Call for Leadership," *Quality Progress*, March 1987, p. 11.

(g) "Quality is the degree to which a specific product conforms to a design or specification." (Gilmore, "Product Conformance Cost," p. 16)

(h) "Quality refers to the amounts of the unpriced attributes contained in each unit of the priced attribute." (K. B. Leffler, "Ambiguous Changes in Product Quality," *American Economic Review* [December 1982], p. 956)

4. Comment on the following statement: "We could meet this customer's requirements, but so could other suppliers. In this case, just meeting requirements was not the whole story; meeting the customer's *needs* was better. . . . So, our goal was to get beyond the actual specification and find out about the customer's needs." (Bob Kukla, "Meeting Customer Needs," *Quality Progress*, June 1986, p. 15)

5. Apply the criteria of Section 6.3 to each of these "definitions" of quality:

    (a) A quality product is one that weighs between 2 and 4 pounds.

    (b) A quality product is one that consumers accept as such.

    (c) (De facto old USSR definition): Every product is a quality product.

6. Ask several people to read Feigenbaum's definition of quality and explain it to you. Compare and contrast their replies.

7. Read David A. Garvin, "What Does 'Product Quality' Really Mean?" *Sloan Management Review*, 26, No. 1 (1984), pp. 25–43. Summarize Garvin's approach to defining quality.

8. Ask several people without prior training on quality to give you a definition of "a quality product." Analyze their responses; compare them to the definitions reviewed in this chapter.

9. How do *you* define "quality"?

10. Discuss the following: "Simply 'meeting requirements' doesn't sound like quality. Shouldn't a producer 'go the extra mile' toward giving the customer what will delight her?"

11. Discuss the following: "What if I know product requirements are wrong. Am I producing a quality product if I conform exactly with wrong requirements?"

12. Discuss the following: "Our company's employee appraisal has three standards: outstanding, exceeds requirements, and meets requirements (the minimum for continued employment). But 'meets requirements' is doing quality work. What more does management want?"

13. Discuss the following: "I'm in charge of building large products that require dozens of workers and take several months to complete. On my projects, I'm responsible for time, cost, and delivering a product that meets all requirements. It seems to me that quality means meeting all three of these objectives."

PART II

◆ ◆ ◆

A Process View of Quality

Before a product can be produced, one needs to establish the production process. A production process entails a transformation process, which consists of equipment and facilities required to produce the work and policies and procedures on how work is accomplished, and a control process, which guides workers and managers in operating and checking the process. These topics are discussed in Chapters 7 and 8.

The production of quality products requires effective work processes. In order to create an effective work process, it is useful to bear in mind the following conceptual model of how work is accomplished. The production of any product, large or small, requires four steps: First, the requirements must be understood; second, a plan must be developed for accomplishing what is required; third, the basic work of constructing the required product must be carried out; and finally, it must be checked whether the product meets the established requirements. The four steps of this paradigm—specify, design, create, and examine—are discussed in detail in Chapters 9 through 12.

The specification (or analysis) process has to do with assessing the customer requirements; one must determine what the customer truly wants. Several useful tools for making this assessment are reviewed in Chapter 9. Design is the creative process of converting customer requirements into a design concept and into a set of product requirements that are complete, clear, and consistent; quality function deployment, discussed in Chapter 10, can help accomplish this task. The actual construction of the product has a huge impact on quality, and these issues are discussed in Chapter 11. The examine step has to do with checking whether the created product meets its requirements; several useful tools for examining products and processes are discussed in Chapter 12.

The Production Process

◆ 7.1 Introduction

To create an effective work process, it is helpful to have conceptual models of how work is accomplished. We will present such a model, a paradigm of work. Following that, we will describe briefly the four major steps of a production process: specify, design, create, and examine. We conclude the chapter with some comments about the management of work and the work process.

A Historical Note

Work is a condition of humankind. Amazingly, however, the first scientific study of work did not take place until almost 1900, when Frederick W. Taylor (1856–1915) introduced the notion of "scientific management." Taylor was the first person not to take work for granted, but to study it in order to understand it and improve the work process.

Taylor introduced many important concepts that are common knowledge today: delineation of authority and responsibility, management by exception, separation of planning from operations, functional organization, use of standards in control, and task specialization. Some of Taylor's disciples continued his analysis of work: Henry Gantt (1861–1919) concentrated on work as a process and introduced the concept of a Gantt chart for work scheduling; Frank and Lillian Gilbreth (1868–1924, 1878–1972) conducted extensive time and motion studies to improve work standards.

In spite of his pioneering effort, in some circles today it is fashionable to discount Taylor's work as being mechanistic and inhumane—emphasizing job design at the expense of human factors. But perhaps that is a little like blaming the Wright brothers for not inventing the jet airplane. Taylor made great contributions toward making work productive; it remained for others to concentrate on making workers achieving.

Note on Terminology

Until recently, there was no standard terminology for the people involved in providing goods and services to others. However, ISO 9000 has provided terminology that is likely to be adopted by quality professionals and those who audit firms for compliance with ISO requirements. Therefore, we have elected to use it in our detailed discussion of production processes, which we begin here.

In the ISO 9000 terminology, an organization or person providing a product to another is referred to as a *supplier*. The person or organization receiving the product is called a *customer*. In providing a product to a customer, a supplier may receive goods or services from another supplier, who is called a *subcontractor*. Thus, the product chain is from subcontractor to supplier to customer.

◆ 7.2 Production Process Components

Performing work in an organization requires a production process that is capable of developing the required product. Such a process consists of two components. One is a *transformation process* consisting of the machines, equipment, and facilities needed to produce the product, together with the policies, procedures, and instructions relating to the work activities to be performed. The other basic component is a *control process* to guide workers and managers in operating the process and to collect information on their accomplishments.

A production process can be very complex, and quality problems can and do arise with all aspects of the process. A quality problem with a transformation process might mean altering the equipment or changing subcontractors. A quality problem in controlling the work effort might involve debugging the information system used to plan and control production. A quality problem associated with operating the process might mean correcting the work instructions or altering worker motivation, recruitment, or training.

In analyzing quality, we might consider the entire company as a production process. Alternatively, we might consider separate production processes of, say, marketing, manufacturing, service, information systems, finance, and personnel. Or we might consider a specific production process, say, the process for assembling a particular component or for processing an order.

◆ 7.3 The Status of Production Processes

Quality is an attribute of a product, and it takes a quality process to produce a quality product. Some quality problems have to do with the *work process itself.* Typical situations are the following.

◆ The process was not designed, it just grew.
Years ago a need arose in the office to handle some matter; a secretary was assigned the task and devised a way to do it. As secretaries came and went, this process was passed from one to another. It was also adjusted over time to handle variations of the original need. Eventually, people followed the process because "this is the way we do it." But is it the way it should be done?

◆ The process is not documented.
Lack of process documentation is a common problem. A usual assumption is that long-term employees know the process and new hires can learn from them. One danger with this approach is that everyone may think they know the process, but they may not all be performing it in the same way. Another danger is that over time the process can "shift" without anyone really being aware. What was once a very good process can degenerate into a mediocre one.
One of the authors once knew a first sergeant in charge of an Army regimental office. On being given the assignment, his first undertaking was a complete change of the office filing system to a new, undocumented one. He was the only person who understood the new system—which he regarded as job security and an excellent way to keep away from the battlefield.

◆ Quality records are not kept.
In the past, many organizations have been remiss in keeping quality records—that is, records of the management reviews of their quality system, records of reviews of contracts with customers, records of their assessment of subcontractors, inspection and test records, employee training records, and the like. But this situation is starting to change because having such records is a requirement of the ISO 9000 standard, with which many firms throughout the world are attempting to comply.

◆ Process responsibility is not always clear.
A root cause of many process problems is that authority over the process is not clearly defined. If a process exists entirely within a functional area, the head of that area generally has responsibility for the process. A prob-

lem arises, however, with processes that cross functional lines. For example, who has responsibility for an order entry system: Sales (which enters orders), Information Systems (which builds and maintains the system), Production (which makes major use of the system), or Accounting (which tracks billing and payments)?

Sometimes the problem involves the *operation of the process:*

◆ A process is documented, but the documented process is not followed.
Most IS departments have a documented procedure for developing new software systems, called a Project Methodology. When you ask to examine their methodology, it is not uncommon for some searching to go on until a dusty document is retrieved from the bottom of some cabinet, the dust is blown off, and it is handed to you for perusal.

◆ Operators of the process are not properly trained.
Sometimes training is left to the manager, but the manager is too busy to do it properly. Sometimes more seasoned workers do not want to share their know-how with the newcomers—a form of job security. Sometimes the training program is inadequate. Sometimes a new employee has exaggerated his ability in order to get the job and now doesn't want to admit that training is needed.

◆ A process is adjusted for convenience, not effectiveness.
Even when a process is documented, some people cut corners for convenience or in an attempt to conserve resources or reduce production time. Sometimes this is a sign that the process is not optimal and needs to be improved; sometimes it is a sign that the person who is to follow the process is not aware of the importance of the step and the adverse effect of trimming it.

Some problems involve the *management of the process:*

◆ Management does not have a process focus.
A prevalent cause of process problems is the lack of management attention. Their interest is in getting an order, not in the process of getting orders; or in producing software, not in the software development process.

◆ Processes are not measured.
Measurement is viewed as too costly, too disruptive. But without measurement, how does one know how the process is performing, and what might be done to improve performance?

◆ Processes are not reviewed.
Every process should be reviewed on a regular basis to determine whether it should be modified or replaced. A common problem is a failure to conduct such a review. Using an outmoded process can be a competitive disadvantage. Moreover, it is an open invitation for people not to follow the process or to make unauthorized changes.

- ◆ Processes are not improved.
  Some processes are universally known to be inefficient or ineffective, but nothing is done about them. No mechanism or management support exists for making process improvements.
- ◆ Quality is not a paramount concern; time, quantity, and budget are more important.
  A root cause of many process problems is the failure of top management to make a firm commitment to quality.

◆ 7.4 The Basic Paradigm of Work

The production of any product, large or small, requires four steps. First, the requirements must be understood; second, a plan must be developed for accomplishing what is required; third, the basic work must be done to produce the required product; fourth, a check must be made to determine that the product does meet the established requirements. This basic paradigm for work means that any work process can be viewed as consisting of four subprocesses:

- ◆ Specify requirements.
- ◆ Design the product.
- ◆ Create the product.
- ◆ Examine the product.

Because these four subprocesses are executed sequentially, they are sometimes referred to as the four *phases* of the work process. From the first initials of these subprocesses, for simplicity we shall refer to this as the *SDCE paradigm* (see Display 7.1).

Requirements specification brings an understanding of *what* the customers require. Design entails research and development, architecting the product, and determining *how* the customer's requirements will be met. Create covers manufacturing, construction, or whatever is done to bring the product into existence. Examine entails verification that the product meets requirements.

DISPLAY 7.1 ◆ Basic Paradigm of Work

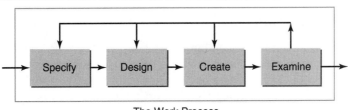

The Work Process

Example. For the task of writing a term paper, all four activities are accomplished by the same person. Specifying requirements is a matter of understanding the assignment and applicable standards; design involves gathering facts and deciding how the assignment can be accomplished; create covers writing the paper; and examine is a review to see that the paper satisfies the assignment and applicable standards.

For a large product, each step of the work paradigm is a significant activity requiring specialized knowledge and experience. Separate departments, such as Market Research, Design, Production, and Testing, might be established to perform the four activities. Each major step results in a product; for example, specification results in a set of customer requirements. Thus, each major step can be viewed as an activity itself, to which the basic paradigm can be applied.

The effort required for each of the basic steps is not the same from one situation to the next. For a task that is well understood, requirements and design might be perfunctory; the major effort would be in creating the product and examining it for correctness. For another task, specification of requirements might be a major effort; producing the product might be easy once requirements are established.

Ordering of Subprocesses

Often the four subprocesses—specify, design, create, and examine—of the basic paradigm will be accomplished sequentially, as depicted in Display 7.1. At times, however, it is preferable to have some phases operate in parallel.

Example. In constructing a large computer software system, it can be effective to establish broad requirements for the system, create a high-level design for the system, and identify the major components to be constructed. These components then might be created somewhat independently, so that one component might be in the detailed requirements phase while another is in a test phase.

This example illustrates that the basic paradigm of work should be regarded as an effective model for accomplishing work, not as a straightjacket that stifles creativity. It is a conceptual view of work that can be applied to any situation. Perhaps its greatest benefit is to emphasize that one must understand all the requirements for a product before jumping into creating it.

The PDCA Cycle

PDCA is an acronym for Plan, Do, Check, and Act. It describes a cycle of actions based on a product life cycle. The PDCA cycle is the creation of Walter A. Shewhart (see Section 2.9). It has gained considerable attention, much of it stemming from the fact that W. Edwards Deming presented the cycle in Japan as part of his introduction of quality concepts. Because of these presentations, the Japanese call

DISPLAY 7.2 ◆ The Shewhart
    (Deming) Wheel: PDCA

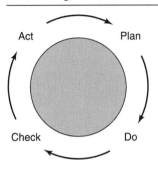

the PDCA cycle the *Deming Cycle* or sometimes the *Deming Wheel*. Those names
are used by many people; Deming, however, always referred to PDCA as the
Shewhart Cycle.

The phases of the PDCA cycle are shown in Display 7.2. They are:

◆ *Plan:* Plan for change. What changes are desirable? What data are available?
   Are other data needed? On the bases of all available data, decide on actions
   to be taken; plan for actions.

◆ *Do:* Carry out the actions that have been planned—make the planned change.

◆ *Check:* Observe the effects of the change. Determine if the change has the
   desired effect.

◆ *Act:* Observe the results. What has been learned? What does this experience
   suggest about future needs? future changes?

The PDCA cycle can easily be mapped onto the basic paradigm: Plan corresponds to Design, Do to Create, Check to Examine, and Act to Specify. Of course,
our basic SDCE paradigm begins with Specify, which is the last step listed in the
PDCA cycle. But because it is a cycle, the starting point is artificial; no matter where
you start, you continue through the four steps in a cyclical manner. Starting with
Act, the PDCA corresponds step by step to our basic paradigm.

◆ 7.5 Production Steps

The paradigm of work can be applied to view a production process as comprised
of four subprocesses, as depicted in Display 7.3:

1. *Specify:* Translating what the customer wants into customer requirements, that
   is, specifying the customer requirements. This step answers the question,
   "What does the customer require?"

DISPLAY 7.3 ◆ Steps of the Production Process

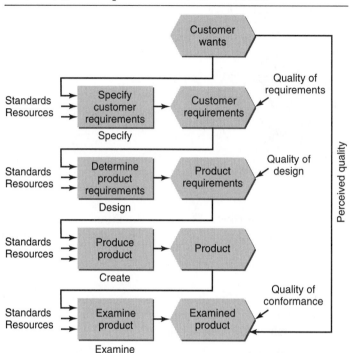

2. *Design:* Translating customer requirements into product requirements, that is, specifying product requirements. This step answers the question, "How can the customer requirements be met?"

3. *Create:* Creating the product to product requirements.

4. *Examine:* Validating that the created product meets customer requirements.

The first two steps of production have to do with determining requirements for the product; together they are referred to as the *requirements specification* or *requirements determination* process. The last two steps are referred to as *build* and *test*, respectively.

For a physical product, such as a car, it is relatively easy to distinguish the four steps of production and their various outputs. Specifying customer requirements involves market research and other activities to learn as nearly as possible what the customer wants in a car. These wants must be expressed in writing—a statement of customer requirements. The second step is to design a product that meets these requirements. This involves balancing quality aspects, such as function, against price and delivery date. The outcome of this step is a detailed description of the car that is to be built—the product requirements. The third step is to assemble the necessary components into the final product—the car. The fourth step is to validate that the car meets the customer requirements.

◆ 7.6 Customer Wants

Customer wants are desirable attributes or characteristics of a product that the customer would like to have. Some of these wants are very specific and can be described clearly by the customer: "I want a red car" or "I want a fish sandwich." Another example is a Request for Price Quotation issued by a company describing in detail a computer system it wants to purchase. But some wants are vague and can be expressed only in general terms, followed by "you know what I mean." Many are wants that a customer is not even aware of until an appealing product brings out his or her latent desire. In Japan, customer wants are referred to as *true requirements* because they reflect what the customer truly wants.

Example. Customers always have latent wants of which they are unaware. In the mid-1960s, few customers for cars expressed a desire for an error-free product—a car with no "bugs"—because nothing like that was then available. Today, even though quality might not be openly expressed as a requirement, pity the car manufacturer who brings out a lemon.

Suppliers want to produce products that delight customers at a price they are willing to pay. To do this, however, they cannot simply consider the wants that a customer openly states. They must go further and attempt to determine what the customer really wants.

Example. Customer wants for hotel accommodations vary with customer type. The want of a business traveler might be for a hotel near the business district with a reasonable room, fine restaurants, and fast check-out facilities; price might be a secondary consideration. On the other hand, the want of a foreign tourist might be for a hotel with a reputation for dependability that is located near tourist attractions.

◆ 7.7 Specify

Customer requirements are a written statement of what the supplier thinks the customer wants. The process of converting customer wants into customer requirements is called *specification* or, sometimes, *analysis*.

Customers always have both specific and general requirements; they require an information system that will supply certain reports (a specific requirement) and is easy to use (a general requirement). It would be convenient for suppliers if customers could state exactly what they require, but most of the time, they can't do this. In the information area for example, customers might ask for a system with new function, increased complexity, and one that makes fundamental changes in the way information is processed. They ask for something entirely new that has never existed before; how can they know precisely what it is they want?

In determining customer requirements, it is important to consider *all* customers for a product. Who are the customers for a car? Certainly the person who buys the car and his immediate family. But what about the mechanic who repairs it? He has requirements, too. And the community in which the car is driven has requirements concerning safety, pollution, and use of resources.

Customers might state requirements that are conflicting—one customer wants the product to be blue, the other green. During the requirements determination process, such conflicts must be resolved. The final set of customer requirements should be complete and nonconflicting.

◆ 7.8 Design

Product requirements are a written statement of *what* is to be produced. *Design* is the process of converting customer requirements and product standards into product requirements. It is the process of creating a description or representation of the product to be built.

> **Example.**   For a house, an architect often handles the design process. The customer requires a three-bedroom ranch-style house with certain heating, plumbing, and so on. The architect examines the customer requirements, the building code, and other regulations, and then creates blueprints and other documents that serve as requirements for the builder.

> **Example.**   A professor wants you to write a term paper. After analyzing the assignment, selecting a topic, and deciding what points to make, you design the term paper. That is, you decide how your points will be presented and perhaps construct an outline of the paper.

As these two examples suggest, design is a process requiring skill and special knowledge of the production area involved.

All product requirements must be specific because vague, nonverifiable requirements lead to product variability. If the person who actually builds the product must interpret a requirement, then the product will be shaped by that interpretation. For example, you can be certain that an IS professional's view of a user-friendly information system is a far cry from that of the typical customer of the system. All product requirements must be specific, yet they must be specified so as to support all customer requirements, specific and general.

> **Example.**   An automobile manufacturer might decide that a customer requirement is for fast acceleration. Then in the design process, all factors affecting acceleration—engine power, transmission performance, body weight, air resistance, and so on—must be specified with this requirement in mind.

Contrasting Customer Requirements and Product Requirements

Customer requirements describe *what* a product should be like—the function to be provided by the product, its appearance, how it can be used, its performance characteristics, and so on. Product requirements must embody all of this information and more. Because they will guide the people who do the actual building, product requirements must state *how* desired attributes will be provided.

◆ 7.9 Create

Create is the process of actually producing the required product. Whether the product is a house, a gourmet meal, a term paper, or a clean office, this stage involves the creation of a product according to the product requirements.

The terminology commonly used for this stage of a work process varies depending on the product being produced. One *builds* a house, *manufactures* a product, *operates* a machine, *delivers* a lecture or *teaches* a class, *sells* a product, *drives* a truck, *acts* a part, *cooks* a meal, and so on.

Although the general process is the same, the actual work done in the create stage varies, and the skills required depend on the product involved. For creating a term paper, the producer must be skilled at expressing ideas in writing. For creating a house, the producer must be skilled in the use of construction equipment.

◆ 7.10 Examine

The fourth step in the production process is to examine the product to learn if it meets all requirements. Basically, examination is done in one of two ways: you look at the product or you operate the product. Often you do both.

If the product is a house, you walk through it to observe if there are any visible defects: Is the paint applied properly? Are there any cracks in the plaster? Does everything look level? Then you operate the various systems in the house: Does the heating system work? Does the water system work? Does the lighting system work? Does the house leak when it rains?

If the house passes inspection, you celebrate. If it doesn't, you start a new process called "correcting the mistakes."

◆ 7.11 Quality Terminology

The production process calls for creating three major work products: customer requirements, product requirements, and the product. Traditional quality control has focused on the third task: creating the product, a task performed on the production line for manufactured products. Insufficient attention was directed to the specify and design tasks. But all three tasks—specify, design, and create—must be performed well for the final product to satisfy the customer, who is the ultimate judge.

We know what it means to do production well: It means producing a quality product, one that meets requirements. But *exactly the same is true of the first and second tasks*: Doing quality specification means producing a set of customer requirements that meets the standards and customer wants for that product. Doing quality design means producing a set of product requirements that meet standards and customer requirements for that product. For each process, one measures quality according to whether or not the product produced meets the requirements and standards established for it. Thus, "meets requirements" is a single standard for the quality of all activities.

For a product to meet the wants and true requirements of a customer, it is necessary to do a quality job of specifying requirements, a quality job of design, and a quality job of production. We can use the terms *quality of requirements*, *quality of design*, and *quality of conformance*, respectively, for the degree to which these tasks are performed correctly.

◆ 7.12 Examples of Producing Products

One general type of work is to operate a system; another is to produce a work system. Both operating a system and producing a work system accomplish work by employing the basic paradigm. However, the terminology involved and the complexity of the work efforts differ significantly for the two. To illustrate these differences, let's look at several examples.

Producing a Custom Product

First, let's examine how the SDCE paradigm applies to the task of producing a typical custom product. We will consider the task of building a house.

Specify the Requirements
The first step in building a house is to determine customer requirements. This involves interviewing the buyer; examining the local building code and ordinances, learning the various standards for safety, health environmental protection, and the like; learning the requirements of insurance companies and mortgage agencies; and learning requirements for utility, waste disposal, and other agencies that will provide service to the new house. The result of this step is a set of requirements for the house.

Design the Product
The second step is to create a design or architecture for the house. Often done by an architect, this involves analyzing the requirements and conceiving a satisfactory,

perhaps elegant way of meeting the requirements. The output of this step is a design consisting of sketches, blueprints, and other documents that meet the specified requirements for the house. This design is a major input to the create process.

Create the Product
The third step is to build the house: lay the foundation, frame the house, install major utility systems, finish the interior, and so on.

Examine the Product
The fourth step is to examine the product. If all goes well, the buyer, building inspector, and possibly a mortgage agency inspect the house and give their approval. In practice, as most home buyers know, it doesn't run that smoothly; that's another way of saying that in practice the house-building process has quality problems.

Producing a Consumer Product

Next, consider the task of producing a consumer product. The basic SDCE paradigm also applies to this task, but there are several significant differences in the complexity of the effort. Let's examine the work effort required to produce an automobile and highlight how this differs from producing a custom product.

Specify the Requirements
For a commodity product such as a car, there are no buyers in the beginning—only potential buyers. Moreover, these potential buyers, whoever they are, have few specific requirements and many general wants. The challenge in determining requirements for a commodity product is to anticipate the marketplace while still meeting the legal needs, environmental requirements, and needs of other customers, such as governmental agencies, insurance organizations, and consumer groups.

Design the Product
A major aspect of producing a commodity product such as a car is that you really need two products: the car and the car production process. These must be designed in tandem because the design of the car will directly impact the car production process and vice versa. Failure to coordinate the design of the product and the design of the production process can have tremendous adverse consequences.

Designing a car is a complex task, but in theory it is similar to designing a house. Designing a production line is another story, and we will examine this in more detail in Chapter 8.

Create the Product
Producing a consumer product means operating the production line. For some products, this is a simple, routine task. For building a car, this is a complex task requiring various skills, careful control of quality, and considerable coordination.

Examine the Product

It is impractical to examine thoroughly each car coming off the production line. Doing so would be very costly; moreover, some examinations are by nature destructive. Examination usually means making an exhaustive test of a few initial cars, making a cursory inspection of all, and randomly selecting others from the production lines for more extensive checks.

◆ 7.13 Applying the Paradigm Recursively

Production is a *recursive function* in that it can be applied repetitively to divide work. For example, building a product is accomplished through specification, design, creating, and examination. But the specification activity itself can be viewed as a production process. One obtains customer requirements (the output of the specification step) by determining what requirements are needed (specify) and how they should be determined (design). Then requirements are gathered (create) and checked (examined) to see that they are complete and nonconflicting. Moving down a level, each of these four activities can be divided further into basic steps.

Quality Control

The fact that the basic paradigm can be applied recursively helps explain what at first appears to be a contradiction: Quality is everyone's job; therefore, every product should be verified against its requirements. Doesn't that imply that there should be a block to indicate a test activity after the activities of specify and design in Display 7.1 as well as after create?

Such additional blocks are unnecessary because the tasks of specify, design, create—even examine itself—will be accomplished by applying the paradigm iteratively to each subtask. This means that there will be an examine activity as part of specify, one as part of design, one as part of create—even one at the end of the examine phase to check that the examine activity was performed correctly. In effect, *an iterative application of the basic paradigm ensures that quality control is built into every activity.*

◆ Exercises and Additional Readings

1. Describe the steps of the SDCE (specify, design, create, examine) paradigm for interviewing a job applicant.

2. Describe the steps of the SDCE paradigm for taking a vacation.

3. The *management cycle* consists of four steps:

   Plan work.

Organize to accomplish it.

Execute the work plan.

Evaluate and take corrective action.

Discuss this cycle as an application of the work paradigm.

4. One variation of the basic paradigm of work is a procedure described by Lauchland Henry for accomplishing a job assignment in a professional manner[1]

Phase 1. Defining the assignment
Phase 2. Planning how to accomplish the assignment
Phase 3. Executing your plan
Phase 4. Reviewing at the end

(a) Discuss how this is an application of the work paradigm.

(b) People sometimes jump into action without fully understanding an assignment. Give an example.

5. IDEA is an acronym for inspect, devise, execute, and affirm, the four steps of a problem-solving procedure developed by one of the authors[2]

Step 1. Inspect the problem.
Step 2. Devise a strategy.
Step 3. Execute the strategy.
Step 4. Affirm the solution.

(a) Discuss how this is another application of the paradigm of work.

(b) A person recently moved into a new community and has a problem in meeting people. Describe how the IDEA strategy might be employed to solve the problem.

6. What are the four basic steps of the paradigm of work as applied to the task of filling an order?

7. The create process of SDCE is described in various ways: You write a term paper, construct a design, and perform in a play. What are some other examples of the create process for goods? information products? services?

8. (a) State your customer requirements for a hamburger. (b) State producer requirements that will meet these customer requirements. (c) Match each producer requirement with the customer requirement(s) to which it relates.

9. Repeat Exercise 8 for a taxi ride.

---

[1]A. Henry Lauchland, *The Professional's Guide to Working Smarter*, (Tenafly, N.J.: Burrill-Ellsworth Associates, 1988), Chapter 3.

[2]J. Ledolter and C. W. Burrill, *Statistical Quality Control: Strategies and Tools for Continual Improvement* (New York: John Wiley, 1999), Chapter 3.

10. For a term paper that you have written recently, list the steps you took to construct it. Could your process have been improved? How?

11. (a) Map the course registration process at your institution onto the basic paradigm of work. Describe clearly the product of that process.

(b) Do the same for the add-drop process.

12. List additional problems associated with production processes, beyond those discussed in Section 7.3.

13. Imagine yourself as a manufacturer of apparel items. Outline the various steps of your production process.

14. Following the SDCE paradigm, describe a process for

(a) Cutting your lawn.

(b) Going on a date.

15. Summarize the new concept in production processes described in the article "Reconfigurable Manufacturing Systems to Help U.S. Firms Compete," *Quality Progress*, August 1996, p. 14.

16. Read "More Retailers Are Embracing Customer-Focused Operations and Technologies," *Quality Progress*, November 1996, p. 21. Summarize how some retailers are modifying their production processes.

17. Read "Employee Involvement Helps Honeywell in Branch Integration," *Quality Progress*, February 1995, p. 18. Describe how a team of employees helped Honeywell to integrate three separate branch offices into one.

18. In this book we talk about a four-step production process, consisting of specify, design, create, and examine. In the book *Juran on Planning for Quality* (published by Macmillan, 1988), Juran discusses an alternate system. Discuss the major steps in his system and relate them to the framework in this book.

Creating a Production Process

Accomplishing work in an organization requires a production process that is capable of turning work inputs into quality outputs. Creating such a process is the subject of this chapter.

◆ 8.1 Source of Production Processes

Many production processes were never designed; they just grew. For instance, most college professors have had considerable instruction on the content they deliver, but few of them have had instruction on the process of delivering it—they just started teaching. The same is true of many office processes and service processes—people just started doing things, and that became the accepted process. Many work processes were designed in much the same way as the streets of many old cities were designed by cattle looking for the nearest watering hole.

Major Processes

The situation is different for an organization's major processes. For example, manufacturing companies typically have a Production and Operations Management Department that is responsible for building and maintaining the manufacturing processes. And most firms have an Information Systems (IS) Department with similar responsibility for the organization's automated information systems. But even in manufacturing companies, who builds the processes for Marketing, Accounting, and Personnel? And who builds the processes for universities, local governments, and the local mom and pop shops?

Departmental Processes

Many processes are built and maintained by department managers or staff who have little training or experience in doing so. Because most processes have a heavy information component, the IS Department becomes involved in some of these efforts and, by default, tends to wield a strong influence on the entire development effort. As a result, the information component of the process gets attention from professionals, but the noninformation component does not. Because IS personnel generally are not highly sensitive to human factors, the result can be a very user-unfriendly process.

One way to lessen the problem of poor production processes is to encourage every manager to gain the ability to build effective, user-friendly work processes. Even if managers don't use this ability to actually construct a process, it will help them to manage and improve processes.

◆ 8.2 Some Process Fundamentals

Process Ownership

Every production process should have a designated *process owner* or *process manager* who is responsible for managing the process: overseeing construction of the process, monitoring process performance, authorizing process improvements, and replacing the process when warranted. This position is especially necessary for processes that cross organizational lines, making the natural authority over the process unclear. The process owner should be a manager whose major assignment is related to the process in an important way. The major duties of a process owner are to see that the process is properly documented, maintained, improved, and replaced when appropriate. However, the process owner is not necessarily responsible for operating the process.

The department manager is a logical candidate for ownership of a process that falls primarily within that department. But who should own some of the automated processes? or some of the major personnel processes? Part of the task of top management is to decide such matters.

Process Management and Project Management

Building or making a major change to a process should be treated as a project. A distinction must be made between managing the process and managing such a project. For illustration, let us consider the process used by the IS Department to develop information systems.

> *The process for creating a computer software system (computer program) might be described in a document called the* IS Development Methodology. *The manager of this methodology typically is the manager of the IS Department. An individual effort to create a software system is a project; the person in charge of this effort usually is called the* project manager. *The project manager is responsible for managing the development effort following the guidelines in the IS Development Methodology.*

Building a Production Process

Building a production process is a complex undertaking that requires specialized skills. In outline, the important steps in building a process are:

◆ Determining all customer requirements for the process
◆ Selecting a principle of production (discussed in Section 8.4)
◆ Building the transformation and control processes
◆ Verifying that the production process meets all customer requirements

◆ 8.3 Production Process Requirements

A production process has many customers, some internal and some external. The first step in determining process requirements is to identify all customers. The next step is to determine all requirements of these customers. Quite likely, there will be conflicts in the customer requirements, and such conflicts must be resolved so as to arrive at a complete, consistent set of requirements. A useful technique for determining customer requirements is to conduct a JAD session; it is discussed in Section 9.9.

Production Process Standards

A production process must comply with certain *process standards*. Process standards relate to such things as work methods, tools, controls, or operator qualifications. Standards can be viewed as a form of process requirements. Standards are of two types: internal standards established by the organization itself and external standards established by various laws, regulations, and industry associations.

Some process standards are merely guidelines to good practice; others are legal requirements or requirements that must be met to gain customer acceptance of the process products. Examples of the latter are the ISO standards and standards for a firm's quality control procedures imposed by an important customer. However they arise, standards can be viewed as a form of process requirement.

The purpose of process standards is to maintain a uniform way of conducting the organization's business. This provides many benefits: Training can be more uniform; people can be transferred from process to process more readily; less confusion arises when different groups discuss their processes.

Process standards also help to improve quality. Having a process standard that applies throughout an organization sends a message that quality concepts apply to everyone, even such "nonproduct" areas as marketing, accounting, and food service.

Example.   The mills of a large American steel company are located in several states. Acting independently, the IS departments at these different locations developed methodologies for their application development process. Although these were satisfactory for local use, differences in the methodologies among the locations caused intercommunication problems and hampered the development of common information systems. To correct this problem, the company adopted IS standards to be used at all locations.

Example.   Robert's rules of order is a standard adopted by many organizations to regularize the process of conducting a meeting. It arises from customer requirements that are both general (the need for a fair and orderly way to conduct discussions) and specific (the need for a process for adopting resolutions).

This example suggests how powerful a process standard can be. Robert's rules structure the entire meeting; they impose limits on debate, allow for shifting the order of business, and so on. In the same way, process standards help establish how the work of that process is to be accomplished—the methods, procedures, sequence of work, and plans and controls. Process standards deal with matters that are vital to the organization and the quality of its products.

An organization also needs a *standard for standards*. This should state what product and process standards are required, who is responsible for monitoring and recommending standards, how standards are adopted, and how people who need to know about a standard are kept up to date. Included in this document should be a statement on the responsibility of top management to see that appropriate standards are adopted and managed. Standards are at the very heart of quality, and the responsibility for quality must start at the top.

◆ 8.4 Principles of Production

To be effective, a production process must be based on some logical principle of production. Three such principles can be distinguished:

◆ Stage production
◆ Assembly production
◆ Process production

Each is suitable for some products and not for others, and each makes its unique demands on skills and resources. And each has its own characteristics regarding the quality of process products.

Stage Production

Stage production is based on homogeneous stages of production. A familiar example is the production of a house. Typical stages for this production are laying the foundation; framing the house; installing major systems of plumbing, wiring, heating, and so on; and finishing the interior. Another example is the production of an information system. Typical stages for this production are requirements determination, systems design, systems build, and systems test.

Characteristic of stage production is the view that the product is more important than the process—usually the quality emphasis is on checking the quality of the house rather than on the quality of the building process. Consequently, the building process is not improved, and the cost of quality stays relatively constant. Another characteristic is that the production process must be able to accommodate a large variety of products (each house might be different); this presents another quality challenge. Finally, changes in requirements are fairly common because customers have difficulty in visualizing what the final product will be like. This makes requirements change control extremely important.

Assembly Production

Assembly production is based on assembling a product from standard parts. A good example is a process used to assemble a personal computer from components. There are two subprinciples of assembly production. In *rigid assembly*, the product is standard; in *flexible assembly*, standard variations of the product are produced. Rigid assembly is used to produce standard catalog products, and flexible assembly is used for products available in standard variation.

> **Example.** Traditionally, information systems have been developed by stage production. An object-oriented approach allows development by flexible assembly.

Rigid assembly production is well suited to mass production. On the other hand, flexibility offers customers more choice, which translates into economic benefits. The advent of computers has done much to lessen the difficulty of building flexible assembly lines.

From a quality perspective, the work process plays an important role in assembly production. A well-designed, well-constructed assembly line is a good foundation for quality. But some degree of randomness is found in every assembly line:

variations in input supplies and materials, in operator actions, in measuring equipment, in product handling, and so on. An important task is to monitor the process to detect quality problems and remove their causes; statistical process control plays a part in this effort.

Process Production

Process production is an integrated system; it has no stages of production and no parts to assemble. In process production, the product is defined by the process and vice versa. The two subprinciples of process production are *flow production* and *service*.

The classic example of a flow process is an oil refinery. The end products produced by a refinery are determined by the process used; defining the process defines the product. Other examples of flow processes are telephone systems and transportation systems. A flow process generally is highly capital-intensive. And it is inflexible; once built, it is not easily modified. On the other hand, a flow process runs almost automatically, employing relatively few people in production.

Examples of service are medical, government, educational, and financial activities. Unlike flow processes, service processes generally are labor intensive. Consequently, they require careful control. The capital requirements for a service process might be low, as for a barber shop; but they can be very high, as for a hospital or a research center.

From a quality perspective, similarities and differences exist between flow production and service. For both, quality is heavily dependent on the process design—if the process is right, the product is likely to be right. This is particularly true for flow production, where the product can easily be distinguished from the process. Here control charts and other monitoring tools are standard tools for monitoring quality and adjusting the process to attain quality.

In judging the quality of service products, it is difficult to disassociate the product from the process. For example, a hamburger from a fast-food outlet is not the same as a hamburger from a fancy restaurant, even if the physical products are identical. Moreover, a hamburger provided in a fast-food outlet by one server in one set of circumstances might not be the same product as that provided by another server in different circumstances, even though the food items themselves are identical.

In the service industry, the importance of the process is sometimes stressed by saying "the process is the product." Quality is provided by having the right process and the right operation of the process; process design and operator training are essential. Service is the industry least touched by the modern quality movement, but this is changing rapidly.

Quality and the Three Principles of Production

The three different methods of production have been presented in order of increased complexity. Moving from stage production to assembly to process production, we see that the focus on the process and its operation tends to shift.

Stage production tends to rely heavily on workers' skills, and lack of proper worker training is a frequent cause of quality problems. In addition, stage production can accommodate a large variation in product design, generating a relatively strong focus on inspection to check individual products for conformance to requirements.

For an assembly process, the quality focus tends to balance between the operation of the process and the process itself. Operator selection and training tend to have less importance than for stage production, and proper management of the process becomes more important. Because output tends to be more uniform, random sampling of output often is sufficient to give assurance of quality products. Quality of the product becomes more dependent on the quality of process inputs; this places a greater burden on processes for selecting subcontractors and inspecting incoming products.

Flow production tends to be heavily automated. Operating the process amounts to "setting up" the process and monitoring it to see that all is proceeding according to plan. With process production, managing product quality shifts very much from checking products to checking the process. If the inputs are right and the process is right, the products will tend to be right. From the operations point of view, a critical concern is that the process be properly adjusted for each product to be produced.

The quality of service depends heavily on both the production process and its operation. And the operation, in turn, depends heavily on all people-oriented processes—employee selection, employee training, and management of employees. Service is the method of production that offers the greatest quality challenge.

◆ 8.5 Coordination of Work

A single artisan building a product has full responsibility for quality at each step of production. There is no need for coordination or cooperation with others; quality depends only on one individual. But work being done in an organization is another matter. Quality then depends not just on each individual's work effort; it also depends on these efforts being properly coordinated.

The design of work systems poses two basic and complementary requirements: (1) the division of tasks into subtasks, and (2) the coordination of subtasks to accomplish the required result—*analysis* and *synthesis*. A fundamental problem is: How should work be subdivided so as to facilitate coordination and promote quality? To resolve this problem, three coordinating mechanisms are employed: standardization, direct supervision, and mutual adjustment.

Standardization

Work can be coordinated by standardization. There are four major standardizing mechanisms, and each can have a very large impact on product quality.

Standardization of work outputs involves establishing product requirements for each product to be produced by the work effort. A waiter must be told what constitutes acceptable service; a welder what constitutes an acceptable weld; a programmer what constitutes acceptable code; and a manager what constitutes an acceptable work completion report. This usually is the simplest of the four standardizing mechanisms and the first to be implemented.

Standardization of the work process involves standardizing the tasks to be accomplished. It standardizes the *process methodology*, that is, the methods and procedures for accomplishing and managing the work effort. Standardization of the work process often is the second standardizing mechanism to be employed.

Standardization of work inputs involves establishing standards for each product that is used by the process. This includes all parts, information, and other components required for operating the process. The task of standardizing work inputs involves assurance that a subcontractor to a process provides inputs that meet requirements; the ISO 9000 initiative focuses on this area.

Standardization of work skills involves establishing job descriptions and skill requirements for each task to be performed. It also involves educating and training workers to make them proficient in performing the required tasks. Of the four standardizing mechanisms, many organizations find the standardization of work skills to be the most difficult to implement. This is particularly true for organizations or industries with heavy labor turnover.

Direct Supervision

Direct supervision achieves coordination by having one person take responsibility for the work of others. Under direct supervision, the coordinator issues instructions to the others and monitors their performance. Direct supervision often is practiced in a hierarchy, with groups of coordinators reporting to higher level coordinators.

The effectiveness of direct supervision depends heavily on the interpersonal relations of the work group and the skills of the coordinator. Supervision can have a negative impact on the satisfaction members of the work group gain from working, and it can be a major source of quality problems. To be effective, it is necessary to train supervisors in how to supervise properly.

Mutual Adjustment

Mutual adjustment achieves the coordination of work through the informal communication process. Under this mechanism, responsibility for coordinating work rests with the workers who perform the task. This simple coordinating mechanism works well and is used almost automatically when a small team is involved with a well-defined task.

Mutual adjustment also can be used effectively to supplement more formal coordinating mechanisms on a large, complex work effort. For example, the construction of a large information system involves many people, some with technical knowledge of information systems (the builders) and others with knowledge of the system requirements (the users). Much of the construction effort involves a division and coordination of labor between these two groups. Although there are formal procedures for coordinating work, often there are unforeseen problems and tasks that cannot be anticipated. In such situations, the success of the work effort often depends on the participants' ability to coordinate their efforts through informal communication.

Heavy reliance on mutual adjustment, however, carries the risk of increasing process variability. With no formal guidelines to follow, mutual adjustment can result in the same general problem being solved differently each time. The result can be great variation in the time and cost of coordinating work efforts and in the quality of resulting products.

◆ 8.6 The Transformation Process

Section 7.2 introduced the notion that a production process consists of a transformation process and a control process. While these processes must be constructed in tandem to ensure that they mesh properly, it will be convenient to discuss them separately. Our discussion starts with the transformation process.

Two basic activities are involved in creating a production process. One is to develop an understanding of the work to be done; this is called *analysis*. It starts with a clear understanding of the products to be produced and the fundamental work effort required to produce those products. This high-level work effort is then subdivided or broken down into smaller tasks, and then into still smaller tasks until one reaches a set of basic work tasks that can be assigned to people.

The second basic activity in creating a process is that of *synthesis*—combining these basic tasks into an effective and efficient work process.

Work Analysis

A standard technique for accomplishing a work activity involves breaking it down into simpler components. This activity is called *process decomposition, function decomposition,* or *work breakdown.* It is a technique used to subdivide a complicated process into pieces that are more easily understood, performed, and managed. It is employed for many reasons: the work effort is too large to consider as a whole, different skills are required for different aspects of the work effort, work is to be done in different places or at different times, and so on.

Clearly, a process can be subdivided in many different ways, and the skillful application of process decomposition is the mark of an expert systems analyst. One standard method for decomposing a work activity is to divide it into activities that will be performed *sequentially.* The paradigm of work and the basic division of a process into specify, design, produce, and examine are examples of this method. Another standard method for decomposing a work activity is to divide it into activities that can be accomplished *in parallel.* For example, work might be divided by required knowledge and skills, as is done in a hospital, or by geographic region, as is done by the post office. Obviously, a combination of these methods also can be used; the work breakdown of a multinational organization is a good example.

Work Synthesis

After work has been analyzed and broken down into basic tasks, these tasks must be arranged into an efficient production process. The ordered set of tasks represents a *production line*, and by executing these tasks (operating the line), one produces the required product. The tasks form the backbone of the work process; all other features of the process (jobs, controls, reports, etc.) are designed around the work breakdown structure.

The system must meet a number of major requirements.

◆ Work flows logically through the process.
It isn't easy to define a "logical" work process, but it isn't difficult to recognize one that is illogical. Government agencies supply many excellent examples. The logic behind some college registration processes is baffling. And information systems that require identical information to be entered several times by different operators are illogical and frustrating.

◆ Work can be planned and controlled without undue effort.
Is it necessary to get two levels of management approval just to buy a book? Is the annual planning process so complex that the plan isn't in final form until the first quarter has ended? Does the purchase of a hammer go through the same planning and control procedures as does the purchase of a new fighter aircraft?
A general system principle is that it takes a relatively complex system to control a complex system. Since a modern production process generally is very complex, it follows that the planning and control effort associated with such a process will not be simple or cheap. Nevertheless, an attempt must be made to make the work management system as simple as possible.

◆ Each worker can be assigned a well-defined, satisfying job.
Having a well-defined job means that you know what you are to do. The job may be fairly routine, or it may be one with great variety. But, routine or varied, the job must be clearly defined. A real problem arises, however, if you know what you are to do but hate doing it. A challenge in designing a work process is to devise a structure so that each worker has a well-defined and satisfying job.

◆ The manner in which work is accomplished supports the organization's goals and objectives.
The goals and objectives are a statement of what the organization hopes to accomplish. The work process and its operation should be aligned with those targets.

◆ 8.7 Building a Transformation Process

The process of building a transformation process follows the SDCE paradigm described in Chapter 7.

Specify the Requirements

A major effort must be undertaken to identify all elements that must be produced by the process, to identify all customers of each product, and to obtain all requirements of each customer. Parts and components must be available for assembly at the appropriate time and place; equipment must be available as required; and information must be provided to those who do the work and to those who plan and control the process. If the transformation process is to produce a new product (say a new model car), it will be necessary to determine the production requirements for the new product before it is possible to specify all requirements for the transformation process.

Design the Transformation Process

The first decision during the design of a transformation process is the selection of the principle of production. Is stage, assembly, or process production the best principle to employ? This decision has a dramatic impact on all aspects of the work process.

Design tends to be an iterative process. Two problems during design are the coordination of efforts and the arbitration of disputes that arise from conflicting requirements. As the design evolves, one gains insights that suggest better ways to do things. As a result, it is necessary to modify some of the work done earlier, thereby creating a new version of the earlier design element. This gives rise to the problem of *design control*—that is, controlling the evolving design so that everyone knows exactly which elements of the design are current. Maintaining proper control of the design is a major problem on any large, complex design project.

Create the Transformation Process

Of the four phases, the building phase often takes the longest and consumes the most resources. If the requirements and design phases have been done well, theoretically there should be few problems during the building phase. But inevitably omissions and changes must be handled. Change control often is a major problem during this phase.

Examine the Transformation Process

Decisions on how to examine or test the transformation process and the preparations for testing should all have been made prior to the test phase. In theory, all should run well. But errors of omission are not uncommon. And the worst nightmare during the test phase is the discovery of a problem that requires major changes. In extreme situations, the test phase becomes a major rework effort; it might be called "test," but it really becomes respecify, redesign, rebuild, and retest.

An entirely different problem occurs when testing fails to reveal all the defects in the process. The effect is that the installed process is faulty and must go through a costly period of "debugging" after it has been placed in operation.

◆ 8.8 The Control Process

A control process is superimposed on a transformation process for the purpose of guiding its operation. Examples are a management control process for guiding the work of an organization and a production control system for helping to produce quality products.

A control system has four components, which are the activities to

1. Plan performance
2. Observe actual performance
3. Compare actual and planned performance
4. Adjust as required

To illustrate these activities, let us consider a system for controlling the temperature of a room in winter. Assume that the room is heated by a furnace (this is a production process). The basic input to this process is fuel, and the basic output is heat. Attached to this production process is a control system that relies on the use of a thermostat, which turns the furnace on and off.

Let's review how the control system works (see Display 8.1). First, the system user decides on a temperature setting. The thermostat reports the actual temperature in the room and compares this temperature with the desired setting. The thermostat turns the furnace on or off whenever the temperature is, respectively, below or above the target.

In common parlance, the first of these activities is called *planning*, and the other

DISPLAY 8.1 ◆ Temperature Control System

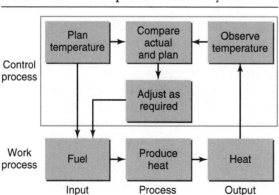

three are called *controlling*. The planning and controlling functions taken together constitute the *control function*.

Control of Production

Production work is controlled along three dimensions: time, cost, and quality. The time dimension of production is controlled by the production management system, which calls for planning activities, tracking results, and comparing actual results to plans. The cost dimension is controlled largely by the accounting processes, which call for budgets, collection of actual costs, and comparison of the two. The quality control system is a similar process and focuses on the control of product quality.

The principles of control are the same for all three dimensions of work, and the three must be coordinated to have an effective work system. Since our interest is primarily in the control of quality, our discussion will be limited to that dimension.

◆ 8.9 Control Principles

Control of work is essential. But unfortunately the word "control" has a bad ring to it, bringing to mind the terms *constrain, check, inhibit,* and *regulate.* We control crime, control pollution, control narcotics—all these uses of the word "control" contribute to the negative impact the word carries. But we also control an airplane, safely guiding it to its destination. It is this notion of control that should be applied to work. The following fundamental principles form the basis for building an effective control system.

1. *Work is controlled—not workers.*
   The aim of a control system is to assist in producing a quality product on time and within budget. To achieve this objective, control must focus on work, not on workers.

   The traditional approach has been to control production by controlling the workers. This was effective when workers were performing a simple repetitive task. Today, many control systems are based on the same principle, even though the character of work has changed significantly.

2. *Control is based on completed work.*
   To be effective, control should be based on completed work. Requiring people to estimate what portion of a task has been completed is asking for "creative reporting."

   But basing control on completed work generally requires more careful planning. The work effort should be divided into many small work efforts, all about the same size and each with a well-defined end product. The control of the total effort can then be accomplished by tracking the number of small work efforts completed relative to the total number to be accomplished.

3. *Control of complex work is based on motivation and self-control.*
Complex work is very difficult to control; a motivated worker is best equipped to exercise control.

A good example of complex work is computer programming. The quality of a program can be checked by operating it (testing) or by observing it (measuring, inspecting, reviewing). But the best assurance of quality is to have a well-trained, highly motivated programmer create the program and exercise control over its quality.

Self-control is part of the job of every knowledgeable worker, and workers must be trained and motivated to perform this function. However, worker training usually does not stress this point. Another problem is that quality and work control do not interest workers unless the general culture of the organization promotes this view. Such problems must be solved to make self-control effective.

4. *Controls for capturing control data must be built into a work process.*
It is not possible to control a work process without proper information. To control quality, resource utilization, and the time required to produce a product, it is necessary to embed controls into the work process for the purpose of capturing the required control data. For quality, typical means of capturing relevant data regarding products and processes are reports, inspections, tests, and reviews.

5. *Control data must go to the right people.*
To be effective, control data must be given to those who need it. The person who produces a product needs to know about product defects. The process owner needs information about process problems. If the product design is faulty, the design department needs to know. If quality problems are rampant throughout the organization, top management needs to know.

Unfortunately, people who need to know often are not given the information. Final test discovers a consistent problem, passes faulty parts back to production for repair, but does not notify engineering that the manufacturing process has a problem. Fixing the product is fine. But to fix the process, control data must go to the right people.

6. *A control system is designed to handle the routine.*
A control system is designed to handle routine situations, not every possible contingency. For example, a thermostat will adjust the production process (furnace) for fluctuations in temperature but will not cope with problems such as a power failure.

In designing a control system, a decision must be made as to what is routine (and to be covered by the system) and what is not. Having made this decision, it is important to assign responsibility for handling all nonroutine problems.

7. *Control of a complex work process is achieved through levels of control.*
One principle of general systems theory is that a complex work system requires a complex control system. Because work in an organization is complex, control of work efforts is achieved through several levels of control.

The first level of quality control is the individual worker—each individual is responsible for the quality of his or her work effort. If a worker is a member of a work group or team, the second level of control probably is the team. A third level of control might be the head of a department or the production supervisor. Responsibility for quality control passes up the hierarchy to the division and finally to the corporate level.

As one goes up the control chain, responsibility and authority for quality change. An individual worker is responsible for operating a production line properly. The head of manufacturing might have responsibility for the quality of raw materials, products, and the production process. And the chair of the board is responsible for every aspect of quality. The most important quality-related responsibility of top management is to establish the company's quality policy and to provide an environment that fosters the implementation of that policy.

◆ 8.10 Characteristics of a Control System

An effective control system must have the following four characteristics:

1. *A control system must be responsive.*
   A control system is ineffective if control signals do not result in timely action. To be responsive, a control system must provide each person with the control data they need at the time they need it. And the data must be presented in a useful form.

2. *A control system must be user friendly.*
   A control system must be easy to use. Instructions should be clear and simple; training should be provided in its use. The system should be designed for the convenience of people, not machines.

3. *A control system must be flexible.*
   A control system must be flexible enough to accommodate the special needs of different departments, different products, and different circumstances. One size doesn't necessarily fit all. For example, the control needs for constructing a people house are not the same as those for constructing a bird house. Similarly, the needs for controlling a large information systems project are not the same as those for a small project to modify an existing system.

   Over time, control requirements change, and the control system must be modified to reflect this change. Therefore, it is necessary to fix responsibility for review, evaluation, and improvement of the control system.

4. *A control system must strive for simplicity.*
   A control system should be as simple as possible. Control costs money; a control system should call for expending the least effort needed to achieve the required results. Unnecessary controls annoy people. And they are counterproductive because they focus attention on the control process and away from work. Unnecessary controls do not provide better control, only higher cost.

But make no mistake: a simple control system is not necessarily a small system. A control system requires a certain amount of redundancy to resolve ambiguities, errors, and omissions. An effective control system consumes a nontrivial amount of resources; our point is not to waste resources needlessly.

◆ 8.11 A Quality Control System

A quality control system is a special case of a control system. It is grafted onto a transformation process to prevent nonconforming products from being used or shipped. In principle, a quality control system is the same as a thermostat for controlling heat, but in practice it is much more complex. Some causes of complexity are as follows.

- ◆ The products to be controlled are more diverse and more complicated than the simple product, heat.
- ◆ Quality control responsibilities span all layers of the organization from the individual worker to top management.
- ◆ Quality control involves people—their attitudes, abilities, and emotions; these attributes are not as easily measured and controlled as are physical elements.
- ◆ Quality control is applied to a variety of product types: goods, information, services, production processes, operating processes, and management processes.

Components of a Quality Control System

As with a thermostat, the basic components of a quality control system involve four activities: plan, observe, compare, and adjust (see Display 8.2). Planning means

DISPLAY 8.2 ◆ Quality Control System

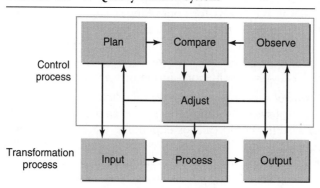

establishing the requirements for the product to be produced. Observing is done by examining the product or operating it. Comparing is a matter of checking to see if the product meets requirements. Generally, these three steps—plan, observe, compare—are more complex in a quality control system than in a heat control system, but the basic principles are the same.

The major conceptual difference between controlling heat and quality has to do with the adjust function. A problem with temperature requires adjusting only the input to the process. But a quality problem might require adjusting any part of the production or control process.

> *Suppose there is a problem with the process of filling a container with a quart of skimmed milk. If whole milk is incorrectly used, it might be because the instructions were wrong (planning problem) or they were not followed correctly (input problem). The process might underfill the container (process problem), but this error might not be caught (observation problem). Or the underfilling might be correctly observed but not recognized as an error (compare problem). Or it might be correctly noted as an error, but nothing is done about it (output problem).*

◆ 8.12 Quality Problems in Production and Their Possible Causes

Quality problems can arise during any part of the production process. We will discuss such problems throughout the book; here we will look at a few to get an overview of the situation.

Some Management Problems

Since management is responsible for processes and their operation, fundamentally all quality problems are due to management. The root cause of many problems is that management does not understand quality or has not made a real commitment to it. Generally, managers vow that quality is a top priority. In practice, however, time and cost often receive the greatest share of management attention. Some typical signs that quality is not a top priority are:

- ◆ Workers are measured on the basis of time and cost, not the quality of their output.
- ◆ There are no quality objectives in worker appraisal systems, and therefore workers have no incentive to achieve quality.
- ◆ Employees are afraid to report errors; they sense that production is more important than quality.
- ◆ Quality control procedures are slighted, particularly when there is an urgent need for output.

Quality starts with management understanding and commitment. Without that, achieving quality is an uphill battle.

Some Process Problems

Problems can plague any aspect of a production process:

◆ Product requirements are incomplete or unclear.

◆ The transformation process is not documented, or the documented process is not followed; as a result, high product variability is inherent.

◆ The control process is not documented, or the documented process is not followed. Reviewers are not well trained. Test coverage is not adequate; tests are not conducted properly, or results are not properly analyzed.

◆ The process is inappropriate; it is simply not capable of producing quality products.

Often the root cause of such problems is that production managers are judged on the quantity of process output, not its quality—and certainly not on the quality of the production processes or on process improvement. So, as usual, the old rule applies: An organization gets the behavior it rewards.

Another source of production problems is poor performance by the workers. One cause might be poor procedures for worker selection, training, and compensation—problems that are relatively straightforward to identify and solve. But the root cause might be an inappropriate organizational culture. This is a serious problem that can be solved only by top management—or a new top management.

The root cause might well be that a process manager has not been appointed. People are busy operating the process, but no one is managing it.

Some Quality Control Problems

Quality control has no great appeal; generally, people get more pleasure out of building something than checking to see that it is built correctly. Unfortunately, the way quality control is conducted in many organizations does little to change this attitude.

In many organizations, product review processes are faulty. There may be no written review procedures, or the written procedures may be inadequate or out of date. Sufficient time and resource are not allocated to performing reviews, giving a clear indication to workers that management is not convinced that quality control is an important part of the job. Other times the product review procedures are appropriate, but workers are given no training in performing reviews—and reviewing a product is not the same as creating it. In some organizations, review information is used in the worker appraisal process. This can easily generate a culture of fear and an attitude that the way to survive is to beat the system. Reviewers overlook problems to keep friends from looking bad, and they pray that the favor will be returned. Or the review process is skipped with the excuse of insufficient time or resources.

Many control problems can be traced to management's failure to understand what an effective review requires: proper review procedures, trained reviewers, adequate time and resources for reviewing, and absolutely no connection between review results and employee appraisals.

If review rules are reasonable and an employee is trained but is unwilling to follow the rules, it could be time to suggest he might prefer other employment.

Product-Specific Problems

Quality problems vary with the type of product being produced.

Goods

The production of goods generally involves heavy use of components and parts obtained from outside subcontractors, and the quality of the incoming material is of concern. Because production depends on physical equipment, another concern is the variability in output caused by equipment wear or changes in the operating environment (temperature changes, dust, moisture, etc.). Depending on how highly automated production is, operator ability and training can also be a critical issue.

Because quality control of goods usually involves measurement, the calibration of measuring and test equipment is an important concern. Identification and storage of products—particularly the segregation and control of nonconforming products—are also major concerns.

Service

For every service product, the production process itself is a critical determinant of quality. But what distinguishes service from goods and information is that the production process is apparent to the customer. Customers don't know how good or bad an automobile assembly line is; they judge quality by the cars that are produced. But a poor, inefficient process for serving a restaurant meal can create a bad impression. To compound the problem, blame for poor service might incorrectly be attributed to the server, so the process isn't improved.

Another feature of service is that, unlike goods and information, quality control can take place while the product is being delivered to the customer. For example, a nursing supervisor might observe how a patient is being treated (quality control) and use this information to make suggestions to the nurse providing the treatment (improve the process).

A major determinant of service quality centers on the people providing the service. Employee selection, training, motivation, supervision, and reward—all processes relating to employees—have a significant impact on quality.

Information

The production of all products depends heavily on information processes, and these processes are a fertile source of quality problems. Some causes of problems in automated information systems are these:

- Typically, the process for developing information processes (system development process) is not well documented.

- The analyst/programmers who develop information processes lack the discipline to follow a documented development process, and their managers do not correct this situation.

- Workers enjoy creating information processes but generally dislike reviewing completed work—particularly the work of others. So product review often is not very effective.

Modifying existing information processes usually is an even greater source of quality problems because

- Information processes are not well documented; therefore, analysts cannot easily understand the full impact of the changes they make.

- The change process itself is not well documented.

Generally, quality is best served by restricting requests for information system changes to those that are necessary. In many organizations, however, this does not happen because a faulty accounting system fails to charge back the full cost of a system change to the department requesting it. This is a good example of how complex and convoluted quality improvement can be.

◆ 8.13 Measuring Process Performance

A serious challenge in any organization is for management to gain a clear picture of what is really going on in the organization. People don't like to admit their mistakes; quality problems are concealed from management out of fear for its effect on careers. No matter how freely information generally flows in an organization, it is useful to have a mechanism for informing management of problems that can affect quality.

Management Evaluation

Managers might be a serious cause of quality problems, and their incompetence and ineptitude should be brought to the attention of upper management. But employees are understandably reluctant to tell upper management that the real problem with quality in their area is that the manager is a turkey. To elicit such information, a scheme must be developed for gathering such information without jeopardizing the employee's career or exposing the manager to unnecessary embarrassment. Two such schemes are executive interviews and employee opinion surveys.

An *executive interview* is a scheduled meeting, required by company policy, between an employee and the manager of the employee's manager. That is, it is a meeting that skips the immediate level of management. An employee is required to meet with his manager's manager on a regular basis to discuss whatever concerns the employee or the manager might have. Generally, such an interview focuses on career opportunities, avenues for improving the employee's ability, or whatever else the employee wishes to discuss. Such interviews give the employee an opportunity to discuss anything, including problems caused by his immediate manager. It gives the manager conducting the interview an excellent opportunity to assess the people and the general atmosphere of the level one step below his immediate level of responsibility.

Executive interviews tend to focus on personnel issues; indeed, the interview is an opportunity for bonding and career counseling. But it also offers an excellent opportunity to discuss quality issues. The troops usually know where the quality bodies are buried; an executive interview is an effective mechanism for passing that information up the line, which gives support for corrective action.

Executive interviews can be conducted right up the management chain, giving management at any level the opportunity to assess the quality of management by those reporting directly to that level, as seen by those directly being managed.

An *employee opinion survey* is a tool for appraising work conditions, including the performance of management. It is a good vehicle for getting feedback on the quality environment and the performance of the quality system. It is a tool for gathering information that might not be offered through normal channels of communication, suggestion schemes, executive interviews, or other "open" schemes where the employee's identity is known. An opinion survey tends to focus on how the company is managed because this information is essential, yet difficult to obtain because there is a fear of management retaliation.

The challenge for conducting an effective employee opinion survey is to obtain the required information without jeopardizing those who provide it or embarrassing those exposed by it.

To conduct an opinion survey, it is necessary to design a survey instrument, administer it, and collect, analyze, and use the information.[1] Designing and administering the survey will not be discussed here because it follows the usual pattern for surveys. The major issue in conducting employee opinion surveys involves collecting, analyzing, and using the information. And the top concerns with all of these activities are security, security, and security.

Employees will give frank opinions about management, working conditions, concerns about quality, and other issues provided they trust the organization not to use the information against them. To establish this trust, it is not enough to say,

---

[1]"Surveys are discussed in Chapter 18." For a detailed discussion of surveys, see our other book, *Solving Quality Problems: Tools for Continuous Quality Improvement*. (NY: John Wiley, 1999).

"Trust us." It is essential to establish a guard for the information supplied by employees as if it were the gold stored in Fort Knox. Information must be collected and stored with absolute security. Rules must be established for the use of information that will not reveal the identity of those who provide it. For example, information might be summarized to avoid revealing individual opinions. Moreover, rules should be established for disclosing group opinions only for groups that are above a certain size. If a manager has only two employees, and the average opinion is that the manager is ineffective, it isn't difficult for the manager to know what each employee thinks! In the same way, information from different groups reporting to a given management level should be reported in summary form to prevent the manager from differentiating among the groups.

People will give frank opinions about management when asked, but only if they are absolutely certain that the information will not be used against them. Properly used, employee opinion surveys can be an effective tool for identifying quality problems—particularly problems relating to management, which might be difficult to uncover by another mechanism.

◆ 8.14 Process Improvement[2]

Building a production process is a major effort. But no matter how successful the effort, any production process will need continual improvement to make corrections or to adapt the process to changing process requirements. This need imposes a requirement on the process owner—namely, the requirement to collect data on process performance and to make needed corrections in the process.

Process improvement generally is accomplished on a project-by-project basis. It is an activity quite separate from the activity of building the process; however, it requires similar skills and a similar methodology to those employed in the building process.

The need for continual process improvement imposes requirements such as these:

- ◆ Build controls into a production process to measure process performance.
- ◆ Build a system to collect data on the defects of products produced by the production process.
- ◆ Build a system for analyzing the collected data and making process improvements.

Example.   Fast Food, Inc. has a process for producing hamburgers; we want to analyze and improve the quality of the products produced by this process. To do this for each hamburger requirement, we need to know (1) how many

---

[2]A detailed discussion of process improvement is given in Part V of this book.

hamburgers were scrapped because they failed to meet the requirements and (2) how many were served to customers but did not meet their requirement (information that is not easily obtained). What is needed is a system to collect these defect data, analyze them, and take corrective actions.

Note that building the data collection system is part of building the hamburger production process; collecting defect data is part of operating the production process; analyzing the defect information is a separate activity; and this activity results in individual projects to make improvements in the hamburger production process.

◆ Exercises and Additional Readings

1. Compare the four basic activities of a control system with those of the Shewhart PDCA cycle.

2. Discuss how standards help to improve

   (a) Planning work

   (b) Educating workers and managers

   (c) Communication in the organization

   (d) Product quality

3. Standards are not an unmixed blessing. What are some of the costs of

   (a) Establishing and maintaining standards?

   (b) Enforcing standards?

   (c) Overly detailed, bureaucratic standards?

4. Feedback control is the use of process control data to make process adjustments. Describe how feedback control might be used to improve the processes of (a) writing a term paper; (b) applying for a job; (c) going on a date.

5. Any process can be subdivided into a collection of smaller processes, which are called *subprocesses.*

   (a) List some major subprocesses for the task of providing a Thanksgiving dinner.

   (b) List some major subprocesses for the task of writing a term paper.

   (c) List some major subprocesses for the task of operating a university.

   For each major subprocess, list a few subprocesses of it.

6. What are some of the pros and cons of having a process operator designated as the process owner?

7. Most quality control systems focus on finding and fixing errors in products but ignore potential problems in the production process. What steps might be taken to correct such a situation?

8. It is often useful to break a complex task into smaller, related tasks. Apply this strategy to the government, universities, stage plays, and football games.

9. Give a few examples of stage, assembly, and flow production.

10. Discuss the difference between effective feedback control and process tampering. (You may want to refer to our discussion of tampering in Section 5.11.)

11. In addition to an organization's internal standards, certain external standards must be observed. One example is environmental standards. List some others.

12. Consider a major assignment you have completed recently, for example, a term paper.

(a) Describe your transformation process—the major steps that you took in completing the assignment.

(b) Critique your transformation process. How could it have been improved?

(c) Describe the quality control process you employed in producing your product.

(d) Could your quality control process have been improved?

13. For some activity that you perform routinely,

(a) Describe your transformation process.

(b) Describe your control process.

(c) What suggestions can you make for improving these processes?

14. Contact a local firm and ask it to describe one of its production processes (marketing, manufacturing, a personal process). Is there a process owner? Is the process documented? How is it monitored and improved? Write a brief report and assess your findings.

15. Construct a process that a college student could use to get a job upon graduating.

16. Construct a process for (a) buying a new car, (b) buying a used car.

17. Contact a local fast-food franchise (McDonalds, Burger King, etc.) and ask it how it controls the quality of (a) its food products and (b) its service.

18. Discuss the differences between direct supervision and mutual adjustment. Give examples for each.

19. An important aspect of any production process is the disposal of waste products (by-products) arising from the process.

(a) Describe the waste products arising from the process of preparing a meal.

(b) How does the consideration of waste change the four steps of the process of preparing a meal?

(c) How does the consideration of waste generate requirements for related processes?

Chapter 9

The Specification Process

A Japanese manufacturer of industrial sewing machines had no complaints from their customers. In spite of this, they had their design engineers spend some time with customers to observe their machines in action. They discovered that machine operators had difficulty sewing the wing tip in collars, causing some shirts to be downgraded. Armed with this information, the engineers designed a sewing machine that produced perfectly stitched collars even when used by inexperienced operators. This machine became a profitable new product for the company.

—Brian L. Joiner[1]

This is the first of four chapters in which we examine in detail the four steps of a work process. In this chapter we will explore the process for specifying customer requirements that reflect customer wants.

---

[1]Brian L. Joiner, "Quality, Innovation, and Spontaneous Democracy," *Quality Progress*, March 1996, p. 51.

◆ 9.1 Custom and Consumer Product Requirements

The processes for determining requirements for custom products and for consumer products are sufficiently different to require some discussion.

Custom Products

A custom product is developed for specific customers, who can express their needs directly to the product builder. By observing customers, interviewing them, displaying prototypes or other examples, the builder can arrive at a set of requirements that reflect the customers' needs.

When there are many customers for a custom product, it is inevitable that they will have different requirements. To satisfy everyone, sometimes the product is loaded with so many features that it becomes unwieldy. At other times, it is impossible to satisfy everyone because requirements conflict. It's vital to have some procedure for resolving such conflicts because they are bound to arise.

A technique that has been used successfully when there are many customers for a custom product is to appoint a *product administrator.* This person's job is to handle the product-related administrative work for the customers. This includes such tasks as convening all meetings related to the product, recording all customer requirements, serving as the customer interface with the group that is producing the product, and helping to resolve conflicts. The product administrator need not be the person who has responsibility for the requirements, nor need he have any decision-making authority. Rather, the administrator is the customers' focus for all product-related matters; the administrator does the staff work for the decision maker.

The agreement between the supplier and customers for a custom product typically is documented in a contract. The contract might well describe the customer requirements in general terms and stipulate that part of the supplier's task is to develop detailed requirements. This might be done, for example, when the customer does not have experience with the requirements process.

> **Example.**   Internal customers for information processes usually rely on the IS Department to determine detailed requirements for their automated information systems.

To assure that contract provisions are clear, complete, and correct, and that the organization has the capacity to provide the required product, the supplier should conduct a contract review prior to accepting an order for a custom product. The procedure for such a review should identify the authority responsible for conducting the review and specify the review record to be produced.

Consumer Products

A consumer product is developed for a class of customers, not specific individuals. The product (including standard product variations) usually is developed before the identity of specific customers is known. This means that the process for determining customer requirements must differ from that for a custom product.

The problem facing those who build consumer products is to determine the product features that people want and are willing to pay for. Some techniques used to ascertain these features from potential customers are discussed in Section 9.8.

◆ 9.2 Related Products

The development of a product can generate the need for an array of related changes. For example, a new product may generate the need for a new or modified production process, a process for operating the line, a process to hire and train the operators, and appropriate management processes to direct and control the production process, the time and cost of its operation, and the quality of its products. And there may be a need for processes to market the product; handle, store, and ship the product; service the product; account for transactions concerning the product; and so on.

Our intent in this chapter is to explore the process for determining customer requirements for a good, service, or information product. The point of this brief section is to emphasize that the production of a new product might require concomitant changes in related processes.

◆ 9.3 Customer Wants

Customer requirements are a product—a product of the specification process. Let us illustrate this process by examining a simple product: a writing instrument.

The first question in determining customer requirements is: Who are the customers for the product? A major class of customers consists of those who might buy or use the product. Another are the internal customers, who are involved in the marketing, production, and delivery of the product. A third customer is society, which is impacted by the production and disposal of the product.

The second question is: What does the customer want? As a potential buyer of the product, how would you answer this question? Perhaps your reply would be something like this: "It must produce good writing—smooth, the right thickness. It should be convenient to use and carry—not too large or too heavy. It shouldn't leak or damage my clothes. It should look nice; there should be a choice of colors and styles." What else would you want?

As in this example, the customer wants are often expressed in general terms: how the product should look, what function it should provide, and other very general statements. And, of course, the expressed wants usually are based on an assumption that the price for the product will be acceptable in relationship to the wants it will satisfy.

What are the wants of internal customers? Even for a relatively simple product such as a writing instrument, this is not a simple question. An attempt to answer it usually starts by listing all the internal customers. This list might include design, production, material suppliers, receiving, advertising, marketing, finance, and shipping. And, of course, personnel might be involved in adding new people to build and sell the product; education might need to retrain the production and sales forces if the product is revolutionary. The new product might well require some modification of the production process; it might even require building a new plant or subcontracting some portion of the manufacturing. And management and quality assurance are involved in the entire effort. The wants of all these customers must be considered, too.

Society is a customer for most products. What does society want of this new writing instrument? Are there any regulations or standards promulgated by various regulatory bodies, trade associations, civic groups, environmental groups or others that should be considered in producing this new product? If this instrument is to be sold internationally, are there requirements in other countries that should be taken into account?

Anticipating Wants

But this isn't the entire story on requirements. It isn't enough just to learn what customers want today, one must also attempt to anticipate what they will want tomorrow. Three important areas to consider are technology, fashion, and the law. Are you gathering requirements for a better buggy whip when technology is about to replace the horse-drawn carriage with a car? Are you gathering requirements for a better hoop skirt when fashions are about to change? And are you overlooking changes in the legal environment that will have a major impact on your product line?

> *In the 1970's, a sudden interest in product safety and new laws spawned a rash of product liability suits. Rice-Barton Corporation, a manufacturer of paper-making and textile machinery, was notified in 1976 of claims by users of two of its presses for damages arising out of industrial accidents. One of the presses was built in 1895, the other in 1897. The company claimed: "We have no records going that far back, and these presses probably have been resold and modified many times. But we still may be liable."*[2]

The moral is that often it pays to anticipate wants, not just to follow what is customary and required today.

◆ 9.4 Specific and General Customer Requirements

Having identified the wants of all customers, the next step is to convert these wants into a complete set of nonconflicting customer requirements. Even for a simple product, this can be a complex undertaking.

---

[2]*Business Week*, May 31, 1976, p. 60.

A *customer requirement* for a product is a written description of a feature or trait the product should possess. Requirements describe a product's function, physical characteristics, operational characteristics, and other important features. Well-conceived requirements reflect what the customer is looking for in the product.

Some customer requirements for products are specific; there is no question about what is wanted in the product. Examples of specific requirements are:

◆ The diameter of this part must be 5 cm, plus or minus 0.05 cm.

◆ Phones must be answered within four rings 95 percent of the time.

◆ This computer program should have no more than two reported bugs per thousand lines of code in the first three years of operation.

All these requirements have something in common: It is possible to verify whether or not the requirement is met. By measuring a part or by counting phone rings, spelling errors, and program bugs, it is possible to verify that the requirements are met. Requirements for which there is a verification procedure are called *specific requirements*. A specific requirement, therefore, is a written statement of

◆ An attribute or function that a product is to possess

◆ The performance standard for that attribute or function

◆ The measuring process to be used in verifying that the standard is met

Not all requirements are specific; some examples are:

◆ The car must provide a smooth ride.

◆ The information systems program must be maintainable.

◆ Table service should be fast, efficient, and friendly.

◆ Lectures must be interesting and informative.

◆ The computer should be reliable.

These customer requirements are not precise. There is no clear way to verify whether or not a product meets any of them. Requirements for which there is no verification procedure will be called *general requirements*. Buyers of cars might ask for power steering (a specific requirement), when what they really want is ease of use (a general requirement). Users of an information system want it to be user friendly; they don't know how to be more specific than that, but they can judge the relative "friendliness" of two products.

Importance of General Requirements

General requirements are very important. Their study basically is an attempt to view the product from a customer perspective—to express quality requirements as a customer sees it. Customers tend to view quality in general, nonspecific terms.

They don't have a formal definition of quality, such as a manufacturer must have to produce consistent products. Customers use value-laden terms: easy to use, quick response, nice appearance, comfortable. They speak of wants and problems, not solutions. While general customer requirements are not specific and are often difficult to measure, it is a grave mistake to ignore them.

The point of focusing on general requirements is to offer products that go beyond simply having no flaws. The aim is to produce products that give customers what they really want. The aim is not just to meet requirements but to do one's best to have the right requirements to meet.

◆ 9.5 Standards

Some requirements apply to a class of products; these are called *product standards*. An example is a building code that applies to all houses built in a community; another is the format to be used for all interoffice correspondence. Product standards arise from two sources. *External standards* arise from outside the producing organization, possibly from a customer, but more often from some agency such as the Food and Drug Administration or Underwriter Laboratories. *Internal standards* are established by the producing organization itself.

Some standards are adopted by a supplier by choice, some by necessity. For example, products must meet standards such as these:

- ◆ *Laws*. Building codes, environmental laws, privacy legislation, national security regulations, and so on.

- ◆ *Industry standards*. Most industries have professional groups that establish standards for products of the industry. An example is the automotive industry.

- ◆ *Customer standards*. Large concerns, such as the government, McDonalds, and Ford, establish product standards that subcontractors must meet.

- ◆ *De facto standards*. A single product can become so successful that it establishes what amounts to a de facto standard for its market sector. An example is the Qwerty keyboard for typewriters.

◆ 9.6 Problems with Requirements

Incomplete or improper customer requirements are the cause of many quality problems. Some problems related to customer requirements are these:

- ◆ *The requirements process is slighted.*
  Many organizations slight the entire requirements process. They are so anxious to "get on with it" that they don't stop to define what "it" is. Most

information processing professionals will agree that specification of requirements is the weakest, most error-prone part of the development process. Most will agree that errors made during requirements definition are the most expensive to repair. And most will also agree that we should spend more time on requirements determination.

◆ *The focus is on what can be done, not what is wanted.*
Frequently, organizations don't start by asking: "What does the customer want?" They start by asking "What technology and processes do I understand, and how can I use these to build something the customer wants?" The process is driven by the developers' capability, not by customer wants.

◆ *Some requirements are missing.*
Because customers are not totally familiar with the product area, they assume the supplier will fill in the features they have in mind but failed to specify. This is particularly true when the customer and supplier are closely related; they are members of the same overall organization, or they have done business together for years.

◆ *Sometimes requirements are sketchy.*
We were once told about three development contracts that were awarded to an organization that builds large software systems for customers. One contract, with an American retail firm, was for $10 million; it was based on a five-page requirements document (about par for contracts of its type). The second, with a U.S. government agency, was for $100 million; it had a 10-page requirements document. The third, with a Japanese firm, was for $10 million; it had a 500-page requirements document. Will it be a surprise if the Japanese firm is the one that is most satisfied with its product?

◆ *Validation procedures are missing.*
Customers tend to state requirements without specifying how to validate the requirements. Customers have in mind what they expect when they specify a requirement, and they assume that the supplier has the same vision. However, to avoid confusion and conflict, a validation procedure must be specified.

◆ *Not all customers are considered.*
Specific customer requirements generally are oriented heavily toward the primary customer and often ignore important needs of secondary customers. It is important that all customers be considered.

◆ *Relying on past practice.*
Many times requirements are simply based on previous requirements. "Like the last lot you sent us." "The way we've always done it." In effect, no real thought is given to the requirements; it's just business as usual.

◆ *Conflicting requirements.*
No two customers have the same requirements. Conflict among requirements is the norm, not the exception. A good part of the specification process involves making hard choices as to which requirements are to carry the most weight.

◆ *Designs are specified, not requirements.*
It is very common for customers to confuse requirements and design. They have a need for transportation, but they ask for a car because that's the way they have always satisfied their need. Maybe roller skates, a taxi, or an airplane would be a better solution; but the supplier won't consider those solutions if the solution is expressed as the need.

◆ 9.7 Methods for Determining Custom Product Requirements

Requirements for custom products can be obtained by asking, deriving, synthesizing, or discovery. Which approach is used depends on the situation; sometimes it is more effective to use more than one. In establishing requirements, it is important not to overlook relevant standards; these might be learned from the customer, trade associations, government organizations, consumer groups, and similar bodies.

Results are summarized and organized into a *requirements document.* This document forces a sequential ordering of requirements, which helps to ensure that nothing is overlooked. The completed requirements document should be circulated to appropriate customers for their approval. Discrepancies, disagreements, and problems must in some way be resolved; the revised document then will serve as the statement of customer requirements.

Asking

A basic tool for determining requirements is the interview. Individual interviews, group interviews, brainstorming sessions—all are means of asking customers what they require.

Obtaining requirements by interviewing customers is not as simple as it may appear. First of all, it is necessary to select the right people to ask. Who has knowledge and insight into the product? Who has political power and cannot be overlooked? Who understands the needs of secondary customers? It is also necessary to prepare for the interview. What questions should be asked? Can a checklist be used to assure that all is covered? Conducting an interview requires special skills—the ability to establish rapport and elicit truthful responses, even while probing into matters that the interviewer might be reluctant to discuss. While keeping the interview "flowing," the interviewer must keep an accurate record of responses to avoid misinterpretations and omissions.

Deriving

A second approach to obtain requirements for a custom product is to derive them from a similar, existing product. The existing product might be one that is to be replaced by the new product; or it might be a product someone else has that is to be copied; or it might just be a description in a book or magazine.

A new computerized information system for an organization rarely plows completely new ground. Generally, there is an existing process—perhaps just a manual one—that provides at least part of the function that the new system is to provide. Documentation of the existing process saves reinventing functions that are already in place and working. It helps the builder understand the human interfaces to the existing system, thereby making for a more intelligent transition to the new system. And it helps everyone to understand better the manual procedures, which may be impacted by the new system.

Synthesizing

Still another approach to determining requirements for a new product is to synthesize them from characteristics of the utilizing system, that is, to develop the requirements from the uses to be made of the product. This approach asks how the product is to be used, and then it infers the requirements from the answer.

Normative Method of Synthesizing

One way to synthesize requirements is to start with a normative (or standard) set of requirements and then to tailor these to nonstandard needs. Essentially, this is what a contractor does in determining your requirements for a new bathroom. This is the method used when a product is designed by following a checklist of specific requirements to be discussed.

The normative method is based on the fundamental similarity of classes of products; a standard set of requirements is developed for each class. An advantage of the method is that it imposes a structure on the requirements process. It also tends to result in complete requirements.

Critical Factors Analysis

Another way to synthesize requirements is to elicit the critical factors that can be used in deriving requirements. An example is the Critical Success Factors (CSF) method.[3] It is a method for determining information requirements by asking people to define the factors that are critical to the success of their organization. An advantage of critical factor analysis is that it requires relatively little effort to find the ways to view the requirements problem.

Process Analysis

When the product is information, one method for synthesizing requirements is process analysis. Business Systems Planning (BSP) is an example of a process-based methodology for obtaining information requirements.

BSP is an IBM methodology that has been widely used to determine information requirements.[4] A comprehensive methodology, BSP derives information re-

---

[3]John F. Rockart, "Chief Executives Define their Own Data Needs," *Harvard Business Review* (March–April 1979), p. 81.

quirements by examining business objectives, business processes, and data requirements. From this a proposed information architecture and major applications are defined.

Input-Process-Output Analysis

For any process, a standard method of synthesizing requirements is input-process-output analysis. It considers a process as a transformation that accepts inputs and produces outputs. Starting in a top-down fashion with an object process, it systematically decomposes each process into subprocesses, analyzing the inputs and outputs of each. Analysis can be carried to as low a level as one likes.

Input-process-output analysis is a systematic and comprehensive method for determining requirements. Moreover, it is a straightforward method that is easily learned.

Discovery from an Evolving Product

A final way to synthesize requirements is to discover them by experimenting with an evolving product. The approach is to obtain an initial set of requirements and implement them in a prototype or model. Customer reaction to the prototype will then generate a new set of requirements, resulting in a new prototype. After as many iterations as are deemed necessary, a set of actual product requirements will emerge.

This method of obtaining requirements is very effective for complex products or highly innovative products. It is also helpful when the customer doesn't really know what is wanted or cannot easily visualize the final product. Architects frequently use the method to display the characteristics of a building. Under the name of "prototyping" it is a popular method for specifying requirements for the user interface to information systems. In a modified form, it has been a traditional practice in IS because written descriptions of requirements for information systems have been supplemented with examples of the forms and reports associated with the system.

9.8 Methods for Determining Consumer Product Requirements

For consumer products, other techniques are used to determine customer requirements. Not that they couldn't be used for custom products; some are quite suitable.

- *Literature search*. Insight into customer requirements can be gained by reading magazines, newsletters, consumer reports, and similar publications.

---

[4]*Business Systems Planning—Information Systems Planning Guide,* Application Manual, GE20-0527-4, IBM Corporation.

- *Trade groups.* For most product areas, established trade groups collect information on consumer attitudes. These organizations sponsor trade shows, which are a good source of information on product trends.

- *Competitive analysis.* Most suppliers in rapidly changing industries pay close attention to product announcements of competitors; in fact, they have groups within their organization whose job is to analyze the offerings of competitors.

- *Data analysis.* For many product areas, there is a large amount of data available that can be related to customer demand. These data range from government demographic statistics to internal company data on customer reaction to past products.

- *Surveys.* Sometimes companies interview or survey potential customers; sometimes these surveys are conducted by outside agencies. Surveys can be used to get reactions to specific questions relating to a new product.

- *Focus sessions.* In lieu of an interview, a company might gather a representative group of potential customers and ask them to express opinions on subjects relating to the new product. At a group session, the discussion might be nondirected ("What features would you like to see in a word processor?"), or it could be directed to the requirements that the supplier is thinking about using ("If a word processor had this feature, how would you like it?").

- *Test marketing.* For some products, consumer views of requirements are obtained by test marketing—the product is offered for sale in a limited region, and the supplier measures customer reaction to it. Of all methods, test marketing is probably one of the most effective for determining customer opinion. It has the drawback, however, of being suitable only for products with a short development cycle. Also, it might tip your hand to your competition, who probably monitors your test marketing as carefully as you do.

Clearly, the methods available for market research do not lead to crisp, precise statements about specific customer requirements. Moreover, the methods can lead to conflicting requirements. Consequently, the supplier must use a great deal of skill, intuition, and insight in establishing specific customer requirements.

◆ 9.9 Establishing Information Requirements

It is a much more complex task to obtain requirements for a production process than for a commercial product such as, say, a house. This is because production processes also involve the flow of information. A methodology that can help obtain process requirements is *JAD (Joint Application Design).*[5]

---

[5]In spite of its title, JAD is a requirements methodology, not a design methodology. The title does illustrate, however, how much confusion exists among professionals in the business world about basic process concepts.

In automating information flows, it is good practice to document the current information system. JAD is a methodology for doing this. The general concept, however, can be applied to other processes, which is why we examine it here.

JAD is based on the philosophy that the personnel who will develop the automated system are partners with the people in the business area who will use the system (called "users" by the IS community). To determine requirements for the system, a small JAD team of users and IS people meets regularly to conduct workshops following the JAD steps:

1. Familiarization workshop
2. Workshop preparation
3. JAD workshops
4. Joint application design review (JAR)

Familiarization Workshop

The first workshop is a one-hour briefing attended by all team members. The objective is that the JAD team understand the current business environment and the information problems facing the application area being studied.

After the workshop, the team leader visits the business site, talks with management and workers, and observes the work process. The leader then documents the present system and prepares a report describing it.

JAD Workshops

Next, a series of JAD workshops are held to explore each business activity in depth. The purpose of these workshops is to develop a requirements document for the new system and to have it validated. Following the flow of work in the application area, the JAD team explores eight activities: planning work, receiving work, tracking and initial processing work, assigning work, processing of work, recording work, sending work, and evaluating performance.

Application familiarization is in depth. Among the points covered are information requirements, volumes, peak loads, interfaces, external communication, the eight activities listed in the preceding paragraph, problem areas, bottlenecks, issues and concerns, constraints, sample forms, documents, terminology, jargon, backup and recovery, and security. Familiarization activities might include:

◆ Conducting sessions to review business functions of work area
◆ Visits to work sites to interview, observe, and photograph users at work, as well as to document key observations
◆ Creating data flow diagrams and other documents of the current system

The output of the workshops is a detailed requirements document for the work area. Included in the documentation are: the organization structure, mission, and objectives; performance indicators; a summary list of work areas; a glossary of user terms; and an action list of issues and problems. The business area then reviews this output and lists corrections, comments, additions, and changes.

Workshop Results

JAD is a practical means of determining comprehensive requirements. It requires considerable effort, but in the long run it saves time and effort by greatly reducing the number of changes required during development of a new system to accommodate requirements that typically are missed by following traditional requirements processes.

JAD has been used extensively with excellent results. It is an effective way to obtain requirements and is overwhelmingly preferred to traditional methods. Success factors for the method are top management commitment and involvement, the ability of the session leader, and the rapport between the session leader and the requirements specification team.

Although designed for obtaining requirements for information systems, the technique clearly can be adapted to obtain requirements for any production process.

◆ 9.10 Dynamics of Requirements

In our treatment of customer requirements, we have not attempted to discuss the dynamics of requirements specification. Without saying so, our approach to the topic might leave the impression that the customer specifies his requirements, hands them to the supplier, then goes away and simply waits for the product to be produced. This might happen for a simple, well-understood product, but it is not likely for involved, innovative products. For these products there are complex interactions among the specify, design, and production processes. Let's examine some of these interactions.

One interaction is that every new product spawns new customer requirements. This is quite natural because customers' wants are driven by their existing state of knowledge. In stating the wants for a new product, customers can visualize certain attributes for their products. But as the new product unfolds, their knowledge expands. As they understand the full capabilities of a new product, they visualize even more features they would like. One reason for using prototypes as part of the process for defining requirements is to help customers visualize the final product and add any new requirements early in the specification process.

Requirements are also influenced by the design process (which is discussed in the next chapter). During the design stage, for example, it might be discovered that a certain customer requirement will preclude the use of a standard component in the product. Changes in requirements that would allow use of such a component might avoid a more costly "roll-your-own" part (and, incidentally, might also improve product quality).

Outside influences during product development are also a source of change to requirements. A new law, a change in the competitive environment, a change in the management structure—all can lead to changes in customer requirements. Often these outside influences are unpredictable and must be accepted as a fact of life.

Because customer requirements are dynamic, an organization needs effective procedures. At a minimum there must be:

◆ An established *specification procedure* for determining customer requirements

◆ An effective *change procedure* for monitoring changes in customer and supplier requirements

◆ A *version control* procedure for tracking and controlling the requirements on various versions or releases of the requirements document

With these and appropriate customer involvement, the organization can establish useful customer requirements. The next step is to translate these into product requirements, which we discuss in the following chapter.

◆ Exercises and Additional Readings

1. From your collection of articles on quality (see Exercise 1, Chapter 1), give examples of quality problems that are due to poor requirements or examples that illustrate an effective requirements process. What lessons can you learn from these articles?

2. List two goods, two services, and two information products that you are provided by various organizations. For each product, (a) list your requirements, (b) assess how well these requirements are met, and (c) for those requirements that are not met, suggest what might be done to change the situation.

3. Read Susan Helms and Coretta H. Key, "Are Students More Than Customers in a Classroom?" *Quality Progress*, September 1994, p. 97.

(a) In your view, are university students customers? employees? what?

(b) How does the answer to this question change the requirements for the product of university education?

   The student/teacher relationship may be far more complex than a simple business exchange. Note that the instructor is also the customer of the student when the student submits exams, papers, and project reports for evaluation. It is the student's "job" to learn the material to the extent that he can satisfy or even delight the instructor with his work product.

4. Bob Kukla, division quality manager for the Specialty Products Division (SPD) of the National-Standard Company, describes a requirements specification process in "Meeting Customer Needs," published in the June 1986 issue of *Quality Progress*, p. 15. Compare and contrast that process with JAD.

5. Read Michael F. Masterson, "Buying Radios Is Adding Quality to Madison's City Government," *Quality Progress*, January 1995, p. 50. Describe the city's requirements process for purchasing radios. How did this differ from prior practice? What was the result of the change?

6. Read and summarize Section 14.3, "Specification of Quality Requirements for Suppliers," in J. M. Juran and Frank M. Gryna, *Quality Planning and Analysis*, 3rd ed. (New York: McGraw-Hill, 1993).

7. Discuss the following as it relates to requirements: "Quality in a product or service is not what the supplier puts in. It is what the customer gets out and is willing to pay for. . . . Customers pay only for what is of use to them and gives them value. Nothing else constitutes quality." See Peter F. Drucker, *Innovation and Entrepreneurship: Practice and Principles* (New York: Harper Business, 1993), p. 22.

8. Discuss the following: Customers judge quality against their *wants*, not against what we call *customer requirements*. Quality should be defined in terms of wants, not customer requirements.

9. Discuss the following: It is not practical in most jobs for a supplier to get his requirements from the customer; instead he must rely on his manager to supply customer requirements along with the resources and tools needed to do the job. And the manager might have to get those requirements from the sales force. Quality, therefore, should mean producing what the manager wants.

10. Discuss the following: "Customers do not judge quality, they judge *relative perceived quality*—their perception of how a product compares with competing products. But suppliers need something more than relative perceived quality as a target for their production efforts. How can this dilemma be resolved?"

11. Ask a friend to list his or her requirements for a one-week vacation. Critique the list. Can you think of a vacation that would meet the listed requirements but would not satisfy your friend?

12. List the requirements you were given for a recent class assignment. Then list some *unstated* requirements you were expected to meet. Are there any unstated requirements for which noncompliance might affect your grade?

13. For an entertaining and enlightening discussion, read Donald C. Gause and Gerald M. Weinberg, *Exploring Requirements: Quality Before Design*, (New York, NY: Dorset House Publishing, 1989). Summarize the book.

14. Read and summarize "PDM: A Requirements Methodology for Software System Enhancements," *IBM Systems Journal*, 1985, p. 134.

15. The primary customer for a car is the person who buys it.

    (a) List external customers for a car (that is, people outside the organization that manufactures and sells the car).

    (b) List internal customers for a car (that is, people inside the organization that manufactures and sells the car).

    For each customer in (a) and (b), describe some of their requirements.

16. The Center for Quality Education at the Wright-Patterson Air Force Base used a certain technique to learn who its customers are. Discuss that technique and its effectiveness. (Reference: Gerald R. Tuttle, "Cascading Quality Through the Training Process," *Quality Progress*, April 1993, p. 75.)

17. Discusss why there are differences in establishing customer requirements for custom and consumer products.

The Design Process

> *Improvement in the quality of design is the first step toward higher sales and profits and lower cost.*
>
> —Kaoru Ishikawa[1]

◆ 10.1 Introduction

Design is the creative process of converting customer requirements into a product concept and capturing that concept in a set of product requirements that are complete, clear, and consistent. Starting with customer requirements, the designer makes successive transformations until a satisfactory set of product requirements emerges.

Two Sony products offer good illustrations of a design concept as contrasted with a product requirement. One was the concept that the Walkman portable radio should be small enough to fit into a man's shirt pocket, making it easy

---

[1]Kaoru Ishikawa, *What Is Total Quality Control?* (Englewood Cliffs, N.J.: Prentice-Hall, 1985), p. 105.

to store and retrieve. The other is that the cassette for the Betamax video recorder should be the size of a typical paperback book.[2]

Of the four steps of the basic SDCE (Specify, Design, Create, Examine) paradigm, design is the most dependent on worker talent and imagination. Superior products depend on superior designs, and the best designs tend to be produced by people who have a good understanding of the product area.

But many designers, like other creative people, dislike being constrained to follow rules. They tend to view their work as an art, not a science. They look on formal design procedures and instructions as constraints on their creativity rather than as a system to channel and direct it toward meeting the organization's needs. As a result, it is common to find that there is no formal plan for design efforts; interfaces for design efforts are informal with insufficient checking of steps; designs are not documented properly; there is insufficient design verification; and so on.

A real challenge to managers of design efforts is to convince designers that they must adhere to and improve the design process. A difficulty is that managers themselves came from the design ranks and have much the same view of the process as the people being managed.

The key to improving the design process is to view design as a production process where the output is a design. One way to overcome designer resistance to the process is to assign competent designers to the task of monitoring and improving the design process. It also helps to have the design function managed by someone who has the designers' respect.

Related Products

The design of most any product generates the need for additional products, all of which must be designed and built. There might be a need for manuals to assemble the product, instructions for using or repairing it, advertising material for selling it, and so on. And the new product might require new processes or a change in existing processes for marketing, building, shipping, and servicing the product; new procedures and material for training people to run the new processes; and so on. The design of a new product influences and is influenced by the requirements for all of these ancillary products. It can be a real management challenge to coordinate all of the required efforts.

Cost

A designer must balance among competing parameters and costs. Almost always there are several designs that will satisfy all stated customer requirements, and the

---

[2]Akio Moreta, *Made in Japan*, (Glasgow: Fontana Paperbacks, 1988), pp. 71, 112. A product concept is not a precise statement. For example, the original Walkman was slightly larger than a standard men's shirt pocket; to compensate, Sony provided their salesmen with shirts that had slightly larger than normal pockets.

experience and judgments of the designer are major factors in determining which is selected. Cost usually plays a role in that selection.

> *GE executives say 70% of the cost of manufacturing truck transmissions is determined in the design stage. A study at Rolls-Royce reveals that design determines 80% of the final production cost of 2,000 components.*[3]

Design and Information

Design is largely an information process, as can be seen from the growing use of computers in the design effort. At an early stage, physical models and prototypes may be produced, but the output of the design process involves words, charts, and diagrams—information products. Thus, the quality of a firm's design efforts is inextricably linked with the quality of the information systems that support the design process. And there is a lot of information to control:

> *The design documentation for a Boeing 747 weighs as much as the aircraft itself.*[4]

In recent years, there has been a move to replace the traditional empirical design process with formalized, quantified approaches. Automated CAD/CAM (Computer Aided Design/Computer Aided Manufacturing) systems for design engineers and CASE (Computer Aided Software Engineering) systems for IS professionals help to speed the design process. More importantly from the quality view, such systems also help to enforce design procedures and standards, increasing the practicality of planning and controlling the design process. In addition, computers help to ensure the consistency of designs and naming conventions within a design team.

Design and ISO 9000 Standards

The chief difference between the quality standard ISO 9001 and ISO 9002 is that ISO 9001 extends quality assurance to the design function. Because of this, it is customary for the lead auditor to cover the design department during an ISO certification audit.[5]

Statistics compiled by ISO certification bodies show that most serious failures to fulfill quality system requirements are found in the design area. Other studies show

---

[3]Daniel E. Whitney, "Manufacturing by Design," *Harvard Business Review* (July–August 1988), p. 83; I. J. Corbett, "Design for Economic Manufacturing," *Annals of C.I.R.P.*, No. 1 (1986), p. 93.

[4]*Datamation*, June 1, 1986.

[5]Jack Kanholm, *ISO 9000 Quality System*, (Los Angeles: AQA Co., 1994), p. 29.

DISPLAY 10.1 ◆ Traditional versus Modern Products

Aspects of Products	Traditional	Modern
Simplicity	Simple, static	Complex, dynamic
Precision	Low	High
Need for interchangeability	Limited	Extensive
Consumables or durables	Mainly consumables	Mainly durables
Environment for use	Natural	Unnatural
User understanding of product	High	Low
Importance to health, safety, and life	Seldom important	Often important
Life of design	Long	Short
Scientific basis of design	Largely empirical	Largely scientific
Basis of reliability, maintainability, etc.	Vague	Quantified
Volume of production	Usually low	Often high
Usual cause of field failure	Manufacturing errors	Design weakness

that the most expensive quality problems are due to design deficiencies. Some of the most common reasons for quality problems in design are:

◆ Failure to understand the customer requirements

◆ Failure to understand how quality system principles should be applied to the design area

◆ Unwillingness of designers to conform to established design procedures[6]

Another reason for design problems is that modern products present the designer with a much more difficult task than did traditional products. This can be seen from the comparison Juran and Gryna made of traditional and modern products, as shown in Display 10.1.[7] Today, customer requirements are complex. In addition to the inherent features and functions of the product, the designer must also design for reliability, manufacturability, and marketability.

◆ 10.2 The Design Process

In practice, the design process is less structured than the build process. Traditionally, design quality has been achieved largely by product control. Little attempt was

---

[6]Ibid., p. 29.

[7]J. M. Juran and Frank M. Gryna, Jr., *Quality Planning and Analysis*, 2nd ed. (New York: McGraw-Hill, 1983), p. 168.

made to use defect information to improve the design process, but this, too, is changing.

Project Methodology

Design is accomplished project by project. To do design work effectively, an organization needs an effective design project methodology and an effective design project management process.

A design project methodology states how an organization's design projects are to be accomplished and the interface of a project with other organizational functions. Typical major steps of a design methodology are these:

- Review project inputs.
- Develop a design concept (functional design) of a product that will meet customer requirements; define completion criteria for these functional design components.
- Develop a plan for producing the required design components.
- Develop a quality plan for reviewing project products.
- Develop the design according to plan, reviewing work products at each step according to the quality plan.
- Conduct a final review to verify and approve the design.

Project Management

The design project methodology describes the design process. To operate this process and produce an actual design, it is necessary to assemble a group of qualified designers and provide them with necessary resources (including time) to accomplish the task. Generally, a project manager is appointed to plan and direct this effort. The project plan describes specific steps to be taken, a schedule for accomplishing these steps, and specific responsibilities for accomplishing the steps. Often the planning effort is supported by computerized tools, such as PERT or CPM programs (see Section 17.3). Included in the plan are appropriate quality check points.

An important task of the project manager is to make work productive; another is to make workers achieving.[8] Requirements to accomplish productive work include:

- An environment that fosters work
- Properly defined work requirements
- Effective plans and controls

---

[8] Peter F. Drucker, *Management: Tasks, Responsibilities, Practices* (New York: Harper and Row, 1974), p. 40.

- ◆ Proper and stable work procedures
- ◆ Adequate resources

For workers to be achieving, they need

- ◆ A well-defined job
- ◆ The knowledge and skills necessary to do the work or provisions for obtaining them
- ◆ Proper facilities and materials
- ◆ Free and open communications, both formal and informal
- ◆ Opportunity for satisfaction and reward from contributing to the organizational goals

The project manager is responsible for supplying these factors.

Design Manager

In addition to the business aspects just described, an important task on a design project is to control the design and the design products. Because design changes are the rule rather than the exception, it is essential that the evolving design be managed to assure that it is consistent and remains focused on the design concept. The task of managing the design is quite different from project management—the task of managing the project work effort. On a large project, the task of managing the design might be assigned to a design manager (lead designer), who reports to the project manager. On a small project, however, the project manager usually is assigned both tasks. Unfortunately, the result often is that project management demands all the manager's time and design management suffers.

Project Personnel

Because design is a creative process, the quality of a design is critically dependent on the ability of the designers. An organization should have established requirements and criteria for designers and should include only qualified people on the design team.

◆ 10.3 Design Inputs

The customer requirements that are input to the design process originate from various sources and are expressed in various formats. The first step in establishing the design input is to identify all customers for the product and collect all of their requirements. These must then be reviewed for completeness, clarity, currentness, and possible conflicts, which must be resolved. Then the design requirements must be organized; they should be expressed in a single document if possible.

Reference Material

A second type of input to the design process are the reference materials used in the design process or used to validate designs. This includes catalogs, design manuals, design rules, magazines, design textbooks, component descriptions, examples of designs, old designs, information on competitive products, and so on. It is not uncommon for this material to be in a jumble: it is stored in various places, including desk drawers; much of it is not current; the material may be conflicting; and there is no standard way to discover what information is available. This manner of handling reference material usually slows the design effort and increases the odds of design errors. And certainly it is an open invitation for an ISO auditor to look for design problems.

Design reference materials should be organized, controlled, and centrally stored. A retention policy should be established for materials, textbooks, magazines, and similar items to assure that current materials are being used. Obsolete materials should be clearly marked as such and stored in a special area for possible reference in repairing or modifying old products.

Computer Software

Computers are central to many design efforts. CAD/CAM systems are used in developing or verifying designs. In addition, computers might be used to store and retrieve design products and to plan and manage a design project.

Whether developed in house or purchased, computer software that is used in a design effort should be validated to prove that it works properly. Master copies of such design software and the related user manuals should be controlled. The location of all copies of the software should be recorded so that program corrections and changes are provided to all users.

Proper control of design software requires coordination between the Design Department, which uses computer programs to do design work and store design products, and the IS Department, which usually controls major decisions concerning the CAD/CAM system.

◆ 10.4 Design Quality Control

The techniques used to control the quality of designs include development testing, design reviews, and product qualification. For IS products, these three controls are essentially the same as unit test, system test, and final test.

Development Testing

During the development process, individual design components are tested to identify and correct design defects. These tests tend to be informal and are conducted to demonstrate conformance to requirements. Development testing generally is done by and for the benefit of the designer.

Each requirement should be reflected in a quality test specification. A common problem, however, is that the requirements document is vague or deficient, leaving it up to the designers to interpret requirements. Because individual interpretations are not coordinated, the final product might not meet requirements. Design might get the blame, but the problem often is with the requirements process.

Design Reviews

A *design review* is a formal procedure[9] for the review of design products by a qualified group of people who are independent of the design team; it is held for the purpose of identifying design defects and recommending design improvements. A series of such reviews should be held to review output of a design project. For design reviews to be successful, management commitment is essential.

Scheduled design reviews should be mandatory after each major phase of a design project. Such reviews are comprehensive; they cover compliance with customer requirements and other quality-related issues. The reviews are open to all concerned people of the organization, including the internal customers of the process and designers of related design components.

Design reviews should address only quality-related issues. If needed, separate management reviews can be held to discuss business matters, such as the schedule and cost of the design project. Combining design and business reviews often results in the business matters of time and cost dominating the review session, to the detriment of quality.

Product Qualification

Product qualification is a formal phase of testing conducted to prove that the design meets requirements. Design reviews look at design components; product qualification looks at the total design as an entity. It covers requirements for performance, appearance, size, environmental constraints, reliability, safety, operability—all the requirements for the product.

◆ 10.5 Design Control

Design control concerns control of the design process and the design concept, not just the design documents. The easy part of design control is to verify that individual drawings and specifications meet requirements. The difficult part is to verify that an evolving collection of individual design documents is complete,

---

[9]A *formal* procedure is a procedure that has been a established by an organization and transmitted in writing.

consistent, correct, and supports the design concept. To help assure this, everyone involved in the design activity must understand the logic of the design concept.

When a design is complete, it is released for production of the product. There should be established criteria to be satisfied by a design before it can be released and a release procedure for reviewing a design against these criteria. There should also be a procedure for assigning a unique identity to design elements so they can be traced.

◆ 10.6 Change Control

Design is a creative activity, and a certain amount of trial and error is inherent in the design process. A design change might be required because of a change in customer requirements, a need to correct a design flaw, a sudden inspiration, a new law. . . . Because change is the rule, not the exception, change management is an extremely important part of the design process, as well as all other stages of the SDCE paradigm. For a complex product, version control (the control needed to assure that everyone is using the same version of a design) is also necessary. Problems in managing change and control of released documents is one of the leading causes for firms to fail their first ISO 9000 audit.

A change procedure should explain how to:

- ◆ Initiate a change request
- ◆ Evaluate and approve a change request
- ◆ Plan and allocate resources for designing a change
- ◆ Verify that a proposed change is satisfactory
- ◆ Implement the change
- ◆ Verify that the change is effective and has no adverse consequences
- ◆ Update all documentation to reflect the change and to remove all obsolete documents
- ◆ Update the history file

It is important to keep a permanent record of all design changes because occasionally there is a need to "back out" a change.

◆ 10.7 Control of Released Designs

Once a design has been reviewed and released for production, another problem arises: uncontrolled changes in the design during the production process. A common situation is that an operator discovers a (usually minor) flaw in the design, understands how to correct it, and does so by simply writing an appropriate adjustment on the copy assigned to the operator. Such changes are not authorized, not controlled, and might not be done uniformly by all operators. They are a fertile area for quality problems and one that quality auditors look for.

Changes in released designs should be handled by a procedure similar to the one used for the design process. In theory this presents no problem; in practice it can be a frustrating experience because there can be many copies to be traced and modified.

◆ 10.8 Subcontracting

One step in the design process is to decide if products or subproducts will be built by the organization or obtained from an outside source—a subcontractor. This "build or buy" decision clearly affects the product requirements to be specified. Conversely, the decision is affected by what requirements the subcontractor can meet; the decision also is limited by the subcontractor's ability to produce, his cost of producing, and the lead time required to produce the product. And his limitations will depend on whether the product that is specified is "off the shelf" or custom made.

The decision to "build or buy" raises another important issue: how the quality of subcontractor-supplied products is to be assured. The ISO 9000 standards were established to address this very issue.

◆ 10.9 Quality Function Deployment

Quality Function Deployment (QFD), also known as the *House of Quality*, consists of a set of planning and communication routines for coordinating cross-functional planning. It fosters communication among units, especially design, manufacturing, and sales. QFD is an organized way to bring together marketing, design, and manufacturing managers. In many companies these units act rather independently, despite ample evidence that much can be gained by coordinating their efforts. Sales has marketing data on customers, and they usually know what customers want and don't want. This information is very important when it comes to designing a new product or redesigning an old one. The design group depends on marketing data because it needs customer requirements, which it then translates into product requirements. Also, since production needs to manufacture the product according to the plans of the design group, it is important that design and manufacturing interact closely. Certain designs may be quite difficult to manufacture, and slight changes in the design (which may impact the customer requirements only slightly) might lead to substantial savings. In short, much can be gained by coordinating the information and the knowledge that resides in the design, manufacturing, and marketing groups. However, coordination doesn't just happen. It takes a truly *interfunctional team* consisting of marketing, design, and manufacturing, and a *systematic roadmap*, or procedure, to bring this coordination about. This is where QFD comes in.

Quality function deployment originated in Japan at Mitsubishi Corporation and was further developed by Toyota and its suppliers. Today it is widely used by manufacturers of a variety of products, in Japan as well as in the United States. Ford and General Motors are two U.S. companies that make extensive use of this technique.

Assessment of Product Attributes Desired by the Customer

The House of Quality begins with the assessment of product attributes that the customer desires. In QFD terminology, these requirements are called *customer attributes*. These requirements are expressed in the customer's language. Information on product attributes might come from customer surveys, customer complaints, or focus groups that are specifically conducted for this purpose. Usually, the marketing group is heavily involved in making this assessment. The first steps in Quality Function Deployment is to listen to the *voice of the customer*, that is, to determine the product attributes the customer desires and to group these attributes into logical bundles. We discussed this issue in the previous chapter.

To illustrate QFD, we will use an example involving car doors, taken from the paper by Hauser and Clausing.[10] Desired product attributes for a car door include good function (that is, the car door should be easy to open and close), good isolation (that is, the door should keep out rain and road noise), and comfortable support for one's arm. Display 10.2 lists, in the customers' language, the attributes they desire together with the relative weight or importance they attach to each attribute. These weights are relative; that is, if all were listed, they would sum to 100 percent. Not all preferences are likely to be equally important, and the first task is learn what the customer wants most.

Usually, marketing has data on the competition and knows how well in-house and competitive products score on the various attributes. Comparisons between our own product and products of competitors can tell us much about the relative position of our product in the marketplace. Such data, if available, are usually displayed next to product attributes, often in the form of a display that ranks the satisfaction of customers with regard to the various product attributes on a scale from worst to best. This information shows whether there are opportunities for our product. It may be that all cars score low on one attribute (for example, "door staying open on hill"). Then that would provide a good opportunity to improve our position relative to the competition. If, on the other hand, all cars score high on an attribute, then there is not much room to do better, and improvement would not add much competitive advantage.

---

[10]An excellent discussion of QFD is given in John R. Hauser and Don Clausing, "The House of Quality," *Harvard Business Review* (May–June 1988), pp. 63–73. Note that in our introduction to QFD we only focus on the operation of the door; we ignore issues that relate to its appearance.

DISPLAY 10.2 ◆ Customer Attributes for a Car Door As They Relate to Good Operation and Use

| | | | Customer Perceptions | | | | |
		Relative Weights	Worst 1	2	3	4	Best 5
Easy to open and close door	Easy to close from outside	7	●		BA		
	Stays open on a hill	5					
	Easy to open from outside	3					
	Doesn't kick back	3		B●A			
	Easy to close from inside	7					
	Easy to open from inside	4					
	.						
	.						
Isolation	Doesn't leak in rain	3			AB●		
	No road noise	2					
I	Doesn't leak in a car wash				BA		●
	No wind noise						
	Doesn't drip water when opened						
	Doesn't rattle						
	.						
	.						
Arm rest	Soft, comfortable						
	In right position						
	.						
	Sum of relative weights	100					

Note: Relative Weights, if summed over all customer attributes, add to 100. Here we have not shown all customer attributes.

Customer Perception is illustrated for four attributes (● refers to our car; A—competitor A; B—competitor B)

Engineering Characteristics

Marketing tells us *what* to do, but engineers tell us *how to do it*. To develop a product that will satisfy customers, it is necessary to translate the product attributes desired by the customer into the language of engineers.

Engineering characteristics are aspects of a product that are thought to influence the product's attributes desired by the customer. For example, the "energy to close the door" and the "door seal resistance" are engineering characteristics that are likely to impact customer satisfaction. Engineers know whether these engineering characteristics should be increased (+) or decreased (−) to have a beneficial effect on satisfaction. The relevant engineering characteristics must be determined, and they must be related to the desired product attributes. This step usually is performed by engineers because it requires technical knowledge; also, it will be their task later on to translate the desirable engineering characteristics into product requirements.

The Relationship Matrix

The next step is to start constructing the House of Quality. This is done by linking product attributes desired by the customer and engineering characteristics in the form of a *relationship matrix*. The product attributes are arranged as the rows of the matrix; the engineering characteristics are listed across the top as columns. The relationship between engineering characteristics and product attributes is indicated by marking appropriate cells in the matrix: If an engineering characteristic has a beneficial impact on a product characteristic, then the cell of the matrix determined by the intersection of the respective row and column is marked with a check mark (✓); if it has an adverse impact, the cell is marked with an ✗.

For example, in Display 10.3 there is a check mark in the cell where the product attribute ("Easy to close from outside") intersects with the engineering characteristic ("Energy to close the door"), indicating a positive association among these two variables. Decreasing the energy that is needed to close the door will make it easier to close the door from the outside. As an embellishment on the diagram,

DISPLAY 10.3 ◆ The House of Quality: The Relationship Matrix-Car Door Example

Source: John R. Hauser and Don Clausing, "The House of Quality," in the *Harvard Business Review* (May–June 1988), pp. 63–73.

different colors or thicknesses of characters can be used to indicate the strength of the relationship.

Note that an engineering characteristic may affect more than one product attribute, and the effect may be positive on one and negative on the other(s). Consider "door seal resistance"; the "+" sign in the column indicates that this engineering characteristics should be increased. Increased door seal resistance will prevent the door from leaking in the rain; the positive association among these two variables is displayed through a check mark in the relationship matrix. Increased door seal resistance will also help with road noise (another positive effect). However, increasing the door seal resistance will make it more difficult to close the door; the negative effect is characterized through the "X" in the intersecting cell.

The cross-functional team, consisting of marketing, design, and manufacturing, fills in this relationship matrix, which is also known as the "body of the house." Engineering knowledge, customer data, and results of prior statistical studies and controlled experiments are used to complete this matrix. Group discussions within a cross-functional team often lead to initially conflicting ideas, but it is important that a consensus be reached.

Objective measures on the engineering characteristics, which are used by our company as well as by our competitors, are added to the bottom of the table. These are benchmarks and indicate current practice. The measures are expressed in the appropriate engineering units. For example, 11 foot-pounds of energy are needed to close our car door, whereas only 9 and 9.5 foot-pounds are necessary for the competitors' doors. Road noise reduction is expressed in decibels (db); our current design achieves 9 db, while our two competitors are at 5 db and 6 db, respectively.

Completing the House

The final step in constructing a "house" is to build a triangle on top of the relationship matrix to summarize how the various engineering characteristics interact. This is also known as the *roof of the House of Quality*. The completed House of Quality for the car door example is shown in Display 10.4.

A change in one engineering characteristic often affects other engineering characteristics. For example, strengthening a certain mechanism of the door (for example, the gear mechanism for raising and lowering the window so that the window will open and close faster) makes the door heavier. Consequently, one needs more energy to open and close the door. These two engineering characteristics, energy to open the door and the strength of the gear mechanism, exhibit a negative association: doing something good for one engineering characteristic implies something bad for the other. As a further example, an increase in the door seal resistance requires more energy to open the door and a higher peak closing force. These two engineering characteristics exhibit a negative association: what's good for one (seal resistance) is bad for the other (requiring more force). Check marks (✓) are used for beneficial impacts, and X for adverse ones.

The roof of the House of Quality displays the associations and helps the design

DISPLAY 10.4 ◆ The Completed House of Quality: Car Door Example

House of Quality matrix — Engineering characteristics grouped under "Open-close effort" and "Sealing-insulation":

Customer attributes		Relative importance	Energy to close door (−)	Check force on level ground (+)	Check force on 10° slope (+)	Energy to open door (−)	Peak closing force (−)	⋯	Door seal resistance (+)	Acoustic transmission, window (+)	Road noise reduction (+)	Water resistance (+)	⋯	Customer perceptions (Worst 1 2 3 4 5 Best)
Easy to open and close door	Easy to close from outside	7	✓				✓		✗					• BA
	Stays open on a hill	5		✓	✓									B•A
	Easy to open from outside	3				✓			✓					
	Doesn't kick back	3	✓	✓	✓				✗					
	⋮													
Isolation	Doesn't leak in rain	3							✓			✓		AB•
	No road noise	2							✓	✓	✓			BA •
	⋮													

Objective measures:

	Energy to close door	Check force on level ground	Check force on 10° slope	Energy to open door	Peak closing force	Door seal resistance	Acoustic transmission, window	Road noise reduction	Water resistance
Measurement units	ft-lb	lb	lb	ft-lb	lb	lb/ft	—	db	psi
Our car door	11	12	6	10	18	3	.10	9	70
A's car door	9	12	6	9	13	2	.10	5	60
B's car door	9.5	11	7	11	14	2	.10	6	60
Technical difficulty	4	5	1	1	3	1	3	3	5
Imputed importance (%) (all total 100%)	10	6	4	9	1	6	2	4	3
Estimated cost (%) (all total 100%)	5	2	2	9	5	6	6	9	2
Targets	7.5 ft-lb	9 lb	6 lb	7.5 ft-lb	12 lb	3 lb/ft	.10	9 db	70 psi

Source: John R. Hauser and Don Clausing, in "The House of Quality," *Harvard Business Review* (May–June 1988), pp. 63–73.

team specify the various engineering features that have to be controlled "together." Sometimes a targeted feature impairs so many other features that the team decides to leave it alone. In some respects, the roof of the house contains the most useful information for the engineers because it allows them to see how to make trade-offs when attempting to satisfy the various product attributes that the customer desires.

A conceptual display of the House of Quality is given in Display 10.5.

Using the House of Quality

The completed House of Quality helps the team set targets on the engineering characteristics, which are then entered on the bottom of the table. QFD is not a cookbook procedure, and it does not relieve any group of making difficult decisions, often in the context of considerable uncertainty. However, it does bring the groups together to debate priorities. It makes sure that the voice of the customer is heard; it gives engineers a structured procedure for eliciting engineering characteristics and their inner relationships, as well as their relationship to product attributes. And it gives managers a better chance to discover strategic opportunities.

Display 10.4 shows that customers believe that our doors are much harder to close from the outside than are those of our competitors. Marketing thinks that "ease of closing the door from the outside" is an important attribute, as shown by its relatively high importance weight. We should do something about it! The relationship matrix shows that this product attribute is affected by the energy to close the door, the peak closing force, and the door seal resistance. Energy to close the door and peak closing force are good candidates for improvement; changes in these two factors are strongly related, and reductions in either will make the doors easier to close. The roof of the House of Quality shows that several other engineering characteristics are affected by changes in these two factors. The energy to close a door is related to the energy needed to open it. The association is posi-

DISPLAY 10.5 ◆ The House of
        Quality: A Conceptual View

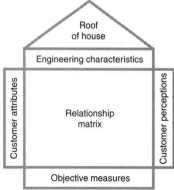

tive, which means a change in one is also beneficial for the other; a reduction in the energy to close the door lowers the energy to open the door, which is beneficial for other customer-desired product attributes (such as ease to open door from outside; door doesn't kick back). However, the roof of the House of Quality shows that changes in these two engineering characteristics have an impact on several other engineering characteristics (such as door seals, window acoustic transmission, road noise reduction), and for these factors the association is negative; what's good for making doors easier to open/close is bad for isolation. One must decide whether the benefits of doing better on some variable outweigh the costs of doing worse on others.

In this particular example, it was felt that the benefits of doors that are easier to close outweigh the drawbacks. After some discussion, the group set the target for energy to close at 7.5 foot-pounds. Targets for the other engineering characteristics governing the open/close effort were set similarly.

What about other desired product attributes; for example, road noise? Display 10.2 shows that road noise is only marginally important to the customers, and, furthermore, customers already perceive our product as the best. The relationship matrix shows that a reduction in the acoustic transmission would decrease road noise. However, such redesign would probably increase the weight of the door, which in turn would impact negatively on the ease to open and close the door. Hence it was decided to leave the old targets unchanged.

◆ 10.10 Designing a Production Process

Up to this point, we have discussed the design of custom and consumer products to be supplied to customers (internal or external to the providing organization). In many cases, these products can be produced by making minor adjustments in an existing production process. In other cases, however, it will be necessary to construct a new production process or to make drastic alterations in an existing one in order to create the new process.

Design of a major production process—an auto assembly plant, an oil refinery, an air traffic control system—is a highly complex task requiring years of training, experience, and apprenticeship. However, most production processes are *not* overly complex, and most were designed by people with no formal training to guide them. For example, consider the process for filing correspondence in the Dean's Office, or your process for writing a term paper, or a process for handling customer complaints, or all of the processes you operate day after day at home, in the classroom, or on the job. Most of these were never "designed"; they simply grew and were handed down as "the way to do it." And for those that were "designed," the attempt might well have been to find some way to accomplish the task, not an efficient or optimal way.

Any manager in an organization might be required (usually implicitly) to design a production process. Some points that should be remembered in doing so are these:

1. Determine *all* customers for the process: customers, suppliers, operators, managers, support groups (building maintenance, personnel, finance, . . .).

2. Determine all requirements for each customer: functional requirements, physical/ergonomic requirements, psychological requirements, financial requirements, ... Resolve conflicting requirements and gain universal acceptance of the requirements statement.

3. Decide on the technology to be employed. For example, is a report to be prepared by hand, typewritten, or coordinated on the internet, . . . ?

4. Design a transformation process; sometimes the easy way to do this is to work backward from the required output to the beginning of the process. Examine variations of this design and alternative designs. Select the transformation design that seems most suitable.

5. Design a control process. Build in control points to check product quality and points to collect information for process improvement. Coordinate this process with processes for controlling time and cost.

6. Review the design. Include potential operators of the process, suppliers, and customers in the review effort. Also include impartial, knowledgeable people who will have no direct involvement with the completed process.

7. Document the process. Gain management approval of the design.

Despite your best efforts, your process may well experience "teething problems." The process should be monitored carefully to detect and correct problems and make adjustments. Some person should be designated as process owner with responsibility described in Section 8.2.

◆ 10.11 Concurrent Engineering

Very often the design and introduction of a new product require changes in related processes, such as marketing, manufacturing, installing, and servicing products. *Concurrent engineering* is defined as "a systematic approach to the integrated, concurrent design of products and their related processes, including manufacturing and support. This approach is intended to cause developers from the outset to consider all elements of a product life cycle from conception through disposal, including quality, cost, schedule, and user requirements."[11]

Quality Function Deployment, discussed in the previous section, and concurrent engineering are related, but they are not the same. QFD is a technique for designing *products* so as to balance the conflicting requirements of various organizational units, such as product planning, production, marketing, accounting, IS

---

[11]R. I. Winner, J. P. Pennell, H. E. Bertrand, and M. G. Slusarezuk, "The Role of Concurrent Engineering in Weapons System Acquisition," IDA Report R-338, Institute for Defense Analysis, Alexandria, VA.

support, and personnel. Concurrent engineering is a technique for designing the manufacturing and support *processes* to be used in producing products. It requires the interaction of diverse groups of individuals, information sharing, and coordinated, collaborative work. Use of the concurrent engineering process can accelerate the time it takes for a product design to mature, and it can reduce the number of product design changes after a design is released to manufacturing.

To illustrate concurrent engineering, let us consider a much simplified example of producing a new line of cars. This requires us to produce cars (products) and calls for methods for producing, selling, and servicing cars (production processes). Let us assume that the requirements for the cars have been determined. (In practice, these may be modified during the concurrent engineering process.)

Our first step is to make a preliminary design of the car. Next, we make a preliminary design of the production processes. Typically, certain features in the car design will cause problems in operating some production process; so the next step is to modify the car design, if possible, so as to simplify its production. Next, the production processes are redesigned to reflect the product change. If all is well, the process is stopped. But there may still be problems with the production processes that require additional iterations of the planning process.

As just described, concurrent engineering appears to be a simple process. However, it can be complicated by conflicting demands, say, between marketing that demands a particular feature and manufacturing that finds it difficult to provide. Or between marketing that wants a particular feature and service that must provide it. And it can be complicated or made ineffective by the way that power is distributed in the organization. Moreover, for concurrent engineering to be effective, there must be a strong level of cooperation and communication among the participants in the process.

Improvements from applying concurrent engineering techniques can be impressive. For instance, Pitti Laminations Ltd. of Hyderabad, India, reduced the development time for a new set of press tools from 140 days to 50 days. The number of individually designed components was reduced from 80 to 40. Tool sizes, which had varied considerably, were standardized to six ranges, and tool change time was reduced due to quicker clamping, faster location, and faster setting.[12]

◆ Exercises and Additional Readings

1. From your collection of articles on quality (see Exercise 1 in Chapter 1), give some examples of quality problems due to poor product design. What lessons can you learn from these articles?

---

[12]Major Suneel S. Bhamburkar, "Concurrent Engineering in Manufacture of Press Tools," *Proceedings of the Concurrent Engineering in Manufacture of Press Tools*, 48th Annual Quality Congress, May 1994, Las Vegas, NV, pp. 400–406, ASQC.

2. Design a procedure for planning a spring break vacation.

3. (a) Design a procedure for interviewing an applicant for a job. (*Suggestion:* Use the basic SDCE paradigm.)

    (b) Construct checklists to assist you with the first and last steps of the SDCE approach.

    (c) Design a procedure that you can follow when you yourself are interviewed for a job.

    (d) Did part (a) help you produce a better answer for part (c)?

4. Two design concepts for a government are:

    (i) Of the people, for the people, and by the people.

    (ii) From each according to his ability, to each according to his need.

    (a) Comment on the impact of each design concept on the general welfare of the population.

    (b) Comment on the Internal Revenue Service (IRS) design relative to these two concepts.

5. A large university has a spread-out campus, and many students complain that there is insufficient time to go from class to class. You have been given the task of devising several approaches to designing a system that will improve the situation; from these, one will be selected for actual design and implementation.

    (a) List several such approaches.

    (b) List the pros and cons of each approach.

6. Design a procedure to survey students on some campus issue.

7. Design a procedure for writing a term paper.

8. Read Michael R. Hunter and Richard D. Van Landingham, "Listening to the Customer Using QFD," *Quality Progress*, April 1994, p. 55. Briefly describe how QFD can be used to define feature differentiation for market segmentation.

9. (a) Read and summarize Section 4.4 on Design Control in the American National Standard ANSI/ASQC Q9001-1994 (the U.S. version of ISO 9001).

    (b) Read pp. 25–34 in Jack Kanholm, *ISO 9000 Explained*, 2nd ed (Los Angeles: AQA Co., 1994). Summarize his discussion of the ISO requirement cited in part (a).

10. Read and summarize Section 5.6.2 on Design in ISO 9000-3, a guideline for the application of ISO 9001 to the development, supply, and maintenance of software.

11. (a) Read and summarize Section 12.5 on Design Control in Watts S. Humphrey, *Managing the Software Process*, (Reading, MA: Addison-Wesley, 1989).

    (b) Compare Humphrey's design control requirements with those of ISO 9000-3.

12. Read Section IV of Chapter IV, in Kaoru Ishihawa, *What Is Total Quality Control? The Japanese Way* (Englewood Cliffs, NJ: Prentice-Hall, 1985). Summarize the three stages of quality assurance in postwar Japan.

13. A bank's policy is to pay interest on savings accounts quarterly. Their annual interest rate is 4 percent on accounts with a balance under $10,000 and 4.4 percent on accounts with a larger balance. A computer programmer designed the following procedure for adding the quarterly interest to all accounts. (Note that $A(n)$ is the balance in account n.)

Is this a quality design? (Support your answer.) If not, correct the design.

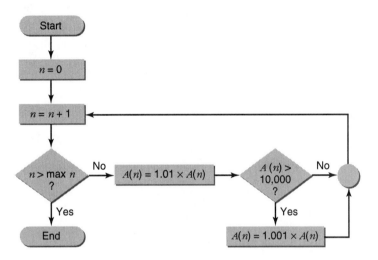

14. Design a food delivery process that delivers food from several restaurants.

15. Describe and evaluate the design of the health care management organization (HMO) to which you belong.

16. If you mail a change of address to a financial institution, it is likely to send its acknowledgment to your *old* address. Critique this aspect of the design for the change process.

17. Read and summarize Donald S. Ermer, "Using QFD Becomes an Educational Experience for Students and Faculty," *Quality Progress*, May 1995, p. 131. Describe the application of QFD to the mechanical engineering undergraduate curriculum at the University of Wisconsin–Madison.

18. Read Karen Bemowski, "Ceremony Honors the 1992 Baldrige Award Recipients," *Quality Progress*, February 1993, p. 27. Summarize ATT's Transition Business Unit's success in applying QFD concepts.

19. Discuss the benefits and drawbacks of using Quality Function Deployment.

20. If you were the manager of a fast-food restaurant specializing in hamburgers, how could you use Quality Function Deployment to improve your op-

eration? How would it help you see strategic opportunities? What data would you need to carry out the approach?

21. Read John R. Hauser and Don Clausing, "The House of Quality," *Harvard Business Review* (May–June 1988), pp. 63–73. Summarize the steps in QFD. Comment on the difficulties that one may encounter in its implementation.

22. Use an internet browser and search for articles and discussion materials on "Quality Function Deployment." Relate this material to the discussion in this book. Review examples of successful applications of Quality Function Deployment.

23. Repeat Exercise 22 for "concurrent engineering." There is a website that contains a bibliography on concurrent engineering; see "http://mijuno. larc.nasa.gov."

24. Read Pete Hybert, "Five Ways to Improve the Contracting Process," *Quality Progress*, February 1996, p. 65. Discuss the ideas in this paper as they relate to concurrent engineering.

The Create Process

The problems of today are not in finance, but in how to build a high-quality low-cost product. Whoever solves them will be at the top of tomorrow's companies.

—Lester Thurow, Dean of the Sloan School at MIT[1]

◆ 11.1 Introduction

The actual construction of a product obviously has a big effect on the product's quality. Many factors are at work, and their effect depends on the production process being employed. In this chapter, we will present a general overview of the quality situation, but each product, each production situation is unique.

Requirements specification and design are basically information processes. Neither process depends very much on the type of product being produced; be it a good, information, or service, the process of determining customer wants and

---

[1]Christopher W. L. Hart and Paul E. Morrison, "Students Aren't Learning Quality Principles in Business Schools," *Quality Progress*, January 1992, p. 26.

their synthesis into a set of product requirements is fairly similar. But the process of creating a product does depend on the type of product being produced.

Every task can be viewed as the operation of a process. The specification and design tasks, however, usually are not seen in this light. People tend to think of these as creative acts, not as the operation of a process that results in a product (the requirements or a design). Moreover, the create process often is viewed as a repetitive action—operating a process. In fact, sometimes the create process is referred to as "Operations."

In most organizations, the create process employs more workers than all other steps of the production process. Moreover, it is the process most apparent to customers. Blame for problems with product quality often is attributed to operation of the create process even though the fault might be poor product requirements or a poor product design—or a poor design for the create process, a poor training process, a poor management process, or a problem with some other process that "feeds" production. The create process might rightly claim, "I get no respect."

◆ 11.2 Three Dimensions of Production

Production is monitored along three dimensions—cost, time, and quality. How do these three dimensions interrelate?

Cost and Quality

Traditionally, cost has been the major concern of management, and elaborate accounting systems have been established to record and track costs. The government has had a major influence on these systems through the imposition of an array of federal, state, and local tax regulations. The financial controller has become a key member of the top management team, vested with power to influence many decisions concerning products and production processes.

What is the relationship between cost and quality? That depends on whether one takes a short- or long-term view. In the short run, production cost has little impact on customer buying decisions. Customers have requirements for quality of product, time of delivery, and price, but not the cost. In fact, the customers don't know the cost, and they don't care what it is as long as they view the product as worth the price asked.

But in the long run, cost is vital because a company with high costs cannot compete on price, and this is where quality enters the picture. There is mounting evidence that striving for quality cuts the cost of production and increases product demand. Striving for quality on the production line is a sound business practice.

Time and Quality

For goods, customers are not concerned with how long it takes to create a product, only with when they receive it. Customer demand can be met by offsetting a slow production process with large in-process and finished goods inventories. But this is costly and, as the Japanese learned some time ago, it also allows production problems to go unnoticed.

A customer's time requirements also can be met by "running the line faster," but this means creating defects at a faster rate. A better strategy is to change the production process. Quite often, quality improvement also accelerates the production process. With fewer defects, less time and effort is spent in making repairs or in handling products that later are simply scrapped.

◆ 11.3 The Work Environment

Culture

If one factor can be said to have the dominant, most pervasive influence on the quality of an organization's products, it is the organization's culture. Top management's commitment to quality, the organization's concern for customer and employees, and the organization's attitude toward quality and continual process improvement—all have a major impact on the creation of products. Generally, the organization's culture has a greater impact on the quality of the output from the create process than those of the analysis and design processes. One reason for this is that analysis and design are inventive, challenging activities, which tend to be interesting and carry intrinsic rewards for producing quality products. Another reason is that analysis and design tend to require skills that are regarded as "more professional"; they require more education and give the operators professional standards for product quality that are applied even in the absence of organizational standards.

Infrastructure

Production sometimes appears to be a chaotic arrangement of operations performed amid accumulated scrap, trash, and unused materials in a facility with broken windows, obstructed passageways, and poor lighting. Such conditions can impact product quality directly, for example, through contamination or by causing the inadvertent use of the wrong components. And they can impact product quality indirectly by impeding workers' ability to perform properly and by causing them to doubt the sincerity of management's stated commitment to quality.

Production facilities and production equipment must be suitable and effective. There should be appropriate lighting, ventilation, temperature control, noise control, and good housekeeping. An appropriate physical and psychological environment is a prerequisite for quality production.

◆ 11.4 Some Production Process Problems

Problems in creating goods, information, or services can be attributed either to the production process being used or to the operation of that process. First, let us consider problems arising from the process itself.

Some quality problems can be traced to the fact that the production process is not documented. In effect, there isn't a single process but a collection of processes that are more or less the same, depending on the particular process operator doing the work. The result is that products more or less meet requirements, which means that the quality of production is uneven.

Another problem situation is a production process that is documented, but the documented process is not being followed. This failure might be traced to a lack of training—people don't understand what they should do. Frequently, however, it is due to a lack of discipline.

A third situation is that there is a documented process and it is followed, but the products fail to meet requirements—the process is not effective. This sounds like a real disaster: Like lemmings marching to the sea, process operators regularly produce defective products even though they are following all the rules. In fact, this situation is not as bad as it first appears. It can become the basis for building an effective process that consistently produces quality products. What is needed, of course, is an effective improvement effort to make adjustments in the process so as to bring the products in line with requirements. Such improvement efforts require process owners that have a solid understanding of process and quality concepts, and have access to pertinent, timely data on process performance—data that must be collected during the create and examine processes.

◆ 11.5 Some Process Operation Issues

Next, let's consider some quality-related issues arising from the operation of a process.

Management Stereotypes

The traditional management stereotype of the workforce is that it consists of white-collar workers in the office, who tend to be allied with management, and blue-collar workers in the plant. Traditionally, management and blue-collar workers in many industries have viewed each other with basic distrust and animosity. However, a management attitude of "we versus them" is not conducive to quality. Changing such an attitude requires rethinking the fundamental role of management and labor, and rethinking the authority, responsibility, and information each must have to do a better job of meeting customer requirements. And it requires building trust, which only develops from working collaboratively over time.

Enabling People

But the right attitude is not enough; people also must have the *ability* to do the required work. Human factors must be considered in designing jobs; in turn, this requires that products must be designed for manufacturability. Selection and training of people, motivation, evaluation, reward and recognition (on and off the job)—all influence product quality.

Empowering People

People must also have the authority (power) required by the task they are to perform. Workers who do analysis and design generally are regarded as "professionals". Their specialized knowledge generally gives them the power they need to work effectively. The tradition in the create process, however, is that managers manage and workers work. That traditional division of labor served reasonably well when tasks were simple, such as digging a trench. But for much of today's complex work, workers need the power to make certain decisions concerning their work efforts.

The documented success of self-directed work teams in improving quality and productivity confirms the benefit of empowering workers to shoulder a certain responsibility for their work process in addition to their traditional responsibility for operating it. But empowering workers often is seen by supervisors and managers as a threat to their power. The transition to self-directed work teams requires considerable effort and can take several years, but the reward can be improved quality.[2]

Organized Labor

In organizations where workers are represented by a union, management must work with the union in making process changes to improve quality. At a bare minimum, management should keep union officials informed of changes that affect workers.

Some union leaders are suspicious that quality improvement is just another ploy by management to gain benefits at the expense of workers. To forestall such suspicions, management must help union leaders understand the reasons for their quality initiative and the benefits it will bring to workers. And they must make certain that union leaders are fully aware of the potentially adverse effect on employment that can result from a failure to improve quality.

◆ 11.6 Creating Goods

The main focus of the quality movement has been and continues to be on the production of goods. And increasingly the dominant factor in the quality of goods is the production process. Selection and training of process operators is important,

---

[2]Jack D. Orsburn, Linda Moran, Ed Musselwhite, and John H. Zenger, *Self-Directed Work Teams*, (Homewood, IL.: Business One Irwin, 1990). A detailed discussion of self-directed work teams is given in Section 16.7.

but increased automation is lessening the dependence on their skills. In assembly-type operations, the quality of incoming products is also important. In recent years, the ISO initiative has focused attention on this area.

Some other quality issues relating to the production of goods are:

- Selection and qualification of subcontractors
- Calibration of the measuring devices used in production
- Product traceability through the production process
- Control of nonconforming products to prevent their inadvertent use
- Maintenance of production equipment
- Process monitoring, using statistical process control
- Gathering defect data for process improvement

11.7 Quality of Goods

The quality of goods has improved tremendously in the past twenty years, but problems still remain. A few dramatic examples of problems are these:

- Schwan's Sales Enterprises of Marshall, Minnesota, conducted a massive re-call of their ice cream products after receiving reports of food poisoning from many states. Some 400 cases were confirmed, and a total of 3000 to 5000 were suspected. Cases were from as far distant as Delaware, Georgia, New York, Washington, and Oregon. The problem could have been caused by the ingredients (milk, sugar, and cream made into a pasteurized mix), or the transportation system of ingredients to the plant. Investigators looked inside pipes, checked loading docks, and so on, in an attempt to determine the bacteria's source.[3]

- A giant earthquake struck Japan in January 1995 killing more than 1800 peo-ple, injuring more than 11,000, leaving over 70,000 in shelters. The quake was centered at Kobe, an important port, and it disrupted the country's vaunted just-in-time delivery system. Expressways that had been built to en-dure a shock as severe as the 1923 earthquake in Tokyo fell. But the Tokyo quake registered a magnitude of 8.3 on the Richter scale, whereas the Kobe quake was of magnitude 7.2. (Recall that on the Richter scale a quake of magnitude 8.0 is ten times as severe as one of magnitude 7.0.)[4]

- Of 86,000 artificial heart valves manufactured by Pfizer, about 450 have frac-tured, leading to nearly 300 deaths. Investigation revealed that at least part

---

[3]"Minnesota Ice Cream Is Linked to Salmonella Illness in 15 States," *New York Times*, October 16, 1994.

[4]*Daily Iowan*, January 18, 1995, p. 11A.

of the problem was that manufacturing records were falsified. As one example, the wire struts welded to the valves sometimes developed cracks during manufacturing and had to be rewelded. Records showed that a certain employee rewelded nearly 1900 valves. But in fact, records revealed that this employee left the company many months before these particular valves were manufactured. Moreover, in an interview, this ex-employee said he never welded valves while he worked in the plant.[5]

◆ 11.8 Creating Information

Information is an essential ingredient of every production process. Policies, procedures, instructions, rules, directives, requirements, designs, production plans, test plans, completion reports, employee evaluations, paychecks, advertisements, orders, shipping documents—we truly are an information society.

The Information Systems Department

Many information products are created by individuals using a pen or a word processor. Others are generated by using systems developed and operated by the IS Department, and it is mainly these information products we consider in this text.

Information Systems Departments (IS Departments) are found in all industries. Their mission is to develop, maintain, and operate the basic information systems of the organization and to provide support for "end-user" computing—users building and operating their own programs. Developing and maintaining an information system amounts to building and maintaining a production process. Operating the information systems involves assembling input information, processing information, storing and retrieving information, and delivering information.

Originally, the work of IS was accomplished on centralized, mainframe computers. Much of it still is today, although data input and output usually are handled through a large data communications network, which also may be built and maintained by IS. The data input and output procedures, however, often are under the control of individual departments.

IS personnel usually are classified as managers, professionals, and operators. Operators run the IS systems; their work consists largely of loading appropriate disks, tapes, and supplies (paper, forms. . . .) and unloading products that have been produced. Operators often are trained on the job by managers or fellow workers.

IS professionals develop and maintain computer programs and the data communications systems used to process and transmit information. They are well educated, usually having a college degree in computer science. Generally, they are

---

[5]*New York Times*, November 7, 1991, p.A1.

not very people oriented—some can rightly claim that their computer is their best friend.

The IS Development Process

There is a saying in IS: It's easy to make a mistake, but to really screw up, you need a computer. Some quality problems can be traced to the operation of processes—perhaps the wrong form was used or the wrong tape mounted—but these problems are relatively easy to identify and correct. The real "screw-ups" usually can be traced to the application (program) development process or the application change process—processes operated by IS professionals.

Some typical problems with the development process are these: It is not clear, steps are not correct, and needed control points are missing. But a more common problem is that, whatever the process, it is not followed. Under constant pressure from customers to have the system "tomorrow," steps are skipped, documentation is omitted, tests and reviews are curtailed, and so on.

> *A former product manager for Lotus Development Corp. said that Lotus typically found 5,000 bugs per product. Practice was to fix serious flaws before shipment, but minor bugs were ignored or put off fixing. His excuse was, "If every software vendor tried to sit there and ship bug-free software products, we would never have any software."*[6]

The only thing unique about the Lotus experience is that they actually seem to know how many bugs they typically ship!

Because of the recent interest in ISO 9000, the QA manager in the manufacturing area has gained considerable stature. But not the QA manager in the IS area. In part, this lack of respect arises from the fact that an organization can be certified as in compliance with ISO 9001 without any check being made of the IS area—in spite of the fact that IS might be processing data related in some way to the design and create processes! And it might be processing much of the information relating to the quality system! As interest grows in complying with the ISO 9000-3 software standard, more attention will be paid to the software development process and the stature of the IS QA manager will undoubtedly improve.

User-Developed Software

The major computer systems of an organization, such as the order entry system and the payroll system, typically are built, maintained, and operated by the IS Department under policies that cover quality and data security. Increasingly, however, managers and professionals throughout an organization are building and operating their own

---

[6]*New York Times*, January 18, 1995, p. B1.

systems. We will refer to these as "user-developed" software systems. Some of these are built "from scratch" using a program such as Basic or C; others are built by using "packages" that are modified to suit the user's requirements.

It is not uncommon to find user-developed programs that are poorly documented, poorly tested, and poorly controlled. Generally, there is no independent review or verification of such programs. Little thought is given to backup and recovery or security of the programs and data associated with them. Badly needed in most organizations is a policy covering software that is not managed by the IS Department.

◆ 11.9 Quality of Information

Some examples of poor quality information products are the following.

◆ The Brazilian government reported that the country's trade deficit for December 1995 was underestimated by up to 1 billion U.S. dollars because of a series of mishaps and errors. As the *Financial Times* observed, "[The error] will also raise doubts about the quality of Brazil's official statistics." One banker was somewhat more relaxed. "Economics is easy in Brazil. The deficit is somewhere between $47m and $1.3bn." After all, what's a billion dollars between friends?[7]

◆ Fidelity Investments, America's largest mutual fund manager, announced in December 1994 that an accounting mistake meant that investors in the $39 billion Magellan fund would not receive $2 billion in year-end dividends that had been promised earlier.[8]

◆ On July 19, 1994, 967 automated teller machines of Chemical Banking Corporation refused to shell out money. On a typical day, the machines would have handled about 80,000 ATM transactions. Officials attributed the failure to "what should have been a routine software revision."

In February of that year, the machines deducted too much money from some customer accounts; one day in May, some customers could not get at their funds. Although officials did not know the specific cause of the July malfunction, they said there was no reason to expect future breakdowns. Would they like to bet?[9]

◆ But, of course, the Denver airport takes the prize. A software problem in the baggage-handling software delayed opening of the new airport for over a year.[10]

---

[7]*Financial Times*, January 17, 1995, p. 1.

[8]*The Economist*, December 24, 1994–January 6, 1995, p. 93.

[9]*New York Times*, July 20, 1994, p. A4.

[10]*The Economist*, October 19, 1994, p. 99.

◆ 11.10 Providing Services

The service industry is large and diverse; it includes such areas as health care, government, education, and financial services. Clearly, these industries differ widely in the products they deliver, the requirements of their customers, the skills required of process operators, and the customer's concern about the quality of products. Because the service sector is so broad and nonhomogeneous, anything we say about services will not apply across the board. But with this caveat, we will make a few general remarks about service.

Quality is an attribute of a product, but what is the product of a service? To explore this question, consider the service of providing a meal in a restaurant. The customer receives two types of products: tangible products (information in the form of a menu and a check, and a good in the form of the meal) and an intangible product (the service itself). But these two are intertwined—excellent presentation can mask mediocre food, and the best food might leave a sour taste when the service is surly. For some services, the tangible aspect is the more important to customers—if you have your car serviced, you are more concerned that the car is in proper shape than having a smile with your bill. For others, the intangible aspect might be paramount—you might go to a movie to be entertained, not informed.

For the most part, the literature on quality does not attempt to distinguish the tangible from the intangible aspects of service. Nor shall we. But if you ever are dealing with the quality of service, remember that it consists of "body and soul."

Characteristics of Service Products

A feature that distinguishes service from goods and information is that for many services "the process is the product." More accurately, it is the operation of the process that is the product. This applies, for example, to the performance of a play and to the serving of a meal in an upscale restaurant. The product is judged by the production process and how well it is operated. For goods and information, we really don't know or care how the product was produced, just that what we get is "as advertised." But often the service process is in full view of the customer, making process management and control even more important and more difficult.

Unlike producers of goods and information products, those who provide services often have direct contact with the external customer of the product. This contact precludes the possibility of producing products and verifying them before delivering them to the customer. "Right the first time" must be the rule.

Because service providers have direct contact with external customers, the quality of service depends greatly on the provider's ability and personality—they largely control the intangible product and, to some extent, the tangible. And what customers want is not always what they say they want.

What is a good college lecture? This question was explored by "Dr. Fox," who was really a professional actor to whom were ascribed phony degrees and publications. He delivered six 20-minute videotapes on the biochemistry of memory. Three were delivered in a "seductive" style—with enthusiasm, humor, expressiveness, friendliness, charisma, and personality. Of the three, one lec-

ture was high in content, one medium, and one low. The content was low-ered by removing substantive material and substituting short stories, discussion of what "will be covered," circular discussions, etc. The other three lectures consisted of the same high, medium, and low content, but were low in seduction—flat and dull. Each lecture was shown to a group of students at the Southern Illinois University School of Medicine (a different group for each lecture); the students were asked to evaluate the lecture by completing a typical faculty rating form. Among the results of the study was that students receiving seductive lectures covering only four teaching points gave the same rating as to the dull lecture covering 26 teaching points.[11]

Providing good service means going back to basics: First, there must be a clear statement of customer requirements. Next, there must be a well-documented work process—procedures, work instructions, standards of performance, and appropriate quality controls. Process operators should be selected not only for their technical competence, but also for their "service attitude"—the willingness and ability to satisfy customers. They must be well trained and properly motivated to do an excellent job. And they must be properly compensated for their efforts.

Work supervision, too, is more demanding for service than for other products because it focuses more on the operation of the process than would be the case for goods or information. And much of it must be accomplished in the presence of customers.

Of the basic requirements for good service just listed, it appears that the hardest to fulfill in the United States is a good "service attitude" on the part of employees. We conjecture that there are at least two reasons for this difficulty. Americans have a strong feeling of equality; they stand ready to help one another, but any suggestion that they should be servile or submissive rubs against the grain. A more basic reason, perhaps, is that most Americans have never received excellent service. But some American organizations manage to provide excellent service; here is an outstanding example of one that does.

At the travel management firm Rosenbluth, Inc., employment begins with a two-day visit to corporate headquarters to meet top officers and learn what's really important to the company. The culmination of the visit is afternoon tea elegantly served to the new associates by the top officers of the company. The purpose of the tea is to show the new employees that they are important to the company, management is happy they have joined the team, and that people come first in the organization. Also it is to support a company belief that people cannot provide good service until they themselves experience it. By providing their employees with excellent service, they are instilling the habit of providing such service to their customers.[12]

---

[11]"Bogus Dr. Fox Cited in a Study of 'Seductive Lecturing'," *Chronicle of Higher Education*, IX, 9:3, November 18, 1974, p. 3.

[12]Hal F. Rosenbluth and Diane McFerrin Peters, "*The Customer Comes Second*," pp. 19-20. Rosenbluth, Inc. is also discussed in Section 4.2.

From Rosenbluth's basic belief have flowed many other innovations, including new ideas on hiring, perpetual training, use of technology, and enhancement of services.

Status of Service

Service industries are behind manufacturing and information providers in recognizing the importance of quality. Some firms are still in the denial stage, claiming that service is different and quality principles don't apply. In general, firms do not yet understand basic concepts of quality. Some service industries even fail to have a proper perception of their customers' requirements. For example, a survey of airline passengers, airline executives, and officials in the U.S. Department of Transportation asked about the importance of 60 quality dimensions of airline travel.[13] The partial results shown in Display 11.1 indicate that neither the airline managers nor the officials overseeing the industry understood the main concerns of passengers. Of the top ten passenger concerns of passengers, only four were among the top ten concerns of airline managers and only two among the top ten concerns of officials.

Many service organizations fail to take a process view of their operations. For example, historically the patient care delivery systems of health care organizations has been structured on managing departments rather than production processes. It has been focused on outcome (did the patient improve or not), not on the process. As a result, techniques such as process simplification and process improvement have not been employed. This situation is beginning to change. But as recently as 1992, only 5 percent of U.S. health care organizations always or almost always used process simplification techniques, and 66 percent used such techniques occasionally or never. Quality problems still tend to be blamed on people, not the process.[14]

DISPLAY 11.1 ◈ Order of Quality Concerns

Order	Passengers	Managers	Officials
1	Airline responsive to lost bags	Airlines must earn a profit	Security screening before boarding
2	Prompt information on delayed flights	Cabin attendants must be courteous	Safety announcements made
3	Bags handled carefully	Flights depart on time	Airlines must earn a profit

---

[13]Timothy J. Kloppenborg and Kent N. Gourdin, "Up in the Air about Quality," *Quality Progress*, February 1992, p. 31.

[14]Craig A. Anderson, "Curing What Ails U.S. Health Care," *Quality Progress*, April 1992, p. 37. This issue is devoted entirely to quality of health care.

◆ 11.11 Quality of Services

Service quality is improving. The Ritz-Carlton, Federal Express, and the Madison city government are examples of high levels of service quality.[15] But, in general, quality in the service sector is such that examples of good service are lost among examples such as the following.

> *In the 1960s, the Cunard liner* Queen Elizabeth II *(QE II) was one of the grand ladies of the sea. Plying between Southhampton and New York, she provided luxurious service in the best British tradition to her first class passengers. But in the decades that followed, jet travel cut the time for the passage from almost a week to under a day, and the days of luxury liners were over.*
>
> *In 1994, Cunard decided to modernize the QE II for use as a cruise ship. An ambitious schedule was established for the refit effort, calling for it to be completed in time for a Christmas cruise. A number of contractors fell behind schedule, so it was decided that workmen should remain on board and finish the refitting during the journey. The result was a disaster for the passengers.*
>
> *Many confirmed reservations had to be canceled to make room for the extra workmen. Those canceled were the lucky ones, being given some compensation and a free cruise the next year. Those who sailed did not find the luxury they expected. Some reported water slopping in the entrance of their room, no carpet, and building materials in the middle of the floor. Others reported it was three days before they could get their toilet to flush. Others found their cabins had no water, no air conditioning, and no flushing toilet.*
>
> *On docking in New York, passengers filed a $62 million class action suit in New York against Cunard. And to top it all off, sailing from New York to the Caribbean was delayed because the US Coast Guard refused to give a safety certificate to the ship until obstacles were cleared from passage ways.[16]*

The *Wall Street Journal* reported on the quality of English-language advertising in signs observed in various countries.[17] Here are some examples:

◆ Hotels in many countries attempted to display their friendliness. A Japanese hotel posted the sign, "You are invited to take advantage of the chambermaid." A Paris hotel suggested, "Please leave your values at the front desk." And a Zurich hotel advised, "Because of the impropriety of entertaining guests of the opposite sex in the bedroom, it is suggested that the lobby be used for this purpose."

---

[15]Chapter 24 gives a detailed discussion of service quality at these organizations.

[16]*Financial Times*, December 24/25, 1994, p. 4.

[17]*Wall Street Journal*, November 19, 1992, p. B1.

- Many foreign restaurants are justly proud of their offerings. One in Switzerland announced, "Our wines leave nothing to hope for." And a hotel in Acapulco emphasized their quality control by claiming that "The manager has personally passed all the water served here."

- But foreigners also requested Americans to observe a certain decorum. A Norwegian cocktail lounge drew a line: "Ladies are requested not to have children at the bar." And a Budapest zoo asked: "Please do not feed the animals. Instead, give suitable food to the guard on duty."

- And, of course, firms advertised their services. A Hong Kong dentist promised to "extract teeth by the latest Methodists." A Swedish furrier claimed its "fur coats are made for ladies from their own skin." And a tailor in Rhodes asked that orders be submitted early because "in a big rush we will execute customers in strict rotation." A Bangkok dry cleaner claimed you should "Drop your trousers here for best results." And to enjoy Rome, a laundry urges, "Ladies, leave your clothes here and spend the afternoon having a good time." After such a lively visit, Americans might want to fly home from Copenhagen, where an airline office promises to "take your bags and send them in all directions."

◆ 11.12 Creating Better Production Processes Through Reengineering

A newly founded organization must create all of the production processes required to build, sell, and deliver its products, as well as the processes required to operate and administer everything—a massive undertaking. Recall that the term *production process* does not merely refer to manufacturing but to all processes of a firm.

The creation of a production process was discussed in Chapter 8. Most organizations, however, have been in existence for some time. Their problem is not to create production processes but to modify them to improve product quality. One method for this is to *reengineer* their processes.

Hammer and Champy coined the term *reengineering* in their 1993 book, *Reengineering the Corporation.*[18] They define it to be the fundamental rethinking and radical redesign of business processes (production process) to achieve dramatic improvements in critical contemporary measures of performance, such as cost, quality, service, and speed. Reengineering is about work and about the creation of redesigned work processes that are far better than the original processes.

The process owner is responsible for reengineering a production process. The reengineering effort must be guided by a committed individual who has profound knowledge of the process and who has the authority to make changes to the process. In order to reengineer the process, the process owner assembles a team

---

[18]Michael Hammer and James Champy, *Reengineering the Corporation* (New York: HarperCollins, 1993).

of experts consisting of insiders who bring knowledge and expertise about the current process, as well as outsiders who can provide a fresh perspective on the problem.

Reengineering is not simply a technical activity to be carried out solely by engineers. Instead it creates a redesign of the process to better meet the customer's requirements. It has little to do with traditional industrial engineering techniques, which focus on optimizing individual tasks and activities. Instead, it has to do with the process as a whole, the sum aggregate of the various individual activities. It is about work and cross-functional work processes. Also, it is not about how an organization is structured. In practice, however, the organizational structure of a reengineered organization usually is quite different from the traditional organizational structure. A good way to understand the ideas behind reengineering is to look at an example.

> *Hammer and Stanton[19] discuss the maintenance and repair system at GTE, the largest provider of local telephone service in the United States. The old system for handling complaints about nonfunctioning phones was complex. You called the company and were connected to a repair clerk. The repair clerk recorded the information but did nothing more than pass it to a line tester, who checked to learn whether the problem was in the central office or on the line. Depending on which it was, the line tester then passed the information to a central office technician or to a dispatcher, who in turn passed the information to a service technician, who eventually arrived at your premises to make the necessary repairs. Because of the time all of this took and the uncertainty about when their phone would be back in service, the whole process was totally unsatisfactory to the customer.*
>
> *The reengineering solution had a strong customer focus. The process was reengineered so that a* single *person handled the maintenance and repair. This person was given the ability and tools to test the line, modify central software, and locate the problem on the network—all while still talking to the customer. GTE refers to this person as the customer care representative. If the problem cannot be fixed immediately, the customer care representative consults the schedules of repair technicians, schedules the repair job, and promptly tells the customer when the repair person will come to fix the problem. And all this takes place in a single call. Under the old system, less than 1 percent of the problems could be fixed through a single contact. Under the new, reengineered system, the proportion increased to 40 percent and, as a result, customer satisfaction increased. At the same time, the company realized significant savings because of the reduced number of handoffs and the employee time involved.*

---

[19]Michael Hammer and Steven A. Stanton, *The Reengineering Revolution* (New York: HarperCollins Publisher, 1995), p. 6.

Reengineering often leads to a reduction in the workforce. Some employees lose their old jobs and are either laid off or retrained to carry out other tasks. Reengineering also can create new job classifications (such as the customer care representative) that require new, expanded skills.

Reengineering and technical innovations frequently go hand in hand. Reengineering is often possible only through innovations in technology. Handling the telephone repair through a single customer care representative, for example, was made possible by the new switching and computer technology, which allowed the customer care representative to carry out tests right from his terminal and to have on-line access to the work schedules of repair personnel. The impact of the new technology and radical redesign can be much more dramatic than the incremental improvements one gets by "tweaking" an old system.

Most reengineering efforts are focused on order fulfillment, product development, and post-sale services. This makes sense since these activities are of great concern to the customer. As the previous example shows, restructuring a repair service function can increase customer satisfaction and, at the same time, result in savings for the company.

The "just-in-time" (JIT) production system developed by Toyota Motor Company is another good example of reengineering. JIT changed the way manufacturing was carried out, and it had a major impact on the company's financial bottom line. In the old days, companies kept large inventories of parts required for assembly into finished products. This investment in inventory tied up funds, and it took a lot of needed plant space—a very expensive way to manufacture. The reengineered system, where subcomponents are delivered at the very time they are needed ("just in time"), is obviously cheaper—there is no need to hold expensive inventory. Of course, one must take the right actions to make this new, "just-in-time" system work. One needs to develop relationships with reliable subcontractors so that one can be sure that subcomponents are delivered right on time. New developments in shipping play an important role in JIT. Today it is very easy for a U.S. manufacturer to ship a component within 24 hours to virtually any place within the United States.

JIT has yet another benefit. Because JIT calls for little or no inventory, one has better, more cost-effective control over necessary changes. For example, assume that you build radios. If you decide to modify the radio, then under the old system you would have unused inventory to cope with. Under the JIT system, you can institute the change immediately without incurring a large cost for scrapping your old inventory.

Replacing an "inspection" approach to quality, where outgoing end products are inspected prior to shipping, by an approach that focuses on the production processes, is another example of reengineering. The old approach to quality was to first produce and then screen out bad parts before shipping products to the customer. A better, reengineered strategy addresses the processes that lead to the products and checks the stability and capability of these processes over time.

Reengineering can also be applied to product development processes. As an example, consider an automobile company introducing a new model into the market. Just a few years ago the design of the car was quite separate from the manufacturing function, and interaction between these two groups took place quite late in the game—namely, at the point when the design team was finished with its work and was ready to pass it on to the manufacturing group. Often the problem was that some designs were very difficult to manufacture. Also, it wasn't always clear whether some of the requested, and difficult to manufacture, design features were all that important to the customer. Reengineering the process of introducing a new model so that there is closer interaction between the design, manufacturing, and consumer research functions in the company would help to reduce the time required to introduce a new product. Quality Function Deployment, or the House of Quality, provides a blueprint that can be used for this purpose; see our discussion in Section 10.9.

Quality Improvement and Reengineering

Quality improvement and reengineering share many characteristics: both focus on customers and processes, and both are driven by a commitment to make things better. Quality improvement stresses incremental improvements through various methods of problem solving, while reengineering attempts to bring about improvement through radical process redesign. Continual, incremental improvement of processes is an important component of quality improvement. However, Hammer and Champy argue that more dramatic improvements can be obtained by taking a fresh look at the process and by starting with a new slate. Reengineering does exactly that. It leads to a complete rethinking of the entire production process. Reengineering is akin to Juran's breakthrough achievements.[20] As the following example shows, such breakthroughs can lift the quality of a process to dramatically higher levels.

> *Many years ago, motorists from New Jersey had to pay tolls entering and leaving Manhattan (either over bridges or through tunnels). Collecting tolls at either end of the bridges and tunnels caused rush hour traffic jams on both sides, but the effect was considerably worse on the crowded Manhattan side. Much thought went into improving this system; the customers' perspective of having as few traffic jams as possible was a driving force behind all improvement efforts. The traffic department experimented with varying the number of lanes, the number of toll booth operators, the approach routes to the entrances, and so on. Continual incremental improvement of the system led to improvements, but the situation was still far from being acceptable. The breakthrough came through the reengineering of the system. The reengineering idea was to get rid of toll booths in Manhattan and to charge the double amount on bridges and tunnels leading from New Jersey into Manhattan. This worked well because virtually all traffic between the two goes over bridges and*

---

[20]Juran and Gryna, *Quality Planning and Analysis*, International Edition (New York: McGraw-Hill, 1993), pp. 52–77.

through tunnels. The payoff from this rather simple innovation (or break-through, or reengineering concept) was large; it eased the congestion in Manhattan because traffic was no longer slowed down by toll booths. It also led to savings for the Transportation Department because half of the toll booths (namely, those on the Manhattan side) could be removed.

While radical changes or innovations in business processes and technology can indeed lead to dramatic benefits, it would be a mistake always to count on such quantum leaps to happen. Furthermore, it is often the case that innovations reach their full potential only after a subsequent sequence of continual improvement steps. Even if a total redesign is the correct strategy for improvement, it usually takes a sequence of continual and incremental improvement steps to "iron out the kinks." Hence, reengineering of processes and continual quality improvement strategy must be viewed as partners, not competitors. It's not a question of whether you should use one or the other; these two techniques complement each other.

Dangers Associated with Reengineering

Radical redesign, if successful, can lead to dramatic improvements. On the other hand, radical changes can also lead to major busts if they don't work out. The opportunity is there for major improvements, but major setbacks are also possible. With incremental small improvement steps, the changes are usually small, but the potential losses also are small. As with any radical change, the opportunity for changes in either direction is large; one needs to be especially careful when redesigning processes from a clean slate.

The ability to make truly radical changes is usually slowed by our present knowledge of the processes. Prior knowledge acts like an "anchor" or a "weight" that doesn't let us stray too far. In fact, it is usually quite difficult to break from previous assumptions and go beyond the current thought framework. In some ways, this is bad because it acts as a drag on our ability to introduce a radically new solution. On the other hand, the prior knowledge acts as a safety net, and it may prevent us from going too far astray. There are dangers associated with tearing down old conventions and starting from a clean slate. Hence, whenever possible, one should test the reengineered process on a smaller scale before implementing it throughout an entire organization. It is also important that one follows an organized approach in (re)designing the process; the discussion of the design process in Chapter 10 should be helpful.

Reengineering, Downsizing, and Human Factor Implications

Some organizations are turning to reengineering as a tool to *right-size* (mostly *downsize*) their businesses and to be able to do more with fewer employees. A fresh look at business processes should bring about improvements in these processes and should ultimately translate into savings. No doubt, reengineering efforts affect employees, and, as with any process change, certain jobs may become obsolete. This is where the human factor issues come into play. Reengineering efforts are typically employee-involved improvement projects; therefore, their effectiveness depends to a large degree on how the company treats the employees that are impacted by the reengineering results. If the company's attitude is to fire affected employees (and hence downsize the workforce), the reengineering effort is unlikely to get the employee support needed for it to succeed. Employees are rational; if the company doesn't look out for their well being, they will not be eager to reengineer themselves out of a job. On the other hand, if a company reassigns impacted employees to other areas of the company, it will be much more successful in its reengineering efforts. This strategy is followed by Toyota, and it is a major reason why Toyota has been so successful with its employee-involved improvement projects.[21]

◆ Exercises and Additional Readings

1. From your collection of articles on quality (see Exercise 1, Chapter 1), give some examples of (a) quality problems due to product construction and (b) quality products resulting from improving the requirements, design, or production processes. What lessons can you learn from these articles?

2. Strict cleanliness standards must be observed in producing computer disks. List some other products for which there are strict requirements for the production facility.

3. The April 1992 issue of *Quality Progress* is devoted to quality of health care. Select one of the articles from this issue and report on the delivery of health care.

4. Read one or more of the references on reengineering. What other points and features that are *not* mentioned in our brief review are important? Present other examples of the possible benefits of reengineering, and mention some of its dangers.

5. Hammer and Stanton, in their book *The Reengineering Revolution* (New York: HarperCollins Publisher, 1995), discuss several applications of reengineering in what they call "mission-driven organizations." By that they mean organizations whose mission goes beyond economic concerns such as profit or stock price. Examples are nonprofit organizations, such as Planned Parenthood, Right to Life, or Greenpeace; schools and universities; governmental organizations such as the U.S. army; and churches. Reengineering applies to all organizations, profit or nonprofit, because it applies to work processes. Summarize their discussion.

---

[21]G. Dennis Beecroft, "Reengineering and Downsizing an Organization," *Newsletter of the Institute for Improvement in Quality and Productivity,* University of Waterloo, Fall 1995.

6. Think about reengineering the introductory statistics course at your educational institution (or any other pet course that you would like to discuss). (a) Start with the desired objectives of the course. Here you may run into a problem, because it may not be obvious who the customer really is. Should one try to satisfy the objectives of the students who are taking the course, or those of instructors of higher-level courses that build on the foundation, or those of the future employer of the students? (b) Think about how the current process achieves these objectives and how it falls short. (c) Start with a clean sheet and redesign the process. Discuss how you would implement the new design and how you would evaluate it.

7. Describe present attempts to reengineer the U.S. health care delivery system. Discuss the impact of reengineering on the quality of the health care delivery as seen by the customer, as well as from a cost perspective. Discuss how this reengineering effort will affect health care providers. Who are the winners and losers of the restructuring of the health care delivery system?

8. How would you reengineer the processing of insurance claims? Describe the current system and comment on possible improvements.

9. Consider the process by which consumer goods are delivered from the manufacturers' plants to the shelves of retailers. This process involves hundreds of manufacturers and countless retail stores, numerous wholesalers and distributors, and many trucking firms. Describe the current system and discuss how this process could be reengineered to function more efficiently. Keep in mind that new information technology is now available that can transmit information almost instantaneously. Contact a local Wal-Mart store and learn about its distribution system.

10. Read and summarize Mahesh P. Desai, "Implementing a Supplier Scorecard System," *Quality Progress*, February 1996, p. 73.

11. Read Timothy J. Kloppenborg and Kent N. Gourdin, "Up in the Air About Quality," *Quality Progress*, February 1992, p. 31. Summarize their message about airline quality.

12. Read Richard B. Keith, Jr., "MIS + TQM = QIS," *Quality Progress*, April 1994, p. 29. Summarize how Management Information Services can become a leader in process reengineering.

13. Discuss Ishikawa's recommendation on how to interact with external suppliers and subcontractors. See K. Ishikawa, *What Is Total Quality Control? The Japanese Way* (Englewood Cliffs, N.J.: Prentice-Hall, 1985), pp. 159–162.

14. Look for additional examples of failures: inferior goods, service, and information products.

15. Read and discuss J. S. England, "Reengineering: Texas Instruments Revamps Its Order Fulfillment Process," *The Quality Observer*, March 1996. It describes several successful reengineering efforts at Texas Instruments.

16. Read and discuss Lawrence P. Leach, "TQM, Reengineering, and the Edge of Chaos," *Quality Progress*, February 1996, pp. 85–90. (a) Write a paragraph to support Leach's position. (b) Write a paragraph to refute his position.

17. Read the book by James Champy, *Reengineering Management: The Mandate for New Leadership* (New York: HarperCollins Publishers, 1995). Discuss the main differences with his other books on reengineering.

18. Read and discuss Gary K. Gulden and Robert H. Reck, "Combining Quality and Reengineering Efforts for Process Excellence," *Information Strategy: The Executive's Journal*, (Spring 1992), pp. 10–16. In this paper, the authors state: "Although business reengineering appears similar in technique and result to quality improvement, reengineering is a far different approach to process management with far different results." What reasons do they give that justify this claim?

19. Search the web for materials on "reengineering." List and discuss examples where the reengineering process has helped turn around companies.

20. Read the paper by Howard Eisenberg, "Reengineering and Dumbsizing: Mismanagement of the Knowledge Resource," *Quality Progress*, May 1997, p. 57. Summarize the author's comments on the negative side that reengineering can have on a company.

Chapter **12**

The Examine Process

The proof of the pudding is in the eating.

When Pump Division of Imo Industries receives a defective product from a supplier, they videotape someone describing the problem and actual close-up footage of the defective part. The videotape is sent to the supplier to help them prevent the problem recurring.

—Robert J. Tracy[1]

◆ 12.1 Quality Control

Examine is the fourth and final stage of the production process. For all production processes, the emphasis always should be on doing things right the first time.

---

[1]Robert J. Tracy, "Use Video for Corrective Action," *Quality Progress*, March 1994, p. 184.

But examination is a necessary stage because this lofty goal cannot be met every time, and often even a single mistake can be disastrous.

In an organization, control is exercised over three dimensions of production: time, cost, and quality. Control systems for the three dimensions involve similar steps: You plan what you want to do, observe what you have done, compare the two, and make adjustments as necessary. A manager of production must consider all three dimensions. Here we focus on quality control.

The primary purpose of quality control is to prevent nonconforming products from being shipped to the customer. A secondary purpose is to gather information on defects for use in directing process improvement efforts. Quality control information most definitely should not be collected for the purpose of employee evaluation; doing so is an open invitation for employees to protect themselves by thwarting the quality control system.

Problems with Quality Control

Some typical problems with the examination process are these:

- Examination is not enforced.
  The emphasis is on production; examination is viewed as a bothersome detail. After all, nothing is perfect, so why spend a lot of time looking for minor problems. Besides, customers will complain if they aren't happy with the product.

- The examination process is not effective.
  Attention is given to how the product is built, and the examination process is tacked on as an afterthought. Methods and procedures for examination are not given much thought; examination equipment is not properly calibrated and maintained. Or, at the other extreme, a reasonable examination process is put in place; then it is left untended and becomes ineffective over time, but nobody bothers to check.

- Examination equipment is faulty.
  Measuring equipment is not properly calibrated; automated measuring equipment is not properly monitored and maintained.

- Examiners are not effective.
  Examiners are not properly trained and motivated. They view their job as production, not examination. Why spend time examining products when we are paid by how many we produce?

- Product requirements are not clear.
  Sometimes product requirements are not clear, leaving it up to the inspector to decide what is acceptable. Tolerances might not be clearly established; standards for computer programs are loosely defined; service standards concentrate on what to do, not how to do it.

- Poor examination environment.
  The environment is often to blame for a poor examination process. One of

the worst problems is that discovered defects are blamed on the people operating the process, not the process itself.

◆ Poor control of nonconforming product.
When nonconforming products are discovered, they are not properly tagged, segregated, and handled. Quality records for nonconforming products are faulty.

◆ Defect information is not collected for use in process improvement.
A step in every examination process should be the collection of defect information gained while operating the process. This step is often overlooked, but it is very important and deserves some attention.

◆ The examination process fails to take the human side of the enterprise into account.
An examination process generates fear and resentment if it is seen to be directed at people. To avoid this, the rule should be that the process is to blame, not the operators.

The fact that a product does not meet requirements can be used to reject the product until it can be corrected and reinspected. It is very important to understand, however, that the "reject" information also can yield valuable insights into the characteristics of the production process. Thus, although this chapter focuses on examinations of a product, the results of such examinations must be collected and analyzed to assist in making process improvements—a topic we will address in Part V.

Golden Rule of Quality Control

The golden rule of quality control is:

Every quality problem is a process problem.

If an operator makes a mistake, the problem might be with the production process (inappropriate procedures or tools), the operator selection process (wrong person for the job), the training process (doesn't know how to do the job), the reward system (extrinsic but no intrinsic reward), the management process (too much control, too little control), the communications process (manager doesn't know of a worker's pressing personal problem), and so on.

Errors should be "blamed" on processes, *not* people. Once in a while this will be wrong. But when you have the occasional "turkey" on your hands, the people will let you know, or they will find their own way to handle the situation.

◆ 12.2 Defect Database

Some defects are discovered during the process of examining products; other defects go undetected and are discovered by customers who use the product.

It is important to collect information about each defect: a description of the defect; when, where, and how it was discovered; and probable cause if known. The defect should be classified by type. Then all of this information should be entered into a *defect database*. On a regular basis, these data should be analyzed and used to make improvements in the processes that allowed the defects to occur (the production process, training process, management process, etc.).

It is extremely important that the information in the defect database *not* be used for employee evaluation. Doing so almost guarantees that some discovered defects will go unreported and valuable data will be lost.

◆ 12.3 Planning for Quality Control

Two general techniques are used to detail quality control activities within a production process. One technique is used for routine products—those whose production can be viewed as the routine operation of an established production process. The other technique is used for unique, complex products, such as a manufacturing production line or the development of the space shuttle.

Controlling Routine Products

For routine products, quality control activities are incorporated into the production process. At appropriate points in the process, various inspections and tests are included as process steps. Such a step might call for 100 percent inspection of products or for a sample inspection. Quality control can and should be viewed as just another step of the production process.

Quality Plan

For a unique product, quality control activities should be tailored to the product and detailed in a *quality plan*, which is "a document setting out the specific quality practices, resources, and sequence of activities relevant to a particular product, project, or contract."[2] This plan should specify the quality practices and activities to be carried out, including instructions for receiving, processing, and final inspection and testing of the product. A quality plan is especially useful for complex products and for stage production involving unique products.

◆ 12.4 Examination Techniques

Basically, there are two ways to examine a product: you observe it or you operate it. You examine a plan by observing it. You examine a Broadway play by operating it through rehearsals and performances. For many products you examine

---

[2] ISO 8402.

both by observing and operating; for example, you examine a computer program by reading each instruction (observing) and by testing (operating) it.

Observing Products

Observation is the primary technique for examining products during the specify and design phases of development, but it can also be used in the build and test phases. Various observation techniques are employed; all are used to establish that the product meets requirements.

- *Measurement*
  Observation often involves measurement, such as measuring a part with a micronometer, counting the number of items in a box, or weighing a sack of flour. Sometimes measurement is automated, such as spell-checking a document. Measurement commonly is used to check products during the production process.

- *Individual review*
  Each individual is responsible for the quality of his or her output. Individuals should review their work products before asserting that they are completed and meet requirements.

- *Peer review*
  For complex work products, the producer sometimes is so "close" to the product that he cannot review it effectively. For example, often the writer of a letter cannot discover flaws as easily as a disinterested person. Sometimes it is useful to have a product reviewed by someone other than the producer. A common procedure for accomplishing this is for peers to review each other's work.

- *Review*
  After a work product has been subjected to individual and peer reviews, it might be subjected to an additional observation under the direction of management. We shall call such an assessment a *review*. (The basic and vital difference between a peer review and a review is that the peer review is "owned" by the producer of the product, the review by management.) Generally, a review is an assessment of a significant, related collection of work products. It is held under the direction of management, and it is conducted under formal rules. For example, the customer requirements for a product typically are reviewed before design commences, and the product design is reviewed before production is started.

- *Quality System Audit*
  An audit is a formal review conducted by an independent group, called auditors. Traditionally, audits have been held to verify financial matters; our interest, however, is in the more recent practice of conducting audits to verify the status of an organization's quality system. Quality System audits are discussed in Section 13.11.

Operating Products

Some products can be examined by operating them. To learn if it meets requirements, you drive a car, run a computer program, preview a Broadway play, rehearse a courtroom trial, and operate a production line. In all cases, you are testing the product to learn how it performs: Does the product do what it should; does it meet its operating requirements?

Testing is a vast subject with many technical aspects. A few observations will give you a flavor of what is involved:

◆ Testing is done by different groups of people.
  Testing might be done by people producing a product, by customers of the product, by government agencies, and by independent testing groups, such as Consumer Reports and the Underwriter Laboratories.

◆ Testing is conducted at different levels of product development.
  In building a car, one tests parts from subcontractors, components, subassemblies, and then the final product. In building a computer program, one conducts unit tests, integration tests, final tests, and user tests. In testing a play, one tests parts, scenes, acts, and the total production. Testing is done during development to *verify* that the product is correct; it is done at the end of development to *validate* that the product is correct.

◆ Testing can be destructive or nondestructive.
  The only way to see if an atom bomb works is to try one—and, of course, that is no real proof that another bomb of the same type will work. On the other hand, you can test a computer without destroying it. Sometimes it isn't clear just how destructive a test is. Probably you would not want to buy a car that a manufacturer had put through the paces on a test track. On the other hand, would you want to buy a computer terminal that had *not* gone through a "burn-in" test?

◆ Testing is not a trivial topic.
  Is the test coverage adequate? Is the sample representative? How much testing is enough? Is the test environment representative of the likely operating environment? Shouldn't there be just one more test? In many fields there are experts who specialize in answering such questions.

◆ 12.5 Examining Requirements

Very often customer requirements are stated in a written document, sometimes called a *contract*. Occasionally, there will be a requirement that a product "looks like this object" or "performs like this device," but usually the desired characteristics of the product are reduced to a description in text or to drawings. The examination of customer requirements generally is an examination of the contract to learn if the stated requirements meet customer wants.

Some major issues to be examined are as follows:

- *Clarity and accuracy.* Do the customer requirements clearly and accurately reflect the wants of the customers?
- *Completeness.* Are the customer requirements complete? Were all of the customers for the product considered? For example, in addition to the potential buyer of a car, was consideration given to the needs of other family members? the mechanic who will service it? the community in which it will be driven?
- *Consistency.* Are the requirements consistent? Has the potential conflict between the requirement for gas mileage and the requirement for fast acceleration been resolved?
- *Feasible.* Does there seem to be some feasible way to meet all of the customer requirements? Will we be handing design an impossible task?

For a custom product, the customer can be asked to examine the requirements; for a consumer product, the examination most likely will be made by the supplier. Examination of customer requirements should cover some of the potential problems discussed in Section 9.6.

◆ 12.6 Receiving Inspection

Incoming products should be examined. A typical process for receiving inspection is the following.

All Products

As part of the receiving process, all products should be given a visual inspection. This should involve verifying that a product matches its order in type and quantity, and making a check for any signs of damage or tampering. If the visual inspection reveals a problem, the product should be marked "not passed" and segregated pending resolution of the problem with the subcontractor.

Custom and Critical Products

Custom products and those that are critical should undergo a second stage of inspection, the amount and scope of which will depend on the status of the subcontractor supplying the product. If the buyer is assured that the subcontractor has a satisfactory quality system, the product might be exempted from further inspection.

Incoming products might be subjected to a sample inspection to assure that they are satisfactory. Today, however, many product defect rates are measured in parts per million; this means that sample sizes must be very large for a sample inspection to be effective. Many companies have stopped using sample inspections. Instead, they rely on the fact that their subcontractors are registered as in compliance with the relevant ISO 9000 standard.

Control of Products

It is very important that at each stage of production the inspection status of each product be clearly identified. This is necessary to prohibit the use of nonconforming products in production. Nonconforming products should be segregated to prevent their inadvertent use. The identification of inspection status starts at the receiving platform and continues throughout the production cycle and final storage pending delivery to the customer.

◆ 12.7 In-Process Inspection

Because the basic paradigm of work is applied recursively, every task of creating a product is followed by an examination of the product to see that the task was done correctly. Sometimes this examination is very thorough; sometimes it is cursory. In-process inspection saves money by catching errors early in the production process; but it costs time and resources to conduct inspections—balancing cost of inspection against savings is part of the challenge in defining a production process.

Sampling Frequency

The products of the specify and design phases of the production process generally are subjected to 100 percent inspection. There are two reasons for this. First, the earlier one is in the production process, the more costly an error becomes and the more it is worth to avoid one. For example, if a customer requirement is wrong, it might mean that some subcontractor requirements are wrong, so the product will be wrong—everything must be corrected. But an error in production, serious as that may be, impacts only the final product.

The second reason for 100 percent inspection in the early phases is that specify and design are accomplished once, but production may continue indefinitely. It isn't until one gets to the production stage that there is a need for relief from the cost of inspecting every product.

If a process is performing well and is reasonably stable, it might not be necessary to examine every product of the process to have reasonable confidence that all products meet requirements. One decision to be made in the examine process, therefore, is whether 100 percent of the products will be examined or whether it will be satisfactory to employ *random sampling*—that is, to examine a suitably selected sample from the process and use this to make inferences about the lot from which the sample was taken.

◆ 12.8 Final Examination

Because of the basic paradigm of work, the create stage ends with an examination of the created product. Is it really necessary, then, to have a separate final examination? Isn't final examination repetitious and a needless expenditure of resources? As the following example shows, the answer is: No. Final examination is required.

> *The create stage for producing a car consists of four subprocesses: specify, design, create, and examine. The last of these subprocesses ("examine") answers the question, "Is the car defect-free?" It does not directly address the question, "Does the car provide what the customer wants?"*

Final examination addresses the question: Does our product provide what the customer wants? For a custom product, one way to answer this question is to involve the customer in the final inspection. For a commercial product, one way to gain insight into the answer is to ask a representative group of customers.

Another way to look at the distinction between these two examinations is this: If you are producing dog-food, the examination at the end of the create process is to see that the dog-food meets the supplier requirements established for it. The final examination process answers the question, "Will the dog eat the dog-food?"

◆ 12.9 Examining Goods

The basic process of examining products does not change from one product type to the next. However, some features of the process and some tools employed do vary from product group to product group. Therefore, we will look at the three major product groups separately, starting with goods: cars, electronics, and so on.

Examining Subcontractor Products

Most manufacturing processes require components, parts, and other products from outside subcontractors and vendors. Because the quality of these subcontractor products has an impact on the quality of the finished product, it is necessary to assure that the subcontractor's products meet requirements.

The traditional way to assure the quality of incoming products was to conduct receiving inspection (goods-inward inspection in the more descriptive British terminology). One important aim of the ISO 9000 series of standards is to replace the traditional receiving inspection with a system whereby subcontractors are audited and certified to be in compliance with a satisfactory quality system. This certification should nullify or at least lessen the need for traditional receiving inspection.

The benefits of the ISO certification scheme are that a manufacturer need not devote resources to inspecting a subcontractor; and perhaps more importantly, a subcontractor would not have to offer separate proof to each customer that his quality system was satisfactory.

Measuring Devices

The manufacturing process often must produce products to extremely close tolerances. To assure that these tolerances are met, various measuring devices are employed throughout the process. But what happens if the measuring device is not adjusted properly? A mess. To avoid this, it is necessary to *calibrate* all measuring equipment, that is, to adjust equipment to assure that the instrument provides accurate readings. Keeping inspection, measuring and test equipment properly calibrated and maintained is so important to the quality of manufactured products that the ISO quality standard devotes more discussion to this topic than any other.

Inspection

The production of goods often entails very large quantities of output. Random sampling gives some relief to the inspection problem by providing reasonable assurance of quality based on checking only a portion of production. More recently, advances in automating the inspection process have made 100 percent inspection again feasible in some industries.

A shift in the focus from products to processes decreases the need for inspection. On the one hand, consumers are ever more intolerant of poor quality. On the other, initiatives such as the Deming Prize, the Baldrige Award, and ISO 9000 are showing that quality can be improved dramatically by improving production processes. Who knows? One day processes may be improved to the point that inspectors will be as lonely as the Maytag repairman in the TV ads.

◆ 12.10 Examining Services

The examination of service differs fundamentally from that of goods because often the examination and production of service take place simultaneously. For example, a critic reviews (examines) a play while the play is being performed; the maitre d' observes the waiters and waitresses while they serve customers. For many services, it is impractical to insert a separate quality control step between the production of the service and its delivery to the customer—the create and examine steps must be fused.

Examination of service is primarily by observation. Individual servers check their own performance. Further examinations might be made by the server's work group and supervisor. Customer feedback might be obtained through a survey, and service delivery might be videotaped and used for improvement.

Some problems surrounding service quality are:

- High subjectivity on the part of the customer as to what is good service.
- High variability of the service provided.
- Lack of a service attitude by many service providers.
- Lack of experience with good service on the part of many customers.

Some of the root causes of service problems are:

- The service process is not clearly defined.
- Service standards are lacking.
- Employee training is poor or lacking.
- Quality control is not embedded into the service process.

◆ 12.11 Examining Information

Most products from personnel, market research, finance, legal, information systems, and corporate headquarters are information products: plans, directives, operating procedures, letters, reports, and so on. Generally, information products must be examined by observation, although on occasion it might be possible to examine them by some other means, say, building a prototype to examine a design. Examination of some aspects of information products can be automated (spelling and syntax checking), but content generally must be checked by careful review.

◆ 12.12 Examining Production Processes

An important technique for examining the quality of a production process is *statistical process control* (SPC). This technique (discussed in Chapter 20) helps us determine if a process is stable over time and can produce products that satisfy their requirements.

Another important technique is to analyze the information in a defect database (Section 12.2) in an attempt to find defect patterns and to learn the cause of the most frequent types of defects. With this information, the next step is to make changes in the process to eliminate the defect cause.

Responsibility for defect analysis and defect cause removal should be assigned to the process owner. Capturing data on defects is an ongoing activity; defect analysis and defect-cause removal usually is managed as a project.

Examining Information Systems

Today most organizations are extremely dependent on computerized information systems to facilitate most of the major processes of the organization. The quality of these systems is critical to the sales, manufacturing, inventory, shipping, servicing, billing, personnel, and administration systems of the organization.

Some appreciation of the effort that goes into the building of these systems to assure their quality can be gained from the following list of typical examinations that are made during the building process:

- Examination of individual program modules (desk checking)
- Group checking of individual modules (peer reviews)
- Unit testing of individual modules
- Integration testing of groups of modules
- System testing of the completed system

Some of the quality-related efforts that go into the operation of these systems to assure the quality of the output are these:

- Operator check of input (right data sets, right hardware, software, communications configuration, and so on)
- Machine checking of input (check of input data, exception reports)

But in spite of all these efforts, information systems errors are not rare. In many organizations, defect removal, defect analysis, and defect-cause removal is a thriving business.

◆ 12.13 External Examiners

In addition to internal examinations, the facilities, production processes, and products of an organization might well be subject to examination by outside agencies. Generally, these agencies are concerned with health, safety, and environmental matters. Some examples of outside examiners are:

- Building inspectors
- Federal Aviation Agency
- Federal Food and Drug Administration
- Occupational Safety and Health Administration

The facilities and production processes of an organization are also of great concern to its important customers, who might require that their examiners monitor your production. Increasingly, however, these customers are accepting 9000 certi-fication in lieu of conducting their own assessment of subcontractor production processes (see also Section 12.6).

◆ 12.14 Desk Checking

Many techniques are available for examining a product. We conclude this chapter with several sections, each describing a popular technique.[3] We start with desk checking.

Desk checking is a structured procedure that an individual can use to control the quality of a work product he has produced. Although originally designed for checking computer code (which you do while seated at a desk), the procedure is general and can be applied to any information product: requirements documents, designs, plans, operating instructions, book manuscripts, inventory lists—all can be desk checked.

We will describe a typical procedure for desk checking; this procedure is "owned" by the individual doing the checking, so it can be modified to suit individual styles.

Preparation for Desk Checking

Most people tend to have favorite errors that they make repeatedly—they forget to perform a certain operation, or they do it incorrectly, and they make the same mistake time after time. To catch such mistakes, for each of your product types you should maintain a *checklist* of the errors you frequently make. These lists, which can be referenced while doing desk checking, should be updated to add new types of errors that arise; old errors that have been overcome can be dropped.

It is important to separate "doing" from "checking." Desk checking is an activity quite distinct from producing the product. Desk checking should be scheduled, preferably not immediately after the product was produced. If there is a time lag—even an overnight gap—you are more likely to look at your actual work product rather than subconsciously reviewing your *perception* of what is there. Sufficient time must be allowed for the review—with experience it will become easy to judge how much time is required. Allowing insufficient time or scheduling desk check-ing just before some important event is likely to cause an anxiety that will inter-fere with effective checking.

It is important to eliminate distractions that might interfere with desk checking. Noise and interruptions can interfere with the process. If possible, arrange that desk checking be done in a quiet place, say the office library or some other shel-tered spot.

Finally, before starting to desk check, assemble all the materials that will be re-

---

[3]Our discussion is detailed. On initial reading, you might want to skim these sections.

quired: the product to be checked, requirements and standards that apply to it, any tools that might be required—and your appropriate checklists.

Performing Desk Checking

The following guidelines will help you to make desk checking an effective product review technique. They are not meant as an inflexible list; as you gain experience, you might well discover modifications or additional guidelines that will work well for you.

Develop a proper attitude. Take desk checking seriously—view it as an integral, important part of producing a quality product. Try to take a detached view of the product; pretend it was produced by someone else and that you are seeing it for the first time. This will make it easier for you to examine the actual product, not just your memory of what you think it is. A detached view also will make it easier for you to critique the product.

Study the requirements and standards. A common mistake is for people to read product requirements, set them aside, and then rely on their memory as to what the requirements are. Don't do this. Read the requirements as if you were seeing them for the first time. Also, review the relevant standards.

Review relevant checklists. A review of these checklists will alert you to possible problems in the product you are about to review.

Check the product. With this preparation, you are now ready to review the product. Exactly how you do this will depend on the product. For a product that is reasonably large, the following procedure might be used. First, make a macro check of the product to determine if it is complete and generally satisfies the requirements. Then divide the product into logical components. Check each component in detail. For most information products, this amounts to a line-by-line review. Next, check groupings of components, verifying that they interface properly. Finally, check that all requirements have been met. As you check the product, make a note of exceptions and concerns.

Record results. Even though you are checking your own product for your own benefit, record the results of your review formally. Make note of any problems found and any concerns that require further investigation.

Remember, desk checking is a search for problems, not a problem-solving process. Do not let your desk-checking activity be sidetracked by attempts to solve problems and correct the product; that comes later. Just record the problems and go on.

After Desk Checking

After desk checking, make necessary corrections in your work product and improve your production processes. Furthermore, use the information gained from desk checking to improve your desk-checking process. In particular, update your checklist of errors. If you have spotted an error that you are likely to make again, add it to your checklist as a problem to be avoided.

A Critique of Desk Checking

Deck checking is an effective tool for workers to improve the quality of their own products. It helps to catch mistakes soon after they are made when the cost of repair is usually much less than after the faulty product has been combined into a larger assembly. Another distinct benefit of desk checking is that errors are caught and corrected by workers before they release their products. Errors that are discovered after that are known to management and inevitably have weight in appraisal decisions. Errors found during desk checking are known only to the worker; there is no way that management can be swayed by such errors when appraisal time rolls around.

◆ 12.15 Peer Reviews

At times it is very difficult for you to find an error in your own work—you are just too close to it. But colleagues can spot the error, and you can find errors in their products. An effective way to improve quality is to take advantage of this natural trait. One technique for accomplishing this is the peer review.

A *peer review* is a structured review of work; its purpose is to detect errors and highlight concerns that can lead to errors. An important characteristic of a peer review is that it is conducted in a *penalty-free* environment. This means that errors and concerns uncovered by such reviews are used only for improving products and processes; in particular, this information is not to be used for employee evaluation.

A peer review is a supplement to, but not a substitute for, a review of work by individual workers. The philosophy behind peer reviews is that, although each individual is responsible for his own work product, the individual's work group is responsible for all products produced by its members. Peer reviews of individual work products help to ensure the quality of the work done by all group members.

Peer reviews are widely used in the information systems area to control the quality of product requirements, program designs, computer code, test plans, and user documentation. They also can be used to review project plans and other documents produced by managers. A variation of the procedure can be used to review many service products. Universities evaluate the teaching effectiveness of their professors through peer reviews. Scientific results must go through several peer reviews before they are published.

Characteristics of Peer Reviews

Peer reviews are *formal*, meaning that they follow a written procedure that is regularly applied and requires written output. Peer reviews are structured. They are scheduled, and attendance is by invitation from the reviewee.

Peer reviews focus on error detection. Their purpose is to uncover and record errors, problems, and concerns that a reviewer has about the adequacy of the product.

Peer reviews address correctness, not style. The only concern is that the product meets the requirements; questions of the approach used or style are inappropriate. The comment, "This is a better way to solve your problem," might be appropriate in an informal, friendly discussion but not during a peer review.

The primary purpose of a peer review is to help the producer build a quality product; a secondary purpose is to provide information that will help improve his production process. Because the aim is to help the producer, the review "belongs" to him. Results of the review can be used by the producer to correct his product before submitting it to management. As viewed by management, peer reviews are part of the process of producing work, not part of the control process.

It also must be stressed that peer reviews are not a tool for employee evaluation. To avoid any possibility that the review results could be used for that purpose, the review report should not be sent to management. Only the reviewee and members of the review team should know what was found.

Peer reviews are most effective when all work is reviewed. Some organizations believe that this is too expensive, so they use them only for more complex products. Evidence shows, however, that peer reviews more than make up for their cost by improving the quality of products. They are particularly cost-effective for reviewing product requirements, where an error is very costly if it is not discovered until the design or build stage.

Peer reviews should not be optional. Peer reviews are most effective when they are a standard procedure applied to all work products. If reviews are optional, they will be skipped because most people prefer to "do work" rather than "check work." And they will argue that they don't have time to do both.

Peer reviews must be psychologically open. People involved in a review must feel completely free to express their opinion about the product being reviewed. There should be no fear of recrimination from fellow team members or from management. On the other hand, reviewers must not "hold back" for fear of hurting the reviewee's feelings or making him lose face. Reviewees must understand that nobody is perfect; they must learn how to take honest, well-intended criticism of their work. Quality products must be viewed as the overriding goal, not individual egos.

Peer Review Procedure

A peer review involves three to five people, who play distinct roles:

- *Reviewee*: The person who produced the product to be reviewed.
- *Reviewers*: Several (usually between two and four) peers appointed by the reviewee to review the product.
- *Moderator*: One of the reviewers appointed to conduct the review.
- *Secretary*: One of the reviewers (other than the moderator) appointed to record errors and issues raised at the review.

Peer review tasks can be divided into three groups. First are the tasks required to arrange for the review. These tasks are: Schedule the review and appoint reviewers, including the moderator and the secretary; define the tasks of reviewers and provide them with instruction and training if necessary; and distribute the product to be reviewed, its requirements, and an agenda for the review. These documents should be distributed early enough to allow reviewers time to study them before the review is held.

Second are the activities of the review itself. The reviewee gives the group a general overview of the product, stating its general nature and the general approach taken in producing it. Reviewers present major concerns they have with the product. (An example is a concern that a certain standard had been overlooked.) The reviewee makes no attempt to refute these major concerns; only clarifying discussions are allowed. Following a logical pattern, the reviewee then "walks through" the product step by step. As each portion of the product is encountered, reviewers voice any problems or concerns they have with it. Again, discussion is restricted to clarification of the remarks. The secretary records all issues, major and minor, as they are voiced.

The third set of activities are those that follow the review. Soon after the review, the secretary gives the reviewee and each reviewer a list of the issues that were raised during the review. The reviewers should check this list to see that it is accurate and complete. The task of resolving all issues falls to the reviewee. Errors should be corrected. Concerns, however, must be evaluated and judged as to their validity and importance. After addressing the issues raised, the reviewee sends each reviewer a report showing how each valid concern was dealt with and giving reasons for ignoring those concerns that he judged not to be problems.

Advantages of Peer Reviews

Peer reviews can be applied in any situation where a team of people is involved in producing a product. Such teams are quite common. Moreover, there is a growing interest in treating workers as a team because it has been found that a team spirit helps promote better quality. Thus, the opportunity and need to employ team review mechanisms, such as peer reviews, is growing.

Peer reviews are an effective technique for reviewing products that cannot be checked by being operated; examples are requirements, designs, operating instructions, and various management products. It is also a useful technique to review products with subjective requirements, such as restaurant service, the taste of food, and the smoothness of a car ride.

A distinct advantage of peer reviews is that they can be used in the early stages of a product's life cycle. There is a growing awareness that errors in plans, requirements documents, designs, and other early products of the production cycle are extremely costly to correct. Peer reviews can be used to improve their quality, thus generating substantial savings and resulting in greater customer satisfaction.

Peer reviews are usually adopted as a device for detecting errors; but, interestingly enough, they also prevent errors! It stands to reason: If you know that your peers are going to review your work, you are likely to be more careful about what you produce. You don't want a reputation among fellow workers for building sloppy products, so you take more care to see that your products are correct.

In evaluating the effectiveness of peer reviews, it is important for management to be aware of this effect. One organization installed peer reviews on a trial basis and then stopped using them because management had the impression that "The reviews weren't catching any defects." Efforts by outside consultants to convince management that this was not a proper measure of effectiveness fell on deaf ears.

The proper way to measure the effectiveness of peer reviews is to compare the error rate in products before peer reviews were used with the error rate after their use. If the shipped products are better, does it make any difference whether peer reviews catch defects or prevent defects? In fact, might not prevention of defects be better than increased detection?

Another side benefit of peer reviews is that they can be used as a communication and training device. Allowing inexperienced workers to participate in reviews of work done by experienced people is an excellent way to improve their skills. But even experienced people can learn from each other. In the service industry, where requirements are very difficult to formulate, critically observing the work of a peer can help workers to view their own work more critically. Moreover, it can help the group and management improve the requirements for the service products they provide.

The peer review is a primary tool for quality improvement. It deserves to be more widely applied.

◆ 12.16 Inspections

The term *inspection* is used in the quality literature to describe two different procedures for examining products. One is a procedure for examining products of so-called knowledge work; an example would be the examination of information systems. The other is a procedure for examining manufactured products, for which product requirements are verified more routinely.

Inspections of Knowledge Work

As applied to knowledge work, an inspection is an examination procedure that is similar to a peer review; it is a structured review held for the purpose of detecting errors. Generally, an inspection examines the product of a single person, and it is conducted by that person's fellow workers. Inspections are more formal and more structured than peer reviews, but the major difference is that they are conducted as part of the management control process. Thus, inspections "belong" to management; a manager might attend an inspection, and information about defects in the product is reported to management.

Because defect information from inspections is known to management, it is likely to enter the employee appraisal process. Employees are aware of this prospect, and this awareness can affect their performance during an inspection. For example, to help a friend, a reviewer might neglect to mention a very minor error at an inspection, intending to tell the reviewee "off-line." But then the reviewer forgets, and the defect goes uncorrected. On the other hand, some reviewers take great pleasure in reporting every little blemish, acting on the premise that the way to rise in the organization is to push others down.

In spite of these problems, inspections are a popular method of controlling knowledge work. One possible reason is that managers still don't understand the impact their presence has on the review process. Another is that managers, who bear responsibility for all work produced in their departments, want to see for themselves that products are correct; they don't want to take someone else's word for it.

Inspections in Manufacturing

For manufactured products, an *inspection* is any process for assessing the product. Often the inspection is by observation, but it also can involve the operation of the product.

Reviewing manufactured products differs substantially from the review of knowledge work. One difference is the volume of products. It might take a knowledge worker a week to produce a product that requires inspection. In the same period, a production worker might produce thousands, perhaps millions, of products. The total volume of output for certain manufacturing processes can be staggering.

Another difference is in the nature of products. Requirements for knowledge work usually are loosely defined and leave much to the worker's professional judgment. Inspection of knowledge work, therefore, is partly a check on that judgment. For manufactured products, on the other hand, the requirements are much more precise. This and the discipline imposed by automated production processes result in a more uniform product and call for less worker judgment.

A third difference is the nature of inspection tools. Only a few tools are available to assist in inspecting knowledge work (an example is a spell-checker), but many are available for most manufactured products. Often automated inspection is possible.

◆ 12.17 Reviews

A *review* is an assessment by a group; it is a procedure for one group to scrutinize products produced by another. Informal reviewing takes place regularly; our concern is with reviews that are structured and planned.

A review is an effective quality control technique. Unfortunately, reviews of product quality frequently are held in conjunction with reviews of schedules, budgets, and other business concerns. This tends to divert the attention from quality issues. The best practice is to hold separate reviews for quality and business issues; somewhat different groups should hold these two types of reviews because of differences in interests and expertise.

Quality reviews can serve various purposes: inform management; obtain information for decision making; provide an objective assessment of status; identify and define problems; identify improvement opportunities; improve communication, education, and motivation; and enforce policies, procedures, and standards.

A review can be a means of providing a production group with advice and specialized information they cannot reasonably be expected to have. For example, a design group cannot possibly have the specialized knowledge of experts from market research, production, sales, legal, technical writing, and many other areas of a company. A design review is a means of using such knowledge to detect errors and suggest product improvements.

To be useful, a review requires an effective process, which should be formally prescribed by an organization standard. This standard should define the roles and responsibilities of all parties to the review process; qualification required of reviewers; scheduling, distribution of relevant information, and other pre-review activities; the general agenda or plan for a review; and post-review activities.

In addition to these technical aspects, a review requires careful attention to human factors. Matters of power, pride, and prejudice can easily mar the review process. Cultural resistance of a group being reviewed can prevent their taking advice from outside authorities. A quality review can easily become a compromise based on whose ox is being gored.

Characteristics of a Review

The term *review* is used differently from organization to organization—even within different units of a single organization. This means that there is no such thing as a "typical review." The following characteristics, however, are fairly common:

- ◆ *Mandatory*: Reviews generally are compulsory, required by a methodology, a standard, a regulation, or by contract.
- ◆ *Formal*: A review is an assessment that follows a written procedure that is regularly applied and requires written output.
- ◆ *Investigative*: A review is conducted by highly experienced, objective specialists who were not involved in creating the product being reviewed. Penetrating, in-depth questions are common.
- ◆ *Extensive*: Generally any quality-related issue can be raised in a review. Product, production process, requirements, planning and management of the production—all might be scrutinized.
- ◆ *Time consuming*: Usually, much time is required to prepare for a review; the review process itself can be lengthy; and post-review time can be required to comply with suggestions generated during the review.
- ◆ *Expensive*: A review can be costly. Much time and many people can be involved in a review.

Types of Reviews

One type of review is that held as a regular management activity. A department manager might hold a weekly review of the department's performance; a higher level manager might hold monthly or quarterly reviews. Such regularly scheduled reviews might touch on quality, but mostly they are concerned with the business issues of schedule and budget. Exceptions are periodic reviews held by a quality council or some other management group with a quality-oriented charter.

Another type of review is that held as part of a product development project. For example, an IS project development methodology typically calls for milestone reviews, phase reviews, and reviews of major components.

> **Example 1.** The National Computer Board of Singapore (NCB) is a government agency with major responsibility for computerizing various Ministries of the Republic of Singapore. Their IS development methodology calls for nine checkpoint reviews during the eight phases of their development cycle. A review process is provided, detailing activities to be performed by the project team and the reviewers prior to, during, and following each review. For each review, there is a checklist covering the major questions to be answered. Characteristics of reviews are described, requiring them to be formal, structured, and psychologically open, with an emphasis on reviewing products, not people. The Guide also contains a glossary and examples of review output.
>
> The Guide has proved to be a useful tool in helping NCB realize its commitment to delivering quality products and services to their customers.

> **Example 2.** A *design review* is a formal evaluation of a design to assure that a product is manufacturable, maintainable, and will perform satisfactorily. It is conducted by a group of experts in fields that relate to the product. Based on the assumption that the designer cannot possibly be expert in all fields, the review helps the designer by providing expert advice on a range of topics. Design reviews are conducted at several points of the design process—for example, at the concept stage, at the prototype stage, and at the final design stage.

Still another type of review is that held to examine a major process. A review might focus on a manufacturing process, an order entry process, or a major function, such as security or disaster recovery. Reviews of this type usually are ad hoc, triggered by some special concern.

◆ 12.18 Testing

As we said before, testing is not a trivial topic. Our aim is not to cover the topic but merely to review a few aspects of testing—enough for you to see that it is a very complex topic. There is a large literature on testing that you should consult if you need to know more about testing a particular good, service, or information product.

Tests can be classified in many ways. A test might be destructive or nondestructive. It might be classified by the size of the product being tested, for example, a part, a component, an assembly, a final product, or by who conducts the test—the seller or the buyer.

Test Purpose

The first question to ask in testing a product is: Why are we testing this? What do we hope to learn? Some product aspects you might examine are:

- Appearance—Does the product look right? Is it as attractive as it should be? Is it the right size? color? texture?

- Performance—Does the product operate as it should?

- Environmental impact—Will the product operate under the expected conditions? Will it suffer under other than a perfect operating environment? On the other hand, will the operation of the product have an unfavorable impact on the environment?

- Stress—Will the product operate under extreme conditions, such as extreme loads, extreme speeds, extreme handling?

- Reliability—Can one count on the product to meet requirements every time, over time?

- Maintainability—Is it easy to keep the product in good working order?

- Life—Will it last and operate as long as it should?

- Manufacturable—Can it be made?

Test Considerations

There are many questions to ponder when designing a test. A few are these.

Is the test to be conducted under normal or extreme operating conditions? in a lab or in the field? Is the test equipment properly calibrated, or does it introduce a bias or excessive randomness in the test results? Is the test equipment functioning properly?

Usually, not every product is tested—only a selected few. Is the sample of selected products random, or is there a bias? Is the input to the test typical or handpicked? Is the test coverage proper? Is the operator conducting the test a person with typical or special skills? Are the test results viewed impartially or with rose-colored glasses? Is the sample large enough and random enough to reflect the actual operating conditions of the process?

For a complex product, one of the hardest questions to answer is: How much testing is enough? Testing can prove only the presence of an error, not the absence of errors. "Just one more test" is a common cry. One way to minimize this request is by careful test planning.

◆ Exercises and Additional Readings

1. From your collection of articles on quality (see Exercise 1, Chapter 1) give some examples relating to quality control, that is, the examination process. What lesson can you learn from these articles?

2. Some external examiners of product quality are listed in Section 12.13. List some others.

3. Comment on the fact that managers want to inspect products because "they don't want to take someone else's word for it." (see Section 12.16.)

4. What steps would you take in examining

    (a) Instructions for the assembly of a personal computer system?

    (b) Requirements for a quality cup of coffee?

    (c) A term paper on the subject of quality improvement?

    (d) Requirements for a course on quality?

5. How would you examine the quality of these processes:

    (a) The service process at a student cafeteria?

    (b) A process for training machine operators?

    (c) A company's process for recruiting MBA students?

6. What steps would you take to examine the quality of

    (a) Modules of computer code?

    (b) A process for creating modules of computer code?

    (c) A process for examining modules of computer code?

7. For each of the following products, (i) list some quality problems that go uncorrected; (ii) state your opinion as to the reason they go uncorrected; (iii) list steps you might take to help correct the problems:

    (a) Service by your local restaurant/cafeteria.

    (b) Information about registering for a course at your educational institution.

    (c) Service provided by the computer facilities at your institution.

    (d) Service provided by your place of lodging.

8. Read Rafik H. Bishara and Michael L. Wyrick, "A Systematic Approach to Quality Assurance Auditing," *Quality Progress*, December 1994, p. 67. Describe each of the five steps in the QA audit cycle.

9. Skim Allan J. Sayle, *Management Audits* (Allan J. Sayle Ltd, UK, 1988). Compare a "management audit" (page 1-6 of this book) with a quality audit as described in the article cited in Exercise 8.

10. Assume that you have just received excellent service in a restaurant. What can you do to reward the server other than leave an appropriate tip?

11. Discuss with the local building inspector the inspection of new homes. Determine the purpose of the inspection, the requirements used, and the inspection process. Comment on this process from the view of (a) the builder and (b) the potential buyer of the house.

12. Read Section 18.9, Errors of Measurement, in J. M. Juran and Frank M. Gryna, *Quality Planning and Analysis*, 3rd ed. (New York: McGraw-Hill, 1993).

  (a) Define "precision" and "accuracy" of a measuring instrument.

  (b) Illustrate the results that might be obtained from an instrument that is (i) unbiased and precise, (ii) unbiased and not precise, and (iii) biased and precise.

13. How would you examine a Broadway production?

14. How would you examine a physician's decision to prescribe a certain drug for an ailment?

15. How would you examine the quality of advice offered by a stockbroker?

16. In spite of 100 percent inspection, customers still receive defective products. What might be the reason?

17. You are buying a house. Describe your procedure to examine the house.

18. Read and summarize Deming's ideas on "all-or-nothing" inspection. (See W. E. Deming, *Out of the Crisis*, (Cambridge, Mass.: Massachusetts Institute of Technology, Center for Advanced Engineering Study, 1986, p. 410.)

19. Devise a procedure for inspecting a term paper. In your procedure, include actions relating to (a) preparing to make the inspection, (b) inspecting the product, (c) preparing an inspection report, (d) evaluating and improving your procedure.

20. At one time, the contract between the teachers union and the State Colleges of New Jersey prohibited college administrators from assessing a teacher's ability and effectiveness by direct observation of a teacher's performance in the classroom. Discuss the pros and cons of this rule, and how it affects the quality of instruction.

21. Read and discuss Carol A. King, "Service Quality Assurance Is Different," *Quality Progress*, June 1985, pp. 14–18. Discuss why the techniques for measuring service conformance to standards are different from those for goods.

22. Give several examples of destructive testing.

23. Comment on the differences between a peer review and a (management) review.

24. Describe how you would apply desk checking to control the quality of a term paper.

25. Contact several local companies engaged in providing goods, services, or information products. Ask them about their examination processes. What methods do they use? Are they satisfied with their approach? If not, how could examination be improved?

◆ ◆ ◆

Management Issues in Achieving Quality

The chapters in Part II dealt with the production processes of an organization. Part III discusses the quality system and the culture that must be established to support production.

Chapter 13 lists the requirements that a quality system should meet. It discusses the documentation needed to describe the quality system and to provide evidence that it is being operated properly. The quality system should be assessed regularly by management; in addition, it is helpful to have it reviewed or audited by an independent authority. The chapter introduces and uses the ISO 9000 terminology for the parties involved in business transactions. It covers the ISO 9000 requirements and the four-tiered documentation of a quality system. The chapter concludes with a discussion of the quality audits and the ISO registration process.

One of the duties of management is to establish a culture of quality. Chapter 14 discusses management actions needed to achieve this goal: establishing quality as a basic belief, showing quality leadership, and building a culture of excellence. Also discussed are strategies for achieving quality and undertaking organizational change.

The quality organization comprises the quality professionals of the organization, who are charged with oversight and coordination of quality-related matters. Chapter 15 discusses Quality Assurance and its role in initiating, introducing, and enabling a firm's quality efforts. It discusses the measures an organization can take to track the progress of a quality effort, and it examines the special role the Information Systems area can play in that effort.

Through the years, various theories have been advanced as to what motivates people. Chapter 16 reviews some well-known theories and the link between motivation and quality. It examines the connection between quality and job characteristics, such as task variety, job content, and job authority. Self-directed work teams have proved to be very effective in motivating employees and in improving quality. The introduction of such teams, their benefits, and the ways Quality Assurance can assist teams in improving quality are discussed. The chapter concludes with a discussion of the relationship between quality and rewards—rewards that can be enjoyed on the job, off the job, and in retirement.

Several cases in the Appendix illustrate the concepts explored in Part III. *Case 1: Hank Kolb, Director, Quality Assurance* describes a typical quality problem and the complex network of affairs that must be altered if the cause of the problem is to be eradicated. *Case 2: Acme Electronics* is an example of a quality program that seems to be ineffective. It helps to illustrate that achieving quality requires more than simply hiring a Director of Quality and adopting a quality policy. *Case 3: The Budapest* illustrates a typical problem facing an organization that is starting a quality program—the physical plant is in place, but a quality policy and process documentation are missing. Because most students have some familiarity with restaurant operations, the case provides an opportunity for them to formulate procedures and instructions that should be reasonably realistic. *Case 4: Toyota Supplier Development* describes an effective program for dealing with suppliers (subcontractors in the ISO terminology).

Chapter 13

The Quality System

◆ 13.1 The Quality Policy

In any organization, cultural expectations and patterns of behavior guide what people consider to be appropriate conduct, and they guide what people do. For an organization to provide quality goods and services on a consistent basis, the expectations and behavior patterns of the organization must clearly indicate that quality is a top priority. The responsibility for establishing these expectations and behavior patterns falls squarely on top management.

The first step towards a successful quality program is for the top management of the organization to define and document the organization's policy, objectives, and commitment to quality in a *quality policy*. Management should ensure that this document is understood, implemented, and maintained by all levels in the organization.

The quality policy should clearly indicate that management supports quality and that quality is the task of every individual. The quality policy should be clear and succinct so that everyone in the organization can understand and remember it. A common question in a quality audit is to ask an employee, "What is your organization's policy on quality?" The auditor expects to hear a statement of the policy, or at a minimum a statement as to where the policy can be found.

There is no standard format for a quality policy; the important issue is that it be an accurate reflection of management's belief and intent. A quality policy must contain a commitment to quality. In addition, it might address such topics as the organization's general approach to quality, a general statement of responsibility for quality, the general standard of the quality level to be maintained, their general approach to achieving quality, and statements of the activities the organization will undertake to achieve quality. It might also address wider issues, such as employee involvement and training, the customer's need for quality, or the needs of society. Several examples of quality policies are given in Display 13.1.

Although the quality policy is issued by top management, it is imperative that there be wide support in the organization for it. Asking for wide participation among top management in formulating the policy is one way to overcome resistance and ensure ownership. When the policy is issued, it is vital that everyone in the organization receive orientation at once as to its purpose, intent, and potential impact. This instruction should be part of a larger effort in quality training, which is discussed in Section 16.5.

Quality and Responsibility

Everyone in an organization is responsible for quality, but responsibilities differ. Top management's first responsibility is to establish a quality policy and to infuse this policy in the organization. Other important top management responsibilities are to establish a quality assurance function to support the organization's quality effort, to oversee the construction of a quality system, and to review the quality system periodically and make required improvements.

All levels of management are responsible for managing the operation of the quality system, managing the products produced by the system, and managing the quality system itself. Everyone in the organization is involved in operating aspects of the quality system. And customers and the community benefit from the products produced by the system.

Management should clearly define the responsibility, authority, and interrelation of all personnel who manage or perform work affecting quality or who review products produced by the quality system. This is particularly necessary for those who need organizational freedom and authority to prevent nonconformities, identify and record quality problems, initiate and verify solutions to problems, and control nonconforming products. Management should also provide the resources needed for them to do their job.

◆ 13.2 Organizing for Quality

Recall that in the ISO 9000 terminology, if you produce a product, you are a *supplier* to your *customer* and are provided products by *subcontractors*. Keep this terminology in mind as you read this chapter.

DISPLAY 13.1 ◆ Examples of Quality Policies

Burroughs Corp., now a part of UNISYS:[a]

We shall strive for excellence in all endeavors.

We shall set our goals to achieve total customer satisfaction, and to deliver error-free, competitive products on time, with service second to none.

IBM[a]

We have established a quality policy for the corporation—which gives direction to quality efforts. The policy makes five basic points:

1. Quality is our cornerstone.
2. The objective is to provide products and services that are defect-free.
3. Each of us must learn to do things right the first time.
4. Each job—each stage of the process—must be defect-free.
5. Quality is truly everyone's job.

United Brands Co.[a]

1. A key factor in consumer value is quality, and the consumers are the judges of quality.
2. The goal of the company is to deliver to the consumer products of consistent, uniform quality meeting specifications based on consumer values and produced at affordable costs.
3. The determination of the quality attributes that result in superior consumer value (satisfaction) will be determined by consumer surveys that will be updated every three years.
4. Written quality specifications will be prepared, which include the permissible levels and tolerances for each quality attribute.
5. The permissible tolerance for each quality attribute will be based on data—reflecting system capabilities and consumer preferences.
6. Quality standards (specifications) will be reviewed at least once each year.

XEROX[b]

Xerox is a quality company. Quality is the basic business principle for XEROX. Quality means providing our external and internal customers with innovative products and services that fully satisfy their requirements. Quality improvement is the job of every XEROX employee.

Logiciel Systems[c]

Logiciel is committed to quality and to error-free products. Quality is an organisation and individual responsibility.

To further this policy, the management of Logiciel shall:

1. Ensure that the organisation measurement and evaluation system rewards quality performance.
2. Ensure that definitions and measures of quality are established.
3. Provide work standards and procedures to achieve a quality-oriented operating environment so as to ensure effective use of human, machine, software, and material resources.
4. Ensure all personnel receive proper training in concepts, methods, and procedures for producing quality work.

The Ritz-Carlton Quality Policy[d]

The Ritz-Carlton is a place where the genuine care and comfort of our guests is our highest mission. We pledge to provide the best service and facilities for our guests who will always enjoy a warm, relaxed yet refined ambience. The Ritz-Carlton experience enlivens the senses, instills well-being, and fulfills even the unexpressed wishes and needs of our guests.

[a]Richard B. Stump, "Quality Management and Planning," Chapter 22 in *Tool and Manufacturing Engineers Handbook, Vol. 5: Manufacturing Management*, (Dearborn, MI: Society of Manufacturing Engineers, 1988).

[b]David T. Kearns, CEO of XEROX Corp., "Chasing a Moving Target," *Quality Progress*, October 1989, p. 29.

[c]The quality policy for Logiciel, a Singapore company, was taken from their quality manual for ISO certification.

[d]Quality at the Ritz-Carlton is discussed in detail in Chapter 24.

Each supplier must establish, implement, and maintain a documented quality system in order to ensure that products conform to requirements. This system should consist of appropriate processes, procedures, and instructions required to produce conforming products. The supplier should also identify and provide adequate resources and trained personnel for the management and operation of the quality system, including verification and audit activities. Generally the quality system is documented in a *quality manual* and *quality plans*. The system also identifies the *quality records* that must be prepared to demonstrate the achievement of required quality and the effective operation of the quality system. Management should periodically review the quality system to ensure that it is suitable and effective.

Management Representative

A management representative should be appointed with authority and responsibility to ensure that the quality system is implemented effectively. This representative typically is the Quality Assurance Manager. The QA Manager should have the authority to speak for management in matters relating to the quality system. It is important that the QA Manager report directly to the top management of the organization to give the position the authority required and signal to the organization how important quality is to top management.

The Quality Organization[1]

Although quality is everybody's job, certain quality-related tasks are best done by a special group, which we are calling Quality Assurance (QA). QA is best described as an in-house consulting organization that focuses on the quality system. It evaluates the quality system, makes recommendations for its improvement, and gives advice, suggestions, and instruction on making improvements. The QA function of an organization should report directly to top management to give them the independence required to serve the entire organization.

It is important to recognize that QA is an advisory function, not a police function. QA is not responsible for the quality system, it does not operate the system, and it does not do quality control. The planning, organizing, staffing, directing, and controlling of the quality system is in the hands of top and line management. QA may audit the system, make recommendations for its improvements, and provide assistance in making improvements, but responsibility for the system and its improvement rests entirely with management.

QA is responsible for the quality of its own work efforts, but it is not responsible for the work of others. In particular, QA is not responsible for the quality of the products the organization provides to its customers.

There is a vast and growing literature on concepts, tools, and techniques relat-

---

[1]Quality Assurance was discussed briefly in Section 4.3. Section 15.2 gives a detailed discussion of QA's organization and specific responsibilities.

ing to quality; part of the QA's task is to monitor this literature and bring the best ideas to management's attention.

The QA department need not be large to be effective. In fact, a very large QA department might indicate a problem with the quality program.

> *In the late 1980s, Florida Power & Light (FP&L) engaged in an extensive program in an attempt to win the Deming Prize. In the process, they developed an 85-person quality group and established 1,900 quality teams involving three-quarters of the employees. In 1989 they did win the Deming Prize, becoming the first American company to do so. But customers saw only marginal improvement in service—insignificant improvements compared with the scale of the effort that had been extended. One utility regulator noted that FP&L employees seemed more interested in the appearance of quality than in quality itself.*
>
> *After a top management change in FP&L, the quality department was reduced to six employees and most of the quality teams were disbanded. The company then focused on the customer, making real, effective improvements in providing what the customer required.[2]*

◆ 13.3 Quality System Documentation

To provide quality products, a supplier requires an effective production system. Some assurance that a system is effective can be had by documenting it, maintaining control over the documents describing the system, maintaining records to establish that the documented system is followed, and auditing periodically to verify that plans are followed. These documents should describe the processes for producing products and the various controls, inspections, measurements, reviews, and standards to be applied. They also document the effective implementation of those processes. In addition, the quality system typically requires the preparation of such elements as quality plans, quality controls, quality measurement systems, standards to be applied, and records of performance. We discuss the arrangement of this documentation in Section 13.10.

Quality Manual

The organization's quality policy and the descriptions of its processes are contained in a document typically called the *quality manual.* Composition of that manual varies from organization to organization. Typical contents include:

- ◆ The quality policy of the organization
- ◆ Documented organizational processes, procedures, instructions, standards

---

[2]*The Economist*, April 18, 1992, p. 67.

- Controls, such as inspection equipment, check points, measurements required, reviews
- Identification of measurements required
- Identification and preparation of quality records

Document Control

There is a need to control all of the documents and data describing the quality system. Prior to use, documents should be reviewed and approved by authorized personnel. Changes to documents should be controlled according to an established document control procedure. Appropriate documents should be available at all work locations where required; obsolete documents should be removed to prevent their inadvertent use.

Quality Records

Quality records must be maintained as objective evidence of the achievement of quality and to demonstrate the effective operation of the quality system. Rules must be established for the storage and maintenance of records so that they can be retrieved to demonstrate compliance. Quality records are used by a quality auditor to confirm that the organization is in compliance with its quality system. Also, purchasers might arrange contractually to use the quality records to verify the conformance of the supplier's products to requirements.

(Note that the term *document* is being used for items that describe the quality system, and *records* for evidence to demonstrate effective operation of the system. A description of a process is a document; a test report is a record.)

Internal Quality Audits

The supplier should carry out planned internal audits to verify that quality activities comply with plans and to determine the effectiveness of the system. Auditors should prepare for the audit by examining the quality system documentation for the area being audited, and they should prepare a schedule for the audit and a checksheet of questions they will ask. Their task is to document objective evidence that can be used to assess the effectiveness of the system being audited. Observed nonconformances should be reported, and corrective actions should be taken by those being audited. Audit findings are an important input to adjusting and improving the quality system and to management's review of the quality system. Quality audits are discussed in more detail in Section 13.11.

◆ 13.4 Managing Production

In addition to having an effective process, it is necessary to operate it properly. Some assurance can be had that production will result in quality products by conducting contract reviews, controlling designs, controlling the process and its operation, and maintaining procedures to show that service meets requirements.

Contract Review

The supplier should have procedures to review contracts with customers. The review should establish that the requirements in the contract are clear and that the supplier has the capability to meet these requirements. Records of contract reviews should be maintained.

Design Control

The supplier should have procedures to control the design of products. These procedures should cover design and development planning, organizational and technical interfaces between the various groups dealing with the design, and the design input and output. Procedures should also be in place to verify that the design meets requirements and to control any design changes or modifications.

Process Control

The supplier should control all processes that directly affect quality and ensure that these processes are operated under controlled conditions. Controlled conditions should include documented work instructions, suitable equipment, samples or criteria for workmanship, and compliance with relevant standards and quality plans. Operations should be conducted in a suitable environment. Process and product characteristics should be monitored during production and installation.

Servicing

If servicing is required by contract, the supplier should establish and maintain procedures to verify that service products meet specified requirements.

◆ 13.5 Managing Products

Quality production also depends on acquiring suitable products from subcontractors and on effective management of all products. Some assurance that quality will not be compromised by poor product can be gained by controlling purchased and customer-supplied product, by properly identifying and tracing product, and by maintaining proper procedures for handling product through all stages of production and delivery.

Purchasing

Purchase orders should contain a complete description of the product and quantities required; orders should be reviewed and approved prior to release. The supplier should assure that the purchased product conforms to requirements. Subcontractors should be assessed based on their having an effective quality system installed and their ability to meet subcontract requirements, including quality requirements.

Customer-Supplied Product

The supplier should conform to appropriate procedures for the verification, storage, and maintenance of items that the customer furnishes to be incorporated into the product. Any such product that is lost or unsuitable should be reported to the purchaser.

Product Identification and Traceability

Where appropriate, the supplier should maintain procedures for identifying product during all stages from requirements through delivery and installation. Different versions of product resulting from changes in requirements, designs, or purchased components should be carefully segregated and controlled.

Handling, Storage, Packaging, and Delivery

The supplier should maintain suitable procedures for handling product. Product should be packaged according to requirements. Storage areas should be secure with controlled access.

◆ 13.6 Controlling Quality

Quality control involves the inspection and testing of product to determine if it meets requirements. This control process uses various inspection, measuring, and test equipment; and it can employ various statistical techniques. It is necessary to have procedures to maintain inspection and test status, control nonconforming product, and take corrective action to eliminate potential causes of nonconforming product.

Verification Resources and Personnel

The supplier should provide for in-house verification of product. This requires identifying verification requirements, providing adequate resources for verification, and assigning trained personnel to make the verification. Verification might be by inspection, test, or monitoring processes involved with building the product. Verification should be made by persons not directly involved with the production of the product.

Inspection and Testing

Testing should be carried out in accordance with documented procedures or the quality plan for the product. Usually, this would mean that incoming product should not be used until it has been inspected or otherwise verified as conforming to specified requirements. During processing, product should be inspected and tested in accordance with documented procedures or the quality plan. Conformance can also be established by monitoring appropriate process variables. Final inspection should provide evidence that the finished product meets specified requirements. Nonconforming product should be identified and properly controlled. Inspection and test records should be maintained.

Inspection, Measuring, and Test Equipment

Equipment used in inspecting, measuring, and testing to demonstrate conformance of product to specified requirements should be properly controlled, calibrated, and maintained. Equipment should be used so as to ensure that measurement uncertainty is known and consistent with requirements, and to ensure that its fitness for use is maintained. Calibration records should be maintained.

Statistical Techniques

Where appropriate, statistical techniques should be used to verify product characteristics and to verify and improve process capability. Examples of such techniques are statistical process control, sampling inspection, and design of experiments.

Inspection and Test Status

The inspection and test status of a product (indicating the conformance or nonconformance) should be suitably identified and maintained throughout the production, storage, and installation of the product. Records should be maintained to indicate test status and release authority.

Control of Nonconforming Product

The supplier should establish procedures to ensure that nonconforming product is prevented from inadvertent use and should also establish authority for dealing with such product. In accordance with procedures, nonconforming product should be reworked, accepted by concession, regraded for alternative application, or scrapped.

Corrective Action

The supplier should establish documented procedures for taking corrective action to eliminate potential causes of nonconforming product. These corrective action procedures should include error-cause investigation, error-cause removal, controls to assure that corrective actions are effective, and the change in documented procedures required to implement the corrective action.

◆ 13.7 Managing Workers

Quality requirements and standards generally focus on the product; after all, quality is a matter of a product meeting requirements. And with the exception of some aspects of the service industry, quality requirements generally do not refer to people. Yet people are an extremely important part of most production processes, and the actions of people can be a dominant influence on product quality.

Worker Qualifications

People should be qualified for tasks based on appropriate education and training, appropriate experience, or both. Their qualifications should include knowledge of quality concepts as well as ability to perform assigned tasks.

Training

Task and skill requirements change so frequently in some industries that continual education and training are required to keep worker qualifications up to requirements. This means that most organizations have a need for training and retraining their personnel. There is a need, therefore, for procedures to determine training requirements and procedures to meet those requirements.

Training records should be maintained to demonstrate worker qualifications to perform assigned tasks.

Job Structuring

Personnel policies and practices have a large influence on worker performance, and there is a large management literature on effective personnel practices. One important influence is the actual definition of the job. One effective practice is to assign workers a whole job, the task of creating a product that they can relate to. Another is to structure a job with appropriate job variety to prevent boredom and carelessness.

Empowering People

Personnel practices in many industries were shaped at a time when it was assumed that workers worked and managers managed. Redesigning jobs to empower people can improve quality. Empowerment might mean more emphasis on product requirements and a change in process requirements. Another way to empower people is to shift some of the responsibility for quality control from managers to the workers.

Supervision

Supervision can have a strong influence on job performance and product quality. Is the supervisor like the traffic cop, and is the challenge to slip defective products by him if you can? Or is the supervisor there to fight battles for you when problems arise, even to be a mentor?

Reward

Reward also has an influence on job performance. Is the job satisfying? Can employees have pride in the quality of the organization's products? Does the community recognize that the employee is working with a company with a deserved reputation for quality?

In the larger picture, quality and reward are definitely correlated. If a company has a reputation for quality, then it is very likely to survive and prosper. Increasingly, this "if-then" statement is becoming an "if and only if" statement.

◆ 13.8 Quality System Review

Sections 13.1 through 13.6 specify quality system requirements for producing products to suppliers' requirements. At appropriate intervals, management should conduct reviews of the quality system to ensure its continuing suitability and effectiveness. These reviews typically include the assessment of any internal audits that have been conducted. Records of these management reviews should be maintained. Results of audits and management reviews are an important input to process improvements activities.

◆ 13.9 Quality System Requirements

At this point, we would like you to review all of the quality system requirements we have discussed in Sections 13.1 through 13.8 and to form your own opinion about them. Do you think these requirements are reasonable? Do you see anything in the requirements that look unnecessary? Or do they all look fairly reasonable, describing requirements you would expect to be met by any organization that supplies *you* with goods, services, or information?

****(This symbol indicates a pause while you go back to skim through the previous sections of this chapter and answer these questions.)

Now a second question for you: Do you think most companies in America comply with the requirements you have just reviewed? Just form an opinion, a snap judgment.

**(Only two stars because forming a snap judgment doesn't take much time.)

It is our view that all of the requirements we have discussed are reasonable, yet fairly comprehensive. Indeed, we believe that these requirements represent a minimum set; there is nothing in the set that you would want to omit on the grounds of it being unnecessary or unduly burdensome. If there is a shortcoming in the requirements, it is that they focus more on the production process and infrastructure of an organization than on its culture. But that is because it is more difficult to establish clear requirements for an organization's culture. Culture is more an ethical issue than a matter of methods and procedures.

ISO 9001 Requirements

The requirements listed above are reasonable, and their implementation provides a firm foundation for an organization to supply quality products to their customers. Essentially, what we have presented in Sections 13.1 through 13.8 are the requirements for a quality system as specified in the ISO 9001 quality standard.[3] If an organization has a quality system that meets the requirements we have described and can present objective evidence of compliance with that system, then they can be certified as being in compliance with the ISO 9001 quality standard. An outline of the ISO 9001 standard is given in the Appendix to this chapter.

Was your snap judgment that, because these requirments make common sense, most organizations probably meet them? If that were so, then most companies

---

[3]The correspondence between the Sections of this book and the ISO 9001 standard are as follows:

Section	ISO 9001 Requirement
13.1	4.1.1, 4.1.2.1
13.2	4.2, 4.1.2.2, 4.1.2.3, 4.1.3
13.3	4.2, 4.5, 4.16, 4.17
13.4	4.3, 4.4, 4.9, 4.19
13.5	4.6, 4.7, 4.8, 4.15
13.6	4.10, 4.11, 4.20, 4.12, 4.13, 4.14
13.7	4.18
13.8	4.1.3

You will discover that we have included some requirements that are not in the ISO standard, particularly in Section 13.7 regarding the management of people.

could obtain ISO certification with very little effort. The fact is, however, that most companies seeking certification must go through an extended period getting their house in order before they can demonstrate that they meet these requirements. Typically, companies find that their quality system is very weak in some areas, much of it is not documented, operation of the system is not consistent, and records of conformance are in poor shape. A company can easily spend a year or two preparing to demonstrate to auditors that they do, in fact, meet requirements of the type we have described. In many organizations, quality is like the weather: everyone talks about it, but nobody does anything constructive about it.

◆ 13.10 Documenting the Quality System

In Section 13.3 we discussed the documentation that is required to provide assurance that a supplier's quality system is effective. Here, we discuss how that documentation can be organized in a systematic, orderly, and understandable manner.

Rudyard Kipling once wrote:

> *I keep six honest serving-men*
> *(They taught me all I know),*
> *Their names are What and Why and When*
> *and How and Where and Who.*

Essentially, Kipling's serving-men can be used to document a quality system.

Common practice in documenting a quality system is to arrange documentation into four levels ranging from general policies and procedures to records of performance. These four levels cover:

First: Why the organization has a quality system
Second: The what, when, where, and who aspects of quality-related tasks
Third: How these tasks are to be performed
Fourth: Records of what actually was done

Kipling's six serving-men define the system; "what" works overtime, describing what to do and what was done. This hierarchy of documentation gives increasing detail about the organization, its operations, its methods, and its accomplishments.

Specifically, the levels are these:

Level 1: Quality manual
The quality manual expresses the organization's total commitment to quality, how it is organized to fulfill that commitment, and its approach to fulfilling it. The purpose of the quality manual is to outline the quality system and to serve as a reference. Supporting the quality manual are procedures and instructions detailing the quality system.

Level 2: Procedures

The second level of the quality system is a collection of procedures that specify the major activities of an organization and the way these major activities are to be performed. A procedure is "a specified way to perform an activity."[4] Procedures describe what is to be done, who (by organizational title) is responsible for doing it, where it is to be done, and when (that is, the order in which procedures are to be accomplished). Procedures reflect the principles and practices expressed in the quality manual; they detail how those principles and practices are to be fulfilled.

Level 3: Work Instructions

Work instructions detail how work is to be accomplished. They are detailed instructions for specific tasks; they might be known as operating instructions, service instructions, flow diagrams, process charts, activity charts, review or inspection instructions, and so on. Work instructions always relate to a procedure; they provide the detailed instructions for accomplishing the procedure. Work instructions ensure consistent working methods and help to ensure consistent work products. Also, they are a basic element in worker training.

Level 4: Records

Procedures and work instructions describe what is to be done and how, whereas records describe what was done. Records document the output from a procedure or work instruction and may also include other documents referenced in an individual work effort, such as inspection and test records, audit results, and referenced design charts. Records provide objective evidence of conformance to specified requirements.

Structuring quality system documentation into levels has many advantages. For one, it serves different requirements. A potential customer of an organization might examine the quality manual in judging the organization's capability to produce quality products—understanding there is a commitment to quality and a general structure for achieving it might be sufficient assurance to use the organization as a source. Managers of an organization need to have a general idea of how the entire organization functions; Levels 1 and 2 provide it. Operators of a process must understand Level 3 documentation to do their work properly. And quality auditors will use Level 4 documentation in determining whether or not the organization is in compliance with their documented quality system.

Another great advantage of structuring quality systems into levels is that a change in one level may well affect the levels below, but it is very unlikely to affect a higher level. The quality manual (which is the customer's view of the system) rarely changes after a "shake-down" period. Changes in procedures affect only a few departments. Changes in work instructions, which are the most frequent changes, usually affect only the work done within a department.

---

[4]ISO 8402.

◆ 13.11 Auditing the Quality System

Once a quality system is installed, the question immediately arises as to how good it is. Each person with responsibility for a portion of the system should conduct regular assessments or reviews of the suitability and effectiveness of the quality system and its operation. Such reviews are a normal part of good process management. In addition, there should be a systematic review of the quality system by an authority that is not directly responsible for the process or its operations; we shall refer to such a review as a *quality audit.*

A *quality audit* is a planned, systematic examination of a quality system and its implementation to determine the adequacy of the system and the degree of conformance to it. It is a management audit that concentrates on the quality-related aspects of production. A quality audit is conducted by examining a representative portion of the quality system and drawing an inference about the total system based on this sample. It is to the quality system as a financial audit is to the financial system.

There are two types of quality audits: internal audits and third-party audits. An *internal quality audit* is a review conducted by employees of the organization. A *third-party audit* is conducted by an outside organization—for example, an audit by an outside party for the purpose of ISO 9000 certification or for the Baldrige Award. In this section we discuss internal quality audits. For convenience, we sometimes refer to an internal quality audit simply as a *quality audit,* or an *audit.*

Quality audits have been a requirement of companies working on defense contracts since Military Standard Q-9858 was first invoked in the early 1960s. A renewed interest in audits has been generated by ISO 9000, which requires them for registration. Specific requirements for the performance of audits and the actions to be taken on audit findings are described in the ISO Standards. Also, in order to attain registration a company must allow a third party to visit and evaluate the compliance of activities to the standards. Such *compliance audits* are discussed in Section 13.12.

Section 17 of ISO 9001 discusses internal audits. Although the standard does not explicitly require them, internal audits may be relevant to satisfying the requirements of other sections of that standard. Aside from ISO, however, quality audits are a useful tool. They help management obtain factual statements about the status of the quality system and identify opportunities for improvement. They also improve communications, and they can be used as a vehicle for training personnel who participate in audits as observers.

Every organization should conduct quality audits on a regular, scheduled basis. Top management should establish a policy to this effect and commit the organization to conduct quality audits, report the results, and follow up with corrective actions as appropriate. The quality manual should contain this policy statement.

If an organization intends to use audits as a regular management tool, it certainly pays to train a group of internal people to conduct such audits. Because people should not audit areas they are closely associated with, this group should represent various areas of the organization. This diversity of personnel will allow making audit assignments that neither create a conflict of interest nor cause an auditor to "pull punches."

Managing Internal Quality Audits

Responsibility for managing internal quality audits usually is assigned to an Internal Audit Department. Internal Audit focuses on quality and is separate and distinct from the Internal Financial Audit function. Internal Audit is the eyes and ears of top management; its task is to make an independent assessment of the compliance to standards and procedures and to assess whether those standards and procedures are adequate, effective, and efficient.[5]

In a small organization, Quality Assurance might also handle the internal audit function. If at all possible, however, QA should *not* have responsibility for managing internal audits. This is to avoid the potential conflict of, on the one hand, giving advice concerning process improvement and, on the other, auditing results stemming from that advice.

Auditors should examine the overall system as well as the individual elements (processes) of the system. An organization should plan and schedule internal audits so that every element of the quality system is audited periodically.[6] For a mature system, it might be sufficient to audit each element once a year, but newly implemented elements should be audited more often. One way to plan is to divide the audits according to the sections of ISO 9001; another is to follow the organization chart.

The members of an audit team are employees of the organization who are trained and qualified to conduct an audit. Team members should be independent of the process being audited; at the same time, they should be familiar with the process. One way to gain familiarity is to study the process documentation. This study might be augmented by including the trainee in an audit team as an observer; this gives the trainee an opportunity to learn about both the process being audited and the auditing process. Being an auditor is an excellent way for a person to understand the requirements for a quality system and the objective evidence that must be collected to demonstrate the effectiveness of the system.

Conducting an Audit

Audits should be planned, and the unit being audited should be notified of a planned audit well in advance of the scheduled date. The audit should not be a surprise visit to catch wrongdoing. If the auditee gets everything in ship-shape and passes the audit with flying colors, that's fine. Audits are a tool to help the organization, not to "catch" people.

Every process is accomplished through an interconnected collection of procedures. A process is audited indirectly by auditing the procedures that accomplish the process. This is done because a procedure is detailed; it specifies not only

---

[5]Internal Audit also is discussed in Section 13.11.

[6]Section 4.17 of ISO 9001 explicitly requires planning and scheduling of internal audits but places no restrictions on their frequency.

what work is to be accomplished but also where and who will do it (by title or position).

During an audit, the auditor will ask specific questions concerning the quality system. Do you know the company quality policy? May I see the record for the quality review of this product? Please show me the work instruction for this job; now show me the report required by it. The auditor's task is to gather objective evidence concerning the implementation of the quality system and the degree of conformance to it.

If the auditor finds a problem with the quality system, it will usually warrant the issuance by the auditor of a *Corrective Action Request (CAR)*. This CAR will be directed to the proper level of management, which should take appropriate action to improve the quality system and report this correction back to the auditor. The specific problem that was found should also be corrected.

The Audit Report

The audit report should describe any nonconformances that were observed. It should also report any observations of potential nonconformances, lack of effectiveness, or lack of relevance of process steps. The report should not, however, make suggestions for solving a problem; that should be left to the local manager.

◆ 13.12 Quality System Registration

The ISO 9000 series are generic standards for quality management and quality assurance.[7] They apply to all types of companies, large and small, in all sectors of the economy. Registration is a process that involves the audit and approval of an organization's quality system against ISO 9001, ISO 9002, or ISO 9003 by an independent body known as a *third-party registrar*, who then includes the organization's name in an appropriate, publicly available list. *Registration* assures potential customers that an organization at least meets the scope of the stated ISO standard and that each quality system element is adequate and consistently deployed. Note that registration does *not* concern the quality or the properties of the product being produced; it concerns the processes used in production and the conformance to these processes.

Once top management has decided to pursue registration, it takes the typical organization several months to prepare for a registration audit. Employees must be trained, and a high-level flowchart of the organization's processes must be developed. Then more detailed flowcharts must be developed to identify all procedures, many of which will need to be documented. Procedures for creating and handling

---

[7]The reference for this section is Robert W. Peach, ed., *The ISO 9000 Handbook*, 2d ed., Fairfax, Virginia: CEEM Information Services, 1994.

records will also be required. Because the registration effort touches most parts of the organization, the registration process usually requires considerable employee training and much assistance from outside consultants.

According to Lionel Stebbing, a leading UK expert on quality systems, five primary problems recur during management system audits:

1. Document Control (ISO 9001, Clause 4.5): Inadequacies include out-of-date versions of procedures and work instructions; document changes without proper authority; copies of important documents not available where needed.

2. Calibration (Clause 4.11): Outdated calibration stickers; responsibility for the calibration system without the authority to make it work effectively; calibration equipment used but not included in the calibration process; and inadequate paper trail of all equipment used in calibration.

3. Training Records (Clause 4.18): Failure to record on-the-job training; training records restricted to production personnel and other technical staff—missing for others, including executive management.

4. Planning for Customers (Clause 4.3): Failure to have evidence of contract review between the customer and supplier; no record of changes in shipping dates.

5. Management Review and Audit (Clause 4.1.3 and 4.17): An inadequate procedure for internal audit that diminishes the effectiveness of the corrective action system.

Appendix ◆ An Outline of ISO 9001 (1994) Requirements. Section 4

◆ Management Process

Quality System

4.1 Management Responsibility

Formulate quality policy

Define and document responsibility and authority

Provide adequate resources

Appoint a management representative

Review the quality system regularly

4.2 Quality System

The supplier shall establish, document, and maintain a quality system to ensure quality products.

4.5 Document and Data Control

The supplier shall establish and maintain procedures to control all data and documents relating to the ISO standard.

4.16 Control of Quality Records

The supplier shall establish and maintain procedures for the handling and disposition of quality records.

4.17 Internal Quality Audits

The supplier shall establish and maintain procedures for holding internal quality audits and recording the results of these audits and of corrective actions.

Control

4.8 Product Identification and Traceability

Where appropriate, the supplier shall establish and maintain procedures to identify and trace products from production through installation.

4.9 Process Control

The supplier shall establish and maintain procedures for the production, installation, and (where relevant) servicing of product and carry these out under controlled conditions.

Other

4.14 Corrective and Preventive Actions

> The supplier shall establish and maintain procedures for taking preventive and corrective actions.

4.20 Statistical Techniques

> The supplier shall identify the need for statistical techniques and shall implement and control needed techniques.

◆ Production

Specify

4.3 Contract Review

> The supplier shall establish and maintain procedures to review and amend contracts.

Design

4.4 Design Control

> The supplier shall establish and maintain procedures for the design process; in particular, these must cover design planning, design input and output, design reviews, design changes, and interfaces of the design group with other units.

Build

4.7 Customer-supplied Products

> The supplier shall establish and maintain procedures for handling customer-supplied products to be incorporated into the final product.

Test

4.10 Inspection and Testing

> The supplier shall establish and maintain procedures for receiving, in-process, and final inspection and testing, and for maintaining inspection and test records.

4.11 Control of Inspection, Measuring, and Test Equipment

> The supplier shall establish and maintain procedures to control, calibrate, and maintain equipment used in product verification, ensure the equipment is used properly, and maintain related records.

4.12 Inspection and Test Status

The supplier shall establish and maintain a procedure to identify the conformance or nonconformance of a product throughout production, installation, and servicing to ensure that delivered products have passed required inspections and tests.

Control

4.13 Control of Nonconforming Product

The supplier shall establish and maintain procedures to prevent unintended use of nonconforming product.

◆ Other Processes

4.6 Purchasing

The supplier shall establish and maintain procedures to evaluate subcontractors and ensure that purchased product conforms to requirements.

4.15 Handling, Storage, Packaging, Preservation, and Delivery

The supplier shall establish and maintain procedures for handling, storage, packaging, preservation, and delivery of product.

4.18 Training

The supplier shall establish and maintain procedures for providing needed training and maintaining training records.

4.19 Servicing

If required by contract, the supplier shall establish and maintain procedures for performing and verifying servicing.

◆ Exercises and Additional Readings

1. From your collection of articles on quality (see Exercise 1, Chapter 1) give some examples relating to a quality system or a quality audit.

2. Read Carol A. King, "Service Quality Assurance Is Different," *Quality Progress*, June 1985, pp. 14–18. Summarize how quality assurance systems for service differ from those for manufacturing.

3. Read Eugenia K. Brumm, "Managing Records for ISO 9000 Compliance," *Quality Progress*, January 1995, pp. 73–77.

   (a) What does the author mean by the statement "quality records provide strong inferential evidence"?

   (b) What is the meaning of "documentation" as it relates to ISO 9000?

(c) What does she mean by "implied records" as contrasted with "specified records"? What does the author mean by:

(d) Record, document, documentation, and document control?

(e) Implied versus specified records?

(f) Management's responsibility regarding the quality system?

4. Read and comment on the article "Survey Finds ISO 9000 Registration Is Market Driven," *Quality Progress*, March, 1996, p. 23.

5. Read and comment on a software company's strategy for achieving ISO 9001/TickIT registration described in Malcolm L. Macfarlane, "Eating the Elephant One Bite at a Time," *Quality Progress*, June 1996, p. 89.

6. Read and summarize Australia's experience in requiring that all suppliers be ISO 9000 registered in Joseph L. Orsini, "What's Up Down Under," *Quality Progress*, January 1995, pp. 57–59.

7. Summarize the benefits of ISO 9000 registration described in the Standards Department compiled by Jon Brecka, *Quality Progress*, January 1994, p. 26.

8. Consider several companies in your immediate area. Get copies of their quality policy and their quality manual. If some of the surveyed companies are ISO certified, ask them about their certification experience. Summarize the results of your efforts.

9. Ask your surveyed companies from Exercise 8 about their quality system documentation.

10. Ask your surveyed companies from Exercise 8 about their processes for

(a) managing production

(b) managing products

(c) managing workers

(d) controlling quality

11. Ask your surveyed companies from Exercise 8 about their Quality Assurance group. How large is it? How is it organized?

12. Quality systems documentation serves many purposes; for example, it provides a basis for a uniform, consistent understanding of the quality system. List some other needs that it satisfies.

13. Quality systems documentation helps in achieving product quality. List some other benefits it brings to an organization.

14. Critique the example of a quality policy given by Philip Crosby, in *Quality Is Free* (New York: McGraw-Hill, 1979), p. 67.

15. Critique the quality policies in Display 13.1. For each statement, discuss how much is policy and how much is practice. Are the two clearly distinguished in the policy statement?

16. Formulate a quality policy statement that would be suitable for (a) an educational institution, (b) a copy center, (c) a student cafeteria (treated as a separate institution).

17. Determine if your educational institution has a quality policy statement. If so, critique it. If not, would it be suitable for them to adopt one?

18. Read James P. Corrigon, "Is ISO 9000 the Path to TQM?" *Quality Progress*, May 1994, p. 33. Summarize the author's views on how ISO 9000 and TQM can be integrated and used to improve an organization's production process.

19. Read Elizabeth Potts, "Steps in the Registration Process," in Robert W. Peach, ed., *ISO 9000 Handbook*, 2nd ed., published by CEEM Information Services. Summarize each of the six steps in the process for ISO registration.

20. In many companies, the Quality Assurance Manager has less clout than the Comptroller. Discuss how this impacts product quality.

21. Read and summarize Bonnie Holzer, "Quality Auditing in a Public-Sector Service Environment," *Quality Progress*, June 1994, p. 61.

22. Read and summarize Kymberly K. Hockman, Rita Grenville, and Suzan Jackson, "Road Map to ISO 9000 Registration," *Quality Progress*, May 1994, p. 39.

23. Read and comment on the articles in the Special Issue, "World Quality: Making Connections Through Standards," *Quality Progress*, June 1990, pp. 16–54. The papers included in this special issue address various aspects of the ISO 9000 series of standards.

(a) What are the benefits of the ISO registration?

(b) Describe the road to ISO registration.

(c) Discuss the effect of ISO 9000 on quality.

For another point of view, read the letter by P.D.T. O'Connor, "ISO 9000 Does Little to Ensure Product Quality," *Quality Progress*, June 1990, p. 6. Who do you think is right?

24. Read "Phases of the Audit: PERC" in Robert W. Peach, ed., *ISO 9000 Handbook*, 2nd ed., pp. 146–155. Summarize the four basic phases of a quality audit.

25. Summarize the objectives of a quality audit.

26. Use the internet to obtain information on the ISO 9000 standards. Locate and discuss the ISO requirements.

27. Most large companies have websites. Use an internet browser to access the home pages of several companies and look for their quality policies. Discuss and examine their quality policies.

Establishing a Culture of Quality

If employees are to think differently, act differently, and be motivated differently, they must not be allowed to do so in an environment that is diametrically opposed to new thinking because there will be a great deal of frustration and little success. It is up to management to replace these hostile systems with ones that will support the desired culture. By doing this, the lifeline to old culture is cut, disabling it and opening the way for the new one to take its place.

—Ralph L. Liberatore[1]

◆ 14.1 Duties of Management

Management Tasks

Henri Fayol (1841–1925) was the first to develop a rational approach to the enterprise, and his ideas established a pattern followed to this day in the West. Fayol identified the tasks of managing work to be:

---

[1]Ralph L. Liberatore, "The Culture Factor and Quality," *Quality Progress*, December 1993, p. 63.

- ◆   Planning—Establishing goals and courses of action
- ◆   Organizing—Structuring and arranging employees and processes
- ◆   Commanding—Leading, motivating, and directing employees
- ◆   Coordinating—Harmonizing work efforts
- ◆   Controlling—Monitoring results against goals

Other authors include such tasks as establishing policies, staffing, making decisions, focusing on objectives, and supervising and developing people.

Fayol's tasks are widely recognized and are the basis for much of today's management training, say, the typical MBA program. The tasks can be applied to quality as well as to goals for time and cost.

Empowering Workers

Although Fayol's tasks must be performed to accomplish work, they need not all be performed by management, as has generally been assumed since Fayol formulated them. It is now generally acknowledged that the people who operate processes know them the best and are best equipped to make meaningful process improvements if empowered to do so. The quality movement did not spawn the modern move toward worker empowerment; the roots go back to workers at the Tavistock Institute, who conceived the idea in 1949.[2] But the quality movement has done much to support and encourage employee involvement in what was once considered to be management prerogatives. Japanese use of quality circles, which started in the 1950s, was another factor that injected the concept of employee empowerment into the quality improvement effort.

Beyond Fayol

The modern quality movement focuses on a management function that might be classified as "organizing" but is sufficiently different to be listed as a sixth basic management function: *continual process improvement*. This function lifts management from "business as usual," which a Fayol view accommodates, to a dynamic view of a production process. Obviously, continual improvement can be directed at improving production time and production cost as well as product quality, but it is primarily this last objective we are concerned with in this text. It should be recognized, however, that improvement of any one dimension might well bring about improvement in the other two.

---

[2]The Tavistock Institute of Human Relations in London became involved in examining the social consequences of technological change in the British coal mining industry. Several of their studies found that meaningful tasks and social organization arranged with task completion in mind were critical for productive and satisfied workers.

Data for Improvement

Recognition that continual process improvement is a basic management function requires an addition to the task of operating any process: gathering data on process performance to guide improvement efforts. One example is to gather data for use in statistical quality control; another example is defect information for use in directing improvement efforts. To assure that performance data are gathered, it is necessary to modify processes by inserting data-collection activities. And it is necessary to install new processes for analyzing data, devising improvements, and installing them in the process.

Process Management

Traditionally, Fayol's five tasks were applied to the management of *products*. Until recently, rarely was it said in Western management literature that a manager's duties include *process* management. This activity, however, is at the heart of the quality issue.

In Japan, the collection of tasks associated with running the operation—all of the tasks listed in Western management books—is called *maintenance*. It is recognized that maintenance is one major function of management. The other major function to the Japanese is *improvement*, making the products and operation better—improving quality and productivity. Maintenance has to do with today, improvement with tomorrow. Under the maintenance function, managers establish policies, standards, and plans for everybody to follow. Under the improvement function, they innovate to introduce new products and better processes.

Every job in Japan, not just those of managers, involves both maintenance and improvement, but the relative importance of the two changes with one's level in the organization. Most workers, especially relatively inexperienced ones, are involved primarily with maintenance; improvement might take place mainly through quality circles or work improvement teams. For managers, the nearer to the top, the more effort is spent on improvement, and the top manager might well spend his full time on this task.

The Japanese view of management's function contrasted sharply with the traditional Western view. Today, however, managers in the West widely recognize that quality improvement requires innovation and improvement of products and processes. All Western managers and prospective managers must learn that this is an important part of their job if they are to compete in the quality arena.

◆ 14.2 The Business Environment

In the 1950s, customers expected new cars to have defects. By the 1980s, they expected a new car to be relatively error-free; for manufacturers, the emphasis was on the production line and turning out a consistent product. Today, competition is fierce. Customers take it for granted that a new car will be defect-free; their concern is that it "fits their life-style." This means a manufacturer must place heavy emphasis on customer requirements and the design process, as well as on manufacturing. And in today's highly competitive world, a manufacturer must react swiftly to the ever-changing demands. Today's business environment and the challenges facing managers in implementing quality are aptly described by Professor Rosabeth Moss Kanter:

> *In considering the relationship of the environment to the dramatic need for quality, innovation, and better management in American corporations, I think the game that best describes most business today is the croquet game in* Alice in Wonderland. *In that game nothing remains stable for very long. Everything is changing around the players. Alice goes to hit the ball, but her mallet is a flamingo. Just as she's about to hit the ball, the flamingo lifts its head and looks in another direction. That's just like technology and the tools we use. Just when employees have mastered them, they seem to change, requiring different learning and competencies.*
>
> *When Alice finally thinks she's mastered the flamingo and goes to hit the ball, the ball becomes a hedgehog. It walks to another part of the court. That's just like our employees and customers, who are no longer waiting for us to whack them. Instead, they have minds of their own and will in fact walk off to another part of the court to choose another option in a heightened competitive environment.*
>
> *And finally in that croquet game, the wickets are the card soldiers being ordered by the Red Queen. This is perhaps a great metaphor for government. Just as Alice thinks she understands the tools, her employees, and her customers, the Red Queen barks out another order and the wickets reposition themselves. The very structure of industry, the structure of regulation, the structure of international competition, are changing at the same time that we're trying to get people to do a better job. That, to me, is the ultimate quality challenge. It's not only to improve what we're already doing, but it's to build into our organizations the capacity to improve and change direction as conditions change all around us.[3]*

◆ 14.3 Management's Interest in Quality

For years, quality was not very high on the list of major concerns of most managers in the West. One reason was that many subscribed to various management myths about quality:

- ◆ Quality is expensive; it lowers productivity.
- ◆ Quality is intangible; it can't be pinned down, so it can't be managed.

---

[3]Rosabeth Moss Kanter, "Quality Leadership and Change," *Quality Progress*, February 1987, pp. 45–51.

- ◆ Poor quality means poor workers.
- ◆ Quality is the responsibility of the quality professionals.
- ◆ Quality is not a major issue; it has little impact on the company.

All of these myths provided reasons for doing nothing about quality. But there were attitudes, too, that hindered quality improvement. Some of these attitudes were as follows.

- ◆ Some managers honestly didn't think they had a quality problem. They had no measures of quality, and that gave them a false sense of security. No news was interpreted as good news.
- ◆ Some managers faced so many problems that they didn't have time for another one. They didn't see quality relating at all to their other worries.
- ◆ It never occurred to some managers that quality could be used as a competitive strategy.
- ◆ Some managers are excellent salesmen, and excellent salesmen must believe in their product. To question the product's quality is just not in their makeup.
- ◆ Some honestly thought they had solved their problem because they had assigned responsibility to Quality Assurance.

For years, managers could subscribe to these myths and attitudes about quality without adverse consequences because consumers had few real alternatives. However, the world was changing. Around the mid-1980s increased competition, both domestic and foreign, gradually caused attitudes to change. Success stories, such as those we discussed in Section 2.7, as well as the positive publicity generated by the Baldrige Award, made managers realize that quality can be used as a competitive strategy. Today most large manufacturing companies take quality seriously, and interest in quality is spreading very rapidly to all other sectors.

◆ 14.4 Making a Commitment to Quality

Understanding quality is one thing; making a firm commitment is another.

A top manager's commitment to quality is a prerequisite to attaining quality. By a top manager we mean the person or group who has ultimate power in the enterprise. If the top manager is committed to quality, it is very likely to improve; if he is not, improvement is unlikely.

It is hard to find a top manager who openly admits a lack of commitment to quality. That would be the same as admitting a lack of commitment to motherhood, the flag, and apple pie. Everyone *says* they are committed to quality, but this doesn't fool their organization. The organization understands when the commitment, like beauty, is only skin deep; the customers understand it, too.

Commitment comes only after an understanding of quality and a realization that quality is an attractive strategy for becoming competitive. Managers must make a concerted effort to learn as much as they can about quality so that they can understand the benefits of quality and their part in achieving it.

Practical Experience

To understand quality completely, top managers must become involved. They can read about quality and be briefed on quality, but true appreciation only comes after participating actively in a quality effort.

The processes that top managers work with most closely are information processes. They can gain experience about quality by improving the quality of the information supplied to their (mainly internal) customers. How complete and understandable are management directives? How consistent are their goals? basic plans? Do they really know what their customers require? Some other ways top managers can gain practical experience are:

- Instruct those reporting to them on the principles of quality.
- Promote the company's quality image to the outside world.
- Constantly learn more about quality.
- Listen to their customers.
- Observe companies that are role models of quality.
- Link manager's compensation to quality performance.

A Decision for Quality

I know nothing more important to our survival and prosperity than quality.
—Douglas D. Danforth, Chairman, Westinghouse Electric Corp.[4]

Top managers need to go beyond understanding to conviction—quality is an act of faith, not something one accepts from proof. Japanese leaders are convinced; so are many American leaders. But others are not—they still view quality as a desirable feature, not a central strategy. They talk a good game, but their lack of real commitment is spotted immediately by subordinates. Subordinates hear quality, but they know promotion depends on today's results.

Conversion to quality can be likened to a religious conversion—a person believes or has lingering doubts. A belief in quality is preceded by an intellectual understanding of the subject, but this is not enough. Ultimately, belief depends on a visceral feeling that it is the right thing to do. We can discuss what a top manager

---

[4]Douglas D. Danforth, "At the Helm," *Quality Progress,* April 1986, p. 17.

needs to know about quality and what he should do to promote it, but we cannot convert anyone to the belief that it is the right strategy to adopt. Commitment is a personal matter.

As with religion, commitment to quality must be unswerving—a person can't just go to church once a week and sin the rest of the time. But, like religion, there is always the danger of backsliding. This can be a disaster—if a quality program fails for any reason, reviving it is extremely difficult. Top management can't let up simply because last quarter's earnings were down; this would be a clear signal to the troops that what counts is time/budget/profits, not quality.

> *The heart of quality is not technique. It is commitment by management to its people and product—stretching over a period of decades and lived with persistence and passion.*[5]

◆ 14.5 Quality as a Basic Belief

An organization's commitment to quality needs visible expression. There must be a document that states clearly that producing quality products is the standard, expected mode of operation. Some call this basic statement a goal, others a policy, and still others a basic belief. Whatever it is called, it should clearly express the commitment to quality, and everyone in the organization should be familiar with this commitment.

The commitment to quality is usually expressed as part of a package of beliefs or convictions. Some examples are these.

Hewlett-Packard

Hewlett-Packard's quality culture has five dominating characteristics:

- ◆ Respect for the customer
- ◆ Excellence in engineering
- ◆ Superior workmanship
- ◆ Universal commitment to produce quality products
- ◆ Values and beliefs of the company's founders

These characteristics describe a corporate culture known to HP veterans as the "HP Way" and have been described as "a golden rule of financial/business behavior and employee relations."[6]

---

[5]Quoted by Dana M. Cound, "A Call for Leadership," *Quality Progress*, March 1987, p. 12, but taken from Tom Peters and Nancy Austin, *A Passion for Excellence*, New York: Random House, 1985.

[6]Henry J. Kohoutek and John Hamish Sellers, "From Criticism to Partnership," *Quality Progress*, May 1988, p. 18.

Singapore's Ministry of Defense Information System

The Systems and Computers (S&C) section of the Ministry of Defense of Singapore expresses its belief in quality as part of its basic S&C philosophy:

- Objective 1: To improve defense capability through the application of information technology and management science.
- Objective 2: To make striving for excellence a way of life in our organization.
- Objective 3: To provide our people with meaningful, challenging, and rewarding careers.
- Objective 4: To make S & C a great place in which to work.
- Objective 5: To be a responsible corporate member of society.

IBM

For IBM, quality is embedded in the basic beliefs of the organization:

Service to the customer, respect for the individual, and excellence in all we do.

These three beliefs are the principles guiding employee actions, and they were the foundation for IBM's success.

Quality and Other Beliefs

Running through these and many similar examples of basic beliefs is the theme that quality is part of a triad: concern for customers, concern for employees, and concern for quality. There is strong evidence to suggest that quality cannot be separated from the other two. Quality involves satisfying customers, and quality results from the people who produce products. To strive for quality while ignoring customers or producers makes no sense; Watson of IBM saw this clearly, as did many others. Quality of product, perceived quality, and quality of work life are intertwined. One might even visualize the customer, the supplier, and quality as an indivisible trinity.

◆ 14.6 Quality Leadership

The job of management is not supervision, but leadership. . . . The required transformation of Western style of management requires that managers be leaders.[7]

---

[7]W. Edwards Deming, *Out of the Crisis*, Cambridge, Mass.: Massachusetts Institute of Technology, Center for Advanced Engineering Study, 1986, p. 54.

Quality conviction is not the same as quality leadership. Conviction has to do with personal beliefs and values, whereas leadership has to do with instilling those beliefs and values in an organization. Leadership also has to do with organizational commitment and cultural change, and with building an understanding that "quality is our way of life—the way we do things around here."

> *Leadership is "the power of individuals to inspire cooperative personal decision by creating faith.". . . "Faith in common understanding, faith in the probability of success, faith in the ultimate satisfaction of personal motives, faith in the integrity of objective authority and faith in the superiority of common purpose."[8]*

Leadership is an essential ingredient in the makeup of the modern, successful organization. It is so essential to building a quality discipline in a company that the Malcolm Baldrige National Quality Award criteria require that competing companies begin their application with a section dedicated to the leadership function. Leadership is described as the "driver" of the dynamic relationships and interactions that make up an organization's quality system.

Most employees try to do a good job. Most try to do what they perceive management wants them to do. They gain their perception directly from what managers say and indirectly from what they do: the way they spend their time, the topics that capture their attention, the actions they reward. Employees gain their perception from the grapevine and informal organization as well as from official statements and the formal organization. If top management talks about quality but does not lead the way, the troops will perceive that they, too, should pay lipservice to quality.

If management's approach to quality is tentative or ambiguous, it will be reflected in the organization's behavior: People will go through the actions of hanging the banners and will mouth the words, but they will conduct their business as usual.

Characteristics of a Successful Leader

For an organization to achieve quality, its leader must

- ◆ Understand the situation, know what needs to be changed, and when change is possible.
- ◆ Be able to formulate a clear vision and communicate it.
- ◆ Be able to "rock the boat"—to challenge traditional beliefs and practices.
- ◆ Be an empowering person (be able to provide power to others).

---

[8]Quoted by Dana M. Cound, "A Call for Leadership," *Quality Progress*, March 1987, p. 13, but taken from Chester J. Barnard, *The Function of the Executive*, Cambridge, Mass.: Harvard University Press, 1968, first published over 50 years ago.

- ◆ Be able to build coalitions to support proposed changes and have the political skill to cope with conflicting requirements of various groups.
- ◆ Place heavy emphasis on intangibles, such as vision, values, and motivation.
- ◆ Be authentic.
- ◆ Have energy.

You almost have to have a messianic view of this. You must be willing to travel, to go and see people, and talk. You can't communicate or show your commitment on a videotape or in written form all the time.

—James ("Jamie") R. Houghton, chairman and CEO of Corning Glass Works[9]

Signs of Poor Leadership

People are very quick to see through a management charade. They are very adept at reading the tea leaves to learn what the organization really values and rewards. Here are some of the things leaders do that signal to people that quality is really not that important:

- ◆ Appoint a loser to the post of quality manager—someone the group does not respect.
- ◆ Forget to emphasize quality when speaking about organizational directions.
- ◆ Reward people who meet schedules but deliver poor-quality products.
- ◆ Invest little or no personal time and effort in quality improvement activities.
- ◆ Give a speech on quality that is high on clichés ("quality is our top priority") and low on specifics ("here is an improvement we have made").
- ◆ Ship a product that is knowingly bad in order to meet the schedule.
- ◆ Push productivity instead of quality.
- ◆ Don't spend time on quality, spend it on something important.

Leadership Tasks

An important task of top management is to establish the vision and values of the organization. What business are we in? What business should we be in? What are our attitudes and basic beliefs? Part of the answer to those questions must be: We are in the business of providing quality products that delight our customers. To promote this basic vision, top management must establish and deploy a *quality policy*; see Section 13.1.

---

[9]Nancy Karabatsos, "The Chairman Doesn't Blink," *Quality Progress*, March 1987, p. 23.

Next, management must adopt a basic strategy for achieving quality. Frequently, this is a "crawl, walk, run" strategy. The first tactic is to *stabilize* production processes to make their output more predictable. Process documentation and training are among the techniques used to achieve stability. The second tactic is to *improve* production processes. This involves measuring processes to learn their capability and conducting projects to make improvements. This tactic can be employed indefinitely. The third tactic is *innovation*—making a basic change in a process or replacing it with a new, improved process. An example is the introduction of self-directed work teams.

Leadership involves the handling of change, and change is necessary to create and sustain a new quality culture. Robert Galvin, the CEO of Motorola, observed that quality consistently slipped to the end of the agenda for major planning sessions. To make a point, he insisted that quality be the first topic on the agenda and that no other discussion precede it. Sometimes he would leave the meeting right after the report and discussion on quality. The message was clear: "If our quality is 'right,' the rest of our business will take care of itself."

◆ 14.7 A Culture of Excellence[10]

The purpose of an organization is to provide customers with quality products. To accomplish this purpose, the organization requires people, structure, systems, and resources. But more fundamentally, it must establish a proper *culture*, that is, a set of values and patterns of behavior that focus on customers, quality, and individuals of the organization. The culture shapes the organizational structure, the access to and flow of information and other resources, the patterns of behavior, the reward system—all aspects of the organization that make it possible to serve the customer.

Organizations with a reputation for quality display many common characteristics that can be called a *culture of excellence*. Among these characteristics are the following:

- ◆ *Attitude.* The organization views itself as a select group of people—an elite corps of capable people, one for all and all for one. Patterns of behavior and unofficial dress codes tend to reinforce their belief that they are different and special.

- ◆ *Structure.* The organization has a relatively flat structure with easy access up, down, and around the hierarchy. Task forces and other problem-solving coalitions are used to bridge organizational barriers that might

---

[10]This section includes many ideas that come from Rosabeth Moss Kanter. We refer you to her books *The Change Masters* (1983), *When Giants Learn to Dance* (1989), *The Challenge of Organizational Change* (1992), and her paper "Quality Leadership and Change," in *Quality Progress*, February 1987, pp. 45–51.

impede collaboration. Self-directed work teams accept ownership and management of processes.

◆ *Information.* Information is regarded as an important resource. Internal information, technical information, competitive information, industry information—all are openly available for those with a need to know. Information is made accessible and is shared.

◆ *Empowerment.* People are empowered to take initiatives and explore new paths. Information, support, and resources are available for exploring new ideas. People are encouraged to collaborate and build problem-solving coalitions. Personnel policies and the organizational culture encourage innovation without a fear of failure.

◆ *Career Development.* Organizations with a culture of excellence spend heavily in career development. Training, seminars, tuition reimbursement programs, and other devices are used to encourage career development. Company executives act as mentors to exceptional employees who are selected to be on a "fast track." Newsletters and other house organs encourage all employees to engage in self-improvement.

◆ *Recognition.* Organizations with a culture of excellence are quick to give recognition for special achievement. Praise, awards, plaques, desk trinkets, a Friday night beer party around the pool, a "dinner for two"—all are used to mark accomplishment.

◆ *Family Bond.* Organizations with a reputation for quality have a cohesiveness that can be compared with a family bond. They provide support for their people that extends well beyond the business perimeter. An outstanding example of a family bond took place during the Iranian revolution in 1979. Two employees of Electronic Data Systems (EDS) were jailed in Ghasr Prison in Teheran by the revolutionaries. Ross Perot, then CEO of EDS, recruited a team of employee volunteers (mostly Vietnam veterans). He then organized and directed a storming of the prison and got the men safely back to the United States.[11]

◆ 14.8 Quality as a Goal

A statement that quality is a basic belief helps to establish the identity of an enterprise, it helps to tell employees and customers how the enterprise conducts its affairs. To support such a belief, it is necessary that the enterprise establish goals and objectives to point the direction for quality improvement.

Goals and objectives describe what the enterprise wants to accomplish, but management literature is not clear as to which should be used for a long-range target

---

[11]An account of this event was published in the March 5, 1979 issue of *Newsweek*, p. 47.

and which for a short. We choose to use the term *goal* for a long-range end to be accomplished. Usually a goal establishes a general direction; often it is a qualitative statement of what the enterprise wants to accomplish. An *objective*, on the other hand, is a short-range target, for example, something that the enterprise would like to accomplish in the next three to five years. Objectives usually are quantified, enabling measurement of their accomplishment.

Quite frequently, goals are established concerning customers, work processes, and employees. A goal might be to make products that satisfy or even delight a customer. For processes, the goal might be to produce error-free products or to do things right the first time. The goal for employees might be to improve the quality of work life or to enhance job satisfaction.

Some goal statements have a marketing ring; they seem to be designed more for external consumption than as an internal guideline. Some statements are more functional; they definitely give direction to the internal staff.

Error-free Products

The goal of producing error-free products has been adopted by many organizations without an explanation. This has caused considerable confusion, even resistance to the entire quality program.

On first hearing that the goal is error-free products, some workers (and some managers) incorrectly think it is a mandate that applies at once; they panic because they know they cannot comply. If a process is producing an average of 5 percent defective products today, there is little hope it can be adjusted to produce error-free products tomorrow. This, of course, is not the intent of a goal. The goal is designed to point the general direction; in all likelihood, this particular goal will never be reached because every process allows a defect once in awhile. The idea, of course, is to establish an achievable objective that leads toward the goal, say the objective of 4 percent defective products. Once that objective is achieved, people celebrate; then they set a new objective of, say, 3 percent defective, and go on from there. Error-free products is the goal; this means that no matter how low the error rate gets, one is not satisfied and tries to make it even lower.

Conflicting Goals

Goals for quality are only part of the direction that the managers of an enterprise must establish. Other areas where goals are established include marketing, innovation, human organization, physical plant and resources, financial resources, quality and productivity, social responsibility, profit requirements for survival, and others.

Clearly, it is no simple task to establish nonconflicting goals for all these areas, and goal conflict is quite common. The goal for quality might well interfere with a financial goal for short-term profits or with a marketing goal of shipping products on time in spite of their defects. When goals conflict, which is to be dominant? Management must be prepared to answer those questions if their quality goal is really to mean anything.

◆ 14.9 Quality Strategy

Strategy refers to management's general approach to attain outcomes consistent with the organization's mission and goals. A quality strategy can be formulated for a general tactical level or for an operational level.

An organization's strategy for quality should be broad enough to cover the entire organization—this helps everyone to move in the same general direction toward the goal. It might be necessary to "tune" aspects of the strategy to the terminology and other special characteristics of certain units, but for the most part a single statement should suffice for all.

Hewlett-Packard's strategy for Total Quality Control, as their quality improvement program is known, consists of three basic elements:

- ◆ Customer satisfaction goals directed at exceeding both internal and external customers' needs and expectations
- ◆ Universal participation of employees in all areas of the company
- ◆ Continual process improvements using statistical quality control methods[12]

Strategic Elements

As this example illustrates, a quality strategy usually has several elements directed at the specific areas where improvement is to be stressed. An element might be very general, placing little restriction on the work plans that follow; the first two elements of HP's strategy are of this type. Or an element can be quite specific—for example, emphasizing the use of a specific technique, as does HP's third element.

As in the Hewlett-Packard example, it is usual for an organization's strategy to focus on three important elements: customers, employees, and processes. The customer element might refer to satisfaction, service, the quality of the products provided, competitive advantage—whatever the organization views as the benefit it provides customers. The employee element might refer to participation, respect, or some other terms describing employee treatment and their value to the organization. The third element might refer to what the organization does and how well it is done—process improvement, process excellence, or process operation.

An enterprise's quality strategy basically establishes the long-term direction of its quality improvement process. The elements of a strategy must be tailored to the needs of the enterprise and are likely to be adjusted as the improvement effort matures.

Quality and Other Strategies

An enterprise establishes a strategy for each of its goals. Thus, there may be a strategy for achieving a financial goal, one for building a workforce, one for market

---

[12]Henry J. Kohoutek and John Hamish Sellers, "From Criticism to Partnership," *Quality Progress*, May 1988, p. 17.

penetration, and so on. These goals and strategies must mesh, or the enterprise will be working at cross-purposes with itself. In particular, the quality strategy must mesh with the overall direction of the enterprise. Frequently it does not.

A newly established quality strategy for an enterprise generally will be in conflict with other, long-established strategies because it calls for a change in the direction of the enterprise. A common planning problem is the failure to face this issue adequately. There is only one effective way to do so: Quality must be established as the primary goal of the organization, and all other goals and strategies must be realigned to match. If an enterprise procrastinates over this important step, quality will lose out because it is aimed at "tomorrow"; quality will simply be pushed aside by "today."

> *Placing primary emphasis on quality achievement requires basic changes in management concepts and company operations, brings me to what I call "the new global quality strategies."*
>
> —Feigenbaum[13]

Strategic Quality Planning

Strategic planning is a process that follows a written procedure, is regularly applied, and produces a written document, called the *strategic plan.* This plan establishes a direction for the enterprise and is a means of communicating that direction to all who should know it.

The *strategic quality plan* consists of those sections of the strategic plan that deal with quality issues.[14] Thus, the strategic quality plan consists of the identity and mission for the enterprise; the goals and objectives for quality; the strategy, programs, and projects for meeting those goals and objectives; and the plan for tracking actual quality progress. We will discuss strategic quality planning in Section 15.4.

◆ 14.10 Undertaking Organizational Change

> *I come from an environment where, if you see a snake, you kill it. At GM, if you see a snake, the first thing you do is organize a committee on snakes. Then you go hire a consultant who knows a lot about snakes. Then you talk about it for a year.*
>
> —H. Ross Perot[15]

---

[13]Armand V. Feigenbaum, "Quality: The Strategic Business Imperative," *Quality Progress*, February 1986, p. 29.

[14]We use the term *strategic quality plan* to distinguish it from the *quality plan* discussed in Section 12.3.

[15]Maryann Keller, *Rude Awakening*, (New York: Harper Perennial (paper), 1990), p. 181.

Installing quality is an instance of undertaking an organizational change—in spades! The key to making such a change is the ability to deal effectively with people. A small group of specialists can't do it. Establishing a culture of quality requires the participation and cooperation of the various interest groups to determine improvement requirements, resolve all conflicts in requirements, design the required process changes, and install them.

Initiating Change

Installing quality requires a radical change that impacts both managers and workers. The hardest part is to change the culture and people's attitudes. The more mechanical part is to change processes and procedures. Another difficult part, however, is to change people's habits and skills to make them effective and contented in the new environment.

To accomplish this change, the organization must adopt a new philosophy and develop a new management system. Salient features of the new philosophy are:

- Management leadership of the quality effort
- Focus on customers, obtaining their confidence
- Focus on employees, earning their trust and support
- Excellence in every aspect; striving for world-class quality
- Applying quality concepts to all products and all processes
- A focus on process improvement
- Building an environment of contribution
- Adopting a structured approach to solving quality problems
- Making quality a permanent way of doing business

Organizational change is a complex process that

- Takes time—on average about four years
- Involves many interest groups with different objectives and agendas, which must be reconciled
- Requires information and knowledge that are widely disbursed among process customers, subcontractors, and operators
- Is likely to encounter resistance. One way to cope with resistance is to remember that change is a threat when it's done to me or imposed on me; but it's an opportunity if it's done by me.

Care must be taken to distinguish between real (permanent) change and superficial change. One way to tell the difference is to remove the change agent and observe the results. If things revert to the old ways, the change was superficial; if they stay the same or continue to improve, the change is real.

Many quality programs start out with good intentions and make immediate headway. But then things fall apart. Top management initiates the program, and then turns it over to others to implement—a clear signal that it is merely the "flavor of the month." Or people lose interest and stop making improvements; they take it for granted that success will continue because of the program's merits. Or people who feel threatened find subtle ways to sabotage the effort. Or a crisis causes people to revert to old, trusted ways rather than new, unfamiliar ways.

For most processes that undergo a significant change, the performance dips before it shows steady improvement. This dip sometimes is called the "valley of despair"—it is a time when management sees the cost of change but has yet to reap its benefit. This dip can cause some managers to abandon the change effort and revert to the old, well-known ways. But this is a serious mistake because the need for quality does not vanish, and any attempt to reinitiate improvement will not be easy. Each time a quality improvement effort is allowed to expire before its work is done, the time cycle for real change starts all over again.

Time to Accomplish Change

It takes time for a quality improvement effort to show significant results. Of course, there will be a few spectacular success stories right in the beginning, but it will take at least four or five years to show substantial improvement. And it will take ten years before the effort really takes hold. The Japanese quality improvement effort started in 1945 with the American occupational forces. Twenty years later, the Japanese had established a quality leadership position in several industries. Thirty years later, their reputation for quality was well known to many American business leaders, whose markets had been taken over by Japanese firms. Forty years later, their reputation for quality was well known to the American man in the street.

Quality Improvement Projects

Introducing quality is one project that must be undertaken. Beyond that, there is no limit to the type of improvement that an organization might undertake. To help stimulate thought, we have listed examples of improvement projects in Display 14.1.

◆ 14.11 Summary

In summary, installing quality is not a simple program—not like building a new factory or doubling the workforce. It requires a total overhaul of the organization's culture moving toward an attitude of accomplishment, pride, team spirit, acceptance of challenge, and a trust in people and their ability to excel. It also requires a total overhaul of the organization's processes to enable them to meet new, more demanding standards.

DISPLAY 14.1 ◆ Some Examples of Improvement Projects

Organizational Projects
 Establish QA, Quality Council
 Establish Standards Committee
Awareness and Communication
 Provide quality orientation
 Improve quality communications
 Publicize quality accomplishments
Management Processes
 Exhibit commitment and leadership
 Change culture
 Communicate the quality message
 Practice participatory management
 Develop champions
 Break down barriers and drive out fear
 Control work, not workers
 Be a trainer to your people
 Develop better customer and subcontractor contacts
 Reward quality
Education and Training
 Teach basic quality concepts
 Orient on standards and available tools
 Train managers in how to
  —Establish employee improvement groups
  —Develop customer-supplier partnerships
  —Install self-directed work teams
 Provide technical education and training, on
  —How to develop standards
  —How to develop defect information systems
  —Process improvement techniques
  —Statistical concepts
Process Improvement Projects
 Establish process ownership
 Document processes
 Establish employee improvement groups
 Develop customer-supplier partnerships
 Develop a defect information system
Assessment Projects
 Determine quality status
 Assess quality measurement system
 Establish recognition projects
 Devise and review recognition schemes

DISPLAY 14.2 ◆ Management Elements Applied to Climbing Kilimanjaro

Basic Belief:	Fundamental concept we believe to be true. ("Man does not live by bread alone.")
Mission:	This is our calling—our overall purpose. ("To climb mountains.")
Goal:	This is what we want to accomplish as part of our mission. ("Climb Kilimanjaro.")
Objective:	A milestone toward reaching a goal. ("Get to the first set of huts.")
Leadership:	Direction and inspiration. ("A guide will lead me.")
Strategy:	The general approach we will take. ("Let my daughter make arrangements, don't carry too much, walk early in the morning when the volcanic ash is partly frozen, etc.")
Strategic Plan:	The general plan for accomplishing my goal. ("Arrange trip; go to Tanzania; get near the Park; hire guide and other base arrangements; go up; come down; celebrate; go home.")
Detailed Plans:	Specific objectives, actions, schedules, resources, etc. ("Get in shape, plan what to take, arrange transportation, contingency plans, etc.")
Other Plans:	Annual plans ("Not for Kili—once was enough."), departmental plans, quality improvement plans, . . .
Commitment:	I will do it. ("My daughter and I will do it.")
Records:	Evidence of accomplishments. ("A certificate signed by the guide.")

In this chapter we discussed many elements of management that affect quality. Sometimes it is difficult to see the differences among them. In Display 14.2 we illustrate these differences for the "business" of climbing Kilimanjaro.

◆ Exercises and Additional Readings

1. In *What Is Total Quality Control?*, p. 122, Ishikawa states: "Unless the person in charge, the one who has the full power, that is, the president or the chairman, takes the initiative and assumes leadership in implementing quality control, the program cannot succeed." Comment on this statement; give reasons to support it and reasons to refute it.

2. In *What Is Total Quality Control?*, p. 122, Ishikawa states: "QC is an acquired taste. Taste is acquired only after eating. A chief executive officer can appreciate the taste of QC only after he has taken active leadership in its implementation." Discuss this statement.

3. In the paper "IBM's Quality Focus on the Business Process," *Quality Progress*, April 1986, p. 28, Edward J. Kane states that IBM's quality improvement plans were based on five concepts:

    Quality improvement results from management action.

    Everyone must be involved.

    Focus for improvement must be on the job process.

    No level of defect is acceptable.

    Quality improvement reduces total costs.

Comment on these concepts. Are they understandable? anything you might change? anything you might add?

4. Read Dennis P. Grahn, "The Five Drivers of Total Quality," *Quality Progress*, January 1995, pp. 65–70. Summarize the five drivers of quality that are discussed in the article.

5. Read "When GM's Robots Ran Amok," in *Economist*, August 10, 1991, p. 64. Summarize the lessons GM learned from (a) their efforts to automate production and (b) their partnership with Toyota.

6. Read Harold S. Page, "A Quality Strategy for the 80s," *Quality Progress*, November 1983, pp. 16–21.

    (a) List the major areas of concern within the corporation.

    (b) List some steps that management should take to improve the situation.

    (c) What is needed to take each of these steps?

    (d) Is the quality strategy for the 1980s still relevant for the 1990s and beyond?

7. Select three organizations in your community. For each organization, talk with a few employees to learn about the organization's culture as it relates to quality. Compare and contrast your findings.

8. (a) In *The Customer Comes Second* (published by William Morrow and Co., 1992), Hal F. Rosenbluth and Diane McFerrin Peters describe the two-day orientation that new associates receive at Rosenbluth Travel (pp. 17–20). Summarize the approach.

    (b) Ask some employees of your educational institution to describe the orientation they received when they were hired.

    (c) Write a short paper describing what you learned from these activities and how this might influence you as a manager.

9. Read Terry R. Sargent, "The Pygmalion Effect on Quality," *Quality Progress*, August 1986, p. 34. Summarize Sargent's message.

10. Give examples of leadership, basic belief, goal, objective, and strategy as they relate to quality.

11. Assume that your summer job involves running a day-camp for 10-year-olds. How would you establish a culture of quality?

12. Your summer job involves the management of five paint crews of college students, who paint houses in town. How would you establish a culture of quality?

13. In addition to going to your classes, you are a manager of five apartment buildings of eight apartments each. How would you establish a culture of quality?

14. Select a few companies in your immediate area. Describe their culture of quality. How did these companies go about establishing this culture.

15. Read Jayant V. Saraph and Richard J. Sebastian, "Developing a Quality Culture," *Quality Progress*, September 1993, pp. 73–78. Summarize the major points made in this article.

16. Read and summarize Samuel C. Welch, "Total Quality Management in the Performing Arts," *Quality Progress*, January 1993, p. 31.

17. Consider your own institution and the way it delivers instruction. Is there a culture of excellence? Is there a strategy to improve instruction? Is there quality leadership? Does your institution have documents that speak to these issues?

18. Access the websites of several large companies and look for their commitments to quality, their quality beliefs, and their quality leadership.

Managing Quality

In today's competitive environment, ignoring the quality issue is tantamount to corporate suicide.

—John A. Young, CEO of Hewlett-Packard[1]

◆ 15.1 Quality-Related Activities

Every organization should perform these six quality-related activities:

◆ *Quality planning* is the collection of activities designed to identify customers, determine their requirements, and develop the capability to meet these requirements in a cost-effective manner.

◆ *Quality control* is the collection of prevention and appraisal activities within a process designed to ensure that defects are neither made nor shipped. The term is also used for the act of performing prevention and appraisal activities.

---

[1]"The Renaissance of American Quality," *Fortune*, October 1985, p. 166.

- ◆ *Quality improvement* is the activity of changing a process to improve the quality of products produced by that process.
- ◆ *Quality assurance* is the collection of activities designed to facilitate quality control and quality improvement.
- ◆ *Quality audit* is the function of checking compliance with the requirements, standards, and procedures of the quality system.
- ◆ *Quality assessment* is the critical review of an organization and its processes to assess their ability to produce quality products. Whereas an audit checks compliance to the system, an assessment is a critique of the system.

For each activity, it is necessary to define responsibilities for performing the task and procedures for doing so; it is also necessary to supply resources (including time) to accomplish the task, and training to do it properly.

◆ 15.2 The Quality Organization

An enterprise of any size must have quality professionals on its staff. If nothing else, they must serve as a focus for quality and as advocates, seeing that quality is given equal time by management. Generally, they are also charged with internal coordination and oversight of quality-related matters, as well as with training and assistance to support the quality improvement effort.

In this section, we will examine the roles, responsibilities, and organizational structure for these quality professionals. We assume that the new view of quality prevails.

Organizational Structure

An enterprise of fewer than a hundred people might have only one quality professional. A large enterprise will have quality professionals in each major section; however, their total number will not be large. Our discussion in this section will be geared to the large enterprise, but it also will serve as a guide for a small one. Rather than talk abstractly, we will assume an enterprise with three major divisions: manufacturing, marketing, and administration.

We will use the term *Quality Assurance* (QA) for the organization that houses the quality professionals, but various terms are used in practice.[2] We will describe one organizational structure for QA, but obviously many others might be used.

If quality is to be the primary goal of the organization, the head of the quality organization should have the title of Vice President and report directly to the President of the enterprise. In headquarters there should be a small staff to assist

---

[2]The quality assurance organization was discussed in Section 13.2.

the Vice President. Similarly, each division should have a small staff of quality professionals reporting to the division head and supporting the quality efforts of the division. The head of the divisional staff might be called the divisional Director of Quality. The divisional QA staff will promote quality in the division and will assist and consult with the line as required, but responsibility for the quality of divisional products rests squarely with the line organization.

The quality professionals in the enterprise are staff personnel with responsibility for assisting the line in quality-related matters. Although they do not report to him, the divisional quality staffs should have a strong tie to the Vice President for Quality; this usually is described as a "dotted line" relationship. Thus, the divisional quality staffs look to the Vice President of Quality for direction and assistance, and they support his programs.

This organizational structure is depicted in Display 15.1.

Staffing

Among the most critical decisions in a quality program is the choice of QA personnel, particularly the choice of the person to head the effort. The enterprise will examine personnel decisions carefully in an attempt to learn just how important the effort is. If respected, valued employees are chosen, people will believe the effort is serious. If appointments are given to those who are judged (rightly or wrongly) to be mediocre or poor, it will send a signal that quality is "just another program" and people will not expect it to last.

There is another fundamental reason for putting the best people in QA. Making quality a reality can transform an enterprise into a world-class competitor. It can mean the difference between failure and success. An enterprise needs some of its top people in QA because a well-done QA job will have a significant impact on

DISPLAY 15.1 ◆ Quality Organizational Structure

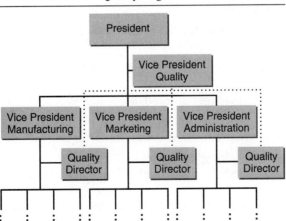

profitability and survival. If top management doesn't believe that, then it really shouldn't start the quality effort because it will not be successful. If top management doesn't believe, no one else will, and it won't happen.

Vice President for Quality

The Vice President for Quality should report to the President and should have a strong voice in selecting the divisional quality staffs, even though they do not report directly to him. This will help to avoid the common problem that local managers who make QA appointments often do so before they themselves are thoroughly familiar with the potential of the quality program. Instead of appointing their best people to the job, they tend to appoint people who can most easily be spared.

> One QA manager we know (who, as it happens, is very competent) told us, "I was pregnant at the time and about to go on maternity leave and they didn't know what to do with me; so they made me the QA manager."

The Vice President for Quality is charged with specific responsibilities; a typical list of these responsibilities is as follows:

- ◆ Serve as a focal point for quality matters, including corrective action and continual improvement activities.
- ◆ Formulate and recommend enterprise policies, strategies, tactics, goals and objectives relating to quality.
- ◆ Review and help to coordinate quality aspects of line plans.
- ◆ Assist and counsel top managers on quality matters.
- ◆ Exercise dotted-line authority over QA groups in the units.
- ◆ Concur with the appointment of unit QA directors.
- ◆ Serve as a resource for information in the quality area, including competitive information.
- ◆ Foster awareness of quality and help to gain credibility for the quality improvement effort.
- ◆ Monitor quality and report to top managers on the status of quality in the enterprise.
- ◆ Coordinate the efforts of standards committees, quality improvement teams, and other groups whose activities touch on the quality area.
- ◆ Interface on quality matters with external bodies, including government agencies and professional associations.
- ◆ Provide leadership for the quality function as necessary.

This list of responsibilities can be taken as the charter for the quality organization. It clearly describes QA as a support function, leaving responsibility for quality to the line function. Charters for line organizations should be adjusted to make their quality responsibility explicit.

The QA charter does not place restrictions on the method to be employed in improving quality. Most vice presidents choose process improvement as the basic tactic. They support this tactic by interpreting their mandate to include these further responsibilities:

- Maintain high professional standards for manning quality units.
- Provide education and training relating to quality.
- Install effective quality programs, projects, procedures, and information systems.
- Recommend recognition plans.
- Foster the development and use of standards.
- Conduct special studies of tools, techniques, and procedures that might improve quality.
- Promote appropriate and effective quality audits.
- Assess the enterprise's quality relative to competitors.
- Recommend appropriate corrective actions.

No matter how clear the charter, the boundary between QA responsibility and line responsibility must be established through practice. For example, QA might take responsibility for providing basic training in quality, and the line might take responsibility for technical training in their area. But teaching, say, a course on structured design to a computer analyst will improve both his technical competency and the quality of his work products. Who teaches the course? Answers to questions such as these must be worked out between the line organization and the unit's QA group.

Quality Professionals

Quality professionals should be viewed more as consultants and facilitators than as technicians. It is essential, therefore, that they are people-oriented and able to establish rapport with all levels of the enterprise. They should be familiar with the technical aspects of the units with which they work and understand basic quality concepts; ASQ certification (such as CQA, CQE, etc.) are often good indicators of engagement in the field. However, the skills quality professionals are most likely to use are the abilities to organize, teach, counsel, and communicate. They should understand something about organizational and team dynamics and behavior. And they should know how to deal with resistance to change.

Traditionally, quality professionals have been engineers and worked mainly in the manufacturing area. The problems they solved dealt more with manufacturing processes than the workers, so their technical backgrounds served them well. Today, quality improvement is applied to all processes, and people are recognized as part of those processes. A strong technical background might still be needed in some areas, but in others—the office, for example—dealing effectively with people is the main instrument of change.

Many companies have observed the changing role of quality professionals. The following comments are typical:

- ◆ "Our QA managers are on their way to becoming facilitators and change masters, not policemen and administrators."
- ◆ "Our quality professionals are growing out of their narrow administrator or technician roles and becoming cross-functional."
- ◆ "Our QA professionals are highly qualified individuals playing the dual role of quality assurance technicians and general consultants."

QA Activities

QA is a small organization and has its hands full attempting to fulfill all the responsibilities of its charter. Typical activities undertaken by them can be grouped into several categories.

Start-up Activities

Start-up is the first order of business for a newly formed QA group. This activity involves establishing and manning unit quality organizations, designing operating procedures, and working out the mechanics of doing business. It also involves discussing the quality direction with all top managers to make certain there is consistency in management pronouncements.

The first major activity after start-up is indoctrinating the entire organization on the enterprise's quality direction and introducing them to the fundamentals of quality. This is a massive effort; often it is undertaken with assistance from outside consultants because it requires temporary manpower to cope with the teaching load.

Education and Training

The primary effort of many QA groups involves education and training. Much of their effort focuses on conducting classes and otherwise meeting the organization's educational needs. However, more than half the education in an enterprise takes place on the job, not in the classroom. One task of QA is to encourage workers, supervisors, and managers to include quality concepts in their training efforts.

Education and training are needed on the basic beliefs, culture, and traditions of the enterprise, the fundamentals of quality, quality improvement, the fundamental concepts of processes, technical topics, management and supervisory practices, and quality leadership. An organization must have a mechanism for providing this required education and training. It must also have a mechanism for keeping informed about external quality developments that are pertinent to their organization.

Process Improvement

In many enterprises, important business processes—processes that the enterprise depends on for survival—are neglected. People are so busy operating the processes that nobody stops to look at them. If no one in the organization takes responsibility for an important process, it sometimes falls de facto to QA. They might attempt to improve the process; alternatively, they might attempt to introduce the enterprise to the concept of process ownership and then help the owner to make improvements. No matter how they are involved, process improvement is a major concern of QA.

Standards

An enterprise should have procedures for developing and reviewing internal standards and for tracking external standards with which they must comply. Often such procedures are lacking. Many QA organizations spend considerable effort in helping standards committees with their work.

Special Projects

Many QA groups undertake efforts relating to quality that no one else wants to tackle. Examples of such projects are as follows.

- Collecting and analyzing of data related to quality.
- Forming and leading corrective-action teams to make specific improvements.
- Integrating decisions and actions concerning quality that are being taken within the enterprise.
- Facilitating quality actions of others.
- Evaluating tools, techniques, procedures, standards, and so on.

Consulting

QA frequently serves the enterprise as a consultant. They might assess a process and recommend improvements, help a department in its efforts to improve a subcontractor's quality, evaluate and recommend changes in a unit's quality program, and so on.

Monitoring Quality

To discover opportunities for improvement, QA monitors quality both inside and outside the enterprise. Internal monitoring is done with the knowledge and support of line organizations in order to avoid any connotation that it is a police action. This is a tricky area, and it takes much effort to monitor quality without creating tensions. External monitoring focuses on issues relating to subcontractors' quality and external quality developments.

Coordinating Quality Activities

As the focal point for quality matters, QA expends much effort in coordinating the activities of others and keeping everyone informed about events surrounding the quality effort.

Gaining Credibility

Even though QA makes it clear that quality is the responsibility of producers and they are there to help, people will be suspicious. They will be concerned that error information might find its way into the appraisal system, and they will wonder how QA with little experience can teach them something about a job they've been doing for years. QA must earn trust and credibility. If you are a QA professional, here are a few things you can do to earn it.

- Know what you're doing. You must understand quality concepts thoroughly and know how to apply them.

- Learn something about the processes you deal with. You don't have to become an expert, but you should attempt to understand the terminology and tasks in the areas you serve.

- Ask "How can I help you?" Make very certain people understand you are there to help and advise, not to "fix" them.

- Cultivate the managers in the areas you serve. They are likely to be more frightened than the workers because they have more to lose.

- Market quality. Most people like the product.

- Try to help someone solve a single problem, even a small one. Then publicize the fact that it has been solved. Let the other person take the credit; chances are he will share some with you.

- Be flexible. Consider new ways of doing things. If you run into a stone wall, back off and try something else.

- Get exposure. Drop around and talk with people. Don't sit in your office waiting for the phone to ring.

- Believe in quality. If you don't, ask for a transfer.

◆ 15.3 Quality Units

Quality improvement requires an organizational structure. Superimposed on the regular line organization is the typical three-tiered arrangement:

- A *Quality Council* drawn from the organization's senior levels. Its concern is policy, goals, and other broad issues relating to quality.

- *Quality advisory committees* drawn from middle and operational levels. Their concerns are major improvement projects and oversight of lower level improvement efforts.

- *Quality teams* consisting of people at the task level. Their concern is improvement of the processes they operate.

Various modifications of this basic structure are encountered. For example, membership in these committees might also include officials of all unions representing workers. A small organization might have only two of the three tiers, omitting the middle one. Also encountered are various standards committees and task forces that supplement the work of the committees and tackle specific tasks. ISO 9000 has had a substantial impact on companies as they structure to implement the activities required by the standard.

The third tier of the quality structure has received much popular attention. Known as *quality circles, work improvement teams, employee involvement teams,* or a similar name, teams of workers have been established in many organizations to discover problems and solve them.

Quality advisory committees at a divisional level coordinate the efforts of all quality teams in the division. In particular, they help teams solve problems that lie within the division, but which extend beyond the unit in which the team works. For example, the solution of a problem that involves two departments of the division might be coordinated by the advisory committee. The advisory committee might also be assigned a role in developing the quality plan for the division.

For most, membership in the quality advisory committee is a part-time effort. One member, however, may work full time on quality matters. This person's job is to act as adviser to the work teams of the division, teaching team building and problem-solving techniques, advising, and facilitating their efforts. This adviser might also have responsibility for keeping records of team accomplishments and administering a recognition program. An alternative to having such a full-time adviser is to assign these responsibilities to the divisional QA team.

Quality Council

The *Quality Council* is an important body; let us examine it in some detail.

A Quality Council is a high-level committee of a major enterprise unit. Its responsibility is to oversee and advise the unit head on quality matters. It consists of the head of a large unit and his major advisers. In the organization chart depicted in Display 15.1, it would consist of the President, Vice Presidents (including the Vice President for Quality), and other top-level managers of the company. The Quality Council can be likened to the budget committee of the major unit.

The Quality Council meets monthly or bimonthly, usually just before or just after the regular meeting of the top officials. Although the two meetings are attended by the same members, the Quality Council devotes its entire meeting to quality matters. It is here that top officials discuss quality plans and actual accomplishments, review problems and plans for solution, discuss recognition programs, and so on. One responsibility of the Quality Council is to establish policies and other broad issues relating to the quality advisory committees and quality teams.

The Council establishes the ground rules for quality teams: Do teams meet during work hours? Is the unit's manager to be involved in the team? What procedure will be followed to approve and implement team solutions to problems? How will team accomplishments be recognized? The Council also establishes the ground rules for advisory committees, fixing their procedure for managing quality teams and their role in the overall quality effort of the enterprise.

QA plays a leading role in the Quality Council. Although meetings usually are chaired by the unit head, the chief QA person (the Vice President of Quality in the Display 15.1) has major input into the agenda and assumes the major administrative burden of the meeting. Thus, the Quality Council is a major tool for coordinating quality matters and for keeping the top managers' focus on quality.

Other Quality Units

In addition to the three quality units just discussed, various groups are formed to install and maintain standards. Overseeing this work is an organizational unit we will call a *Standards Committee*. Here we merely introduce this committee; a further discussion appears in Section 17.4. QA is heavily involved with assisting the Standards Committee. The Director of Quality or a senior QA professional represents QA on the Standards Committee; however, the QA representative usually tries to avoid chairing the Committee because the job is too time consuming.

Another organization involved with quality is *Internal Audit*, discussed in Section 13.11. The concerns of Internal Audit—procedures, instructions, standards, and compliance—overlap the concerns of QA. There are two very good reasons why these two units should cooperate:

◆ There are far too many processes for Internal Audit to assess them all in any detail. By working closely with QA, scarce auditing resources can be used more effectively.

◆ QA usually has regular contact with various areas and knows their processes better than does Internal Audit.

◆ 15.4 Planning for Quality

To achieve quality it is necessary to establish a detailed plan of action—a strategic quality plan, which was introduced in Section 14.9.

Quality planning is the process of identifying the actions needed to achieve quality goals. It consists of identifying objectives that will support the long-term goals and then devising programs and projects for achieving those objectives. The quality plan is part of the total plan for the enterprise. This must be the case because quality improvement competes for the same scarce resources needed for ongoing operations and for other special projects.

Some enterprises use a two-year planning horizon, some use five, and some ten or more. Although the planning horizon depends on many factors, not the least of which is tradition, a five-year horizon is quite suitable for a quality plan: It is long enough to force speculation and planning for the future, but not so long that it encourages pure guess-work about the most distant planning years.

To make the description of the planning process easier to follow, we will again assume the organizational structure of Display 15.1.

The first step in planning is taken by top management. Based on their assessment of the present situation and prospects for the future, management establishes quality objectives to support their long-term quality goals and describes their general tactics for achieving them. (Of course, management establishes objectives in other areas, but here we are concerned only with the quality portion of the plan.) Because the language of top management usually is dollars—the common denominator for measuring all aspects of the enterprise—they might, for example, establish an objective of lowering the cost of quality to a specified percent of the total costs. For this objective to be meaningful to the lower levels of the organization, where the emphasis is on "things," it must be translated into their quality language: scrap rates, re-run rates, total defects, and so on. After this translation, each division has specific objectives it is to reach. For example, the Information Systems area might have targets for defect rates, re-run rates, ABEND (abnormal endings) rates, response times, and employee education. Product development's target might be a lower defect rate for a new product, lower than that for the product it replaces and lower than the rate for any competitive product.

Next, it is the divisions' turn. They must devise projects and programs that will take them from today's reality to the objectives established for them. Division plans are assembled from plans of their individual departments. Along with others, QA departments must propose projects and programs to improve the quality of their processes; they also propose improvements that cut across departments and benefit the entire division. Division plans must assign responsibility for accomplishing these efforts and establish that allocated resources are sufficient to get the job done.

When a division's plan is complete, the division's QA group assesses it. Did the division face the most pressing problems? Will the planned actions accomplish the objectives? Can the planned actions be accomplished? Are the resource estimates realistic? Do the plans of the various departments of the division mesh and support one another?

With QA's stamp of approval, the division plans are passed to the corporate level, and these plans are merged to produce the enterprise plan. Usually, this total plan contains contradictions: required resources far outstrip those available; actions by one division conflict with those of another; a support activity required by one unit of another unit is not in their plan, and so on; some objectives are overlooked. The Vice President of Quality checks the quality portion of the plan, noting any such irregularities. These errors, omissions, and excesses typically require adjustments, calling for an iteration of the planning process. But after a few adjustments, the plan is complete.

Initiating a Quality Program

The planning steps just reviewed tacitly assume that QA is in place and that quality planning is an ongoing activity. Initiation of a quality program also requires planning; essentially it requires steps that precede the regular planning cycle just described.

For top management even to consider a quality program seriously, strong support and advocacy for such a direction must come from one or more senior executives or very highly regarded senior staff members. We will refer to such people as the *advocates* of the program. If the enterprise is lucky, one advocate will be the top executive officer; if not, some senior official who has the ear and confidence of the top executive can and must win his support. The advocates need a plan for making their concept a reality. Typical steps they must take to initiate the quality effort are as follows.

Step 1. Gain Top Management Support

The first step the advocates must take is to gain the commitment of the top executive officer and his promise to lead the quality effort. The aim is to have the top executive commit to quality as the primary goal of the enterprise. Sometimes this support can be gained through persuasion and education. Sometimes it requires a pilot study to produce convincing evidence.

In one large multinational corporation, a senior manufacturing official became an advocate for quality. He conducted a cost of quality study in his area and then embarked on a quality improvement effort. For a year, his effort showed no decrease in the cost of quality; in fact, there was a slight increase because additional cost factors were discovered as his group gained experience. But after a year, his cost of quality started slowly downward. After a year and a half, the downward trend was clearly evident; and it was reasonable to project huge savings if his programs were enacted throughout the company. This evidence caused top management to commit to quality and to make the organizational changes necessary to support the effort.

Step 2. Assemble the Corporate Quality Group

Considerable staff work is needed before the organization can make a major change, such as pushing for quality. After the top executive commits to the direction, the next step should be to assemble a group to plan for the transition; members of this group will then become the nucleus of the Corporate Quality Assurance Group. The future Vice President for Quality should be identified as soon as possible and asked to work with and guide the group.

Step 3. Develop a Constituency for Quality

Next, the top executive, quality advocates, and quality group must win over a critical mass of top executives and other opinion makers to the new direction. The aim is to develop a constituency with a shared vision about the need and potential of a quality direction. The broader and more committed this constituency, the more likelihood the adoption of a quality direction will be supported, not sabotaged.

Step 4. Develop a Quality Policy and Goals

The next step is to develop a clear policy about quality and to incorporate general, long-term quality goals with the other long-term goals of the enterprise. This step actually takes place in parallel with Step 3 because part of developing a consensus among top officials is the process of coming to agreement on exactly what a "quality direction" means. And it is not an easy step; many an ox will be gored because making quality the primary goal means displacing previous goals.

Step 5. Plan for Announcement

Before an announcement of the new direction can be made, many decisions must be made. What structure should the quality organization have? What responsibilities? Who will occupy the key positions in the divisions? What old policies need be scrapped because of the conflict with the new direction? What tactics will be used to achieve quality? How will the program be introduced to all employees? What changes must be made to the enterprise planning cycle to incorporate quality planning? What is required to phase quality planning into the planning cycle?

After announcement, planning for quality follows the general planning steps that were discussed at the beginning of this section. A transition period will be required; but if that is properly defined in Step 5, regular planning for quality should be underway.

◆ 15.5 Introducing Quality

How should a newly adopted policy of striving for quality be introduced to an organization? Opinions differ.

Philip Crosby advocates that it be done in a quick, total emersion baptism. He argues that "The establishment of ZD (Zero Defects) as the performance standard of the company should be done in one day. That way, everyone understands it the same way. Supervisors should explain the program to their people, and do something different in the facility so every one will recognize that it is a 'new attitude' day."[3]

Crosby's cookbook procedure for improving quality has been widely followed. Scores of companies have introduced their commitment to quality to employees with the special day Crosby advocates. Following the scenario presented in his book, they have gathered everyone in a large hall or a park, had speeches from dignitaries (Crosby himself has appeared at many) and company officials, provided refreshments and entertainment, and asked people to sign ZD pledges, all with the intent of making people realize that there has been a change in the organizations' attitudes and practices concerning quality.

---

[3]Philip B. Crosby, *Quality Is Free*, (New York: McGraw-Hill, 1979), p. 137. The Zero Defects concept is discussed in Section 22.1.

What is the result of such an introduction? As far as we know, no objective study has been made. W. Edwards Deming, who is never shy about expressing an opinion, states:

> *A quality program for a community, launched by ceremonies with a speech by the governor, raising of flags, beating of drums, badges, all with heavy applause, is a delusion and a snare.*[4]

We agree with Deming. People might enjoy the day—it's a nice break from work—but it probably has little long-term effect on their performance. Moreover, it can backfire badly if the extravaganza doesn't come off. We were told by one person: "They held our Quality Day in a large hall. There was a big banner behind the speaker's podium with a quality slogan on it, and during the ceremony it fell down. That's what they mean by quality!" A comment from a person in another organization: "When they kicked off the program, they gave us all ball-point pens with our quality slogan printed on them. Within a week mine had broken. That's the commitment to quality around here." Experiences such as this are quite common because, to cut the cost of Quality Day, cheap, poor quality merchandise is used for a memento. (Ponder what this says about commitment!)

Quality professionals soon realize that they are judged more harshly than others. As advocates of quality, they are expected to be paragons, not mere mortals who aim at perfection but sometimes miss. If you want to witness a nervous crowd, observe a group of quality professionals before any public assembly they are conducting. They realize that if 99.9 percent of the program is flawless, one slip will be remembered and widely discussed. That's why many like to use videotapes in their programs; flaws can be edited out. (But then they fret about the projecting equipment!)

A new emphasis on quality needs publicity, and people need motivation. But motivation that is not followed closely with education, training, and appropriate resources is most likely wasted; in fact, it can be counterproductive. This has been the problem with many Zero-Defects Days—after the event people went back to business as usual. The gap between the hoopla and meaningful instruction was too great. But it is almost inevitable that this gap will be large because the motivation reaches everyone at once, while education and training is parceled out slowly because of resource limitations.

What other ways are there to introduce a quality program? Just about anything you can think of probably has been tried. Some organizations publish a raft of policy statements, organization plans, and other official documents and at the same time announce the new direction in their house newsletter. That's their announcement! Some organizations gather their managers, pass the message to them, and instruct the managers to pass it to the troops. A fairly consistent outcome of this method is that what the managers tell the troops differs considerably from

---

[4]W. Edwards Deming, *Out of the Crisis*, (Cambridge, MA: MIT Center for Advanced Engineering Study, 1986), p. 21.

what they were told to say. Some organizations make a general announcement with no great fanfare and then proceed to indoctrinate all employees by sending them in groups to a several days-long class on quality.

But rather than talk generally about introducing quality, it might be best to review a few successful examples.

Motorola

The initial and continuing emphasis at Motorola has been on training each associate (employee) in the essentials of Motorola's approach to quality. Formal sessions are held to introduce each associate to Total Customer Satisfaction (TCS), the tenets of Motorola's quality beliefs. This is followed with education on Six-Sigma Quality,[5] a formal, structured approach to measure quality-oriented efforts, and on a quantified report on how customer satisfaction objectives are being met.

Originally, each associate received at least 40 hours of training in quality annually. But this number has been increased, indicating Motorola's conviction that the value of providing these seminars far exceeds the costs!

National Computer Board (NCB) of Singapore

The NCB is a government agency that employs all computer professionals who work for the various government ministries. It established a Quality Assurance function in the mid-1980s. Misguided by literature in American professional journals, this group followed the old view of quality and attempted to inspect and verify the output of all professionals. Soon realizing that this was an impossible task, it switched to the view that quality is everyone's responsibility. To mark this transition, it hired an American consulting firm to teach the fundamentals of quality and basic quality improvement techniques to all professionals. Through the years, newly hired professionals have been given the same training. An effect of this approach to introducing quality is that TRADENET, which was produced by the NCB staff, was one of two computer programs in the world selected in 1989 for recognition by the Society of Information Management (SIM).

◆ 15.6 Enabling Quality

It is management's job to enable quality. Most of this effort just amounts to "good business practice"; it requires nothing special. To enable quality, management must provide funding, an appropriate organizational structure, delegation of authority and accountability, specific targets, and tracking performance, and must appraise and reward accomplishments. All of these are standard tasks; what is new is that they are directed toward quality.

Management has one additional task, which is not standard: It must create an environment that is favorable to quality. Often this means changing the culture of

---

[5]The Six-Sigma Concept is discussed in Section 20.8 in the context of capability indexes.

the organization. This is the major challenge facing top management; all others are more mechanical.

There is no cookbook for changing a culture, but certain actions can lead in that direction.

A Coalition for Quality

People embarking on a new venture need security to keep from feeling isolated. Knowing that they are supported by others and are part of a team helps them take the initial steps in the new direction. The greater the change, the more they need the comfort of knowing they are not sticking out like a sore thumb.

To make quality the primary goal of the organization, it is necessary to form a strong coalition of people who will espouse this view and actively work toward its attainment. The leader must find disciples who, in turn, will convert others. To learn how to build a coalition of people committed to a common belief, study IBM, Hewlett-Packard, and Namura Securities of Japan, but don't overlook the Marines and the church.

In building a coalition, don't forget the informal organization. The support of a few natural leaders can make a world of difference.

A Supporting Environment

To establish a culture of quality, the work environment must be supportive. For one thing, the signals people receive from the identity, mission, and goals of the enterprise must be consistent; people receiving mixed signals tend to sit on the fence until they understand clearly that quality is the primary goal.

More mechanical aspects of the work environment must also support the quality direction. If workers are to be responsible for their own quality, they will require information that might previously have gone only to management. Improved communication, access to information, understanding the plans, and knowing how the firm is doing—all of these help.

Deming correctly stresses the need to break down barriers. The "us versus them" attitude that prevails in parts of most organizations must be replaced with cross-functional cooperation. Fiefdoms directed more at personal benefit than company goals must be dismantled. First, of course, they must be ferreted out because they are carefully sheltered from upper management's gaze; but all the workers can identify them.

Deming also stresses the need to drive out fear. This advice is extremely important because fear can result in restrictive labor practices, acceptance of atrocious management, overlooking dishonest actions, and a "don't give a damn" mentality. None of these is consistent with a quality focus. Some fear stems from economic concerns; stable employment can help drive this out. Some fear concerns treatment on the job; opening communication channels to higher levels of management can help to ensure fairness.

Adjustment of Management Processes

Management processes must be in line with the quality direction. For example, it is one thing to change the charter of the Quality Department from inspection and control to advise and assist; it is another to change the control habits of all managers. But if quality is to be everybody's responsibility, managers must learn to pass the quality responsibility to those who do the work. This requires that the employee be helped to learn how to accept the control responsibility, and it requires that the manager have trust and confidence in employees. More than that, it means overcoming managers' doubts about the ability of employees to step up to this challenge; it strikes at the heart of Taylorism.

In many organizations, the employee appraisal system also needs a complete overhaul. An important concept in quality is teamwork; traditional appraisal systems are directed at individuals and cannot cope with appraising a team.

Middle management can be a big block to a quality effort, and a special effort is needed to win them over. A basic problem is that middle managers are very successful people. It is quite an achievement to become a middle manager in a large organization; the management triangle gets very narrow as you move toward the top. Middle managers have been successful playing by the rules of the past. But an emphasis on quality changes the rules. Middle managers are adaptable; they can easily learn to play by the new rules. The trouble is, they don't know if the new rules are real and permanent or are just another passing fad like so many they have witnessed during their climb up the ladder. If they join the quality movement and it fades in a year or two, they will be left out on a limb and their careers might be damaged. If they play it safe and only stick a toe in the water, they can bide for time and avoid making a serious mistake.

The only way to overcome middle management caution is to convince them that the quality direction is permanent. The only person who can accomplish this is the chief executive officer.

Management Style

The importance of a participative style of management has already been stressed as a factor in achieving quality. If that style is to prevail, it must be adopted and promoted by top management. If top management believes in worker participation and encourages its practice, then most of the organization will follow the example.

But not all will. There are bound to be pockets—sometimes large pockets—in the organization that will use an authoritative style: People are units of production; if quality is poor, slap on more controls; if people still don't shape up, fire them! Chances are that in these pockets, quality will not be good. There is also a danger that poor products in these areas will have an adverse effect throughout the enterprise.

In addition to setting the management style, top management must monitor the enterprise to determine if their lead is being followed. Employee opinion surveys should contain questions relating to quality and management style. When searching for the cause of poor product quality, management style should be considered as a possible causative factor. Every effort must be made by top management to promote throughout the organization a management style that is conducive to quality.

Education

If one were attempting to identify the single most important "special" quality-promoting activity, education probably would be it. Education about job requirements, how to perform the job, how to communicate with people about the job, and so on—all contribute directly to quality of products. Equally important is education about improving the business processes used to create products.

Managers influence education in several ways:

- ◆ How much is spent on education.
  Education is expensive, mainly because of the time spent "off the job." Managers must decide what portion of the organization's resources will be spent on it. They must resist the temptation to cut funding for education every time business turns down.

- ◆ How much education actually takes place.
  Education is for tomorrow; line managers are measured on what happens today. Faced with difficult targets to meet, managers find it easy to put off education in favor of "getting the product out of the door." Upper managers must monitor to see that workers get the education called for in the plan.

- ◆ How education is perceived by the organization.
  Every manager should consider that an important part of his job is to develop the people who report to him—education of subordinates. Every manager should view himself as a teacher—at least, part time. Education should be perceived as an indispensable part of the management function.

- ◆ How education is delivered.
  A manager should educate subordinates on a one-on-one basis, helping them to perform actual work. This takes time. But once the subordinate learns the work, the time can be regained by delegating authority for the work to the subordinate and giving him the freedom to do it.

Displaying Quality Leadership

Top management sets the tone for quality improvement. For the quality effort to be successful, it must be apparent that top management is *solidly* behind it. Employees are quick to perceive lip service, and there is so much of that about quality—so much advertising hype—that they are especially skeptical about quality improvement efforts.

To get the organization behind quality improvement, top management must:

- Show that they really understand what quality is about and really believe it is vital to the organization. Anything less will spawn an ineffective improvement effort, and it is probably worse than doing nothing because it will turn believers into skeptics. Unfortunately, too many top managers are too busy rearranging the deck chairs to see that the ship is sinking.

- Convince people that the quality improvement effort is meaningful.
  To do this, top management must invest significant portions of their own energy in the quality improvement effort. Lip service to the effort with the idea that others will carry it out will not produce meaningful results. For many companies, quality improvement is a matter of survival, and top management knows this. To instill a sense of urgency in the troops, top management must be actively and visibly involved in making improvements. A videotape won't do.

- Convince people that the quality focus is permanent.
  People must believe that quality improvement is not just this year's fad, soon to be replaced with another spectacular program. People must be made to understand that the emphasis on quality improvement marks a new, permanent change in the organization's direction.

Quality improvement starts with two strikes against it because so many abortive efforts have been made in the past. People have seen too many banners waved, heard too many speeches, and have not seen enough real, sustained action. For quality improvement to be a success, top management must visibly lead the way.

◆ 15.7 Monitoring Progress

As part of its system for controlling quality, an organization should have a system for measuring and tracking quality. The quality control system should provide timely data, make it available to the proper people, provide for levels of control, and all the other features of a good control system. Building a quality measurement and tracking system is another of those activities that can be classified as "special" to the quality program.

Judah Lando observes that there are four generally useful categories of measures:

- Measures that are indicative of outgoing quality. This category would indicate the defect rate in final inspection, measures of customer satisfaction, repair and recall rates, and so on.

- Measures that are sensitive to changes in quality within the time frame of measurement. Examples are control charts, records of production cycle time, task defect rates, and other quality measures within the production process.

- Measures that are meaningful to at least two or three, preferably more, levels of supervision. The cost of quality and unit assessments are examples.

- Measures that can be used for intradepartmental or intraplant comparison. Measures of outgoing quality, the cost of quality, top management assessments, and cycle times are among those that can be used to make cross-unit comparisons.[6]

Top managers must play an important role in setting the tone for the quality measurement and tracking system. They must provide guidelines for the type of data that is collected and the way the data is used.

If you say "data gathering" to most people, they think "accounting department." They think "green eye shades" and "down to the last penny." Much data collected in an organization is used, in part at least, in the financial accounting system; therefore, its accuracy is governed by accounting standards, IRS requirements, and the habits of accountants. Generally, data about quality need be nowhere nearly as precise as accounting data. Whether the cost of quality is 29.3 percent or 29.6 percent of manufacturing cost makes little difference; in fact, if you can justify 29.3 percent, you can probably find some way to justify 25 percent or 35 percent. It makes little difference if the IS "bug" rate is 5.1 per thousand lines of code or 5.3. All you are counting are *discovered* bugs, the true rate might be much higher. The point we are making is that data about quality need not be precise. It is much more important that data be related in a meaningful way to the requirement for the product and that it be collected in a consistent manner. Top managers must influence the data collection system, direct it toward these goals, and guard against the inherent tendency of people to be overly precise.

But more important than what is collected is how the data is used. If data is used to appraise and reward people, then you can be sure that they will find some way to influence the data to their advantage. People are very adept at beating the system. One case we heard about is typical.

A programming group in one company delivers its completed code to an independent test unit. But when the test unit reports a bug, the programming group often refuses to acknowledge it (their reporting system permits this behavior) because they are appraised on the test results. The net effect is that the programming group gets a good appraisal, and a known (but unacknowledged and unrepaired) defect is left in the system. But whose fault is this nonsense?

There is a dilemma regarding data about quality. On the one hand, one wants to reward people who produce quality products, and that argues for using such data for appraisal. But on the other hand, as soon as data is used for appraisal, you can be absolutely certain it will be distorted. Top managers must set the tone for how data on quality is to be used. A reasonable guide is as follows: Data collected

---

[6]Judah L. Lando, "Launching the Corporate Quality Function," *Quality Progress*, November 1985, p. 74.

by the quality measurement and tracking system should be used to judge business processes, not the people. It should be used to understand how well the processes are performing and to help direct process improvement efforts. It should *not* be used in the appraisal process; other means should be found to reward worker performance. For example, all employees can be given a bonus based on profits, which can be increased significantly by a successful quality improvement effort. In addition to providing a tangible reward, a properly structured bonus system can promote teamwork, give profits a lift (which brings the added bonus of increased job security), and give the workers a real stake in the company.

◆ 15.8 IS Role in Managing Quality

The importance of information is slowly but surely coming to management's attention. People gradually are understanding that most organizations are basically information processing factories, with units for physical production grafted on. Their corporate identity might say correctly that they are in, say, the manufacturing business, but most of their people might well be spending their time pushing pieces of paper, handling electronic files, handling telephone calls, attending meetings, or having informal discussions over coffee.

Information is an important part of every process in an enterprise. And every product delivered to a customer, internal or external, is accompanied by an information product of some sort.

Information is integral to the quality movement, too. In the previous section we discussed the need for data to track the quality effort. But data is also needed to discover problems, find their cause, and verify their solution. Without effective quality-related information systems, meaningful quality improvement is not possible.

The quality of any major process of the enterprise depends critically on the quality of the IS applications that support it. For that reason, enterprises should pay particular attention to quality in the IS area.

How IS Is Different

Managing IS offers special challenges because the area is different in many respects from the more traditional areas of marketing, manufacturing, and so on. These are some of the major differences:

- ◆ Information is power, and IS applications redistribute power. It follows that IS gets entangled in the internal politics of every unit it serves.

- ◆ Information is not viewed as a product. People don't know what to make of it or how to think about the quality of information.

- ◆ People have difficulty describing their information requirements. They know what parts they need to assemble a physical product, but they have difficulty saying exactly what information they need for the product and the production process.

- ◆ The ownership of IS applications frequently is unclear. Who owns the automated accounting system? If Accounting claims to be the owner, can they even describe what it is they own?

- ◆ IS systems are subject to very rapid obsolescence. Technology changes rapidly. A bigger problem, however, is the continual demands for change made by some internal customers.

- ◆ Information technology drastically changes customer processes. CADCAM (Computer Aided Design, Computer Aided Manufacturing) systems have made major changes in the design process. Point-of-sales terminals have changed the balance of power from grocery suppliers to grocery chains because it is now the grocery chains that have the most up-to-date market information. The introduction of robots in manufacturing has moved the opportunity for creating defects from the plant floor to the IS Department.

- ◆ Continuing education is essential. The half-life of IS information is at most five years, probably less. There are heavy demands on people's time just to stay current with the IS field.

- ◆ Because IS is relatively new, their processes are not well understood. The distinction between product and process is difficult for some to comprehend because they both consist of information. Still regarded as an art form by many IS professionals, there is a reluctance to standardize methods and procedures.

- ◆ Newness also makes it difficult for top managers to understand IS. Gradually, a new breed of IS managers is emerging who can communicate with other managers, but many still speak the foreign language of technical jargon.

Because IS is quite different from most other departments, both in processes and its strong need for highly qualified professionals, the QA function in IS has tended to grow independent of the general enterprise QA function, which typically had its roots in manufacturing.

IS Role in Quality Improvement

IS has three major roles in a firm's quality improvement effort. First, IS is directly involved with most of the major processes of the firm (sales, production, inventory control, production scheduling, payroll, etc.) because it processes data that is critical to the process. Improving the quality of, say, the production system might well be a matter of IS improving the data flow and data availability for that system.

Second, the quality system *is* an information system consisting of procedures, instructions, documents, and records. Except for very small companies, an organization's quality system is maintained and updated by IS.

The third involvement of IS in a quality effort is optional. The business of IS is to build, document, operate, and maintain systems. Because of this, IS generally is the part of the organization with the most knowledge of process concepts and the most experience in documenting processes. They should be used as a source of information on flowcharting and other documentation techniques.

Recently, a manufacturing company that was applying for ISO certification needed to document all of its production processes. The Quality Manager (an engineer) told one of the authors that he was having great difficulty in finding people who could teach the machine operators how to flowchart. It was suggested that he contact his own internal IS Department for assistance because they did that sort of thing for a living. He had never thought of that.

◆ Exercises and Additional Readings

1. A responsibility usually not assigned to QA is to be a surrogate for the external customer. Discuss the pros and cons of such an assignment.

2. Read Jon Brecka and Laura Rubach, "Corporate Quality Training Facilities," *Quality Progress*, January 1995, pp. 27–30. Summarize the benefits that accrue to Motorola from its corporate training center, Motorola University.

3. Summarize the views on the software quality issue expressed in Chapter 1 of Edward Yourdon, *Decline & Fall of the American Programmer* (Englewood Cliffs, NJ: Yourdon Press, 1993).

4. Read Allan J. Sayle, *Management Audits* (United Kingdom: Allan J. Sayle, Ltd., 1988), Chapter 1.

   (a) List the eight reasons Sayle gives to justify a management audit.

   (b) What type problems does he say are the vast majority?

   (c) What does he list as the six real causes of these problems?

5. Read Robert Wettach, "Function or Focus?—The Old and the New Views of Quality," *Quality Progress*, November 1985, p. 65. Summarize the views of quality management expressed in the article.

6. Read Henry J. Kohoutek and John Hamish Sellers, "From Criticism to Partnership," *Quality Progress*, May 1988, p. 17. Summarize the views of quality management expressed in the article.

7. Discuss the statement: If an organizational process does not impact product quality in some way, it should be eliminated.

8. (a) Read and summarize the section headed "Rehearsal of some of the problems" in W. Edwards Deming, *Out of Crisis*, (Cambridge, MA: MIT Center for Advanced Engineering Study, 1986), pp. 149–155.

   (b) Do you believe the situation is the same today as it was when Deming wrote it? (Support your answer.)

9. Read the following statement and find articles or examples that support or refute the statement:

   A review of the sources of power suggests that Quality Assurance in an organization is in a weak position. Their legitimate power, functional power, and expert power carry little weight. Their coercive power, report power, location power, and resource power are insignificant. To have an effect, QA must rely heavily on its personal power and especially on its ability to build coalitions. It is essential for QA to get those with legitimate power—especially the top executive—behind the quality effort. Otherwise the quality effort will be like whistling into the wind.

10. Read J. M. Juran, "The Quality Trilogy," *Quality Progress*, August 1986, p. 19.

    (a) What is the underlying concept of the quality trilogy? How does the trilogy relate to the concepts of finance?

    (b) At the time the article was written, which parts of the trilogy were not functioning well in American companies?

    (c) What major changes does Juran suggest were needed to improve quality?

11. Discuss your ideas about enabling quality.

12. Contact one or two companies in your area. Describe their quality organization and discuss how it is staffed. Describe their QA activities.

13. Ask the surveyed companies whether they have a quality council.

14. Access the homepages of several large companies. Look for information on their quality units and discuss the role of their Quality Assurance groups.

Quality and People Management

Quality is very much a people issue. In a respect-driven environment, all employees work together in a spirit of fairness, respect, trust and teamwork. The Eastman Way describes a culture founded on these and other key beliefs and principles concerning people. Having this foundation is necessary to reach the level of excellence described in our quality policy and to achieve our vision to be the world's preferred chemical company.

—Eastman Chemical Company[1]

Effective work involves two tasks: planning work and accomplishing it. For most of recorded history, the accepted view was that these tasks should be divided between those who direct the work and those who actually do it. The Pharaoh had his overseers and his slaves; the army had officers and enlisted ranks; offices had managers and clerks; and plants had white- and blue-collar workers. It is only in the twentieth century that this traditional view is being seriously challenged.

---

[1]Weston F. Milliken, "The Eastman Way," *Quality Progress*, October 1996, p. 57.

There is an extensive literature on the management of people, and most of it has implications for quality. In this chapter, we will attempt to present an overview of this topic and discuss some implications for quality.

◆ 16.1 Theories of Human Behavior

Although there is no clear consensus on what motivates people, there are many theories and strong support for the notion that proper motivation contributes greatly to achieving quality. For example, John W. Gardner, a former Secretary of Health, Education and Welfare, and a respected writer and thinker, stated:

> *I come down very hard on the motivational side. . . . If you're not working on giving your employees a sense of identity with your product, you're never going to improve quality.*[2]

Most quality professionals would agree that motivation is strongly linked to quality. There are many theories concerning the link; here are a few.

Scientific Management

For decades, motivational theory in America was dominated by the scientific management views introduced around the turn of the century by Frederick W. Taylor.[3] Taylor concentrated on work, efficiency, and order. He took a mechanistic view, assuming the goals of employees were aligned with organizational goals, that people responded positively to authority, and that they were motivated solely by monetary rewards. Taylor's views seemed appropriate at that time when the workforce included many immigrants and farm workers with low educational levels and, in many cases, a limited grasp of English. Today, these views seem inappropriate to many, but they still hold a powerful grip on management attitudes and actions.

Under Taylorism, quality was based primarily on inspection. The aim was to meet acceptable quality levels; striving for defect-free products was deemed to be too expensive. Control charts and other statistical techniques were used to detect errors and make process adjustments. These tools involved "thinking"; therefore, quality control was a task for managers and professionals, with only the actual inspection activity being performed by workers. Responsibility for quality was assigned to the quality organization; workers rarely were consulted for their ideas on process improvement.

The principle of quality control developed under Taylorism was widely adopted during World War II, and it proved to be better than the alternative at the time,

---

[2]*Quality Review*, Summer 1987.

[3]Frederick W. Taylor, *The Principles of Scientific Management* (New York: Harper's, 1912).

which was no principle. An unfortunate outcome, however, is that old habits die hard; installing more effective quality control concepts sometimes runs into resistance by those with vested interests in the old.

Hierarchy of Needs

In 1954, Abraham Maslow published his well-known hierarchy of worker needs

1. Physiological, stemming from hunger, thirst, sex, and so on.
2. Safety, providing protection against danger, threat, deprivation, and the like.
3. Social, the need for belonging, acceptance, giving and receiving love and friendship.
4. Ego, the need for self-esteem and reputation.
5. Self-fulfillment, the need to realize one's potential, for creativity, continued self-development, and so on.[4]

What need, if any, is filled by producing a quality product? For a convict in a harsh prison, it could be a physiological need—do quality work or no food. For some workers it could be safety—do quality work or see your job migrate to the Far East. But the higher levels of social, ego, and self-fulfillment needs undoubtedly are the motive for many.

A manager might find it useful to view Maslow's hierarchy from another perspective: What need should be appealed to in order to spark workers' interest in doing quality work? The most successful companies see quality as a means of self-esteem or self-fulfillment. But they also attempt to build a strong social bond with employees and provide them with the means required to satisfy their physiological and safety needs.

Management Beliefs and Worker Motivation

In 1960, Douglas McGregor published his Theory X and Theory Y sets of management beliefs and their influence on managerial behavior.[5] According to McGregor, a Theory X manager assumes people are lazy, dislike work, and avoid it. People do not want responsibility; therefore, they must be made to work by use of a carrot or a stick. In contrast, a Theory Y manager assumes people are intelligent, creative, and want to work. They are naturally motivated and want to achieve, and they gain satisfaction from doing a job well.

McGregor also called attention to the self-fulfilling prophecy: People tend to do what is expected of them. Theory X managers expect people to dislike work and be lazy, treat them accordingly, and then discover that their expectations are real-

---

[4]Abraham H. Maslow, *Motivation and Personality* (New York: Harper & Row, 1954).

[5]Douglas McGregor, *The Human Side of Enterprise* (New York: McGraw-Hill, 1960).

ized. On the other hand, Theory Y managers treat people as if they are creative and achieving, and then discover that they are.

A Theory X style of management is not suited to an organization that is attempting to achieve quality by prevention and process improvement as contrasted with placing a heavy reliance on quality control. Prevention of errors and process improvement require a Theory Y view of people and the ability to align the personal goals of workers with the organizational goals.

Behaviorism

Inspired by Pavlov's work on dogs, B. F. Skinner studied factors in the environment that contribute to human behavior.[6] His emphasis was on *operant behavior*, that is, behavior that is voluntary, learned, and a function of its consequences.

One learns to make certain responses because of the consequences those responses will bring about. In a work environment, these consequences can be influenced by managers through adjustment of the reinforcement factors. Managers may give a positive reinforcement (give an "attaboy" for a job well done) or a negative reinforcement (public rebuke). Managers can also intervene by punishing you (not giving you a raise) or do nothing in the hopes that an unwanted response will eventually disappear. In Skinner's view, the most effective long-range strategy is positive reinforcement.

Today, few would question that strong links exist among learning, reward, and quality. The link is complex and difficult to understand, but managers must attempt to do so.

Expectancy Theory

The *expectancy theory* formulated by V. H. Vroom provides a link between behavior and reward.[7] According to Vroom, people are motivated to achieve a goal. The course of action taken by people in achieving a goal depends on:

1. Their assessment of the perceived outcome or consequences of an action
2. The worth of that outcome to them
3. Their expectation of their ability to perform at a desired level

In other words: What will happen if I do it? Is that outcome worth the effort? Can I do it?

As it applies to quality, expectancy theory suggests that a manager should ponder: Do I provide workers with processes that are capable of producing quality products? Do I share the rewards of improved quality with them? Do I provide what is necessary (tangible and intangible) for them to do the job properly?

---

[6]B. F. Skinner, *Beyond Freedom and Dignity* (New York: Alfred Knopf, 1971).

[7]Victor H. Vroom, *Work and Motivation* (New York: John Wiley, 1964).

Eastern Cultures

The theories of human behavior presented to this point were developed in Western cultures. But many of the leading providers of quality products are located in the East: the quality of the Toyota and other Japanese cars forced Detroit to push for quality; Singapore Airlines consistently is ranked at or near the top in terms of airline service; some Indian software organizations are world-class in terms of quality products. What can be learned from Eastern cultures about human behavior as it relates to quality?

Ishikawa has given us his assessment of Japanese thinking: "If you delegate authority freely your subordinates will use their abilities to the fullest extent and grow in their jobs."[8] "The fundamental principle of successful management is to allow subordinates to make full use of their ability. . . . Management based on humanity is a system of management that lets the unlimited potential of human beings blossom. . . . The Swedish people have observed the way we handle management. They termed it 'industrial democracy.' That says it all."[9]

Indeed it does.

Implications for Quality

There are lessons to be learned from all these management theories. Taylor called attention to the work process. Maslow and Vroom concentrated on worker motivation. McGregor pointed out the importance of management's assumptions about workers. And Ishikawa discusses the power given to workers.

All of these theories rest on assumptions about human behavior. Every manager makes such assumptions and bases management actions on them. Frequently, however, a manager does not examine his assumptions carefully; they are just "inherited," in much the same way that most people "inherit" a religious belief.

Every manager should contemplate these questions: What do *I* believe motivates *our* people? Fundamentally, are they lazy? achieving? Have we ever asked for their opinion? How can these motivating factors be used to improve quality?

◆ 16.2 Managing People

People management is a process. To achieve quality, people management should be studied as is any other process; but too often this is not done. People management is a good example of a service process for which there often is more concentration on the activity and product than on the process.

---

[8]Kaoru Ishikawa, translated by David J. Lu, What Is Total Quality Control (Englewood Cliffs, NJ: Prentice-Hall, 1985), p. 132.

[9]Ibid., p. 112.

Management of any resource requires a means of determining the requirements for the resource, acquiring the resource, maintaining stewardship of the resource while you employ it, and disposing of the resource. As it applies to people management, this means there must be effective methods and procedures to

- Structure jobs
- Hire and assign employees
- Train, educate, and grow employees
- Motivate employees
- Evaluate employee performance
- Reward performance
- Retire employees

While all these processes are key to a well-run business, they cannot remain static. They must be updated continually to meet the needs of industry, competitive pressures, changing worker requirements, and changing government regulations. Restructuring the business has become a mania for some businesses in their attempt to remain competitive. For example, Motorola has reorganized continually in recent times to keep pace with the changes in their product mix and the challenges presented by the marketplace. For them, restructuring has been almost an annual event. The same was true of IBM during its rapid growth in the 1960s and 1970s.

The people management process must be intertwined with the work management process because both aim at the same objective—making work productive. The two processes, however, deal with different aspects of productive work. The work management process deals with the work to be done, whereas the people management process deals with those who do it. The two processes also have different emphases. The focus of the work management is on the production line. Is the work process operating properly? Are input materials timely and do they meet requirements? Is the line producing quality products on time and within budget? Are there ways that the work process can be improved to make it more efficient and to improve the quality of its output? The focus on the people management process is on the people who operate the process. Do they have well-defined jobs? Are employee abilities and work assignments well matched? Do people have proper information, resources, and tools to do the job? Are the workloads appropriate? Is the employee evaluation and reward system appropriate? Are workers motivated to be achieving?

We are dwelling on the distinction between work management and people management to emphasize that these are two different, but related, activities. Many problems in the quality area result from the failure to make this distinction. For example, it is almost "standard practice" in some organizations to blame employees for poor products when, in fact, the failure lies in an inappropriate work process. Another common problem is to judge employees by whether work is completed on time, when the failure might be a poor work plan. Of course, people must be evaluated, but care must be taken to build a people management system that does not penalize workers for failures of the work process.

When quality problems occur, the question should *always* be "What is to blame?" not "Who is to blame?"

◆ 16.3 Structuring Jobs

Process management concerns procedures, instructions, and the machines and equipment required for an effective production process. Job structure concerns the tasks that people will perform in operating a production process. Thus, job structuring is the link between process management and people management.

People are a resource, but they are a unique resource in that they react to the process, and their reaction influences their effectiveness. Therefore, jobs must be structured so as to motivate workers to be achieving and produce quality products. Good procedures are necessary but are not sufficient to ensure motivation. Leadership, communications, reward—all play a role. Just what *does* motivate people to be achieving is a controversial topic. But "people" includes *you*—what motivates you to be achieving? What motivates you to produce quality products? Do you think other people are much different?

It is difficult to quantify the link between the structure of jobs and the quality of products produced. But it seems a safe assumption that people who like their jobs and find them interesting are more likely to produce better products. Some ways to make jobs more satisfying are to provide task variety and to increase job content and job authority.

Task Variety

What can be duller than a bland job calling for the mechanical repetition of some simple task? One way to motivate people and prevent boredom is to introduce more variety into the working process. This can be done by building task variety into the job or by rotating workers from task to task.

One way to achieve task variety is to give each worker a whole job, not just some small part of it. For example, some insurance companies structure work so that each individual is to perform a small task on a large number of policies—simple, repetitive tasks that make boring jobs. Other companies structure work so that each individual does all the necessary tasks for a small set of policies—whole jobs that are more interesting and in which workers can take pride.

Adding variety to jobs requires workers to make decisions about the order in which tasks will be performed and the time to be allocated to each task. In other words, workers must be involved in the management of work as well as in working. This change adds further variety to the job. More fundamentally, it blurs the traditional line between the tasks of managers and the tasks of workers; it also generates the need for a different work structure, a different distribution of power, different rewards, and more worker training.

Job Content

Traditionally, jobs were structured into simple, repetitive tasks; workers worked and managers managed their work efforts. But the old *command style* separating management from doing does not work well in the new business climate that must cope with much more complex products, an increased demand for quality, greater competition, and a better educated workforce. The challenge today is to structure jobs so that they tap the full potential of workers and bring them job satisfaction. Today's more *participative style* calls for workers to be structured around small work teams. Members of these teams have a clearer knowledge of the organization's goals and objectives, broader-based jobs, and more power and ability to cooperate and work with one another than did workers under the command style of management. They are multiskilled, engage in continual learning, and take pride in the team's accomplishments.

Job Authority

To be effective, workers require certain authority or power. *Power* is the force others perceive you to have that gives you the capacity to influence them. Power depends on perceptions that people have of one another and the situation they are sharing. Three key power tools in any organization are information, support, and resources. The sources of power are:

- ◆ Authority: Power of position, power based on fear, power based on reward
- ◆ Process power: Power of the function being performed, position in the work flow, power over scarce resources
- ◆ People power: Expert power, power from an unofficial coalition of people, personal power from appearance, ability to persuade, or other personality features

The general trend since World War II has been to give workers increased authority. We will have more to say about job authority in Section 16.7.

◆ 16.4 Employee Recruitment

People are one of the most important resources for organizations, often costing between 40 percent and 60 percent of sales. And it can be argued that no personnel process is more important than the employee selection process—if you hire the wrong people, you may never be able to recover. As Drucker states, "ability to perform is the foundation of willingness to work,"[10] and ability depends very much on what the worker brings to the job.

---

[10]Peter Drucker, *Practice of Management* (New York: Harper & Row), p. 300.

The quality literature has very little to say about employee recruitment beyond such advice as "pick the best candidate for the job." Or "select based on what the organization needs to serve its customer." For practical advice from *Quality Progress*, one must go back to the August 1985 issue and an article by John A. Berger, then manager of human resources of the Chicago office of W. A. Golomski & Associates.[11] Many of our comments were gleaned from that article.

The first step in employee selection is to develop a *job description* describing the task to be performed and the required qualifications: skills, experience, education, and personal characteristics. Don't overstate requirements because it might result in your hiring the wrong person. To develop the job description, you must analyze what causes people to succeed or to fail in the job. In addition to its use in recruitment, the job description can be used later in coaching and counseling the new hire.

For each candidate, you should build a specification sheet listing the candidate's abilities, skills, personal characteristics, qualifications, and experience. Some of the required information will come from references and other documents supplied by the candidate, and some from a job interview. Be careful in judging references because there might be bias either for or against the candidate.

In a job interview, practice active listening—treat the interview as the important activity it is—don't let your mind wander. Get past the candidate's "social mask" to discover the real person. In addition to hearing *what* is said, hear *how* it is said. And remember that nonverbal communications account for about two-thirds of the communication message and the actual words only about a third. Body language and eye movement can speak volumes.

For an important job, the candidate should be interviewed by several people—three is a good number because it avoids "ties." All interviewers should be in substantial agreement before the candidate is hired. For a more routine job, a simple majority will do, with the provision that dissenting interviewers can escalate the decision to the next level of management if they feel strongly that an error is being made.

An old rule in hiring was that good employees can be counted on to recommend good job candidates; the selection process was easy—just get your best workers to bring in their friends. Unfortunately, this rule can also result in unintentional discrimination because people who are friends tend to belong to the same ethnic and economic groups. Whatever selection procedure you design, be certain that it complies with all the laws regarding employment. If in doubt, consult a lawyer or an expert in labor relations—better to be safe than sorry.

◆ 16.5 Quality Training

In 1986, the United States spent $6 billion annually on training and development; this is inadequate to keep America competitive.[12]

A serious quality effort in an organization requires a large, effective effort to educate and train people in quality concepts and practices. An organization's train-

---

[11]John A. Berger, "Human Resources Tools for Quality Improvement," *Quality Progress*, August 1985, p. 21.

[12]*Business Week*, September 29, 1986, p. 70.

ing process, therefore, is a critical element in quality improvement. What can be done to improve the training process? An example worth emulating is provided by the Center for Quality Education at the Wright-Patterson Air Force Base in Ohio.

The Center was established in 1990 to provide TQM training to the 13,000 employees of the Air Force Logistics Command (AFLC). The 20 instructors had little or no experience in training and few had experience with TQM concepts. It was decided by center management that the way for the instructors to learn TQM was to apply the concepts to their own training processes.

To accomplish this, management empowered the instructors through self-directed work teams. The teams were given process ownership and control over their teaching schedules, and they started on their improvement effort.

Their first effort was to benchmark their performance against three educational institutions in the Dayton area by reviewing student critiques. This effort provided them with data to plot control charts of customer satisfaction, which they used to discover and correct problems. Another outcome of the effort was the realization that they really didn't know who their customer was. After some study, they decided that their primary customers were the organizations of AFLC and their secondary customers were the students in their classes.

Their next step was to use quality function deployment to translate their customers' needs into behaviors, the behaviors into objectives, and the objectives into course content. They found a mismatch of about 20%, forcing an adjustment in course content.

Next, they transferred responsibility for quality from QA to process owners. The process owners then undertook to make continual process improvement and established measures to monitor performance.

AFLC has changed the military bureaucracy and is now being benchmarked by other training schools in the federal government. Many training schools in the private sector should be doing the same thing.[13]

◆ 16.6 Motivating Workers

When you are motivated to perform a task, don't you do a better job? produce a better product? Worker motivation and product quality go hand-in-hand. But there is no simple prescription for "turning people on"; job content, job control, the workplace, reward—all have an impact on product quality. And what works in one country might not in another. However, one factor that is likely to be effective with today's workers is a *people-oriented management style*.

---

[13]Gerard R. Tuttle, "Cascading Quality Through the Training Process," *Quality Progress*, April 1993, p. 75. Further discussion of this example is given in Section 16.7.

With a people-oriented management style, people are respected and valued. They are encouraged to participate in the planning of a job as well as its execution. This style is based on the assumption that people want to be achieving, they want to do a job well; and the purpose of the management system is to provide them with an opportunity to contribute to organizational goals while simultaneously pursuing their individual goals.

These are but a few ideas for motivating workers.

- ◆ *Control Work*
  Control work, not workers.

- ◆ *Explain the Purpose*
  How many workers understand how their actions fit into the larger picture? Explaining "why" something is to be done in addition to "what" and "how" can be a strong motivating force.

- ◆ *Job Design*
  Don't treat people like robots, endlessly performing some simple, repetitive task. Give people the whole job, some task variety.

- ◆ *Two-way Communication*
  Too often, communication is only from management to workers. Suggestion programs, executive interviews, management by walking around, and other feedback mechanisms allow workers to share their ideas with management.

- ◆ *Career Development*
  Workers are more achieving if they feel they are growing in their jobs and can see their careers advancing. Attention to career development can help workers to be more achieving.

- ◆ *Stable Employment*
  Job security and stable employment are motivating factors. Moreover, firms providing these also take a long-term view and invest in employee education and career development—added benefits to employees.

You should also reward the behavior you want. We will say more about rewarding people in Section 16.8.

◆ 16.7 Self-Directed Work Teams

The Wright-Patterson team described in Section 16.5 is an example of a *self-directed work team* (SDWT).[14] This is a highly trained group of employees who are fully responsible for producing a set of work products. The group usually consists of from 6 to 18 people who work together as a team, not "for" someone. Such

---

[14]The reference for this section is Jack D. Orsburn, Linda Moran, Ed Musselwhite, and John H. Zenger, *Self-Directed Work Teams* (Homewood, IL: Business One Irwin, 1990), Chapter 1.

teams have better access to information, greater decision-making authority, a wider range of cross-functional skills within the team, and more resources than is traditionally assigned to workers. Transforming traditional work groups into a fully committed, fully trained work group requires a drastic change in management and worker attitudes and skills, but the benefits are great: Most fully trained, fully committed team have 20 to 40 percent higher productivity after 18 months, and exceptional benefits range as high as 250 percent. Companies that have formed such teams include Xerox, General Motors, Federal Express, Aid Association for Lutherans, and Shenandoah Life.

Introduction of Work Teams

The decision to implement the SDWT concept requires a major change in an organization—changes in the structure, function, and responsibilities, the distribution of power, and the reward system. Teams are given the resources and authority to perform many activities that previously were the responsibility of management. This requires them to have the information, education, and training to manage work and work processes in addition to their traditional task of operating work processes. Instead of the traditional practice of rewarding individual accomplishment, workers must adjust to the fact that recognition and reward will be based on team performance.

The role of managers, too, is drastically altered. In place of directing and controlling work through controlling workers, first-level supervisors must learn to relax their grip and function at a distance. As work teams assume responsibility for their processes, much of the old bureaucracy can be eliminated and layers of the old management chain trimmed.

Fundamental changes such as these cannot be accomplished easily. Both workers and managers will be apprehensive about the direct impact on their lives. Management resistance to work teams can be lessened by pointing out the benefits of work teams to them. Among these are the opportunity it offers to act more as entrepreneurs than administrators, focus more on tomorrow than on today, be concerned more with strategy than operations, focus more on customers and less on workers, and manage upwards more than downwards. As these benefits become translated into profits, managers' jobs should be more, not less, secure.

It takes much time and effort to design and implement new processes and a cultural environment that encourages teamwork. None of this can be accomplished without first building a trust that in the transformation all employees will be treated fairly. To accomplish such a massive change, the top manager must be a leader who understands the enormity of the change to be made and has the trust and support of the employees.

Foundations for Work Teams

The installation of SDWTs requires a champion among upper management who is committed and has the respect of the organization. The champion must be willing to risk making a complex, disruptive change in order to improve quality and productivity. The champion also must ensure that resources will be available over the several years it will take for the SDWT concept to mature and show benefits.

Managers in general must understand that SDWTs require a drastic change in management style. In place of controlling workers, their task will be to encourage them to use their initiative. They will spend their time listening, advising, compromising, and building consensus, trust, and esprit de corp.

Work Teams and Power

To participate in managing their efforts, work teams must have power, which they derive from the authority granted to them, the control they exercise over their work processes, and their enhanced personal skills. Most workers welcome participation and the added power it gives them. Managers, however, sometimes see work teams as an invasion of their territory and a usurpation of their power. Trade unions, too, might dimly view work teams as a management device for destroying worker solidarity, and their own power in the bargain. Even some workers might resist work teams, preferring to do as told rather than assuming added responsibility.

Benefits of Work Teams

The concept of work teams changes the job of workers from that of "do as you are told" to that of running a small business. This change promotes employee commitment and ownership. Teams take increased pride in the quality of their products and in the efficiency and productivity of their processes.

SDWTs offer workers greater task variety than they had before. They learn new skills and generate real problem-solving abilities. And they have more latitude to experiment and use these abilities to solve production problems and make process improvements. Because teams have the skills and the information and are highly motivated, they are able to respond quickly to changing conditions in the company and in the marketplace—which translates into increased job security.

Commitment and ownership, increased pride in their products, new skills, and problem-solving abilities—all these have a beneficial impact on quality. Teams also eliminate many of the "turf" issues at the local level that can inhibit quality. And they improve the interface between technical and administrative functions because teams are responsible for both.

SDWTs help to improve quality in every part of the organization. It becomes a matter of professional pride to seek opportunities for quality improvement and to act on them. It is interesting to note that of the eight companies cited by Orsburn, Moran, Musselwhite, and Zenger as having launched and nurtured self-directed work teams, three are Baldrige Award winners (Xerox, General Motors, and Federal Express).[15]

---

[15]Ibid., p. 16.

Strategic Issues

Several strategic issues must be handled correctly if SDWTs are to be successful. First, there must be a consensus on the goals to be achieved and how these goals will be aligned with personal interests. If the workers are represented by a union, it is essential that the union be part of this consensus.

Second, there most likely will be a need to adjust the organizational structure to be in line with the SDWT concept. Generally, this will result in a flatter structure with fewer managers.

Third, the organization's performance measurement and reward systems must be aligned with the SDWT concept.

Operational Issues

Where teams have been successful, managers have been closely involved and have learned to use teams as a resource for accomplishing their business objectives. To do this, they have had to gain a better understanding of how the processes under their management support business goals and the roles of the people involved with those processes. They have learned to focus on the important processes rather than take a traditional, narrow departmental view. And they have learned that teams need a relatively large responsibility to make real quality and productivity improvements possible.

While the concept of teamwork has generally been honored, many organizations have not been practicing it in a structured professional way. Management had talked teamwork, but the cultural environment and employee appraisal systems did not encourage it. Nor had workers been provided with the skills and power needed to make teamwork work. Successful teams were provided training in interpersonal and technical skills, such as team building, process analysis, and problem solving. And they received help and assistance in learning to apply these new skills.

Role of Quality Assurance

Product quality is an important goal for SDWTs; this presents the Quality Assurance organization with a real opportunity to be a major facilitator of change. QA can provide education on the concepts and techniques of quality, processes, and process improvement. They can also be a resource for the team to scan the outside environment and introduce new concepts. QA should be viewed by the SDWTs as their consultant on quality issues.

◆ 16.8 Rewarding Employees

Rewarding employees is a very broad topic, and we will attempt only to touch on it here. By *reward* we mean not just monetary compensation, but also the pride, satisfaction, and other general benefits that employees derive from their work efforts. Reward relates to matters such as job satisfaction, pride and self-esteem, plea-sure, security, freedom from fear, and financial well-being, or any other benefit that employees value and desire.

For our discussion, it will be convenient to view rewards as comprised of two types: job-related rewards and general rewards. By *job-related rewards* we mean those that are enjoyed primarily on the job. All others are *general rewards* that can be enjoyed on or off the job.

The reward system of an organization is an important factor in spurring and guiding worker performance. It is also a very complex system that is shaped by the organization's basic beliefs and is empowered in the organization's strategy, structure, policies, and practices. A constant challenge to top management is to align the reward system with requirements of the marketplace and the objectives and goals of the organization, including those for quality.

Job-Related Rewards

Job-related rewards are directly related to work, working, and the workplace. They come in the form of safety and comfort on the job, job pride and satisfaction, in-creased skill and worth, job security and freedom from fear, and similar elements that bring pride and satisfaction.

Rewards are generated by providing employees with task variety, education and training to improve their skills, and a safe, pleasant work environment. A more major reward, however, is for employees to have the power to control elements of work management: the scheduling of work activities, assignment of duties and responsibilities, and tracking of actual progress against schedule—even the redesign of the work process itself.

General Rewards

The general reward that receives most attention is employee compensation. The guiding principle for this is perceived equity: "A fair day's pay for a fair day's work" is viewed by most people as just. Workers expect top management to be paid more than line workers, but they also expect the differences to be "reasonable." A per-ception by workers that salaries are equitable may not be a strong motivating fac-tor, but a perception of inequity is a strong demotivating one.

Related to compensation are other rewards that have monitory value. Examples are job security, health insurance, wellness programs, scholarship programs for em-ployees' children, and similar benefits.

A strong motivating factor is the perception that one is a member of a winning team—an elite corps. The feeling is that "we are the best," and the perception is that others agree. The foundation for such a perception is the ability to deliver su-perior products and services, and it is constructed through the culture, practices, and reward system of the organization.

To build a strong social bond and a sense of belonging to a team, organizations establish employee clubs, hold family dinners or beer parties, and arrange for top managers to mix with and meet employees. Attention is also paid to career development, with easy access and support for education and career management for young "fast track" managers.

Another strong motivating factor is praise and recognition. This can be in the form of substantial financial awards or promotion for significant accomplishments. Or in the form of recognition and thanks at a staff meeting or in the internal news publications. It can also come in the form of trophies, wall plaques, desk ornaments, and other trinkets. A problem with awards is that what "turns on" some employees might well "turn off" others—what pleases a marketing representative might cause an information systems person to wonder about the sanity and sincerity of management.

Reward Schemes

In an attempt to improve quality and productivity, organizations are experimenting with various reward schemes. Some examples are these:

- Developing people by linking pay to acquired skills and knowledge
- Offering group incentive and award schemes in place of individual awards
- Providing resources for improvement by funding quality circles and proposals by individuals
- Encouraging innovation by providing time and resources for developing new ideas
- Giving sabbatical leaves, long a practice in the academic community, which might be an idea whose time has come for the business community.

Employee Retirement

New employees who enter an organization directly from high school or college have very little interest in an organization's retirement policy. But as the years go by, questions of job security and the retirement policy become important. Moreover, the way an organization treats people who retire after a long term of employment is a good indicator of their general view of people.

There is considerable variability among organizations with regards to their retirement benefits. Display 16.1 lists the benefits provided by IBM.

Rewards and Quality

It seems intuitively obvious that there is a link between employee rewards and product quality, but that link is not easily quantified. One can observe that companies with a deserved reputation for quality, for example, Baldrige Award winners, generally take very good care of their employees. And one can think of examples of poorly rewarded employees whose only concern is to do what is nec-

DISPLAY 16.1 ◆ IBM Retirement Benefits

IBM Adoption Assistance Plan
IBM Employee Assistance Program (professional counseling services)
IBM Group Life Insurance
IBM Medical and Dental Plans
IBM Major Medical Plan
IBM Surgical Plan
IBM Retirement Education Assistance Plan
IBM Retirement Plan (pension plan)
Child Care Referral Service
Company publications
Credit Union
Elder Care Referral Service
Employee Sales Program
Fund for Community Service
Home Mortgage Availability Option
IBM Clubs
IBM Money Market Account
Matching Grants Program
Quarter Century Club if a member prior to retirement
Speak Up Program
Suggestion Plan
Thomas J. Watson Memorial Scholarship Program

essary. So we leave it to you, the reader, to judge. If you worked for an organization that valued employees and provided attractive job-related and general rewards, wouldn't you respond by doing your best to produce quality products? Don't you think others would react in the same way?

◆ Exercises and Additional Readings

1. A document circulated on an electronic bulletin board of a large organization contained the comment: "It is a fact that some people will hesitate to report quality data accurately when they FEAR how that data will be used. . . . It is that perception (of fear) that has found its way into the minds of some (of our) employees." Discuss how electronic communication has changed the manager's task of dealing with issues that impact quality. As a manager, how would you view this change? How would you attempt to cope with it?

2. Ishikawa expresses his views as to why people work in his book, *What Is Total Quality Control* (pp. 26–28, bottom p. 65). Do you agree with him?

3. Summarize W. Edwards Deming's views on fear expressed in *Out of the Crisis* (Cambridge, MA: MIT Center for Advanced Engineering Study, 1986).

4. Read Lee Branst and Agnes Dubberly, "Labor/Management Participation: The NUMMI Experience," *Quality Progress*, April 1988, p. 30.

    (a) Summarize the employee recruitment process at NUMMI.

    (b) Summarize the "andon" system and what it says about management's beliefs.

5. List several possible reasons for the slow acceptance of self-directed work teams. For each of your reasons, suggest a possible remedy.

6. Read and summarize Thomas A. McLaughlin, "Six Keys to Quality," *Quality Progress*, November 1985, p. 77. How does this article relate to the material in this chapter?

7. Read and summarize Karen Bemowski, "What Makes American Teams Tick?" *Quality Progress*, January 1995, pp. 39–43.

8. Read and summarize Chapter 1 of Orsburn, Moran, Musselwhite, and Zenger, *Self-Directed Work Teams* (Homewood, IL: Business One Irwin, 1990).

9. Read Ronald D. Snee, "Listening to the Voice of the Employees," *Quality Progress*, January 1995, pp. 91–95. For each of the five subsections of the article (e.g., An Improvement Tool), write a sentence to summarize the author's message.

10. You may have had experiences being a player on a soccer team or on a Little-League baseball team. Describe the coach's approach to managing the team. Did he practice some of the principles we discuss in this chapter? Where did he fall short? Did he have another successful principle?

11. Good colleges need good students. Describe your experience with the college recruitment process at your institution. Is it successful?

12. Locate information on the difference between CEO compensation and worker salaries; between university administrators and university professors. Interpret and comment on the information.

13. In some of your college courses, you will be assigned to teams. Describe your experience and comment on why teams in a college course might work differently from those in the workplace. How could your instructor have improved the work processes of a team?

14. Survey several companies in your area and ask them about their employee training programs. Ask them about their reward structure and about their work teams.

15. Read John A. Young (CEO of Hewlett-Packard Co.), "Teamwork Is More Easily Praised Than Practiced," in *Quality Progress*, August 1985, p. 30. What factors led to successful teams at HP? What does Young say are the five prerequisites for organizationwide teamwork?

16. Read and discuss the major message of Peter R. Scholtes, *The Team Handbook*, (Madison, WI: Joiner Associates, 1988).

17. Read and discuss John Guaspari, "The Role of Human Resources in 'Selling' Quality Improvement to Employees," *Management Review*, March 1987, pp. 20–24. What should the human resource function do in support of quality?

18. Read and discuss John E. Rehfeld, "What Working for a Japanese Company Taught Me," *Harvard Business Review* (November–December 1990), pp. 167–176. Comment on his 10 specific management techniques that can improve any company's performance. Comment on some of the major differences between U.S. and Japanese management strategies.

19. Do peer reviews get more out of employees than the old merit system? What are the possible benefits and drawbacks of tying raises to performance reviews? What do the quality gurus, such as Deming, have to say about this issue? What is the current practice at most companies? Discuss.

20. Reflect on some of your previous job experiences. What was your strongest motivation for doing a good job? List some attributes of a job that would motivate *you* to be achieving.

21. Reflect on some of your previous job experiences. Comment on the way your job was structured. Was there a documented procedure that you were to follow? Comment on possible ways of improving the job structure.

PART IV

◆ ◆ ◆

Stabilizing Quality

A basic strategy for achieving quality is: stabilize, improve, innovate. This can be described as "crawl, walk, run." In Part IV, the focus is on the first stage—stabilizing the quality system so that it produces uniform products.

Chapter 17 discusses various tools and techniques for stabilizing a process to make its output more consistent. An early effort in process stabilization is to document a process. Tools are discussed for documenting work structure, work flow, and work management. The introduction of standards for products and processes represents another useful stabilization tool.

Quality control—checking to see that products meet their requirements—is a method of ensuring that customers do not receive faulty products. Chapter 17 discusses quality control both as a technical system and as a social system. Also discussed are the levels of control from self-control of products produced by each employee, to team control, to control as a separate step in the production process.

To know whether or not a process is satisfactory or to make process improvements, you must know how it is performing. Chapter 17 concludes with a discussion of several techniques for process evaluation.

Decisions about quality must be based on data. Quality cannot be assessed nor improved without having access to the relevant data. Chapters 18 through 20 discuss various aspects of data collection and data analysis. Chapter 18 reviews data and their importance for quality. It examines various ways of using data, and it discusses the collection of data and their classification into meaningful groups. It addresses some of the problems that arise with data, such as data accuracy, and incorrect and useless data.

Chapter 19 reviews basic principles of statistical analysis, including the graphical display and the numerical summary of data. It illustrates how to organize defect data in the form of Pareto charts, and it shows how to display measurement data through time-sequence plots and histograms. It reviews summary statistics, such as the average as a measure of the center, and the range and standard deviation as measures of variability. Chapter 19 discusses scatter plots for displaying the association among two variables and the correlation coefficient as a numerical measure of the association. The normal distribution, probably the most important model for variability, is reviewed. Statistical inference, where one uses the results of a random sample to make assessments about the whole population from which the sample was drawn, is introduced in this chapter.

Chapter 20 introduces statistical techniques that are important for stabilizing and improving products and processes. It includes an introduction to acceptance sampling. There one uses the information from a small sample to make an assessment of the quality of the much larger lot from which the sample was taken.

Chapter 20 includes a discussion of statistical process control and control charts for monitoring the stability of processes, and capability indexes for assessing the capability of processes. Control charts are useful for checking whether a process is stable over time. One takes small samples from the process at consecutive time periods, obtains the relevant measurements, and displays the summary information from the samples in the form of time-sequence charts. Control limits are attached to these charts; these limits help us assess whether a certain sample is consistent with what can be expected from a stable, unchanged process.

Monitoring processes through control charts is important, and it can lead to much useful information. However, even more can be learned by actively changing factors and observing how the process reacts to changes that are introduced deliberately. In a monitoring situation one does not exert control over the factors; therefore, one never really knows whether the observed changes in the output are due to one particular factor that happened to change, or whether they are due to some other factors that happened to change at the same time. Changing the factors in a deliberate, planned fashion and observing the resulting effect give a more direct assessment of the causal relationship. Chapter 20 gives an introduction to the statistical design of experiments. This is an important area; one must understand how to carry out experiments in the best possible way.

Case 5: The Pancake Dilemma in the Appendix presents an example of a typical quality problem. The discussion questions take you through the steps that arise in the analysis of the problem.

Chapter 17

Stabilizing the Quality System

◆ 17.1 Introduction

The three stages of successful quality management are stabilization, improvement, and innovation. In this chapter, we discuss tools and techniques that can be used to stabilize a process. It should be noted, however, that many of these tools and techniques can also be employed for improvement and innovation, topics we discuss in Part V of this book.

Process stabilization and product control are closely related topics. In Chapter 12 we discussed testing and quality control with the view that the data from these activities can be used to prevent faulty products from being shipped to customers. However, the same data can be employed to stabilize the quality system and make it less error-prone. Conversely, the techniques for stabilizing the quality system help prevent the production of nonconforming products. Thus the material in this chapter is closely related to that in Chapter 12, and our division of the material is somewhat arbitrary.

The first step in stabilizing a quality system is to designate a process owner who is responsible for stabilizing and improving the process. The discussion in this chapter assumes that this has been done.[1]

Stabilizing techniques center on controlling product quality and standardizing the work process so as to reduce its variation. Examples of stabilization techniques are given in Display 17.1.

◆ 17.2 Stabilizing Through Process Documentation

An amazing number of processes were never designed—they just grew. An early step in most stabilization efforts is to document the process and the methods used to accomplish work. Documentation makes requirements and responsibilities more explicit, more uniform, and more repeatable. And it provides the necessary foundation for process analysis and improvement. The process owner should have responsibility for documenting a process, but the actual documentation should be done by those who best understand the process.

The ISO 9000 requirement for documenting a quality system was discussed in Chapter 13. Although the ISO standard is designed primarily for manufacturing processes, the basic concepts can be applied to all processes. But we must use common sense. For example, we wouldn't worry about calibrating the test equipment if we were documenting an office process; on the other hand, we would make certain that the process for controlling the quality of office products is producing valid measurements.

In addition to the basic ISO 9000 series, other ISO standards can assist in documenting processes, including

- ◆ ISO 9000-3, which applies to software.
- ◆ ISO 9000-4, which applies to program management and is suitable for products such as transportation, electricity, telecommunications, and information services.
- ◆ ISO 9004-2, which applies to services and such matters as customer interaction and customer assessment.

◆ 17.3 Work Documentation Tools

Many tools are available to help document a work process. In this section we review several of the most commonly used tools.

---

[1]Process ownership was introduced in Section 8.2.

DISPLAY 17.1 ◆ Some Process-Stabilizing Techniques

◆ Clarify process ownership.

◆ Document the process.

◆ Install policies and standards. Install standards and requirements for subcontractor quality, the work process, inputs and outputs, the resource management system (including inventory), and the quality management system.

◆ Verify compliance to procedures and instructions.

◆ Reduce variability. Reduce input variability, human variability, environmental variability, and management system variability.

Work Structure

A *work structure chart* (also called a *work-breakdown chart*) is used to provide an overview of work decomposition. A good example is an *organization chart*; another is a chart displaying the calling sequence among computer modules. For each unit of work (process, subprocess, task), the documentation should address (a) the inputs, (b) the outputs, (c) the procedures and instructions for performing the tasks, (d) the tools to be used, and (e) the control procedures.

Work Function

Another tool for process documentation is an *input-process-output diagram*, which was discussed in Section 5.3. This tool can be used to document the process from a functional view.

Work Flow

In Section 5.5, *flowcharts* were introduced as a tool for mapping the sequence of events in a process. A very simple example of a flowchart is the basic paradigm or work, discussed in Chapter 7. Another example is the diagram in Exercise 13 of Chapter 10. Flowcharts help us understand a process and, in doing so, detect possible problems. If a flowchart maps the *process as it actually is* (and not as it should be), then it can help us locate problem areas. Problem areas within a process might include unneeded complexity, redundancies, and unnecessary loops. A flowchart helps us identify improvement opportunities, and its use can lead to simplification and standardization of the process.

We don't mean to imply that any flowchart will *automatically* contain all the inefficiencies and redundancies that are actually part of the system. Most of the time the people's first attempt to flowchart a process produces a flowchart of "the way things are supposed to work." It usually takes some effort to get people to draw in all the absurd things that actually go on in their processes. Only if one is successful in getting people to draw "the way things really are" will the flowchart reveal problems in the system.

Another good use of flowcharts is to ask people to draw the *process as it actually should be*. A flowchart of "the way things should be" can reveal whether the process can actually be implemented and whether unforeseen negative side effects are present.

Example:[2]   An assembly operation was supposed to work as follows: Get a kit of components consisting of parts A, B, and C; put them together; and move the assembled product to the stock area.[3] The flow diagram at the top of Display 17.2 shows how the assembly is supposed to work. However, it turned out that the kits were not always complete; quite often one of the parts was missing. If a part was missing, employees would use what parts they had to construct a partial assembly, log the information into a computer database, and store the partially completed assembly on a shelf. When a part arrived, they would go to the computer, find a partial assembly that was missing that component, retrieve it from the shelf, and complete the assembly. The work process that was used in actuality is documented in the flowchart in the top diagram of Display 17.2. The broken line on that diagram separates the "real work," which are the steps that are necessary when everything works perfectly, from the "added complexity," which is introduced because not all parts are always available. The work below the broken line represents the steps that could have been avoided if the kits were complete.

Work Management

Documentation should also describe the process for managing work. It should include procedures for planning work, controlling work including quality control, and reporting completed work. It should also include measures of quality and process performance and productivity. Several tools are used for these purposes.

Bar Charts

A *bar chart*, or *Gantt chart*, can be used to portray a work schedule. Such a chart consists of a collection of horizontal bars plotted against a calendar scale. Each bar represents an activity. The beginning and end of the bar represent the scheduled start and finish dates of the activity.

Bar charts are easy to construct and serve as an effective tool for communicating a work plan to all involved groups. A problem with bar charts, however, is that they do not display interdependencies among work activities. This can cause scheduling errors. More importantly, it makes it difficult to assess the impact that

---

[2]This example is taken from Brian L. Joiner, *Fourth Generation Management* (New York: McGraw-Hill, 1994), p. 17. Joiner attributes this example to Tim Fuller.

[3]In realistic assembly processes, the assembled product will consist of many parts, say 100 or so.

DISPLAY 17.2 ◆ Flowcharts: Assembly Operation. The top chart shows the idealized assembly operation; the bottom chart displays the actual operation.

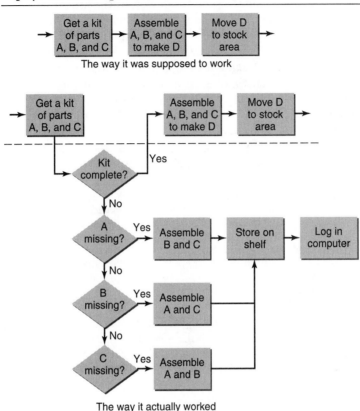

a change in schedule for one activity can have on other activities included in the chart.

Network Diagrams

During the 1950s, two closely related tools evolved to overcome the deficiencies of bar charts: CPM (Critical Path Method) and PERT (Project Evaluation and Review Technique). Over the years, a technique emerged that employs the common planning and scheduling methods of CPM and PERT. Today that technique might be called PERT/CPM, or simply a *network* technique which is the term we will employ. This technique is commonly used in operations management to schedule the tasks that lead to a finished product. It also is employed to schedule the activities of a project.

The network technique can be used to schedule the tasks to be performed by a group of workers so that the total operation is completed in the shortest possible time. It can also take into account resource constraints—for example, the constraint that no more than three people are available to work on any day or the constraint that only certain people can perform certain tasks.

Using a fairly simple procedure, we can construct two schedules for a network. One calls for completing each activity as early as possible, and the other for completing each activity as late as possible while still meeting some preassigned deadline. For each activity, the difference between the earliest and the latest completion dates is called the *slack* for the activity. Activities for which the slack is zero are called *critical activities* because any delay in such an activity will delay the completion time of the total work effort. The identification of critical activities is useful to the manager of the work effort because it highlights potential problem areas.

The following example illustrates the basic steps in constructing PERT and bar charts. Assume that your job is to schedule the production of a play. A simplified list of activities, shown in alphabetical order, is as follows

A	Hold advanced rehearsal	I	Obtain costumes and props
B	Arrange hall	J	Select business manager
C	Design and construct scenery	K	Select director
D	Erect scenery	L	Select play
E	Stage final dress rehearsal	M	Select stage manager
F	Generate publicity	N	Sell opening night tickets
G	Hold initial rehearsal	O	Try-out and select actors
H	Give opening night performance		

The PERT chart for scheduling the production of a play is given in Display 17.3. The work activity starts with the selection of the play. Next, the management team (director, business manager, and stage manager) must be hired; these three activities can be carried out simultaneously. Arrangements for the hall are made by the business manager. Scenery, costumes, and actors are selected once the management team is in place. An initial rehearsal is scheduled after the actors are selected; this can take place before the scenery is designed. Scenery can be erected only

DISPLAY 17.3 ◆ Example of a PERT Chart: Scheduling the Production of a Play.

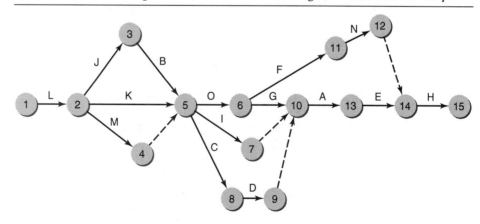

after its design is completed. Publicity can begin right after the actors have been selected; this can start before the initial rehearsal and before the costumes and scenery are in place, . . . , and so on. Standard PERT charts also display the times that are scheduled for each activity. The chart in Display 17.3 shows the flow of the activities, and, in order to keep the discussion simple, we have omitted the times. The bar chart for the same activity is given in Display 17.4.

A PERT chart constrains the order in which tasks are performed, but it might not completely determine the actual work schedule. For example, activity L in Display 17.3 is called an *immediate predecessor* of activities J, K, and M because these activities cannot be started until L is completed. Note, however, that in the bar chart shown in Display 17.4 only K is started immediately after L is completed. Also note that M is scheduled after K, even though this is not required by the PERT chart.

In constructing a bar chart, the only constraint imposed by the related PERT chart is that you cannot schedule an activity to start before all of its immediate predecessors are scheduled to be completed. However, the bar chart schedule might be constrained by other conditions. For example, perhaps only one person can perform tasks K and M, so they are scheduled consecutively. Or, there are only two people who can perform J, K, and M, so that the three tasks cannot be performed concurrently. Note also that task J does not start immediately after L is finished; perhaps the person to perform J will be away for the first part of week 2.

Computer programs for constructing PERT charts are capable of taking resource constraints into account. For a more detailed discussion of this tool, you can consult any book on operations management.

DISPLAY 17.4 ◆ Example of a Bar (Gantt) Chart: Scheduling the Production of a Play.

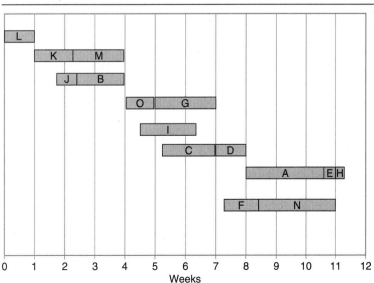

◆ 17.4 Stabilizing Through Standards

Standards are requirements for products and processes. For example, ISO 9001 is a standard for processes; the Food and Drug Administration issues standards for regulated products; and organizations establish standards to support their policies.

The purpose of a standard it to reduce the variability in products and processes. Producing a quality product means meeting product standards as well as specific product requirements. One route to quality improvement is to upgrade standards.

Like most aspects of an organization, standards must be managed. Left unattended, obsolete standards will remain on the books, necessary new standards might not be installed, and enforcement of standards might be haphazard. Each standard should have an "owner" who is responsible for any necessary maintenance, modification, and retirement or replacement of the standard.

A viable way to manage standards is to form a *Standards Committee* that is responsible for establishing standards for the products and processes of a specified organizational area. The Standards Committee should be the driving force behind a standards program. It should consist of experienced professionals of a unit who should be given the responsibility for managing the unit's internal standards. All the major products and processes of the area should be represented; major internal suppliers and customers might be represented as well.

Quality Assurance should be represented on the Standards Committee to provide advice and coordinate QA activities with those of the committee. However, QA should not be a major doer—and certainly should not chair the committee—because generally they do not have the specialized knowledge required. QA definitely is *not* in the business of enforcing standards. Enforcement of standards follows the usual line of authority from the individual through the management chain.

◆ 17.5 Stabilizing Process Operation

In addition to having a well-documented process for accomplishing work, it is necessary to assure that work is carried out correctly. Appropriate employee selection and training processes must be in place to equip workers to perform the required tasks. Necessary instructions, information, equipment, and tools must be available. And the reward system must encourage the proper operation of all production processes. An important task of management is to provide conditions and incentives that promote quality.

◆ 17.6 Stabilizing Through Quality Control

Quality control is the process of checking products to determine whether they meet requirements. Quality control helps stabilize the process output by catching products that are faulty so that they can be scrapped or improved to meet requirements, thereby making the output more consistent.

Several remarks should be made about the control process. First, it should be recognized that one cannot inspect quality into products. Quality comes from improving the underlying process. However, data collected during the control process is put to several uses. Primarily, it is used for product evaluation. But the data might also be used for product improvement, process evaluation and improvement, employee evaluation, and management evaluation; see Section 17.7.

Second, a control process is not always perfect; in fact, it might be quite error-prone. Requirements can be ignored or misinterpreted; incorrect or incomplete observations can be made of actual performance; and important data can be ignored in judging whether or not requirements are met. And the greatest neglect quite often is in the failure to examine the control process itself to ascertain if it is appropriate and being operated effectively.

A third matter of importance is the issue of "ownership" of a control process. The basic question concerning ownership is: Does the control process belong to the people responsible for producing the product, or does it belong to some other group, such as the Quality Control Department or management? The answer to this question is fundamental to any discussion of quality control; see Section 17.9.

Exercising Evaluation and Control of Quality

For effective control of quality, an organization must understand how to design and operate a control system.

The *design of a control system* requires certain information: The designers must understand the organization's products, processes, people, and its operational environment. They must understand what to control and why, and where to imbed control points into the process. They must understand what evaluation techniques to use. They must be aware of the human side of control and know how to gain employee acceptance of the control system. And they must understand the tools, methods, and practices of control.

The *operation of a control* system requires knowledge of the product requirements and applicable standards—one must know what "good" is. It also requires knowing how to examine and measure the product properly, having properly calibrated measuring equipment, and knowing how to interpret the results of the measurements.

Views of Evaluation and Control

Evaluation and control can be viewed from a technical or a social perspective. Viewed as a *technical system*, the concern is with such matters as methods and procedures, tools and techniques, and measurement. Viewed as a *social system*, the concern is with such matters as the alignment of the control system with the basic beliefs of the organization, the power structure within the organization, and the feedback between the control and the personnel system.

Levels of Quality Control

The first level of quality control is that exercised by the *individual* who creates a product; quality control is part of every job. This level of control should not be part of the formal employee evaluation process; instead it should be viewed as a component of the basic paradigm of work.

The next level of control is the work *team*. To promote openness and a team spirit, this level of control, too, should not be part of the formal appraisal process. As the level of control increases, so does the size of the unit being controlled. Individuals exercise quality control on the small products they produce. Teams generally integrate these small products into larger units, and they exercise quality control of the integrated unit.

The *department* is the next major level of quality control, although there might be intermediary levels if the department is very large or segmented. At this level, the department manager assumes responsibility for product quality; he "owns" the quality control process. Quality control information automatically becomes "official," part of the formal records of the department.

Higher levels of quality control generally track the organization chart. A plant manager is responsible for the quality of all products produced by the plant. The Vice President of Manufacturing is responsible for the quality of all manufactured products. The President and Board of Directors are responsible for everything produced by the company.

◆ 17.7 Uses of Control Information

The information from product control serves several purposes. The most obvious use of control information is to identify products that do not meet requirements to prevent their being shipped to customers. In some cases, information about a defect in one product can be used to locate defects in similar products. For example, the discovery of a serious defect in one car triggers a reinspection of similar cars to determine if they, too, are defective.

The quality of a process is measured largely by the quality of the products it produces. Hence, a second use of defect information is to monitor the production process to learn if it meets requirements or needs adjustment. Statistical process control, discussed in Chapter 20, helps in making this decision. Thus, *product control* and *process control* are interwoven through dependence on the same basic data.

A third use of control information is for improvement. Defect information is studied to learn the cause of the defect and to suggest ways to improve the production process so as to remove that cause. Defect information is also utilized to find ideas to improve the design of successor products.

Yet another use of control information is its use in evaluating the control system itself. The control system will detect some defects; others will be discovered later when the product is in use. The effectiveness of a control system can be measured by the proportion of errors that are discovered by the control system.

Somewhat different defect information is required for the various purposes just listed. In evaluating products, it is sometimes useful to classify errors by their severity. In evaluating the production process, trends in defect rates are important. For product and process improvement, the cost of defects, likely causes of defects, and suggestions for improvement are all useful. For evaluating the control system, information on the defect rate by defect type is needed.

Because control information is used by many different individuals and for many different purposes, great care must be taken in recording the information so that it will be useful to all. A good *defect database* is an important asset to an organization, and its design requires considerable thought.

◆ 17.8 Social Aspects of Quality Control

To stabilize a process, it is necessary to evaluate and control its operation. Traditionally, evaluation and control has been concerned mainly with procedures, techniques, and tools for measurement. However, several people have argued that evaluation should be regarded more as a social system and less as a technical system. Inadequate concern for social aspects can overwhelm and cause the failure of an evaluation system that otherwise is technically sound.

Evaluation and Subjectivity

Evaluation is subjective, especially in the service industry. This point is illustrated well in the following example.

While on a business trip to Los Angeles I had dinner one night at a Japanese restaurant. This was an up-scale place with up-scale prices to support leisurely dining. The decor had the quiet, tasteful simplicity one associates with Japan.

My waitress, dressed in traditional Japanese attire, greeted me with a small smile and a slight bow. She placed the menu on the table and, with the same motion, made an almost imperceptible adjustment to align it perfectly parallel with the edge of the table. Her manner and her careful attention to detail made me think this was going to be a pleasant, memorable dining experience. And it was.

My meal impressed me so favorably that I returned three nights later. This time I was served by a waiter. While approaching my table, he continued to talk over his shoulder to a fellow waiter. Without acknowledging me, he tossed the menu on the table and wandered back to continue his conversation. Obviously, I was in for beer service at champagne prices.

That night nothing seemed quite right. The same food; but it was delivered, not served. The restaurant was the same, yet it was different; there was no magic. I might just as well have been in the coffee shop getting the same service at much a much lower price.

The waiter who served me probably would have been shocked to learn that I regarded his service as completely unsatisfactory. After all, he had attended to me promptly, gotten the order right, delivered the food when it was ready— what more is required? I suspect it never occurred to him that people entering a Japanese restaurant might have completely different requirements than those he assumed. And it's a good bet that no one ever explained this to him.[4]

Evaluation, Politics, and Special Interests

Organizational politics can so influence evaluation that many writers have concluded that evaluation is meaningless. Beer observes that evaluation can be made to support any position simply by selecting an appropriate evaluation technique.[5] Suchman has pointed out that two types of evaluation can be effective in supporting political ends:[6] "eye wash," used to show things in a favorable light, and "white wash," designed to conceal the truth. Evaluation by accomplished politicians often amounts to "hog wash," which is an old-fashioned phrase for garbage.

Evaluation is also vulnerable to hijacking by strong interest groups who can distort the control system so as to make it serve their special interests.

In 1967, the B. F. Goodrich Company received an order from LTV to supply brakes for a new Air Force plane. They were elated because this initial order promised lucrative follow-on contracts during the life of the aircraft.

Testing the new brake fell to a young, inexperienced engineer named Lawson. Kermit Vandivier, a technical writer, was to incorporate the test results into a formal qualification report; this was to serve as official proof that the brake had met all requirements.

After several tests failed, Lawson concluded that the design was faulty. His suggestion that the brake was not up to the task was rejected by management; he was told to continue the qualification testing. It was clear that at least three levels of Lawson's management wanted the brake qualified regardless of what it did on tests. Twelve attempts by Lawson to qualify the brake failed; on the thirteenth attempt, he ignored the prescribed testing procedure and "nursed" the brake through the required simulated stops.

Through examination of the test data and conversations with Lawson, Vandivier became convinced that the test results had been deliberately falsified. But two levels of his management (a different management chain from Lawson's) disclaimed any control over the situation and advised him to com-

---

[4]Claude W. Burrill, "Quality, Value, and Profit," *International Journal of Value Based Management*, Vol. 1, No. 1 (1988), pp. 65–69.

[5]"Questions of Metric," in R. Mason and B. Swanson, eds., *Measurement for Management Decision* (Reading, MA: Addison-Wesley, 1981).

[6]C. Suchman, "Action for What? A Critique of Evaluative Research," in T. O'Toole, ed., *The Organization, Management and Tactics of Social Research* (Cambridge, MA: Schenkman, 1970).

plete the report. Reluctantly he did, but he refused to sign the report. (In fact, it never was signed by anyone.)

With the qualification report issued, actual test flights were undertaken. On these, brake failure resulted in several near crashes; in one incident the plane skidded 1,500 feet before coming to a halt.

Vandivier, a high-school graduate with no technical training and seven children to support, liked his job at Goodrich; he knew that resisting his superiors would place his job in jeopardy. Nonetheless, he decided he would not become party to the fraud, so he reported the entire matter to the FBI. Shortly thereafter the military rescinded their approval of the qualification report and demanded to see the test data.

In the ensuing investigation, both Air Force and General Accounting Office investigators testified that the brake was dangerous and had not been tested properly. Goodrich managers, however, maintained they had done nothing wrong, that any problems were a matter of interpretation of data. They did, however, recall the brake and replaced it with a larger brake at no cost to LTV. Goodrich essentially blamed the problem on the inexperience of Vandivier and Lawson, saying it was incredible to assume that higher managers would stand by and see reports falsified.

In the end, Vandivier and Lawson resigned from Goodrich. All the Goodrich managers who subverted the control system remained secure in their old jobs except two, who were promoted. And the brake business continued to do well at Goodrich.[7]

◆ 17.9 Responsibility for Quality Control

A basic question regarding the evaluation process is: Who owns the quality control process: workers, managers, or both? Let us explore this issue.

Years ago, product control was the responsibility of independent *inspectors* who reported to an independent inspection group. The rationale for this arrangement was that "two heads are better than one," but in reality management did not trust workers to check their own work. Workers resented the arrangement, and animosities developed. For many workers the task became not to produce a quality product, but to produce a product that would get past the inspectors.

Transferring responsibility for quality from workers to inspectors irritates workers but is technically feasible if the work product is very simple. With the complex products routinely produced today, however, it is difficult and costly to transfer responsibility. For example, for you to check a computer program I have written might take you longer than it took me to write it. Similar problems arise with, say, checking the design for a complicated computer chip.

---

[7]Kermit Vandivier, "The Aircraft Brake Scandal," *Harper's Magazine,* April 1972.

Self-Control of Quality

Juran and Gryna point out that self-control is possible only if three criteria are met:

1. People know what they are supposed to do.

2. They know what they actually do.

3. They are empowered to take corrective actions if necessary.[8]

Using these three criteria for self control, Juran classifies defects into two categories:

- A defect is *operator-controllable* if the three criteria for self-control have been met.

- A defect is *management-controllable* if one or more of the three criteria for self-control is violated. Only management can provide an environment in which the three conditions for self-control exist. Thus any failure to meet these criteria is a failure of management.

Based on an extensive study, Juran stated that 80 percent of all defects are management-controllable. When the study was made years ago, his observation was controversial; it caused much discussion and prompted many organizations to alter their entire evaluation and control philosophy. But even today, Juran's 80–20 rule is unknown in many circles.

Joint Control

An alternative to choosing between self-control and control by inspectors is to have both. The idea is that if two people check a product (that is, 200% inspection), then it is highly unlikely that both will miss a defect.

Deming strongly disagrees with this contention. He observes that 200 percent inspection, as it is usually carried out, is less reliable than 100 percent inspection.[9] The reason is that each inspector depends on the other to do a proper job. Divided responsibility means that nobody is responsible.

Team Control

Another approach is to assign responsibility for product control to a team of workers. Often this is practiced in conjunction with self-control; each individual is responsible for his own work, but the team is responsible for the total product of all team members.

---

[8]J. M. Juran and Frank M. Gryna, Jr., *Quality Planning and Analysis*, 3rd ed. (New York: McGraw-Hill, 1993), p. 100.

[9]W. Edwards Deming, *Out of the Crisis* (Cambridge, MA: MIT Center for Advanced Engineering Study, 1986), p. 30.

Team control has proved to be very effective. It can result in better quality products for two reasons: defects are less likely to go undetected, but, more importantly, defects are less likely to be created when workers know they might be discovered by fellow workers whom they want to impress favorably. Team control can also help build a team spirit, thereby improving the quality of work life.

◆ 17.10 Establishing a Quality Control System

Social Steps

The difficult part of establishing a quality control system is dealing with people. Building quality checks into a computer program or a production process is relatively simple; building them into a people process is another matter.

Before designing a quality control system, it is necessary to gather information about the requirements, benefits, and probable consequences of the proposed system. Then much time must go into building a coalition of influential people who will support the control effort. It is necessary to sell managers and workers on the concept, and convince everyone that the system will not conflict with their interests. The attempt to establish a quality control system usually encounters apathy and resistance; dealing with these is an important and difficult task.

The actual building of a control system is people-intensive. Power positions, work habits, social customs, and many other aspects of human behavior are likely to be threatened by a new quality control system. So far, no one has devised a textbook solution for dealing with these threats; certainly skills in listening, communicating, compromising, and smoothing ruffled feathers are important. But so are determination, firmness, and constancy of purpose.

People issues are paramount in installing a control system and gaining its acceptance. Explaining what the system is, why it is important to those who will be affected by it, and the benefits that will accrue to them are every bit as important as the more customary instruction on how to operate the system. Monitoring compliance, detecting and dealing with sabotage, and maintaining commitment to the system all require effort; very often more effort is expended in prodding managers on these issues than in convincing workers.

The social issues just mentioned are not peculiar to the introduction of a quality control system; they are encountered in varying degrees by any attempt to introduce innovation and change into an organization.

Technical Steps

A typical set of steps or phases for implementing a quality control system are as follows.

1. *Determine requirements for the control system.*
   The first step after a control system is authorized is to develop a detailed set of requirements for the system. One must establish the scope of the control

system, that is, what is to be included in the system and what is not. Next, one identifies the levels of quality control and the control requirements for each level.

Requirements are of two general types: operating requirements and improvement requirements. Unless the improvement requirements are recognized before the system is designed, valuable improvement information will be lost.

2. *Create the control system.*

The second major step is to create the control system. This step can be subdivided into four tasks that must be performed for each level of control.

The first task is to decide which key attributes are to be controlled. For most processes, there is usually a dominant factor that strongly influences quality. We can distinguish between:

◆ Input dominance: Product quality is dominated by the quality of products from suppliers, such as the meat supplied for producing a steak dinner.

◆ Set-up dominance: Product quality depends largely on the way the process is established for a particular lot or batch of products. Printing a batch of business cards is a good example.

◆ Equipment dominance: Product quality depends on whether machines are functioning properly; producing copies on an office copier is an example.

◆ People dominance: Product quality depends primarily on the skills of people. Examples are many services, such as teaching and pulling teeth.

◆ Information dominance: Product quality depends heavily on supplying the appropriate information and on processing it correctly. Examples are financial services and the publishing industry. Many processes are more dependent on information than process operators realize.

The second task is to select the control (inspection) points. There are certain "natural" locations for control points. Some examples of locations are as follows: at receipt of an order for products to be produced; at receipt of incoming products used in production; during the running of a critical or costly operation; before an irreversible operation; after an appropriate unit of work has been completed; after an individual work effort, an assembly, or major phase of production; before passing a product from one organizational unit to another; and before shipping a final product to a customer.

The third task is to construct the control system. This requires specifying exactly which attributes are to be controlled at each control point and the requirements for these attributes. For each of these attributes, a detailed control system must be designed and built.

The final task is to install the system and verify that it works as intended. Testing a large quality control system is a nontrivial task. It might be done with a pilot operation, or it might be done by operating in parallel with the old system until the new one proves itself.

17.11 Stabilizing Through Process Evaluation

Process evaluation is an ongoing effort. It helps us determine if a process is stable—that is, operating properly and producing consistent quality products time after time. Process evaluation is accomplished in many ways; one evaluation technique is a quality audit, which we discussed in Section 13.11. Another is statistical process control, which consists of techniques for assessing the stability of processes; it is discussed in Chapter 20. In the remainder of this chapter, we will examine three additional evaluation techniques: surveys, quality reviews, and process reviews.

Process evaluation is an essential prerequisite to process stabilization and improvement. If you don't know where you are, it is very difficult to get to where you want to be.

17.12 Surveys

By a *survey* we mean a study of a process or product, usually conducted by asking people a series of questions. Surveys are used to gather consumer reactions to products or services; the survey cards used by restaurants or hotels to gather comments on the quality of their services are examples. People are surveyed to assess their views and opinions, firms are surveyed to assess the future business outlook, and voters are asked about their voting intentions. Some surveys are repeated at regular time intervals so that changes over time can be assessed.

A survey can be conducted in one of two ways: The total population can be surveyed, in which case we talk about a *census*. Or the survey is conducted on only a sample group taken from the population, in which case the sample results must be extrapolated to the entire population; this is referred to as a *sample survey*.[10] Conducting a sample survey is similar to sample inspection for determining whether an entire lot of products should be shipped. The two are done for the same reason: Sampling cuts the cost and time required to do the survey with little loss of accuracy, provided that the sample is properly chosen.

Surveys can be afflicted by many problems. A low response rate can bring survey findings into question. Bias in the responses may be a problem. The bias can be introduced by selecting a nonrepresentative sample. For example, in a survey where participation is voluntary, disgruntled and extremely pleased customers are more likely to respond than others. The accuracy of responses to survey questions may be an issue. Two people might answer a question differently not because they hold different opinions, but because they interpret the question differently. Ambiguity in the survey instrument is an issue that must be considered, and it is one

---

[10]Chapter 19 discusses statistical inference and shows how to assess the sampling error that is associated with such extrapolations.

reason why survey questions must be thoroughly tested before they are used. The accuracy of responses can also be influenced by the perceived use to be made of the responses. For example, a survey of employees' attitudes would be useless if people believed that their responses could be seen by their immediate managers.

A simple survey on "where we should go on the annual company outing" can be handled easily by anyone. But conducting a serious survey requires training and experience, particularly in the design and testing of the survey instrument, the selection of the sample group to be surveyed, and the statistical interpretation of results. Anyone who must conduct a serious survey and does not have this technical background is well advised to seek professional assistance.

Conducting a Survey

A survey should not be conducted unless there is a strong possibility that some action will result. To do otherwise builds expectations that, when left unfilled, can lead to resentment.

A procedure for conducting a survey is given in Display 17.5. You will find that it resembles quite closely the procedure for conducting a review, which will be

---

DISPLAY 17.5 ◆ A Procedure for Conducting a Survey

Step 1. Plan the survey
◆ Establish and orient survey team
◆ Identify survey objective: process to be studied, reason for study
◆ Scope survey: define population, estimate size
◆ Make preliminary announcement to population
◆ Fix manner: survey sample or entire population
◆ Estimate completion date
◆ Estimate resources and cost

Step 2. Prepare for the survey
◆ Identify population: list the population by an identifier
◆ Fix sample size
◆ Determine sample (which might be the population)
◆ Develop survey instrument
◆ Test survey instrument: plan and conduct test
◆ Train respondents: plan and conduct training for completing the survey instrument
◆ Plan report outline

Step 3. Conduct the survey
◆ Administer survey instrument
◆ Follow up on unanswered and incomplete surveys
◆ Accumulate and analyze results

Step 4. Develop report
◆ Check all results
◆ Summarize results
◆ Develop recommendations
◆ Write report
◆ Present report
◆ Thank all concerned

---

discussed in Section 17.13. This similarity, however, covers up an important difference: a survey can be conducted from one location, whereas a review should be conducted in part, at least, at the site being examined. This difference in location points out a difference in technique: All of the information gathered from a survey must derive from the survey instrument. For a survey, it is not possible to overcome planning deficiencies by "winging it." Planning and preparation steps are essential for a survey, much more so than for a review.

Training is also very important; studies show that the validity of survey results increases when a more thorough job is done of explaining the intent and purpose of a survey, and the correct way to complete the survey instrument.

Survey Report

The format and contents of the final report will depend on the purpose of the survey. The survey might be for the purpose of internal planning or for external analysis by, say, a customer or a government agency. It is important to decide on the format and general contents of the report very early in the survey (Step 2) in order to ensure that the data gathered will be sufficient to address the questions that are of interest.

A report can be of almost any size. The 1990 U.S. Population Census, for instance, had only a few questions, but these were analyzed by various demographic breakdowns, generating many lengthy reports. An employee attitude survey can ask 50 questions or more covering topics ranging from local management to the benefits package. The report for such a survey can also be very lengthy. On the other hand, a study of the cost of quality might be reported in a one-page document.

The survey report should state the survey objectives and the process or the product being surveyed. In the case of a sample survey, the report should describe the population and the mechanism for selecting the sample. Survey results should be included; a graphic display of the findings usually has more impact than a table or verbal statement. Conclusions and recommendations should be clearly stated and highlighted.

◆ 17.13 Quality Reviews

A *quality review* is a formal study done to assess the status of a quality system within an organizational unit. A quality review can cover status, compliance, or improvement questions—the present quality of products and what is being done to improve quality. The unit being reviewed can be a single process, a department, an entire organization, or a subcontractor. Typically, a quality review would include an examination of quality policies and objectives, relevant processes and products, problems, plans, suggestions for improvement—all aspects of quality.

A quality review might be held by a supplier to evaluate its own performance or the performance of a subcontractor. The purpose of the review might be to determine quality attainment or to establish a basis for quality improvement. A review seeks to learn the present level of quality, the need for improvement, the effectiveness of improvement efforts, the problems that hinder quality, the right direction for the future, and facts relating to the quality effort.

A quality review is *not* an audit. An audit is concerned largely with compliance to standards and requirements. Although a review is concerned with compliance, it goes much further and asks: Are standards and requirements *right*? Are processes right? Also, a review of quality is not part of the quality control process. Quality control has to do with meeting requirements and standards. A review of quality examines quality control data, but it also seeks suggestions, looks at industry practice, and gathers any other information that will serve the purpose of the review. To hold an effective review, an organization needs a formal process for assessing the present status of quality, diagnosing findings, and generating suggestions and recommendations.

A quality review generally has these characteristics:

- ◆ *Authorized*. A review must be authorized by an appropriate authority.
- ◆ *Formal*. A review is conducted according to a written procedure; it produces written output and is regularly applied.
- ◆ *Scheduled*. A review is scheduled in advance; it is not a surprise visit.
- ◆ *Purpose*. A review fulfills a specific, quality-related purpose.
- ◆ *Objective*. A review attempts to be an objective assessment.

◆ 17.14 Process Reviews

An important type of quality review is a *process review*—a review of the quality status of a process authorized by the process owner. The review is conducted to identify problems and establish a baseline from which improvement objectives can be established and improvements measured.

A process review sometimes is restricted to the portion of a process that resides in a specific department. In this event, it might be called a *departmental review*.

A process review covers the actual situation, attempting to determine the most critical problems facing the process and suggestions for dealing with those problems. A basic premise behind such a review is that those operating a process know more about its details than does management—they usually know what's right, what's wrong, and how the process can be improved.

The charter of a process review term is generally very broad. To determine process status, the review covers all aspects of the process, including:

- ◆ The work of the process. This includes such matters as the process purpose and objectives, the structure of the process, the products and customers of the process, its status, and the control and tracking process.

◆   The people of the process. This includes staffing, training, appraising, rewarding, the work environment, and other human conditions of those involved with the process. Communications is another important people aspect, as are power and decision making.

A process review looks for both conformance and nonconformance. It examines organization, procedures, techniques, and tools associated with the process under review. While the major objective is to find facts and quantify the process, opinions are also gathered, particularly opinions about problems and suggestions for improvement.

A procedure for conducting a process review after its authorization is given in Display 17.6.

The Review Team

A simple process review can be conducted by gathering a few people who know the process well and listening to their comments. A larger review should be conducted by a team consisting of several people who do not operate the process

---

DISPLAY 17.6 ◆ A Procedure for Conducting a Process Review

Step 1. Plan review
◆   Establish leader and nucleus of review team
◆   Make preliminary announcement to unit
◆   Study objective: process to be reviewed, reason for review
◆   Scope review: estimate size and effort of review
◆   Complete review team
◆   Determine requirements: define conformance and nonconformance
◆   Estimate completion date
◆   Resources: estimate cost

Step 2. Prepare for review
◆   Train the team in conducting a review
◆   Orient the team to the process and the review
◆   Prepare and send advanced questions to unit
◆   Schedule visits
◆   Prepare scripts and checklists for visits
◆   Plan report outline

Step 3. Conduct review
◆   Conduct interviews
◆   Schedule and conduct additional interviews as required
◆   Analyze results

Step 4. Develop report
◆   Check all results
◆   Summarize results
◆   Develop recommendations
◆   Write report
◆   Present report
◆   Thank all concerned

---

being studied. At least one team member should be highly experienced in the type of process being reviewed and able to ask penetrating questions, understand the answers, facilitate the identification of problems, and, at the same time, understand and be sympathetic to the disruption that the review is causing. The team leader should have had previous experience on some review team; having been a team leader would be even better. The team should report to the person who authorized the review.

For review findings to be a true reflection of attitudes, the review team must be sensitive to human concerns and to human behavior. Fear, ego, insecurity, exhibitionism, defensiveness, cultural differences—all these can and do distort review results. Reviewers must have the ability to establish a level of trust with respondents so that they will speak freely. This requires that reviewers be sensitive to the climate within the organization and respect the concerns of all involved. It also means that reviewers must learn to maintain confidentiality when appropriate, even in the face of threats from powerful people.

Conducting a Review

Group and individual interviews are the fundamental tools used in reviews, and the skill with which they are conducted will largely determine the outcome of the effort. Interviews should be planned and scheduled. Questions generally cover process requirements and objectives, the status of the process, problems, and possible solutions. Distributing questions prior to interviews will allow people to prepare for the session, thereby making it more effective. Interviews are best conducted on site so that reviewers can observe what's going on and hold casual conversations with process operators.

Group dynamics make group interviews more difficult to conduct than individual ones. Many times the people with the most information will say the least. In the presence of some managers, no one else will speak; but this in itself speaks volumes. Questions must be directed to those who are quiet, and efforts must be made to keep one or two from dominating the discussion. Getting the group to think objectively about where they are and what they must do provides a framework for people to express their problems and concerns without seeming to admit failure of management.

Look for positive as well as negative results. This can yield valuable information, and it makes the survey seem less a police action or a search for the guilty. Public praise is in order if appropriate, or sympathy and understanding; a remark that "We had the same problem" makes the group feel less foolish.

Interviewers should practice nondirective listening instead of "hearing" only what they anticipate. By listening clearly to what people are saying, it is possible to pick up insinuations and innuendoes, or to glean some common themes. Body language, too, can pass messages that go unspoken.

Reviewers should spend at least one-third of their time in one-on-one interviews with workers and first-line managers to gain grass-roots information about the process and the workings of the organization. Also, interviews should elicit suggestions for improving the process.

Reviewers should identify common themes that appear throughout the review.

The review of a testing process involved four levels of management. But during the review, no mention was made of the third level. This clue to organizational conflict ultimately required the transfer of two managers.

Other clues to common concerns include disagreement on facts; disagreements with customers; crisis management; a very low or very high turnover rate; unclear roles and responsibilities; absence of product or process ownership; failure to track critical items; a "Caine Mutiny" management style that goes by the book but destroys morale and group effectiveness.

Reviewers should also attempt to uncover taboo topics that will not be aired openly. Examples are overstaffing, favoritism, slackers, contempt for management, failure of decision making, and corruption. Concern about taboos can be learned simply by raising the possibility of a problem and observing people's reactions. They may talk it out, or they may show an uneasiness that betrays concern.

After the interviews, the results must be summarized and recommendations formulated. Remember that the purpose of a review is to discover and correct problems with a process. Stay clear of evaluations of individuals; blaming the people rather than the process usually misses the point. Moreover, it is a reasonably certain way to ensure that the report will bring no lasting benefit.

The review findings and recommendations should be given to individuals for validation and comment before being submitted to higher management. This increases the support that individuals will give the report and the probability that some action will be taken.

Done badly, a review can be seen as an intrusion, as a waste of time, a burden, or even a threat. On the other hand, a well-conducted review can have a very positive impact apart from its specific findings and recommendations. It can help the group being studied to be more reflective about their process and lead them to make continuing improvements. And it can build team spirit and individual pride; many times the reaction to a review is, "That's great. Nobody ever asked my opinion before!"

Process Review Compared with a Survey

A major advantage of a process review over a survey is that it provides two-way communication. This communication allows the clarification of questions and responses, making it more likely that real understanding is developed. An interviewer can adjust questions to the responses being given and re-ask a question in a slightly different way so as to elicit a response that otherwise might not have been forthcoming. The best results of a review are achieved when the review team can act as a catalyst to draw out latent recommendations from the respondents.

The personal contact provided by a review is much more likely than a survey to build trust between management and workers. When the two groups meet face to face and hold frank discussions, each is more likely to understand the other. Workers gain a better understanding of their jobs and management's aims. Managers learn some of the grass-roots knowledge that workers possess. Junior people learn good practice from those more experienced, and managers learn how they are perceived by their people. Groups learn to get the support from each other that they require. And this learning helps to generate mutual respect.

But the review technique does have disadvantages over surveys. One is that a review can be more expensive than a survey, particularly if opinions are solicited from many people.

A more difficult problem for many organizations, however, is the skill level needed by reviewers. This problem frequently goes unrecognized; in fact, many assume quite the opposite—that constructing and administering a questionnaire require more skill than conducting a series of interviews. This view stems from the fact that the questionnaire requires technical knowledge and involves a procedure with which few are familiar, whereas conducting interviews appears to be nothing more than holding a series of meetings.

Process Review Compared with a Quality Audit

A process review differs from a quality audit[11] in several respects. A process review is authorized by the process owner; a quality audit generally is authorized by top management. A process review is conducted to identify problems and opportunities for improvement; a quality audit is conducted to determine conformance to procedures, whether the procedures are good or bad. An audit determines if things are being done right, whereas a review determines if the right things are being done.

◆ Exercises and Additional Readings

1. In Japan, a *presidential assessment* is a quality assessment conducted by an outside consultant. At the conclusion of the assessment, the consultant addresses all employees and includes in his remarks some comments on the performance of the president.

   (a) Do you think American top executives would ask a consultant to do this?

   (b) Do you think most American consultants would grade a top executive honestly in public?

2. (a) Compare and contrast the four-step procedure for constructing a survey (Display 17.5) with the PDCA cycle (in Section 7.4) and the IDEA procedure (Exercise 5, Chapter 7).

   (b) Do the same for the four-step procedure for conducting a process review (Display 17.6)

---

[11]Quality audits are discussed in Section 13.11.

3. List some reasons why prevention is not practiced and reliance is placed on control.

4. Read and summarize Dale H. Myers and Jeffrey Heller, "The Dual Role of AT&T's Self-Assessment Process," *Quality Progress*, January 1995, p. 79.

5. What are the advantages and disadvantages of having a control process "owned" (a) by management? (b) by the Quality Control Department? (c) by the workers who operate the process?

6. Document your process for brewing your morning coffee; for cleaning your car.

7. Document several processes of your choice.

8. Employees of organizations travel frequently in their jobs. Construct a flowchart for the travel reimbursement process. For further reference, read Steven C. Hillmer, "A Problem Solving Approach to Teaching Business Statistics," *The American Statistician*, August 1996, pp. 249–256.

9. Construct a flowchart that describes the process for analyzing whether potential causes are root causes. For further reference, see Steven C. Hillmer (Exercise 8).

10. Read and summarize Michael J. Taylor, "Process Product Integrity Audits: A Hardware Auditing Technique for the '90s," *Quality Progress*, February 1996, pp. 81–83.

11. Read and summarize Kris A. Rasmussen, "Flowcharts Can Show Process Improvements in Action," *Quality Progress*, February 1992, p. 112.

12. Examine the flowchart for Corrective Action Decisions and accompanying notes on page 17-5 of Allan J. Sayle, *Management Audits*, 2nd ed. (Allan J. Sayle, Ltd.). According to the flowchart, what action should an auditor take upon discovering a persistent problem of which the auditee is aware and there is objective evidence that the auditee is taking action to remedy the situation?

13. Read Dwight Kirscht and Jennifer M. Tunnell, "Boise Cascade Stakes a Claim on Quality" *Quality Progress*, November 1993, p. 91. Summarize how the flowcharting procedure was used to gain better understanding of a process and greatly simplify it.

14. Ask several people who provide service for you in restaurants, stores, libraries, and so on, whether they follow a *documented* process. Ask what instruction and training they have received in how they operate their processes. What conclusions can you draw from their responses?

15. What problems might you encounter in documenting an existing process

   (a) in a department whose manager you report to?

   (b) as an outside consultant to the department manager?

16. Read and discuss Leland R. Beaumont, "Sticking with Flowcharts," *Quality Progress*, July 1993, p. 168. Describe Beaumont's flowchart of the flowcharting process.

17. Read Ronald D. Snee, "Listening to the Voice of the Employee," *Quality Progress*, January 1995, pp. 91–95. Discuss the value of surveys and summarize Snee's ideas on how to plan and conduct surveys.

18. Read and discuss E. H. Melan, "Process Management in Service and Administrative Operations," *Quality Progress*, June 1985, pp. 52–59. This paper reviews several useful tools for process management. Relate these tools to those we have discussed in Chapter 17.

19. The creation of a certain product requires 11 activities: A, B, . . . , K. The time required for each activity and the constraints among the activities are as follows:

Activity	Immediate Predecessors	Time to Accomplish (days)
A	—	3
B	—	4
C	A	2
D	B	4
E	B	6
F	B	2
G	F	2
H	C,D	5
I	E,G	5
J	F	3
K	I,J	2

(a) Draw a PERT chart to display the activities.

(b) Determine the minimum time required to complete all tasks (assuming no resource constraints).

(c) Assume that it requires one worker to accomplish each activity and that each worker can perform every task. Build a schedule for accomplishing all activities with three workers. Can you improve on your schedule (that is, reduce the total time required)? What if only two workers are available?

20. In serving a meal, you must carry out the following activities:

Activity		Immediate Predecessor	Time (minutes)
A	Clean dining room	—	20
B	Fix menu and select beverages	—	20
C	Shop for food and beverages	B	60
D	Prepare ingredients	C	20
E	Prepare meal	D	70
F	Prepare coffee	C	5
G	Set table	A	10

H	Serve and consume meal	E,G	60
I	Clear table	H	10
J	Serve and consume coffee	F,I	20
K	Clear table and dining area	J	15
L	Wash dishes	K	30

(a) Construct a bar (Gantt) chart for the process of preparing and serving a meal.

(b) Construct a PERT chart for the process of preparing and serving a meal.

(c) Determine the early start, late start, and slack for each activity, assuming that there are no labor or other constraints.

21. A job consists of the following tasks:

Activity		Immediate Predecessor	Time (days)
A	Forecast sales	—	10
B	Price sales	A	3
C	Schedule production	A	4
D	Cost production	C	3
E	Prepare budget	B,D	3

(a) Construct a PERT chart.

(b) Determine the early start, late start, and slack for each variable.

(c) Assume that task A is done by the Sales Department, tasks B, C, and E by Accounting, and task D by Manufacturing. Also, assume it takes two days to transform information from one department to another. Then how long will it take to perform the job? [*Suggestion:* Include additional two-day tasks to the network as appropriate.]

22. Summarize the differences between a quality audit and a quality (process) review.

23. Give examples of operator-controllable and management-controllable defects. Discuss why it is important to make this distinction.

24. Summarize and discuss the various uses of control information.

25. Contact one or two local companies. Ask the managers of these companies about the control systems they have instituted. Assess their understanding of the technical and the social issues surrounding control. Can you think of improvements to their adopted strategies?

Managing by Facts: Data Gathering and Data Classification

In God we Trust—all others must have data.

Quality cannot be assessed, and quality cannot be improved without having access to the relevant data. This and the next two chapters in this book discuss aspects of data collection and data analysis. Chapter 18 discusses data and their importance for quality, the collection of data, and their classification into meaningful groups. Chapter 19 reviews basic principles of statistical analysis, including the graphical display of data and the numerical summary of information. Chapter 20 introduces statistical techniques that are important for stabilizing and improving products and processes. It includes an introduction to acceptance sampling; it covers statistical process control and control charts for monitoring the stability of processes and capability indexes for assessing the capability of processes; and it reviews basic principles of the statistical design of experiments, which is important for product and process improvement.

Our presentation in these three chapters is introductory. If you want to learn more about these topics, we recommend that you consult our other book, *Statistical Quality Control: Strategies and Tools for Continual Improvement.*

◆ 18.1 The Need for Data

The manager of an IS Department wanted to learn about the quality of a newly installed system, so he decided to ask several people what they thought. The first person he questioned was one of the people who had developed the system, and his reply was that the system was *outstanding*—by far the best the department had ever produced. Next, the manager encountered a customer who used the system. This particular person was unhappy because his request to include certain functions in the system was not fulfilled. His opinion was that the system was *really bad*; it doesn't do what it should, and it gives all sorts of problems. The manager next questioned a maintenance programmer whose job was to make corrections and enhancements to the system. No matter what the quality of a system, a maintenance programmer usually spends the full day making changes. If the system is bad, more maintenance people are needed; if it is good, fewer. Not surprisingly, then, the maintenance programmer said the new system was *about the same as any other*. What was the IS manager to believe? Is the new system good, bad, or in between?

This story is meant to illustrate that opinion not backed by facts often is of no value. People use evaluative words in different ways—one person's "good" is another person's "bad." To judge things impartially and make fair comparisons, it is necessary to have facts—*data*. In the following chapters, we will discuss several basic activities involved in dealing with data, including *data collection, data classification, data analysis*, and *data use*.

An important source of data in any organization is measurement. Products are measured against requirements, projects are measured against deadlines, people are measured against performance plans, and entire organizations are measured against targets for return on investment and profit per share. Whatever is important to management must be measured. In effect, measurement is management's way of saying, "We care enough for you to do your very best."

Whatever is important is measured, but it is also true that whatever is measured becomes important. For example, if the number of pages in a manuscript is measured but quality is not, people will produce big, fat documents of mediocre merit. In establishing a measurement system, careful thought must be given to the consequences of every single measurement that is made.

The importance of having effective tools for measurement can be seen from the history of science. Measurement has always been an important precursor to scientific advancement. The precise astronomical measurements by Tycho Brahe allowed Kepler to discover the elliptical orbits of planets. Similarly, inventions such as the thermometer and barometer led to important scientific advances. Much the same phenomenon holds in a business organization. A sure prescription for reducing problems in an organization is to establish effective measuring systems for gathering data about problem frequency and severity. Gathering, classifying, analyzing, and making appropriate use of problem-related data is an important tool for problem solving.

◆ 18.2 Data and Quality

Our concern in this book is with the quality of products. A product is produced by some process, and the most effective way to achieve a quality product is to improve the process used to produce the product—in other words, to improve the capability of the process. But the capability of a process can be judged only by its products. Thus, the fundamental question in the quality area is: Does a product meet its requirements? If the answer is consistently "Yes" for the products produced by the process, then the process is satisfactory. If not, then the process needs improvement. Data is needed to help us decide which state our process is in.

A requirement for a product must specify not only an attribute or function, but it must also state the standard against which the attribute or function will be judged and the process to be used in measuring the product. This is where data comes on the scene. The action of checking a product to see if it meets requirements (the quality control action) generates data or information about the product. This data relates directly to the fundamental question: "Does the product meet requirements." But it also serves as the foundation for answering a host of other questions that relate to the capability of the process used to produce the product. Some of these product- and process-related questions are these:

◆ What are the most pressing problems in our department?

◆ Is a certain new technology an improvement over the old way of doing things?

◆ What do defects cost?

◆ What causes most of our defects?

◆ Which parts of our products are the most error-prone?

◆ What is our defect rate?

◆ What is the defect removal efficiency of our quality control activities?

◆ In what phase of product development are most defects injected? most removed?

◆ What proportion of our defects are severe?

◆ Do we have many invalid defect reports?

◆ How severe is the problem of getting multiple reports of a defect?

◆ What is the average cost of repairing a defect?

All of these questions require data for a proper answer. Collecting the proper data is not a trivial task; sometimes it is downright difficult. But once proper data is collected, it provides an objective yardstick for judging production and business processes.

◆ 18.3 Quantitative and Qualitative Data

Data can be quantitative (expressed in numbers) or qualitative (verbal, or nonnumeric). Quantitative data often arises through using some tool to make measurements, say a clock, a scale, a ruler, or some similar instrument. Time to failure, time to repair, length, weight—all are quantified and all depend on the use of some measuring device. Another way that quantitative data arises is through the use of some automated collection procedure. Examples are the data obtained by automatically taking measurements on certain dimensions, automatically logging machine malfunctions, or data on cost taken from the accounting system. Quantitative data can also arise through the simple act of counting, say by counting the number of trouble reports on some system, the number of calls to a helpline or the number of machine jams.

It is easy to become enamored with numbers and hence ignore any measurement that cannot be quantified. In fact, a reasonable argument can be made that "any" measurement can be quantified if there is sufficient motivation to do so, and therefore only numbers are important. The fact is, however, that for many important characteristics of products the benefit of quantification is less than its cost, so the practical approach is to work with nonquantified data. The user-friendliness of an information system, the attractiveness of a car, and the service provided by a hotel may be quantified to a very fine degree, but doing so may not be beneficial.

An important source of qualitative data are the opinions about product quality that are expressed by those who build the products and by those who use them. Sometimes attempts are made to quantify this type of data by asking people to rate products on a scale, say, from 1 to 10. Another source of qualitative data is the output of a brainstorming session—for example, the responses to the question: "What are our quality problems?" For such data, there usually is no obvious way to introduce quantification; attempts to do so generally result in a significant loss of information. Usually, it is much better to work directly with the qualitative statements, attempting to classify, group, and otherwise arrange the data so as to understand more clearly their underlying message.

◆ 18.4 Uses of Data

There are many good reasons why an organization should collect data. We will look at four: to manage a process, to understand a process, to control a process, and to improve a process.

Managing a Process

Managers need data to do their jobs effectively. One use of data is to direct management attention to significant problems and avoid wasting time on insignificant details. A relevant measure is the *cost of quality*, which we introduced in Chapter 3. Recall that the cost of quality for an organization is the amount of money the organization spends to ensure that it produces quality products, as well as the costs that arise if the quality is unsatisfactory. It consists of three components: the cost or prevention, the cost of appraisal, and the cost of failure.

For some manufacturing areas, the cost of quality is about 30 percent of the total manufacturing budget. A quality improvement effort can cut this cost in half. In the information systems area, most organizations do not know their cost of quality; many are *afraid* to know what it is. Some years ago, it was estimated that for the average IS Department in the United States the cost of quality was 50 percent of the department's total budget. (See Claude W. Burrill and Leon W. Ellsworth, *Quality Data Processing* [Tenafly, NJ: Burrill-Ellsworth Associates, 1980].) Evidence suggests that even this estimate was extremely conservative. Moreover, it did not include costs that were incurred by users' departments and that were not charged against the IS budget. Knowing that the cost of quality is 50 percent certainly focuses management's attention on the fact that there is a problem somewhere in IS. It helps to strengthen the resolve to improve the quality of the major processes that are used by the information systems groups.

Management also uses data to allocate resources. Return on assets, cost-benefit comparisons, and similar sets of numbers are used to decide how resources will be deployed. Once resources are deployed, data is needed to track progress against plan and to measure the attainment of targets.

Still another management need for data is to sell ideas. It is one thing to say that "We have problems with our billing system," but it is quite another to say that "Ten percent of the bills we send to customers are wrong." One way to get people's attention is to have facts—data.

Understanding a Process

A second, and related, use of data is to help people understand the processes with which they work. Consider again the quality of a large software system or some other process that is operating in an organization. The quality of such a system frequently is measured by the number of defects that are found in the system during its operational life. Now, to have a defect in an operational system, two things must happen: First, the defect must have been injected into the system—it didn't just happen on its own; and second, the quality control system designed to eliminate defects from the system prior to its implementation must have failed to catch the defect. The following simple equation relates the number of defects injected into a product, defects removed from a product, and defects remaining:

Defects injected − Defects removed = Defects remaining

If few defects remain in the system, does this mean that the injection rate is low or the removal efficiency is high, or both? Without data, the answer is anyone's guess. Yet the action taken to improve the process would be quite different if it were a problem of high injection rate, rather than a problem of a poor quality control system.

In order to gain insight into the situation in a typical IS Department, we examine data given by Capers Jones in his book *Programming Productivity* (New York: McGraw-Hill, 1986), p. 30. He states that for large software systems written in Assembler language, the number of bugs injected often exceeds 50 per thousand lines of code (KLOC). He also states that defect removal is only 85 percent efficient; that is, quality control catches only 85 out of every 100 defects actually present in the system. Putting these figures together, we can see that the average number of bugs in the system when it is placed in operation is about 7 per KLOC. Several conclusions can be drawn from this data:

- ◆ The process for building large software systems allows an unacceptable number of defects, and it must be improved.

- ◆ The quality control process for detecting and removing defects from large software systems is not efficient enough.

- ◆ The number of defects shipped to customers in a large software system is often alarmingly high and must be reduced.

These three assertions might be contested if we had no figures to back them up. However, with our data at hand (injection rate of 50 per KLOC; efficiency rate of 85%; and number of shipped defects of 7 per KLOC), few would quarrel with these statements. This data makes us realize that (1) we must make serious efforts to improve the application development process so as to inject fewer defects into products, and (2) while this is being done we must improve the efficiency of our quality control efforts. The data helps us gain a much better feeling for the capability of our processes than we would have otherwise.

Controlling a Process

A third use of data is for process control. Many manufacturing processes use feedback data to adjust an input, such as temperature, in order to keep the output at the desired level. In much the same way, feedback data from quality control activities can be used to make adjustments that result in more products meeting their requirements.

Improving a Process

A fourth use of data is in making process improvements. Some improvements are made for the purpose of increasing productivity, and for this we would need data on the inputs and outputs of the process. If our interest is in the improvement of quality, then we need data on defects. Analysis of defect data is an important component in process improvement.

What we have discussed in this section are some representative uses of data, but we have hardly scratched the surface of potential uses. For all the different uses of data, however, we find that essentially the same activities are performed: data collection, data classification, data analysis, and data presentation. These four basic activities provide the foundation for using data in solving quality problems.

◆ 18.5 Collecting Data

It might seem that the first step in using data to solve a problem is to collect some data, but this is absolutely wrong. The most common error made by people who are not trained in statistics is to gather data before asking what you will do with it once you have collected it. The secret in using data effectively is to start with a *plan*. Before collecting anything ask:

- ◆ What is the purpose of collecting the data?
- ◆ What data do I need?
- ◆ How will I collect it?
- ◆ How will I analyze it?
- ◆ What conclusions am I attempting to draw?
- ◆ How will I present those conclusions to achieve my objective?

You may need to cycle through these questions several times before you have a clear understanding of what you want to do. When you have reached that understanding, lay out your plan; *then* start gathering data.

Collection Process

Sometimes the data needed to solve quality problems is gathered as part of a special project. For example, an attempt might be made to learn the effectiveness of a particular tool in preventing defects or to look into the cause of a particular defect. For such problems, data might be gathered through a research effort, a library search, a brainstorming session, surveys of knowledgeable people, or many other means. For such special projects, there is no simple, well-defined data collection process—how data is to be gathered is part of the problem being solved.

Another way that quality-related data is gathered is through quality control efforts, and here there is a more standard approach to data collection. Quality control has to do with examining products that are produced by some process, so the starting point for a quality control effort is a study of the production process. Usually, a process can be decomposed into a collection of interconnected subprocesses. Such a decomposition is depicted in Display 18.1, where a rectangle

DISPLAY 18.1 ◆ Data Collection Points in a Process. Rectangles represent subprocesses. Triangles represent quality control points.

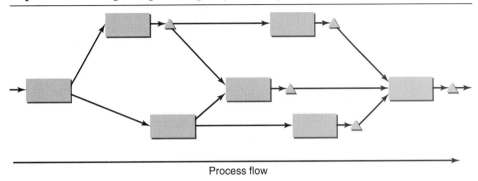

Process flow

indicates a subprocess and an arrow indicates that the output (product) of one
subprocess is an input to another. The entire figure represents the process under
consideration. Once the process is well understood, the next step is to determine
where quality control points (indicated by the triangles in Display 18.1) should be
inserted in the system and what data is to be collected at each such point. Usually
this data is about dimensions and properties of products, and quite often it is about
defects: how many defects, descriptions of defects, probable causes of defects, and
so on. The data is collected through actions such as reviews, inspections, and testing.

The actual collection of quality control data is part of a detection procedure,
and an important step in a quality control effort is to design such a collection
mechanism. Design of the detection procedure includes detailing the mechanism
for capturing all of the required data and deciding how that data will be collected,
recorded, stored, and made available for subsequent use.

A data collection mechanism is a system itself. Like all systems, it should meet
user requirements, which, of course, are specific to a particular system. Generally,
however, people who are responsible for entering data want such systems to be
simple, very easy to understand and use, and sensible. People who will use the
data from such systems want to be certain that the appropriate data will be gathered and that it is defect free. Design of a system to meet all these requirements
sometimes takes considerable ingenuity.

Some points to keep in mind when building a data-collection mechanism are
these:

◆ Understand clearly all uses that will be made of the data before designing
   the system. Will it be used to fix the product? improve the process? measure productivity? make product improvements?

◆ Organize data collection to ease the task of recording data and transcribing
   it for subsequent use.

- ◆ Collect data so as to simplify the task of analysis. Before designing the data collection mechanism, plan how data will be organized, analyzed, and presented; and by whom it will be done.

- ◆ Keep a clear record of where data came from and important circumstances surrounding its collection.

Collection Problems

Don't be surprised if you have difficulties in collecting the data you need. People know that they are supposed to record something, but they forget to do it and later they make up an estimate. So you wind up working not with actual observations but with estimates of actual observations. If data collection is to extend over a long period of time, you should make an effort to have the collection process standardized and perhaps automated. It may be that what you want can be obtained automatically from computer monitoring. It may be that you can get what you want by having a small change made in the system used to record accounting data, say the time-reporting system. It's a fairly safe rule that if you need a consistent, regular flow of data, then the data-collection routine must be built into the work procedure, preferably in an automated manner.

Sometimes it requires ingenuity to collect the data you need. We have a friend who made a study of tape handling in the operations area of a very large computing center. The people doing the job and from whom he had to get the data were newly hired, lowly paid employees who stayed on the job about six months and then got promoted if they were performing satisfactorily. Naturally they were skeptical when our friend discussed gathering data; they were concerned that the data might be used to evaluate their performance rather than to improve the process. So our friend had to work side-by-side with the people for some time just to gain their confidence. Once this was accomplished, he asked them to record their activities for his analysis; then he ran into another problem. The floor of an operations area is a very busy place; so much activity was going on that no one could remember at the end of a shift what they had been doing. Our friend solved that problem by getting a timer from the hardware store—the kind used in cooking—and placed it in the work area. Every 15 minutes the clock would go off, the workers would record what they had been doing for the past 15 minutes, rewind the clock, and go back to work until it went off again. In this way our friend got data that allowed him to make a significant improvement in the tape-handling process. Moreover, the people on the floor were pleased and felt important to have been part of a successful improvement effort.

Data Accuracy

A problem you will encounter as you start to deal with data is the question of accuracy. Many people suffer from the belief that data is not useful unless it is very accurate. Because of this belief, they tend to concentrate only on measurements that can be made precisely, and this can lead them into a trap. What they end up doing is measuring things that can be measured accurately and ignoring things for which the measurement is only approximate. Often this leads to being overly concerned with the trivial, while overlooking the important.

A few years ago one of us worked with a professional group in an effort to learn the cost of quality in the information systems area of several large companies. Our aim was to publish an average figure for the cost of quality, in that way providing the information systems community with useful data while protecting the confidentiality of individual companies. The project never reached the desired goal. Among the several reasons for this was the fact that many of the investigators got hung-up on measuring prevention costs (which were a small part of the total cost) and ignored failure costs (which were the dominant figures). The reason for their actions is that prevention costs (education, installing standards, and so on) could be determined by examining accounting records, whereas failure costs (rework, losses, and so on) were not identified as such in the accounting system but had to be estimated. Since they felt estimates were not accurate, they shied away from making them.

The rule on accuracy should be that the need for accuracy depends on the use to be made of the data. If one were testing a potent new drug for side effects, accurate data would be required. But if the problem is to determine the most serious cause of defects in order to eliminate that cause first, it doesn't matter too much if you make a mistake and attack the second most important problem rather than the most important one. You probably will get to the most important cause in a subsequent improvement effort, and meanwhile you have made an improvement that needed to be done anyway. Fortunately, most uses of data for solving problems are like this. You need data that reflects the true situation, but accuracy usually is not an overriding issue.

Representative Data

More important than accuracy is the need to be certain that the data you use is representative, that it really reflects the situation you are studying. There is a famous story about nonrepresentative data on the U.S. political scene; it goes like this.

In 1936 Alfred Landon was running as the Republican candidate for president in opposition to the Democratic incumbent, Franklin D. Roosevelt. This was the period of the Great Depression; Roosevelt was running on a New Deal program that appealed to the common man whereas Landon was viewed as representing the conservative establishment. In those days there was a very well known magazine called Literary Digest. *This magazine decided to conduct an opinion poll—one of the early political polls—to predict the winner of the election. They carefully designed an experiment and randomly selected names from telephone directories and lists of car owners. They conducted their survey, and announced in their publication that Landon would win with*

57 percent of the vote against 43 percent for Roosevelt. Instead, Roosevelt won by a landslide with 62.5 percent of the vote, and Literary Digest *became a laughing stock. What was their error? Nonrepresentative data. After all, who owned a telephone or a car in 1936? Only the well-to-do, who tended to be Landon supporters. The adopted sampling procedure never reached those without telephones, and this systematic (nonsampling) error biased their results.*

In collecting data, you must make certain that it represents the true situation. There is no simple rule to tell you how to judge this. It is easy, however, to spot situations where the data is very likely to be nonrepresentative. If you collect data about one production team and suggest that this is representative of all other production teams in your organization, you probably have a problem. If you collect data about one department and try to use this for all departments, you may be wrong. In general, if you intend to make a statement about an entity, then you should collect data or at least randomly sample from that entire entity. If you apply common sense and are aware that nonrepresentative data can cause problems, you will probably be alright.

Time Series Data

One final point about collecting data. You should be aware that the analysis of data about an event often involves knowing just when the event took place; this information is used in an attempt to match cause and effect. For such problems, time-related information must be recorded, otherwise the rest of the data is worthless. If you follow our earlier injunction and plan before you collect data, you should have no problem. You should automatically collect time-related information when that is required.

◆ 18.6 Problems with Data

Having collected data, you must next ask, "What do I really have?" You may have some surprises.

False Data

Some of the data you have will, in fact, be false. Would you believe that people deliberately lie? It happens all the time. For example, a professional, who gets no extra pay for overtime work, frequently will record on a time card that the time worked for the week was "standard hours" when in fact the time worked was really 50 percent more than that. The reported time is then put into an estimating database as the actual time worked. When it is time to estimate the resources required for the next project, the new estimate is based on the false data from the earlier activity. Not surprisingly, the new project turns out to require a lot of un-recorded overtime, too—in fact, about 50 percent more than the estimate!

Sometimes false data arises from more conscious efforts to deceive. We heard a story recently about an information systems development group that had an in-dependent testing unit to make a final check of all developed products. In one in-cident, a development group handed their product to the testing group, that group discovered an error, and they reported the error to the development group. Instead of repairing their mistake, the development group reported to their management that there were no errors and sent their product on to their customer. In effect, they knowingly reported no defects when, in fact, they knew one existed; and worse yet, they knowingly released a faulty product. The reason for their behav-ior was the appraisal system: If they reported an error, it was held against them during appraisal and salary review. In their own best interest as they saw it, they lied.

Although this example is blatant and extreme, it is not isolated. Whenever peo-ple must report data that they expect might be used in appraising and rewarding them, they are likely to slant it in their favor. That goes for every level right up through top management. Data about quality is particularly susceptible to being shaded because, although the data is being collected to measure the process, the people who operate the process will be concerned that the data might also be used to measure them. Unfortunately, often it is.

The reasons for falsifying data, however, are not always clear. In one instance, a medical doctor working for the Forensic Toxicology Research Unit of a federal agency routinely falsified results of drug tests made on employees involved in rail-road accidents. In 16 cases, the doctor submitted negative readings where other tests, which were not disputed, showed positive results. Investigators speculated that the doctor was careless, tired, lacked in the right equipment, or was unable to use the equipment properly. It was also speculated that he was too embarrassed to admit his inability to provide correct results, or perhaps was concerned that he might suffer financially if he admitted his problem. Interestingly, these reasons and motives are universal; they can be present in any data-gathering situation.

Mistaken Data

Another problem you will encounter is mistaken data. The effect is the same as with false data, only the motive for the data being wrong is different. People sup-plying mistaken data don't know they are doing it; hence, they can't even suggest that you view it with skepticism.

A good example of mistaken data occurred with an employee who was con-cerned about computer programs that ended abnormally (abended), that is, with programs that ended before useful results were produced. To judge the serious-ness of the problem, he collected information from the system about the time that programs had run before abnormally terminating, applied a cost figure to this time, and obtained a dollar amount, which turned out to be quite significant. After using this figure for several weeks, he suddenly realized it was wrong and greatly overstated the real loss. It dawned on him that when a program terminates abnormally, it does not have to be restarted from the beginning; most programs have "check and restart" points at various places. The only time lost from an abend was the time from the last check point to the time of abnormal termination, typically a small fraction of the total time from start to abnormal termination.

A variant of mistaken data are numbers that purportedly measure one thing when, in fact, they measure something very different. The grade an instructor assigns to an examination purports to be a measure of the students' knowledge of the subject; in fact, it might simply be a measure of the student's willingness to memorize a collection of facts. Conversely, when a student evaluates a course, it is purportedly on the value of the material and the educational experience; in fact, it might simply be a measure of the entertainment value of the course.[1] In the quality area, one must be particularly careful of mistaken measures. Much of the data that purportedly relates to quality can be seen on close examination to measure productivity, total volume, some narrow aspect of quality, or even worse some totally unrelated phenomena.

Incorrect Data

Some of the data you encounter will be incorrect. People misread instructions, measure poorly, and make recording errors. Sometimes they don't even bother to measure. There was a case of an oil field where people tried in vain to change the production level. No matter what they tried, production remained the same. Eventually someone discovered the problem: The person recording the production level simply marked it as equal to the previous production level. The recorded data bore no relationship at all to the true production level. But even when data are gathered and recorded properly, the computer programs used to manipulate it can have defects that cause distortion.

Because errors can and do occur, you should make a habit of scanning the data you work with to see if it appears to contain anomalies—outlying values, clusters of data that cannot be explained, or numbers that just seem wrong. If you spot something unusual, investigate. Satisfy yourself that nothing is wrong; otherwise, edit the data and remove those values that are clearly wrong.

Unavailable Data

A common problem with data is that frequently what you would like to have is not available. Suppose that a company has an on-line order entry system or a computer-controlled production line system that is resident on a central computer. The central computer goes down, leaving dark screens throughout the company and clerks with nothing to do but talk to one another. You might like to know the cost

---

[1]See our discussion of Dr. Fox's lectures in Section 11.10.

of this failure, but chances are it is not available. You can estimate or guess at the cost, but you probably cannot use the accounting system to obtain it.

In the information systems applications development area, people must test the programs they develop. If a defect is found, it is repaired, and the program is retested; sometimes this cycle of repair and retest is repeated many times. If you asked about the total time spent in retesting (an activity required only because tasks were not done right the first time), most likely you would be told that the information is not available. Most development areas can tell you exactly how much time is spent in testing, but the available database can't tell you what fraction of that time was for retesting.

You will find that much of the data required for studying a problem is not available. It stands to reason that this will be so. If data on the problem were readily available, then most likely someone would have looked at it, recognized the problem, and have done something about it. Many problems persist precisely because there is no readily available data that highlights them.

If you really want to measure something, you can always find a way to do it. If you really want data on some problem, you can always find a way to obtain it. The catch, of course, is that the costs of getting the data can be extremely high. So one must compromise. Measure what you can and make reasonable estimates where such estimates will suffice.

Useless Data

Let us conclude this section by acknowledging that a large part of the data currently being collected by organizations, perhaps with the exception of the accounting data that serves a financial reporting function, is useless. The usual problem is that it has been collected because it *could* be collected and for no other reason. The attitude "Let's collect it because some day we might be able to use it" is the organizational equivalent of collecting string. Don't add to the pile of useless data by violating the basic rule we started with: Collect no data until you have planned what you will do with it.

◆ 18.7 Classification of Data

Several of the techniques described in this book call for gathering data. Data are collected to gather ideas for improvement, potential causes of problems, or major inhibitors of quality. Data on processes and their products are taken routinely to monitor performance. Off-line and on-line experiments are carried out, resulting in valuable information on how processes are affected by changes in the input variables. All these activities generate data. To understand the underlying message in the data, it needs to be organized, summarized, and interpreted.

How data is organized and manipulated depends largely on whether the information is *quantitative* or *qualitative*. Quantitative data is analyzed with the use of statistical tools such as those discussed in the next two chapters (Chapters 19 and 20). Qualitative data is analyzed through appropriate data classification; that is, it is arranged into one of several classes according to characteristics the elements have in common. In the following sections of this chapter, we discuss how one goes about making such a classification.

Before you can classify a collection of data, you must select the classification scheme—the system for grouping the data. No matter what the data, there are always many ways to classify. Usually there is no right or wrong way to look at the data. The basic test of whether a classification scheme is appropriate is: Does it serve the special purpose you have in mind when analyzing the data?

To describe classification in a formal way, assume that we have a set of objects under consideration. They can be physical objects such as eggs or fruit that are graded and sorted according to size, or manufactured products that are classified as regular or seconds. If you are dealing with information products, then the objects will represent verbal data, such as words, phrases, or descriptions. A *classification scheme* for a set of objects is a collection of subsets or classes that are mutually exclusive and exhaustive. *Classification* is then the assignment or labeling of the elements according to the classes to which they belong. A useful classification is one where the classes are reasonable in number and serve the purpose of a particular investigation.

Let's examine the meanings of these terms. To say that the classes we are using are *mutually exclusive* simply means that they do not overlap. This means that each object under consideration can be classified in at most one way—no object belongs to two or more classes. To say that classes are *exhaustive* means that each element under consideration belongs to some class. This requirement is easily (and frequently) met by having a catch-all class called "other," "not elsewhere classified," or "miscellaneous." Having a collection of mutually exclusive and exhaustive classes simply guarantees that each object to be classified fits into one and only one class.

The purpose of classification is to group "like" things. Therefore for each class, there must be some characteristics that are possessed by all members of the class and not possessed by objects that are not in the class. An object is in a class if and only if it possesses that characteristic.

How many classes should one select? There is no simple rule as to the "right" number of classes. If one has too few, distinctions among the things being classified are lost. If one has too many classes, useful patterns may fail to materialize. For the kind of problems we consider in this book, from four to ten classes might be reasonable; but this is certainly not a hard and fast rule.

The key element in having a useful classification scheme is the purpose for which classification is done. For defect data, the purpose might be to improve a product or to improve a process. If the focus is on a product, classification might be by the location on the product where the defect is found. If the focus is on a process, classification might be by the cause of the defect. Whatever it is, the purpose of an investigation must be understood clearly before a particular classification scheme is selected.

18.8 The Many Uses of Classification Schemes

Classification schemes are used in several ways. One of the simplest uses is to define an object. Attaching the statement "This is a book on problem solving" to an object helps to identify the object. Here the object is a member of a class of objects called "books" and, moreover, a member of a subclass of books that deals with problem solving.

Another use of classification is to produce systematic order on a set of objects. An organization chart, for example, places a person or a department within the total company structure. A statement of responsibility for action, say, action on solving a quality problem, imposes an order on the set of quality problems.

Classification in the context of problem solving helps us locate problems by going from the general to the specific. For example, suppose there is a problem with a car. Use of a classification scheme may tell us whether the problem is with the engine. Going from the general to the specific, the problem may be narrowed down to the cooling system, and from there to a defective gasket. Similarly, a problem with an information system might first be classified as a hardware, software, or communications problem; further classification might trace it to a specific component.

For problem solving, classification can also help in the opposite direction: going from specific problems to general ones. Consider the area of systems maintenance. Repair activities typically are small, and each single activity requires relatively little resource. Unless these activities are aggregated, it is easy to overlook patterns. By classifying maintenance activities into a few major classes, it is often possible to discover areas where a little preventive work will lessen the amount of maintenance activity in the future.

The use to be made of a classification scheme and the structure of the scheme are closely tied together. For one information system, for example, defects were classified by the phase in the applications development process in which the defect was injected. This revealed no particular information and surprised the group doing the analysis. Then they decided to classify the data according to who had responsibility for the step in which the defect was injected. To their surprise, they discovered several defects for whom there was no responsible authority. This finding made them change certain aspects of their project procedures.

In summary, classification schemes can be used in a variety of ways. Much of the time you do this so naturally that you don't even notice yourself doing it; it is all tied up with the way you think and work. Try, however, to think more consciously about how and when you classify objects; this should help you to use the tool of classification more effectively.

18.9 Building a Classification Scheme

Classification schemes can de defined in two ways: *enumeratively* and *faceted.* The enumerative method of defining a classification is the traditional method. It postulates a universal class of all objects under consideration, which then gets divided into successively narrower classes until an appropriate level of detail has been established. The resulting classes frequently are arranged to show a hierarchical structure. One of the most familiar enumerative classification schemes is the Dewey decimal classification used by libraries. Another example is the scheme of classifying IS development defects by the phase in which the defect is created. Enumerative classification schemes are pre-built and static in that they are devised before examining the specific collection of data that is to be classified.

The faceted method of defining a classification scheme is to synthesize classes from the actual objects being classified. This is the method used in library science to build a computerized database in which documents are filed and retrieved based on key words. For such a database, classes are defined by looking at documents sequentially. The first document is examined, and this becomes the nucleus for the first class. The second document is then examined. If it is sufficiently like the first document, it is placed in the first class; otherwise, it becomes the first member of a new class. This process is repeated: Each document is examined in turn and either is added to an existing class or, if it does not "fit" in an existing class, is used to start a new class.

The faceted technique for defining a classification scheme is dynamic in that the scheme evolves from the data itself. One feature of the technique is that the actual classes that evolve depend on the order in which the data is examined. This can cause problems.

For the type of data that you are likely to examine, a faceted classification scheme is constructed in a less formal way. A person generally starts by looking at a large amount of data—or all of it if it is not too extensive—in an attempt to find similarities. As such similarities are spotted, data elements that share characteristics are grouped together. If a first examination of the data results in too many classes so that patterns are not easily understood, the level of abstraction is raised by further grouping similar classes together. Eventually, a point is reached where the process of grouping (and redefining classes where necessary) results in an appropriate number of classes of a reasonable size. There might also be a number of classes containing only one or two members, and these usually are collected into a single class called "miscellaneous" or "not elsewhere classified."

When you are faced with the problem of classifying a collection of data, a question you will probably ask is: Should I build my own classification scheme, or can I avoid reinventing the wheel by using a scheme someone else has devised? Sometimes you can find a scheme, perhaps by searching the literature, that will serve your purpose; sometimes you can use a very standard scheme, such as classifying numerical data by magnitude. Often, however, your problem will have a special twist that will make other schemes inappropriate. What one tends to do, then, is borrow general ideas, even some specific elements, from other schemes but devise actual classes in either an enumerated or a faceted manner.

◆ 18.10 Schemes for Data Classification

One of the best ways to get a feeling for what might be a useful classification scheme for data about problems is to review what others have done. Many classification schemes for defect data are based on *temporal aspects* of a situation. The classification may involve the time an activity is started or completed, or the time taken by an activity. More specifically, such schemes might classify defect data by

◆ Hour, day, or month some action takes place

◆ Time to failure, repair time, and so on

◆ Development phase in which the defect was created

Often the purpose of a temporal classification is to help find the cause of the problem. By relating the defect to other activities that took place at the time the defect was created, the cause of the defect sometimes can be determined.

Another group of classification schemes for defect data are those based on *location*. Such examples include:

◆ Component of the product in which the defect occurred

◆ Team or unit creating the defect

◆ Team or unit discovering the defect

◆ Team or unit responsible for removing the defect

◆ Team or unit responsible for improving the process to prevent the defect in the future

Other classification schemes for defect data are based on some *characteristic of the defect* of the production process. Examples of such classifications by "type of defect" include:

◆ The activity producing the error (for example, design, coding, etc. in the development of a computer software; or the assembly line, paint shop, etc. in a manufacturing process)

◆ The function of the defective product (logic, input/output, etc.)

◆ The severity of the defect (stops system, wrong result, cosmetic. Or acceptable, scrap, rework)

Frequently, a classification by type attempts to identify the most serious defects, the idea being that these will be addressed first.

Let us look at an actual scheme that has been used in finding the causes of problems. It consists of classifying defect data into four classes:

◆ Communication problem ("I did not understand what I was to do")

◆ Education problem ("I did not know how to do it")

◆ Transcription problem ("I was doing it right, but something went wrong in the process")

◆ Oversight ("I just forgot")

This scheme illustrates several points. First, a scheme need not be elaborate to be useful; with only four classes, the scheme is very simple. Second, a scheme should be easy to use; employees understand this scheme and use it consistently with no difficulty. Third, the classes selected for a scheme should relate to the investigation at hand; knowing which class a problem falls in gives an immediate clue as to how the problem can be eliminated.

The classification approaches discussed here do not exhaust the possibilities for classifying defect data; many others can be devised. If one considers other than defect data, the possibilities for classification are equally great. For example, ideas generated in brainstorming some topic can be classified by similarity, by area of responsibility for action, by importance, by tool or technique involved, and by dozens of other ways.

◆ Exercises and Additional Readings

1. Give several examples of quantitative and qualitative data.

2. Give several examples each for the various uses of data (data to manage, understand, control, and improve processes).

3. Discuss why the style of management can have an impact on the quality of the data that is being collected. Illustrate with examples.

4. Imagine that you are the manager of a fast-food franchise and that you are interested in the quality of your delivered food products as well as your service. What data would you need to assess the current situation, and what data would you need to chart improvements?

5. Assume that you are a dean of the university at which you are pursuing your education. You are concerned about the quality of instruction. What data would you need to assess and improve the quality of instruction, and how would you go about obtaining that data? Which institutional factors do you believe have an influence on the quality of instruction?

6. Consult newspapers and find examples of misleading data.

7. Devise a scheme for classifying the defects that you create in (a) writing term papers; (b) using the computer; (c) managing your time.

8. Devise a scheme for classifying the defects created by people who play your favorite sport.

9. Contact a local firm and ask the Quality Assurance manager what past data is essential for their process improvement efforts. How do they collect it? classify it?

10. Contact a local service organization (restaurant, grocer, . . .) and ask what data they collect for process improvement. Find out how they use the information. How much of their data is geared towards managing, understanding, controlling, or improving some process?

11. Devise a scheme for classifying your daily expenditures. Using this scheme, record your expenses for two weeks. Do the data suggest that you should alter your spending habits?

12. Read and discuss Coreen Casey, Vicente Esparza, Clinton J. Graden, and Paul J. Reep, "Systematic Planning for Data Collection," *Quality Progress*, December 1993, pp. 55–59. Relate the ideas in this paper to the material on Quality Function Deployment that was discussed in Section 10.9.

13. Read and summarize the basic ideas in the following:

    (a) Laura Struebing, "Measuring for Excellence," *Quality Progress*, December 1996, pp. 25–28.

    (b) Mark W. Morgan, "Measuring Performance with Customer-Defined Metrics," *Quality Progress*, December 1996, pp. 31–33.

14. Classroom exercise:

    (a) Select a quality problem that interests the class.

    (b) Brainstorm ideas for solving the problem. Summarize each suggestion in a few words. Write the suggestions on separate slips of paper.

    (c) Use the faceted method of data classification to group the suggestions into categories.

15. Give several examples of false, mistaken, incorrect, unavailable, and useless data.

16. Read James H. Drew and Tye R. Fussell, "Becoming Partners with Internal Customers," *Quality Progress*, October 1996, p. 51. Discuss how surveys can facilitate internal customer relationships.

Chapter 19

Data Analysis and Data Presentation

◆ 19.1 Introduction

The next step after data collection and classification is the analysis of the information. The data need to be summarized and displayed so that its meaning can be shared with all parties involved.

A basic principle that applies in many situations, the so-called 80-20 rule, describes the fact that in many situations, 80 percent of what you are interested in is concentrated in 20 percent of the observations. For example, 80 percent of a company's sales are likely to be to the top 20 percent of their customers. For a complex product, often 80 percent of the defects are found in 20 percent of the components. In almost every society, 80 percent or more of the wealth is concentrated in the hands of 20 percent of the people. This 80 percent and 20 percent rule is not meant as an exact measure, but only as a rough rule of thumb. We mention the 80-20 rule because it also holds for the analysis of data. Many techniques are available for analyzing data: the entire field of statistics deals with this subject. But for most types of problems, 80 percent of what you want to do can be done with the simplest 20 percent of the techniques. For the data you are likely to encounter with quality problems, relatively simple statistical techniques will suffice most of the time, and it is these simple techniques that we study in this and the next chapter.

This discussion is included because we believe that basic statistical principles must be understood by everyone in the organization. If you need to go beyond what is discussed here, there are many books on statistics that can guide you. Our book on statistical techniques for problem solving (Burrill and Ledolter: *Statistical Quality Control: Strategies and Tools for Continual Improvement*, Wiley, 1999) gives a thorough but easy-to-follow introduction to these topics; numerous other well-written introductions are available. If faced with a difficult statistical question, you should also consider seeking the advice of a competent statistician. It often takes a great deal of study to be able to make meaningful statistical inferences; unless you have plenty of time to devote to this, you might be better off employing someone who already has made that investment.

The topics discussed in this and the next chapter deal with the organization, summary, and graphical display of data; summary statistics, such as averages and standard deviations; scatter diagrams and correlation coefficients for displaying and measuring the association among variables; the normal distribution as a useful model to describe the variability in measurement data; statistical inference for estimating population characteristics from sample statistics; sampling issues and acceptance sampling plans; time-sequence plots and control charts for monitoring processes over time; capability indexes to express the capability of processes in meeting required specifications; and principles of statistical design of experiments.

◆ 19.2 Organizing Data—The Pareto Diagram

In many situations, all that is required to gain insight from data is to classify and organize the data properly. For example, suppose you have gathered data from a certain process regarding the defects that originated during the past six months. You want to improve the process by eliminating the causes of some of these defects but have only limited resources to devote to this problem. Where should you start? One approach is to start with the most frequent problem, and you can learn which this is simply by classifying the data and seeing which class has the highest frequency.[1] For example, IBM found that in a large Information Management

---

[1] If you know the cost of each defect, then you can also rank the categories by their total cost (that is, number of defects multiplied by the cost per defect).

System, 31 of the 425 modules accounted for 57 percent of all defects. Similarly, an engineering organization classified their data on the design errors in their engineering drawings. The data in Table 19.1 show that their most frequent error, "callouts," accounted for almost 40 percent of all errors

It is easy to organize data by the type of defect. You simply,

1. Collect data for the problem under consideration.

2. Classify the data into about a half-dozen categories, one of which might be "Other."

3. List each class and the number of its members in order starting with the most frequent class.

Conceptually, this is a very simple exercise; but don't let its simplicity fool you into thinking that it is a useless exercise. People spend a great deal of time and effort working on problems that are inconsequential—time that could be better spent working on important problems. The difficulty is that most people do not know which are the important problems. They need data, hard facts, to guide their efforts.

In Table 19.1 we have also calculated relative frequencies (that is, the number of errors in each class divided by the total number of errors) and the cumulative relative frequencies. For example, $100(329/836) = 39.4$ percent of errors were "callouts"; and $39.4 + 24.2 = 63.6$ percent of all errors were due to the two most frequent errors, "callouts" and "general notes." A simple, but useful, graphical display of the information in Table 19.1 is given in Display 19.1. The (relative) frequencies are displayed in the form of a bar chart, with the heights of the bars representing the frequencies of the various groups. Such a chart is known as a *Pareto diagram,* named in honor of the Italian economist Vilfredo Pareto who encoun-

TABLE 19.1 ◆ Frequencies of Various Design Errors. Errors are ordered from the most frequent to the least frequent one.

Error Category	Number of Errors	Relative Frequency	Cumulative Relative Frequency
Callouts	329	39.4	39.4
General notes	203	24.2	63.6
Dimensions or tolerances	137	16.4	80.0
Parts list	95	11.4	91.4
Symbols	47	5.6	97.0
Drawing practices	23	2.8	99.8
Diagrams	2	0.2	100.0
	836	100.0	

DISPLAY 19.1 ◆ Pareto diagram

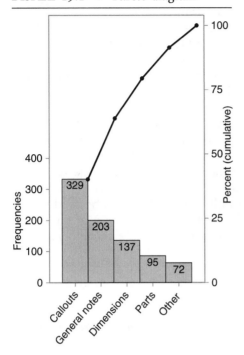

tered distributions of this type in his study of income. In a Pareto diagram, the data is presented in the order of its importance; the data class with the most members is listed first, the second largest class is second, and so on.

In Display 19.1 we also graph cumulative relative frequencies; the scale on the right-hand axis goes from 0 to 100 percent. It shows that the two most common errors represent 63.6 percent of all errors, the three most common 80 percent, and so on.

A Pareto diagram highlights the most important data class and shows its importance relative to others. Use of Pareto diagrams is promoted as a standard tool for quality improvement.

◆ 19.3 Data Presentation

Many people do not feel comfortable with numbers, especially when they are presented in the form of a table or as part of a computer printout. They don't relate to them; they don't examine the entries to learn what interesting story they might tell, and they don't explore the interesting comparisons that might exist. Some people just see the table as a thing, and an uninteresting thing at that. But if the same information is presented graphically, people at once grasp meanings and implications that aren't easy to gain from a table.

Table 19.1, which presents data on defects classified by types, is a good example. Most people find the graphical representation in Display 19.1 more informative than the tabular presentation of the same data.

Just a few years ago, constructing graphs and plotting data was a chore, and a book such as ours would devote several pages of instructions on how to make the various kinds of graphs. With the advent of interactive desktop computers, all of that has changed. Today, one simply uses one of the large number of programs available. It is easy to construct histograms (or bar charts) to display the variation among a set of data, scatter plots to display the association among variables, and time-sequence plots and control charts to display the variation over time. Countless modifications and combinations of these graphs are easily constructed.

Because of the ease with which graphs can be produced now, one can experiment and determine the best way to present a given set of data. The ease and flexibility of building graphs today has done much to improve the format in which data is presented.

◆ 19.4 Graphical Displays of a Data Set: Time-Sequence Plots, Dot Diagrams, and Histograms

In a *time-sequence display*, we plot the measurements against time, or the order in which measurements are collected. To emphasize the time series nature of the observations, it is common to connect successive observations. Since the time order is a very common feature of so many of our measurements, it is important to construct and study such displays. Just think about observations that arise in process control (see Chapter 20 for a detailed discussion). There we take consecutive small samples of observations each hour, or each half hour, depending on the particular application. The first thing we want to do with data of that sort is to plot it against time. Time-sequence plots will tell us about unusual observations, shifts, trends and runs in the data, cycles, periods of increased variability, and unusual time patterns.

Consider as an example the daily attendance figures for lunch at the largest dormitory at the University of Iowa during the fall semester of 1995, given in Display 19.2. Note the decreasing trend in the data. After an initially high attendance at the start of the school year, the number of students eating in the cafeteria trails off. Also note the seasonality in the data; attendance on Saturday and Sunday is usually low as many students are away from campus. This information is of interest to the food services department, for it helps them decide how much food to prepare.

How much variability is there in the process? How can we best describe this variability? Dot diagrams and histograms, which are discussed next, are simple, yet very useful graphical displays of the variability among measurements.

DISPLAY 19.2 ◆ Time-Sequence Plot of Daily Attendance for Lunch: University of Iowa cafeteria, Fall 1995. First point represents a Monday.

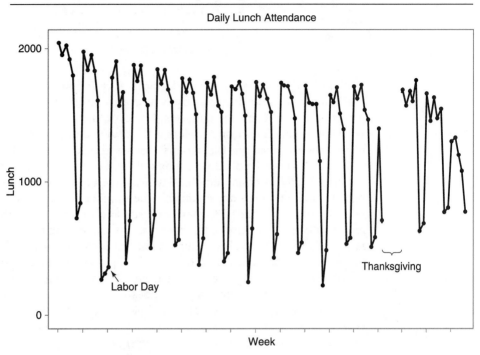

In a *dot diagram* each measurement is represented on a horizontal line by a dot that indicates its magnitude. For small data sets, such diagrams are easily drawn by pencil and paper. For larger data sets, we can use one of the many available statistics software packages to create these displays. The 20 measurements on kathon (in ppm) given in Table 19.2 are used to illustrate the construction of a dot diagram. Kathon is a chemical additive that prevents the growth of bacteria. The measurements were obtained by taking samples from 20 batches of a certain liquid component that goes into the production of shampoo. In this particular case, the manufacturer had set the specification limits for kathon at 3.95 and 6.05 ppm. The dot diagram in Display 19.3 shows that the 20 measurements range from a low of 4.20 ppm to a high of 5.35 ppm. The center of the distribution is around 5.0 ppm. The observations are well within the specification limits 3.95 and 6.05 ppm; there is no apparent problem with the amount of kathon in these batches.

TABLE 19.2 ◆ Measurements on Kathon (in parts per million)

4.82	5.13	5.16	4.85	5.16	5.11	4.86	5.35	5.03	4.97
4.20	4.93	4.70	4.75	4.72	4.89	4.64	4.58	4.98	4.83

DISPLAY 19.3 ◆ Dotplot of Kathon (in ppm)

Kathon (in ppm)

A dot diagram gives a detailed graphical description of the information. Since the numerical value of each observation can be inferred from such a graph, no precision is lost. For large data sets, however, the dot diagram tends to be somewhat too detailed and one prefers a larger degree of summarization (or smoothing) of the information. Histograms, discussed next, do exactly that.

In a *histogram* we divide the range of our observations into nonoverlapping intervals, usually of equal length. A typical rule takes the square root of the number of observations as approximately the number of intervals. Let us illustrate this with the data in Table 19.3 where we list 100 observations on the pH value of different batches of shampoo; the observations range from 5.82 to 6.55. We select 11 nonoverlapping intervals for our histogram, each with a width of 0.07. [Note that the number of intervals, 11, comes very close to the suggested square root rule, $\sqrt{100} = 10$.] The first interval goes from 5.795 to 5.865; the midpoint of this first interval is 5.83. The second interval goes from 5.865 to 5.935, with a midpoint of 5.90. The last interval goes from 6.495 to 6.565, with a midpoint of 6.53. We then count the number of observations that fall into the various intervals. Note that the boundaries of these intervals have three significant digits, which is one more than the significant digits in the observations. Thus, there is no ambiguity as to the interval in which an observation falls. If boundaries are selected such that an observation can fall right on the boundary, then one needs to specify a rule about the allocation. A common convention is that an observation that falls exactly on one of the class boundaries is allocated to the class that has this value as the lower boundary.

The number of observations that fall into each of these classes are called the (absolute) frequencies, and they are denoted by $f_1, f_2, \ldots, f_k$, where k is the

TABLE 19.3 ◆ Measurements on pH of Shampoo

6.19	6.30	6.19	6.02	6.27	6.22	6.31	6.10	6.29	6.36
6.24	6.31	5.97	6.26	6.22	6.26	6.09	6.30	6.03	6.38
6.43	6.15	6.23	6.31	6.19	6.18	6.06	6.36	6.30	6.30
6.43	6.24	5.98	6.39	6.12	6.36	6.55	6.41	6.45	6.45
5.99	6.19	6.47	6.22	6.09	6.01	6.55	6.12	6.43	6.17
6.32	6.24	6.12	6.19	6.23	6.25	5.95	5.82	6.21	6.18
6.23	6.23	6.21	6.41	6.35	6.32	6.14	6.09	6.45	6.08
6.13	6.33	6.15	6.29	6.14	6.20	6.31	6.13	6.15	6.13
6.38	6.40	6.15	6.16	6.30	6.05	6.11	6.02	6.29	6.20
6.27	6.16	6.33	6.05	6.22	6.00	6.42	6.17	6.15	6.03

TABLE 19.4 ◆ Frequency Distribution: pH of Shampoo

Interval	Midpoint	Frequency	Relative Frequency	Cumulative Frequency	Cumulative Relative Frequency
(5.795,5.865)	5.83	1	0.01	1	0.01
(5.865,5.935)	5.90	0	0.00	1	0.01
(5.935,6.005)	5.97	5	0.05	6	0.06
(6.005,6.075)	6.04	8	0.08	14	0.14
(6.075,6.145)	6.11	14	0.14	28	0.28
(6.145,6.215)	6.18	20	0.20	48	0.48
(6.215,6.285)	6.25	16	0.16	64	0.64
(6.285,6.335)	6.32	17	0.17	81	0.81
(6.355,6.425)	6.39	10	0.10	91	0.91
(6.425,6.495)	6.46	7	0.07	98	0.98
(6.495,6.565)	6.53	2	0.02	100	1.00
		100	1.00		

number of classes. In our case $k = 11$; $f_1 = 1$, $f_2 = 0$, ..., $f_5 = 14$, $f_6 = 20$, and $f_{11} = 2$. The absolute frequencies of the various classes sum up to the total number of observations; in this case $n = 100$. One can also calculate the relative frequencies, f_1/n, ..., f_k/n. For example, $f_1/n = 1/100 = 0.01$ and $f_5/n = 14/100 = 0.14$. The sum of the absolute frequencies is one. The frequencies for the 11 selected intervals are given in Table 19.4. Cumulative relative frequencies are given in the last column; they are obtained by cumulating the relative frequencies. For example, the value 0.28 in the fifth row indicates that 28 percent of the pH measurements are smaller than 6.145.

A histogram is a picture of these frequencies; it is given in Display 19.4. We call it a frequency histogram if we display the frequencies. We call it a *relative fre-*

DISPLAY 19.4 ◆ Histogram: pH of Shampoo

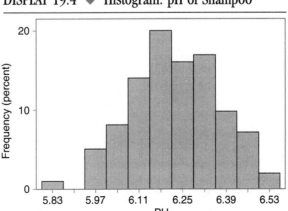

quency histogram if we display the relative frequencies. The only difference is in the labeling of the *y*-axis in the display.

The visual appearance of a histogram may change if one selects a different set of intervals. The interval width controls the smoothing of the information and determines how much detail is shown by the histogram. However, it is not always true that an extra level of detail provides more information. The extra precision may be just noise that is better smoothed out by taking wider intervals.

When constructing histograms of continuous data, one must decide on the number of intervals as well as on the midpoint of the first interval. Computer software packages usually have "automatic" (and usually quite good) procedures that make this decision for you, but also include options that allow you to make your own selection if that is needed.

Histograms for categorical data are constructed similarly. They are even easier than those for continuous data because it is not necessary to make any decisions on how to group the data; for categorical data the categories are already given. An example of a histogram (or bar chart) of a categorical variable is given in Display 19.1, where we display the Pareto diagram. We should mention that there are other ways of displaying frequency distributions of categorical data. The pie chart, for example, displays the frequencies in the form of a "pie" in which the area of each segment is proportional to the frequency of that category.

◆ 19.5 Summary Statistics of a Data Set: Descriptive Statistics

Often one collects so much data on a problem that it is impossible to assimilate and understand it all; one cannot see the forest for the trees. In such cases, instead of working with all the data, it is useful to consider a few well-selected *descriptive statistics* that indicate the general tendencies of the data. We generally distinguish between descriptive statistics that measure the *central tendency* and those that measure the *variation* or *spread*.

Measures of Central Tendency

Measures of central tendency attempt to describe the central point about which the data is arranged. These measures include

◆ The *mean* or the arithmetic *average* of the data, which is defined as the sum of the data elements divided by the number of data elements.

◆ The *median* of the data, which is the middle-most data element after the data have been arranged according to size; half of the data elements are at the median or below, and half are at the median or above.

◆ The *mode* of the data set, which is a data element that appears with the highest frequency. Of course, there can be several elements all appearing with the same maximum frequency, in which case there are several modes.

The concept of a mode is applicable, especially if the data set is already grouped in classes; then the mode is the middle of the interval with the highest frequency.

A histogram with two distinct and separate peaks (modes) is referred to as a *bimodal distribution*, even if the two peaks are not of the same height. Bimodal distributions can arise from measuring two processes that differ in terms of their centers. Imagine items produced by two different machines; on one machine the product dimensions vary around 3.9 inches, while on the other they vary around 4.1 inches. The distribution of all items taken together is bimodal with peaks at 3.9 and 4.1 inches. The frequencies of the two modes depend on the proportion of items that are taken from the respective machines. It is worth pointing out that such "mixtures" are encountered in many other situations: heights of workers (men and women); education of workforce (high school, college); freshness or quality of vegetables (different growing regions or suppliers).

The *average* is the most popular measure of central tendency primarily because the behavior of averages has long been studied by statisticians and is well understood. Also, it is easy to compute the average of a set of numbers by hand, and it is no problem at all to do so with a computer. The average is a good indicator of central tendency if the distribution of the data is symmetric. For example, it would give a reasonably good indication of the central tendency of the heights of adult females in the United States, or of fillweight of an industrial process. We would like to point out, however, that the average can be affected by a few extremely small or large outlying values.

The average of a set of observations is usually denoted by the same symbol that is used for data elements but with a bar placed over it. For example, if the n elements of a data set are denoted by $x_1, x_2, \ldots, x_n$, then the average is denoted by

$$\bar{x} = (x_1 + x_2 + \ldots + x_n)/n$$

The *median* of a set of observations, Md, is defined as the middle value in the data set after the data have been ordered from the smallest observation to the largest. That is, we first order the data from the smallest to the largest: $x_{(1)} \leq x_{(2)} \leq \ldots \leq x_{(n)}$; $x_{(i)}$ is called the *i*th *order statistic*, and the number in parentheses is called the *rank of the observation*. Then the median is defined as

$$Md = x_{(n+1/2)} \qquad \text{if } n \text{ is an odd observation, and}$$
$$Md = (x_{(n/2)} + x_{(n/2+1)})/2 \quad \text{if } n \text{ is an even number}$$

The median is also easy to compute; the observations are ordered, and the median is the middle of the ordered sequence. The median is less affected by extreme values. For example, the median is 3 for the numbers 1, 3, and 8. (Here n is odd and $(n + 1)/2 = 2$; the median is the second smallest observation, that is, the observation with rank 2.) The median is also 3 for the numbers 1, 3, and 100.

Measures of Variability

The second class of descriptive statistics in common use consists of measures of variability or spread. These measures describe the extent to which the data is concentrated about its central point. The larger the value of such a measure, the more spread or variability in the data. Three common measures of variability are:

- ◆ The *variance*, which is based on the squared difference between the data elements and the average.
- ◆ The *standard deviation*, which is the square root of the variance.
- ◆ The *range*, which is the difference between the largest and the smallest data element.

We included the variance in our list for two reasons. First, you will hear reference to both variance and standard deviation, and you should be aware of their relationship. Second, the calculation of the standard deviation is based on the calculation of the variance—the standard deviation is the square root of the variance.

To find the *variance* of a set of numbers, subtract the average from each number, square the resulting differences, add them, and divide the sum by one less than the number of data elements; the result is the variance. To write this in symbolic form, assume that the n observations are denoted by $x_1, x_2, \ldots, x_n$. Then the variance, which is denoted by s^2, is given by

$$s^2 = [(x_1 - \bar{x})^2 + (x_2 - \bar{x})^2 + \ldots + (x_n - \bar{x})^2]/(n - 1)$$

Because it is a sum of squares, the variance is never negative; the closer the variance is to zero, the more the data is concentrated about the average.

The *standard deviation*, denoted by s, is the square root of the variance; that is, $s = \sqrt{s^2}$. Before the use of computers, calculation of the standard deviation was a chore because of the need to take a square root. Today, however, all that has changed because we use hand-held calculators or computers.

A few remarks will help explain the calculations leading to the variance and the standard deviation. First, let us consider the differences between the data elements and their average (the numbers calculated in deriving the variance). These differences indicate how much the observations deviate from their central point. It might seem that an average of these differences would be a good measure of spread, but it is not because that average is always zero. This is because the positive differences exactly cancel the negative ones. (If you are in doubt, try it with a simple example, say with the elements 1, 2, 3, and 6, which have an average of 3.) To prevent such canceling, we square the differences; the squares are all nonnegative so there is no canceling effect when we average them.

To calculate the variance, squares of the differences are added; then the sum is divided, not by the number of observations, but by the number of observations less one. The reason for subtracting 1 from the number of data elements is not easy to explain; suffice it to say that it is compensation for the fact that we do not square differences from the "true" center but only from an estimate of it. Subtracting "1" from the number of data elements compensates for this mathematically.

An intuitive feeling for why a square root should be involved in measuring spread can be gained by looking at the dimension of the data. Say, the data is measured in feet. Because the data is in feet, the average of the data is in feet, and the differences from the average are again in feet. But then these differences are squared and more or less averaged, which means that the variance has a dimension of "square feet." To get back to feet, it is necessary to take a square root, and this leads us to the standard deviation, s.

Because a standard deviation (unlike the variance) has the same dimension as the data elements and their average, it makes good sense to compare the two; for example, it makes sense to ask how many data elements lie within one standard deviation of the average. It turns out that for many data sets, roughly two-thirds of the observations will lie within one standard deviation from the average. Roughly 95 percent of the observations will lie within two standard deviations from the average, and almost all observations will lie within three standard deviations from the average.

One other measure of spread listed above is the *range*, which is the difference between the largest and the smallest observation. The range is easy to calculate. Before computers were commonplace, this advantage made the range a very popular measure, particularly when calculations were made right on the factory floor. With computers, this advantage has disappeared; nonetheless, the range has retained a certain popularity, especially in statistical process control (see our discussion of the range control charts in the next chapter).

To illustrate the descriptive statistics just discussed, consider the 20 measurements on kathon (in ppm) listed in Table 19.2. A simple dot diagram of the data was given in Display 19.3. The descriptive statistics for this set of 20 observations are

Average: $\bar{x}$ = 4.883 ppm
Median: Md = (4.86 + 4.89)/2 = 4.875 ppm
    (Since n = 20 is an even number, we average the observations with rank 10 and 11.)
Variance: s^2 = 0.06467 (ppm)^2
Standard deviation: $s = \sqrt{0.06467}$ = 0.254 ppm
Range: R = (5.35 − 4.20) = 1.15 ppm

You may want to recalculate these values as a check on your understanding of the measures we have discussed and how they are computed. Using statistical computer software, you may also want to check the summary statistics for the n = 100 observations on the pH value of shampoo that are listed in Table 19.3. The histogram of this data set was shown in Display 19.4. The summary statistics are: Average $\bar{x}$ = 6.223; median Md = 6.220; variance s^2 = 0.0197; standard deviation s = 0.14; and range R = 0.73.

◆ 19.6 Uses of Descriptive Statistics

In pursuing quality many questions arise. At what rate are defects being produced by our department? Are we consistently performing at that particular level? Which of two competing processes results in fewer defects? Are some parts of a particular system more error-prone than others? To answer questions such as these, it is necessary to gather relevant data and analyze it with appropriate statistical tools. Simple descriptive statistics about the average performance and the variation in performance usually are all that are needed to gain an improved understanding of a process or a product.

Descriptive statistics also help us track performance over time. A decrease in the standard deviation of the number of defects can indicate that a process is becoming more consistent. Knowing that the average defect rate of a process decreases over time can be convincing evidence that a quality improvement program is working. Several examples of this are given in the next chapter when we discuss control charts.

In tracking a process over time, you need to understand that a measure of central tendency gives different information than does a measure of spread. The level of a process can change over time, yet its standard deviation can remain more or less constant. An example of this is given by the daily temperature readings in, say, Chicago. Through the year, the average monthly temperature will cycle up and down. But the monthly standard deviation of temperature remains about the same; there is about as much variation in temperature in January as in July, though at quite a different level. On the other hand, the average for a process might remain more or less constant while the variation fluctuates. Readings of a seismograph registering the earth's tremors show this pattern—the needle centers on the same point but gyrates about that point in proportion to the earth's motions.

◆ 19.7 Scatter Diagrams and the Correlation Coefficient

Until now we have looked at just a single variable. Sometimes, however, one wants to know whether two or more variables vary together. For example, does the defect rate of a production process vary with the size of the product being produced? Does the number of defects on a particular production line change with the speed of the line? Does the purity of a certain product vary with the temperature and humidity in the plant? Does the weight of a product increase with its moisture content? Does the price of an appliance depend on its quality rating? And so on. We shall confine our attention to two variables, but the discussion of this section extends to several variables.

Let us consider two variables. One variable is denoted by X, and it is plotted on the horizontal, or x-axis. The other variable is denoted by Y, and it is plotted on the vertical, or y-axis. The question of interest is: Is there a relationship between these two variables? Do these two variables vary together, or are changes in one variable unrelated to or independent of changes in the other?

As an example, consider the data in Table 19.5 listing measurements on the moisture content (X) and weight (Y) of 20 items. We obtained this data by selecting an item, measuring its moisture content x and its weight y, thereby obtaining a pair of values (x, y). This procedure was repeated until $n = 20$ such pairs were obtained. The 20 observations listed in Table 19.5 are plotted in the *scatter diagram* shown in Display 19.5; there we plot weight (Y) against percent moisture content (X).

We must now decide whether these two quantities are related. We are looking not for an exact, deterministic relationship but for a tendency or trend. Is there a general pattern showing that as X increases, Y generally does, too? Or as X increases, does Y tend to decrease? If X and Y vary together, we say the variables are *correlated*.

A simple way to assess linear association[2] is to add to the scatter plot a vertical line at the sample average $\bar{x}$ and a horizontal line at the sample average $\bar{y}$, and number the four quadrants as indicated in Display 19.5. Then check whether the number of points in the resulting four quadrants is about even (in which case there is no association), or whether there are more points in quadrants I and III (in which case the association is positive), or in quadrants II and IV (in which case the association is negative). Most points in Display 19.5 are in quadrants I and III. It is pretty obvious that a rather strong positive association exists among the two variables; the larger the moisture content of an item, the larger the weight.

A simple numeric measure of linear association is given by the *sample correlation coefficient*. There one calculates, for each item i, the product $[(y_i - \bar{y})/s_y][(x_i - \bar{x})/s_x]$. Here $\bar{x}$ and $\bar{y}$ are the sample averages, and s_x and s_y are the respective sample standard deviations. The product is positive for points in quadrants I and III and negative for points in quadrants II and IV. Also note that the quantities in

TABLE 19.5 ◆ Moisture (in percent) and Weight for a Sample of 20 Items

Sample	Moisture	Weight	Sample	Moisture	Weight
1	9.2	8.19	11	8.9	8.17
2	8.6	8.15	12	9.5	8.16
3	8.5	8.10	13	8.7	8.12
4	8.9	8.15	14	8.2	8.06
5	9.9	8.23	15	8.3	8.10
6	8.0	8.07	16	9.7	8.22
7	8.9	8.11	17	9.1	8.13
8	9.1	8.16	18	9.1	8.17
9	9.4	8.19	19	8.5	8.08
10	8.4	8.11	20	9.7	8.21

---

[2]The restriction to linear association will become clear in a moment.

DISPLAY 19.5 ◆ Scatter Diagram of Weight (Y) Against Moisture (X). The added coordinate lines intersect at the point that is determined by the sample averages $\bar{x} = 8.93$ and $\bar{y} = 8.144$.

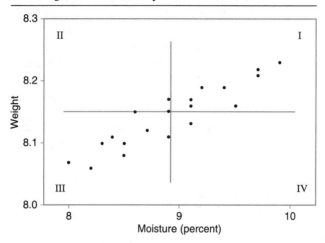

the above expression that get multiplied together are standardized; the division by their standard deviations gives them unit dimensions (in other words, makes them dimensionless). The correlation coefficient is given by the "average" of these products; that is,

$$r = \frac{1}{n-1} \sum_{i=1}^{n} \frac{(y_i - \bar{y})}{s_y} \frac{(x_i - \bar{x})}{s_x}$$

where the summation symbol indicates that we calculate the sum of the n cross-product terms. (As with the variance and standard deviation, we divide the sum in the numerator of the expression by the number of items minus one.) The calculation of the correlation coefficient is a standard feature of any statistics package; hence, there is no need to calculate this coefficient by hand.

The correlation coefficient has several very useful properties. (a) It is always between -1 and $+1$. (b) Its *sign* tells us about the direction of the association; a positive value indicates a positive (or direct) association, whereas a negative value indicates negative (or indirect) association. (c) Its *absolute value* tells us about the strength of the association. The correlation coefficient $r = +1$ means that all points (x_i, y_i) are on a straight line with a positive slope. The correlation coefficient $r = -1$ implies that all points lie on a straight line with negative slope. The correlation coefficient $r = 0$ means that there is no linear association among the two variables.

We want to emphasize that the correlation coefficient measures *linear association only*. You can understand this fact by considering the situation where the observations lie, equally spaced, on a circle of a certain fixed radius. Such a picture reflects a perfect deterministic, but nonlinear, relationship. However, the numbers of observations in the four quadrants of the scatter plot of Y against X are the same, and the (linear) correlation coefficient is zero. The correlation coefficient fails to capture the nonlinear component of the association. This is a limitation of the correlation coefficient, and it suggests the following approach. We recommend that you always supplement the correlation coefficient with a scatter plot of the data. The scatter plot includes more information because it is not always possible to characterize a graph by just a single number. The scatter plot can tell us whether the relationship between the two variables is more complicated than a simple linear association.

The correlation coefficient for the data in Table 19.5 is 0.92. It is positive and quite strong. This says that weight (Y) increases with the moisture content (X) of the product. Or, to say this differently, if the moisture content of an item is higher than average ($\bar{x} = 8.93$), then weight also tends to be higher than average ($\bar{y} = 8.144$); if moisture content is lower than average, then also weight tends to be lower than average. The correlation coefficient confirms what is expressed by the scatter plot in Display 19.5.

Some other questions you might try to answer with scatter diagrams and correlation coefficients are these: Is the cost of quality correlated with the amount spent on prevention? Is there a relationship between defect rates and the speed of the line? Is there a relationship between defect rates and the impurity of the raw materials? Is there a correlation between defect rates and the experience of process operators?

One word of caution: The fact that two variables are correlated does not mean that a cause-and-effect relationship exists between them. The fact that Y tends to increase with X cannot be interpreted as revealing that X "causes" Y to rise. Many examples can be given that show that correlation and cause-and-effect must not be confused. For example, one study showed that the consumption of alcohol is positively correlated with teachers' salaries; the higher the salaries, the greater the consumption of alcohol, and vice versa. But it isn't that teachers rush out and blow their latest pay rise at the nearest bar. Hence there is no causal effect; rather, it seems that underlying economic factors affect both variables. In good times, people spend more on alcohol as well as on teachers.

A little learning can be a dangerous thing; be careful with correlation. Use correlation to find relationships; *treat cause-and-effect as a separate issue.* Only if you can experiment and can change the variables according to a plan that is under your control can you be sure that the correlation comes from a causal relationship. The next chapter shows how to design such experiments.

◆ 19.8 The Normal Distribution: An Important Model to Describe Variability

The measurement value of a certain characteristic (such as a product's length, weight, density, or strength) usually varies from item to item. The production process is subject to many influences and changes; therefore, all products are not exactly the same. Furthermore, the measurement process itself is subject to variability; measuring the same item twice quite often will lead to different results. In other words, the measurement of the characteristic is subject to variability, which may be due to the process (that is, process variability) or to the measurement system (that is, measurement variability). Statisticians describe the variability with probability distributions, and they refer to a measured characteristic that is subject to variability as a *random variable*. This variable might assume only integer values; then we call it a *discrete random variable*. Or it might take on any value in some interval; then we call it a *continuous random variable*. For example, consider a document selected from those produced by a word processing center. The number of typing errors in the document is a discrete random variable; the number of errors can be 0, 1, 2, and so on. On the other hand, the weight of an item, such as the weight of a loaf of bread, is a continuous random variable. Many types of discrete and continuous variables and their distributions have been studied; a detailed description of many of them can be found in introductory statistics books.

The most commonly encountered continuous random variable is the normal random variable. A *normal random variable* is one whose values are distributed according to a bell-shaped curve, the "normal" distribution shown in Display 19.6. As with any distribution function (the function drawn in Display 19.6), the area between an interval on the horizontal axis and the curve immediately above it is equal to the probability (i.e., the chance) that an observation of the random variable will fall within that interval. For example, in Display 19.6, the area under the curve between *a* and *b* is about 0.5. This means that the probability is 0.5 that a value of the random variable is somewhere between *a* and *b*.

The normal distribution depends on only two parameters, the mean and the standard deviation of the distribution. The maximum height of the curve is attained at the point that is the mean of the distribution, and the curve is symmetric about this point. If the standard deviation is small, the curve rises steeply and has most of its area near the mean. For a large standard deviation, the curve is flat and spread out. Because of the close tie between the spread of the curve and its standard deviation, it is possible to make the following statements about a normal population:

◆   68 percent of the population lies within one standard deviation of the mean.

◆   95 percent of the population lies within two standard deviations of the mean.

◆   99.7 percent of the population lies within three standard deviations of the mean.

DISPLAY 19.6 ◆ The Normal Distribution

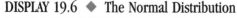
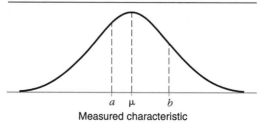

Measured characteristic

Let's see how you can use this information. Suppose that, on the basis of past experience, you believe a certain population is normally distributed with a mean of 10 ppm (parts per million) and a standard deviation of 1.3 ppm. With this assumption you can expect 95 percent of the observations between 7.4 ppm and 12.6 ppm (that is, within two standard deviations from the mean), and about two-thirds of them between 8.7 ppm and 11.3 ppm (that is, within one standard deviation from the mean).

If we know the mean and the standard deviation, then we understand a lot about the entire distribution; of course, these statements only "work" if the normal distribution is an appropriate model of the variability. Luckily, it turns out that the variability of many continuous measurement variables can be described extremely well by such a normal distribution. An important theorem in statistics, called the *central limit theorem*, states that under very mild conditions, a random variable that is affected by many small random factors will follow a normal distribution.

◆ 19.9 Random Sampling and an Introduction to Statistical Inference

Many of our data-gathering activities have to do with sampling. Quite often we are interested in learning about certain characteristics of a whole universe of elements. In statistics, the universe of all elements is called the *population*. For example, the population may consist of all items of a very large shipping lot, all tubes of tooth-paste that were filled during the last shift, all customers who purchased from us during the last year, all students at the University of Iowa (28,000 of them), or all registered voters in the United States. The characteristics that we are interested in may include the proportion of defective items in the shipping lot, the mean or the median income of our customers, the mean grade point average of University of Iowa students, the mean fillweight of our production during the last shift, or the standard deviation among the fillweights.

Most of the time it is not practical to examine each and every member of a population. One hundred percent inspection may be much too expensive or physically impossible as in the case of destructive testing. Instead, we select a small number of elements from the population, measure the attribute on the selected elements, calculate summary statistics from these measurements, and use those to estimate the characteristics of the entire population. The process of selecting members from the population is called *sampling from a population*, and the selected elements represent a *sample* from the population. The number of elements selected is referred to as the *sample size*, and it is common to denote it by *n*.

Most data that gets collected can be viewed as a sample from some population. When viewed in this way, the terms that are used for the descriptive statistics of a set of observations usually have the word "sample" tacked on in front of them. Thus, what we called the average and standard deviation is also referred to as the "sample average" and the "sample standard deviation." This is done to distinguish the statistics that are calculated from the sample from corresponding statistics of the entire population.

Sample statistics are used to estimate population parameters. The sample average is used as an estimate of the population mean, the sample standard deviation is used as an estimate of the population standard deviation, and the sample proportion (of defective items, for example) is used as an estimate of the population proportion. We refer to this process as *estimation* or, more generally, *statistical inference*. For the inference to be accurate and useful, we must select the sample from the population in a fair and representative manner. Now there are many ways of selecting a sample of size n from a population that consists of N elements. Usually, the population size N is quite large and the sample size n is small. For illustration, assume that the population consists of $N = 10$ elements, and suppose that we want to sample $n = 2$ of them. We can select elements 1 and 2, 1 and 3, . . . , 1 and 10, 2 and 3, 2 and 4, . . . , 9 and 10. Convince yourself that there are 45 different samples of two elements each that we could select.

If each of the possible samples has the same chance of being selected, then we say that we have a *random sample*. Random samples give a fair picture of the population as each possible sample has the same chance of being selected. For random samples it is possible to make an accurate inference about the population characteristic, and, as we will illustrate shortly, it is also possible to quote margins for the estimation error. Note that without random sampling the inference could be quite misleading. Assume, for example, that an estimate of a 65 percent satisfaction rating resulted from 100 report cards that customers had left in their hotel rooms prior to checking out. This number may not be a very good estimate of the average satisfaction level for all our customers. Note that here we are not dealing with a random sample. The opinions of people who fill out such cards on their own may not be representative of all customers who stay in our hotel; people filling out these cards usually are extremely pleased or quite upset.

How do you draw a random sample? Imagine that the elements of the population are already numbered; from 1, 2, . . . through N; for the population of customers this is easy because the sales department will have the required list. A simple conceptual approach to drawing a random sample is as follows: Enumerate all elements of the population, prepare N slips of papers with each slip representing an element, put the slips into a bowl, and draw n slips of papers one after the other and without replacement (that is, once you select a slip, you do not return it to the bowl). The elements that correspond to the selected slips are the ones that make up your random sample. This procedure is instructive and easy to carry out, but not convenient because it involves making up many slips of papers. There are easier ways of doing exactly the same thing; this involves the use of random numbers (see Section 20.10).

In certain situations it will be difficult to enumerate the elements of your population. For instance, it is difficult when you sample from a process that produces many items. Enumerating all tubes of toothpaste that were produced during the last shift is probably impossible because the tubes will already have been packed into larger shipping units. It is impossible to enumerate the population when sampling one pound of iron ore from a ton of ore that goes into the production of a batch of steel. While it may not be possible to draw a genuine random sample in such cases, you should always try to make the sampling as random as possible.

This means giving each part of the population a roughly equal chance of being selected. In the case of iron ore, you could approximate random sampling by selecting small ore samples at more or less random times.

Let us consider a few more examples. Suppose you are interested in the proportion of defectives in a lot that consists of many items. Since it is impractical to examine each single element of the population, you draw a random sample of, say, $n = 100$ elements and determine the sample proportion of defective elements. Suppose the sample proportion of defectives turns out to be 4 percent. Then you take this as an estimate of the proportion of defectives in the whole population. Of course, another sample of 100 different items may lead to a different estimate; it may be 6 percent in the second sample and 3 percent in the one after that. However, with random samples and with a reasonably large sample size, you can expect that your sample estimate is close to the proportion of defectives in the population. Similarly, you may be interested in the mean time it takes your customers to pay their bills. Instead of looking at the records of all your customers, you select a random sample of size $n = 30$, and calculate the sample average from these 30. Again, sample averages for different samples will not be the same; however, for reasonably large samples one can show that the sample estimate will be close to the mean of the population. For this to hold, one must make sure that the sample is indeed a random sample, and not just a sample that represents a very specific part of the population.

A reason for discussing sampling is to give you a better conceptual base for interpreting the data you might gather. For example, suppose you collect defect data from a certain process that is stable, meaning that its mean and standard deviation are constant. Even if the process remains unchanged from one time period to the next, there are many random factors that introduce variability into the observed defect rates; you just cannot expect that the observed defect rates will be identical. For example, the raw materials for your process may vary somewhat; the conditions in the plant may show some variability; the workforce may not always function exactly the same way; and so on. All these factors cause the number of defects to vary from time to time. So you shouldn't take slight variation as evidence that the process has changed and that corrective action must be taken. Instead, you can adopt the view that the process is stable and regard the variation in your observations simply as the result of chance or "noise," not a change in the underlying process. If the variation is large (larger than what is indicated by the usual process variability), then you need to take action.

How large is the *margin of error* in our estimates? *Confidence intervals* are typically used to express the uncertainty in our sample statistics as estimates of the unknown population characteristics. The sample average is an estimate of the population mean. Furthermore, it turns out that for random samples of reasonably large sample size n, the interval ($\bar{x} - 2\ s/\sqrt{n}$ to $\bar{x} + 2\ s/\sqrt{n}$) is a *95 percent confidence interval*. We are 95 percent confident that this interval will cover the unknown population mean. Similarly, the interval ($\bar{x} - 3\ s/\sqrt{n}$ to $\bar{x} + 3\ s/\sqrt{n}$) is a 99.7 percent confidence interval; we are extremely confident (almost certain) that this interval will cover the unknown population mean. For us to have this confidence, the information must be collected through a random sample. This is a very important assumption; these intervals might be wrong and misleading if you sampled only from a particular segment of the population.

As an example of a confidence interval, assume that a random sample of $n = 30$ accounts reveals that the average time to pay is 18.2 days, and the sample standard deviation is $s = 6.0$ days. A 95 percent confidence interval for the (population) mean time to pay goes from $18.2 - (2)(6.0)/\sqrt{30}$ to $18.2 + (2)(6.0)/\sqrt{30}$, or (16.0 days to 20.4 days). This says that we are quite confident that the mean time to pay is somewhere in this interval; in other words, we are quite confident that the mean time to pay is from 16 to 21 days.

Similarly, we can calculate confidence intervals for an unknown population proportion. A 95 percent confidence interval goes from $p - 2\sqrt{p(1-p)/n}$ to $p + 2\sqrt{p(1-p)/n}$, where p is the sample proportion that is obtained from a random sample of size n. A 99.7 percent confidence interval extends from $p - 3\sqrt{p(1-p)/n}$ to $p + 3\sqrt{p(1-p)/n}$. As an example, consider a random survey of 100 hotel customers showing that 65 percent of the surveyed people are happy with the service they received. We take these 65 percent as an estimate of the population proportion of satisfied customers. But what is the margin of error? The 95 percent confidence interval from $0.65 - 2\sqrt{(0.65)(0.35)/100}$ to $0.65 + 2\sqrt{(0.65)(0.35)/100}$, or (0.602 to 0.698) shows that we are 95 percent confident that the unknown population proportion is somewhere within this interval. In other words, we are quite sure (95 percent to be exact) that the level of satisfaction is larger than 60 percent but also less than 70 percent. Again, these calculations depend very critically on the fact that our results have come from a random sample and that every one of our customers had the same chance of being selected in our sample. It does not apply to sample information that is obtained from *convenience surveys* such as the completed survey cards that customers leave on restaurant tables or in hotel rooms.

◆ 19.10 Things to Watch When Displaying Information

Because graphs are such persuasive tools, there is ample room for their misuse. Sometimes this is done unconsciously, but sometimes people deliberately use statistics to shade the truth. Among several standard tricks is the "bottom trick." It involves omitting the dull, equal bottoms of bars in a histogram and concentrating only on the tops, which display the difference. Display 19.7 is an example. Notice the great improvement of the "After" over the "Before." The second bar is half the length of the first, suggesting incorrectly a 50 percent cut. But if one troubles to look at the label on the vertical axis, it can be seen that the improvement is more like 10 percent.

Another standard trick is the "dimensional effect." It usually involves a picture graph, and the importance of the objects is depicted by the size of the picture. Display 19.8 shows a typical example, expressing a reduction in the total number of defects from 445 to 231. Since the defects were cut more or less in half, the

DISPLAY 19.7 ◆ A Misleading Graphical Display:
Cutting Off the Bottoms of a Bar Chart

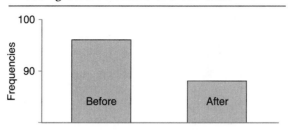

second square has one-half the width of the first. Fair enough. But that means that the area covered by the second picture is only one-fourth the area of the first, which introduces an unconscious bias toward overemphasizing the importance of the achievement.

Symbols, too, can be used to mislead. Once we saw a beautiful example of this in an advertisement for an annuity. Under a large banner headline, "How long will $39,000 last these days?", two hourglasses were shown as in Display 19.9. One hourglass had little sand left, while the other one was full. Each proclaimed that for an investment of $39,000, a person would receive $279.25 per month. The first hourglass, representing payments from a bank account, carried a caption stating that the payment was for 11 years; the second, representing the annuity, proclaimed that payments were for life! Fantastic. Except that the fine print stated that this applied only if you are 60 years old; obviously, payments for life at that age don't mean the same as they do at age 25. No doubt the two schemes are actuarially equivalent, but the hourglasses certainly were not.

DISPLAY 19.8 ◆ Misleading Graphical
Display Using a Wrong Display of
Area

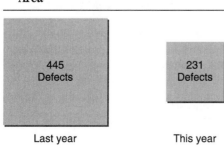

DISPLAY 19.9 ◆ Another
    Misleading Graphical Comparison

How long will $39,000 last?

Bank payments   Annuity
for 11 years   payments for life

◆ 19.11 More Discussion on Measurement Problems

Without attempting to distort the truth, we can still get into difficulties when sum-
marizing or displaying data. Often this is because there is just no single good way
to describe a situation, only many less-than-perfect ways. Several examples will illustrate what we have in mind.

Example 1.   One corporation constructed measures of the quality of individual computer programs that had been developed by their company. They
wanted an overall measure of the effectiveness of their application development process, and they decided to base the overall measure on the data for
individual programs. Assume that there are two programs (in the actual example there were many more) with individual defects as shown in Table 19.6.
For an overall measure of quality, they averaged the defect rates for the individual programs. Using the data in Table 19.6, we see that this amounts to
an overall measure of 5 defects per KLOC (thousand lines of code).
    Many other organizations obtain an overall defect rate according to the
same way: by averaging the defect rates for the various components that
make up the overall product. But suppose that in our example Program 1 is
large, say 100,000 lines of code, and Program 2 is moderate, say only 35,000
lines of code. Then the total number of defects is 805—700 from Program 1
and 105 from Program 2. Since the two programs contain a total of 135,000
lines of code, the true average defect rate in the total package of code is
about 6 per KLOC.

TABLE 19.6 ◆ First Paradox: Defect
    Rates of IS Programs

Program	Defects per KLOC
Program 1	7
Program 2	3

But is this really the correct way to average the defects of the two programs? Let us suppose further that Program 1 is accessed very frequently (it may be an active component of the operating system), while Program 2 is used only infrequently, perhaps as part of the year-end closing. Then how should the average be calculated? Isn't then the true average essentially the 7 defects per KLOC of Program 1?

The point of this particular example is that often there is no simple best way to measure a process. One uses a measure that seems reasonable, but any measure must be examined carefully to learn its shortcomings and the tricks it can play on you.

Example 2. Measures taken for one particular purpose are often used for another. This, too, can lead to confusion, as the following example shows. Capers Jones, in his book *Programming Productivity* (New York: McGraw Hill, 1986), studied the effect of the programming language on productivity and quality. The data in Table 19.7 compare the costs of building a particular function for each of three different languages; Assembler, PL/I, and APL. His results show that APL represents by far the cheapest alternative.

A commonly used measure of programming productivity is the number of lines of code that is produced within a unit of time, say a person-month. This measure is much used and much debated because there are questions about what constitutes a line of code, whether this is a valid measure of accomplishment, and so on. Let us assume that it is a useful measure for comparing programs that are written in the same language. Even so, the data of Table 19.7 show that this measure can give paradoxical results when used to compare productivity across languages. As measured by lines per person month, Assembler language is twice as "productive" as PL/I and four times as "productive" as APL. This measure is contrary to the costs given in line 3 of that table, which shows that APL is the cheapest alternative. The paradox is easy to explain. For example, consider APL. It cuts the total number of lines by 90 percent, but it cuts the total cost by only 40 percent. This difference in percentages arises because a change in the code language does not

TABLE 19.7 ◆ Second Paradox: Lines of Code per Person-Month and Cost per Line—Two Dubious Productivity Indicators

	Assembler	PL/I	APL
Source lines	100,000	25,000	10,000
Total person-months	200	100	80
Total cost	$1,000,000	$500,000	$400,000
Lines/person-month	500	250	125
Cost/line	$ 10	$ 20	$ 40

impact all other noncode-related activities such as design, testing, documentation, and project planning. The number of lines per person-month goes down because the decrease in the numerator (the number of lines) is so much greater than the decrease in the denominator (person-months).

Using cost per line in the last line of Table 19.7 suffers the same fate and for a similar reason. For example, compare APL with Assembler. While APL cuts the total programming cost by 60 percent, it cuts the total number of lines even more (by 75%); thus, cost per line increases.

Example 3. Table 19.8 presents data on number of defects per KLOC. It, too, shows that this measure can give paradoxical results when applied across programming languages. The paradox is similar to that discussed earlier in the context of a productivity measure. APL, for example, cuts the total number of defects in half, but it cuts the total number of lines by 90 percent. Hence the number of defects per line soars. This is because a change in the programming language will not change the number of defects in nonprogramming areas.

Jones estimates that of the 7000 defects occurring during the creation of the Assembler program, about 3000 are in nonprogramming areas. This number is not changed by changes in the programming language. So while APL drops the number of programming errors from 4000 to 500 (almost the same as the percentage drop in the number of lines of code), the total number of defects only drops by half.

What moral can we draw from all of this? We definitely will need data for a better understanding of a problem, but data can be tricky. Some of it does not describe the true situation, so you must be careful to examine your data and gain confidence that it is representative and useful. For most of what you will be doing, simple classification and analysis will probably be sufficient, but if you need to go beyond that, don't hesitate to look for professional assistance. When you use your data, do so with common sense. Remember that the way you present it can make a big difference in how effective you will be in communicating your ideas. Finally, never accept data or measures blindly. Examine them to learn their shortcomings. Don't reject a measure because it isn't "perfect"—no measure is. But don't accept it simply because it is easy to calculate or generally used. Make certain you feel comfortable with it, too.

TABLE 19.8 ◆ Third Paradox: Defects per KLOC—A Dubious Quality Indicator

	Assembler	PL/I	APL
Source lines	100,000	25,000	10,000
Total defects	7,000	4,000	3,500
Defects/1000 lines	70	160	350

◆ Exercises and Additional Readings

1. The following table lists the percent yields of 25 consecutive batches (read across rows). Construct a time-sequence plot and comment on its appearance. Construct a dot diagram and calculate the summary statistics discussed in Section 19.5

72.4	75.3	72.7	74.2	75.6	75.0	73.3	73.1	74.4	77.5
75.8	74.0	73.2	74.8	76.2	72.7	68.2	79.1	73.8	55.5
74.7	75.7	72.9	72.1	77.7					

2. In the production of shampoo it has long been speculated that the pH level is a major factor in controlling the color of the product. The following data were obtained by sampling several batches and determining their pH and their "B-color." Interpret the data. Construct a scatter plot and calculate the correlation coefficient.

Batch	pH	B-Color
1	6.4	5.50
2	6.4	6.33
3	6.6	6.09
4	6.3	3.54
5	6.5	7.14
6	6.5	9.41
7	6.4	8.61
8	6.4	9.81
9	6.4	7.46
10	6.5	6.99
11	6.3	6.29
12	6.5	8.32
13	6.3	9.81
14	6.4	9.95
15	6.3	8.48
16	6.5	9.84
17	6.5	8.57
18	6.5	9.90
19	6.4	9.53
20	6.4	8.86
21	6.3	8.70
22	6.5	5.40
23	6.3	9.40
24	6.5	8.72
25	6.4	8.72

3. Consider the data on the gain of 120 tested amplifiers. The design of the amplifier had called for a gain of 10 decibels. This means that the output from the amplifier should be about 10 times stronger than the input signal. Construct a dot diagram and an appropriate histogram. Describe the distribution. Is it symmetric? Calculate the summary statistics, including the average, median, variance, standard deviation, and range.

8.1	10.4	8.8	9.7	7.8	9.9	11.7	8.0	9.3	9.0
8.2	8.9	10.1	9.4	9.2	7.9	9.5	10.9	7.8	8.3
9.1	8.4	9.6	11.1	7.9	8.5	8.7	7.8	10.5	8.5
11.5	8.0	7.9	8.3	8.7	10.0	9.4	9.0	9.2	10.7
9.3	9.7	8.7	8.2	8.9	8.6	9.5	9.4	8.8	8.3
8.4	9.1	10.1	7.8	8.1	8.8	8.0	9.2	8.4	7.8
7.9	8.5	9.2	8.7	10.2	7.9	9.8	8.3	9.0	9.6
9.9	10.6	8.6	9.4	8.8	8.2	10.5	9.7	9.1	8.0
8.7	9.8	8.5	8.9	9.1	8.4	8.1	9.5	8.7	9.3
8.1	10.1	9.6	8.3	8.0	9.8	9.0	8.9	8.1	9.7
8.5	8.2	9.0	10.2	9.5	8.3	8.9	9.1	10.3	8.4
8.6	9.2	8.5	9.6	9.0	10.7	8.6	10.0	8.8	8.6

4. Brian L. Joiner, "The Key Role of Statisticians in the Transformation of North American Industry," *The American Statistician*, 1985, pp. 224–227, emphasizes that one must have relevant data to manage effectively. Discuss this paper. What other fundamentals are needed?

5. For an excellent guide on how to display data graphically and for many examples of outstanding graphical displays you should consult the following books by Edward R. Tufte: *The Visual Display of Quantitative Information* (1983) and *Envisioning Information* (1990). These books, published by Graphics Press (Cheshire, CT), should be available in your library. Summarize Tufte's guidelines for creating good and truthful displays.

6. You are told that the pH value of a certain liquid ingredient that goes into shampoo varies according to a normal distribution with mean 6.30 and standard deviation 0.15. Describe the variability to someone who doesn't know about distributions.

7. The fillweight of 10-ounce tubes of toothpaste varies according to a normal distribution with mean 10.20 ounces and standard deviation 0.10 ounce. Describe the variability to someone who doesn't know about distributions. What proportion of your tubes will be underfilled?

8. Looking at newspapers and magazines, find several examples of misleading tables and displays.

9. Your population consists of a carton of 12 extra large eggs; here the population size is $N = 12$.

   (a) Determine the mean weight of eggs in your population. You can do this by putting all 12 eggs on the scale and dividing the weight by 12.

   (b) Your objective is to estimate the mean weight of an egg from a sample of size $n = 2$. Select a random sample of two eggs. You can do this by numbering your eggs, writing out 12 slips of papers, putting the slips into a bowl, and drawing two slips without replacement.

The two selected slips will tell you which eggs to measure. Weigh the eggs and calculate the average weight. How close to the population mean did you get?

(c) How can you explain the difference between your estimate and the population average? Discuss. What would happen if you had selected a different pair of eggs? How many ways are there to select two eggs from among the 12?

10. Consider the following data on rain during the harvest season (rain in August and September, in total millimeters), average temperature during the growing season (April through September, in degrees centigrade), the age of the vintage, and the average price for the Bordeaux vintage relative to the year 1961. Data for the years 1952 through 1980 are listed at the end of the exercise. The prices for the 1954 and 1956 vintage are missing. Relative prices for these two vintages could not be established because these were poor vintages and very little wine is now sold from these two years.

The objective is to predict the price of the vintage as a function of its age, rainfall, and temperature. How successful is this approach? Interpret the data through appropriate scatter plots (such as plots of price against the various explanatory variables) and summary statistics. One informative plot shown in the reference given below is a scatter plot of harvest rain against summer temperature where each point in the scatter plot is displayed by one of two symbols: a solid circle if the price of that year's vintage is above average, and a square if the price is below average. Such a graph allows you to display three variables. *Hint:* It may be beneficial to transform the response, price, into logarithm (price).

One advantage of the statistical approach is timely prediction; the quality of the current year can be rated immediately without having to wait for several months before the vintage can be evaluated. Even then, in March of the following year when the vintage is first evaluated by experts, the ratings are rather unreliable because the four-month-old wine is a rather foul mixture of fermenting grape juice and little like the magnificent stuff it can become years later.

Source: Orley Ashenfelter, D. Ashmore, and R. Lalonde. "Bordeaux Wine Vintage Quality and the Weather," *Chance Magazine* 8, No. 4 (1995), pp. 7–14; see also *Barron's*, December 30, 1996, pp. 17–19.

vintage year	summer temp	harvest rain	age of vintage	relat price
1952	17.12	160	31	0.368
1953	16.73	80	30	0.635
1954	15.38	180	29	*
1955	17.15	130	28	0.446
1956	15.65	140	27	*
1957	16.13	110	26	0.221
1958	16.42	187	25	0.180
1959	17.48	187	24	0.658

1960	16.42	290	23	0.139
1961	17.33	38	22	1.000
1962	16.30	52	21	0.331
1963	15.72	155	20	0.168
1964	17.27	96	19	0.306
1965	15.37	267	18	0.106
1966	16.53	86	17	0.473
1967	16.23	118	16	0.191
1968	16.20	292	15	0.105
1969	16.55	244	14	0.117
1970	16.67	89	13	0.404
1971	16.77	112	12	0.272
1972	14.98	158	11	0.101
1973	17.07	123	10	0.156
1974	16.30	184	9	0.111
1975	16.95	171	8	0.301
1976	17.65	247	7	0.253
1977	15.58	87	6	0.107
1978	15.82	51	5	0.270
1979	16.17	122	4	0.214
1980	16.00	74	3	0.136

11. Group project: Crime is an important factor that affects the quality of life. Obtain crime data for your community (state, or country) and display that data graphically. Interpret the results.

12. Group project: Obtain data on traffic accidents for your state or the country as a whole. Most likely this data will already be classified into several logical groupings (such as severity of accident, age of driver, etc.). Display the data. Obtain data for two successive years. Discuss whether there has been a change.

13. Group project: If you are a student at a public university, then the salaries of your professors will be public information. Most likely, you can look them up in the library.

(a) Select the professors in the Mathematics Department. List the salaries. Display them graphically (using a dot diagram); calculate summary statistics such as the average and the standard deviation.

(b) You will notice variability among the salaries. One reason for variability in salaries is differing experience and productivity. Academia distinguishes three main categories of professors: assistant, associate, and full professors. Repeat your analysis in (a), but carry it out for each category separately. That is, construct three dot diagrams. For ease of comparison, it is best to stack these diagrams and to draw them on the same scale. Also, obtain summary statistics of salaries for each of the three categories.

(c) You are asked to estimate the mean salary of all professors at your university. You use the salary average that you calculated in (a) as your estimate. You argue that the professors in the Mathematics

Department represent a sample of professors at your university, and you contend that the sample average should be a reliable estimate of the population mean. Discuss why or why not this is true.

14. Among the 120 defects from a lens-polishing operation, we found 12 lenses with incorrect dimensions, 33 scarred lenses, 8 cracked lenses, 15 unfinished lenses, 44 poorly coated lenses, and 8 where the defect could not be classified ("other"). Construct a Pareto diagram. Assuming that each type of defect is equally costly, which defect would you attack first?

15. Collect defect information on the delivery of instruction in one of your classes. You can do this with a survey of your fellow students by asking them to list the three most useful changes that could be made to this course. Organize your information and develop an appropriate Pareto diagram.

16. A random sample of 50 current customers shows that 30 of them would definitely buy from us again. Obtain and interpret a 95 percent confidence interval for the proportion of customers who would buy from us again.

17. The breaking strength of leads for mechanical pencils is an important quality characteristic. The test for breaking strength is destructive. A random sample of $n = 100$ leads was taken from today's production. It was found that the average breaking strength was 5 pounds, with a standard deviation of $s = 2$ pounds. Calculate and interpret a 95 percent confidence interval for the mean breaking strength of today's production.

18. Read Marti Benjamin and James G. Shaw, "Harnessing the Power of the Pareto Principle," *Quality Progress*, September 1993, p. 103. Discuss the Pareto diagram and the flowchart of the payment process.

19. Consider the daily lunch attendance at the Burge residence hall cafeteria at the University of Iowa for the fall of 1995. This is the data set that was used to construct the time-sequence display in Display 19.2.

    (a) Calculate weekly totals and construct a time-sequence plot of these data. Repeat this for weekly weekday totals (Monday through Friday) and weekly weekend totals (Saturday, Sunday). Discuss your findings. Note that attendance on Monday, September 4 is unusually low; September 4 was a holiday, Labor Day. You may want to adjust the weekly total for this unusually low number.

    (b) Compare the attendance for the various days of the week. Discuss the seasonal (that is, the weekly) attendance figures. What are your findings?

    (c) Attendance at lunch varies from day to day. List the factors that influence attendance.

Month	Day	Day Code	Attendance
8	21	1	2045
8	22	2	1955
8	23	3	2027

8	24	4	1926
8	25	5	1799
8	26	6	732
8	27	7	850
8	28	1	1979
8	29	2	1843
8	30	3	1956
8	31	4	1835
9	1	5	1604
9	2	6	266
9	3	7	300
9	4	1	356
9	5	2	1785
9	6	3	1904
9	7	4	1569
9	8	5	1672
9	9	6	382
9	10	7	711
9	11	1	1887
9	12	2	1757
9	13	3	1875
9	14	4	1617
9	15	5	1575
9	16	6	494
9	17	7	755
9	18	1	1847
9	19	2	1729
9	20	3	1840
9	21	4	1683
9	22	5	1593
9	23	6	524
9	24	7	562
9	25	1	1779
9	26	2	1670
9	27	3	1768
9	28	4	1662
9	29	5	1502
9	30	6	367
10	1	7	571
10	2	1	1738
10	3	2	1649
10	4	3	1786
10	5	4	1564
10	6	5	1521
10	7	6	394
10	8	7	458
10	9	1	1712
10	10	2	1694
10	11	3	1743
10	12	4	1656

10	13	5	1491
10	14	6	238
10	15	7	648
10	16	1	1747
10	17	2	1634
10	18	3	1733
10	19	4	1592
10	20	5	1513
10	21	6	421
10	22	7	600
10	23	1	1734
10	24	2	1715
10	25	3	1708
10	26	4	1629
10	27	5	1468
10	28	6	453
10	29	7	534
10	30	1	1719
10	31	2	1585
11	1	3	1573
11	2	4	1580
11	3	5	1150
11	4	6	214
11	5	7	481
11	6	1	1645
11	7	2	1596
11	8	3	1711
11	9	4	1508
11	10	5	1394
11	11	6	527
11	12	7	570
11	13	1	1715
11	14	2	1618
11	15	3	1728
11	16	4	1541
11	17	5	1463
11	18	6	498
11	19	7	579
11	20	1	1396
11	21	2	716
11	22	3	0
11	23	4	0
11	24	5	0
11	25	6	0
11	26	7	0
11	27	1	1692
11	28	2	1561
11	29	3	1681
11	30	4	1594
12	1	5	1763

12	2	6	622
12	3	7	686
12	4	1	1655
12	5	2	1457
12	6	3	1632
12	7	4	1464
12	8	5	1541
12	9	6	773
12	10	7	804
12	11	1	1301
12	12	2	1333
12	13	3	1199
12	14	4	1079
12	15	5	774

DayCode: 1—Monday; 2—Tuesday; . . . ; 7—Sunday
September 4—Labor Day
Wednesday, Nov 22 to Sunday, Nov 26—Thanksgiving, no classes

20. Read and summarize the main message in Douglas B. Relyea, "The Simple Power of Pareto," *Quality Progress*, May 1989, pp. 38–39. Discuss how Pareto charts were used at Brand-Rex Cable Systems.

21. Read Roger E. Duffy, "Pareto Analysis and Trend Charts: A Powerful Duo," *Quality Progress*, November 1995, p. 152. What can you gain by combining the Pareto chart with time-sequence plots?

22. Read Ron S. Kenett, "Making Sense Out of Two Pareto Charts," *Quality Progress*, May 1994, pp. 71–73. How does the author use Pareto charts for the display of software errors?

23. Read Carolyn K. Amy and Ann Strong, "Teaching the Concepts and Tools of Variation Using Body Temperature," *Quality Progress*, March 1995, p. 168. Repeat this exercise with the students in this class. Construct a histogram and summarize the information. Investigate whether there are gender differences.

24. Read and discuss Bert Gunter, "Surveys: Thank You for Your Support—I Think," *Quality Progress*, December 1990, pp. 111–112. Discuss the difference between sampling variability and survey bias. Confidence intervals for the true proportion are easily calculated; but what assumptions must be met before you can use such intervals as uncertainty measures for your sample estimate?

Chapter 20

Statistical Techniques for Achieving Quality

◆ 20.1 Introduction

For several decades statistical quality control (also called statistical process control, or SPC) has been the main technique for improving product quality in the manufacturing area. As its name suggests, *statistical quality control* is a branch of applied statistics dealing with statistical tools that help control the quality of products and improve the processes responsible for these products.

Broadly speaking, the tools of statistical quality control can be divided into several major groups. One group of techniques deals with sampling inspection. *Acceptance sampling plans* rely on samples of incoming or outgoing material to decide whether a lot should be accepted. While it is still used by many companies, sample inspection has lost some of its appeal in today's climate of emphasizing process improvements and processes with low defect rates. Today the aim is to improve the quality systems so that ultimately such inspections will become unnecessary.

The second group of statistical quality control tools involves *control charts*. These techniques go back to the 1920s, when W. A. Shewhart of the Bell Telephone Laboratories originated the concept of statistical quality control and control charts. Control charts are important tools for monitoring processes through the products they produce. Unusual events can be recognized, their causes can be found, and actions can be taken to prevent these causes in the future. A cycle of recognizing and preventing unusual events improves processes.

The use of control charts spread through the manufacturing segment of the U.S. economy, slowly at first, but rapidly during World War II when sudden heavy demand was placed on industry. After the war, Japan turned to quality as a fundamental strategy for recovering from the devastation wrought by the war and for regaining world markets. American experts, such as W. Edwards Deming and Joseph M. Juran, were invited to help, and they introduced statistical process control and control charts to the Japanese. For at least a decade, this was Japan's chief tool in promoting quality. Gradually, the growth of other notions, such as the importance of management in achieving quality, eclipsed the importance of statistical quality control in Japan. But it still remains a fundamental tool for quality, one that the Japanese thoroughly mastered and regularly apply.

The third group of statistical techniques introduced in this chapter deals with experimentation and the *statistical design of experiments*. We may have certain ideas about which factors affect our processes and products. For example, a pastry chef may be interested in the quality of his popovers but may not know whether and how some of the suspected factors influence the quality. It could be the preheat temperature of the oven, the temperature and the size of the eggs, the consistency of the batter and whether it was stirred by hand or by a mixer, the temperature of the batter before it goes into the oven, and so on. After coming up with a list of factors that may have a possible effect on the results, it is time to experiment. And for this it is important to have a plan—a roadmap. Knowledge of what is important in a process is valuable, but so is knowledge of what isn't. Knowing which factors have no effect helps save time and money, and it frees our attention so that we can better focus on things that do make a difference.[1]

Experimentation is an important step in any problem-solving strategy. Statistical design of experiments provides the roadmap for successful experimentation. The techniques for experimental design go back to the 1920s when R. A. Fisher, through his work at the Rothamsted agricultural research station in England, laid the foundation for future work in this area. Design techniques were later extended to industry, but application has been patchy in the West, usually because of lack of management understanding and support. Experimentation has been inhibited by

---

[1]This example was taken from Brian L. Joiner, *Fourth Generation Management* (New York: McGraw-Hill, 1994).

an attitude of "if it ain't broke, don't fix it" and the fear of being blamed if a change goes wrong. This is different from Japan, where engineers routinely conduct experiments on processes both on-line and off-line. Japanese companies have recognized the importance of statistically designed experiments to further the quality of their processes and products. They are convinced of the value of experimentation, and their well-designed experiments have contributed to the development of many innovative products and processes. The Japanese have placed a relentless emphasis on the value of experimentation, and they have achieved great success.

◆ 20.2 Sample Inspection and Acceptance Sampling Plans

Inspection amounts to checking whether products meet the requirements that have been established for them. If there are only very few items and if each item is very large and complex, then one might check every single one before products are released or shipped to the customer. For example, each manufactured car goes through an intensive inspection before it is shipped to the dealership. But what if the product involved is a fairly inexpensive widget that is produced in large numbers—for example, an inexpensive mass-produced action-figure toy? In such a situation one relies on *sample inspection*. There one takes a small sample of size *n* from each shipment lot, inspects the sampled items, and counts the number of items in the sample that fail to meet requirements. If the number of defectives is large (equal to or larger than a certain rejection number that can be looked up in commonly available tables), then the quality of the lot is considered unacceptable. In this case, one inspects each element of the lot and reworks or scraps each defective item before the lot is shipped. On the other hand, if the number of defectives is smaller than the rejection number of the sample inspection plan, then the entire lot is acceptable and is shipped.

Sample inspection plans such as this inevitably lead to two types of errors: one may reject acceptable lots, and one may fail to screen out unacceptable lots. The number of elements that need to be sampled and the rejection number (which is the number of defectives in the sample causing a lot to be rejected) are selected so that the probabilities of making these errors are not too large.

Sample inspection was quite popular in the past, for it was commonly thought that by "screening out" bad items one could improve the quality of production. While under effective inspection the customer will get only acceptable items, the cost of these items increases because the costs of inspection, rework, and scrap have to be allocated to the good items that are eventually shipped. Furthermore, a realization at the shipping stage that items produced several shifts ago are defective comes too late; many more defective items will have been produced in the intervening time period. In addition, because of the time lag between production and detection, one usually doesn't know what particular circumstances may have caused the defects, leaving fewer clues on how to solve the quality problem. People now realize that in many instances the timely monitoring of the production processes is a better alternative.

◆ 20.3 Control Charts

A control chart is a graphical tool that can be used to understand a production process and help assure that the quality of products produced by that process is consistent (or stable) over time. There are several reasons why these charts have been used successfully for more than half a century. First, control charts are easy to explain and can be applied by everyone, including workers on the production floor. Experience shows that people want a prescribed procedure to assist them in achieving quality, and control charts provide this. Control charts serve as a guide for people who otherwise might not be able to take effective actions toward quality improvement.

A second, and more fundamental, reason for the success of control charts is that they raise important issues and force their resolution. In order to apply control chart techniques, it is necessary to decide specifically what is to be controlled, the standards to be used, the measurements to be taken, how they are to be taken, and what will be done with them. The use of control charts forces communication, and it fixes responsibility on these important issues.

Finally, control charts are successful because they focus attention on the process rather than on the product. There are two basic causes of excessive variation and poor products, and it is important to distinguish between them. Variation can result from improper operation of a satisfactory production process—for example, from worker error or some other special event. More often, however, a poor product is not due to poor workmanship but to a poor production process—a process that simply is not capable of meeting requirements and standards on a consistent basis. The distinction between poor workmanship and a poor process is highlighted by the use of control charts.

◆ 20.4 X-bar Charts

Several types of control charts are in everyday use and are designed for different situations. A chart widely used in manufacturing is the *x-bar chart*, also known as the *mean chart*. This chart is used in situations where one measures a continuous variable—say, the response time of an on-line system or dimensions of a manufactured item.

Most processes exhibit some variation; one does not obtain precisely the same output from the process time after time. The dimensions of products vary from time to time. The fillweights of toothpaste tubes vary, and so do the waiting times until customers are connected to speak with a customer support representative. We experience variability in our products and services because of the many chance factors that affect the process. Observed variation can be consistent—the type of variation one would observe from repeatedly throwing a pair of dice. In such a case we say that the system is *stable over time*, or *in statistical control*. But variation can also shift over time, owing to the influence of outside factors—that is, special effects that are not part of the normal operating system. Examples are a switch to a new supplier for an essential raw material, a sudden change in the plant, or the hiring of a poorly trained worker. A basic question about processes is: Does the observed data suggest that the process behaves consistently (that is, is it stable or in statistical control), or does the process exhibit sudden changes or shifts (that is, is it out of statistical control)? A process can go out of control in several ways. For example, there may be a transitory shift in the process; there may be a shift or a trend in the level of the process; or the variability of the process may change while the level of the process stays the same. The x-bar chart helps us monitor the stability of the process level; the range chart, which is discussed in the next section, helps us monitor the stability of the process variability.

To construct an x-bar chart, samples of moderate size (sample size of $n = 4$ or 5) are taken from the process at periodic intervals—say, every 10 minutes, every hour, or every shift. The resulting information is treated as a random sample of size n from the production process. The average of each sample is computed, and the sample averages are plotted against time on graph paper. Using statistical guidelines, one draws an *upper control limit* and a *lower control limit* on the chart. These control limits are calculated so that for a stable process 99.7 percent of the sample means obtained from repeated samples—that is, practically all of them—will fall between these limits. For a process that is under statistical control, almost all of the observed averages must fall between the lower and upper control limits. We refer to such a process as a *stable process*, a *constant cause system*, or a process that shows *no assignable cause of variation*. What this means is that the process generating the observations is behaving in a consistent manner; the observed variation in measurements is due to the inherent randomness of the process, and not to some outside influence. If the process is under statistical control, then the observed output is typical of what the process is capable of producing.

On the other hand, if an average falls outside these limits of "normal" variability, then one would question that the process is still under statistical control. This means that there was a change in the process and that an *assignable cause* is responsible for the aberrant behavior. In this event, the task is to determine what caused such an unusual result. To assist in this effort, one would start investigating all other process conditions that existed around that particular time.

It is important to note that the definition of statistical control does *not* make mention of the requirements or specifications for the product! This means that a process can be in statistical control (that is, stable and predictable over time), and yet the products that it produces may not meet the requirements. Think of it this way: A process is in control if it produces consistent products; whether or not these products meet requirements depends on the use to which they will be put. For one application where the requirements are lenient, the products might be quite appropriate; for another with stricter requirements, they might not.

To illustrate the x-bar control chart consider the data in Table 20.1 which lists response times of a certain on-line information system. These data were obtained by taking samples of size $n = 5$ at 10-minute intervals. The requirement for this particular system specifies that the response time should be 1.5 seconds or better. Sample averages and sample ranges are calculated for each of the 27 samples. The average of the sample averages is taken as the center line on the x-bar chart; that

TABLE 20.1 ◆ 27 Samples of $n = 5$ Observations.
Response times (seconds) of an on-line system

Sample	Observations					Mean	Range
1	1.41	1.42	1.44	1.47	1.50	1.448	0.09
2	1.45	1.50	1.50	1.52	1.53	1.500	0.08
3	1.40	1.46	1.46	1.54	1.55	1.482	0.15
4	1.44	1.45	1.47	1.48	1.50	1.468	0.06
5	1.42	1.43	1.49	1.49	1.52	1.470	0.10
6	1.43	1.43	1.44	1.50	1.51	1.462	0.08
7	1.44	1.45	1.49	1.49	1.54	1.482	0.10
8	1.44	1.44	1.45	1.50	1.52	1.470	0.08
9	1.47	1.47	1.48	1.49	1.54	1.490	0.07
10	1.39	1.44	1.47	1.49	1.52	1.462	0.13
11	1.42	1.44	1.44	1.49	1.54	1.466	0.12
12	1.44	1.47	1.49	1.49	1.53	1.484	0.09
13	1.46	1.48	1.49	1.49	1.49	1.482	0.03
14	1.44	1.44	1.47	1.51	1.52	1.476	0.08
15	1.42	1.49	1.50	1.51	1.51	1.486	0.09
16	1.39	1.47	1.48	1.51	1.52	1.474	0.13
17	1.44	1.44	1.48	1.49	1.50	1.470	0.06
18	1.44	1.49	1.49	1.50	1.51	1.486	0.07
19	1.42	1.47	1.49	1.49	1.50	1.474	0.08
20	1.43	1.44	1.46	1.47	1.49	1.458	0.06
21	1.45	1.47	1.49	1.50	1.51	1.484	0.06
22	1.46	1.46	1.47	1.50	1.53	1.484	0.07
23	1.44	1.46	1.47	1.49	1.52	1.476	0.08
24	1.41	1.48	1.49	1.50	1.54	1.484	0.13
25	1.44	1.45	1.48	1.48	1.52	1.474	0.08
26	1.45	1.47	1.50	1.51	1.52	1.490	0.07
27	1.44	1.45	1.47	1.52	1.52	1.480	0.08

is, $CL = \bar{\bar{x}} = (\bar{x}_1 + \bar{x}_2 + \ldots + \bar{x}_{27})/27 = 1.476$. The average of the sample ranges $\bar{R} = (R_1 + R_2 + \ldots + R_{27})/27 = 0.08593$ is used to calculate the control limits,

$$LCL = CL - A_2 \bar{R} = 1.476 - (0.58)(0.08593) = 1.427$$

and

$$UCL = CL + A_2 \bar{R} = 1.476 + (0.58)(0.08593) = 1.526$$

The constant $A_2 = 0.58$, for sample size $n = 5$, is obtained from Table 20.5 in Appendix 20A. The calculation of the control limits is summarized in Appendix 20A. If you want to learn why these constants A_2 have to be chosen in this particular way, then you should consult books on statistical process control. The books by Douglas Montgomery, *Introduction to Statistical Process Control*, 3rd ed.,

(New York: John Wiley, 1995), and Richard DeVor, Tsong-how Chang, and John Sutherland, *Statistical Quality Design and Control* (New York: Macmillan, 1992) are good references. For our purposes, it is sufficient to remember that with this particular choice of limits there is a 99.7 percent probability that repeated averages from a stable system will fall within these limits.

The control chart in Display 20.1 shows that the system is under statistical control; none of the sample averages falls beyond the control limits.

The process is predictable, but does it meet its requirements? Clearly not. The histogram of the individual observations in Display 20.2 shows that 28 of the 135 observations in Table 20.1, or $100(28/135) = 20.7$ percent, exceed the required 1.50-second response time. To meet the requirements, the process must be improved or replaced.

It is also possible for a process to be out of statistical control and yet have its products meet the specified requirements. This is most likely to happen when there is wide tolerance for the products. When the products meet requirements, then there is a temptation not to worry about whether or not the process is under statistical control. However, this may be a mistake. The fact that the process is not under control means that some outside factor is causing variation; you really don't know what it is. Since you don't know, what guarantee do you have that the unexplained variation will stay in a range where the products are still satisfactory? If a process is not under control, then you can't be sure what it will produce next!

Other Out-of-Control Conditions

In the preceding discussion, we mentioned only one possible condition that would signal that a process is out of control: namely, if a plotted sample average falls outside the control limits. But several other patterns would not be expected if all the observations were governed simply by randomness. For example, even if all averages were within the control limits, we would not expect to find many crowded near one of the

DISPLAY 20.1 ◆ x-Bar Control Chart for Response Times

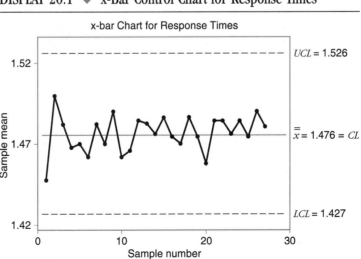

DISPLAY 20.2 ◆ Histogram of Response Times

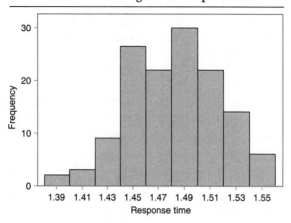

control limits; such a pattern would indicate that the level of the process had shifted. Nor would we expect to find them alternating with, say, the odd sample averages near the upper control limit and the even ones near the lower one. These and other "non-random" patterns would cause us to reject the notion that the process is stable. Appendix 20B contains a list of patterns that signal that a process is out of control.[2]

◆ 20.5 R-Charts

A companion to the x-bar chart is the *R-chart* (or *range-chart*) which plots the ranges of samples taken over time and monitors the variability of the process over time. Both the x-bar chart and the R-chart should be constructed because these two charts look at different aspects of stability: one looks at the levels, and the other at the variability. The sample range is calculated from each sample, and the R-chart is simply a time-sequence plot of successive ranges. The center line for this chart is given by $CL = \overline{R}$, the average of the sample ranges. The control limits are selected such that for a stable process 99.7 percent of the sample ranges (that is, virtually all of them) will fall within the control limits. It turns out that the control limits for the R-chart are given by

$$LCL = D_3\,\overline{R}$$

and

$$UCL = D_4\,\overline{R}$$

where D_3 and D_4 are constants that depend on the sample size n; these can be looked up in Table 20.5 in Appendix 20A. A process is deemed to be out of control if a sample range falls beyond the control limits. We refer the reader to textbooks on statistical process control to learn how to obtain these specific constants.

---

[2]*Statistical Quality Control Handbook* (Western Electric Co., 1956), p. 29.

The R-chart for the response times in Table 20.1 is shown in Display 20.3. The control limits are given by $LCL = (0)(0.08593) = 0$ and $UCL = (2.11)(0.08593) = 0.181$, because for $n = 5$ we find from Table 20.5 that $D_3 = 0$ and $D_4 = 2.11$. The R-chart shows that the variability of the process is stable over time. The process is stable with respect to both its variability and its level.

X-bar and R-charts are used whenever we measure so-called "variable" aspects of a process. They are used when the variable being observed can take on any value in a range. Typical situations are the measurement of time, length, weight, or a variable that for practical purposes can be considered to vary continuously, such as cost. With such variables, it is customary to plot both an x-bar chart and an R-chart because the two provide different information. Stability of an x-bar chart implies that the central tendency of the process (that is, the level) is not changing. However, keep in mind that there could be frequent, wild variations in individual observations that are masked by the averaging process. Such variations would show up in an R-chart, for this chart monitors the stability of the process variability over time. Conversely, a process could have stable variation so that the range of a sample, and hence the R-chart, remained stable. But the process level could be shifting over time, a fact that would show up in an x-bar chart.

◆ 20.6 Another Example of x-bar and R-charts

As a second example of x-bar and R-charts, we consider the fillweights of dentifrice tubes for fill nozzle number 18 on a filling machine. The sample averages and sample ranges in Table 20.2 are obtained from samples of size $n = 4$. The time between samples is 20 minutes; 24 samples are taken during the eight-hour production shift. The average of the sample averages is given by $\bar{\bar{x}} = 21.955$, and

DISPLAY 20.3 ◆ R-chart for Response Times

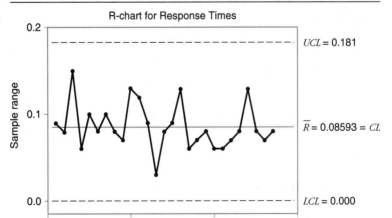

TABLE 20.2 ◆ Data on Fillweight of Dentifrice Tubes for Fill Nozzle Number 18

Sample	Fillweight				Mean	Range
1	22.1	21.9	21.7	22.0	21.925	0.4
2	22.0	22.2	21.7	21.6	21.875	0.6
3	22.2	21.9	22.0	22.0	22.025	0.3
4	21.6	22.2	22.3	22.0	22.025	0.7
5	22.2	21.9	22.1	22.4	22.150	0.5
6	22.2	22.2	21.9	22.3	22.150	0.4
7	22.2	22.2	22.1	21.8	22.075	0.4
8	22.0	22.0	22.0	22.1	22.025	0.1
9	21.9	22.2	21.7	21.5	21.825	0.7
10	22.2	21.8	21.8	22.2	22.000	0.4
11	21.9	21.7	22.5	22.0	22.025	0.8
12	22.3	22.0	21.9	21.8	22.000	0.5
13	21.8	22.2	22.2	21.7	21.975	0.5
14	22.0	21.9	22.1	22.1	22.025	0.2
15	22.2	21.9	22.1	22.2	22.100	0.3
16	22.2	21.9	22.1	22.1	22.075	0.3
17	22.2	21.9	21.9	22.0	22.000	0.3
18	21.9	22.0	22.0	21.8	21.925	0.2
19	22.2	22.0	21.8	21.8	21.950	0.4
20	22.1	22.1	22.0	21.7	21.975	0.4
21	21.5	21.7	21.9	21.9	21.750	0.4
22	21.8	21.8	21.7	21.5	21.700	0.3
23	21.5	21.9	21.7	21.8	21.725	0.4
24	21.5	21.6	21.7	21.7	21.625	0.2

the average of the sample ranges is $\bar{R} = 0.404$. The control limits for the x-bar chart are given by $LCL = 21.955 - (0.73)(0.404) = 21.66$ and $UCL = 21.955 + (0.73)(0.404) = 22.25$; for samples of size $n = 4$, $A_2 = 0.73$ (see Table 20.5 in Appendix 20A). The control limits for the R-chart are $LCL = 0$ and $UCL = (2.28)(0.404) = 0.922$; for samples of size $n = 4$, $D_3 = 0$ and $D_4 = 2.28$. The R-chart shows that the variability of the process is in statistical control. The x-bar chart in Display 20.4 indicates that the levels have gone out of control; a considerable reduction in the fillweight can be noticed over the last few periods. It was discovered that this particular fill nozzle needed adjustment.

◆ 20.7 Control Charts for Attribute Data: p-Charts and c-Charts

Control charts are designed for different situations. Certain charts are used to monitor the proportion of defective items; they are called *p-charts*. Some charts are used to keep track of the number of defects or flaws on a product, such as the

DISPLAY 20.4 ◆ x-Bar and R-charts for Fillweights of Dentifrice Tubes for Fill Nozzle Number 18

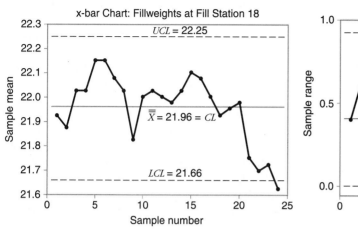

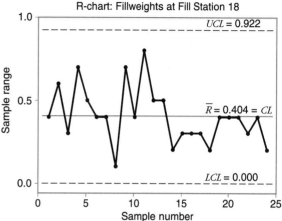

number of defects on a car or the number of blemishes on a section of woven fabric; such charts are referred to as *c-charts*. The p- and c-charts are used for *attribute data*, which is data that describes the presence or absence of a certain characteristic. Such measurements are satisfactory when we are dealing with a very large number of relatively simple products, where it is often sufficient simply to classify each product as satisfactory or defective.

The p-chart is a time-sequence plot of consecutive proportions of defectives. For example, if your company pays bills to its suppliers on an ongoing basis, you may divide the bills into consecutive groups (lots) of say 100 or so and obtain the proportion of late bills for each of the groups. The proportions of late bills for consecutive groups are then plotted on a p-chart.

As an illustration, let us consider the data in Table 20.3, which lists the number of defective cap threads on dentifrice tubes from consecutive samples of size $n = 200$. Samples were taken twice during each shift. The p-chart is given in Display 20.5. The average fraction of defectives is $\bar{p} = 0.08675$. The lower control limit is given by $LCL = 0.08675 - 3\sqrt{(0.08675)(0.91325)/200} = 0.02704$, and the upper control limit is $UCL = 0.08675 + 3\sqrt{(0.08675)(0.91325)/200} = 0.14646$. Appendix

TABLE 20.3 ◆ Number of Defective Cap Threads on Dentifrice Tubes from Consecutive Samples of Size $n = 200$ (read across)

20	19	7	11	11	13	15	16	18	12
16	15	9	10	12	26	30	22	29	36

20A explains the calculation of the control limits.[3] For this choice of control limits, the chance is 99.7 percent that repeated sample proportions from a stable process fall within these limits. The p-chart shows that the proportion of defective threads has increased over the last five samples; a check of the machine indicated that it needed maintenance.

With a large and complex product, such as a car, a tractor, or a large information system, one usually measures the quality of the product in terms of the number of defects that are found on each product. A time-sequence plot of the number of defects or nonconformances from successively selected products is known as the *c-chart*.

As illustration, let us consider the data in Table 20.4 which lists the number of bottle defects for each batch that is received. The number of defects for successive batches are plotted on a c-chart in Display 20.6. The average number of bottle defects per batch is $\bar{c} = 2.407$. The lower control limit is given by $LCL = \bar{c} - 3\sqrt{\bar{c}} = 2.407 - (3)\sqrt{2.407} = -2.25$, or 0 defects because the number of defects cannot be negative. The upper control limit is given by $UCL = \bar{c} + 3\sqrt{\bar{c}} = 2.407 + (3)\sqrt{2.407} = 7.06$ defects; see Appendix 20A for details. The chart shows that the number of defects is consistent over time; the process is in statistical control.

DISPLAY 20.5 ◆ p-Chart for Proportion of Defective Cap Threads on Dentifrice Tubes

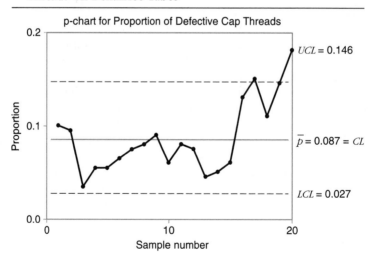

---

[3]The calculation of the control limits is carried out to five decimal points. We have done this to illustrate the steps in the calculations. In practical applications we certainly recommend rounding. In this example, you may want to round to three decimal points, that is, $LCL = 0.027$ and $UCL = 0.146$.

TABLE 20.4 ◆ Bottle Defects per Batch Received (read across)

0	1	4	1	3	6	1	2	2	3
4	1	2	4	2	0	5	1	3	2
2	3	2	1	3	4	3			

A Comment

In most situations, it is fairly obvious whether to consider attribute or continuous measurement control charts (such as the x-bar and R-charts). For example, if we observe the presence or absence of a condition, then we are naturally led to attribute data and attribute charts. However, if we measure the dimensions of a product (such as the length or weight of an item), then we have a choice of what to do: we can control the product on the dimensions, or we can control the product on its attribute of whether the dimensions exceed certain specification limits. In general, continuous measurement data provide more useful information about process performance. With such data we can construct two charts: an x-bar chart to monitor the level and an R-chart to monitor the variability. These charts give us a better chance to detect the potential causes of out-of-control signals. Furthermore, these charts can give us an indication of forthcoming trouble, usually well before the process starts producing defectives. In other words, the x-bar and R-charts are leading indicators of future trouble, while the attribute charts only react to changes in the rate of defective products. Furthermore, the sample sizes that are used with

DISPLAY 20.6 ◆ c-Chart for Number of Bottle Defectives per Batch Received

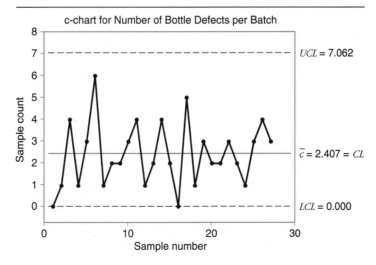

continuous measurement data are usually much smaller (most of the time we sample about $n = 5$ products) than those needed for attribute charts. Hence, there are also economic advantages to using the continuous measurement data.

◆ 20.8 Process Capability

Typically, a product must meet certain specifications that are established by the customer. Product specifications usually are given in terms of a *target value (Tg)*, a *lower specification limit (LSL)*, and an *upper specification limit (USL)*. They are called the "specs" or the "tolerances" of the product. If the products meet the specifications, then we say that we are dealing with a process that is *capable* of producing according to the given specifications.

Probably the simplest way to check process capability is to construct a dot diagram of the measurements (or, if the data set is large, a histogram). The target value and the lower and upper specification limits can be added to this graph, and the proportion of values that are outside these limits can be calculated. Of course, no (or very few) values should be outside these limits.

While dot diagrams (or histograms) are instructive in displaying the capability graphically, it is common practice to calculate *capability indexes*. These indexes quantify the capability or, in other words, the conformance of our process to the required specifications.

A commonly used measure of capability is the C_p *capability index*. It is given by

$$C_p = \frac{USL - LSL}{6s}$$

where LSL and USL are the lower and upper specification limits, and s is the process standard deviation. For most distributions the interval $(\bar{x} - 3s, \bar{x} + 3s)$ covers virtually all of the distribution (99.73 percent if the distribution is normal). Hence, an interval of length $6s$ measures the extent of the process variability; $6s$ is a measure of the actual process spread. The C_p relates the allowable spread (that is, USL − LSL) to the actual process spread. For capable processes we expect that the actual process spread is smaller than the allowable spread and that C_p is at least larger than one. A large value of C_p indicates that the process variability is small compared to the width of the specification interval. The larger this index, the better. Some companies (for example, Motorola) require that this index is at least 2.0.

The C_p capability index assumes that the process is on target, which means that the process level and the target value are the same. The index can be very misleading when the process is off-target, as illustrated in Display 20.7. There the process is off-target, causing a considerable fraction of defectives. However, the actual process spread, $6s$, is small when compared to the allowable spread. The large value of C_p is deceptive because the process is not capable of meeting the specifications. Because C_p makes no reference to the target value, we recommend against its use.

DISPLAY 20.7 ◆ Illustration of the Shortcomings of C_p as a Measure of Capability

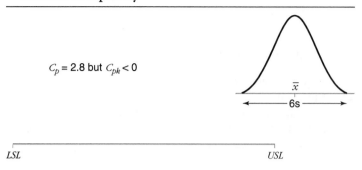

$C_p = 2.8$ but $C_{pk} < 0$

$\bar{x}$

$6s$

LSL   *USL*

The C_{pk} *capability index* is a measure that takes into account process variability as well as departures from the target value. It is given by

$$C_{pk} = \text{minimum}\left\{\frac{USL - \bar{x}}{3s}\;;\;\frac{\bar{x} - LSL}{3s}\right\}$$

C_{pk} relates the distances from each specification limit to the process mean to three standard deviations. For capable processes we expect that the difference between the upper specification limit and the process mean is at least three standard deviations. We expect the same for the difference between the process mean and the lower specification limit. Therefore, we expect that the smaller of these two is larger than one—hopefully much larger than 1.

The C_{pk} is a much better measure of capability than the C_p. For the case displayed in Display 20.7, convince yourself that the C_{pk} index is, in fact, negative even though C_p is large. The C_{pk} capability index shows that this particular process is unacceptable.

The C_{pm} *capability index* is another useful index. It is defined as

$$C_{pm} = \frac{USL - LSL}{6s^*}$$

It is similar to C_p, except that s^* measures the variability of process measurements around the target Tg, and not around the process mean $\bar{x}$. The distance of a measurement x from the target Tg can be written as $(x - Tg) = (x - \bar{x}) + (\bar{x} - Tg)$. We can think of it as the sum of the distance of the observation from the process mean and the distance of the process mean from the target; the second component is referred to as the bias. It can be shown that $s^* = [s^2 + (\bar{x} - Tg)^2]^{1/2}$. Hence

$$C_{pm} = \frac{USL - LSL}{6[s^2 + (\bar{x} - Tg)^2]^{1/2}}.$$

Both the C_{pk} and the C_{pm} incorporate a possible bias into the capability measure; these two indexes are similar and clearly preferable to the C_p, which ignores the fact that a process may be off-center. For capable processes, we expect C_{pk} and C_{pm} to be large—hopefully much larger than one. The examples in Display 20.8 will help you appreciate the differences among C_p, C_{pk}, and C_{pm}.

An Illustration of Capability Indexes

Consider the measurements on pH in Table 19.3. The sample mean and the sample standard deviation for the $n = 100$ observations are given by $\bar{x} = 6.223$ and $s = 0.14$. In this particular application, the target value for pH was 6.10, with lower and upper specification limits given by $LSL = 5.75$ and $USL = 6.55$, respectively. The C_{pk} capability index is

$$C_{pk} = \text{minimum} \left\{ \frac{6.55 - 6.223}{3(0.14)} \; ; \; \frac{6.223 - 5.75}{3(0.14)} \right\} = \text{minimum} \{0.78, 1.13\} = 0.78$$

DISPLAY 20.8 ◆ C_p, C_{pk}, and C_{pm} for Four Different Situations.

Here we have assumed a normal distribution for the quality characteristic. In the first situation, $USL - LSL = 6s$. In the other three, $USL - LSL = 12s$.

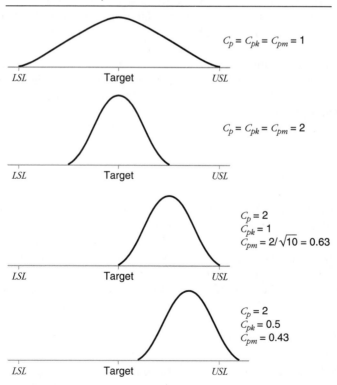

$C_p = C_{pk} = C_{pm} = 1$

$C_p = C_{pk} = C_{pm} = 2$

$C_p = 2$
$C_{pk} = 1$
$C_{pm} = 2/\sqrt{10} = 0.63$

$C_p = 2$
$C_{pk} = 0.5$
$C_{pm} = 0.43$

The C_{pm} capability index is

$$C_{pm} = \frac{USL - LSL}{6 \, [s^2 + (\bar{x} - Tg)^2]^{1/2}} = \frac{6.55 - 5.75}{(6)[(0.14)^2 + (6.223 - 6.10)^2]^{1/2}} = 0.72$$

The capability of the process, with respect to keeping the pH values within the required specifications, is quite poor. The process spread is just too large compared to the tightness of the desired specifications.

Motorola's Six-Sigma Concept

Motorola, in announcing the achievement of Total Customer Satisfaction as the corporation's fundamental objective, introduced the concept of "Six Sigma" as a statistical way of measuring quality. Motorola views its failure rates in terms of parts per million (ppm). Motorola's Six-Sigma goal is a 3.4 ppm defect level!

How does the six-sigma requirement translate into a defect level of 3.4 ppm? Obviously, Motorola requires very capable processes. In fact, it requires that processes are on target and that the specification limits are at least six sigma away from the target, hence the name "six sigma." Such a requirement on the process translates into a capability index C_p of 2.0; this is better than the usually adopted standard.

Motorola, however, also realizes that the process is not always exactly on target. In practice, mean levels shift dynamically over time. Motorola allows drifts away from the target of at most 1.5 sigma. Under the six-sigma goal and assuming that the observations are from a normal distribution with (shifted) mean $Tg + (1.5)\sigma$ and standard deviation σ, we can calculate the probability that an individual observation falls outside the interval $(Tg - 6\sigma, Tg + 6\sigma)$. This probability is given by 0.0000034, or 3.4 parts per million. (Note that these calculations require detailed tables of the normal distribution, which are not shown here.)

Some Further Comments on Capability Indexes

Capability indexes depend on the specifications, which usually are determined by the customers and engineers. It is important that careful thought goes into the selection of the specifications. It is wrong to select them too wide because this allows inferior products. Usually, products are part of a complicated assembly that involves many components. If there is too much variability in a component (because specification limits or tolerances are set too wide), the parts may not fit together as they should. Take, for example, car doors and car frames. If there is too much variability in the door and the frame, the door will not close correctly. We refer to this as tolerance stack-up. However, the specifications should not be taken as too narrow either. Unnecessary expenses are incurred with narrow specification limits if tight tolerances are not needed.

Keep in mind that specification limits and control limits are not the same. The specification limits reflect the requirements of the customer, whereas the control limits reflect the process behavior and provide bounds on the common-cause variability of the process. These two sets of limits must not be confused! Furthermore, a process should be in control first, before its capability is assessed. A capable process that is not in control is not very reassuring. It is capable of surprising you! The fact that the process is not under control means that some outside factors are causing the process to be unstable. Since you don't know what these factors are, there is no guarantee that the unexplained variation will stay in a range where the products are still satisfactory. If the process is not in control, you cannot predict its future performance.

◆ 20.9 The Statistical Design of Experiments

In studying and improving processes, we need answers to questions such as these: Which raw material leads to better products: material 1 or material 2? Which one of five identified methods gives the most satisfactory results? Can the yield of a chemical process be improved by varying the temperature and the pressure of the reaction? If so, what are the optimal levels for temperature and pressure? Which settings of the input factors ensure that the process yield is maximized? Which factors affect the hardness of steel flats that are produced in our rolling mill? How should we select certain input factors so that our product achieves a specified target value, with as little variability as possible?

Information can be collected in an *active* or a *passive* manner. In a passive way of collecting information, we merely observe the process without actively intervening. The control charts discussed earlier are good examples of passive data collection. There the process is sampled at periodic time intervals, and the results are displayed on charts for everyone to see. Special events can be identified quickly, and actions can be taken to prevent these special events from reoccurring.

An active way to collect data is to intervene in the process by deliberately changing some of the factors that are thought to influence the process. Preliminary studies may have tentatively identified several important factors. For example, we may have identified the temperature of the reheat furnace and the time the billet spends in it as possible factors that influence the strength of the rolled steel flats. Or we may have tentatively identified five different ways of carrying out a certain operation, and we want to learn which one of the five is best.

Monitoring processes (that is, listening without active intervention) is important, and it can lead to much useful information. However, even more can be learned by actively changing factors and by observing how the process reacts to changes that are introduced deliberately. Relying on data that are obtained by "listening" to the process is often inefficient because it might take quite a long time before changes in important process factors occur on their own. Also, in a monitoring situation one does not exert control over the factors; therefore, one never really knows whether the observed changes in the output are due to one particular factor that changed or to some other factors that happened to change at the same time. Changing the factors in a deliberate, planned fashion and observing the results of deliberately planned changes give a more direct assessment of the causal relationship.

We must understand how to carry out experiments in the best possible way. Data need to be collected according to a well-thought-out plan; we call this an *experimental plan*. In terms of the information to be gained from experiments, there are good ways of changing factors and there are bad ones. Bad experimental plans increase the cost of obtaining relevant data and, in the worst case, may result in data that is totally irrelevant for answering the posed question. In this text, we introduce you to the *statistical design of experiments*, and we discuss several important principles of experimental design. A more detailed discussion can be found in our other text, *Statistical Quality Control: Strategies and Tools for Continual Improvement.*

◆ 20.10 Important Principles in the Design of Experiments

In *comparative experiments*, we compare the effects of several different methods. For example, we may compare a currently used raw material A with a competitive one, material B. We may compare the effectiveness of two different methods of teaching statistics, one method using a "mathematical" (that is, a theorem-proof) approach and the other using a "project-driven" approach (where students have to collect and analyze data of their own choice). We may study three different temperature settings in the reheat furnace (say, 1500, 1750, and 2000 degrees) and assess the effect of temperature on the steel's breaking strength. As the following simple example shows, *randomization* in the assignment of the methods to the experimental units plays an important role.

Consider the situation in which one is interested in comparing the effectiveness of two different methods of teaching statistics: the mathematical approach versus the project-driven approach. Assume that there is a good measurement instrument (that is, a test at the end of the semester) that can tell us how much students learned in each course. The experimental units in this comparative experiment are the 100 students who have signed up for the introductory statistics course. We divide these 100 students into two groups; 50 students receive instruction according to method 1, and 50 according to method 2. How should this division be carried out? Obviously, it would not be very wise to put all males in one group and all females into the other because this would confound our variable of interest, the teaching method, with gender. Even if we found a strong difference in the test scores among the two groups, we wouldn't know whether this difference was due to the teaching method or to gender. What if we assigned the students in the front rows of the lecture room to method 1 and those in the back rows to method 2? This assignment is not very clever because the choice of seating may be confounded with how people respond to the two methods of instruction. Such may not be likely, but we don't really know.

The safest and fairest way to divide the 100 students into two groups is to carry out the division at random. One hundred slips of papers are cut out; each slip contains the name of one of the students. The 100 slips of paper are placed in a bowl, and slips are drawn without replacement. The first 50 selected slips (students) are assigned to teaching method 1; the remaining ones are instructed according to method 2. *Randomization* is important here because it avoids possible biases in the assignment of the experimental units (that is, the students) to the methods that are being compared. Under the randomized scheme, each student has the same chance of being assigned to either method. This is much better than assigning to method 1 only male, or front-row students, or letting the students pick their own group. Such assignments should be avoided because they might bias (or skew) the comparison. Biases are avoided by randomizing and giving each student the same chance of being assigned to one of the groups. We call the resulting design a *completely randomized design.*

Using a bowl with slips of papers and drawing slips at random without replacement represents a very descriptive model of the randomization. This procedure makes sure that every possible allocation (that is, every possible arrangement of these 100 students into two groups of 50) has the same chance of being selected. However, a drawback of this procedure is the work of cutting out the slips of paper and physically drawing from the bowl. You can avoid these physical aspects by using a random number table instead.[4]

Randomizing the run-order of experiments is another good example of randomization. Assume that you are changing a process factor, such as the raw material, in a certain batch operation. You are willing to experiment on the next 40 batches, and you are planning to run 20 batches with material A and 20 batches with material B. It would be most "convenient" to run the first 20 consecutive batches with material A and the rest with material B, for this involves only one "switchover." However, such a strategy could be dangerous because a difference in the results for group A and B could be due not only to the difference in the raw material, but also to time or run-order. Some other factors, unrelated to raw material, might change over time and be responsible for the observed difference. You just don't know. Again, it is much safer to randomize the run-order. You can do this by writing batch numbers 1 through 40 on 40 slips of paper, placing the slips in a bowl, and randomly drawing one slip after the other. The numbers on the first 20 slips identify the batches that are run with material A; all others are run with material B.

Randomization is important because it avoids the introduction of biases. However, there is another important principle in the design of experiments that can improve the efficiency of a randomized design. This is the principle of *blocking the experiment.*

Consider the following example. Assume that we are interested in comparing the wear characteristics of two different materials used for shoe soles: material A

---

[4]A random number table is a random arrangement of the digits 0 through 9. Each digit is equally likely; furthermore, there are no groups of adjacent digits that are more likely than others. Statistical computer software and most spreadsheet programs include routines that allow you to generate such tables of random digits.

made of rubber and material B made from a mixture of certain plastic components. The 100 students mentioned earlier are the experimental units. Using the procedure of drawing slips from a bowl, we divide the 100 students, at random, into two groups of 50. One group gets pairs of shoes with material A, and the other pairs with material B. After four weeks, we measure the wear on their shoes and, for each student, average the wear on their right and left shoes. The results of these 100 observations (50 averages with A and 50 averages with B) would, in all likelihood, show tremendous variability. You could see this by constructing dot diagrams to display the measurements of wear for the two groups; for ease of comparison it would be best to put these two dot diagrams on the same scale. It would be virtually impossible to say which material shows the greater wear. Sophisticated statistical analyses won't help either. The averages of the two groups will be slightly different, but the small difference in the averages will most likely be swamped by the large variability that is present in both groups. The reason for so much variability in each group is quite simple—it is there because of the varying activity levels of the subjects in each group. The variability in the activity levels is the major source of the variability in wear.

In order to make more precise statements about the wear performance of materials A and B, we should control the activity level of the experimental units. It is easy to do this by assigning *both* materials to each experimental unit. With two materials and two feet on each person, this is easily done. We put material A on one foot and material B on the other. Each participant in this study is viewed as a unit (or, as it is called in statistical terminology, a *block*) and is assigned both materials. In order to avoid a possible "right/left foot bias" in our results, we randomize the assignment. We flip a coin: if the coin comes up "heads," we put material A on the right foot; otherwise we put it on the left foot. Randomization within each block is important because we want to avoid a possible right-left allocation bias within each block. We call a design such as this a *randomized block design*.

This particular plan results in 100 pairs of measurements. The natural approach to analyze these data is to calculate for each subject the *difference* of wear under A and B. It is true that every pair of measurements includes a very large "activity" component; both measurements will be high if the student is very active, and both will be small if the student is inactive. However, the difference between the two measurements on the same subject "cancels" out the activity component, and a direct comparison of the two materials can be made by looking at the differences. An average of these differences that is very different from zero implies that the two studied materials exhibit different wear characteristics. Note that the differences could not have been calculated if the experiment hadn't been blocked (that is, carried out in pairs). Knowing that the experiment was carried out in pairs helps tremendously because we can compare the two treatments within each block directly.

In this section we discussed two important principles. The principle of blocking and the principle of randomization. Here is a brief summary.

Randomization.   Many background factors affect a response variable. For example, the effectiveness of a particular teaching method is influenced by the personal traits of each student and previous experiences. Similarly, process and production conditions are affected by many small factors that vary over time and that are unrelated to the factors under study; these conditions may change according to patterns that we can't even anticipate. In order to be fair to the various factor levels under study and in order to avoid biases from unrelated factors that we don't control in our experiment, we should assign the experimental units to the treatments at random. Randomization, in some sense, compensates for the many factors that cannot be controlled.

Blocking.   If there is an important factor that separates the experimental units (such as the activity level of our subjects), then we should utilize this factor and think about running the experiment in blocks (or pairs). In our particular example, the subject served as the block, and we assigned both methods (materials A and B) to each block. A block is a region (or a group) of experimental units that provides fairly uniform conditions for the comparison of the factors of interest. While there may be large differences with respect to wear between the subjects, the differences within each subject (that is, the wear on the two different feet) are small.

A good rule of thumb for any experimental design is: "Block whatever you can block, and randomize whatever you can't block."

Generalizing the Results of an Experiment

You must be aware of the *range of validity* of an experiment and of the risks that are associated with extrapolating the findings of one experiment to other circumstances. Experiments are often carried out off-line (that is, in the lab and outside the normal production process) and under tightly controlled conditions. You must also examine how these experiments perform on the factory floor (that is, on-line), where many other factors and conditions are not controlled so tightly. One needs to investigate, through further confirmative experiments, whether the results are *robust* with respect to changes in environmental conditions, variability among raw materials, and variability among the workers

Sequential Nature of Experimentation

It would be wonderful to have unlimited time and resources to find optimal answers to questions of interest. However, this ideal never exists because there are always constraints on time and budget. It is essential to think very carefully about the use of one's resources. It would be quite unwise to spend the whole budget on just a single comprehensive experiment. It is much better to carry out a sequence of smaller-sized experiments because the information that is gained during each step allows one to improve the experimental plan for the next step. Gaining knowledge is a sequential process, and one must make sure that the experimental strategy permits learning to take place. For that reason, we prefer a *sequential approach to experimentation* and a sequence of smaller-sized experiments to one giant all-encompassing experiment.

Factorial Experiments: The Importance of Changing Factors Together

Response variables are usually affected by more than one factor. Take the yield of a certain chemical reaction that depends on both the temperature and the pressure. Often the factors interact; for instance, the effect on yield of a change in temperature (say from 200 to 220 degrees) depends on the pressure of the reaction.

In order to learn about the effects of these two factors on the response, we should conduct a sequence of experiments in which temperature and pressure are changed *together*. *Factorial experiments* in which each level of one factor is combined with each level of the other(s) are particularly useful. Consider a *two-level factorial experiment* in which each of the factors is studied at two levels, a low one and a high one. For two factors (temperature and pressure, in our example), a two-level factorial design calls for experiments at four factor-level combinations. For illustration, suppose that temperature is studied at 200 and 220 degrees and pressure at 90 and 110 psi. Then the four factor-level combinations are given by

(Temperature = 200 degrees, Pressure = 90 psi)—yield = 60
(Temperature = 220 degrees, Pressure = 90 psi)—yield = 70
(Temperature = 200 degrees, Pressure = 110 psi)—yield = 65
(Temperature = 220 degrees, Pressure = 110 psi)—yield = 80

Of course, the order of these four experiments should be randomized; refer to our earlier discussion on the benefits of randomization. The yields from these four experiments, listed in the above table, tell us how to change temperature and pressure in order to increase the yield. In this particular example, we should increase both temperature and pressure. This study should be followed up with additional experiments where the levels of the two factors are varied around temperature 220 degrees and pressure 110 psi. Usually, with a few additional runs, the maximum can be located.

◆ 20.11 Summary

In the last three chapters, we have covered important statistical techniques commonly used in the quality area. Our discussion has gone beyond *Ishikawa's Seven Tools*, which are considered the standard tools for analyzing quality problems. Ishikawa's Seven Tools include Pareto diagrams, cause-and-effect diagrams, histograms, time-sequence plots and control charts, scatter diagrams and correlation coefficients, graphs, and checksheets. Cause-and-effect diagrams will be discussed in Section 21.7.

Appendix 20A ◆ Constructing Control Charts

Take samples of size n at periodic time intervals. The sample (subgroup) size n is usually small ($n = 4$ or 5). Typically, $k = 20$ or 25 such samples are taken in order to determine the control limits of the charts.

For each subgroup, compute the sample average and the sample range. Thus, for $i = 1, 2, \ldots, k$:

$\bar{x}_i$ = the mean of the observations in the subgroup
R_i = the range (largest observation minus smallest observation in subgroup)

The *x-bar chart* is a time-sequence graph of the sample averages $\bar{x}_1, \bar{x}_2, \ldots, \bar{x}_k$. The *R-chart* is a time-sequence graph of the sample ranges $R_1, R_2, \ldots, R_k$.

For the construction of the control limits, one finds the overall mean

$$\bar{\bar{x}} = (\bar{x}_1 + \bar{x}_2 + \ldots + \bar{x}_k)/k$$

and the average range

$$\bar{R} = (R_1 + R_2 + \ldots + R_k)/k.$$

The center line and the lower and upper control limits of the x-bar chart are given by

$$CL = \bar{\bar{x}}$$
$$LCL = \bar{\bar{x}} - A_2 \bar{R}$$
$$UCL = \bar{\bar{x}} + A_2 \bar{R}$$

The center line and the lower and upper control limits of the R-bar chart are given by

$$CL = \bar{R}$$
$$LCL = D_3 \bar{R}$$
$$UCL = D_4 \bar{R}$$

where the constants A_2, D_3, and D_4 are given in Table 20.5. The constants depend on the sample size n. Note that we have used the standard notation that is used in the control chart literature.

For a *p-chart*, we are taking k samples of size n at periodic time intervals and determine the fraction of defectives $p_1, p_2, \ldots, p_k$. For attribute data we need larger sample sizes; the typical sample size n is of the order 100. A p-chart contains a time-sequence plot of the proportion of defectives $p_1, p_2, \ldots, p_k$. The center line is given by

$$CL = \bar{p} = (p_1 + p_2 + \ldots + p_k)/k$$

TABLE 20.5 ◆ Constants A_2,
D_3, and D_4 for Determining
the Control Limits of x-bar
and R-charts

Sample Size n	A_2	D_3	D_4
2	1.88	0.00	3.27
3	1.02	0.00	2.57
4	0.73	0.00	2.28
5	0.58	0.00	2.11
6	0.48	0.00	2.00
7	0.42	0.08	1.92
8	0.37	0.14	1.86
9	0.34	0.18	1.82
10	0.31	0.22	1.78

and the control limits are given by

$$LCL = \bar{p} - 3\sqrt{\frac{\bar{p}(1 - \bar{p})}{n}}$$

and

$$UCL = \bar{p} + 3\sqrt{\frac{\bar{p}(1 - \bar{p})}{n}}$$

The control limits are selected such that for a stable process the probability that a proportion falls within these control limits is 99.7 percent.

For a *c-chart* we select elements at periodic time intervals and count the number of defects on each selected element. Assume that the number of defects on the k selected items are given by $c_1, c_2, \ldots, c_k$. The c-chart is a time-sequence plot of $c_1, c_2, \ldots, c_k$, with center line

$$CL = \bar{c} = (c_1 + c_2 + \ldots + c_k)/k$$

and control limits

$$LCL = \bar{c} - 3\sqrt{\bar{c}}$$
$$UCL = \bar{c} + 3\sqrt{\bar{c}}$$

The limits are selected such that for a stable process the probability that the number of defects falls within these limits is 99.7 percent.

Appendix 20B ◆ Patterns Indicating That a Process Is Out of Control

Divide the area between the lower and upper control limit into six equal zones as follows:

```
UCL ─────────
              Zone A
              ─────────
              Zone B
              ─────────
              Zone C
CL   ─────────
              Zone C
              ─────────
              Zone B
              ─────────
              Zone A
LCL  ─────────
```

Four out-of-control conditions are listed here. In applying these rules, consider only one-half of the control band at a time. Thus, "two points in Zone A" means two points in Zone A on the same side of the center line. Also, a point is "beyond" a Zone if it is further from the CL than that Zone.

A process is not in statistical control if any one of the following conditions holds:

1. An observation lies outside the control limits (beyond Zone A).

2. Two out of three successive observations fall in Zone A or beyond.

3. Four out of five successive observations fall in Zone B or beyond.

4. Eight successive observations fall in Zone C or beyond (eight in a row on one side of the CL).

Also, the following patterns suggest that the process is not completely random. In applying the following tests, consider the entire control band. Thus, "points in Zone C" means points in Zone C, either above or below CL.

1. Hugging the center line exists when 15 consecutive observations fall inside Zone C.

2. Mixture (sampling from two populations) exists when eight consecutive observations fall outside Zone C.

3. Systematic variation exists when a long series of observations alternates between high and low.

4. Trends are indicated by an increasing series of consecutive points or a decreasing series.

◆ Exercises and Additional Readings

1. Consult past issues of *Quality Progress*. Locate and discuss articles on the design of experiments. For example, comment on the papers by

   (a) B. H. Gunter, "Statistically Designed Experiments: Quality Improvement, the Strategy of Experimentation, and the Road to Hell," December 1989 (Vol. 22), pp. 63–64.

   (b) G. E. P. Box, and S. Bisgaard, "The Scientific Context of Quality Improvement," June 1987 (Vol. 20), pp. 54–61.

   (c) T. B. Barker, "Quality Engineering by Design: Taguchi's Philosophy," December 1986 (Vol. 19), pp. 32–42.

2. To learn about simple experiments that can be carried out within a class-room structure, read W. G. Hunter, "Some Ideas about Teaching Design of Experiments with 2^5 Examples of Experiments Conducted by Students," *The American Statistician*, 1977 (Vol. 31), pp. 12–17. Think about simple factorial experiments with two or three factors.

3. Consult past issues of *Quality Progress*. Locate and discuss articles on capability indexes. For example:

   (a) B. H. Gunter, "The Use and Abuse of C_{pk}," January 1989 (pp. 72–73), March 1989 (pp. 108–109), May 1989 (pp. 79–80), July 1989 (pp. 86–87), January 1991 (pp. 90–94).

   (b) P. McCoy, "Using Performance Indexes to Monitoring Production Processes," (p. 49) February 1991 (Vol. 24).

   (c) F. A. Spiring, "The C_{pm} Index," (p.57) February 1991 (Vol. 24).

4. Consult past issues of *Quality Progress*. Locate and discuss articles on control charts. For example,

   (a) A. J. Barnett, and R. W. Andrews, "Are You Getting the Most Out of Your Control Charts," November 1994 (Vol. 27), pp. 75–80.

   (b) L. B. Hare, R. W. Hoerl, J. D. Hromi, and R. D. Snee, "The Role of Statistical Thinking in Management," February 1995 (Vol. 28), pp. 53–60.

   (c) J. W. Leppelmeier, "A Common-Sense Approach to SPC," October 1987 (Vol. 20), pp. 62–64.

   (d) R. G. Maki and M. R. Milota, "Statistical Quality Control Applied to Lumber Drying," December 1993 (Vol. 26), pp. 75–79.

(e) W. McCabe, "Improving Quality and Cutting Costs in a Service Organization," June 1985 (Vol. 18), pp. 85–89.

(f) T. Pyzdek, "A Ten-Step Plan for Statistical Process Control Studies," July 1985 (Vol. 18), pp. 18–21.

(g) J. Stalter, "Process in Control for Conformance," April 1984 (Vol. 17) pp. 18–21.

(h) C. Wozniak, "Proactive vs. Reactive SPC," February 1994 (Vol. 27), pp. 49–50.

5. Consult past issues of *Quality Progress* for articles on sampling inspection. The government has adopted Military Standard Plans (for example, the MIL-STD-105 series) that must be used when certain government contracts are involved. Summarize the steps involved in establishing a MIL-STD sample inspection plan. A good reference is the book by H. M. Wadsworth, K. S. Stephens, and A. B. Godfrey, *Modern Methods for Quality Control and Improvement* (New York: Wiley, 1986).

6. Discuss the disadvantages of sample inspection plans for maintaining and achieving quality.

7. The required specifications for the width and gauge of steel flats are as follows.

　　Width: target 10.00 cm, and specification limits 9.85 cm and 10.15 cm

　　Gauge: target 2.50 cm, and specification limits 2.45 cm and 2.55 cm.

Inspection of $n = 300$ steel flats from today's production led to the following summary statistics.

　　Width: average 10.06 cm and standard deviation 0.024 cm

　　Gauge: average 2.48 cm and standard deviation 0.019.

Calculate and interpret the capability indexes C_p, C_{pk}, and C_{pm}.

8. Twice each shift (one and five hours into the shift) the process operator takes a sample of 100 items and checks the items for surface scratches. The number of scratches on the last 20 samples were as follows (read across):

　　2 3 1 0 5 2 3 4 2 5 1 5 2 2 3 1 2 3 9 8

Construct a p-chart and interpret the results.

9. Why is important to consider both an x-bar chart and a range chart when monitoring the stability of continuous measurement variables? Discuss.

10. Samples of size $n = 6$ are taken every 15 minutes to check the dimensions of steel flats. The target specification is 10.00 cm, and the specification limits are given by 9.85 cm and 10.15 cm.

Width Measurements

1	9.91	9.88	10.13	10.05	10.12	10.02
2	9.94	10.09	10.04	9.98	10.06	10.10
3	10.20	10.16	9.91	9.94	9.94	9.98
4	9.96	10.20	9.96	9.97	10.00	10.09
5	10.09	10.14	10.05	10.05	10.04	9.85

6	9.92	10.00	10.05	9.91	10.19	9.91
7	10.23	10.02	9.99	10.06	9.93	9.85
8	9.82	9.77	9.96	10.05	9.93	10.04
9	10.06	9.89	9.85	9.89	10.07	9.83
10	10.12	9.93	9.90	10.16	9.96	9.88
11	10.04	9.97	9.90	9.73	10.00	10.09
12	10.04	10.28	10.15	10.08	9.98	9.96
13	9.98	9.93	10.12	9.89	9.80	10.13
14	10.03	10.13	9.97	10.05	9.92	10.08
15	9.83	9.99	9.93	9.94	10.09	9.94
16	9.95	10.02	10.24	10.09	10.07	9.96
17	9.82	9.98	9.98	10.13	10.15	9.96
18	10.15	9.86	10.00	9.87	9.99	10.13
19	9.95	9.89	9.88	9.87	10.07	10.05
20	10.20	9.94	9.99	10.12	9.88	9.92
21	10.05	10.04	9.84	10.00	9.93	10.09
22	10.00	9.94	9.93	9.96	10.16	10.06
23	10.10	10.05	9.89	9.97	9.92	10.05
24	10.00	10.06	9.94	10.05	10.00	9.91

(a) Is the process in statistical control? Construct the appropriate control charts and discuss.

(b) Is the process capable? Calculate the appropriate capability indexes and discuss.

11. Motorola Six-Sigma concept: Assume that $C_p = 2$. Furthermore, suppose that the mean of the process variable has shifted away from the target by 1.5 standard deviations. That is, the process variable is centered at $Tg + (1.5)\sigma$. Calculate the implied C_{pk} capability index.

12. Motorola's target for 1992 (set in 1987) was to obtain defect rates of 3.4 per million components manufactured.

(a) It is said that "Six Sigma" is a statistical term for 3.4 defects per million opportunities. Explain this statement.

(b) Discuss the problems of a sample inspection approach to quality if defect rates are in the 1–10 parts per million range.

(c) Six Sigma is a measurement tool. Discuss what is needed to implement Six Sigma.

13. Compute C_p for the measurements on pH in Table 19.3. Compare this with C_{pk} and C_{pm}, given in Section 20.8.

14. Read and discuss Juran Institute, "The Tools of Quality. Part V: Check Sheets," *Quality Progress*, October 1990, p. 51.

15. Read Kevin M. Nolan, "Planning a Control Chart," *Quality Progress*, December 1990, pp. 51–55. Discuss the author's views of the development and maintenance of control charts.

16. Read and discuss Joseph G. Van Matre, "Control Charts and Process Capability," in *Foundations of TQM: A Readings Book*, Van Matre, ed. (New York: Dryden Press, 1995), pp. 99–134.

17. Read and discuss Lynn B. Hare, Roger W. Hoerl, John D. Hromi, and Ronald D. Snee, "The Role of Statistical Thinking in Management," *Quality Progress*, February 1995, pp. 53–60. What is the role of statistical thinking, what are its benefits, and how can one ensure that statistical knowledge is effectively applied?

18. Read Fred A. Spiring, "A Bill's Effect on Alcohol-Related Traffic Fatalities," *Quality Progress*, February 1994, pp. 35–38. How can you use p-charts to assess the effectiveness of a law?

19. Read Brian L. Joiner, "Using Statisticians to Help Transform Industry in America," *Quality Progress*, May 1986, pp. 46–50. Summarize the contributions that a statistician can make to quality and quality improvement.

20. The stability of the velocity of rifle bullets is a main concern in the manufacture of bullets. Small samples of size $n = 5$ are taken each hour from the manufacturing line and test-fired. The velocity of each bullet is measured.

The data given in the following tabulations represent the results for two different types of bullets. Here we only give the average and the range of the chronologically arranged subgroups of size 5.

20 groups of 5 for bullet type 1		19 groups of 5 for bullet type 2	
Mean	Range	Mean	Range
2900	75	2770	50
2855	52	2550	65
2715	182	2660	160
2820	254	2705	130
2790	85	2745	60
2855	162	2660	215
2640	187	2525	150
2955	95	2650	35
2860	80	2720	55
2780	177	2530	175
2730	210	2810	105
2865	135	2605	40
2685	50	2680	80
2870	110	2595	85
2845	120	2720	90
2770	122	2780	115
2775	148	2665	65
2665	80	2725	95
2820	130	2700	195
2960	70		

(a) Construct x-bar and R-charts and investigate whether the production process is stable with respect to average velocity and velocity dispersion. Do this for each type of bullet separately.

(b) Use displays to assess graphically whether there are differences in velocity among the two types of bullets. You may want to construct and superimpose dot diagrams of the velocity averages of the two types of bullets. You can do the same with the ranges.

(c) Why is it important that the processes are stable before you can make comparisons? Discuss.

21. Assume that you want to maximize the yield of a process by varying the levels of two design variables, temperature and pressure. You use the following strategy: You fix one design variable (say temperature) at a certain value and vary the second design variable, pressure, to locate its value where the yield is largest. Then you fix pressure at this optimal setting and change temperature in order to maximize the response. This is referred to as the "change one variable at-a-time approach" to experimentation. Discuss why this approach may fail to locate the optimum, and why it is important to change the design variables together.

22. Read and summarize the first two sections of Chapter 19 (Inspection and Test—Sampling Plans) in J. M. Juran and F. M. Gryna, *Quality Planning and Analysis*, 3rd ed., (New York: McGraw-Hill, 1993).

PART V:

◆ ◆ ◆

Improving Quality

In Part V, we discuss the other two stages for achieving quality: improvement of products and processes, and innovation to make quantum improvements by replacing old production processes with new, more effective processes.

Chapter 21 discusses various techniques for improving quality. The chapter begins with a review of some Japanese techniques that helped them gain a worldwide reputation for quality. Discussed are self-directed work teams and cross-functional management. The first is a technique for helping workers make improvements; the second is a technique for making improvements that cross organizational lines. Some improvements are made through individual efforts. Suggestion systems for capturing employees' ideas and techniques that individuals can apply to improve their own work processes are particularly useful.

Quality improvement is a process; this process is discussed together with principles for solving problems and conducting improvement projects. Some improvements involve making changes in work processes. Three examples are discussed: installing a defect management process, foolproofing a process to make it harder to create a defect, and benchmarking an organization with an outstanding process to gain ideas for improving your own. The chapter concludes with a discussion of the Seven Management Tools for Quality Control.

Through the years, there have been various initiatives for improving quality; in Chapter 22, several of these are reviewed. Some initiatives, such as the zero defects concept, generated much excitement but had little lasting value. Others offer very sound advice, such as Juran's 10 steps to quality improvement and his breakthrough sequence, and Deming's 14 points for management. Chapter 22 concludes with a list of reasons why some quality programs fail. It is not a simple task to accomplish quality improvement in an organizational setting. This list offers advice on some things *not* to do.

Chapter 23 discusses quality improvement through innovation—radical change. Improvement brings about gradual change in quality; innovation can bring quantum improvements. The chapter examines several innovations that an organization should consider adopting. It also discusses how organizational structure, organizational environment, and access to power impact innovation.

Three cases in the Appendix describe mature, effective quality programs and illustrate the concepts explained in Part V. In *Case 6: Xerox Puts the Customer First*, the focus is on dealing with customers. The case discusses how the corporate culture, corporate priority, various production processes, and other aspects of the corporation all have a bearing on customer satisfaction. It also describes some of the tools and initiatives that Xerox uses to maintain a customer focus. *Case 7: Federal Express: The Vision Made Real* describes a mature, very successful quality program. The case provides a detailed discussion of the strategies and systems Federal Express uses to implement its fundamental principle: an intense focus on the needs of the customer and continual quality improvement. *Case 8: Saturn's Blueprint for Success* illustrates the importance of establishing a corporate mission and making the innovative changes needed to fulfill it.

CHAPTER 21

Quality Improvement

It must be considered that there is nothing more difficult to carry out, nor more doubtful of success, nor more dangerous to handle, than to initiate a new order of things. For the reformer has enemies in all those who profit by the old order, and only lukewarm defenders in all those who would profit by the new order, this luke-warmness arising partly from fear of their adversaries, who have the laws in their favor; and partly from the incredulity of mankind, who do not truly believe in any-thing new until they have had actual experience of it. Thus it arises that on every opportunity for attacking the reformer, his opponents do so with the zeal of parti-sans, the others only defend him half-heartedly, so that between them he runs great danger.

—Machiavelli, *The Prince*

◆ 21.1 Introduction

Much of the material in Part IV is directed at achieving process stability. A stable process is *consistent over time.* A stable process is not necessarily a satisfactory process—it might consistently produce substandard products. In this case, the obvious next step is to find ways to improve it. If, however, a process is not stable

469

(that is, not in statistical control), then any attempt at improvement is "fiddling while Rome burns" and is unlikely to be rewarding. Process stability, therefore, is the foundation for quality improvement.

Effective quality programs focus on *process improvement*—making incremental changes in a process in order to bring about continual improvement in the quality of the process products. This means all processes: improving the requirements process to get a better understanding of what the customer requires, the design and build processes to better satisfy customer requirements, and the examine process to ensure that the product has no defects.

Continual improvement can bring tangible results, such as reduced defect rates, a lower cost of quality, and an improved financial picture, as well as intangible results, such as pride, esprit de corp, and satisfaction. Continual improvement has wide acceptance because it is devoid of such emotion-packed words as "control" and "management." Unions, professionals, health-care providers, academics, and other groups have been receptive to using continual improvement as the name for their quality effort.

Some typical symptoms of the need for process improvement are these:

Frequent customer complaints
A large part of production involved with product inspection
Feeling that there is not enough time to do the job right
Excessive rework
Too many missed schedules and too much firefighting
Poor economic performance
Employee discontent and high turnover

To achieve continual improvement, an organization must adjust its strategic and operational planning processes to accommodate quality improvement. Generally, quality improvement is accomplished *project by project*. Strategic and operational plans must identify goals for quality improvement, projects to accomplish these goals, resources for the efforts, and measures of success. Planning for quality is similar to and must be integrated with the traditional plans for running the organization. But you must know where you are before you can plan how to get where you want to be. Thus, the first step in improving a process is to document it—to pin down exactly the current procedures and practices.

Quality improvement is the responsibility of the process owner. Quality Assurance, acting as an adviser/consultant, might provide suggestions and guidance. QA might also serve as a resource, say for teaching quality concepts or facilitating early improvement efforts. However, QA is responsible only for the quality of its own products.

In this chapter we discuss several useful techniques for continual quality improvement. We will discuss other quality-related techniques in Chapter 23 under the heading of "innovation." Quality innovation calls for radical improvement in quality as contrasted with the continual improvement that we discuss here. You should understand, however, that the line between improvement and innovation is blurred and, to some extent, a matter of convenience in presenting concepts.

21.2 Kaizen: The Japanese Approach to Company-Wide Continual Quality Improvement

Kaizen[1] refers to the Japanese approach of continual improvement of products and processes with participation of all employees from all levels of the organization. Our interest is in quality, but improvement need not be confined to that; it can also be aimed at improving productivity and delivery time. Improvements made in the name of quality often have these added benefits. Japanese managers have found that seeking improvement for improvement's sake is the surest way to strengthen their companies' overall competitiveness. Kaizen goes by many names: Total Quality Management (TQM), Continuous Quality Improvement (CQI), or Company-Wide Quality Control (CWQC), a term that is used in Japan.

Kaizen has several goals: (1) to provide products and services that satisfy customers; (2) to steer the organization to higher profitability through improved work procedures, fewer defects, and lower costs; and (3) to help employees fulfill their potential for achieving the organization's goals.

Kaizen emphasizes process-oriented thinking and process improvement. It emphasizes problem awareness and stresses various problem-solving tools. Kaizen's focus is on people; it stimulates and supports their efforts to improve the system. Employees are provided with training and a structure for solving quality problems. Once problems are solved, the improvements are locked in through standardization. Kaizen builds quality into the products by improving production processes.

Kaizen relies heavily on data. Employees are taught skills for collecting and analyzing data. Customer complaints, for example, provide a wealth of data once one gets beyond viewing them as an embarrassment or a nuisance.

Kaizen develops a culture in which everyone can freely admit to problems. Under the Kaizen system, companies develop elaborate suggestion systems in which management offers rewards for useful suggestions. Toyota, for example, receives about 1.5 million suggestions a year; 95 percent of the suggestions are actually implemented.

The following examples illustrate several major improvement concepts.

Example 1. Engineers in western companies usually are not too excited about working on the factory floor; rather, they want to work on research and development problems. Often designs are constructed in offices, and there is little feedback between the design engineers and the workers on the factory floor. But the workers are the people who know how well or poorly a design works in practice, and poor communication prevents this knowledge from influencing the design.

Japanese industry puts a priority on a smooth-running production. Engineers are assigned to the production line and are actively involved in

---

[1]Masaaki Imai, *Kaizen: The Key to Japan's Competitive Success* (New York: Random House Business Division, 1986), is the source for much of the material in Sections 21.2 through 21.5.

production. In addition, the R&D staff is distributed among the production facilities. This allows the engineers and staff to understand production problems, thus helping them design better processes and procedures.

Example 2. *JIT (just-in-time)*[2] is a system for inventory management that has its origin in the Kaizen philosophy. The JIT system is an answer to the traditional system, where multiple copies of required items are held in inventory. The JIT approach is to deliver the exact number of required units to each successive stage of production and to do this at exactly the appropriate time. JIT reduces inventory because only items that are needed "just in time" are brought to the production line. JIT requires that suppliers be trusted to deliver quality products at the right time. If the supplier is late with his delivery or the delivered products are of poor quality, production halts. Supplier quality, therefore, is an important consideration in making JIT viable.

A rule of thumb, says Thomas J. Murrin of Westinghouse Electric, a member of the President's Commission on Industrial Competitiveness, is that each $1 of inventory costs 25 cents a year to carry—half of that for interest, half for storage space, insurance, deterioration, and handling.[3]

Example 3. The Kanban system in Japan is another good example of Kaizen. *Kanban* means signboard or label. It is a simple tool used in Toyota's production system to coordinate the flow of parts to the assembly line.

At Toyota, a card (kanban) is attached to the front body of each car on the assembly line. Depending on codes on the card, each car gets appropriate components as it is assembled. For example, one car may get a steering wheel on the right, another on the left. The worker picks up the parts based on the instruction on this card. The kanban is returned after parts are used to serve as a record of the work done and an order for new parts.

◆ 21.3 Cross-Functional Management

Management-oriented improvement strategies require managers to focus on the work system and the work procedures. Managers must focus their efforts on quality problems that extend across different functional areas of the company, and their problem-solving actions must go beyond the narrow boundaries of individual work areas. Managers must identify and reduce waste on the manufacturing floor, and make workers' jobs less complex. *Cross-functional management*, as practiced by Japanese companies, is an important part of companywide improvement efforts. An understanding of this concept requires some knowledge of Japanese planning.

---

[2]JIT was first mentioned in Section 11.12 in the context of reengineering efforts.

[3]*Forbes*, April 9, 1984, p. 33.

As part of annual planning, top managers formulate two types of annual objectives: maintenance objectives and improvement objectives. Although handled differently, maintenance objectives and improvement objectives are interwoven and coordinated.

> *Maintenance objectives* have to do with business results; they concern profit, market share, and products. These objectives focus on "today," on the need for performance; they are similar to objectives commonly established by top managers in the United States. Generally they are established along organizational lines (product development, production, marketing, etc.). They are the responsibility of line managers, who usually view them as their primary goal, taking priority over improvement.
>
> *Improvement objectives* are established to promote systems improvement. These are aimed at promoting better systems for quality, better systems to identify and reduce cost, and better systems for delivery and volume. Improvement objectives are aimed at "tomorrow"—on an improvement in competitive position. Their purpose is to improve customer satisfaction, product quality, customer service, employee ability, cost control, delivery control, and new product development.

Improvement objectives are also known as *cross-functional objectives* because they require coordinating the activities of different units. The ultimate goal of a company is to make profits, which are required for survival. But after this, cross-functional (improvement) objectives are the most important or "superordinate" objectives. They are established by a high-level cross-functional committee prior to determining unit objectives. The view is that all line managers exist to serve these superordinate objectives because these objectives provide the key to meeting competitive pressures on quality, cost, and on-time delivery.

In addition to objectives (ends), the Japanese planning process also develops specific action programs (means) for meeting the objectives. In Japan, *policy* refers to the ends and the means. *Policy deployment* is the process of implementing plans for improvement directly through line managers and indirectly through cross-functional organizations.

The vehicle for achieving policy deployment is *cross-functional management*. This is a system of matrix management cutting across line functions; its purpose is to realize the cross-functional goals and to assist in deploying the policies for improvement. It evolved from the need to break the interdepartmental barriers that hindered quality improvement.

The concern of cross-functional management is with process improvement, both vertically and horizontally. It requires each manager to interpret improvement plans in light of his or her own responsibilities and to establish criteria for measuring success in meeting these plans.

As we have described it, cross-functional management has a strong focus on process improvement. A good example of a Japanese company that employs cross-functional management with this focus is Komatsu, who is reputed to have one of the best total quality control programs in Japan. But not all companies have this focus. For example, Toyota, which originated the cross-functional management concept, appears to employ it more for quality assurance and cost control than for process improvement.

◆ 21.4 Self-Directed Work Teams

Self-directed work teams (SDWT) were introduced in Section 16.7, where we discussed the benefits they can bring to an organization as well as some operational issues. Here we focus on developing SDWTs and making them an effective agent for quality improvement.[4]

In a typical situation, an executive steering committee conducts a feasibility study before a decision is made to install SDWTs. Management then issues a mission statement or charter for SDWTs, draws up a plan for their introduction, and appoints a group to carry out the plan.

Team development typically proceeds through several phases. The first is a training phase. Team members are given intense instruction on group dynamics, communication, the use of administrative procedures, and other technical and interpersonal skills needed for team activities.

Training is followed by a second phase—general confusion. Team members do not understand their new role. They have difficulty reaching cooperative decisions. They worry about their new roles, managers worry about their security and loss of authority, and unions are concerned about their role in the new order of things.

Gradually, confidence grows, and the team enters a third phase as a natural leader emerges. Most team members welcome this development; they are accustomed to being led and are content with a leader who is one of them. In this stage, there is too much dependence on the natural leader; the group is not truly a team.

Over time, the group enters a fourth stage and becomes a tightly formed team. They learn to establish team goals and schedule team activities. Intense team loyalty builds, even to the point of the group protecting poor performers and being reluctant to accept new team members. Rather than cooperate, teams compete with one another.

In time, the group enters a fifth and final stage: it becomes a true self-directed team. The team develops a sense of commitment, trust, and involvement. Through continual education and working cooperatively, team members broaden their technical and interpersonal skills.

Some critical success factors for developing SDWT's are:

- ◆ Top-level commitment
- ◆ Management-employee trust

---

[4]Jack D. Orsburn, Linda Moran, Ed Musselwhite, and John H. Zenger, *Self-Directed Work Teams* (Homewood, Il: Business One Irwin, 1990), pp. 19–23.

- Willingness to take risks
- Willingness to share information
- Sufficient time and resources
- Commitment to training
- Operations that are conducive to work teams
- Union participation
- Access to help

Based on the experience of Lucent Technologies, here is some practical advice about forming SDWT's.[5]

- *Hire attitude over aptitude.* Look for self-starters and team players; avoid loners and curmudgeons.
- *Create mission from above, methods from below.* Ask each employee to sign a pledge committing to speed, innovation, candor, deep respect for colleagues, and other plainly stated goals; give them latitude in developing the means of meeting the goals.
- *Foster feedback.* Remember that good communications magnify the effect of good changes and curtail the effect of bad ones.
- *Provide information.* Establish written procedures, ratified by those who are affected; post operating statistics everywhere; establish an "urgent board" listing orders that are behind schedule; and ask people to jump in where they are most needed.
- *Unite the inside and the outside.* Put employees next to customers; let people know the destination of every product they touch; encourage employees to know external customers through trade shows, product installations, and conducting customer tours.
- *Reward teamwork.* Base bonuses on individual achievement and team performance; nurture an all-for-one atmosphere.
- *Encourage a sense of ownership.* Be aware that the biggest motivator is feeling that "This business is ours."

◆ 21.5 Individual-Oriented Improvement Efforts

Individual-oriented improvement focuses on the employee's own work area and on improving one's own personal processes. It boosts morale, helps adopt a positive attitude toward change, and improves the way the employee thinks.

---

[5]Thomas Petzinger Jr., "The Front Lines," *Wall Street Journal*, March 7, 1997, p. B1.

Suggestion Programs

Many organizations install suggestion programs designed to encourage the reporting of employee ideas for improvement. Employees are encouraged to submit ideas; in return, they are given a reward, which may be tied to the value of the savings or additional revenue generated by the idea. In practice, most of the suggestions offered through such plans concern product or process improvements; these suggestions are a valuable source of ideas for continual process and product improvement.

The suggestion system is an integral part of Kaizen. For example, Toyota Motors workers provide 1.5 million suggestions per year; 95 percent of those are put to practical use.[6] In 1985 Matsushita topped the list of Japanese companies in number of suggestions with over 6 million suggestions.[7] A 1987 survey of 570 major private Japanese corporations showed that 47 million suggestions were offered by (only) 2 million employees.[8] Japanese companies make every effort to help workers provide suggestions, no matter how primitive. The suggestions system acts as a great morale booster. Also, with more experience and training in analyzing problems, employees provide better and better suggestions, which are ultimately reflected in an economic impact. The main subjects for suggestions are improvements in one's own work and work environment; improvements in tools, machines and processes; suggestions for improved or new processes; and ideas for improved customer services and relations.

Suggestions can come from both individuals and groups. Many of the suggestions that have an economic impact come from groups. Nevertheless, individual-based suggestions are important because they boost the morale of workers and contribute to learning.

Japanese companies have developed a detailed system for handling suggestions; the procedures of Canon and Aisin-Warner, a major automotive supplier, are described in detail by Imai.[9] Employees are actively encouraged to submit ideas. Companies use special forms for suggestions; the suggestions are ranked and cash awards of varying amounts are given. Competitions and games are held to arouse interest in the suggestion system, and accepted suggestions are implemented as soon as possible.

Personal Improvement

Roberts and Sergesketter[10] argue convincingly that quality as practiced by the individual forms the foundation on which companywide quality improvement programs are built. Quality is based on the action of people. Total quality management

---

[6]Imai, *Kaizen*, p. 15.

[7]Ibid., p. 112.

[8]Reinosuke Hara, CEO of Seiko Industries, in *FYI*, University of Iowa publication, September 23, 1988.

[9]Imai, *Kaizen*, pp. 114–124.

[10]Harry V. Roberts and Bernard F. Sergesketter, *Quality Is Personal* (New York: Free Press, 1993).

as a company function cannot be successful unless all people in an organization understand and practice the principles of quality at a personal level.

Total quality management, a people-focused management system that aims at continual organizational improvements, is not an institutional assignment but a *personal priority obligation*. As a manager you cannot delegate quality; you must show the way and lead by example. Similarly, workers must be encouraged to improve their own personal processes. A worker who "puts on a quality hat" from 9 to 5 while on the job, but who forgets all about quality once outside the factory gate, will not be very committed to improvement. Similarly, you, the reader, cannot view quality as a purely academic subject that you study and memorize for a grade; you must apply this information to your own processes.

What about applying some of this material to improving your study habits; finding more time to do things that you always wanted to do but couldn't; improving your free-throw percentage in basketball or your running time; or improving your own health by following good eating and drinking/smoking habits?

Roberts and Sergesketter recommend a *Personal Quality Checklist* as an effective tool to improve one's own processes. They recommend it for (a) its usefulness in training about quality, (b) its astonishing potential for quickly improving work effectiveness, and (c) its impact on improving quality in everyday life outside the workplace.

Before making your own Personal Quality Checklist, you need to identify the processes that you use to do your work. For most of us, this means communicating and interacting with others. Here is our list.

◆ Be on time for meetings. Much useful time is wasted by not starting the meeting at the fixed time. If you are meeting with ten people, and you must wait just one minute for someone who is late, the group has wasted ten minutes.

◆ Eliminate the need to search for something misplaced or lost.

◆ Return phone calls the same or next day.

◆ Respond to letters within a week. This requires that incoming mail be time-stamped.

◆ Referee papers within a month. Peer review is an essential component in the quality review of scientific publications, and every professor spends quite some time reviewing paper submissions. Timely feedback is important, especially for younger colleagues who have to establish a research reputation prior to tenure. Instead of letting manuscripts sit on the shelf for several weeks, why not read the paper within a month!

◆ Exercise at least three days a week.

◆ Read to our young children at least every other day.

◆ Make someone smile every day.

◆ Drink no more than three cups of coffee a day.

◆ Have no more than one dessert a day.

◆ Eat at least two pieces of fruit a day.

For students the list might contain the following.

- Review class notes before each class meeting
- Read the assigned readings before each class meeting
- Watch no more than ten hours of television a week.
- Stick to the subject while studying.
- Follow a good diet.
- Limit party time, alcohol, and smoking

Once your Personal Quality Checklist has been established, you should keep track of the number of daily (or weekly) defects. It is fairly easy to keep track of defects; a simple stroke tally will suffice. It also helps to display the number of defects in the form of a time sequence chart. Just keeping track of defects usually shows that some activities that you originally thought were of no concern come up repeatedly. Counting defects makes one aware that there are problems, and it is surprising how quickly the number of defects will go down.

Simple experiments can also be planned to improve personal processes. For example, different approaches to a basketball foul shot can be investigated. Similarly, one can embark on a systematic investigation of one's golf game or investigate the effects of different exercise programs on weight loss. The material on statistically designed experiments in Sections 20.9 and 20.10 can be put to good use.

Elimination of Waste or Complexity

Tim Fuller uses *work sampling* methods to find activities that serve no purpose.[11] Work sampling involves observing what one is doing at randomly chosen times. Times can be signaled, for example, by the beeper of a digital watch. Fuller's studies have shown that complexity (or rework) caused by internal and external errors account for a big fraction of work time; real work constitutes only a small fraction. Thus, enormous improvements are possible if waste and complexity can be eliminated. The closer you look at work, the more waste you see. Take observations on your own day; locate and discuss the proportion of unproductive activities.

◆ 21.6 The Quality Improvement Process

Enabling Improvement

For quality improvement to be practiced regularly and effectively, it must be given proper management attention. Quality improvement must be in step with the gen-

---

[11]Tim Fuller, "Eliminating Complexity from Work: Improving Productivity by Enhancing Quality," *National Productivity Review* (Autumn 1985), pp. 327-344.

eral organizational direction. People must be supported with appropriate training and equipment. The following requisites are essential to quality improvement.

◆ *Direction*: Quality improvement will not be practiced effectively without appropriate direction. Management goals must be articulated. Process improvement should become part of every job. To be practiced effectively, quality improvement must be embedded in the organization's culture.

◆ *Support*: Quality improvement will not be practiced effectively without appropriate support. Training, supporting services, and tools to bring about improvement have to be made available. A supportive climate, which includes management support, good communication, availability of information, and a risk-free environment, must be established.

◆ *Empowerment*: Employees must be empowered to make suggestions and changes. They must have the necessary information, resources, and backing.

◆ *Recognition*: Quality improvements should be recognized by management. An "attaboy" remark at a departmental meeting, a small gift, a dinner for two—all can show management's appreciation for an improvement.

The Improvement Loop

Improvement is an unending continual loop of finding problems, prioritizing problems, and solving problems.

We *find* problems by talking with customers, understanding the process, studying product requirements and standards, examining the product and gathering data, and measuring performance, such as recording the number and type of defects.

Problems may involve the output of operations: The output may not meet requirements, in which case we talk about quality problems. The input/output ratio may not be satisfactory, in which case we talk about productivity problems. The timing of the output may be wrong, which indicates a problem with timely delivery.

Problems may arise because of poor process flow. The standards for tasks may be unclear, perhaps because of insufficient documentation and training. Some tasks may be redundant; there may be signs of major bottlenecks and "patched-up" processes. Problems may also arise because of inferior inputs, people factors of processes, technical factors of processes, or the control system of processes.

We *select* problems by listing known problems and by determining the worst problem areas. It is important to prioritize problems. The Pareto diagram (discussed in Section 19.2) can help to distinguish the "vital few" from the "many rare" defects.

Several problem-solving strategies can be employed, including the following. For a more detailed discussion, see our book, *Statistical Quality Control: Strategies and Tools for Continual Improvement*, John Wiley, 1999.

The *principle of abstraction* takes the problem out of its real setting. By simplifying facts, it cuts through complexity and gets down to the basic elements. This approach allows imagining a solution without practical constraints of why it won't work. The *divide-and-conquer* strategy solves a difficult problem by dividing it into pieces, attacking each piece separately. It divides a large problem into several subproblems. This strategy works well if the subproblems are more or less independent. The *hierarchical ordering concept* is closely related to the previous approach. It structures the problem into layers where lower layers are not aware of higher layers, but higher layers involve or use the lower ones. *Data* must be part of any problem-solving strategy. Problems must be solved through the scientific method, not on the basis of hunches.

Improvement Projects

Improvement is usually achieved through carefully planned and executed projects. Projects may be small or large, and they may be carried out by an individual or by groups.

The project must have some structure. Usually, the problem needs to be justified in the sense that it is important, a solution likely exists, and the solution is useful to the organization. Boundaries of the project and reporting procedures (to whom, how often, level of detail) have to be established and time commitments have to determined. If a team is involved, the right team must be selected. Experience, attitude, technical skills, and ability to work together have to be considered carefully. A project leader needs to be selected.

A sound project plan must be developed prior to starting the project. Without such a plan the project probably will be poorly managed and will exceed time and budget constraints. Part of the plan must be a strategy for accomplishing the major objectives. A team agreement on the plan and a full commitment to the plan should be obtained before attempting to implement it.

Managing the project involves monitoring accomplishments and comparing them to the plan. Adjustments to the plan should be made if necessary. The final report at the close of the project should review the findings of the project and emphasize its contributions. The project itself should be reviewed with the aim of improving the project process.

◆ 21.7 The Defect Management Process

Because of the basic paradigm of work, every product is examined to determine if it meets requirements. Thus the management of *product quality* is built into the production process. In this section, we discuss the defect management process, which makes use of defect data to improve *process quality*.

Defect management is the process of tracking and analyzing defects for the purpose of making process improvements. The root causes of defects are determined, and these causes are eliminated from the production process; this is sometimes referred to as *defect cause removal*. By ensuring that these defect causes cannot come up in the future, defect management is a natural way to improve processes.

The first step in defect management is to build a *defect database* consisting of data on defects and their possible causes. Some of these data come from the quality control activities performed while the product is being built, some comes from complaints of customers who were shipped faulty products.

The second step in defect management is to classify the defects in some way that is useful for making process improvements. One scheme is to classify defects according to severity. Ishikawa[12] distinguishes among critical defects that compromise life and safety, major defects that seriously affect proper functioning of the product, and minor defects that do not compromise the functioning of the product but that, nevertheless, are not appreciated by the customer. Although a producer might be able to tolerate a small number of minor defects in a product, he should always remove the cause of a critical defect. Another useful way to classify defects is by frequency of occurrence. Obviously, it is better to remove the cause of commonly made defects before turning to those that are rare (assuming, of course, that their costs are about the same).

The next step is to allocate resources and establish projects for "fixing" specific defects. Such a project starts by examining the defect data for patterns that will help determine the cause of the defects. The usual problem-solving techniques are applied: brainstorming to develop an understanding of the defect, Ishikawa diagrams to find possible causes, importance rankings of possible causes, and data analysis to verify the findings. The next step is to remove the cause of the defect so as to prevent similar defects from occurring again. The defect cause removal process is simple, but it requires considerable technical knowledge about the process being improved, ability to communicate with the operators of the process, and familiarity with problem-solving techniques.

Ishikawa Cause-and-Effect Diagrams

The *cause-and-effect diagram* is a useful tool that graphically displays, in increasing detail, all of the possible causes that are related to a problem under study. This diagram is also called a *fishbone diagram* because of its shape, or an *Ishikawa diagram* in honor of Kaoru Ishikawa, who developed this technique.

To construct a cause-and-effect diagram, first find all possible causes of an effect and then classify them into about four to eight categories and into subcategories where appropriate. Draw a horizontal arrow pointing to a box at the right end, which is labeled with the effect under consideration. For each major classification, draw a line slanting into the horizontal arrow so that the resulting pattern resembles the skeleton of a fish; label each slanting line with the name of a major subcategory. Then draw horizontal arrows into each slanting line to represent the causes within the labeled category. If there are subcategories, these are represented by horizontal lines with slanted lines into them to represent their members. A good cause-and-effect diagram shows several major categories with many causes and subcategories attached to each.

---

[12]Kaoru Ishikawa, *What Is Total Quality Control?* (Englewood Cliffs, NJ: Prentice-Hall), 1985, p. 50.

DISPLAY 21.1 ◆ Ishikawa Cause-and-Effect Diagram: Late Pizza Deliveries on Fridays and Saturdays

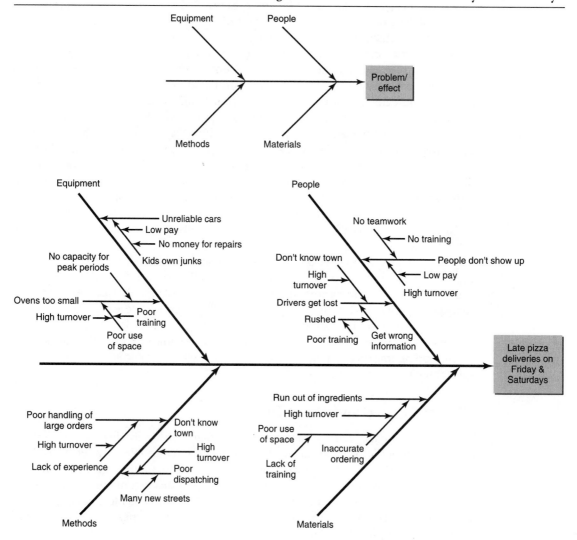

A generic cause-and-effect diagram is shown at the top of Display 21.1; it divides causes into four large categories: equipment, people, materials, and methods. A cause-and-effect diagram that arranges the causes for late pizza deliveries on Fridays and Saturdays is shown at the bottom of Display 21.1.[13]

Cause-and-effect diagrams have many advantages. First, making a cause-and-effect diagram helps you understand the problem. The discipline of categorizing data

---

[13]This example is taken from Michael Brassard and Diane Ritter, *The Memory Jogger II* (Methuen, MA: Goal/QPC, 1994). This is a very useful pocket guide of tools for continual improvement and effective planning. It contains detailed guidelines and many practical examples.

and displaying it graphically helps you see interconnections among causes that are not as clearly evident from a simple list. Second, a cause-and-effect diagram is a focus for discussion; it can be used to direct attention or to encourage a systematic discussion of causes. Most people find it easier to grasp information and concepts if they are presented pictorially or graphically. A cause-and-effect diagram, much like a graph, is a very effective communication tool.

◆ 21.8 Foolproofing or Pokayoke

"Foolproofing" a process means to design a process so that errors are unlikely to occur. Foolproofing a process is an attempt to eliminate error-prone elements in the basic design of the process. The Japanese refer to this as "pokayoke."

For example, an assembly process might be designed so that it is virtually impossible to assemble items incorrectly. Or an operation might be designed so that multiple improbable events must occur simultaneously before a defect can be made. For example, the process might be designed to reduce human fallibility through optical magnification of characters or simultaneous signals to multiple senses. A cash register that computes the amount of change makes the transactions foolproof. Additional examples are different electrical "plugs" for appliances that use 220 volts rather than the usual 110 volts; color coding of components that fit together; gauges that are easier to read; and reducing the number of times breakable goods are handled.

◆ 21.9 Benchmarking

Benchmarking, also known as competitive benchmarking, is a structured approach for evaluating the performance of a process, an organizational area, or a product against that of a recognized leader. The comparison can be with respect to an outside organization or to another part of your own organization. The knowledge that is obtained by benchmarking can then be used to develop and implement a plan to achieve leadership in the marketplace.

Benchmarking uses another unit's achieved results as a standard your unit can measure itself against. Unlike the usual competitive analysis study, benchmarking can take you outside your industry in search of the leading practice. For example, Xerox, which originated benchmarking in the late 1970s, established L. L. Bean's distribution system as the world-class standard and used it to illustrate that there were very real improvement opportunities for Xerox.

Benchmarking broadens your experience base and increases your knowledge. You learn from the practices used by others, and you gain an increased awareness of how your costs and performance compare with others in and out of your industry.

Benchmarking helps you to incorporate best practices into your organization and develop winning strategies. It can be used to develop superiority in all dimensions—quality, reliability, cost, and production time. By using an idea from outside your industry, you can even establish a new standard for performance in your industry.

Companies with effective benchmarking efforts include IBM, Xerox, and Milliken & Company, all winners of the Malcolm Baldrige National Quality Award.

Benchmarking Prerequisites

An organization should not attempt benchmarking until it has satisfied certain prerequisites. Companies need:

◆ *An environment conducive to benchmarking*
Not all organizations can admit that others are better at something than they are. Effective benchmarking requires a certain humility and the recognition that even the best have something new to learn.

◆ *Preparation for benchmarking*
A second prerequisite is that proper preparations must be made for benchmarking efforts. An organization must develop an effective benchmarking process and train people to use it.

◆ *Use of the information gained*
A third prerequisite is that the organization must be prepared to use the information gained from the benchmarking effort. A method for its use should be identified before the benchmarking effort is undertaken. Potential obstacles to the use of benchmarking information should be addressed in advance.

The Benchmarking Process

A benchmarking process consists of four major steps:[14]

1. *Decide what to benchmark.*
The first step in benchmarking is to analyze your current problems and goals and to identify potential topics to benchmark. Some things to consider in making this selection are these: Is the topic important to the customers? Is the topic consistent with the mission and values of the organization? Does the topic reflect an important business need? Is it significant in terms of quality, cost, or other key indicators? Is the topic in an area where additional information could influence plans and actions?

A topic to be benchmarked might be a product, a process, or a functional area. However, to simplify our exposition, we will assume the topic is a

---

[14]Several organizations have established benchmarking processes, which differ in detail. The process we present is essentially that of Alcoa, which is described in Karen Bemowski, "The Benchmarking Bandwagon," *Quality Progress* (January 1991), pp. 19-23.

process; you should have no trouble adjusting our discussion to address the other two.

After a topic has been selected, a *purpose statement* should be prepared stating:

- The process to be benchmarked
- The sponsor of the benchmarking project (usually the process owner)
- The purpose of the study, which will guide the actions of the benchmarking team

2. *Select and train the benchmarking team.*

Next, the benchmarking team should be selected. Those selected should be open minded and willing to accept change, and they should have the respect of their colleagues. At least one team member should be familiar with the process being benchmarked. But it can be helpful for team members to have different backgrounds, enabling them to evaluate and understand the process and its surroundings from different points of view.

After training, team members should understand

- The benchmarking process
- The process to be benchmarked and its performance
- The factors most and least important in influencing process performance

3. *Select benchmarking partners.*

A third preparatory task is to select the appropriate benchmark partners. The temptation and easy path is to select organizations similar to your own. But a much more effective approach is to look outside your industry. Remember, you are benchmarking a process, not a product; order entry is order entry whether it be for General Motors, United Parcel, or Joe's Diner. Moreover, people outside your industry might be more willing to cooperate with you because they have less concern about confidentiality and conflict of interest.

4. *Prepare and conduct study.*

The project sponsor then draws up a plan for the benchmarking project. The usual steps in a plan are the following:

- Refine the purpose statement: Customers of study, scope of study, characteristics to be measured, useful information about topic that is readily available.
- Make project proposal.
- Obtain approval by project sponsor.
- Make detailed preparation: Decide on questions and instruments.
- Conduct study: Perform study, learn from data, write report.

5. *Use findings.*

This is not actually a step in the benchmarking process but a reminder that the entire effort is worthless unless the results are put to use. You should conduct projects to install the improvements suggested by the benchmarking.

Frequently Benchmarked Processes

The scorecard in Display 21.2 ranks the most frequently benchmarked business processes in the United States. These data are taken from a survey conducted by the Benchmarking Exchange (TBE) members.[15] The information on the five business processes described in this section was gathered from a group of more than 300 business subprocesses tracked by TBE. The information spans a five-year period and is presented as a five-year overall rating and an annual rating for 1994 and 1995.

The five processes most benchmarked in 1995 were:

1. *Human Resources.* This process is made up of subprocesses such as employee development, benefits, satisfaction, recognition, training, suggestion programs, and empowerment. A key factor holding this process at the top of the chart is management's commitment to develop employees into long-term contributers.

2. *Customer-related processes*, such as customer satisfaction, service aspects, and help desks. This implies that organizations are investing substantial time and effort in improving their ability to serve customers.

3. *Information systems operated by the IS Department.* This suggests that organizations now recognize the pervasive impact that IS has on their quality system.

DISPLAY 21.2 ◆ Benchmarking Scorecard

Business Process (listed alphabetically)	Past 5 Years 1991–1995	Ranking 1994	1995
Benchmarking	3	16	5
Customer	5	5	2
Human resources	1	1	1
Information systems	2	4	3
Purchasing	4	17	4
Quality	6	2	10
Supplier management	8	3	9

[15]"Benchmarking: Past, Present and Future," *The Quality Observer*, March 1996.

4. *Purchasing*, including general procurement practices, supplier management, and purchase order processing.

5. *Benchmarking processes.* Since resources and information are becoming more affordable, small and medium-sized businesses are breaking into the benchmarking loop.

The TBE study also assessed the costs associated with training people to do benchmarking. It found that, on average, the cost of training someone and maintaining contact with potential benchmarking partners dropped from $20,000 per person-year in 1992 to $2000 in 1995. The cost associated with conducting one benchmarking study dropped from $50,000 in 1992 to $12,000 in 1995.

◆ 21.10 Additional Useful Tools for Continual Quality Improvement

We conclude this section by mentioning several other improvement tools. Ryoji Futami discusses a set of tools that are popular among Japanese companies.[16] He refers to these tools as the *Seven Management Tools for Quality Control*, borrowing his terminology from Ishikawa's Seven Tools, which represent statistical techniques for QC. In this section we describe a few of the more useful tools.[17]

Traditional statistical analysis techniques, discussed in Chapters 19 and 20, are useful if we have access to "hard" or numerical data. In many instances, however, we are dealing with "language" data where the information is represented as linguistic expressions of attributes of products and processes. When selecting improvement projects, when searching for solutions to problems, or when creating strategies, we usually end up with a long list of ideas. This is typical when we are dealing with management issues where "hard data" are often not available. Ideas or statements can be thought of as "soft data." We need tools to elicit the structure among the soft data, similar to the Pareto diagram that was used to find structure in a body of hard data. Given a list of ideas, it is rarely true that they are independent; usually there are a few vital ideas. The ideas are also often interrelated—some of them are causes and some of them are effects. Two tools that help

---

[16]Ryoji Futami, "The Outline of Seven Management Tools for QC," *Reports of Statistical Application Research, JUSE*, 33 (June 1986), pp. 7–26. The Seven Management Tools are the affinity diagram, relation diagram, tree diagram, matrix diagram method, matrix data analysis method, the process decision program chart, and the program evaluation and review technique (PERT). The English-language description of some of these methods is extremely poor, which may help explain why some are not used by U.S. companies. In addition, not all of these methods are totally new, and some of them are known in the West under different names.

[17]We don't cover all techniques. For example, we omit the matrix data analysis method, which is a rather complex statistical technique very similar to principal components analysis in multivariate statistics. This rather sophisticated technique is best left to the statistical specialists. PERT was covered in Chapter 17.

analyze a list of ideas for structure are the *affinity diagram* and the *interrelationship digraph*.

Affinity Diagram[18]

An affinity diagram is a consensus-building tool that groups concepts into categories such that the elements within the same category are very similar. It groups and displays ideas or concepts according to their natural "affinity" or closeness to each other. For example, industry-leading technology, numbers of patents, and affiliated companies with high technical know-how could all be grouped under "high technological ability." A quality level that is higher than that of competitors and the absence of claims filed by customers are expressions of a "well-established system of quality assurance."

The idea behind affinity diagrams is simple. Instead of a chaotic list of many statements (about products, processes, or situations), we can construct a diagram that integrates these statements into a smaller number of groupings that go together in a logical fashion. By integrating data, an affinity diagram organizes thought and directs thinking toward new insights to the problem. Consistent themes and priorities may emerge from these diagrams. The construction of a diagram is usually carried out in groups. Ideas are written down on cards, one card per idea. Ideas that are similar in nature are clustered together by the team. Headers for these clusters are selected to identify the key themes in the groups of ideas.

Interrelationship Digraph

The structure among the clusters can be studied through an interrelationship digraph. There we arrange the clusters in a circle, and we use arrows to express which clusters are linked to and "cause" the other clusters to happen. Each cluster can be labeled with the number of arrows that point toward the cluster and the number of arrows that go away from the cluster. The clusters with a high number of "out" arrows are the key causal factors. As an example, we reproduce in Display 21.3 an interrelationship digraph for "reasons why statistical thinking is not used today."[19] The nine clusters, representing possible reasons why statistical thinking is not used, were obtained from an affinity diagram of a much longer list of reasons. A study of the "in" and "out" arrows shows that there are two key causal factors: "fear of technical tools and methods" and "people's competing priorities." Each of these clusters has zero "in" arrows and five "out" arrows. This analysis suggests that these two issues must be addressed before people in the organization can make greater use of statistics. The interrelationship digraph is quite useful as it identifies the root causes of the problem.

---

[18]The construction of an affinity diagram is essentially the same as the faceted method of classification, discussed in Section 18.9.

[19]Ronald D. Snee, "Nonstatistical Skills That Can Help Statisticians Be More Effective," *ASQC Statistics Division Newsletter* 16, no. 5 (Winter 1997), pp. 12–17.

DISPLAY 21.3 ◆ Interrelationship Digraph: Reasons Why Statistical Thinking Is Not Used Today

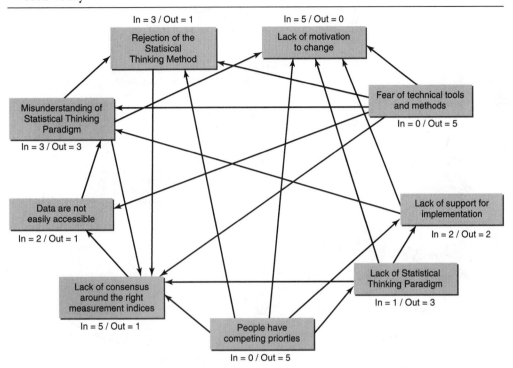

Relation Diagram

The relation diagram discussed by Futami and shown in Display 21.4 is quite similar to the interrelationship digraph.[20] It is used to search for the causes of intertwined problems by means of arranging possible causes as well as their relationships with other causes. It, too, helps to clarify the structure of the problem. In his paper, Futami considers "an insufficient decrease in the number of defectives" as the problem that needs to be sorted out. "Misunderstood instructions" is one major cause of this problem which, in turn, is the result of "insufficient training." Insufficient training, on the other hand, affects the "workers' quality consciousness (or lack thereof)," which in turn affects the likelihood that workers don't pay attention to instructions, which has an impact on the problem of not being able to reduce the number of defectives; and so on. The relationships between the problem and their causes and the causes' causes are complicated. The relation diagram tries to establish some order by writing down causes and effects and examining the relationships. By doing this, we can gain insights into the problem, and these insights help us find solutions.

---

[20]Ryoji Futami, "The Outline of Seven Management Tools for QC," *Reports of Statistical Application Research, JUSE,* 33 (June 1986): 7-26.

DISPLAY 21.4 ◆ Relation Diagram: Problem of an Insufficient Decrease in the Number of Defectives

There are obvious similarities among the relation diagram, the interrelationship digraph, and the Ishikawa cause-and-effect diagram discussed in Section 21.7. All three techniques are ideally suited for team-based efforts. These tools help us understand why certain things happen. The Ishikawa cause-and-effect diagram is used to identify, in increasing detail, all the possible causes that are related to a problem or condition. The interrelationship digraph is a tool to study the cause-and-effect relationships among critical issues, and it is useful for uncovering the root causes of problems. The relation diagram is a way to list the interrelations among factors that are pertinent to a certain problem. A relation diagram with many different items (as is the case in Display 21.4) may be difficult to construct and decipher. It certainly helps to group items into a manageable number of clusters, as was done in the interrelationship digraph in Display 21.3.

Tree Diagram

You are interested in achieving a certain goal, and you want to map out a feasible strategy to achieve that goal. Or you want to solve a certain problem, and you want to determine the feasible actions that are needed for its solution. When we talk about feasible means or actions, we imply they can be carried out and are not just objectives or viewpoints. One approach to problem solving starts by writing down certain primary viewpoints and by drawing lines to connect these to the problem. These viewpoints are usually objectives and not feasible actions. You must look further to find possible ways to achieve them. Often each of the primary viewpoints can be related to secondary viewpoints, which again may be objectives and not feasible actions. Lines can then be used to connect each primary viewpoint to its secondary viewpoints. You can continue to trace the path until you reach feasible ideas that are ready to be used for action. The completed diagram looks like a tree—branching from the problem to primary viewpoints, secondary viewpoints, until the feasible means are reached. An example of a tree diagram is given in Display 21.5. It displays ways of creating a conducive learning environment in the classroom.

DISPLAY 21.5 ◆ Tree Diagram: Creating a Conducive Learning Environment in the Classroom

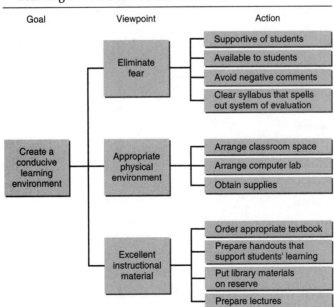

Matrix Diagram

The matrix diagram is a tool used to identify and rate the presence and strength (or type) of pairwise relationships between two or more sets of items. The elements of one set of items are written down as the rows in a matrix, and the elements of the other set of items are written down as the columns. The relationship between each pair of elements is described in the cell where rows and columns intersect. Different symbols are used to express the strength or type of the relationship. The matrix diagram represents an organized way to study the relationship among pairwise combinations of problem elements.

In Display 21.6 we explore the relationships among *three factors*: The orientation of new employees (with elements tour facility, review of personnel and safety policies, . . .), the resources available to carry out the tasks (human resources group, division manager, . . .), and the goals of the orientation (reduce anxiety, resolve practical concerns, . . .).[21] This display shows that the orientation of new employ-

DISPLAY 21.6 ◆ Matrix Diagram: The Tasks in the Orientation of New Employees and Their Relationships to Available Resources and Desired Goals

---

[21]This example is taken from Brassard, Michael and Ritter, Diane: *The Memory Jogger II* (Methuen, MA: Goal/QPC, 1994).

ees should be carried out by supervisors and their associates, and not by the traditional human resources function. The diagram also shows that the most important part of the orientation is the reduction of anxiety.

◆ Exercises and Additional Readings

1. Comment on the book by Robert C. Camp, *Benchmarking: The Search for Industry-Best Practices that Lead to Superior Performance* (Milwaukee, WI: Quality Press, 1989).

2. Read Karen Bemowski, "The Benchmarking Bandwagon," *Quality Progress,* January 1991, p. 19. Compare AT&T's benchmarking process with the process described in Section 21.9.

3. The Postmaster General is concerned about the delivery of U.S. Priority mail (one- and two-day delivery) and wants to benchmark the present system against that of Federal Express, a recognized industry leader. What questions should he ask, and how should he conduct the benchmarking?

4. Administrators at your university plan to benchmark their delivery of education with that of a recognized leader, such as Harvard or Yale University. What questions should they ask, and how should they proceed in their analysis?

5. Discuss other applications of benchmarking. How could a pizza delivery service benchmark its operation? What about a car rental agency or a fast-food restaurant chain?

6. Read and discuss the paper by Ryoji Futami, "The Outline of Seven Management Tools for QC," published in *Reports of Statistical Application Research, JUSE,* 33 (June 1986), pp. 7–26.

7. Read and discuss the material on affinity diagrams in Chapter 7 of Y. S. Chang, G. Labovitz, and V. Rosansky, *Making Quality Work: A Leadership Guide for the Results-Driven Manager* (Essex Junction, VT: Oliver Wight Publications, 1992).

8. Read and discuss the remarks about the Seven Management Tools in David Banks, "Is Industrial Statistics Out of Control?" *Statistical Science* 8 (1993), pp. 356–409.

9. Examine Michael Brassard and Diane Ritter, *The Memory Jogger* (Methuen, MA: GOAL/QPC). This is a convenient pocket guide to tools for continual improvement and effective planning. It gives useful reminders and several examples on many of the tools discussed in this chapter.

10. Read and critique Irving DeToro, "The 10 Pitfalls of Benchmarking," *Quality Progress*, January 1995, pp. 61–63.

11. Read and summarize the message in Sarah Lincoln and Art Price, "What Benchmarking Books Don't Tell You," *Quality Progress*, March 1996, p. 33.

12. Read and summarize the application of TQM in a law firm described in Rolf Hoexter and Mariesa Julien, "Legal Eagles Become Quality Hawks," *Quality Progress*, January 1994, p. 31. In particular, discuss the cause-and-effect diagram.

13. Read and discuss Karen A. Eichelberger, "Leading Change Through Projects," *Quality Progress*, January 1994, p. 87.

14. Read and discuss Robert Burney, "TQM in a Surgery Center," *Quality Progress*, January 1994, p. 97. Which improvement strategies are being used?

15. (a) Read Howard H. Bailie, "Organize Your Thinking with a Why-Why Diagram," *Quality Progress*, December 1985, p. 22. (b) Apply this information to the problem "My study habits need improvement."

16. Read Lloyd Eskildson, "Improving the Odds of TQM's Success," *Quality Progress*, April 1994, p. 61.

   (a) Summarize the evidence of TQM's ineffectiveness.

   (b) Summarize the recommendations for "improving the odds."

   (c) Critique the article.

17. Read Manny Rosenfeld, "Only the Questions That Are Asked Can Be Answered," *Quality Progress*, April 1994, p. 71.

   (a) Classify each of the 23 questions as concerning *mainly* (1) proper process operation or (2) process improvement.

   (b) Be prepared to defend your classification.

18. Read Jesse D. Freese and Emily Konold, "Teamwork Pays Off for Firm," *Quality Progress*, May 1994, p. 53 and summarize the (improvement) efforts of a small software company to gain ISO 9001 registration.

19. Read Duane Meeter and Grant Smith, "Student Quality Improvement Projects" *Quality Progress*, September 1994, p. 111. Summarize the article and critique it.

20. Read Daniel J. Fontaine and Diane B. Robinette, "FCC Makes Dramatic Quality Improvements," *Quality Progress*, November 1994, p. 87.

   (a) Summarize the article.

   (b) How might the process described in the article be applied to a university admission process? a manufacturing process?

21. Construct your own quality checklist.

22. Construct a cause-and-effect diagram that organizes the factors that affect your academic performance in college.

23. Read and discuss H. V. Roberts and B. F. Sergesketter, *Quality Is Personal* (New York: Free Press, 1993).

24. Apply work sampling methods to study the complexity/waste in completing (your) class assignments.

25. Read and discuss the article on suggestion programs in James A. Heath, "A Few Good Ideas for a Good Idea Program," *Quality Progress*, January 1994, p. 35.

26. Read and discuss Michael W. Piczak and Reuben Z. Hauser, "Self-Directed Work Teams: A Guide to Implementation," *Quality Progress*, May 1996, p. 81.

27. Discuss J. Stephen Sarazen, "The Tools of Quality: Cause-and-Effect Diagrams," *Quality Progress*, July 1990, p. 59.

28. Read and discuss Ronald E. Turner, "Cause-and-Effect Diagrams Alone Don't Tell the Whole Story," *Quality Progress*, January 1997, p. 53.

29. Read and summarize Deborah Donndelinger and Barbara Van Dine, "Use the Cause-and-Effect Diagram to Manage Conflict," *Quality Progress*, June 1996, p. 136. What are the benefits of cause-and-effect diagrams in solving conflict situations?

30. Construct an Ishikawa cause-and-effect diagram for "bad-tasting coffee."

31. Read and summarize Harry V. Roberts, "Using Personal Checklists to Facilitate TQM," *Quality Progress*, June 1993, pp. 51–56. Discuss the personal check-lists of Bernard Sergesketter and Harry Roberts. Construct your own personal checklist.

32. Read Franklin P. Schargel, "Teaching TQM in an Inner City High School," *Quality Progress*, September 1994, pp. 87–90. Describe some of the tech-niques that are being used to improve the quality at the George Westinghouse Vocational and Technical High School in New York City. Discuss the Ishikawa cause-and-effect diagram given on page 88.

33. Read and discuss Gary P. Maul and John Scott Gillard, "Solving Chronic Problems with Simple Tools," *Quality Progress*, July 1994, pp. 51–55. Explain their Ishikawa cause-and-effect diagram. Discuss the statistical techniques that are featured in this article and relate them to the material in Chapters 19 and 20. Summarize the recommendations that are made in this article.

34. Read John J. Lawrence and John S. Morris, "Cheese Isn't Just for Eating Anymore: Use It to Introduce Basic Quality Concepts," *Quality Progress*, February 1996, p. 136. Relate the issues raised in this article to the mate-rial that you have studied in this book.

35. Read William A. Golomski "Quality Improvement of Marketing," *Quality Progress*, June 1986, pp. 24–26. Why is it that employees of marketing or-ganizations will benefit by rating each other in the same way that customers rate suppliers?

36. Read Roland A. Shaw, "A Quality Cost Model for Hospitals," *Quality Progress*, May 1987, pp. 41–45. Discuss whether or not industrial quality techniques are applicable in a hospital setting. Which tools and techniques are the most useful?

37. Read Warren L. Nickell, "Quality Improvement in a Marketing Organization," *Quality Progress*, June 1985, pp. 46–51. What does the author mean by the "Marketing Quality Organization?" Which quality management tools are es-pecially useful?

38. Give several examples of foolproofing.

39. Construct one example each of an interrelationship digraph, a tree diagram, and a matrix diagram.

40. Komatsu, a heavy equipment manufacturer, is reputed to have one of the best total quality control programs in Japan. Masaaki Imai, in his 1996 book, *Kaizen*, describes Komatsu's cross-functional management approach (pp. 140–142) and small-group activities (pp. 102–104). Discuss Komatsu's approach.

41. In Appendix E of his book *Kaizen*, Masaaki Imai talks about the *Seven Statistical Tools* and the *New Seven Tools*. Relate these tools to those we have discussed in this book.

42. Use a browser to search for web entries to "benchmarking." Use this information to describe successful applications of benchmarking.

Quality Improvement Initiatives

In the pursuit of total quality improvement, we recognize that good is the enemy of best, and best is the enemy of better.

—Roger Milliken, Chairman and CEO, Milliken & Co.[1]

A company starting on a quest for quality looks to others for guidance. Through the years, various important initiatives have been devised. Although all have strengths and weaknesses, all can give suggestions and guidance to a company that wants to establish its own, unique improvement program. We will examine some of improvement strategies in this chapter.

---

[1]Brad Stratton,"Xerox and Milliken Receive Malcolm Baldrige National Quality Awards," *Quality Progress*, December 1989, p. 19.

◆ 22.1 The Zero Defects Concept

Under the urging of the Department of Defense, many companies (mainly in the defense industry) established zero defects (ZD) quality improvement programs during the 1960s. For the most part, this effort was a failure. It is worth studying, however, because sometimes we can learn more from failure than from success.

Many of these programs consisted solely of motivational propaganda. Indeed, ZD advocates claimed that if workers are properly motivated, they will make no errors—zero defects. As we might expect, such programs had little effect on quality; they did, of course, affect a company's chance of winning Defense Department business. However, programs that went beyond mere propaganda and included some tool or technique for process improvement often were beneficial.

After losing much of its strength, the ZD program was revived in 1979 by Philip Crosby, who made it a central part of the quality improvement program he introduced in *Quality Is Free.*[2] Crosby is a firm supporter of zero defects: indeed, the dust jacket of his book asserts that he created the concept.

Crosby strongly disputes the claim that ZD is a motivational program; instead, he says it is a performance standard. He states that mistakes have two causes: lack of knowledge and lack of attention. Zero defects addresses the second cause. As Crosby states: "To gain the benefits of zero defects, you must decide to make a personal commitment to have improvement in your operation. You must want it. The first step is: Make the attitude of zero defects your personal standard."[3]

As analyzed by Ishikawa, among the reasons for the ZD program's failure are these:

◆ The ZD movement was mostly motivational, based essentially on the assumption that if people do their best there will be no defects.

◆ It was a movement without tools or anything to make process improvements.

◆ The ZD movement was based on the premise that good products would result if standards were followed; no allowance was made for the fact that many standards are inadequate, missing, or just plain wrong.

◆ ZD programs often were announced by a "kickoff" meeting. But Ishikawa asks if "kickoff" isn't just another term for ordering workers to start an effort for which they have very little enthusiasm.

◆ The entire ZD effort was directed at workers, suggesting that mistakes are due to them rather than to the process.

◆ By decreeing that no procurement orders would be issued to businesses that did not participate in ZD, the Department of Defense promoted paper compliance.

---

[2]Philip B. Crosby, *Quality Is Free* (New York: McGraw-Hill, 1979), pp. 127–139.
[3]Ibid., p. 172.

Juran adds to this list by noting that the ZD slogans failed to establish specific goals and did not provide resources needed to make meaningful improvements. He claims that most middle managers found that the exhortation approach created an atmosphere of blame and divisiveness in the enterprise. Juran states that "A number of companies have followed that [exhortation] road, and they're probably worse off at the end than they were at the beginning. They've lost a couple of years, and the idea of quality improvement has lost credibility in their organizations."[4]

Some companies conducting ZD campaigns during the 1960s did succeed in improving quality. From his analysis, Juran found that the successful companies were those that augmented the ZD motivation with training in process improvement.

We can gain some insight into quality improvement by studying the ZD movement of the past, but as Terry Sargent puts it, the zero defects program "died and is better off that way."[5]

◆ 22.2 Deming's Fourteen Points for Management

Deming stated his fourteen points for management in various ways; in fact, there are three variations in his book *Out of the Crisis* (see Display 22.1 for one of his versions). Among the points he stresses are:

- ◆ Unswerving manager leadership in the quality effort
- ◆ Continual improvement of products and processes
- ◆ Training at all levels, particularly for top managers and new employees
- ◆ Driving our fear and breaking down barriers that inhibit communication

We have emphasized the importance of most of these activities in the previous chapters of this book. To accomplish the needed transition, Deming states that management should follow a seven-step action plan:

1. Top managers must understand the new philosophy and agree to follow it.
2. Top managers will break with tradition.
3. Top managers will gain the support of a critical mass for making the transformation.
4. At every stage of each process, there will be continual improvement of methods and procedures.
5. Start to construct an organization to guide continual improvement.

---

[4]J. M. Juran, "Catching Up: How Is the West Doing?" *Quality Progress*, November 1985, p. 19.

[5]Terry R. Sargent, "The Pygmalion Effect on Quality," *Quality Progress*, August 1986, p. 34.

DISPLAY 22.1 ◆ Deming's Fourteen Points for Management[a]

1. Create constancy of purpose for improvement of product and service.
2. Adopt the new philosophy.
3. Cease dependence on inspection to achieve quality.
4. End the practice of awarding business on the basis of price tag alone. Instead, minimize total cost by working with a single supplier.
5. Improve constantly and forever every process for planning, production, and service.
6. Institute training on the job.
7. Adopt and institute leadership.
8. Drive out fear.
9. Break down the barriers between staff areas.
10. Eliminate slogans, exhortations, and targets for the workforce.
11. Eliminate numerical quotas for the workforce and numerical goals for management.
12. Remove barriers that rob people of pride and workmanship. Eliminate the annual rating or merit system.
13. Initiate a vigorous program of education and self-improvement for everyone.
14. Put everybody in the company to work to accomplish the transformation.

[a]This list is taken from the dust jacket of W. Edwards Deming, *Out of the Crisis*. A similar list is given on pp. 23 and 24 of his book, with a detailed exploration of the points on pp. 24–96.

6. Everyone can take part in a team aimed at process improvement.

7. Embark on construction of an organization for quality.

◆ 22.3 Juran's Ten Steps to Quality Improvement

Juran was the first American quality guru to promote the quality function on a businesswide basis. He stressed the need to include a quality discipline in the management of the business right along with the more traditional departments. He likened the activities needed for a formidable quality function (quality planning, quality control, quality improvement) to the activities of the financial function.[6]

Juran formulated ten steps to quality improvement:

1. Build awareness of the need and opportunity for improvement.

2. Set goals for improvement.

3. Organize to reach the goals (establish a quality council, identify problems, select projects, appoint teams and designate facilitators).

4. Provide training.

---

[6]J. M. Juran and Frank M. Gryna, Jr., *Quality Planning and Analysis*, 3rd ed. (New York: McGraw-Hill, 1993), p. 9.

5. Carry out projects to solve problems.

6. Report progress.

7. Give recognition.

8. Communicate results.

9. Keep score.

10. Maintain momentum by making annual improvement part of the regular systems and processes of the company.

◆ 22.4 Juran's Project-by-Project Improvement

Juran popularized the idea that business advances by solving problems on a project-by-project basis.[7] Quality improvement amounts to identifying needs, defining projects, prioritizing them, obtaining authorization and funding, assigning responsibility, and undertaking the projects. Juran points out that major quality problems are interdepartmental in nature, and that their solution requires an interdepartmental project team. It follows that anyone who directs a quality improvement effort should have a solid understanding of projects and project management.

Juran embeds the use of improvement projects in his breakthrough sequence, which is discussed next.

◆ 22.5 Juran's Breakthrough Sequence

The anthropologist Margaret Mead showed that cultural patterns were the root cause of the resistance to change that thwarted efforts to modernize living conditions of primitive societies. On learning of this insight, Juran applied it to the resistance managers face in implementing quality. The result was his managerial *breakthrough sequence*, a procedure for making quality improvements and solving quality problems.[8]

Step 1. Justify the Need for a Breakthrough
Improvement efforts require time and resources, and it is necessary to justify their investment. The objective of this first step is to gain management approval for embarking on an improvement effort. It is necessary to collect, analyze, and organize data that shows the potential benefit of a breakthrough.

---

[7]Joseph M. Juran, *Managerial Breakthrough* (New York: McGraw-Hill, 1995; originally published in 1964.) Also see Joseph M. Juran, "Catching Up: How Is the West Doing?" *Quality Progress*, November 1985, p. 18.

[8]Joseph M. Juran and Frank M. Gryna, Jr., *Quality Planning and Analysis*, pp. 100-129; slightly modified in the 1993 edition.

Step 2. Identify the Vital Few Contributors to the Problem

Generally, there are many contributors or causes of a problem, but only a few of these account for most of the trouble. The second step is to identify the major contributors to the problem (the "vital few" in Juran's terminology, as contrasted with the "trivial many"). This step involves the Pareto principle, which Juran popularized.

Step 3. Organize for Making the Breakthrough

Problem solving in an enterprise usually involves several people, possibly from different departments. The third step is to establish an organizational structure that will allow them to work together on the problem. Juran suggests two structures, a "steering arm" and a "diagnostic arm." The steering arm establishes the aims of the improvement effort, makes suggestions about possible causes of the problem, authorizes the project, and has responsibility for implementing the solution. The diagnostic arm is responsible for problem analysis and solution. For example, the steering arm might be a management committee or the Quality Council; the diagnostic arm might be a quality circle or a special task force.

Step 4. Solve the Problem

The fourth step entails two "journeys," one to determine the cause of the problem and the other to determine a solution—diagnostic and remedial.

In Juran's view, the diagnostic journey is the main source of confusion for chronic problems. One reason for this confusion is that chronic problems frequently cut across organizational lines, and responsibility for their solution is not clear. Another reason is that people dealing with the problem area often confuse symptom with cause. For example, the cause of a "bug" in a computer program might be described as a "logic error," which is really a description of the error, not its cause. The confusion comes from the fact that "logic error" is the cause of the defect that would be created by running the faulty program. Still another reason for confusion during the diagnostic journey is that people confuse theory with cause. Without sufficient data they might assert that they "know" something is the cause, when what they really mean is that they are personally convinced that it is the cause.

Step 5. Deal with Resistance to Change

Resistance to change can inhibit any improvement effort. Juran acknowledges this by devoting his fifth step to dealing with such resistance. He also cautions that, although people might voice objection to *technological* change, the true reason for their resistance usually is the *social* aspect of change.

Step 6. Install the Change

The sixth step is to gain management approval and then to install the solution to the problem.

Step 7. Institute Controls to Hold the New Level of Performance

The final step in Juran's breakthrough sequence is to establish a mechanism for assuring that the problem solution continues to be effective and for dealing with unforeseen problems caused by the solution. An example of such a mechanism would be a periodic audit of the new procedures.

◆ 22.6 Crosby's Quality Improvement Program

Crosby's book *Quality Is Free* was published near the end of 1979 and was an immediate best-seller. The book arrived at a time when businesspeople were just beginning to realize that the United States lagged badly behind Japan in the quality race, and they were desperately looking for solutions to America's quality problem. Crosby's book provided such a solution in the form of a 14-step quality improvement program. These steps are:

1. Obtain management commitment.
2. Establish a quality improvement team.
3. Establish quality measurements.
4. Determine the cost of quality.
5. Make employees aware of quality.
6. Correct identified quality problems.
7. Prepare for zero defects (ZD) day.
8. Train supervisors.
9. Hold zero defects day.
10. Establish quality goals.
11. Establish error-cause removal process.
12. Recognize achievement.
13. Establish quality councils.
14. Repeat the process.

Crosby's program was very popular, well presented, and well received. It was a good vehicle for capturing attention and getting firms started on quality improvement. But it lacked the ability to sustain an improvement effort. People were motivated but then did not have the tools to carry on. The program itself had some serious flaws. We mentioned earlier in this chapter that ZD days often had a circus atmosphere to them; they generated enthusiasm, but there was more sizzle than steak. Also, Step 14 (repeating the process) is not sensible advice; you don't start each school year by going back to kindergarten. One suspects that Deming had Crosby's program in mind when he wrote: "A quality program for a community, launched by ceremonies with a speech by the governor, raising of flags, beating of drums, badges, all with heavy applause, is a delusion and a snare."[9] We agree.

---

[9]W. Edwards Deming, *Out of the Crisis* (1986), p. 21.

◆ 22.7 Juran's Quality Trilogy

In 1986, Juran published his quality trilogy.[10] His introduction to this concept is interesting because it paints a picture of the quality situation at that time, and it provides insight into Juran's very logical thought processes.

Juran wrote, "Several premises have led me to conclude that our companies need to chart a new direction in managing for quality. These premises are as follows:

1. There is a crisis in quality.

2. The crises will not go away in the foreseeable future.

3. Our traditional ways are not adequate to deal with the quality crisis.

4. To deal with the crisis requires some major breaks with tradition.

5. Charting a new course requires that we create a universal way of thinking about quality—a way applicable to all functions and to all levels in the hierarchy.

6. Charting a new course also requires extensive personal leadership and participation by upper managers.

7. An obstacle to participation by upper managers is their limited experience and training in managing for quality.

8. An essential element in meeting the quality crisis is to arm upper managers with experience and training in how to manage for quality, and to do so on a time scale compatible with the prevailing sense of urgency.

9. Charting a new course also requires that we design a basis for management of quality that can readily be implanted into the company's strategic business planning and that has minimal risk of rejection by the company's immune system."

Juran went on to say that forces resisting a unified approach to quality include multiple functions, multiple levels of management, and multiple product lines. Juran's observation made in 1986 still applies to some U.S. organizations today.

Juran proposed a new direction in managing quality, which he called the *quality trilogy.* The underlying concept of the trilogy is that managing for quality consists of three basic processes:

- ◆ Quality planning
- ◆ Quality control
- ◆ Quality improvement

Each of these processes is universal; it is carried out by an unvarying sequence of activities. These activities are described in Display 22.2. Juran describes quality planning as the process of preparing to meet quality goals under operating conditions. Quality control is the process for meeting quality goals during operations. And quality improvement is the process for breaking through to unprecedented

---

[10]"The Quality Trilogy," *Quality Progress,* August 1986, p. 19.

DISPLAY 22.2 ◆ Juran's Basic Quality Trilogy[a]

Quality Planning

Identify the customers, both external and internal.

Determine customer needs.

Develop product features that respond to customer needs.

Establish quality goals that meet the needs of customers and suppliers alike, and do so at a minimum combined cost.

Develop a process that can produce the needed product features.

Prove process capability—prove that the process can meet the quality goals under operating conditions.

Quality Control

Choose control subjects—what to control.

Choose units of measurement.

Establish measurement.

Establish standards of performance.

Measure actual performance.

Interpret the difference (actual versus standard).

Take action on the difference.

Quality Improvement

Prove the need for improvement.

Identify specific projects for improvement.

Organize to guide the projects.

Organize for diagnosis—for discovery of causes.

Diagnose to find the causes.

Provide remedies.

Prove that the remedies are effective under operating conditions.

Provide for control to hold the gains.

[a]Joseph M. Juran, "The Quality Trilogy," *Quality Progress*, August 1986, p. 19. We have paraphrased and condensed Juran's statements.

levels of performance. He compares this trilogy to the finance processes of budgeting, cost control, and cost reduction.

Juran stated that managers rate themselves well on quality control—meeting established goals based mainly on past performance, therefore perpetuating past performance. But they are unhappy about their quality improvement efforts. Juran stated that managers must change priorities regarding the three quality processes, giving more emphasis to quality planning and quality improvement They must adopt the standardized approach of the trilogy to enjoy a beneficial impact from strategic quality planning and quality training.

◆ 22.8 Quality and Organizational Maturity

Both Crosby and Ishikawa have suggested schemes to measure the maturity of an organization's quality effort.

Crosby's Maturity Grid

Crosby proposed the Quality Management Maturity Grid as a tool for measuring the maturity of an organization quality effort.[11] It consists of examining six categories:

Management understanding and attitude
Quality organization status
Problem handling
Cost of quality as a percent of sales
Quality improvement actions
Summary of company quality posture

For each category, a guideline is given for measuring whether the company is in one of five stages of maturity: Uncertainty, Awakening, Enlightenment, Wisdom, or Certainty. Crosby states that even managers who are not professionally trained in quality concepts can determine the quality maturity of their processes.

Crosby proposes the Maturity Grid as a tool for convincing management of the need for improvement and for measuring progress of improvement efforts.

Ishikawa's Three Phases

Ishikawa describes three phases of quality assurance.[12] During the first phase, quality assurance is based on inspection, and only the quality control function is involved. The task is to prevent defective products from reaching customers. In the second phase, quality assurance extends to the entire production process, including purchasing, production engineering, and marketing. In the third phase, quality assurance extends to all areas of the organization and all employees.

◆ 22.9 The Pygmalion Effect

Most improvement programs focus on the mechanics of improvement and the processes of "doing work." But it is also necessary to focus on management processes and the human aspects of improvement.

The concept of a self-fulfilling prophecy, which was popularized by Douglas McGregor, has also been called the *Pygmalion Effect* by Terry R. Sargent.[13] Sargent reminds us about the classical story of Pygmalion, a sculptor who created such a beautiful and lifelike statue of a woman that he fell in love with it. Pygmalion would speak to the statue for hours on end, treating the statue as a real person.

---

[11]Philip B. Crosby, *Quality Is Free* (New York: McGraw-Hill), pp. 49-57.

[12]Kaoru Ishikawa, *What Is Total Quality Control?* (Englewood Cliffs, NJ: Prentice-Hall, 1985), pp. 20-21.

[13]"The Pygmalion Effect on Quality," *Quality Progress*, August 1986, p. 34.

His strong belief in her finally brought about a miracle: She came to life and loved him the rest of his days. Pygmalion's strong belief brought about reality.

Obviously, quality requires more than just strong belief. But a manager's attitude toward quality and the people who are involved in improvement efforts will have a significant impact on the outcomes. And attitude is revealed more by actions than by words. If a manager says that quality is the most important goal of the organization but rewards people who meet deadlines by cutting corners on quality, the people will quickly get the message. As Sargent observes, "It is management's attitude that the worker reads, not the speeches and the glowing articles in the company newspaper, because the attitude is usually much more consistent and is far easier to interpret accurately than verbal language."

Because of the Pygmalion effect, an important part of any successful quality improvement effort must be the education and training of management. Once top managers have a belief in quality, they must use every available opportunity to take actions that convey their belief to middle managers. And they should support these actions by providing all middle mangers with an appropriate education program.

◆ 22.10 Why Quality Programs Fail

Many causes (and excuses) are given for the failure of quality programs. Some of these are listed in Display 22.3. A study of these might suggest some of the things you should *not* do in attempting to improve quality.

DISPLAY 22.3 ◆ Some Causes of Failure for Quality Programs

1. Not concerned about quality
   Problem is a strong dollar
   Problem is unfair competition
   Our troubles lie entirely with the workforce
2. Environment
   Obsolescence in schools
   Unfriendly takeover
   Quality not emphasized in business schools
   Poor teaching of statistical methods in industry
   Mobility of management, workers
3. Leadership
   Flavor of the month; Deming calls this lack of constancy of purpose
   Emphasis on today; short-term profit
   "Our problems are different"
   Emphasis on deadlines, budget
   Lack of understanding of quality
   Support not visible
   Wrong signals are sent

DISPLAY 22.3 ◆ Some Causes of Failure for Quality Programs (*Continued*)

4. Wrong tactics—wrong management direction

   Blame people, not the process; exhortation, pep-talks, firework displays, motivational techniques

   Quick fix; hot-house programs, quality circle fad, instant pudding

   Cookbook; search for examples

   Not total; programs only for factory workers

   View it as a technical problem; buy equipment, technical projects automation, gadgets, and new machinery; overreliance on computer; "We installed quality"

   Emphasis on fire-fighting

   Emphasis on control; use of Military Standards 105D and other standards that are inappropriate for their situation

   Delegate responsibility; "Our quality control department takes care of quality"

   Single solution: quality circles, overreliance on statistical methods, the latest hot idea

5. Interfering organization, policies, procedures, etc.

   Management structure; too many levels

   Management practice; appraisal system; management by the numbers; promotes short-term performance, demolishes teamwork, nourishes rivalry and politics

   Personnel department policies; hiring procedure; individual rating system

   Lack of concern for people; fear in workplace; lack of job security

   Reward system

6. Problems, shortcomings of programs

   Incorrect use of control charts

   Failure to understand process variability

   Failure to appreciate education and training—to invest in them

   Insufficient attention to analysis and design

   Management problems

   Overemphasis on visible figures (accounting figures)

   Not sufficiently people oriented

   Inability to change—were successful with old system

   Inability to use consultants. "Anyone that comes to try to help us must understand all about our business." Knowing how to improve work is not the same as knowing how to do it.

◆ Exercises and Additional Readings

1. Draw up a set of requirements for a quality improvement program; that is, list the requirements you would use to evaluate an improvement program and decide whether or not you would accept it as a guide for an improvement effort. Do this for (a) an overall improvement effort and (b) a single improvement effort (project).

2. Obtain references from the literature (e.g., *Quality Progress* articles) of quality programs and evaluate them.

3. Design a quality improvement program for an enterprise you are currently associated with (for example, the college at which you are taking a course using this book, a past employer, your parent's employer, etc.).

4. Read and critique Crosby's discussion of his "Fourteen Step Improvement Effort" in *Quality Is Free*, pp. 132–139.

5. Read and critique Crosby's comparison of quality and sex in *Quality Is Free*, pp. 15–16.

6. Discuss Juran's Breakthrough Sequence. Compare it with Kurt Lewin's classic "Unfreeze, Change, Freeze" model. See Kurt Lewin, "Frontiers in Group Dynamics," *Human Relations*, Vol. 1 (June 1947), pp. 5–41. For additional discussion, see Peter P. Schoderbek, Richard A. Cosier, and John C. Aplin, *Management*, 2nd ed. (New York: Harcourt Brace Jovanovich, 1991), p. 329.

7. Read and discuss the focus on the customer in John A. Goodman, Gary F. Bargatze, and Cynthia Grimm, "The Key Problem with TQM," *Quality Progress*, January 1994, p. 45. How does their analysis relate to our discussion of quality improvement programs?

8. Discuss and critique Deming's Fourteen Points for Management as a strategy for an organization. Which of his steps will be the most difficult to implement?

9. Discuss and critique Juran's Ten Steps to Quality Improvement.

10. Survey companies in your immediate surrounding area. Show Deming's 14 Points to (a) a manager and (b) a line worker. Ask them which of the 14 points are implemented by their company. Discuss the results you obtain.

11. Repeat Exercise 10, but use Juran's Ten Steps to Quality Improvement.

12. Check whether your surveyed companies use some other special program that has not been mentioned in this book. Compare and contrast the special program with the programs mentioned in the book.

13. Ask your surveyed companies about failures in their quality improvement initiatives. Ask them about the reasons why their programs failed.

14. You have been appointed vice president for quality in an organization. Your first task is to advise management of the actions they must take toward achieving quality. State *your* "Points for Management." That is, produce your version of Deming's 14 Points.

15. Compare Juran's Ten Steps to Quality Improvement (see Section 22.3) with Crosby's Improvement Program (see Section 22.6).

16. As newly appointed vice president for quality, you must develop a strategy for quality. State your strategy. (In Exercise 14 you were asked to develop a quality direction. In this exercise you are asked to discuss the strategy for its implementation.)

17. Read Sections 3.1 through 3.7 in Joseph M. Juran and Frank M. Gryna, *Quality Planning and Analysis*, 3rd ed. (New York: McGraw-Hill, 1993). Summarize their project-by-project approach to quality improvement.

18. Read and summarize John F. Early and A. Blanton Godfrey, "But It Takes Too Long . . . ," *Quality Progress*, July 1995, p. 51. According to a Juran study,

    (a) What are several mistakes people make that cause improvement projects to take too long?

    (b) List the steps the authors give for an effective quality improvement project.

19. Read and discuss Armand V. Feigenbaum, "Quality: The Strategic Business Imperative," *Quality Progress*, February 1986, pp. 26–30. What does he mean by the "four deadly sins" of some approaches to quality?

20. Read Brian L. Joiner and Marie A. Gaudard, "Variation, Management, and W. Edwards Deming," *Quality Progress*, December 1990, pp. 29–37. Summarize Deming's views on variation and its impact on quality. What strategies would you adopt to reduce variation?

21. Take a trip to the business section of your local bookstore. Survey some of the more recent books on quality improvement strategies. Believe us, there is no shortage of books describing "quick fixes."

Quality Innovation

Every management unit of a business should have responsibility for innovation and definite innovation goals. It should be responsible for contributing to innovation in the company's product or service; in addition, it should strive consciously to advance the art in the particular area in which it is engaged: selling or accounting, quality control, or personnel management.

—Peter Drucker[1]

◆ 23.1 Improvement Versus Innovation

Process improvement is an important technique for improving product quality, but it has its limitations. For example, suppose you want to record some material from a book, and the process you use is to "copy by hand." That might do for a short passage, and very likely you will improve your copying technique as you do more work. But no matter how much you improve your hand-copying process, you wouldn't want to copy more than a few pages. Similarly, you might have reached a performance plateau for welding parts manually, and further improvement must come

---

[1]Peter Drucker, *Management: Tasks, Responsibilities, Practices* (New York: Harper & Row, 1973), p. 67.

from innovation. For example, in the production of circuit boards that have hundreds of soldering positions, the innovation comes from robotics—using new wave soldering machines that lay down solder for many individual points simultaneously.

Innovation means *radical change*. It means going beyond the usual job and developing new visions, new policies, new organizational structures, new products, new processes, and new means of operating. Innovation is very important; but so is continual improvement once you have installed your change. In the beginning, an innovation might produce worse results than did the old system. But as you learn more and make needed process improvements, things will get better and better. Each innovation must be followed by a series of improvement efforts to "tune" and improve the process. Innovation links science, technology, and design. Continual improvement links design, production, and the market.

Many innovations improve quality, productivity, and time to market. Examples of technical innovations are the use of a copying machine in place of copying by hand, a new wave soldering machine, and a continuous reheating furnace in the rolling mill of a steel factory.

Everyone in an organization should engage in innovation, but for some innovation is a specific assignment. The task of these people is to determine new markets, new products, new processes, and new ways of doing business. Their objective is to increase the wealth-producing capacity of the organization's resources. Typical innovation tasks might be to build a production line for a new product, redirect the marketing effort, build and install a new computerized accounting system, or design a new product line that delights customers.

It is important that people whose primary task is to operate a process still practice innovation. Those who operate a process know it best; they are in the best position to understand its problems and limitations. Part of their assignment should be the task of making continual improvements and innovations in the process.

Several of the techniques that we discussed earlier are in fact innovations—for example, reengineering, self-directed work teams, and just-in-time production. In this chapter we will mention other examples, but we will concentrate more on the innovation process and the characteristics of an environment that fosters innovation.

◆ 23.2 Examples of Innovation

Innovation can take place with respect to the products, processes, or the management of an organization.

Product Innovation

Product innovation tends to depend on invention and technical progress. Some examples of product innovation are these:

◆ The Han dynasty learned how to cast plowshares, a major basis for their prosperity.

- Writing instruments have evolved throughout history, from the brush, to reed pen, quill pen (seventh century), pencil (seventeenth century ??), steel pen (about 1800), typewriter (shortly after), fountain pen (1884), ballpoint pen (twentieth century), and word processor (late twentieth century).
- High-bred seeds have helped to feed an expanding world population.

Frequently, product innovations come from an outside industry. For example, the watch-making industry was drastically altered by the introduction of digital technology, which developed independently of that industry.

Process Innovation

Good examples of process innovation are:

- Use of standard, interchangeable parts in the manufacture of Remington rifles
- Assembly line pioneered by Sears and Ford
- Transportation from foot, horse carriage, train, car, airplane, to the space shuttle
- Data interchange from voice, print, punched cards, and magnetic tape to electronic data interchange
- Process reengineering. Here is a small example:

In a small town years ago, four boys had routes to deliver the Sioux City Journal *every day of the week. One of the carriers convinced the other three that they should "trade" their Sunday customers for his daily customers so that they could have Sunday free. They agreed and enjoyed their day off. He, of course, had Monday through Saturday off, and the "trade" left him with only slightly less income.*

Management Innovation

Some examples of concepts that lead to innovation in management are these:

- Study of work by Taylor
- Quality assurance in place of quality control
- Participative management
- Self-directed work teams

◆ 23.3 Management Innovation in Action

Rockwell-Collins operates a fairly new production facility in Coralville, Iowa. It is an assembly operation, producing circuit boards for aircraft navigation systems and "black boxes" for civilian and military aircraft. Assembly and testing of various circuit boards is its main line of work. Its workforce of about 700 people is well-educated; all production workers have a high school diploma. In addition, each worker goes through a two-week training session, which covers technical skills (mostly soldering) as well as an introduction to the management philosophy of the plant.

Apart from its emphasis on training, the plant innovated by reducing the number of management layers to just three: (1) the plant manager; (2) product-support teams; and (3) work teams. Work teams are organized around products—for example, a particular type of circuit board. The work team is responsible for the assembly and testing. But work teams also perform several tasks traditionally reserved for management. For example, they schedule their work, make decisions about covering work if someone is absent, schedule vacation time among their team members, and control overtime pay. They can make their decisions within certain established boundaries, which the teams are expected to observe. They might be told, for instance, that overtime pay for a particular month is not to exceed 3 percent of payroll. According to the plant manager, work teams initially had difficulties assuming some of the management decisions. But with growing experience and guidance from the product-support teams, most work teams excel in their new roles.

The function of product-support teams is to assist the work teams. Product-support teams include people who under the old system were managers and members of various departments such as the industrial engineering, testing, human resources, maintenance, and production control. Under the old system they were members of departments, which themselves had various layers of management.

Each product-support team has one member from each of the former departments. Each product-support team is assigned to several work teams and helps them achieve their work goals. Such a structure enhances cross-functional thinking and problem solving.

On top of the new system stands the plant manager. Because many of his old management functions are now assigned to product-support teams, the product manager has more time to look for future opportunities for the plant.

Empowerment of employees and mutual trust are important under this new management system. However, it is not possible to empower employees without telling them what this empowerment allows (expects, enables) them to do and teaching them how to do it. This requires training, as well as guidelines and limits. Empowerment also requires trust. The following two examples illustrate this very clearly.

The Rockwell-Collins plant in Coralville started a cash award system to reward exceptional work. Work teams have a budget from which they can award cash gifts of up to 50 dollars if one team has made a significant contribution to the efforts of another. The first few weeks there were some abuses. In a few instances teams "traded" gifts as favors without making deserving contributions. However, since awards had to be posted for everyone to see, peer pressure took over and led to corrections, and within a few weeks only deserving teams were being rewarded. Upper-level management could have stepped in and put an end to these cash awards. However, such an action would have violated the trust between upper-level management and the work teams. The problem was much better resolved within a system of trust.

Another example at this plant shows the importance of empowerment. Recently, the company purchased a large and expensive wave-soldering machine. Under the old management system, the machine would have been bought by the central purchasing department. It would have arrived one day, and the employees would have been required to figure out how to work with it. Under the new system, the purchasing process worked as follows. Central purchasing identified the four wave-soldering machines it considered to be the most appropriate ones. Then the plant sent several members of their work and support teams to check out these four machines. This group included workers who would actually use the equipment, giving them an opportunity to try it out. The fact that these workers could fly to the various vendors and charge their time and expenses to the company made them feel important and determined to make the right decision for their plant. After all four vendors were visited, the group made its recommendation, and the plant manger purchased the recommended machine. Now do you think that the workers who decided on that particular machine would let it fail? No way! They selected it, and they will do their utmost to make it a success. This is a beautiful example of empowerment—of course, empowerment under guidance because the group was given a list of four to choose from.

◆ 23.4 Innovators

Some people's image of an innovator is a lone Edison working in a cluttered laboratory churning out idea after idea. But innovation can be the result of an individual or group effort, and it can take place anywhere in an organization.[2] Innovators, however, do share certain general characteristics. They view change not as a threat but as an opportunity. They can create a vision and conceptualize how things might be done differently. They are thorough and think through not only their vision, but what it takes to make the vision a reality.

To "sell" their vision, innovators must be able to persuade others that it has merit. This means they must be able to operate on a political level. They must be persistent, yet tactful and practical about compromising to gain as much as they can. Generally, they follow a participative management style.

After selling their vision, innovators have the tough job of making the vision a reality. They must obtain resources, build a coalition to support and assist them, oversee pilot efforts, and overcome resistance and disbelief along the way. Making a vision a reality is a project, and innovators must have the ability to manage a project or enlist a strong lieutenant to manage the project under the innovator's general direction.

To achieve all of these goals, innovators must have the ability to work with people—the ability to command, persuade, cajole, and delegate; and the ability to

---

[2]Much of the material in Sections 23.4 and 23.5 comes from Rosabeth Moss Kanter, and appeared in "Change Masters" (New York: Simon and Schuster, 1983); "The Middle Manager as Innovator," *Harvard Business Review*, January 1982, p. 95, and "Quality Leadership and Change," *Quality Progress*, February 1987, p. 45.

sense which to apply in a particular situation. They must understand how to manage teams and participative employees. And they must have the skill and ability to manage upward.

◆ 23.5 Cross-functional Innovation

Rosabeth Moss Kanter points out that many important business innovations involve crossing organizational lines—for example, a change that involves marketing, design, and manufacturing in launching a new line of products. By Kanter's definition, innovation involves going beyond the job and therefore crossing organizational boundaries. Because more than one organizational unit is involved, the innovator is likely to be a middle manager. Kanter contrasts this with the basic job, which is done within the existing framework and, according to her, requires little inventiveness.

While one can question Kanter's terminology and her assertion that little inventiveness is required for intradepartmental changes, there is no question that an innovation involving several departments is more complex than an innovation within a department. It is such cross-organizational innovation that we discuss in this section.

Cross-functional innovation requires the participation and contribution of appropriate people:

- ◆ The prime mover
- ◆ Those supplying knowledge and ideas
- ◆ Those supplying resources
- ◆ Those sanctioning the innovation
- ◆ Those who might block it
- ◆ Those who provide training and guidance to the innovators

Most likely, these people report to different organizational units; therefore, top management support is necessary to gain their active participation. Top management might agree to lend support, but seldom will it sponsor or champion the effort.

Because innovators go beyond the boundary of their formal jobs, they need additional power. And because innovations cut across organizational lines, they disrupt existing arrangements. All of this makes the task of innovation very difficult.

Examples

Kanter gives several examples of cross-functional innovations, including these:

- ◆ A staff person (with neither subordinates nor budget) collected resources from product line managers, sales managers, and field services by promising each benefits (including recognition) to sell a major new product line.

- The head of a technical department gathered data to show the need for a new measuring instrument and then used this data to convince peers and several bosses two levels up to fund its development. He established a task force and defended them from critics during the development effort. Eventually, this instrument made possible a valuable new technique for the company.

- The head of a purchasing department gathered information from its customers and used this information to reorganize the unit into a cluster of customer-oriented specialists where each staff member concentrated on a particular need. Based on credibility from this success and close contact with customers, he then succeeded in merging three purchasing departments into one; this change resulted in cost-savings and improved the quality of customer service.

◆ 23.6 Environment for Innovation

Innovation is made possible by

- An environment favoring collaboration and teamwork
- Structures that enable and assist change
- The availability of power to achieve innovative change

We will discuss the environment in this section, and structures and power in Sections 23.7 and 23.8, respectively.

The environment, more than individuals, makes the difference in the level of innovative managerial activity. Kanter describes two types of environments. One is a *segmented* or compartmentalized environment in which work units are isolated and people see problems narrowly and independently. People do not go beyond the limits of their jobs, and any change that takes place is isolated. The second is an *integrative* environment in which people see problems as a whole. They actively embrace change, and mechanisms exist for exchanging information among units. People are trusted to make proper use of company-confidential information, and they are team-oriented and cooperative. It is an environment that encourages and supports innovation.

In an integrative environment, change is seen as normal. The culture encourages and supports collaboration and teamwork. Communications are open. People are encouraged to expand their horizons and to think beyond their own area. They are encouraged to experiment, and there is job security to quell fear of failure.

In an integrative environment, the monetary reward is reasonable. But the real rewards are those experienced on the job: gaining more skill, having greater responsibility, enjoying one's work, becoming more promotable, and getting a boost in spirit from being a member of a winning team. An example is provided by the team that developed the Eagle computer (released as the Eclipse MV8000) for Data General:

... many of the team had long since decided that they would never see more than token rewards of a material sort. The bigger game was "pinball." ... You win with this machine, you get to build the next.[3]

◆ 23.7 Structure for Innovation

Structures that facilitate innovation and achievement have features such as these:

- ◆ Assignments are couched in terms of results, not means.
- ◆ Job charters are broad; people are told what they may not do rather than what they may do.
- ◆ There are multiple reporting relationships and matrix management.
- ◆ Resources are decentralized.
- ◆ There are devices to facilitate networking.
- ◆ Territories intersect.

Traditional management hierarchies are maintenance oriented, geared to routine operations. Innovation can be facilitated by adding parallel organizations, thus enabling people to be connected with work organizations in two ways—one for routine work, the other for innovation. Examples of parallel organizations are:

- ◆ A Steering Committee, which can help in securing power, establishing projects, guiding and coordinating improvement efforts, and rewarding achievement.
- ◆ A Quality Council, quality advisory committees, and task forces (project teams), which devise, propose, or accomplish quality-related projects.

Parallel organizations may be permanent or ad hoc. They provide a formal mechanism for people to work together cooperatively regardless of their unit or level. By operating outside the management hierarchy, they can solve problems that cross functional lines.

◆ 23.8 Power for Innovation

Power is the capacity to mobilize people and the resources to get things done. The three basic power tools are

- ◆ Information (knowledge power): Data, technical knowledge, political intelligence, expertise

---

[3]Tracy Kidder, *Soul of a New Machine* (New York: Avon Books, 1981), p. 228.

◆ Resources (economic power): Funds, materials, space, people, time

◆ Support (political power): Endorsement, backing, approval, legitimacy

Quality innovation requires empowerment—the access to power. One means of empowering employees is to have open communications within the organization. Information should be available on a "need-to-know" basis; communications should be open and smooth both horizontally and vertically. Another means of empowering employees is to encourage and facilitate the formation of networks. Some ways to facilitate networking are the extensive use of teams, encouraging the mobility of people within the organization, forming cross-functional task forces, and establishing employee clubs and other social functions. Still another means of empowering people is to decentralize resources. There should be mechanisms for funding special projects that could be beneficial to the organization. There should also be sufficient slack in the system to promote individual self-improvement. Still another means is to have many centers of power, some budget flexibility, and a high proportion of managers in loosely defined positions.

◆ 23.9 The Innovation Process

Innovation can take place by chance. You could sit under an apple tree, see an apple fall, ponder the event, and come up with the theory of gravity, as Newton did according to folklore. On the other hand, you might deliberately attempt to develop and implement a product or process innovation. This attempt can be accomplished as a project involving these activities.

Prepare

Before starting to develop an innovation, you should understand the change process and what it entails. You also should assemble the resources and skills required, gain supporters in affected areas, and establish a power base by building informal networks, recruiting allies, and so on.

Phase 1. Define Problem

The first phase of the project is to define a problem area and determine the innovation required, conceiving what must be done to make the innovation. This phase requires gathering information—technical, political, and information that will help in conceiving and installing the innovation. The need is for information to help you understand the problem and overcome objections to the project.

Phase 2. Build Coalition

Next you need to build a coalition to support your effort. You must get the approval of your immediate manager and the support of the groups that will be affected by the innovation. This will require education, sharing information, enlisting support, overcoming resistance, and maintaining continual communication about the progress of your project. One way to facilitate communication and reduce resistance is to establish a steering committee to assist you. Another is to build something relevant to the project that will suggest the benefits to be derived from it. Still another is to form an advisory committee consisting of senior people to "launch" the project and provide legitimacy and visibility, and to serve as a source of recognition and reward.

Phase 3. Evolve and Install Innovation

The major effort is to evolve and install the innovation. This effort is a project; your task is to manage the project and the project team. This requires knowledge of group dynamics more than technical knowledge about the problem area.

You must assemble the necessary talent and forge them into a team. Teamwork is built by fighting battles together. While they are fighting, you must protect the team, maintain team momentum, and manage expectations. You must also redesign the team and project as required, handle external communication, and provide rewards and recognition.

Phase 4. Institutionalize Change

Left unattended, any process will deteriorate. You must establish appropriate responsibilities to review, maintain, and improve the innovation to prevent affairs from returning to "business as usual." Sharing credit for the improvement with all involved is a good way to build support for the change and to ensure its institutionalization.

◆ 23.10 Generating Innovations

Innovations don't just happen, they have a cause. Some triggers for innovation are these.

- ◆ Crisis or galvanizing event
- ◆ Departure from tradition
- ◆ Strategic decision
- ◆ Institutional mechanism (e.g., a research lab)
- ◆ Individual "prime mover"
- ◆ Simply by asking, "Is there a better way?"

Organizational Changes

Most organizations concentrate on production—doing what they are supposed to do. The focus is on operating processes, not on asking: Is there a better way? One way to foster innovation is to make organizational changes such as the following.

- ◆ Encourage experimentation.
- ◆ Remove inhibitors to new, creative ideas.

◆ Make specialists generalists.

◆ Break down hierarchies.

◆ Make information available.

◆ Reserve some time to think.

Techniques for Generating Innovations

Innovation requires knowing how to innovate as well as requiring time and encouragement. There are many techniques and a considerable literature on techniques for generating ideas; these are a few:

◆ *Examine competitors:* Copying innovations from a competitor won't make you a leader, but it can prevent you from lagging too far behind.

◆ *Employ techniques for generating ideas:* Brainstorming and think opposite are but two of the many techniques for generating ideas and solving problems.

◆ *Examine other industries:* Borrow innovative ideas from another industry. For example, the data processing industry was revolutionized by the computer, which had its origins in the defense industry.

◆ *Think opposite:* If you can't take the horse to water, take the water to the horse. The modern quality movement can be viewed as an example of thinking opposite: Focus on "what does the customer want?" rather than "what can I produce?"

◆ *Expand your range of thinking:* Instead of concentrating only on the needs of those who will buy your product, ask what are the requirements of those who will build it, sell it, install it, maintain it, and dispose of it. And consider the broader need of the society and environment in which it will operate.

◆ *Gather ideas and examine the relevant data:* Listen to customers, your neighbors, and suppliers. Talk with the sales force; go on sales calls to get firsthand impressions. Attend trade shows. Do competitive analysis.

◆ *Solicit ideas:* Look to others for help in generating innovations. Hold group sessions to uncover problems and generate ideas for improvement. Install a suggestion plan and a recognition program for outstanding innovations.

◆ 23.11 Innovation and You

Everyone should practice innovation. You shouldn't wait until you graduate to practice innovation—you should think about making innovations now. Start by thinking of the products you produce right now. Which are the most important? For which products is quality an important consideration?

Of the processes you use to produce your products, which are the most important? Which do you think should be much better? Select one such process and attempt to find a better, innovative way of accomplishing it.

Recently you were assigned a term paper that was due in two weeks time. You thought about it for a while, but didn't really start to work on it until a week had passed. When you went to the library, several references you wanted were checked out, so you had to spend time finding alternative sources. You started writing the paper, but discovered that you hadn't really thought about the issues—so you had to go back and revise much of your efforts. As the deadline neared, you started to panic and that caused you to work ineffectively. But an all-night effort the day before the paper was due gave you something reasonable to hand in. And you vowed to do things differently next time.

OK. Now, how should you "do it" differently next time? Can you innovate and replace your present process for writing a term paper with a new, innovative process?

◆ Exercises and Additional Readings

1. Read Chapter 61 in *Management: Tasks, Responsibilities, Practices* by Peter Drucker. Summarize his comments on an innovative strategy (pp. 791–793).

2. In *Kaizen* by Masaake Imai: (a) Read "The Kaizen Challenge," p. xxix, and summarize his comments regarding innovation and improvement (Kaizen). (b) Read pp. 1–8 and summarize his views of job functions in an organization.

3. In *Kaizen* by Masaake Imai read about just-in-time production (pp. 88–94). What are some of the advantages of just-in-time systems?

4. Read Lawrence P. Leach, "TQM, Reengineering, and the Edge of Chaos," *Quality Progress*, February 1996, p. 85. Discuss how the science of complexity and the study of complex adaptive systems give insights into TQM.

5. Read Herbert W. Hoover Jr., "What Went Wrong in U. S. Business's Attempt to Rescue Its Competitiveness?" *Quality Progress*, July 1995, p. 83. List several specific things management must get right, according to the article, to make a TQM effort successful.

6. Read and summarize Bobbie Ryan, "Naval Station Mayport Jump-Starts Quality," *Quality Progress*, July 1995, p. 95. List the 11 explanations given in the article for the naval station's rapid and successful quality improvement initiative.

7. Read and summarize Brian L. Joiner, "Quality, Innovation, and Spontaneous Democracy," *Quality Progress*, March 1996, p. 51. What does Joiner identify as the three stages of the quality revolution? What does he mean by "Attractive Quality Creation?" What steps are needed to achieve this stage?

8. For a classic article on change, read and summarize Paul R. Lawrence, "How to Deal with Resistance to Change," *Harvard Business Review* (March–April 1986), p. 178.

9. Read and summarize Satish K. Wason and Sushil K. Bhalla, "Managing the

Technological Process," *Quality Progress*, January 1994, p. 81. Summarize the Total Quality Process (TQP) at the Chemicals Division of the J. M. Huber Corporation and discuss its results. Also, summarize the information in the sidebar, "Three Decades of Challenge."

10. From the description in Section 23.3, did the innovation at Rockwell-Collins supply the three prerequisites for innovation listed in Section 23.6?

11. You are a member of a Student Outdoor Club that wants to buy a bus to transport members to various recreational areas. Devise an innovative plan for the Club to raise the necessary money.

12. You are about to graduate from college. Devise an innovative way to get a job that really interests you.

13. List several examples of product, process, and management innovations.

14. Comment on W. Edwards Deming's view on innovation, and how innovation is different from improvement. You may want to read Chapter 14 in Henry R. Neave, *The Deming Dimension* (Knoxville, TN: SPC Press, 1990).

15. Devise an innovative process for some activity that you perform regularly.

◆ ◆ ◆

Conclusion

The outlook for the future of quality is positive. Competition and quality-conscious customers, ISO standards and registration, and the publicity surrounding quality awards are pushing companies to focus on quality. In the final chapter of this book we describe several quality awards, including the Malcolm Baldrige National Quality Award. We feature the accomplishments of several Baldrige Award winners, and we highlight the successes that have been made in recent years. Of course, everything can and should be improved. We conclude our discussion by pointing out opportunities for further improvement.

Chapter 24

Optimism for the Future: Quality Awards and Success Stories

- ◆ 24.1 Introduction
- ◆ 24.2 Quality Awards and Prizes
- ◆ 24.3 Quality Successes
- ◆ 24.4 Opportunities for Further Improvement

I firmly believe that any company that seriously measures itself to the Baldrige Award criteria is a winner. There are no losers in the process.

—Ronald Schmidt, President and CEO of the Zytec Corporation[1]

◆ 24.1 Introduction

Much has changed in the quality area during the last few years, and today's outlook for the future of quality is, in general, positive. More and more companies are becoming aware of the value of quality, and many firms are taking important steps towards establishing and practicing total quality management. As a result, the quality of products has improved tremendously since the post–World War II era.

There are many reasons for this change, probably the most important one being the *impact of competition*: in order to keep up with world-class companies, firms

---

[1] Karen Bemowski, "Baldrige Award Winners Pause to Celebrate Their Success," *Quality Progress*, December 1991, p. 45.

must improve all their business processes on a continual basis. Customers are becoming more and more demanding as they become accustomed to the products made available by quality leaders.

The *ISO 9000 system of standards* is another catalyst that pushes companies into the direction of quality. These standards are used in implementing a compliance system and assessing conformity in company-selected operations. The standards emphasize processes, and the system of certification and registration of companies guarantees that products are produced according to documented standards. Chapter 13 gave a detailed discussion of the ISO initiatives.

A third major force behind an interest in quality is the publicity surrounding the *quality awards* for which companies compete. In the following section we describe three major quality awards: the Malcolm Baldrige National Quality Award which is the premier award for U.S. firms, the Japanese Deming Prize, and the European Quality Award.

◆ 24.2 Quality Awards and Prizes

The Malcolm Baldrige National Quality Award

The Baldrige Award has become one of the most important catalyst for transforming American business; it has had a major influence on managers' thinking and behavior. The Baldrige Award's success as a stimulus for change is in part due to the great publicity it generates; the awards are presented to the winning firms by the President of the United States.

The focus of the Malcolm Baldrige National Quality Award (MBNQA) is on enhancing competitiveness. The award program has three central purposes:

◆ To promote awareness and understanding of the importance of quality improvement to the U.S. economy.

◆ To recognize companies for outstanding quality management and achievement.

◆ To share information on successful quality strategies.

The criteria for the Baldrige Award comprise seven categories. These seven major categories are further subdivided into multiple items of examination that carry different weights. The categories are:

1. Leadership
2. Information and analysis
3. Strategic quality planning
4. Human resource development and management
5. Management of process quality
6. Quality and operational results
7. Customer focus and satisfaction

An applicant for the Baldrige Award is required to submit an application summary that addresses the topics in the examination categories and documents the company's practices and results. Awards applications are reviewed according to a four-stage process by a private-sector, volunteer Board of Examiners. The first stage consists of independent, detailed reviews carried out by at least five examiners. Applications are graded on a 1000-point scale. The top applications are forwarded to a second, consensus stage to refine the first-stage evaluations. In the third stage, top contenders (two to five days) are site-visited by teams of six to eight examiners. Finally, a panel of nine judges reviews the site visit reports and recommends Award recipients. All applicants receive comprehensive feedback reports. Each of the final contenders for the Award receives about 500 hours of review. The Baldrige Award is administered by the Office of Quality Programs at the National Institute of Standards and Technology (NIST).

The Malcolm Baldrige National Quality Award was established by the U.S. Congress in 1987. It is named after former Commerce Secretary Malcolm Baldrige.[2] Companies compete for this award within three eligibility categories—manufacturing, service, and small firms—with a maximum of two annual awards in each category. The first awards were given in 1988. Display 24.1 presents a list of Baldrige Award winners.

The criteria of the Baldrige Award have evolved from the tenets of total quality management. The Baldrige Award focuses on all operations within the company and goes beyond mere management of quality control activities. The criteria call for a steadfast commitment to quality, a strong focus on leadership, and an unwavering commitment to employees. The award criteria encompass activities that influence customer satisfaction, and they go beyond the simple elimination of defects.

The Baldrige Award criteria embody the following values and concepts: customer-driven quality, continual improvement, fast response, long-range outlook, partnership development, design quality, management by fact, leadership, employee participation and development, corporate responsibility, and citizenship. Since companies are judged on these criteria, the Baldrige Award moves companies towards a total quality management philosophy. The award criteria have a large influence on all companies because even nonapplying companies use these criteria in a self-assessment of their quality status.

It is quite instructive to look at the application summaries of some of the winning companies; these are public, and you can get them easily by writing to the companies. For example, in order to document the quality and operational results (Section 6 of the Baldrige Award criteria), Baldrige Award winners track, through the use of time-series charts, factors such as the complaint response within 24 hours, new product cycle time, energy utilization, measures of product variability, performance in meeting shipping times, computer downtimes, and measures of subcontractor quality. In response to human resource development and management (Section 4 of the Baldrige Award criteria), winning companies emphasize teamwork, cross-functional improvement and new-product development teams, partnerships, employee surveys, safety meetings, training and educational devel-

---

[2]N. J. DeCarlo and W. K. Sterett, "History of the Malcolm Baldrige National Quality Award," *Quality Progress*, March 1990, pp. 21-27.

DISPLAY 24.1 ◆ Malcolm Baldrige National Quality Award Winners

1996

ADAC Laboratories (manufacturing): Design and manufacture of support products for health care customers in nuclear medicine, radiation therapy, and health care information systems.

Dana Commercial Credit Corporation (service): Leasing and financing services

Custom Research Inc. (small business): Small national market research firm

Trident Precision Manufacturing Inc. (small business): Manufacture of precision sheet metal components and electromechanical assemblies

1995

Corning Telecommunication Products Division: The world's largest optical fiber manufacturer

Armstrong World Industries' Building Products Operations: Manufacture and marketing of materials for home and commercial interiors

1994

AT&T Consumer Communications Services: Domestic and international long-distance communication services

GTE Directories Corporation: Telephone directory company

Wainwright Industries: Manufacture of stamped and machined products for the automotive, aerospace, and information processing industries

1993

Ames Rubber: Manufacture of rubber rollers used to transport paper in office machines

Eastman Chemical Company: Manufacture and marketing of chemicals, fibers, and plastics

1992

AT&T Network Systems Group: Transmission equipment for telecommunication networks

AT&T Universal Card Services: Credit card company

Granit Rock Company: Production of construction materials

Ritz-Carlton Hotel Company: Business and resort hotels

Texas Instruments Defense Systems and Electronic Group: Manufacture of weapons and electronic warfare systems

1991

Marlow Industries: Production of customized thermoelectric cooling systems

Solectron Corporation: Assembly of printed circuit boards

Zytec Corporation: Manufacture of power supplies for computers

1990

Cadillac Motor Car Company: Manufacture of luxury automobiles

Federal Express Corporation: Air-express industry

IBM Rochester: Manufacture of intermediate computer systems and hard drives

Wallace Co.: Family-owned distribution company primarily serving the chemical and petrochemical industries

1989

XEROX Corporation—Business Products & Systems: Manufacture of document-processing equipment such as copiers and printers

1988

Globe Metallurgical Inc.: Production of ferroalloys

Milliken & Co.: Manufacture of textile and chemical products ranging from apparel and automotive fabrics to floor coverings

Motorola Inc.: Production of communication systems including cellular telephones

Westinghouse Electric Corporation—Commercial Nuclear Fuel Division: Production of fuel-rod assemblies for nuclear industry opment, and employee satisfaction. Leadership (Section 1 of the Baldrige Award criteria) is considered the "driver" of all quality initiatives. Baldrige Award winners emphasize the creation of strategic intent (vision and mission statements) and the development of a company quality policy, with well-specified goals, operational policies and principles. In response to Information and Analysis (Section 2 of the criteria), Baldrige winners emphasize the effective use of data and information at all levels and in all dimensions of the business. Data are used for purposes of planning, control, managing, evaluation, and improvement of quality. This includes data for benchmarking, customer satisfaction measures, and data for eliminating, standardizing, and improving processes.

Even if a company does not plan to submit an application, completing one as if one were an applicant is a very good way to make a self-assessment of the quality system.

Comparison of the Baldrige Award and the ISO System of Registration

The Baldrige Award criteria provide an integrated results-oriented framework for managing all operations. The principal thrust of the Baldrige Award program is customer-driven quality. In comparison, the ISO 9000 standards embrace a somewhat narrower definition of quality. ISO certification guidelines focus on conformity, assuming that customer requirements are already known. The ISO 9000 standards are used in implementing a compliance system and assessing conformity in company-selected operations. Reinman and Hertz[3] conclude that ISO 9000 registration covers less than 10 percent of the scope of the Baldrige Award criteria and that it does not fully address the criteria items of the Baldrige Award. ISO 9000 registration excludes results, improvement, and competitive measures. As a consequence, ISO 9000 registration does not necessarily mean that registered companies have good product quality or that registered companies have better quality than nonregistered companies. Furthermore, the registration and ongoing audit processes do not require that registered companies continually improve their product quality. ISO registration merely means conformity to documented practices, which should result in a more consistent product. If companies are producing junk, then it is consistent junk!

The Deming Prize

The Deming Prize, named in honor of W. Edwards Deming, is awarded each year to organizations that, according to the award guidelines, have successfully applied companywide quality control based on statistical quality control and that are likely to continue doing so. The award is administered by the Deming Prize Committee of the Union of Japanese Scientists and Engineers (JUSE).

---

[3]Curt W. Reinmann and Harry S. Hertz, "The Baldrige Award and ISO 9000 Registration Compared," *Journal for Quality and Participation* (January/February 1996), pp. 12-19.

There are three separate divisions for the award: the Deming Application Prize, the Deming Prize for Individuals, and the Deming Prize for Overseas Companies. The Deming Application Prize was first awarded in 1951. Prominent Japanese Deming Prize winners include Toyota Motor Co., NEC, Shimizu Construction Co., and the Kansai Electric Power Co. Non-Japanese companies were allowed to apply for the first time in 1987. In 1988, Florida Power & Light Company was the first non-Japanese company to be awarded the Deming Prize (see Section 13.2).

The Deming Prize criteria are concerned mostly with the control of processes that ensure the quality of goods and services. One could say that it views quality as defined by the producers. This is different from the Baldrige Award (and also the European Quality Award, which is discussed next), which views quality in terms of the customer. The Deming Prize focuses on the application of statistical control techniques. This is understandable because the primary mission of JUSE, the creator and developer of this award, is to improve and disseminate quality assurance techniques. In addition, the award started at a time when statistical quality control was the major quality improvement tool.

The European Quality Prize

In response to the rapid success of the Baldrige Award, a consortium of large European national corporations established two types of quality awards for firms: the European Quality Prize, given to firms that meet the award criteria, and the European Quality Award, presented to the most accomplished applicant. The first awards were granted in 1992—four European Quality Prizes and an European Quality Award.

Some elements of the European Quality Prize are similar to those of the Baldrige Award: leadership, people management, policy and strategy, resources, processes, and customer satisfaction. However, the European Quality Prize introduces several additional elements: people satisfaction (how employees feel about their organization), impact on society (perceptions of the company by society), and business results (financial and nonfinancial performance of the firm). It takes the view that a firm's quality comprises the view of the customer, employees, and the community at large. The European Quality Prize weighs the various categories somewhat differently than does the Baldrige Award. Another difference is that the European Quality Prize is noncompetitive; all qualified applicants receive awards.

Some Further Comments on Quality Awards

The Baldrige Award, in contrast to the Deming Prize and the European Quality Prize, is competitive. Companies that score well on the examination criteria are not guaranteed receipt of an award; it is a competition rather than a recognition for achieving a certain standard of excellence.

Applicants for the Baldrige Award receive excellent feedback reports. Each final contender for the Award receives several hundred hours of review. Nevertheless, collecting and organizing the application materials takes considerable time, and many small companies may be reluctant to go through this process. For example, Ritz-Carlton reports that the 1991 award submission cost them more than 2000 hours of company time and $7000 out-of-pocket expenses. The costs for the 1992 application, which earned Ritz-Carlton the 1992 Baldrige Award in the service category, were approximately the same. The site visit by the Baldrige Examiners added expenses of another $15,000. In addition, each applicant must pay an application fee of several thousand dollars and, if a winner, must provide information about their application to all who ask for it. This can be a costly burden for a small organization.

◆ 24.3 Quality Successes

We conclude this book by highlighting the successes in quality that have been made in recent years. We feature the accomplishments of several Baldrige Award winners: Ritz-Carlton, Federal Express, Zytec Corporation, and Eastman Chemical. We also discuss the quality improvement efforts at IBM Wisconsin and the quality initiatives by city and state government in Madison, Wisconsin.

Ritz-Carlton

Ritz-Carlton, a privately owned Atlanta-based company operating 27 hotels and resorts in the United States and Australia, won the Baldrige Award in 1992. After Federal Express in 1991, it was the second company that won the award in the service category. Even though running a hotel is one of the most labor-intensive and logically complex jobs, Ritz-Carlton has successfully applied many of the quality control principles that manufacturing companies use to monitor and improve their products. Of course, the challenge in a service company is to create excellence with people rather than with machines and raw materials.

Ritz-Carlton has translated key product and service requirements of the travel consumer into the *Ritz-Carlton Gold Standards*, which include a credo, a motto, three steps of service, and the Ritz-Carlton "Basics," consisting of 20 well-defined employee-empowering basic steps that guide employee actions. Each employee is expected to understand and adhere to these standards, which describe processes for solving problems guests may have, as well as detailed grooming, housekeeping, and safety and efficiency standards.

The Ritz-Carlton Credo

The Ritz-Carlton is a place where the genuine care and comfort of our guests is our highest mission. We pledge to provide the best service and facilities for our guests who will always enjoy a warm, relaxed yet refined ambience. The Ritz-Carlton experience enlivens the senses, instills well-being, and fulfills even the unexpressed wishes and needs of our guests.

The Ritz-Carlton Motto

We are Ladies and Gentlemen serving Ladies and Gentlemen. We practice teamwork and "lateral service" (i.e., employee-to-employee contact) to create a positive work environment.

Three Steps of Service

1. A warm and sincere greeting. Use the guest's name, if and when possible.
2. Anticipation and compliance with guest needs.
3. Fond farewell. Give guests a warm good-bye and use their names, if and when possible.

Employees are aware that excellence in guest services is a top hotel and personal priority. In the company's credo employees are told: "The genuine care and comfort of our guests is our highest mission." To ensure problems are resolved quickly, employees are required to act at first notice; workers are empowered to do whatever it takes to provide "instant pacification" (*sic*). Employees are empowered "to move heaven and earth" to satisfy customer needs.

The company trains, coaches, and encourages employees to prevent breakdowns in service before they happen. Potential employees are put through three intensive days of screening before being employed. All employees receive more than 100 hours of training on quality topics, in particular the Gold Standards. The company trains employees to be "quality engineers" who can spot defects, correct them immediately, and then report their actions to management. Executives are actively involved in employee training. This is especially evident during the seven days leading up to the opening of each new hotel when the company president and senior leaders personally instruct new employees on the "Gold Standards" and on quality management during a two-day orientation.

Ritz-Carlton insists that its outside subcontractors adopt the principles of total quality management. It asks potential subcontractors to conduct a self-assessment of their quality efforts. The company only wants to deal with those who are capable of continual improvement. Ultimately, the company chooses subcontractors on the basis of their quality standards, not just on their price tag.

The company recognizes and rewards employees for their contributions to continual quality improvement. Ritz-Carlton views success as the result of teamwork. Members of teams share in bonus pools whenever solutions to quality-related problems are successfully implemented.

Ritz-Carlton actively collects and uses data on quality. The company meticulously gathers data on every aspect of the guest's stay to determine if the hotels are meeting customer expectations. Quality reports, based on data derived from each of the 720 work areas in the hotel system, serve as an early warning system about problems that impede progress toward meeting customer satisfaction. In addition, Ritz-Carlton conducts mail and telephone surveys on a regular basis to assess the satisfaction of its customers and to learn how the chain can improve its service. It also benchmarks other competitors, such as the Four Seasons hotel company. The company keeps a comprehensive and detailed computerized guest history with profiles on more than 200,000 repeat customers.

Its aim for total quality management is not simply to meet the expectations of guests but to provide them with a "memorable visit." According to surveys conducted for Ritz-Carlton by independent research firms, 92 to 97 percent of the company's guests leave with that impression.

Federal Express Corporation

Federal Express launched the air-express industry in 1973, and it now has over 40 percent of the domestic market, almost twice its nearest competitor. It has almost 90,000 employees at 1,644 sites, and it processes an average of 1.3 million shipments a day. Since 1987, overall customer satisfaction with FedEx's domestic service has rated a satisfaction score of about 94 percent. In an independent survey of air-express customers, 53 percent gave FedEx a perfect score as compared with 39 percent for the next-best competitor. In 1990, Federal Express won the MBNQA.[4]

People

Founder and Chairman Frederick W. Smith has consistently focused on company employees as the source of Federal Express' success, emphasizing people, service, and profit, in that order. The Baldrige Award announcement was no exception:

> Our employees have worked diligently over the years in a concerted effort to achieve 100% customer satisfaction. We believe that our People First philosophy encourages that quest for quality, and this award is clear evidence of Federal Express' employees' dedication to providing quality service to our customers.

FedEx is consistently included in listings of the best U.S. companies to work for. It has a "no layoff" philosophy, and its "guaranteed fair treatment procedure" for handling employee grievances is used as a model in many industries. Federal Express has a well-developed recognition program for team and individual contributions to company performance. Over the five years prior to receiving the Baldrige Award, at least 91 percent of employees responded that they were proud to work for Federal Express.

FedEx has a well-developed management evaluation system called SFA (Survey/Feedback/Action). It involves a survey of employees, analysis of each work group's results by the work group's manager, and a discussion between the manager and the work group. Next, written action plans are developed to aid the manager in improving and becoming more effective. Data from the SFA process are aggregated from all levels of management for use in policy making.

Line managers are responsible for training personnel. Teams assess training needs, and training professionals devise programs to address those needs. All employees are encouraged to be innovative and to make changes that improve qual-

---

[4]Brad Stratton, "Four to Receive 1990 Baldrige Awards," *Quality Progress*, December 1990, p. 19.

ity; FedEx provides employees with the information and technology they need to continually improve their performance.

Technology

FedEx sorts and delivers packages from six sites in the United States and one in Belgium. SuperTracker, a hand-held computer, is used to scan a shipment's bar code each time a package changes hands between pick-up and delivery. The data obtained are used to track shipments; they are also used by quality action teams to determine the root causes of problems.

FedEx's Digitally Assisted Dispatch System (DADS) keeps 26,000 couriers informed about customers' latest requirements through video screens located in company vans. This information allows quick response to pick-up and delivery dispatches, and it permits couriers to manage their time better.

Quality

Company leaders stress management by fact, analysis, and improvement. FedEx has a quality improvement process that focuses on 12 Service Quality Indicators (SQIs), all tied to customer expectations. Measuring themselves against high standards for service and customer satisfaction, managers and employees strive to improve all aspects of the way Federal Express does business.

ZYTEC Corporation

Zytec is a small, employee-owned company located in Eden Prairie, Minnesota. It designs, manufactures, and repairs electronic power supplies that are used in products such as computers, medical equipment, and test equipment. Zytec began in 1984; in 1991, it won the MBNQA and the Minnesota Quality Award.[5]

From its beginning, the company's focus was on Quality, Service, and Value. The cornerstones of their efforts to achieve these goals are Deming's 14 Points for Management, the Baldrige criteria, and a process called Management by Planning (MBP), which was initiated after a 1988 study mission to Japan by Zytec's CEO.

Zytec has several self-managed work groups in place as well as several cross-functional teams. To support these activities, data are collected and used for proactive process improvements. Almost every employee of Zytec is involved in the three-step MBP process that has been a major driver of quality values within Zytec: gathering data, establishing goals, and developing action plans by teams.

Employees are encouraged to contribute to continual improvement and are given extensive quality training. All Zytec employees have been trained in a seven-step problem-solving process. Employees are granted broad authority to achieve team and individual goals. For example, without prior authorization, any employee can spend up to $1000 to resolve a customer complaint. And hourly workers can make process changes with the agreement of only one other person.

---

[5]Zytec Summary of the 1991 Application for the Baldrige National Quality Award; also *Quality Progress*, November 1991, p. 40.

Zytec has made benchmark comparisons with several leading organizations, including Xerox, Motorola, Sony, 3M, and IBM. Senior managers often participate in benchmarking activities. Zytec also shares its experiences with other firms; in 1990, for example, representatives of 47 companies attended Zytec's "noncustomer visit day" to learn about Zytec's quality improvement efforts.

IBM Wisconsin

In 1990, the IBM manufacturing operations at Rochester, Minnesota, received a Baldrige Award. Shortly after that, IBM Wisconsin—a sales and service part of IBM—began applying to its operations the quality lessons learned at Rochester.[6] Its first step was to develop a vision of the organization's role in the 1990s: to help customers gain competitive advantage, to apply all available resources to all aspects of the customers' operations, and to support state businesses and the state government. Next, managers learned quality principles and took four initial steps:

1. Six branch quotas were replaced with a single statewide quota to encourage people to work as a team.
2. The number of managers was reduced to facilitate employee empowerment.
3. Education on quality was included in training for the company's Market-Driven Quality program.
4. In a radical change, compensation was based not just on revenue contribution, but also on improvement in customer satisfaction, process improvement, leadership, and skills development.

Teams were then employed to work on tactical marketing issues and to improve customer responsiveness and employee effectiveness. Organizational changes were made that allowed complicated sales proposals to be developed more quickly with less risk of rejection. Some teams became more involved in community affairs; others developed a strategy to help other Wisconsin organizations with their quality improvement efforts.

An employee opinion survey in Spring 1991 indicated that almost ninety percent of IBM employees in Wisconsin bought into the quality efforts. It also showed very strong (91%) endorsement of management's leadership.

IBM Wisconsin learned four lessons that are applicable to any sales organization:

1. Senior management must give active support to the market-driven quality movement.
2. People closest to the customer know what must be done, and management must trust their judgment.

---

[6]James W. Cortade, "Implementing Quality in a Sales Organization," *Quality Progress*, September 1993, p. 67.

4. Measurement and compensation systems must be aligned with goals.

5. Empowerment and teamwork should be recognized and rewarded by peers.

IBM Wisconsin also learned a very basic lesson: You can apply the Baldrige Award criteria to marketing and sales.

Madison, Wisconsin

Madison, Wisconsin has demonstrated conclusively that quality principles can be applied to government as well as the private sector.

Madison has two major industries, government and education—it is the state capital and county seat, and it is the home of the state university. In 1983, a core group of people from government, education, and the private sector met to initiate a community quality improvement effort. This group consisted of influential government employees and quality experts, such as George Box, Bill Hunter, Brian Joiner, and Peter Scholtes. Their aim was to create a community in which quality is a way of life.

The group started meeting regularly to share their knowledge and experiences and to get other members of the community involved in the quality effort. They started several pilot projects in state and local government. Next we will describe one of them.

A State Service

At one time, a one-page letter sent to the word processing pool at the Department of Revenue would come back two or even three weeks later—with errors. Despite numerous adjustments in the process, the backlog remained high and employee turnover kept rising.

To tackle the problem, a nine-person team was formed consisting of managers, supervisors, operators, and customers. Their first effort was to identify all of the customers and suppliers to the process. Then they brainstormed to list the process problems. The problems were ranked in order of importance, and all team members agreed that quality was the number one problem. To discover possible causes of poor quality, the group constructed a cause-and-effect diagram. From an analysis of this diagram, they concluded that many problems could be traced to the request form that was being used to link customers and operators.

To learn where these problems were occurring, the request process was flowcharted. Next, a customer survey was conducted to learn what users wanted, and a check-sheet was developed by operators to help them locate the cause of errors.

After gathering data for two weeks, the group discovered that the actual workload was 35 percent greater than customers had estimated. Of the requests examined, they discovered that 27 percent had errors caused by the customer. They also discovered that some customers routinely marked *all* requests as "rush," which clogged the normal processing channels.

With data to support their decisions, the section chiefs made several changes: Operators were given new authority to reject illegible or incomplete requests; Saturday overtime was allowed to eliminate the backlog; and typing requests that should have gone to other units were redirected. As a result of these changes, turn-around time decreased to two days; soon after, it decreased to eight hours.[7]

Eastman Chemical Company

Eastman Chemical Company is a leading international chemical company with about 18,000 employees. It produces a broad portfolio of plastic, chemical, and fiber products. In 1993, Eastman Chemical was a Baldrige Award winner.

Eastman has always taken pride in its products, so it was surprised when a key customer stated in the 1970s (at which time Eastman was a division of Kodak) that a competitor had better products. Products that were produced by a process that Eastman had invented, patented, and licensed to the competitor! This was Eastman's wake-up call.

Eastman started making changes. By the early 1980s, customer feedback was imbedded in planning and other operations. A quality policy was adopted in 1983, and employee training in quality principles and tools was begun in 1984. But the company had not driven fear from the workplace. For example, employees were concerned that statistical process control charts would be used to highlight employee mistakes rather than to make process improvements.

Eastman realized that what was needed was not just a change in methods and procedures, but a change in its culture. This led to the development in 1985 of a corporate philosophy that is known as "The Eastman Way." This philosophy expresses the company's beliefs on the following key issues:[8]

◆ Honesty and integrity

◆ Fairness

◆ Teamwork

◆ Diversity of views and backgrounds

◆ Employee well-being

◆ Citizenship and contribution to the community

◆ A winning attitude—excellence through continual improvement

In 1984, a process improvement effort was launched that focused on identifying and adjusting processes to the requirements of all internal and external cus-

---

[7]William G. Hunter, Janet K. O'Neill, and Carol Wallen, "Doing More with Less in the Public Sector," *Quality Progress*, July 1987, p. 19. Also, George E. P. Box, Laurel W. Joiner, Sue Rohan, and Joseph Sensenbrenner, "Quality in the Community: One City's Experience," *Quality Progress*, May 1991, p. 57.

[8]"To Be the Best," Eastman Chemical Company publication ECC-67, January 1994.

tomers. In 1986, senior managers implemented their own quality management process. They identified all of their customers, determined customer requirements, and evolved ways to measure how well those requirements were being met. In 1987, this system was computerized and its information was validated by an outside firm. This exercise had wide impact and was key to the success of their quality effort because it gave evidence that senior managers were "walking the talk."

Later in 1986, the concept of teams was introduced. Each team consisted of workers and their supervisor. Supervisors, in turn, were grouped into teams; and so on up the organization. Teams identified their processes, process customers, and suppliers, and they established measures of process performance.

Employees, however, were still being appraised on a "bell curve," which automatically identified half the people as "below average." Gradually, management realized the shortcoming of this system, and in 1990, this appraisal system was scrapped. The company now expends its energy on developing people, not grading them. Other changes that were made include the following:

- ◆ To alleviate employees' fear of "working themselves out of a job," the company promised never to lay off anyone because of quality improvement.

- ◆ A suggestion system that rewarded individuals was replaced with one that encourages suggestions from teams.

Eastman Chemical's seven steps to continual improvement are these:

1. *Focus and pinpoint.* This involves focusing employee attention on measurable targets. One example is the process MIBE ("making international business easier"), a process to simplify and improve international sales. Another example is MEPS ("making Eastman the preferred supplier"), a process to support the strategic objective of increasing international sales.

2. *Communicate.* Make certain every employee knows what is important and why, and what part they play in achieving goals.

3. *Translate and link.* Translate management goals and objectives, which often are expressed in dollars and percents, into the language of employees—cycle time, reliability, error rates, and so on. Link employee actions to organizational goals.

4. *Create an action plan.* Translate corporate action plans into tasks workers are to perform. Find planning problems before they occur. Identify and remove roadblocks before people encounter them.

5. *Improve processes.* This is a basic technique for quality improvement.

6. *Measure programs and provide feedback.* Eastman has two mottos: "Feedback is the Breakfast of Champions," and "If you don't measure performance, you can't improve it."

7. *Reinforce desired behaviors and celebrate results.* Celebration of results is needed, but at celebrations ask, "How did you achieve this?" By answering

this question, people learn from the result; this reinforces the behavior that led to the result.[9]

◆ 24.4 Opportunities for Further Improvement

Many companies have taken large leaps towards establishing a framework for quality. However, nothing is perfect and everything can be improved. We close this chapter by mentioning some of the areas that limit the realization of the full potential of total quality management.

George Easton, a Baldrige Award senior examiner, has reflected on his experiences in examining and scoring 22 applicants for the Baldrige Award.[10] While his assessment is generally favorable, he concludes that even the best of the best (and one expects that Baldrige applicants are generally far superior to typical companies) have a large number of areas for improvement. He identifies the following weaknesses: lack of a full understanding of process concepts; lack of emphasis on planning; lack of effective systems for implementing the plans; reliance on incentives; failure to apply the principle of management by fact; focus on results to the exclusion of processes and methods; focus on financial measures to the exclusion of direct operational measures; and a sometimes inadequate understanding of customer expectations.

Leadership: Easton concludes that senior management's understanding of total quality management is still quite superficial. Management still is almost exclusively results-oriented, not process-oriented. Management still views the company almost exclusively in terms of financial, not operational measures.

Information and Analysis: Information systems are often inflexible and unable to support the kinds of changes that are part of continual improvement and evolving customer expectations. Benchmarking comparisons are often limited to immediate competitors; they do not take advantage of the fact that benchmarking is most fruitful when carried out on similar process steps in different industries. Quality information is not well organized to support quality management. Most readily available data are still financially oriented, and not always useful to managing operations.

Strategic Quality Planning: Plans generally stop at setting goals and objectives and fail to address the deployment of plans throughout the organization. Most companies lack a well-developed strategic quality planning process.

Human Resource Development and Management: Most teams do not make effective use of team processes, such as problem-solving methods and quality

---

[9]Weston F. Milliken, "The Eastman Way," *Quality Progress*, October 1996, p. 57.

[10]George S. Easton, "The 1993 State of U.S. Total Quality Management: A Baldrige Examiner's Perspective," *California Management Review* 35, No. 3 (1993), pp. 32–54.

tools. There is still too little training, and the effectiveness of whatever training that is given, is not well evaluated. Empowerment is still not understood; in some cases, decisions are still reviewed by multiple levels of management prior to authorization. The performance evaluation system is poorly aligned with the company's quality management system. Much of employee recognition is superficial, and often it is still results-oriented and substantially influenced by factors that are outside the employee's control.

Management of Process Quality: There is still too much reliance on end-of-process defect rates, and not enough emphasis on variables measurements and on driving measurement of processes upstream. Quality improvement teams often fail to use well-developed problem-solving strategies. Documentation of improvement methods and activities, and the dissemination of results, are still limited. There is widespread failure to understand the difference between bringing a process into control and improving the process.

Quality and Operational Results: The scope of the data used to track the results of the quality system is often inadequate. Operational measures and key customer requirements are often poorly linked. Trends are often established on the basis of insufficient data.

Customer Focus and Satisfaction: The understanding of the technical issues behind surveys is limited. Surveys are often left to outside parties. Data on customer preferences and the design process are poorly integrated. All too often customers are still unable to reach someone with authority to make changes.

And remember, Easton is commenting on some of the best companies!

While the outlook for the future of quality is promising, much needs to be done. This means the organizations need people who understand quality and how to achieve it. We hope that our book will provide you with the framework that helps you improve the quality of your processes. We invite you to send us your comments on how we can improve our book. You can reach us through our publisher, John Wiley & Sons, or through the Department of Statistics and Actuarial Science at the University of Iowa, Iowa City, Iowa 52242. Our e-mail address is ledolter@stat.uiowa.edu.

◆ Exercises and Additional Readings

1. Compare the Baldrige Award and the Deming Prize. What are the similarities and what are the main differences? The following articles may help you with this exercise.

   (a) David Bush and Kevin Dooley: "The Deming Prize and Baldrige Award: How They Compare," *Quality Progress*, January 1989, p. 28.

   (b) Behnam Nakhau and Joam S. Neves: "The Deming, Baldrige, and European Quality Awards, *Quality Progress*, April 1994, pp. 33–37.

2. Compare the Malcolm Baldrige Award and the ISO System of registration. An article that may help you with this exercise is Curt W. Reinmann and

Harry S. Hertz: "The Baldrige Award and ISO 9000 Registration Compared," *The Journal for Quality and Participation* (January–February 1996), pp. 12–19.

3. Read and discuss one or more of the following articles on the Malcolm Baldrige National Quality Award:

   (a) Paul Allaire: "Two Years after the Baldrige: Quality and Beyond," *Journal of Quality and Participation* (May 1992), pp. 6–8.

   (b) Suzanne Axland: "Small Wonders," *Quality Progress*, November 1992, pp. 29–34, which describes the experience of the small business recipients of the Baldrige Award.

   (c) Karen Bemowski: "Three Electronic Firms Win 1991 Baldrige Awards," *Quality Progress*, November 1991, pp. 39–41.

   (d) Karen Bemowski: "1994 Baldrige Award Recipients Share Their Expertise," *Quality Progress*, February 1995, pp. 35–40.

   (e) Karen Bemowski: "The Story Might Wander a Bit . . . ," *Quality Progress*, May 1996, pp. 33–42, which describes the 1995 Baldrige Award winners, Armstrong World Industries, and Corning Telecommunications.

   (f) Marion Harmon, "1996 Baldrige Award Winners: A True Cross-Section of American Industry," *Quality Digest,* January 1997, pp. 30–34.

   (g) Brad Stratton: "Xerox and Milliken Receive Malcolm Baldrige National Quality Awards," *Quality Progress*, December 1989, pp. 17–20.

4. The scores and the comments of Baldrige Award examiners are kept confidential. What advantages acrue from this practice?

5. Discuss David T. Kearns, "Chasing a Moving Target," *Quality Progress*, October 1989, pp. 29–31. It describes Xerox's quality experience through the eyes of its CEO.

6. Discuss the articles:

   (a) George H. Labovitz and Yu Sang Chang, "Learn from the Best," *Quality Progress*, May 1990, pp. 81–85, which discusses strategies that are adopted by Deming Prize winners.

   (b) Brad Stratton, "A Beacon for the Worlds," *Quality Progress*, May 1990, pp. 60–63, which describes the Florida Power and Light Co. application process for the Deming award.

7. Read Charles G. Partlow, "How the Ritz-Carlton Applies 'TQM,' " *The Cornell Hotel and Restaurant Administration Quarterly* 34, No. 4 (August 1993). It describes the philosophy at Ritz-Carlton, a 1992 MBNQA winner.

8. The following articles describe the application of a total quality management to the public sector. Summarize the lessons that can be learned from these case studies.

   (a) William Hunter, Jan O'Neill, and Carol Wallen, "Doing More with Less in the Public Sector: A Progress Report from Madison, Wisconsin," Report No. 13, Center for Quality and Productivity Improvement, University of Wisconsin, Madison, 1986. Reprinted in Joseph G. Van Matre, *Foundations of TQM: A Readings Book* (Orlando, FL: Dryden Press, 1995).

(b) George E.P. Box, Laurel W. Joiner, Sue Rohan, and Joseph Sensenbrenner, "Quality in the Community: One City's Experience," *Quality Progress*, May 1991, p. 57.

(c) Joseph Sensenbrenner, "Quality Comes to City Hall," *Harvard Business Review* (March–April 1991), p. 64.

9. Find some articles on the application of total quality management in the education sector. Discuss:

(a) Robert Hogg and Mary Hogg, "Continuous Quality Improvement in Higher Education," *International Statistical Review* 63 (1995), pp. 35–48.

(b) Harry V. Roberts, *Academic Initiatives in Total Quality for Higher Education* (Milwaukee: ASQC Quality Press, 1995).

(c) Stanley J. Spanbauer, *A Quality System for Education*, (Milwaukee, WI: ASQC Quality Press, 1992). This is a case study of Fox Valley Technical College's pioneering application of quality processes to improve educational services.

(d) Assess the efforts and achievements of your institution in this area.

10. Read and discuss the following success stories on the quality of goods, service, and information products.

(a) Richard J. Leo, "Xerox 2000: From Survival to Opportunity," *Quality Progress*, March 1996, p. 65.

(b) Brad Stratton, "How Disney Works," *Quality Progress*, July 1991, p. 17.

(c) Weston F. Milliken, "The Eastman Way," *Quality Progress*, October 1996, p. 57.

11. Read and discuss David A. Kennedy and Barbara J. Young: "Managing Quality in Staff Areas: Part I," *Quality Progress*, October 1989, p. 87.

12. Access the web site of the National Institute of Standards and Technology ("www.nist.gov") and obtain the most recent Award Criteria for the Baldrige Quality Award. Elaborate on each of the seven award criteria. Describe the point system that is used to evaluate applications.

If you don't have access to the internet, you can obtain free of charge individual copies of the Award Criteria and the Application Forms and Instructions (two separate documents) by writing to:

Malcolm Baldrige National Quality Award
National Institute of Standards and Technology
Route 270 and Quince Orchard Road
Administration Building, Room A537
Gathersburg, Maryland 20899-0001

13. The web sites for the American Society for Quality ("www.asq.com"), for the National Institute of Standards and Technology ("www.nist.gov"), and for the Baldrige Award ("www.baldrige.com") contain detailed information on the Baldrige Award. Look for the Applications Summaries of Baldrige Award winners. Discuss how these companies have addressed the seven award criteria. Do you see similarities or differences?

◆ ◆ ◆

Case Studies

We conclude this book with several case studies. These cases can help supplement and reinforce the major points that we have made in our text.

Many other sources for case materials are readily available. The Harvard Business Review Cases are a good source for supplementary class materials. You can contact the *Harvard Business Review* via internet under its address "www.hbsp.harvard.edu." A search with the word "quality" in the case title led to more than 40 cases. Other good sources for cases are the materials published by the International Institute for Management Development (IMD) in Lausanne, Switzerland; its homepage is "www.imd.ch." Several books of cases and readings on quality have been published recently. You may want to refer to the books by Gregory M. Bounds *Cases in Quality* (Business One Irwin, 1996) and by Joseph G. VanMatre *Foundations of TQM: A Readings Book* (New York: Harcourt Brace & Co., 1995). These sources include many useful cases and discussion materials that you can use to supplement our text.

◆ A Note on the Use of Cases

Cases describe business situations and typical problems that managers face. They give students exposure to a wide range of industries, companies, and management situations. By analyzing cases, students develop a better sense of the management function and learn to ask the right questions about problem situations—and asking the right question is usually harder than finding a suitable answer.

Useful as they are, it should be recognized that cases are not the same as real business situations. For one thing, information is delivered to the student in a succinct, written form. In a real situation, gathering useful facts and opinions is part of the problem-solving process. Another difference is that a case is static; real problems are dynamic—attempts to solve one problem can easily create another. A third difference is that a case focuses on a certain type of problem—say, a quality problem—and tends to omit other elements of the real situation. In a real situation, quality problems might be interlaced with problems relating to competition, employees, government regulation—you name it. Still another difference is that students are asked to make decisions concerning cases, but they are not responsible for implementing their decisions.

How to Prepare a Case

There is no standard way to prepare a case; here is one approach.

1. Skim to determine what the case is about and the type of information you are given. In particular, look at a few paragraphs at the beginning and at the end of the case, and at the exhibits provided.

2. Read the case carefully. Visualize the situation; put yourself in the place of the manager; become involved with the manager's problems. Note the key problems as you read through the case.

3. Review the case and sort the relevant facts by the problem(s) to which they relate.

4. Develop recommendations and use your analysis of the case to support them.

Problem definition (Step 2) is a critical step in the analysis process. Sometimes problems are stated explicitly; sometimes they can be inferred from a seemingly casual comment or observation. Sometimes a symptom is given ("defect rates are too high"), and the underlying, fundamental problem must be determined and defined so as to address the explicit issue and the fundamental issue. The scope of the problem should be realistic and within the manager's scope of authority. A broad question ("Should we sell the plant and relocate overseas?") is unrealistic if the manager in the case is not in a position to make such a decision.

Having defined the problem, it is helpful to list relevant areas for analysis. If the problem is "too many defects on the production line," areas for analysis might include:

- The physical production line, its environment, and its management
- Procedures and instructions for operating the line
- Line operator selection and training

◆   Supplies for the line
◆   Management of the operation of the production line

Facts in the case can then be arranged so as to help you understand each area and use this understanding to address the problem.

After analyzing the case on your own, you should discuss it with your group. Present your position and listen to those of other group members. The purpose of the discussion is to help members refine and adjust their own ideas; it is not at all necessary for the group to reach a consensus. The group discussion should improve your understanding of the case so that you will learn more from the class discussion.

In class, you should present and defend your views and recommendations concerning the case. Through discussion and controversy, you will build your analytical and communication skills. You will learn to express and defend your views; you will also listen to the ideas of others and shift your position if this is warranted. Don't judge your progress by whether your ideas were right or wrong; judge it by how much you have learned from the experience.

Hank Kolb, Director, Quality Assurance[1]

Hank Kolb was whistling as he walked towards his office, still feeling a bit like a stranger since he had been hired four weeks ago as director, quality assurance. All last week he had been away from the plant at an interesting seminar entitled "Quality in the 90s" given for quality managers of manufacturing plants by the corporate training department. He was not looking forward to really digging into the quality problems at this industrial products plant employing 1,200 people. Hank poked his head into Mark Hamler's office, his immediate subordinate, the quality control manager, and asked him how things had gone last week. Mark's muted smile and an "Oh, fine" stopped Hank in his tracks. He didn't know Mark very well and was unsure about pursuing this reply any further. Hank was still uncertain of how to start building his relationship with him since Mark had been passed over for the promotion to Hank's job—Mark's evaluation form had stated "superb technical knowledge; managerial skills lacking." Hank decided to inquire a little further and asked Mark what had happened. Mark replied:

Oh, just another typical quality snafu. We had a little problem on the Greasex line last week (a specialized degreasing solvent packed in a spray can for the high-technology sector). A little high pressure was found in some cans on the second shift, but a supervisor vented them so that we could ship them out. We met our delivery schedule!

Since Hank was still relatively unfamiliar with the plant and the products he asked Mark to elaborate. Painfully, Mark continued:

> We've been having some trouble with new filling equipment, and some of the cans were pressurized beyond our acceptable standard on a psi (pounds per square inch) rating scale. The production rate is still 50 percent of standard, about 40 cases per shift, and we caught it halfway into the shift. Mac Evans (the inspector for that line) picked it up, tagged the cases "Hold" and went on about his duties. When he returned at the end of the shift to write up the rejects, Wayne Simmons, first-line supervisor, was by a pallet of finished goods finishing sealing up a cap on the rejected Greasex: the reject "Hold" tags had been removed. He told Mac that he had heard about the high pressure from another inspector at coffee break, had come back, taken off the tags, individually turned the cans upside down and vented every one of them in the rejected eight cartons. He told Mac that production planning was really pushing for the stuff, and they couldn't delay by having it sent through the rework area. He told Mac that he would get on the operator to run the equipment right next time. Mac didn't write it up but came in about three days to tell me about it. Oh, it happens every once in a while, and I told him to make sure the filling machine was adjusted; and I saw Wayne in the hall and told him that he ought to send the stuff through rework next time.

Hank was a bit dumbfounded at this and didn't say much—he didn't know if this was a "big deal" or not. When he got to his office he thought again what Mr. Morganthal, general manager, had said when he had hired Hank. He warned Hank about the "lack of quality attitude" in the plant and said that Hank "should try to do something about this." He had further emphasized the quality problems in the plant. "We have to improve our quality, it's costing us a lot of money, I'm sure of it, but I can't prove it! Hank, you have my full support in this matter; you're in charge of these quality problems. This downward quality-production-turnover spiral has to end!"

The incident had happened a week ago, the goods were probably out in the customer's hands by now; everyone had forgotten about it (or wanted to!); and there seemed to be more pressing problems than this for Hank to spend his time on; but this continued to nag at him. He felt like the quality department was being treated as a joke, and it also felt to him like a personal slap from manufacturing. He didn't want to start a war with the production people but what could he do? He was troubled enough to cancel his appointments and spend the morning talking to a few people. After a long and very tactful morning, he learned the following:

A. From personnel—the operator for the filling equipment had just been transferred from shipping two weeks ago. He had no formal training in this job but was being trained by Wayne, on the job, to run the equipment. When Mac had tested the high-pressure cans, the operator was nowhere to be found and had only learned of the rejected material from Wayne after the shift was over.

B. From plant maintenance—this particular piece of automated filling equipment had been purchased two years ago for use on another product. It had been switched to the Greasex line six months ago, and maintenance had 12 work orders during the last month for repairs or adjustments on it. The equipment had been adapted by plant maintenance for handling the lower viscosity Greasex, which it had not originally been designed for. This included designing a special filling head. There was no scheduled preventive maintenance for this equipment, and the parts for the sensitive filling head, replaced three times in the last six months, had to be made at a nearby machine shop. Non-standard downtime was running at 15 percent of actual running times.

C. From purchasing—the plastic nozzle heads for the Greasex can, recently designed by a vendor for this new product on a rush order, were often found with slight burrs on the inside rim, and this caused some trouble in fitting the top to the can. An increase in application pressure at the filling head by maintenance adjustment had solved the burr application problem or had at least "forced" the nozzle heads on despite burrs. Purchasing said that they were going to talk to the sales representative of the nozzle head supplier about this the next time he came in.

D. From product design and packaging—the can, designed especially for Greasex, had been contoured to allow better gripping by the user. This change, instigated by marketing research, set Greasex apart from the appearance of its competitors and was seen by the designers to be "significant." There had been no test of the effects of the contoured can on filling speed or filling hydrodynamics from a high-pressured filling head. Hank had a hunch that the new design was acting as a venturi when being filled, but the packaging designer thought that "unlikely."

E. From the manufacturing manager—he had heard about the problem; in fact, Wayne had made a joke about it, bragging about how he beat his production quota to the other foremen and shift supervisors. Wayne was thought by the manufacturing manager to be one of the "best foremen we have . . . he always gets his production out." His promotion papers were actually on the manufacturing manager's desk when Hank dropped by, Wayne was being "strongly considered" for promotion to shift supervisor. The manufacturing manager, under pressure from Mr. Morganthal for cost improvements and reduced delivery times, sympathized with Hank but said that the rework area would have just vented with their pressure gauges that Wayne did by hand. "But, I'll speak with Wayne, about the incident."

F. From marketing—the introduction of Greasex had been rushed to beat competitors to market and a major promotional/advertising campaign was now underway to increase consumer awareness. A deluge of orders was swamping the order-taking department right now and putting Greasex high on the back-order list. Production "had to turn the stuff out"; even a little off spec was tolerable because "it would be better to have it on the shelf than not there at all. Who cares if the label is a little crooked or the stuff comes out with a little too much pressure? We need market share now in that high-tech segment."

What bothered Hank the most was the safety issue of the high pressure in the cans. He had no way of knowing how much of a hazard the high pressure was or if Wayne had vented them enough to effectively reduce the hazard. The data from the can manufacturer which Mark had showed him indicated that the high pressure which the inspector had found was not in the danger area; but then again the inspector had only used a sample testing procedure to reject the eight cases. Even if he could morally accept that there was no product safety hazard, could he make sure that this never happened again?

Hank, skipping lunch, sat in his office and thought about the morning's events. Last week's seminar had talked about "the role of quality," "productivity and quality," "creating a new attitude," and the "quality challenge" but where had they told him what to do when this happens? He had left a very good job to come here because he thought the company was serious about the importance of quality, and he wanted a challenge. Hank had demanded and received a salary equal to the manufacturing, marketing, and R&D directors' and was one of the direct reports to the general manager. Yet he still didn't know exactly what he should or shouldn't do or even what he could or couldn't do.

◆ Discussion Questions

1. What is wrong with the way quality is managed in this company?

2. What should be done to improve quality management?

3. What should Hank Kolb do?

Acme Electronics

Acme Electronics is a small supplier of components to manufacturers of television and other electronic equipment. It is located on the East Coast and operates mainly in a six-state region. Acme always has prided itself on its service and fast response to customers, so the president, Dave Borum, was shocked when he learned that a major customer was dissatisfied with the quality of its components and stated they would not place another order with Acme "until they get their act together."

A phone call to the customer did little to soothe the customer or change his mind. But his parting words did make a deep impression on Dave: "You'd better get your quality act together or you'll be out of business."

Dave wasted no time in hiring a director of quality, Rod Larson. With Rod's help, Dave then established a Quality Council consisting of Dave, Rod, all department heads, and the head of the employee union. At their initial meeting a week later, the Council reviewed the situation and agreed that Rod would draft a Quality Policy and a quality improvement plan for discussion at their next meeting, which was to be held in one week's time. Meanwhile, they would all do some outside reading about how to improve product quality.

At their meeting a week later, several ideas were proposed for a quality policy. After some discussion it was agreed that "Our business is quality" set the right tone. After more discussion, it was decided that what they meant by "quality" was producing what you were supposed to produce—that is, meeting requirements. It was agreed that the failure to meet a requirement was a *defect*—a quality product is one that is defect-free. With this definition, each department could measure their quality by measuring their defect rates.

Next, Rod discussed his plan for improving quality at Acme. First, they would inform all employees that Acme was establishing a new direction and making quality a major goal of the organization. In a special Quality Day meeting, employees would be introduced to the new emphasis, told the part they were to play in the effort, and asked to sign a pledge that they would strive to produce quality products. Soon after that, all employees would be given training in the importance of doing things right the first time. Working together, managers and workers would establish measures of quality and goals for quality improvement. Also, there would be a program to recognize individuals who made a significant contribution to quality.

Quality Day was very successful. To mark the event, the families of employees were invited, and the ice cream was a big hit with the children. Because of its size, the event was held outdoors and the weather cooperated beautifully. Everyone had a good time; everything went without a hitch except that the banner with "Our business is quality" blew down in the middle of Rod's speech. The success of the kick-off could be measured by the favorable comments one could hear the next day in the hallways and company cafeteria.

Dave was pleased with the success of Quality Day. This convinced him that Rod was a good choice and that Rod could be trusted to handle quality while he got back to running the business. For his part, Rod was busy working with managers to establish departmental measures of quality and quality recognition programs.

Managers soon came to realize that one way to be popular with Dave Borum was for their department to have a reputation for quality. And this could be done by being generous in assessing quality accomplishments. So gradually there was an increase in recognition awards even though the general level of quality remained more or less constant.

Several months after Quality Day, Dave was again shocked to learn that another major customer was dropping Acme as a supplier because of the quality of their products. "How can that be? We've got a quality program in place." What could Rod Larson say?

◆ Discussion Questions

1. Critique the quality program initiated by Rod Larson. What are its strong points? What are its weak points?

2. Compare and contrast Rod Larson's quality program with that offered by Philip Crosby as described in *Quality Is Free* (New York: McGraw-Hill, 1979).

3. Critique Rod Larson's quality program in light of the three interrelated factors required for corporate revitalization as discussed in Michael Beer, Russell A. Eisenstat, and Bert Spector, "Why Change Programs Don't Produce Change," *Harvard Business Review* (November–December 1990), p. 158. These three factors are coordination and teamwork, high levels of commitment, and new competencies.

4. As an adviser to Ron, list some specific steps you think he should take to improve quality at Acme.

The Budapest

Steve Feketa sat in his closed, dimly lit restaurant and contemplated the events of the day. First, he and his lawyer walked through the restaurant to check that all was in order; then a long meeting was held at the bank with the former owner of the restaurant, lawyers for both parties, and a bank official to transfer the property and grant Steve a mortgage on it. It was a big step and only the first of many that had to be taken to turn his dream into a reality.

Steve was born and spent his early years in a small village not far from Budapest, Hungary. As the war clouds of World War II were forming, his parents attempted to escape the coming conflict by immigrating to the United States. Steve's uncle Piesta in New York City helped them to settle in an apartment in Manhattan on an East Side street that housed many other families from Hungary. Steve went through school and as a teenager worked part time in his uncle's restaurant. Partly for financial reasons and partly to make Steve a "real American," Steve was sent to a Midwestern state university, where both the tuition and cost of living were relatively low.

After college, Steve returned to Manhattan and worked for his uncle. He married and had two children but devoted much of his time to the restaurant. Gradually, Steve took over more and more of the management responsibility; his major influence was gradually to shift the image from that of a family restaurant catering to the Hungarian emigrants to an upscale restaurant catering to the New York business community. Uncle Piesta, who had no children, regarded Steve almost as a son; on his death in 1983, Piesta willed the restaurant to Steve.

Time passed. The children went off to college, then got married; the restaurant prospered; and life fell into a routine pattern of work and home life. Then one day Steve woke up to discover he was 65 years old, and for the first time he began to think about retirement. He realized he was tired of his grueling routine. But he had worked all his life and knew he would be bored to death if he stopped working completely. He must have something to do, but he couldn't keep up his present pace much longer.

As fate would have it, about that time Steve got a phone call from an old college roommate proposing that Steve, several other old college chums, and their spouses get together for a reunion at their old alma mater. After a few calls among the group, it was agreed that they would meet the following summer.

The reunion was great—it gave the men a chance to reminisce about the old days and the wives a chance to meet one another and the men they had heard so much about through the years. Steve found it especially nice to be away from the pressure of New York life and into the relaxed atmosphere of a Midwestern college town. He was impressed with the diversity, quality, and availability of cultural activities. And the fact that, by and large, people still treated one another in a civil manner.

Back in New York, he and his wife discussed their experience and agreed: they would sell the restaurant in New York and move to the college town. Steve had worked all his life; he knew he couldn't just stop "cold turkey." He decided that he would start a Hungarian restaurant in the college town—not a large one, just big enough to keep him occupied and for him to break even financially. By phone, he contacted a prominent realtor in the college town, explained what he was looking for, and waited for something to happen.

The following spring, the realtor called to inform Steve that there was a place on the market that might suit Steve. After a few more phone calls, Steve flew to the college town, inspected the restaurant, and made an offer that was accepted. He then sold the New York restaurant to a small group of loyal employees at a very reasonable price, but a price that nonetheless was several times what he was paying for the new establishment.

Steve and his wife moved from their New York apartment to a spacious, well-appointed house they bought in the college town. Today he closed on the restaurant. He knows that the location and physical plant are excellent and in keeping with his aim of providing a first-class dining experience at an affordable price. To express his aim, he has decided to adopt a modified version of the Ritz-Carlton's statement: "We are courteous people serving courteous people." And he has decided he will call the restaurant "The Budapest." In his mind he is reviewing all the other things he must do. Where to start?

◆ Discussion Questions

1. Formulate a quality policy for the restaurant.

2. List the major processes of the restaurant that will impact the quality of a dining experience.

3. Formulate procedures for
   (a) Selecting and training personnel
   (b) Taking reservations
   (c) Greeting and seating customers
   (d) Ordering kitchen supplies
   (e) Preparing food
   (f) Cleaning the restaurant

4. Formulate instructions for
   (a) Setting a table
   (b) Serving a customer
   (c) Cleaning the restaurant

Toyota Supplier Development[2]

Automobile producers face daunting challenges as they bring together diverse resources to make products. Automobiles contain thousands of parts, many obtained from outside suppliers. To maintain high productivity and quality, automakers must devise complex systems for supplying parts from diverse sources to different stages of production: casting, forging, machining, plastic forming, stamping, body welding, painting, and final assembly.

Toyota uses the Toyota Production System to synchronize activity throughout its own production sequence. Increasingly, the company is working toward having its American suppliers fit into the Toyota Production System, even to having its suppliers apply this system within their own operations.

This case focuses on the role of the purchasing department at Toyota Motor Manufacturing (TMM) in developing suppliers. It also describes the activities of a new organization, the Toyota Supplier Support Center (TSSC), which is beginning to apply the Toyota Production System in a variety of manufacturing settings.

◆ TMM's Purchasing Department

The purchasing department in Georgetown, Kentucky, is engaged in a number of activities to develop its North American supply base. These activities are described below.

Growing the Supply Base

TMM has made significant progress in developing its domestic supply base. When TMM began production in July 1988, it was doing business with 92 suppliers of

---

[2]This case was written by Gregory Bounds. Reprinted with permission of The McGraw-Hill Companies from Gregory Bound (*Cases in Quality*, Homewood, Il: Business One Irwin), 1996.

production parts, components, and raw materials. In late 1991, as TMM launched production of a new model (the 1992 Camry), the number of U.S. suppliers significantly increased to 174 (in dollar volume, that's about $1.5 billion). The introduction of a new model in a few years will allow TMM to involve even more suppliers at the design phase.

TMM is currently expanding its Georgetown, Kentucky, facilities, which will double its production volume and at least double its need for suppliers. The dollar volume of domestic purchasing should be close to $4 billion when TMM reaches full production in the expanded facilities. TMM's domestic supply base grew from roughly 60 percent when it started production in 1988 to around 75 percent in 1992. TMM forecasts that its domestic supply base will be over 80 percent in the near future.

Purchasing Strategy[3]

By operating in Georgetown, Kentucky, TMM is implementing Toyota's worldwide corporate strategy to manufacture in all of its major markets. Toyota also attempts to use as many domestic local suppliers as possible in order to support the economies in which they operate. From a practical viewpoint, it makes more sense to buy parts locally than to ship them from Japan. With domestic suppliers, TMM does not have to deal with massive quantities of rejected material if there is a quality problem. And if there is an engineering change, TMM does not have to deal with large quantities of obsolete materials. Problems are more easily resolved by dealing with suppliers "just down the road" rather than on another continent.

TMM's sourcing criteria are similar to those you might find in any large industrial company. Three very common criteria include quality, price, and delivery. What differentiates TMM from other producers, however, is the extent to which it wants to know how the supplier manages his or her company. As Tom Zawacki, TTM's assistant general manager of purchasing, explains,

> We are very interested in organizations that embrace the concepts of total quality control. We look at how a supplier invests in itself to prepare for the future: how they invest in plant, equipment, technology, research, and their human resources; how they motivate their workforce; and how they keep their workforce on a leading edge of technology and know-how. We believe that suppliers who invest in themselves are the ones who will be there in the future. Most importantly, the automotive industry is fiercely competitive—many suppliers have fallen by the wayside in the last 10 years or so. And many more may continue to fall. Those who make this kind of self-investment stand a better chance of survival than those who don't.

---

[3]We have shortened the comparison of the traditional versus the Toyota purchasing strategies.

Roughly 70 percent of the manufacturing cost of a Toyota vehicle derives from outsourced parts and materials. Toyota does not attempt to control these costs via annual competitive bidding and flip-flopping of sources to take advantage of lower prices. It does attempt to maintain competitive pricing by developing its suppliers: that is, developing relationships that encourage suppliers to become more cost competitive and quality oriented.

Policy Deployment

Each year TMM sets goals and objectives based on its company philosophy, long-term targets, and long-term major activities (see Display 1). As an example, one long-term target may be to manufacture the highest quality vehicle in North America. An annual objective to help reach this target, for example, might be to reduce defects by 10 percent. Each department then develops its goals and objectives to support this annual objective. For instance, the purchasing department might make plans to increase supplier defect detection capability and reduce part defects by 50 percent. Then the parts and components section of the purchasing department develops two objectives to support that specific department objective: 1) prevent incorrect part shipment, and 2) work toward built-in supplier quality. At the assistant manager level, the unit objective is to check the supplier's quality system. Finally, the buyer makes plans to arrange the supplier visitations and to establish a survey check sheet. This is a hypothetical example of how to get from a general target to a specific means of accomplishing it.

DISPLAY 1 ◆ Policy Deployment—Development of Annual Objectives

Supplier Expectations

TMM also translates its annual objectives into broad objectives and expectations for suppliers. The five broad policy categories that TMM sets for its suppliers, along with the 1992 general expectations for suppliers, are listed below:

1. *TMM/supplier relationship development*
    - For suppliers carried over from model 474 we must strengthen our relationship and deepen supplier understanding of TMM's philosophies and expectations.[4]
    - For new suppliers we must build the foundation that will enhance mutual trust and benefit and lead to mutual prosperity.

2. *Production efficiency and delivery capability*
    - Enhance your plant-site management system in order to establish just-in-time delivery to TMM.
    - Rapidly achieve efficient levels of production for 789 by utilizing your experience gained in startup of 787.

3. *Quality assurance for current and new models*
    - Improve supplier built-in quality capability and prevent shipping defects to TMM by improving in-process inspection standards and overall work standards.
    - New-product quality preparation.
        - a. Optimize your quality assurance system for 789 and quickly achieve high levels of quality at production volumes.
        - b. Ensure 088T built-in quality capability for production during the prototype program activities.

4. *Cost reduction and cost control*
    - Strengthen supplier participation in Value Analysis (VA) activities for 787 and 789 programs and other joint cost reduction opportunities.
    - Work on greater localization for your products' purchased components or materials to increase their North American value added and decrease cost.

5. *Other*
    - Encourage utilization of minority-owned businesses.

TMM also sets individual supplier expectations based on the need of that supplier in the areas of quality, delivery, and cost and then perhaps in other areas such as communication. For example, Display 2 lists TMM's expectations for an unnamed supplier. TMM expected this supplier to: ship less than 0.01 percent defects; have fewer than 10 quality problem reports per year; have zero field claims;

---

[4]This number, as well as the following numbers, refer to specific models and parts.

DISPLAY 2 ◆ TMM's Expectations for a Supplier

Supplier name

Expection targets—(OEM parts)

Area	Measurement	Expectation Target	Formula
Quality	Received parts defect ratio	< = .010%	Total number of scrap tag parts / Total number of parts shipped
	Quality problem report	10 per year	Number of QPRs received (per year)
	Critical field claim	0	
Delivery	Delivery performance ratio	100%	Number of unmodified manifests / Total number of manifests
Cost	Design VE/VA proposal dollar ratio (cost of parts)	5.0%	Total accepted dollars of "VE/VA proposals" / Total sales amount to TMM

achieve 100 percent on-time delivery (which TMM expects of all suppliers); and reduce parts costs by 5 percent through value engineering/value analysis (VE/VA) design improvements. Examples of VE/VA improvements include: remove bolt, replace paint with plating, change steel material specification, eliminate rubber insulator, replace specialty fasteners with common fasteners, and eliminate functional quality test.

Monitoring Supplier Performance

Throughout the year TMM provides some checking mechanisms. For example, on a monthly basis TMM gives summary feedback to suppliers in a formal report (see Display 3) and asks them to read it, sign it, and send it back to TMM if they have any disagreement. The report provides suppliers with information they can use to solve problems.

DISPLAY 3 ◆ Supplier Performance Report

Toyota Motor Manufacturing USA
Supplier Performance Report

10/16/92

Supplier name: Supplier code:
Subject: Quality and Delivery Performance for September 1992.
Your performance for this month and YTD (year-to-date):

	Area	Item	Expectation Target	Performance Results This month	YTD
Results	Quality	Total # of defective parts		34	1639
		Total # of parts shipped		197705	1651034
		Defect ratio	0.030%	0.017%	0.099%
		# of QPR	10	1	24
	Delivery	# of unmodified manifests		160	1570
		Total # of manifests		188	1655
		Delivery ratio	100%	85.11%	94.86%
		# of mixed Kanbans	0	1	16

DISPLAY 4 ◆ Quality Problem Analyses for Defects

Defect	Cause Analysis	Countermeasure
Bolt missing	Process skipped by operator	• Additional operator training • Add visual standardized work chart for operator reference • Temporary 100% inspection
Slot/hole missing	Auto press skipping punching operation	Add automatic poka yoke inspection device to auto press
Paint chipping on finished parts	(1) Operator packaging method (2) Packaging design not satisfactory	(1) Additional operator training (2) Propose alternative package design to TMM-PC
Plating adhesion	Plating solution quality problem	• Contact solution supplier for countermeasure • Revise receiving audit/certification standards
I.D. mark in wrong location	Auto mark application equipment malfunction	• Repair mark application equipment • Implement schedule preventative maintenance program

Since problems cannot be solved with old information, TMM also has daily or weekly conversations with suppliers. TMM then requires the supplier to conduct a quality problem analysis, for example, to identify countermeasures the supplier can take to eliminate the causes of defects (as illustrated in Display 4). Similar analyses are expected for delivery problems (as illustrated in Display 5). The supplier also assigns personal responsibility to a manager and a due date for putting in place the countermeasures.

Each quarter TMM also sends a report to the president or the highest appropriate executive of the company. As Tom Zawacki explains, "We want him or her to be accountable for his or her company, in terms of their performance to our expectations. So while we communicate very clearly to the supplier's top managers at the beginning of the year, we also communicate clearly each quarter and ask them to take a look and to get actively involved in making sure their company is meeting Toyota's expectations." For key suppliers (key either in dollar volume or strategic importance), TMM takes additional steps to ensure they are making plans to meet TMM objectives.

DISPLAY 5 ◆ Quality Problem Analysis for Delivery

Problem	Cause Analysis	Countermeasure
Mixed kanban for 12345-67890 and 67890-12345 Qty = 3	• Parts very similar in appearance • Operator did not check part number	• Additional operator training • Monitor standardized work usage • Display sample parts on-line for operator reference
Kanban missing from container when delivered Qty = 6	• Container kanban holder damaged causing kanban to fall from container in shipment	• Immediate 100% inspection/ maintenance of all containers • Establish scheduled inspection/ maintenance program for containers
Mixed kanban for 23456-78901 and 34567-89012 Qty = 7	• Internal process flow (kanban) card placed in wrong parts	• Add TMM kanban card number to internal process flow card for cross-reference

The key purchasing members (vice president, assistant general manager, managers, assistant managers, and the buyer) from TMM meet with the supplier's top management (COO, the sales account representative, and senior sales, manufacturing, and quality managers). They either meet in the Georgetown, Kentucky, facility or the TMM team visits suppliers at their facilities to hold face-to-face discussions. The TMM team and the suppliers top management team discuss their specific expectations. The supplier explains how it has developed an operating policy to meet TMM expectations and discusses the current results.

After the supplier makes its presentation, TMM coaches and advises the supplier. TMM may offer some criticism, but it is constructive and intended to help the supplier improve. Remember, the purpose is to build long-term trust and mutually beneficial relationships. TMM benefits as the supplier becomes more productive and more quality oriented and as it lowers costs. (In fact, TMM recognizes supplier excellence in an annual awards ceremony.) The supplier benefits from the improvements by earning additional business.

At TMM, however, "long-term relationship" does not mean a long-term contract. Ford, for instance, has an increasing number of long-term agreements with its suppliers, which is helping Ford to establish some stability in its supplier relationships. All of TMM's contracts, however, are year to year, and they are automatically renewed unless either side wants to discontinue the contract. So far, TMM has lost only two suppliers, both because of bankruptcy. Remarkably, the rest of the suppliers that TMM started with are still suppliers today. As Tom Zawacki explains, "Our belief is that if we meet our suppliers' needs and they meet our needs, the result of that is long-term relationships."

Networking among Toyota Suppliers

In 1989, TMM established an organization to promote networking, sharing, and learning among its suppliers. The organization, called Bluegrass Automotive Manufacturers Association (BAMA), began with 15 of TMM's key suppliers permanently located in the Bluegrass area (primarily Kentucky). BAMA is patterned after a Toyota supplier network established in Japan in the 1960s.

BAMA was established as an experiment on how to provide Toyota know-how to its suppliers, to support them, and to help them become the best suppliers possible—that is, to be mirror images of Toyota. Through BAMA, Toyota hopes to create enthusiasm and passion for implementing the Toyota Production System (TPS). BAMA representatives are usually top officers in their organizations—presidents, vice presidents, or general managers of manufacturing. They are people with the clout to foster enthusiasm to actually implement TPS. The BAMA education process involves seminars, case studies, and technical presentations on such topics as the following:

High quality and cost control
History of the Toyota philosophy and production system
Various supplier presentations (success stories)

Innovative corrosion resistant materials

Toyota Production System, including topics such as quick die change, teamwork, quality system, human resource management, line stop concept, visual control, Kanban

Quality circle establishment

Suggestion system

BAMA holds quarterly meetings with top managers. Guests who speak at these meetings include TMM's president, Mr. Fujio Cho; Toyota's engineering group from Ann Arbor; motivational speakers; and TMM's public affairs department, which gives legislative updates. TMM also invites suppliers to present case studies on their improvements. TMM has discovered that presenting success stories (cases) on implementing TPS motivates suppliers. Suppliers can identify with other suppliers much more than with TMM preaching to them.

Once TMM determined that the experiment was a success, it expanded BAMA to 40 members in a larger geographic region, including Indiana, Tennessee, Ohio, and North Carolina. TMM recommends BAMA members on the basis of the supplier's interest and the foundation of an already good relationship. BAMA is not intended to fix shaky relationships but to further improve solid relationships.

After the BAMA group was expanded, TMM began also to expand the kind and depth of its activities. In 1993, for example, BAMA formed a "core" group, a working-level group composed of plant personnel (rather than top managers) such as plant managers or foremen. The focus of the core group in 1993 was built-in quality and how that relates to the Toyota Production System. Lance Lewis, a member of TMM's purchasing/technical support staff, guided the core group members in discussions of this topic every two months. TMM hopes eventually to involve all its suppliers in BAMA to some degree, but that expansion is limited by TMM's staff size.

TPS Training

TMM also offers suppliers some of the same training classes that are available to TMM team members. These are conducted by TMM's training and development center (under the Human Resources Department). The training is only for selected suppliers, such as those in BAMA. The training covers such topics as the basics of TPS, problem solving, job instruction, and standardized work. The training is conducted both at TMM and at the suppliers' facilities. TMM charges the supplier a small fee to cover costs of material and travel for the trainer.

Short-Term Support for Problem Solving

TMM closely tracks each company's performance to identify the suppliers that need help. TMM uses various techniques to correct problems that are uncovered. The simplest one is a phone call to get the supplier's attention. If that does not work, or if the situation requires immediate attention, TMM may give the supplier suggestions or help in developing a plan of attack. If that does not work, or if the problem gets very serious, TMM resorts to the short-term approach.

Short-term support is a free service that involves helping suppliers deal with delivery or quality problems that are causing TMM problems. For example, during a startup of a new model a supplier suddenly has trouble meeting the production schedule. In such cases, a TMM team will help the supplier for a limited time, possibly a month or two, by spending time on the floor to correct the problems. Short-term support is specifically focused on a critical line or particular product, with TMM personnel actually directing the problem solving and corrective action. TMM hopes, however, that the managers learn from these troubleshooting activities. As Lance Lewis explains, "We try to involve as many of the management people as possible because even though it might be short-termed and limited, if they absorb some of these ideas, maybe they will start applying the ideas throughout the plant."

Long-Term Support for Development

The last area of support TMM's purchasing department provides is what TMM calls "long-term support" (three or more years) to help suppliers implement TPS, do *kaizen*, and practice *hoshin kanri* (participative strategic planning and goal deployment). The objective is to create a culture in which the management sees improvement as never-ending. For example, Lance Lewis actually goes into suppliers' facilities and teaches them how to implement TPS. The approach is slow, methodical, and nurturing. It takes a long time because TMM has to learn about the change process, learn about the specific company, and experiment to determine what will work with that company.

For various reasons, TMM has picked a handful of companies (8 to 10) for long-term support. One of the main reasons is to gain experience with transforming the American way of manufacturing. TMM also tries to affiliate with various companies from different locations within the United States that supply different types of products and that have different management styles. It tries to mix big companies with small companies, local companies with distant ones, and unionized and nonunionized companies.

To aid TMM in selecting companies for long-term support, the parts and components section and the raw materials and equipment section of the purchasing department categorize the supply base according to the companies' ability, knowledge, and interest in continually improving. There are four categories:

1. No interest: These sell parts to TMM, but they have no interest in improving their organizations.

2. Interest but no knowledge: They want to improve, but they don't know how.

3. Interest and some knowledge: These companies can take suggestions and follow up on them.

4. Ready to implement: These are good companies that have always been successful but still have a lot of waste. TMM can work with these companies and make them excellent practitioners of *kaizen* and *hoshin kanri*.

DISPLAY 6 ◆ Supplier Support Activity Procedure for Selection of Supplier

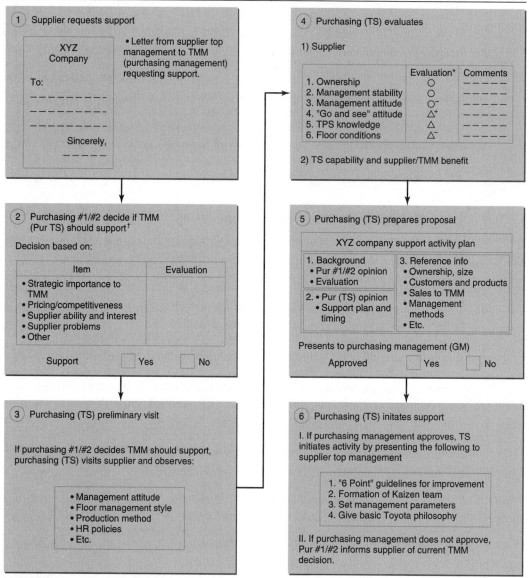

① Supplier requests support

XYZ
Company

To:

_ _ _ _ _

_ _ _ _ _

_ _ _ _ _

Sincerely,

_ _ _ _

• Letter from supplier top management to TMM (purchasing management) requesting support.

② Purchasing #1/#2 decide if TMM (Pur TS) should support[†]

Decision based on:

Item	Evaluation
• Strategic importance to TMM • Pricing/competitiveness • Supplier ability and interest • Supplier problems • Other	

Support   ☐ Yes   ☐ No

③ Purchasing (TS) preliminary visit

If purchasing #1/#2 decides TMM should support, purchasing (TS) visits supplier and observes:

• Management attitude
• Floor management style
• Production method
• HR policies
• Etc.

④ Purchasing (TS) evaluates

1) Supplier

	Evaluation*	Comments
1. Ownership	O	_ _ _ _
2. Management stability	O	_ _ _ _
3. Management attitude	O⁻	_ _ _ _
4. "Go and see" attitude	△⁺	_ _ _ _
5. TPS knowledge	△	_ _ _ _
6. Floor conditions	△⁻	_ _ _ _

2) TS capability and supplier/TMM benefit

⑤ Purchasing (TS) prepares proposal

XYZ company support activity plan

1. Background
   • Pur #1/#2 opinion
   • Evaluation
2. • Pur (TS) opinion
   • Support plan and timing

3. Reference info
   • Ownership, size
   • Customers and products
   • Sales to TMM
   • Management methods
   • Etc.

Presents to purchasing management (GM)

Approved   ☐ Yes   ☐ No

⑥ Purchasing (TS) initates support

I. If purchasing management approves, TS initiates activity by presenting the following to supplier top management

1. "6 Point" guidelines for improvement
2. Formation of Kaizen team
3. Set management parameters
4. Give basic Toyota philosophy

II. If purchasing management does not approve, Pur #1/#2 informs supplier of current TMM decision.

* Circle means good; X means bad; triangle means somewhere in between; plus sign means a little better; and the minus sign means a little worse.

[†] Purchasing #1 refers to Parts and Components section. Purchasing #2 refers to Raw Materials and Equipment section. TS refers to the Technical Support section of the Purchasing Department.

The supplier support activity selection process is depicted in Display 6. Generally, TMM selects companies from the last two categories for long-term development—those that are interested, knowledgeable, and particularly those that are ready to implement.

Long-term support is intended to promote a mutual relationship between the supplier and TMM so that these parties know each other well. TMM would eventually like to use these companies as models to illustrate to others how it can be done. TMM has even pulled the companies together once a quarter or so in "joint supplier activities," enabling them to see each other's plants and each other's problems. This joint activity draws senior executives together and overcomes some of the hesitancy they might have previously had to call one another and request information.

◆ Toyota Supplier Support Center

Despite the growing interest in lean manufacturing across America, success in implementing it has been limited. The Toyota Supplier Support Center was formed in 1992 in response to this increasing interest. The Support Center is an independent organization, not formally a part of TMM or its purchasing department. Currently, the Support Center's mission is summed up in this way: To assist North American manufacturers in implementing their own version of the Toyota Production System. Toyota feels that the Toyota Production System has given it a competitive advantage in the automobile industry. However, they no longer regard TPS as proprietary information. After all, Toyota shared it with General Motors more than 10 years ago when the two companies launched the joint venture NUMMI in California.

The Toyota Supplier Support Center is a bit of a misnomer because its mission is to assist North American manufacturers, not just Toyota suppliers. While TMM's purchasing department is engaged in long-term relationships to improve suppliers, the Support Center takes a more short-term approach. It wants to engage with a company, provide assistance, and then disengage in a short period of time (six months to a year), so it can work with a greater number of companies.

The Support Center wants to begin a project and then end it. Continued improvement, however, does not stop at the end of the project. The company typically has to do much more work to fully implement lean manufacturing. The intervention is very much an education process, not just a troubleshooting exercise. The Support Center wants to leave the company with capabilities to continue the transformation and extend its application of TPS. Although Support Center personnel could enter a supplier's organization, identify solutions with little difficulty, and make the changes in a few weeks, the supplier would not learn much from the encounter. The objective is to leave the company with some real learning that is institutionalized so people can carry on the work.

Why would Toyota want to engage in this type of work? For one thing, the center's mission fits with Toyota's philosophy of contributing to the economy in which it operates, not just by local purchasing but by developing the supplier base. John Shook further explains:

> It is a win-win situation, as everyone gets more involved in doing TPS. Everyone is going to benefit, including us. Will our competitors also benefit? Yes, but we will also benefit. As we expand this throughout the entire supplier industry, it is going to be easier when Tom [or the purchasing department] goes out there and tries to expand this business.

Support Center Activities

The Support Center engages in two basic activities to accomplish its mission: individual consultation and seminars. Individual consultation is the process of working with suppliers on their plant floors to implement TPS. To reach a broader audience, though, the Support Center also offers TPS seminars, which are less intensive and less time-consuming for the Support Center staff. The seminars allow the center to reach a broader audience. For example, in one seminar, the center's staff spent a day talking about TPS, doing a simulation, and further explaining the concepts; the next day the seminar participants visited a supplier to see TPS in practice. The Support Center feels that even the seminars should have some hands-on component to them.

In helping companies change through consultation, the center staff has learned that just talking about the concepts does not help companies change. Sometimes just talking may even cause misunderstandings, no matter how well the staff explains the concepts. So they try to teach the concepts by showing and doing. People learn best through participating in successes.

The Consultation Process

The center begins the consultation process by going to the plant floor and asking, "Where does it hurt? Where are your problems?" Suppliers typically have problems with delivery schedules, defects being returned, and too much overtime. John Shook explains: "We very specifically ask, 'What can you do about these problems?' And we help them come up with a solution that will be a TPS solution. By actually making those changes, they learn how the concepts work. Then we go back and talk with them more about the theory."

Phases of the Consultation Process

The individual consultation process has four phases: evaluation, assessment, *kaizen*, and follow-up. Evaluation means getting to know each other, explaining the center's purpose, and understanding more about the company. Assessment means determining the company's needs and deciding on the goals and targets for a specific project. At this point, the center decides whether or not to go on to phase three, *kaizen*, which is the actual intensive work and where most of the time is spent during a six-month project. Working together, the center and company devise a plan and create a "model," or " ideal" line, one area of the plant that is set up in

TPS fashion. They choose an area of the plant that would be good to learn from and that would serve as a model to expand the concepts throughout the plant and then throughout the entire company.

In the follow-up stage, the center expects the company to do the next project then on its own. During that next project the center takes a more "hands-off" approach, but it still offers advice.

The center develops a set of indicators (such as pieces produced per labor hour, quality defects, inventory) for each project. They also set specific targets. Thus, productivity should go up (by a factor of 2 or 3, or even 5 times), quality defects should go way down (say, from 25 percent to below 5 percent), and lead times should be cut from weeks to hours. It all happens only on this model line and not the entire plant, but the impact of the changes is obvious. One company was shocked that once its buffer or safety stock went away, it was still able to make shipments. In fact, it totally eliminated emergency air freight shipments and shortened lead times so it could meet the production schedules.

The following discussion of Harvard Industries illustrates how Toyota's efforts to improve its supply base can dramatically improve the performance of a supplier.

Consultation at Harvard Industries

Harvard Industries Die Casting Division has a plant in Ripley, Tennessee, about an hour and a half outside of Memphis. It employs about 300 people producing items such as head covers for Toyota and for the Big Three domestic producers. Harvard managers anticipated more business, so they wanted to double their productivity. Staff from the Support Center and Harvard managers have worked together on some specific projects to implement TPS and achieve their productivity goal. The before-and-after conditions are described below.

Work Flow Simplification

Work flows were simplified by eliminating steps between machining and shipping. When the project started, parts came from the machining area, where they were machined, then wrapped in a plastic bag to be sent out to a painter. After the parts returned from the painter, they were unwrapped and shipped back to the assembly process; after assembly, they were inspected and then stored until it was time to ship them. Whole pallets of parts were then wrapped in a plastic film prior to being staged and shipped. Between each step of the product flow, there were piles of work-in-process (WIP) inventory. After the TPS changes, the painting process was eliminated, so the parts now flow from machining directly to assembly and to inspection. They are then immediately wrapped and staged. The parts are shipped one day a week. These changes eliminated several work steps and cleared a lot of formerly cluttered floor space.

Before the intervention, Harvard produced very large batches. It would send an order for production to the die-cast operations, and die-cast might run for four days, building an enormous parts inventory. Machining would then try to run all of these parts through its operations. They then shipped parts to a painter, and the painter required a batch of at least 2,500 parts before he would paint.

The TPS intervention concentrated on what Harvard calls "secondary operations," which includes machining and assembly. The operations are now arranged in a continuous flow line, a U-shaped cell. With flexible manpower, Harvard can run the line with one, two, or three people, depending on the level of demand for products. The only work-in-process inventory in the U-shaped cell resides at the vibratory unit and the washer and dryer. While performing operations, the vibratory unit, which removes burrs that remain after machining, holds about 15 units at one time, and the washer and dryer holds about 30 pieces at one time.

Standardized Work

Another important part of the change to TPS was the introduction of standardized work.[5]

Push System versus Pull System

Harvard's old system of batch production can be characterized as a "push" system, one driven by monthly information flows and production schedules. This system involved excessive lead times to produce 3,200 sets of left- and right-hand pieces for a particular week. Lead times ranged from 2.5 to 5 days in each of the casting, machining, and assembly operations, not to mention the external painting operations, which are not as predictable, and general stagnation in the system.

By contrast, the new TPS approach can be described as a "pull" system. Production information comes from TMC in Japan to Harvard's materials control department, which uses a "leveling board" to keep track and indicate how many boxes should be pulled each 20 minutes. Currently, the department pulls five boxes every 20 minutes. There are five magnets on the board, and every time the material handler pulls one, he or she moves the magnet down and shows it has been pulled. Thus, the board represents the production instruction that feeds into secondary operations (machining and assembly).

Secondary operations and die-cast are linked by a "store" located in die-casting. Whenever secondary operations need parts, they withdraw them from the store. When they pull a certain number, a signal flows back to die-casting to order more production. If the signal does not go back to die casting, diecasting does not produce.

Performance Indicators

The changes at Harvard (from March 1992 to June 1993) resulted in a number of measurable improvements, including the following:

- Scrap percentage is down from 10.6 to 0.5 percent.
- Productivity performance is up from 13 to 118 good pieces per man-hour (due to elimination of wasteful activities such as having to wrap and unwrap parts before and after painting).
- Production lead time (how long it takes to get one pallet of product out) was reduced from 298.7 minutes to 66 minutes. (The before time excludes

---

[5]Here we have omitted several technical details regarding the production layout at Harvard Industries.

the actual painting process and the lead time it took for the parts to be shipped to and from the painter.)

◆ Work-in-process inventory (right-hand parts only) was reduced from 13,140 to 1,000 pieces.

Harvard managers were impressed when they started to see the improved productivity performance, measured in good pieces per man-hour going up (as shown in Display 7), and scrap starting to go down with just a few small changes. Also, the space savings on the formerly cramped and cluttered floor were dramatic. These early positive outcomes rekindled management's interest in further pursuing TPS and *kaizen* improvements.

Harvard has also introduced TPS changes into its other product lines, for example, in the line that produces head covers for the Northstar program of Cadillac. These developments at Harvard illustrate Toyota's intention to set up an ideal line for a company to help it learn and to provide a basis for duplicating the line elsewhere.

DISPLAY 7 ◆ Productivity Performance: Toyota Assembly

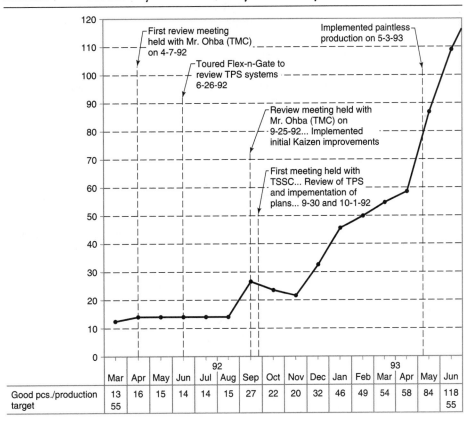

	Mar	Apr	May	Jun	Jul	Aug	Sep	Oct	Nov	Dec	Jan	Feb	Mar	Apr	May	Jun
Good pcs./production target	13 55	16	15	14	14	15	27	22	20	32	46	49	54	58	84	118 55

Review of Harvard's Original Goals

Before introducing the TPS changes described above, Harvard managers anticipated that their volume would increase significantly. They were not confident, however, that they could meet the growing demand. So they wanted to double productivity, and they thought they would have to buy new equipment to do so, which would mean increasing costs. In contrast, the Toyota Supplier Support Center suggested that there was no reason for cost to go up. If anything, costs should go down, since Harvard probably had too many casting machines to begin with and there was no need to purchase more. By eliminating waste and increasing the efficiency of Harvard's operation, Toyota helped increase Harvard's capacity 500 percent at no cost.

Creating the Future

The results that Harvard enjoyed from implementing TPS are not uncommon among other Toyota suppliers. For the suppliers, these results mean an even stronger business relationship with Toyota, improved employee morale, and more financial security and prosperity. For Toyota, these results are encouraging and provide even more impetus for continuing to develop its supply base through various activities of the purchasing department and the Supplier Support Center.

In the long run, Toyota will be supported by a supply base that offers higher quality, lower cost, and exact deliveries. Ideally, all Toyota suppliers will successfully fit into the Toyota Production System and create a smooth, continuous flow, with short lead times and quick response to customer demands. This is the future that Toyota strives to create.

◆ Discussion Questions

1. From the supplier's perspective, describe the pros and cons of being a supplier to Toyota.

2. Describe Toyota's philosophy for dealing with its suppliers by listing a set of principles or general guidelines that the company might use to guide its actions.

3. Explain how the Toyota Production System encourages managers to continually improve quality.

4. How does Toyota's approach to supplier development bring to life the systems view of organizations?

5. Both the TMM Purchasing Department and the Toyota Supplier Support Center are interested in developing better supplier relationships. Describe differences, similarities, and synergism.

6. What are some of the measures used to document success?

The Pancake Dilemma[6]

Harry Cook is the Chief Breakfast Cook at Millie's Diner and Grill. One of the items on Millie's breakfast menu is "Homemade Sourdough Pancakes." Several varieties of these pancakes are offered; plain pancakes, or pancakes with a small variety of fruit in the dough. For example, there are pancakes with blueberries, strawberries, or raspberries, and so on.

The pancakes are cooked on a $54'' \times 26''$ grill that has eight burners. The grill is also used to cook bacon, sausage, and french-toast. Eggs and omelets are pan-fried; the grill is not used.

A good breakfast cook usually has several years of experience. Different items on a plate have different cooking times and should finish cooking at about the same time. Thus, these items should have different start times. In addition, the cook often has to juggle up to six or seven orders at once; he or she doesn't have time to continually look up at the written orders for verification, even though they are placed on clips just above the cook's eye level. Once the plate is loaded, it is put on a warming table along with the written order, and a light is used to notify the waiter or waitress that an order is ready. The cook also has to continually monitor the availability and placement of raw materials; a helper is notified when items need replenishment. The cook's helper also does much of the cleaning and raw material preparation, some of the cooking, and checks the plates on the warming table against the written order to ensure that each order is correct.

Harry has seven years' experience. He is proud of the fact that he can easily handle a fast-paced breakfast rush without allowing the orders to back up or making very many mistakes. He has had the same helper for six months now and privately concedes that his helper is almost ready to become a cook on his own.

One day, Harry walks out into the diner from the kitchen during his customary 10:00 A.M. break, and spots his friend Joe sitting at one of the back booths. Watching

---

[6]This case was written by Martin Broin, Texas A&M International University, Laredo, Texas 78041.

his coffee cup carefully to make sure that he doesn't spill, he heads toward Joe. Harry gingerly sets his coffee cup on the table, plops down across from Joe, and says, "Joe, how's it going?" Joe nods while forking in another mouthful of pancake.

About this time Millie stumps over, thrusts a small card at Harry, and rasps, "Here's another complaint about your pancakes." She heads quickly back to the cash register as a customer begins ringing the small bell for attention.

Harry squints down at the card. "Damn," he whispers. He reads from the customer comment card, "Too tough." He settles back on the bench, takes a noisy sip of coffee, and sighs loudly.

"Is Millie mad at you?" asks Joe with concern.

"Yeah." Harry sighs again. He takes a gulp of coffee, then continues, "She started kidding me about the pancakes a couple of weeks ago. I tried changing some things, but that just seems to make things worse."

Joe frowns at his plate and starts poking the remains of his pancake with his fork. "This one seems alright. Are all of the complaints about tough pancakes?"

"Naw," Harry replies, leaning his head on the bench—back to stare at the ceiling. "One day they're too heavy. Another—they're not done in the middle. They're too thin. They're too cold. One's too small. Too sour. Not brown enough." He trails off with another hearty sigh.

Joe looks up brightly and asks, "Do you or Millie still have the complaints? Maybe we can spot a trend or something."

"Naw, Millie throws them out after a day or so."

Joe asks you to help Harry.

◆ Discussion Questions

1. What characteristics constitute a "good quality pancake?" How would you go about measuring these quality characteristics?

2. What process characteristics contribute to a "good quality pancake?" How would you go about measuring these process characteristics?

3. What are the relationships between the various characteristics identified in questions 1 and 2?

4. Determine a pancake quality improvement plan. What data would you collect? How often? How would you analyze the data? How should the analysis be used to facilitate improvement?

Xerox Puts the Customer First: A Powerful Competitive Strategy[7]

Introduction

The "customer" has become business's key focal point in the 1990s. Everyone is talking about the need to understand customer requirements, capture the words of the customer, and do what's right for the customer. Frequently, too few organizations have put the strategies and systems in place to deliver on this commitment. In addition, most organizations do not really understand the bottom-line benefits of providing excellent customer service and support.

A recent study in the *Harvard Review* has reported that customer service can boost profits from 25 percent to 80 percent, depending on the specific industry. There are many intangible benefits as well, giving a company substantial advantages over its competition.

---

[7]This case was written by Norman E. Rickard, President of Xerox Business. Reprinted with permission from The McGraw-Hill Companies from Gregory Bounds, *Cases in Quality* (Homewood, Il: Business One Irwin, 1996).

Customer Orientation

The heart of Xerox's approach to Total Quality Control (TQC), which we call Leadership Through Quality, is the customer. Our focus begins with the customer—the most important asset a company can have.

The foundation for our TQC approach was laid back in the early 1960s, when Xerox established a philosophy built on six principles:

- We succeed through satisfied customers.
- We value our employees.
- We aspire to deliver quality and excellence in all we do.
- We require a premium return on assets.
- We use technology to develop market leadership.
- We behave responsibly as a corporate citizen.

This philosophy, which starts with a customer focus, also emphasizes our most valuable internal asset, our employees. The remaining principles support the cornerstone of our corporate philosophy of succeeding through satisfied customers. This philosophy has served as our guide since the early 1960s, when it was first written by Joseph Wilson, our founder.

Developing customer orientation and putting it into daily practice, however, is often easier said than done. That was the case with Xerox, and it continues to be the challenge today. In the early to late 1960s, when we were the dominant player in the copier/duplicator business, we lost sight of the customer. As a consequence, competition was able to capture a significant share of the market—a market we created with the introduction of the first plain-paper copier in 1959. Competition increased to the point that it threatened the very survival of Xerox in the early 1980s.

Recognizing the competitive threat at hand, David Kearns, our CEO, called the top 25 Xerox executives together in early 1983, at our Leesburg Training Center outside Washington, DC, to focus on changes required to meet the competitive challenge. During this meeting the senior team agreed to embark on a Total Quality Journey and wrote the Xerox Quality Policy. The policy, which has remained unchanged since 1983, reads:

- Xerox is a Quality company.
- Quality is the basic business principle for Xerox.
- Quality means providing our external and internal customers with innovative products and services that satisfy their requirements.
- Quality improvement is the job of every Xerox employee.

Focusing on the Customer

Our approach is built on the foundation of satisfying customer requirements. Customers can be either external customers or internal customers, whose work outputs form a chain that supports the external customer.

"Customer satisfaction" has been the top, number one corporate priority since 1987, when the three corporate priorities were first ranked. These three corporate priorities are:

- Customer satisfaction
- Return on assets
- Market share

This ranking is driven by the belief that focusing on and satisfying customers and meeting their requirements will drive an improved return-on-assets performance and result in an increase in market share. Said differently, customer satisfaction is our priority amongst priorities, a point that was reiterated by our chairman and CEO, Paul Allaire, in recent communications to the entire Xerox workforce.

At Xerox, we believe that to succeed as a corporation we must establish a customer-first mentality and ingrain this mentality into the corporate culture. To do this first requires an organization to develop and deploy a customer-first direction and establish hard, measurable objectives to ensure goal achievement. The words of the customer must become an integral part of and drive the management process. This is achieved by providing processes—systems that operate within a supportive environment to achieve continuous improvement in customer satisfaction. Lastly, a company must incorporate the words of the customer into its reward system. If the company is successful, repeat business will follow, and customers will say, "These are the people I want to do business with." (See the inset box, Leadership Through Quality.)

But simply telling the workforce that customer satisfaction is a priority is not sufficient. We have established objectives relating to customer satisfaction. First, we want to satisfy our customers by meeting or exceeding their expectations—delighting them. Second, we want to become the benchmark in customer satisfaction in all of our customer interactions. Third, we want to ensure we have year-over-year continuous improvement until 100 percent of our customers rate us "very satisfied" with all of our products and services.

We feel that satisfying customers is not enough. We strongly believe that "delighted" customers provide Xerox a decisive competitive advantage in the marketplace, creating customer and brand loyalty. Delighted customers remain loyal, permitting retention of the customer base and repurchases of your products and services. Ideally, we would like our customers to think only about Xerox! Additionally, a company gains the power of referrals from delighted customers. Recent research shows that customers who are "very satisfied" are six times more likely to repurchase Xerox products—and to recommend the purchase of Xerox products to their colleagues and friends—than those who rate us "satisfied." Hence, the organization's focus is on going beyond just satisfying the customer.

We want to also be able to provide our customers with unique offerings. With these offerings, we are quite often able to enjoy price premiums and reduce nonconformance costs—leading to increased profit margins. These elements combined lead to an expanding market share, which in turn results in an increased return-on-assets performance (see Display 1).

Leadership Through Quality

Leadership Through Quality. The strategy required a transition team and five other mechanisms for change that continue to be used today at Xerox.

The five mechanisms are:

1. Standards and measurement tools and processes provide all Xerox people with new ways of assessing and performing their work, solving problems, and improving quality. Tools to do this include a six-step Problem-Solving Process; a nine-step Quality Improvement Process; Competitive Benchmarking; an emphasis on error prevention and doing things right the first time; and techniques for determining the cost of quality.

2. Recognition and reward ensures that Xerox people are encouraged and motivated to practice the behaviors of Leadership Through Quality. Both individuals and groups are recognized for their quality improvements whether that takes the form of a simple thank-you or a cash bonus.

3. Communications ensure that all Xerox people are kept informed of the objectives and priorities of the corporation in general and their work group in particular and how they are doing in meeting these priorities. Communications includes both formal media, such as magazines, films, and communications events, as well as informal means, such as staff meetings.

4. Training provides every Xerox person worldwide with an understanding of Leadership Through Quality and a working knowledge of the tools and techniques for quality improvement. Training is delivered in "family groups" consisting of a manager and his or her direct reports. The manager, assisted by a professional trainer, conducts the weeklong problem-solving and quality-improvement training.

After training, the manager guides the family group in the use of the quality process in an on-the-job project.

This method of training top managers first and having them participate in the training of their subordinates is called a training "cascade." This enables the management chain to practice the "learn, use, leader inspired" sequence to reinforce the quality improvement objectives of the training.

5. Management behaviors and actions ensure that the management team—at all levels of the corporation—provides the necessary leadership, sets the right tone, and acts as examples for the successful implementation of Leadership Through Quality. Managers must not only espouse the principles of Leadership Through Quality, but also practice them day-in and day-out. In other words, managers must walk like they talk.

DISPLAY 1 ◆ Customer First

Our Vision: Delighted customers provide Xerox a decisive competitive advantage in the marketplace.

Priorities Supported

The corporate priorities are supported annually by corporate objectives developed to enable and support the achievement of the priorities. For 1991, four objectives were established:

- Increase revenue growth with greater focus on awareness and coverage.
- Develop more reliable new products in less time, at less cost.
- Improve productivity by simplifying the way we do business.
- Improve employee satisfaction and motivation through increased empowerment.

These objectives are deployed by the various operating units downward through their respective organizations.

The process Xerox uses to deploy these objectives in the United States Marketing Group (USMG) is called *Managing for Results*. Similar processes exist in major operating units, although they may be titled differently. Within USMG, objectives are deployed from the USMG president to the Field Management Team, then to each of the 65 district partnerships, and finally to hundreds of individuals and teams who have specific goals and targets that support the attainment of the corporate priorities and objectives. Structurally, the Managing for Results process looks like Display 2.

Xerox defines customer satisfaction as meeting or exceeding customer expectations. We call this expected and unexpected quality. We find that when people obtain unexpected quality, they share this by word of mouth with their colleagues and friends. Customer expectations and desires are influenced by the following factors:

- Word-of-mouth experiences.
- Past or current experiences with existing or potential suppliers.
- The images a person has formulated over time of an organization's products through advertising, which influence the way they think and the expectations they develop.

This means that Xerox must live up to high customer expectations to achieve customer satisfaction.

Process Focus

In addition to placing a heavy emphasis on satisfying the customer, our Leadership Through Quality process also focuses attention on the achievement of business results through a disciplined process. We believe it is our work processes that drive business results, and improved business results are a result of improved work processes. We further believe that our work processes begin and end with the cus-

DISPLAY 2 ◆ United States Marketing Group: Managing for Results Process

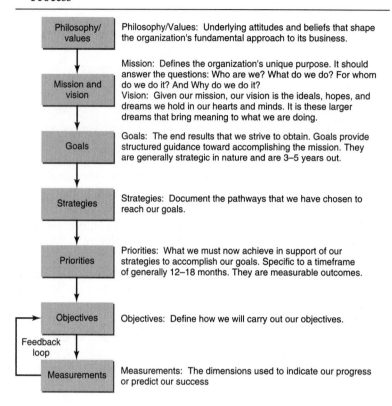

Philosophy/values: Underlying attitudes and beliefs that shape the organization's fundamental approach to its business.

Mission: Defines the organization's unique purpose. It should answer the questions: Who are we? What do we do? For whom do we do it? And Why do we do it?
Vision: Given our mission, our vision is the ideals, hopes, and dreams we hold in our hearts and minds. It is these larger dreams that bring meaning to what we are doing.

Goals: The end results that we strive to obtain. Goals provide structured guidance toward accomplishing the mission. They are generally strategic in nature and are 3–5 years out.

Strategies: Document the pathways that we have chosen to reach our goals.

Priorities: What we must now achieve in support of our strategies to accomplish our goals. Specific to a timeframe of generally 12–18 months. They are measurable outcomes.

Objectives: Define how we will carry out our objectives.

Measurements: The dimensions used to indicate our progress or predict our success

tomer. Meeting and exceeding customer requirements and expectations is a continuous closed-loop process that includes marketing, research and development, manufacturing, and customer operations. Customer operations include all those activities that touch the final customer; at Xerox this includes sales, service, administrative operations, and distribution organizations.

The schematic in Display 3 is an example. It depicts the continuous customer assurance closed-loop process within Xerox. It starts with marketing that performs an integrating function—an essential rote. Marketing obtains the words, the voice, the ideas, and the wants of the customer through a variety of channels, some of which are discussed and reviewed later.

Our research and development organizations then translate the words of the customer into specific products and services. After being developed, products flow into manufacturing, where these are not only manufactured but tested to ensure their quality meets or exceeds identified customer requirements.

After manufacturing, products are installed in customers' locations and are continually monitored to ensure that the customer is using the equipment as it was intended and it is performing to their requirements.

DISPLAY 3 ◆ Continuous Customer Assurance

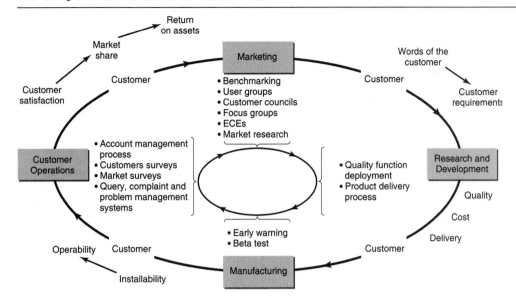

Continuing the Customer Focus

Once the product is installed, we activate an account management process. This process helps us manage the ongoing relationships with our customers. Our sales representatives are required to understand the customer's business, problems, and objectives. With this information, we can then develop solutions for our customers and recommend specific actions. Additional input is provided through customer surveys, and our query and complaint problem management systems (reviewed later) help us to understand issues requiring further attention or improvement.

Our preoccupation with the customer even extends to our new-hire orientation strategy. For the last five to six years, new technical hires entering Xerox have started work at our training center in Leesburg. Following a two-week orientation to the company, which includes being trained in our Leadership Through Quality process and training on some of our products, new hires spend the next six weeks traveling with a Xerox salesperson and service person to experience firsthand the issue of customer satisfaction. Our feeling is that these new hires will enter their technical careers with a customer focus they will long remember. Down the road, as these people begin to design and develop new products and services, they will do so with the mind-set of the customer, based on their early experience.

Gathering the "Words of the Customer"

At Xerox, we feel that any issue we find is a golden nugget that gives us an opportunity to increase customer satisfaction. A number of key approaches have been developed and used to assist in identifying these golden nuggets. Some examples of the ways Xerox captures the "words of the customer" include:

Market segment analysis: Xerox realized early on that different marketplace segments have different customer requirements. To assist us in understanding this difference, we developed and use a process to identify and understand these requirements by market segment. Display 4 graphically displays the process we use.

Starting with the customer, we identify customer samples by specific market segment and develop the process that will be used to capture those customers' requirements. With this information, we then develop a customer requirements profile, while concurrently evaluating the customer's work process. Additionally, we incorporate other sources of customer requirements that come to light—all the time collecting and documenting the "words of the customer."

We analyze, synthesize, and validate these requirements with the customer to ensure they reflect exact needs. Customer satisfaction measurement criteria are then established, and we evaluate our ability to achieve the established targets.

All this information is fed into our marketing and product-planning process, and the cycle repeats itself so that we can continuously refine requirements for that market segment.

DISPLAY 4 ◆ Customer First: Marketing Customer Requirements Understanding by Segment

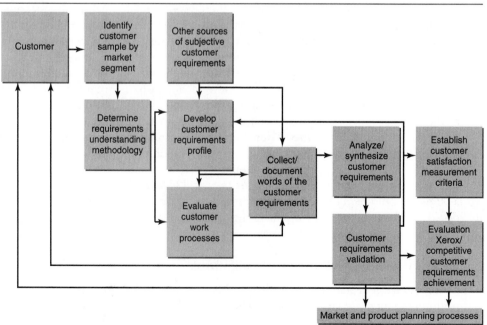

Customer visits: Xerox people continually visit customers to understand their requirements firsthand. This is supported through our Xerox account management process, in which every salesperson develops an in-depth understanding of the customer's needs and work processes. Our Focused Executive Program includes the top 150 Xerox people who are assigned responsibility for interfacing with their assigned accounts and must have at least two meetings per year to gather and understand customer requirements.

Customer councils: We employ councils that bring a group of our customers together so that we can better understand future needs and what we are currently doing right, and, most importantly, identify areas in which we can improve.

Focus groups: Xerox uses this traditional market research technique to understand customer requirements and/or problems in a specific area.

Executive Communication Exchange (ECE): These sessions bring together our customers with our top management and focus on issues the customers wish to discuss, including their future needs.

Surveys: Customer satisfaction surveys provide input from our customers on how they view us and rate us.

Customer queries and complaints: These two mechanisms provide additional sources of input that identify specific areas and opportunities for improvement.

Customer problem management system: This system is employed to identify and address customers' problems with software and systems.

Market research: Extensive market research provides insights on customers' requirements when we have requests for quotations or bids or are considering the development of a new product.

All of these mechanisms provide valuable input on customer requirements—the basis for our approach to Total Quality. Armed with the "words of the customer," we can then begin the product development process, using the customer's requirements as the basis on which to design and develop new product offerings.

Product Delivery Process

Our Product Delivery Process (PDP) is a formal process that enables us to consistently deliver leadership products and systems to worldwide markets. PDP can be defined as the cycle of integrated planning, engineering, manufacturing, marketing, launch, and management review activities that enable delivery of world-class Xerox products to end-user customers. It is important to note that each of the major functions is represented in the PDP process and they play an interactive role throughout the development and delivery process.

Although the PDP process is continuous, its specific phase structure allows timing of program activities and establishes logical decision points at which management reviews, assesses, and approves the progression through the seven phases of the process.

The seven phases of PDP, along with some of the key phase descriptors are:

1. **Preconcept:** This phase begins with identified business need/market opportunities being validated, specific product goals developed, prime architecture and technology sets selected to meet end-customer requirements, and communications established with operating units.

2. **Concept:** Technology readiness demonstrated for hardware, software and supplies; production-intent design plan reviewed and initiated; program quality, cost, and delivery targets (QCD) defined; and business case finalized based on QCD/customer satisfaction targets.

3. **Design:** Production-intent design completed incorporating full-feature set of the proposed product, baseline model built following an iterative development cycle and tested against preestablished QCD performance criteria, integrated program planning completed, program worldwide launch strategy developed and approved.

4. **Demonstration:** Product design stability and production readiness demonstrated through iterative pilot build and evaluation of production commitment baseline model; manufacturing readiness for production scale-up verified by pilot production build.

5. **Production:** Manufacturing scale-up to full production capability completed, product customer acceptability verified through formal acceptance testing, field readiness for worldwide product introduction and market engagement confirmed.

6. **Launch:** Product introduced to end-user market, product performance verified against QCD/customer satisfaction commitments, and field and market performance assessed.

7. **Maintenance:** Production build to meet worldwide demand continues, revenue and profit optimized through product improvement and/or maintenance activities, and asset management/product end-of-life strategies coordinated and translated into plans for ongoing support, and ultimately, product withdrawal and service discontinuance by the operating units.

This disciplined approach assists the Product Delivery Teams, the integrated team of people actually developing new products, to deliver products that meet the needs and expectations of the customer, while achieving benchmark quality, cost, and delivery targets. It further provides the framework that focuses all the individuals' and organizations' efforts into a seamless, worldwide quality process.

Sustaining Customer Satisfaction

Once products are developed and delivered to customers, our job of assessing the level of customer satisfaction and seeking continuous improvement has just begun. We use our Customer Satisfaction Improvement model, illustrated in Display 5, to continually assess and improve at the district level our performance in this vital

DISPLAY 5 ◆ Customer Satisfaction Improvement Model

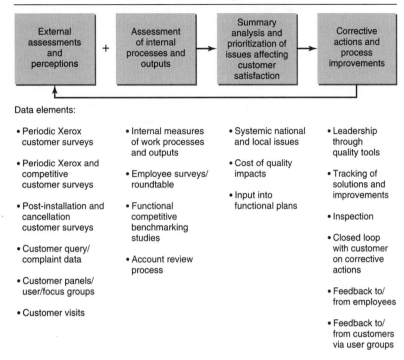

Data elements:

• Periodic Xerox customer surveys	• Internal measures of work processes and outputs	• Systemic national and local issues	• Leadership through quality tools
• Periodic Xerox and competitive customer surveys	• Employee surveys/ roundtable	• Cost of quality impacts	• Tracking of solutions and improvements
• Post-installation and cancellation customer surveys	• Functional competitive benchmarking studies	• Input into functional plans	• Inspection
• Customer query/ complaint data	• Account review process		• Closed loop with customer on corrective actions
• Customer panels/ user/focus groups			• Feedback to/ from employees
• Customer visits			• Feedback to/ from customers via user groups

area. We are intent on continuously improving the ratings customers give us on their satisfaction level with our products and services, until we obtain a level of 100 percent satisfaction.

The improvement cycle starts by collecting assessments and perceptions from our customers from the numerous sources and means reviewed earlier. We add to this information our assessment of internal processes and outputs. This includes internal work processes and their associated measurements, gathered from employee surveys and roundtables to capture input from our people.

Competitive benchmarking studies, in which we evaluate various organizations that we feel have functional expertise that we might learn from, are used. For instance, in the United States, we have benchmarked L.L. Bean, a mail-order house, for its logistics and distribution processes because we felt they were world class. In the process we learned a great deal that assisted us in improving our logistics and distribution processes.

Also, we have an account review process in place, where we formally sit down with customers to understand in greater detail their view of us and areas where we have opportunities to improve.

Using all the information developed from the internal and external assessments, we prioritize the issues impacting customer satisfaction. We evaluate the cost of quality, use Pareto diagrams to identify key issues, and then incorporate these challenges into our functional plans. We develop and deploy corrective actions to improve our work processes, using our Leadership Through Quality process and tools. We track the status of action plans, inspect the work process, and employ a closed-loop process with our customers on corrective actions being taken. This ensures they are addressing and correcting the identified and agreed upon issues.

We also give feedback to employees on their ideas and share information with them from the input we receive from customer user groups and roundtable discussions.

Our customer satisfaction improvement model is a closed-loop model that incorporates the essence of the Total Quality Control process cycle of Plan, Do, Check, and Act.

Another integral part of the Customer Satisfaction Management and Improvement System is the Post Installation Survey. This survey is administered by the district office seven days after a Xerox product has been installed. The focus is on the operator, the person who uses the equipment, and asks the person to evaluate our delivery process, our installation process, and our support activities. The information obtained from this survey is fed into the Customer Complaint Management System, and resulting issues are prioritized using Pareto charts and other statistical tools to drive a continuous improvement cycle.

Another input to our Customer Satisfaction Management and Improvement Systems is the data developed through periodic surveys conducted with customers. Our prime customer survey mechanism is our Customer Satisfaction Measurement System (CSMS). On a five-point scale customers rate Xerox according to their perceptions of our performance against their requirements:

- ◆ Very dissatisfied
- ◆ Dissatisfied
- ◆ Neither satisfied nor dissatisfied
- ◆ Satisfied
- ◆ Very satisfied

The "very satisfied" and "satisfied" categories provide us with the measurement of the percent satisfied. We are not content to have only satisfied customers, we want *very* satisfied customers.

Every customer that has had a product installed for six months or more is eligible. The periodic survey is an ongoing process, with customers surveyed at least every third year. We distribute about 40,000 surveys each month. Of these, we receive between 10,000 and 12,000 completed surveys, or a 25 to 30 percent return rate. Of the surveys sent out, approximately 50 percent go to the operators who use the equipment; about 25 percent go to decision makers, those who made the decision to buy Xerox products; and 25 percent to the administrators who handle the billing and other administrative contacts with Xerox.

Our customer survey response data is loaded into our centralized computer system, and each week the data is downloaded to each of our 65 district offices. This data provides additional input to the District Customer Satisfaction Management and Improvement System.

The heart of this process at the district level is the Customer Resolution Group. This group acts as a focal point for coordinating the resolution of customer issues and analyzes the data for the district management team. They bring issues to management and the workforce so that each can develop countermeasures to ensure that the key issues are being addressed and resolved.

One unique aspect of the District Customer Satisfaction Management Improvement System is the Customer Complaint Handling Process. Within each of the district offices is a Customer Relations Group, commonly referred to as the CRG. This group uses the Customer Complaint Handling Process, which is a cross-functional approach to resolving customers' issues. Once a customer brings an issue to our attention, the individual taking the complaint owns the complaint until it is resolved. The Customer Complaint Management System has been mechanized so customers' issues are electronically downloaded to a closed-loop system, and the system has been enhanced to enable multiple screen capability that shows the specific customer's service history, billing history, and other data.

District Partnership Management Team

Every district is managed by a partnership composed of the managers of sales, service, and business operations. The purpose of this triumvirate is to ensure that we are constantly focusing, across all functions, on customers and doing what is right for them, independent of the specific function involved. The partnership functions as a team and makes the necessary functional tradeoffs to ensure that the voice of the customer is being responded to. The partnership team is appraised and receives bonuses as a team.

The district partnership uses our Management Assessment and Action Process (Display 6) to take the words of the customer, obtained from customer surveys and complaint analyses, and drive an improvement effort. From the percent-dissatisfied information, they identify the key few dissatisfiers using a Pareto analysis. Work is then focused on using an *Ishikawa*, or fishbone diagram to understand the root cause of the problem. If the issues are under the district's control, the district develops an action plan, identifies the responsible person, and finally projects what impact the countermeasures being proposed will have on improving customer satisfaction. This process also identifies activities that are not controllable at the district level, but are controllable at a higher level in the corporation. These issues are then transferred to the organization that has the capability to fix them.

We have closely tied the partnership bonus to their performance, which is measured by customer satisfaction. Each district has a percent customer-satisfied target, and measurements are supplied from our CSMS survey. The CSMS target is tied to the district's past performance, and the target established reflects a year-over-year improvement over the most current level of performance. If the district does not meet the customer satisfaction target, there is no bonus for the district partnership—as a team. The rating factor to achieving a bonus is the attainment of the district's target for customer satisfaction. Additionally, the customer satisfac-

DISPLAY 6 ◆ District Customer Satisfaction Management and Improvement System: Management Assessment and Action

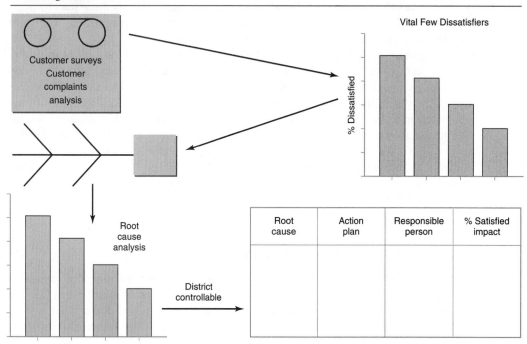

tion element is weighted at 35 percent of the total bonus—making customer satisfaction a significant element in the bonus plan.

Customer Satisfaction Guarantee

The Xerox measure of quality is our customer's satisfaction. To further demonstrate our commitment to our customers, in late 1990 we offered an unprecedented three-year Total Satisfaction Guarantee on all Xerox equipment. This guarantee is based solely on the customer's level of satisfaction with Xerox equipment.

The terms and conditions of the guarantee are simple and written in layman's terms. The Xerox Total Satisfaction Guarantee reads as follows:

If you are not satisfied with your Xerox equipment, at your request Xerox will replace it with an identical model or a machine with comparable features and capabilities.

The term of the Xerox Total Satisfaction Guarantee is three years from equipment delivery. If the newly delivered equipment is financed by Xerox for more than 3 years, the Guarantee will apply during the entire term of your Xerox financing.

> *This Xerox Total Satisfaction Guarantee applies to Xerox equipment acquired by you from Xerox (including sales agents and participating dealers and retailers) and continuously maintained by Xerox or its authorized representatives under a manufacturer's warranty or a service contract. This Guarantee applies to all equipment acquired on or after September 5, 1990, and is not applicable to equipment damaged or destroyed due to an act of God.*

This guarantee assures customers of a long-term level of Xerox support and commitment based on their individual needs and requirements.

Customer Focus Payback

Within Xerox, customer focus has a long history and tradition. In 1964, Joseph Wilson, the founder of Xerox, made the following statement regarding the customer: "In the long run our customers are going to determine whether we have a job or whether we do not. Their attitude toward us is going to be the factor determining our success."

Unfortunately, in our period of very rapid growth and business success, we lost sight of this important value and focus. However, we returned to this basic belief as we became increasingly aware of the important role the customer plays in our success.

Since beginning the Xerox Quality journey with a renewed focus on satisfying customer requirements, Xerox has achieved a substantial turnaround in its business. Since 1985, customer satisfaction with Xerox products and services, as measured by our Customer Satisfaction Measurement Systems, has increased over 42 percent. Perhaps more telling is the turnaround in our return-on-assets (ROA) performance, which has almost doubled since 1986.

At Xerox, the customer is truly king and has our undivided attention. Why? Because it makes good business sense!

◆ Discussion Questions

1. Discuss some of the tools Xerox uses to gather the views of the customer and assess customer satisfaction.

2. Discuss Xerox's process focus and its relationship to business results.

3. Identify the activities and initiatives that Xerox uses to drive a customer focus into the organization. Map each of these onto one or more of the stages of the Managing for Results Process in Display 2. Explain how each relates to the stage where you placed it.

4. What other opportunities does Xerox have for driving a customer focus into the business?

5. Relate the discussion in this case to quality function deployment discussed in Chapter 10.

Federal Express: The Vision Made Real[8]

The next time a teacher gives your most creative paper a grade of C, just remember, that was the same grade Frederick W. Smith received for a Yale undergraduate paper which contained early plans for an overnight air express venture, the original blueprints for Federal Express. Vision is the root of leadership, and Smith's plans were certainly visionary. However, succeeding in business (and making better than a C at Yale) requires more than vision. A leader's vision must also be well executed, else the vision remains only a dream, not a reality.

After a tour of duty as a Marine Corps pilot in Vietnam, Smith returned to fulfill his dream. He and his business partners commissioned two independent market research studies which suggested a market niche for a reliable, time-definite overnight delivery service. Then they executed the vision. The engines of the Federal Express eight-plane fleet first hummed on April 17, 1973, marking the birth of a new company and the genesis of a new service industry, overnight air express.

Seven of the eight packages shipped that first night were trial runs addressed from one Federal Express salesperson to another. This was an inauspicious beginning for a startup that would become the only U.S. company to top $1 billion in revenues within its first 10 years. Although competitors have flocked to the market, Federal Express remains the unquestioned leader in overnight air express, with 45 percent market share and about $8 billion in 1992 revenues. Federal Express

---

[8]This case was prepared by Gregory Bounds. Reprinted with permission of The McGraw-Hill Companies from Gregory Bounds, Lyle York, Mel Adams, and Gipsie Ranney, *Beyond Total Quality Management: Toward the Emerging Paradigm* (New York: McGraw-Hill, 1994).

commands the world's largest air cargo fleet, 420 aircraft, and more than 94,000 employees worldwide to move nearly 300 million packages each year to and from customers in nearly 170 countries. To crown these business successes, in 1990, Federal Express became the first winner of the Malcolm Baldrige National Quality Award in the Service Company category.

What is the secret to such business success? Patented business school answers include: first entrance to the market, product differentiation, innovative systems, leading technological capability, and reliable, high-quality service, These answers are all true; for example, Federal Express pioneered the "hub and spoke" pickup, sorting, and delivery network that allowed it to be the first to transport small packages and documents for customers door-to-door, from one U.S. location to another, overnight. However, the fundamental principle underlying all of these answers, and leading to Federal Express's business success and 1990 Baldrige award, was stated quite simply in its 1991 annual report: "Since our first day of operations, an intense focus on the needs of our customers and an absolute commitment to continuous quality improvement have defined Federal Express."

CEO Smith reiterated the conceptual simplicity of business success in a keynote speech before a national conference on quality and leadership held in conjunction with the Baldrige award ceremonies: "There is no secret to whatever success Federal Express has enjoyed. What we do is all in the books. Our secret, if there is one, is just doing what they say." In other words, the key to a leader's success is execution of the vision. To provide a context for a discussion of how Federal Express refines and executes its vision, we now briefly review Federal Express's current service strategies and systems for executing these strategies.

◆ Current Service Strategies and Systems

The current Federal Express service strategies were summarized in its 1991 annual report: "Our strategies are long-term and focused on one mission—to provide our customers with totally reliable, competitively superior global air/ground transportation of high priority goods and documents that require rapid, time-certain delivery." To provide superior service in an overnight air express market maturing with competition and globalization, Federal Express must continuously improve its service strategies and matching systems. Some recent improvements are discussed below.

Integrated Sales Force

In recent years, Federal Express fully integrated its global sales force to sell all of its services discussed below. Additional resources were added to its global sales force of 17,000 to support this strategy (e.g., 250 extra sales professionals in fiscal 1991). Customers are contacted in a coordinated fashion by a single account team responsible for understanding and responding to their unique needs.

Standard Overnight Service

The FedEx Standard Overnight Service in the United Sates (SOS), with deliveries to most addresses next business day by 3 p.m., was initially limited to five pounds. In 1990, Federal Express expanded the five-pound limit to 150 pounds. This service offers customers next-afternoon delivery at a price that is highly competitive with all other next-day services in the marketplace. This lower-cost option provides customers with a choice: early morning delivery with FedEx Priority Overnight Service, or delivery later in the day at a money-saving price. The customer response exceeded the forecast, and self-dilution (FedEx customers shifting from Priority Overnight to SOS) occurred at an acceptably low rate.

Overnight Freight Service

The FedEx Overnight Freight Service (OFS) was launched in 1991 in the United States to provide next-day-by-noon delivery for individual packages weighing up to 500 pounds. With advance arrangements, Federal Express will accept packages of virtually any weight for OFS delivery. Federal Express continues to offer a two-day freight service with a delivery commitment of 4:30 p.m. Demand for both services has outstripped pre-launch forecasts.

Powership Systems

A Powership system consists of a computer and accompanying devices installed at customer locations. The system allows customers to speed up the shipping process by eliminating the need for airbills. The system also performs numerous shipping tasks-label preparation, online package tracking, daily self-invoicing, and even international paperwork preparation—more quickly and easily than manual methods. The use of Powership systems by customers has grown dramatically over the last few years (e.g., by 60 percent in fiscal 1991). Federal Express plans to continue installing several thousand Powership systems each year. Over one-third of its volume and revenue each day is processed through Powership, saving customers time and saving Federal Express money.

EXPRESSfreighter

In August 1989, a merger with Flying Tigers was completed. As Federal Express integrated two very different businesses, the company's international strategy gained a clearer focus. The schedule and route structure that Flying Tigers flew and Federal Express utilized after the merger were based on a complicated system of collecting and consolidating heavy freight at key terminals around the world. Central to this system was the concept of allocations, which gave each flight a certain amount of transcontinental space allocated to each terminal it served. While this system worked fairly well in the less time-sensitive markets previously served by Flying

Tigers, it proved to be counter-productive in most cases to the time-definite high-value market thought by Federal Express to have the greatest long-term potential.

In January 1991, Federal Express launched a totally new concept called EXPRESSfreighter to change forever the way international shippers look at the air-freight market. The concept capitalizes on Federal Express strengths: global route authorities, enormous lift capacity, worldwide integrated information network, and growing sales and marketing capability throughout the world. EXPRESSfreighter combines the cargo capacity of the Federal Express wide-body fleet (including thirteen new MD-11 wide-bodied jets) with the speed and reliability of international express services to substantially reduce transit times on intercontinental routes.

Federal Express renamed its International Distribution Service to call it FedEx International EXPRESSfreight Service (IXF), a high-yielding, time-definite service for shipments of virtually any size and weight. The service is available two ways: as a time-definite airport-to-airport service, with freight forwarders, brokers, or freight agents handling pickup, delivery, and customs clearance; or as a time-definite airport-to-airport service with customs clearance provided by Federal Express.

FSTCLEAR System

Federal Express offers customers using its International Priority Service and International EXPRESSfreight Service the advantage of a worldwide electronic customs clearance system that speeds up the process of clearing dutiable goods. The FSTCLEAR system has revolutionized the way declared items are cleared through customs. The process starts almost immediately after the package leaves the origin station, and most shipments have been pre-cleared before they reach the destination clearance point. Through electronic manifesting, customs agents can "see" the shipments electronically before they ever arrive, and decide which can be cleared and which need additional examination.

These are some of the recent service strategy and system improvements made by Federal Express to make continual improvements in the value of its services to customers. These strategy and system improvements are important; however, to make the vision real and make the strategies and systems work, Federal Express seeks to improve every facet of its organization. The driving force for all of this continual improvement at Federal Express is its leadership.

◆ Leadership for the Future

A seventeen-year path to service excellence seemingly came to fruition when Federal Express won the Baldrige award in 1990. Federal Express leaders could have been content to view the award as a symbol of their arrival at the end of their journey to service excellence. However, CEO Fred Smith recognized the award as one of many fruits to be earned on the never-ending journey of continual improvement when he called the award "our license to practice." The award was simply a confirmation that Federal Express was putting in place a quality process to continually improve every facet of the company. It confirmed that Federal Express was on the right path, not that they had arrived.

More evidence of progress on that path came in fiscal 1991, when Federal Express achieved its best performance ever on its service quality indicators (SQIs), setting records for daily, weekly, and monthly service. Through quality action teams (QATs) making improvements throughout the company, operating costs were driven down while quality performance went up. In fact, head count during the year grew at only half the rate of package volume. As a result of all the productivity and quality improvements, overall customer satisfaction with Federal Express service increased 12 percentage points from the previous year.

Though he is perhaps too modest to admit it, Fred Smith realizes that such improvements result only from capable leadership. Below, you will read Fred Smith's own words describing the Federal Express vision of how to "provide our customers with totally reliable, competitively superior global air/ground transportation of high priority goods and documents that require rapid, time-certain delivery."

◈ Fred Smith on Executing the Vision[9]

Customer satisfaction is *everything.* "Quality" means nothing if the product we make or the service we give is not exactly what the customer wants. Federal Express was based on that premise from the very beginning of the company. Now, I have to be up front with you. What we do at Federal Express is nothing new, nothing original. We just read the Demings, the Kantors, the Druckers, and work very, very hard to follow their advice. It's not easy.

While we were greatly honored to win the 1990 Malcolm Baldrige National Quality Award, we still have a long journey ahead of us. And so, Total Quality Management will continue to be Federal Express's single greatest management task into the 90s. It has to be, because "quality" is absolutely the only road to a satisfied customer at the end of each and every transaction. Our mission, our strategy, our definition of service are all focused on that one goal, a 100 percent completely satisfied customer, service to *his* standards, and not ours. And that has been our goal from day one.

And so, the Federal Express story is not a typical Malcolm Baldrige winner's story. It is not a dramatic story, like Xerox's, of a giant turnaround and reclaiming of market share from the Japanese. From the beginning, ours has been a story of continuous improvement, of an intense effort to eradicate errors and to reach 100 percent customer satisfaction, and nothing less.

---

[9]This is a speech entitled "Surviving the Global Market" given by Frederick W. Smith, Chairman and Chief Executive Officer, Federal Express Corporation, in Seattle, Washington, and Portland, Oregon, on November 12 and 13, 1991.

In striving for that goal, we have become convinced that customer satisfaction *begins* with employee satisfaction. The processes and programs supporting this concept were noted by the Baldrige examiners as strengths in our application. Our winning in the service category, I hope, emphasizes the necessity of a highly motivated workforce in achieving customer satisfaction. Unquestionably, the efforts, the talents, the commitment of our people are at the forefront of our customers' perception of our quality.

Each positive daily interaction with a customer is priceless, and absolutely impossible to measure. The fact is, interactions with customers are transient. We can't "re-call" a bad experience, like we can a faulty part, fix it and put it back into service so it works right the second time. All the more reason to create a workplace that responds to the human desire to be a part of a greater mission, one in which everyone can contribute and make a difference.

For that reason, we've tried to communicate to our people in a variety of ways that their company's goals are very much in line with their personal goals. We try to do that by answering a set of essential questions:

What's in it for me?
What do you expect of me?
Where do I go if I need help?
Where do I go to get justice if I have a problem involving my career?
Is there opportunity to grow, to be challenged, and to get ahead?

When answers to these questions are reinforced with action, the next question will be from our people and most likely will be, "How can I help? Our corporate philosophy, "people, service, profit," is at the heart of those answers. Three simple words, easy to say, easy to remember, hard to do. Putting people first in every action, every planning process, every business decision requires a tremendous commitment from every manager, indeed, every employee. But because customer satisfaction clearly does start with employee satisfaction, we can't let anything distract us.

Here's the message we try to communicate to our people: the purpose of a business is to gain and keep customers. A courier's job, for example, is to work directly for the customer. Our front-line manager's job is to make the courier's job easier, and her manager's job is to make the front-line manager's job easier, and so on until, for example, you get to me, and my job is to do whatever it takes to help all of our people do their best. The concept is called "servant leadership."

One reason that task is somewhat easier at our company is that we adhere to five layers of management between our nonmanagement people and the executive suite. Now, the way those five layers look is not what you might expect. We have truly made an effort to invert the traditional hierarchical pyramid and put the emphasis where it belongs, where the rubber meets the road, with our customer-contact people. If you look at your organization chart that way, everyone in this room is your top officer's customer [See Display 1].

Do you see what happens when you invert the pyramid? Customers are right on top, where they have to be if our companies are to remain on top. If we're going to expect our people to be the best they can be, to demonstrate a people-

DISPLAY 1 ◆ Maintaining a "Flat" Organizational Hierarchy

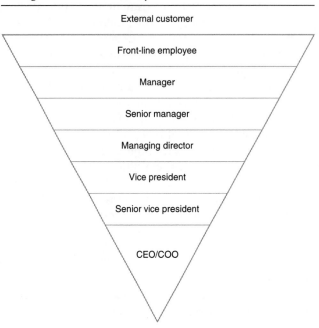

External customer

Front-line employee

Manager

Senior manager

Managing director

Vice president

Senior vice president

CEO/COO

first attitude in everything they do, and to treat every fellow employee as a customer, then we must maintain an environment that encourages it. This is critical to the way our business runs, or any company runs, for that matter. The Malcolm Baldrige examiners cited our people-first philosophy and the processes that demonstrate it as a primary reason for our winning the service award.

The whole idea of servant leadership and the internal customer concept have been practiced from the early days at FedEx, even before they became buzzwords. Of course, there was really no other way we could operate. Consider what we do. We're like a Broadway play. Our curtain goes up on a new performance every night. Unfinished work cannot be postponed, thus, we can't postpone "the last act." This imperative is supported by 92,000 people who perform according to a finely tuned scenario in which timing is everything.

A late plane out of Brussels will affect operations in New York, Anchorage, the far east, and nearly every place in between, and we have over 400 planes in the air every night. Mechanics must maintain these aircraft in top condition so that our pilots arrive on time at airports, where our couriers must sort and deliver those packages, documents, and freight, *on time*, to hundreds of thousands of customers around the world, every day. Customer service agents on five continents must be able to help our customers with their first shipment, or their bulk shipment or their overdue shipment, every day. And they must all work together to make good on our promise to our customers of absolutely, positively on-time delivery, every time.

And adding to that daily challenge are elements beyond our control, a hurricane in England, of all places, volcanic eruptions in Alaska, an earthquake in San Francisco, not to mention the usual rain, fog, sleet, or snow. These are the times when we have to rely on contingency plans, and backup contingency plans, and sometimes no contingency but the human ingenuity to make the right decision on the spot, and to *act* expediently, every time. In short, every employee must be empowered to do what has to be done in the name of customer satisfaction.

We've learned that you've got to let people take appropriate risks to serve customers once in a while, even if it means making a mistake or two once in a while. Well-intentioned efforts are just as important as successes. And, if you hang your sales or customer support people for trying to do something that doesn't quite work, you'll just get people who won't try anything. That's why we make our customer satisfaction policy quite clear:

◆ Take any step necessary to solve customer problems.

◆ Arrange the most expeditious delivery.

◆ Arrange a prompt refund or credit.

Of course, we must pay much more than lip service to empowerment. For example, our customer service agents can solve a customer's shipping problem on the spot for up to $250. And they know how to take care of the unusual; for instance, it was a customer service agent who initiated the special Federal Express delivery of a pump to Waco, Texas, where it saved the life of the little girl in the well, Jessica McClure. Our executive services people can do whatever it takes to expedite a shipment, hire a Lear jet to deliver one package if that's what it takes. And our first-line billing agents can arrange a refund or credit for up to $2,000 while on the phone with a customer. In fact, just one phone call to a managing director will allow an agent to refund up to $10,000. That's a lot of customer satisfaction for a few minutes on hold.

Setting clear goals and reinforcing them by word and action is at the heart of empowerment. Our people/service/profit philosophy guides our goal-setting process and we put teeth in our corporate goals by making management bonuses contingent upon our achieving them. If the goals are not met, no manager, no matter how high gets a bonus, including me. It tends to keep everybody "reality-focused."

Our measurable people goal is the continuous improvement of our management leadership index score, which is drawn from our annual survey feedback action program. You'll hear more about that later. Our service standard is total customer satisfaction: 100 percent on-time deliveries, 100 percent accurate information. But as I'll describe in more detail later, we use customer-focused service quality indicators to measure our service failures in absolute numbers. We call it our "SQI process." Guided by daily report from the SQI process, we focus on reducing those failures. Progress is reflected in reduced SQI points. The profit goal is to improve profit margins by a specified percentage.

Do we put our money where our mouth is? 1990 was the year we won the

Malcolm Baldrige award. It was also the first year that no management bonuses were given. But to actually make the goal-setting process work in a large organization, everyone has to understand thoroughly the corporate mission and goals, and that requires keeping everyone well informed as to how the company's doing.

In addition to our formal communication channels, we employ a variety of programs that encourage two-way communication. The Baldrige examiners cited two in particular: our survey feedback action program (we call it "SFA") and the guaranteed fair treatment procedure (GFT, in short), our internal grievance process. SFA has been a part of our quality process for eleven years. This annual survey gives people an opportunity to express attitudes about the company, management, pay and benefits, and our service. In many ways, it's not unlike most companies' satisfaction surveys.

What is different is the focus of the first ten statements, the statements that comprise the leadership index that determines annual bonuses. Those ten statements do not evaluate how closely managers supervise their people, nor do they assess how well they manage their budget. Instead, the leadership index reveals how well managers support their people and how well they empower them, as *perceived by each manager's customers*, the people who report to him. Allow me to cite three of those questions: "My manager asks for my ideas about work," "I can tell my manager what I think," and, "My manager tells me when I do a good job."

I think you can see that the value we place on our people's opinions is very high, and we send that message in a variety of ways. SFA is just one of them. While individual responses are kept confidential, overall results are passed on to all managers, who must then meet with their work groups to develop an action plan for resolving any problem surfaced.

I think you can see how SFA encourages strong, even-handed leadership and open communication, as does our guaranteed fair treatment process. The aim of the GFT process is to maintain a truly fair environment, in which anyone who has a grievance or concern about his or her job or who feels that he or she has been mistreated (for whatever reason) can have these concerns addressed through the management chain. In fact, every week our chief personnel officer, two rotating senior VPs, and I meet to review GFT cases that have progressed through the three-step internal process to the final stage, the appeals board.

Both the survey feedback action program and the guaranteed fair treatment process promote open communication. These are just two more ways we encourage people to take part, offer suggestions for improvement, question decisions, and surface concerns. Through in-house surveys, we confirmed the notion that most people in the workplace prefer their immediate manager as their primary information source. And so we focus our communications effort on our front-line managers.

As we've expanded across international borders, that strategy has made very good sense. In our case, global dispersion and rapid expansion to 135 countries established a live television network, FXTV, that, so far, reaches our people throughout the United States, Canada, and Europe. FXTV was implemented as an aid to quality deployment with no apparent ROI (return-on-investment) in dollars.

"FedEX Overnight" airs live every morning and is taped at receiving locations for viewing throughout the day. "FedEx Overnight" reports how well we did the night before, recapping operations worldwide. The regular telecast helps our people respond to problems our customers may be experiencing. This program and others fully dedicated to the quality topic give us the opportunity to demonstrate the commitment of our senior management to quality. In fact, each one of our senior officers has had a lead role at some time or other, including me.

The FXTV network has proven invaluable to our managing major changes. We announced our acquisition of Flying Tigers, for example, to our employees immediately after informing the wire services. Then, throughout the integration and final merger process, we used FXTV for live phone-in question-and-answer sessions between senior management and employees. We "go live" with our senior officers any time there is a major event that may affect our people, for example, the day after the Gulf War began, or a few days after our cost containment memos were distributed. FXTV has returned an inestimable return on our investment in people. The Malcolm Baldrige report noted its effective use in the training process along with our extensive use of sophisticated interactive video.

All customer contact people receive extensive training before they assume their jobs. For example, our call center agents are given six weeks of intensive classroom and hands-on training before taking their first call. Then we expect our people to hit the ground running with the ability to handle any customer situation. We want every customer inquiry to be handled by the first person customers talk with. Just think for a minute how frustrating it is to be passed around a company for an answer.

That is why every six months couriers, service agents, and customer service agents participate in a job knowledge testing program. These tests are on-line and can be taken at any computer terminal. This recurrent training has been part of our pilots' FAA requirement for years. And just as the FAA requires pilots who fail the tests to be taken off the line until they can pass, so are our couriers and customers agents. Pass or fail, each person receives a personalized "prescription" that targets areas requiring review with recommended resources, training materials, and interactive video lessons to help them get back up to speed.

We then try to catch people doing something right. We seek ways to reward individual and team quality efforts, and we generally don't have to look very far. For example, the "Circle of Excellence" award, presented monthly to the best performing Federal Express station, underscores teamwork. The winning station has its group photo placed in the lobby of corporate headquarters.

Our "Golden Falcon" is awarded to employees who go above and beyond to serve their customers. For example, Stephanie Flores, in southern Louisiana, hiked through flood water up to her knees to deliver one company's payroll. Maurice Jan't (pronounced Jana) scanned all of the packages he was picking up on the ninth floor of an office building in the middle of the San Francisco earthquake. Then he carried them nine floors down a rubble-strewn staircase so he could get to the airport on time. And do you know how we found out about Stephanie and Maurice? Their customers wrote to tell us about them, as they do about hundreds of other FedEx employees.

The "Bravo Zulu" (a Navy term for "well done") program gives managers the option of awarding a dinner, theater tickets, or cash to any employee who's done a particularly outstanding job.

But what is becoming increasingly more obvious to us is that, for most employees, the job itself is the reward: the autonomy and empowerment to make on-the-spot decisions to meet our customers' needs, the opportunity to design one's job, as our customer service agent task force was able to do, the opportunity to share with engineers the benefit of experience to make new technology work better, as our couriers did when we rolled out the SuperTracker, a vital link in our computer tracking system, COSMOS. COSMOS allows real-time process control of every transaction, 24 hours a day. That means we can capture more than 99 percent of customer data on all packages shipped, and remember, that's over 1.5 million a day.

Briefly, here's how our tracking system works: when a call comes into one of our twenty-four global customer service centers, a courier is dispatched to pick up the package. He or she scans the bar code on the package with the SuperTracker. Then the bar code is scanned again each time the package changes hands: at the station before it leaves your city, in one of our sorting centers before it is placed in a container to be loaded on a plane, at the destination station, before it's placed in a van, and finally, when it is delivered to our customers.

As our couriers are picking up and delivering their packages, they are continually informed through the computer in their vans about other packages to be picked up. The computer is called a DADS unit, and it automatically arranges the pickups in the most efficient order. Upon returning to his van the courier places his SuperTracker in a "shoe" in the DADS unit, immediately downloading the information into the COSMOS system. In this way, our customers can be updated on a real-time basis about the location of their packages.

Data collected through this process allows us to measure our service in absolute numbers, something we realized we'd have to do if we were serious about 100 percent customer satisfaction. As I mentioned earlier, we've been able to maintain service levels of 98 to 99 percent for several years now. However, as our volume grew from thousands of packages to over 1.5 million a day, 98 percent just wasn't good enough in absolute terms.

Just consider what we, as customers, would have to settle for from some of our most important services if things were done correctly even 99.9 percent of the time: two unsafe landings a week at Chicago's O'Hare Airport, 20,000 incorrect drug prescriptions per year, 500 bungled surgical operations each week, fifty newborn babies dropped at birth each day, and 22,000 checks deducted from the wrong bank account each hour. Can you imagine accepting that kind of performance? Why, we'd never get off the ground. We would drive everywhere, keep our money in a shoebox, and practice celibacy the rest of our lives.

We don't want our customers to settle for anything less than 100 percent error-free service from us either. So, starting in 1987, we put the full court press on refining our quality processes. We forgot about percentages and began to look at actual numbers of failures. We identified twelve major causes of customer aggravation, weighting each according to the customer's frustration level. Let me explain.

If you are expecting an important package today, say, a report from one of your international clients that has to be revised before a 10:00 meeting tomorrow morning, and it hasn't arrived by 10:30 a.m. today, as we promised, you might be worried. Maybe enough to call us. Upon hearing that the package is in Portland and will arrive by 11:30 today, you relax. Just an hour later than we promised, just an hour lost. We call this a "Right Day Late" and weight it one point because the "hassle factor" for you is minimal. By the way, we would have chalked up a "Right Day Late" error even if that document were only one minute late.

However, if your report doesn't arrive until tomorrow, the day of your meeting and your deadline is breathing down your neck, the hassle factor increases substantially. We call that a "Wrong Day Late" and give it five points. But should we lose your report, heaven forbid, and you can't begin to prepare for your meeting, then you are really upset and so are a whole lot of other people around you. That rates a ten and just the opposite from what a ten usually implies!

Every day, we add up the failure points and call the total our SQI, service quality indicator. At current package volumes, weighted points give us 60 million chances to fail every day. The first year we instituted the SQI, we averaged 152,000 daily points. The monthly average for August 1991 was 99,959. Our goal is to reduce the number to 15,000 over the next three years. We've set annual SQI goals to help us meet our ultimate goal, and when we reach that, we'll set them even lower. [For more information on the Federal Express approach to measuring service quality, see Appendix I, "Taking the Measure of Quality."]

Our quality action team program, which currently involves 1,000 teams, known as QATs, all over the world, was cited for involving people at all corporate levels. Cross-divisional root cause teams, each led by a vice president, focus on each one of the twelve SQI indexes. Divisional and work group QATs solve hundreds of little problems and come up with solutions that improve our service *and* save money. For example, one quality action team in the hub came up with a plan to reduce the training time of our document sorters, with savings to us of $3,096,000 annually. [For more information on the Federal Express approach to continuous improvement, see Appendix II, "Quality Deployment."]

Through employee involvement, FedEx's Los Angeles metro district improved "Late on the Right Day" and "Late on the Wrong Day" SQI performance by 51 percent. Quite an accomplishment, as you might guess if you've tried to get around in L.A. By fostering strong customer-supplier relationships, our procurement department reduced the number of FedEx vendors from nearly 4,000 to 100, retaining only those who practice quality processes. They saved 40 million dollars over a three-year period. To put that in perspective, our sales division would need to generate equivalent revenue of $668.5 million to have the same effect on our profitability.

When you multiply those kinds of number throughout Federal Express around the world, the vital role of employees becomes abundantly clear. For us, it also represents one more extension of our "people first" philosophy. The question is: how do we know that "people first" management and state-of-the-art technology and the SQI error reduction process really work? How do we *know* that all this is making a difference where it really counts?

The final test of quality resides with our customers. So we survey them continuously. Every day, in fact, an independent company conducts telephone interviews with approximately 150 customers, about 2,400 a quarter. Every question has five possible responses, ranging from 5 for "completely satisfied," 4 for "satisfied," and so on down to 1 for "completely dissatisfied."

Now here's where we make it tough on ourselves. We count *only* the top box, the number of "5" responses, when reporting our customer satisfaction levels. We don't collapse the top two as most surveys do, because we believe there's a lot of room for improvement between satisfied and completely satisfied. For example, how many of you use Federal Express's service? [show of hands] Keep your hands up if you are satisfied with our service. Now, keep them up only if you're completely satisfied. You see, we still have a lot of work to do! Of course, we're very proud of the fact that 92 percent of our customers report being completely satisfied. But it's that 8 percent that will keep quality at the top of our mind until we reach 100 percent.

Do quality processes have any effect on customer satisfaction? You be the judge. [We have data that indicate] the more we reduce the number of errors, the higher customer satisfaction goes. Unquestionably, the factors that will continue to push those lines in opposite directions are the efforts, the talents, and the dedication of our people. Our people made all of this happen. Indeed, employee satisfaction does lead to customer satisfaction.

No matter what business you're in, we believe when people understand the corporate mission, know what is expected of them, and *believe* they can make a difference because they are listened to and are allowed to put their ideas to work, they *will* make a difference. They will go beyond our expectations, and great things will start to happen.

Dan Yankelovich coined the phrase "discretionary effort" and defined it as "the difference between the maximum of effort and care which an individual *can* contribute and the minimum amount necessary to avoid being punished or fired." Discretionary effort is totally within each employee's control, to contribute or withhold as he or she chooses. Our challenge is to create organizations that encourage every person to *use* discretionary effort. We found that the more people are empowered in this way, the more they will freely choose to exert extra effort, and the more ordinary people will produce extraordinary performance.

And the customers? Well, they just keep coming back.

◆ Discussion Questions

1. Describe Federal Express in terms of its

    a. Vision

    b. Strategies for service

    c. Systems

    d. Approach to continuous improvement (including methods and measurements)

    e. Note the synergies among these four aspects of Federal Express. How does each aspect either support or operationalize the others?

2. What incongruities are there between Federal Express's vision, strategies, systems, and approaches to continuous improvement?

3. As a consultant to Federal Express, what changes would you propose to eliminate these incongruities?

4. The industry in which Federal Express operates is increasingly competitive. What should Federal Express do to ensure that it provides superior value to customers in the future?

5. Describe and discuss how Federal Express ensures quality in its operations.

6. How does Federal Express assess customer satisfaction?

Appendix I ◆ Taking the Measure of Quality[10]

We believe that service quality must be mathematically measured.
—Frederick W. Smith, Chairman and CEO, Federal Express

◆ Service Quality Indicators (SQI)

Federal Express developed a twelve-item statistical measure of customer satisfaction and service viewpoint. Display 2 illustrates the twelve SQI items and the relative weighting factor assigned to each. Federal Express tracks these every day, both individually and in total. Note that the greater the weight factor, the greater the impact on customer satisfaction. A customer, for instance, will be less dissatisfied with a package delivered late on the right day than with a damaged or lost package.

Here is a brief description of each SQI item:

◆ **Abandoned calls** Any phone call not answered by a customer service agent (i.e., the caller does not speak with an agent, but hangs up after ten seconds from the receipt of the call).

◆ **Complaints reopened** Any customer complaint reopened after an unsatisfactory resolution of the initial complaint.

◆ **Damaged packages** Packages with visible or concealed damage, or weather or water damage.

---

[10]The following two appendixes were shortened by omitting several technical details.

DISPLAY 2 ◆ Federal Express Service Quality Indicators

Indicator	Weight
Abandoned calls	1
Complaints reopened	5
Damaged packages	10
International	1
Invoice adjustments requested	1
Lost packages	10
Missed pick-ups	10
Missing proofs of delivery	1
Overgoods (lost and found)	5
Right day late deliveries	1
Traces	1
Wrong day late deliveries	5

◆ **International** A composite score of service quality indicators from the company's international operations. Along with many of the SQI categories listed here, the international SQI also includes customs clearance delays.

◆ **Invoice adjustments requested** The number of packages on which customers request invoice adjustments. Federal Express includes invoice adjustments granted, as well as those requested but not granted, because an adjustment request indicates the perception of a problem by the customer.

◆ **Lost packages** Missing packages, and packages that have contents missing through pilferage.

◆ **Missed pick-ups** The number of requested package pick-ups that failed to occur.

◆ **Missing proofs of delivery** The number of invoices that do not include proof-of-delivery paperwork. (Federal Express promises customers proof of delivery with each bill.)

◆ **Overgoods (lost and found)** Packages that lack, or have lost, identifying labels for the sender and the addressee and are sent to the overgoods department.

◆ **Right day late deliveries** Packages delivered after the delivery commitment time (even one minute after) on the right date.

◆ **Traces** The number of "proof of performance" requests from customers that cannot be answered through data contained in a computer system called COSMOS (Customers, Operations and Services Master On-Line System) IIB, the main computer system used to track a package's movement throughout delivery. In other words, traces indicate that a Federal Express employee did not electronically scan a package's identifying bar code into COSMOS IIB at each point in the delivery process.

◆ **Wrong day late deliveries** Packages delivered after the commitment date.

Federal Express has established a goal to reduce by 90 percent the failure points recorded when the company instituted SQI in 1988. It is shooting for 1993 as the target date, five years after SQI start-up. (The initial SQI point figure was approximately 150,000, which represents actual failures within each SQI, multiplied by the weighting factor, then totaled.) The company expects to achieve the goal despite annual increases in package volume.

During the first year under SQI, Federal Express reduced actual service failures by 11 percent, despite the fact that package volume had grown by 20 percent. By the first quarter of 1991, the company's average daily SQI score had been significantly reduced toward the five-year, 90 percent goal.

Each year, the company's service goal has been a set degree of progress toward that five-year SQI reduction goal. Determining exactly the amount of that progress is part of executive management's MBO goal-setting process. To invite widespread employee involvement in the continuous pursuit of lower SQI figures, management reports weekly results to employees via FXTV news programs.

◆ Customer Satisfaction Surveys

SQI notwithstanding, customer satisfaction surveys continue to be a significant barometer of performance. They represent a "reactive" tool for measuring service quality and as such are used to monitor improvement gains within Federal Express.

The company's marketing research department analyzes its customer base by many subjects and niches, including shippers versus consignees, document versus nondocument shippers, domestic versus international, overnight versus second-day service users, package generators (the individuals who want a package shipped) versus service implementors (the persons who actually call Federal Express for service).

Each year, the company conducts numerous customer satisfaction surveys, which consist of the following five major tracking studies.

The Customer Satisfaction Study

This is a quarterly telephone survey of 2,100 customers, chosen at random, with phone calls conducted on a daily basis. By contrast some large service organizations conduct only one customer satisfaction survey annually, interviewing a few hundred customers in the process.

The Federal Express quarterly survey covers four market segments: base business (by far the largest group, comprising the typical customer who phones in a request for pick-up service), U.S. export customers (domestic customers who ship overseas), manned-center customers (those who drop packages at the company's store-front service centers), and dropbox customers (those who drop packages in unmanned receptacles).

During a ten-minute interview, each customer's satisfaction is gauged against a fifty-item list of service attributes. Results also are relayed to senior management on a quarterly basis.

Federal Express uses a five-point satisfaction scale (completely satisfied, somewhat satisfied, neither satisfied nor dissatisfied, somewhat dissatisfied, completely dissatisfied). Unlike some companies, where "completely satisfied" and "somewhat satisfied" responses might be blended into a single satisfaction rating, Federal Express also has chosen to use "completely satisfied" *alone* as its primary measure of improvement in customer satisfaction.

In a first-quarter 1991 survey, the company achieved a 94 percent completely satisfied rating, the highest rating yet under its new five-point system. If it had combined "completely" and "somewhat," the percentage of satisfied customers would have surpassed 99.6 percent.

Says one Federal Express market researcher: "We've decided that if we combine the completely satisfied and somewhat satisfied, that won't leave much room for improvement. This new survey format puts us on track to pursue 100 percent, *complete* customer satisfaction, which is really our main corporate goal."

Targeted Customer Satisfaction Studies

The company conducts a total of 10 targeted studies on a semiannual basis. Each direct-mail survey is designed to measure the satisfaction of customers who, within the previous three months, had an experience with one of 10 specific Federal Express processes, including complaint handling, claims handling, Saturday delivery, and invoice adjustments.

Federal Express goes so far as to survey customers on their satisfaction with its credit-collections handling process. It targets the studies because a random sampling of customers typically would not include a statistically valid sample of those that had recent experience with the process in question. Response rates average between 8 and 18 percent.

Federal Express Center Comment Cards

Each Federal Express store-front business service center invites customer reaction via comment cards. Staff collects and tabulates the cards twice a year and forwards the results to managers in charge of the business service centers.

Customer Automation Studies

Federal Express equips roughly 7,600 of its largest customers with Powership shipping and billing computer systems. The systems allow customers to print airbills and shipping labels automatically, track and confirm package delivery, generate shipping-volume and shipping-management reports, and receive invoices electronically. Powership users account for about 30 percent of the company's total package volume. The annual direct-mail survey, designed to gauge satisfaction with the automated devices, has garnered response rates as high as 45 percent.

Canadian Customer Study

Outside the United States, Canada represents the largest source and destination of Federal Express shipments. Once a year, by phone and direct mail, those customers are surveyed in much the same manner as the Customer Satisfaction Survey.

By way of summary, those who oversee the Federal Express customer-survey process cite the following components as contributing to meaningful measurement:

- Consistent performance of the survey process over time, so results can be compared to identify trends.
- Customer segmentation to a meaningful level.
- Measurement by service attributes that are detailed enough to be actionable. (Professionalism, for example, is not sufficiently detailed. Cleanliness or speed in answering the phone, however, are detailed enough to be acted on.)
- Telephone surveys, as opposed to direct mail, when feasible.

Appendix II ◆ Quality Deployment

If someone called Federal Express asking for the person in charge of quality, I would hope they could speak with anyone.

—James L. Barksdale, Chief Operating Officer, Federal Express

The ultimate quality challenge for any organization is to equip employees with a common quality language and a toolbox of problem-solving skills in order to pursue continuous service quality improvement on an ongoing basis. Federal Express describes this final, never to be fully realized step as the "quality improvement process" (QIP).

Before delving further into the specific QIP strategies and techniques practiced by Federal Express, a brief overview of the Federal Express quality organization is in order.

◆ Quality Structure

The company has created a lean and decentralized quality deployment organization.

At the upper level, the company's leading quality overseer, the vice president of internal audit and quality assurance, has a direct reporting relationship to CEO Smith. Reporting to the vice president is a five-person quality department, responsible for research and development of the new quality improvement techniques, as well as for overseeing major, high-level quality improvement efforts and activities with other organizations.

Along vertical lines, the company's twelve divisions are encouraged to take ownership of quality by establishing yearly divisional quality deployment plans, linking their divisional quality objectives with the company's people/service/profit corporate goals.

Virtually every division employs a quality administrator, point person with direct access to senior division management. The quality administrator is responsible for fostering and overseeing quality initiatives within the division, for managing quality award programs, and for serving as a quality resource to employees within the division. The larger divisions also employ several employee-involvement facilitators. These professionals have been trained in quality improvement techniques and in facilitating quality problem-solving meetings. They also train other employees in those same QIP skills.

Administrators and facilitators share information and quality improvement successes horizontally, across division lines, in biweekly meetings of the quality advisory board (QAB). A similar organization, the executive quality board (EQB), is designed to promote and maintain participation in QIP at the director and senior management levels. The EQB is chaired by the vice president of quality assurance, and includes at least one representative from each division.

Briefly stated, Federal Express has decentralized its quality structure by vesting quality autonomy within divisions while providing horizontal mechanisms (the QAB and EQB) for sharing information and quality successes across organizational lines within the corporation.

Even just a brief description of the Federal Express quality hierarchy would not be complete without the company's often-repeated caveat: a service quality improvement process should not, cannot, be imposed or instilled from on high within an organization and be expected to flourish long term. Instead, the objective is to set clear quality goals for all employees, provide as many people as possible with a uniform set of quality terms, skills, and tools, then allow each of those employees to evolve into what one Federal Express manager described as a "quality zealot."

◆ Quality Training

To convey a uniform set of quality terms and tools to its work force, the company has developed curricula to teach quality theory and skills training to management and hourly employees alike.

The Leadership Institute (LI) offers training for management employees and quality administrators and facilitators, with courses developed by both the company's quality consulting firm and internal sources. To hasten the spread of the quality "gospel" across its broad employee base, Federal Express has created a Quality Academy (QA) to provide similar training to nonmanagement employees.

The extent to which all management and non-management employees receive quality training varies by division, once again in accordance with the Federal Express theory that decisions about quality administration are best made "close to home" within functional business units. Overall, Federal Express's training programs are having their intended organizational impact—to open the same quality dictionary and the same quality toolbox to the greatest number of employees possible.

Quality administrators within each division have been charged with conducting quality improvement surveys of employees who receive training, gauging from their responses the value of the training materials, methods, and instructors. The results of these surveys are used to customize training courses to the needs of each division.

What are all these Federal Express employees learning about quality? Within the company's QIP, employees master fundamentals about quality, important process-analysis techniques and problem-analysis/solution tools and quality management skills. It bears repeating that virtually all of the company's QIP techniques, terms, and tools have been imported and adopted from existing management theory and quality literature, or from an outside quality consulting firm. As CEO Smith noted, "What we do is all in the books. Our secret, if there is one, is just doing what they say."

◆ The Federal Express "Toolbox" for QIP

Quality Action Teams (QATs)

Also described as root cause teams and service teams, the quality action team (QAT) is the primary QIP technique taught in Federal Express's quality-training programs, then practiced hundreds of times throughout the company day in and day out.

At its core, the QAT is typically a four- to ten-member problem-solving team, often comprising both management and hourly employees drawn from multiple work groups or divisions. QATs are formed on either an ad hoc or ongoing basis to identify persistent service-quality problems, pinpoint "root causes," develop action plans to solve problems, then implement and track the effectiveness of solutions.

At any given time, more than 1,000 ongoing QATs focus on matters as local and specific as transporting packages from the Phoenix airport to a nearby sorting station by a more expeditious route, or as global as making major software enhancements to the company's main COSMOS IIB on-line package-tracking system.

"From our quality action teams we've learned," says Barksdale, "that success is seldom the result of a few big, technological or conceptual breakthroughs, but rather, hundreds of small innovations and improvements throughout the organization."

DISPLAY 3 ◆ Focus • Analyze • Develop • Execute (FADE)

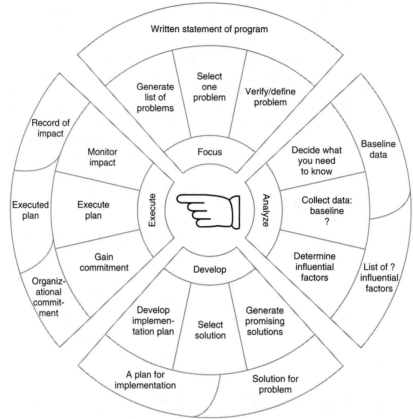

Focus
The focus phase represents the first major task in problem solving: selecting, verifying, and defining a problem on which to work. A QAT selects a single "critical" problem, often from a list of related problems that need to be resolved. Once the problem is identified, the QAT must verify and define it. The end product of the focus phase is a clear, written problem statement, which becomes the foundation for the remaining phases of the process.

Analysis
The goal of the analysis phase is to understand the primary contributing factors, or root causes, that lie at the problem's source. Typically, this analysis includes gathering and evaluating related data stored in myriad information management systems within the company.

Develop
At the development phase, a QAT builds on its analysis to brainstorm promising solutions to eradicate permanently all or part of the problem. Employees evaluate one solution against another, and develop an implementation plan for the most promising one.

Execute
The team seeks commitment to its solution from within the organization, then executes the plan and monitors its effectiveness.

Each QAT follows a four-step problem-identification, assessment, and solution process known as FADE: Focus, Analyze, Develop, and Execute. More specifically, the FADE process involves the steps described in Display 3. All employees are permitted—Federal Express would say "empowered"—to initiate and participate in a QAT. And although FADE is primarily a team problem-solving process, employees are reminded through quality training and by quality facilitators that FADE can apply to an individual's professional and personal circumstances as well.

Significantly, corporate quality action teams have been formed for each of the company's 12 SQI items. Each team, headed by a corporate officer, is charged with tracking and analyzing actual failure data for one of the critical points of value in Federal Express's service process, and then using FADE and other quality tools and techniques to seek improvements in SQI results. Hundreds of smaller, fairly autonomous QATs also function within divisions, guided in their task by quality administrators and facilitators.

To acknowledge QATs that have performed well, employees are encouraged to submit success stories within each division to the divisional quality administrators. Each administrator, in turn, passes along a success story to a committee of the QAT, which reviews all submissions. Once approved, the QAT has the opportunity to present its problem-solution story to executive management during a quarterly quality success story award presentation. Display 4 presents examples of two successful QATs.

Root Causes

It bears repeating that throughout the Federal Express QIP, the primary emphasis is on identifying critical value points within a process or organization, then locating and eliminating the root causes of failures at those points (service failures, communications failures, training failures, safety failures, etc.).

This quest for root causes is drummed home time and again, in innumerable ways, within the company. Often the concept is restated as "working on the main thing." In other instances it's framed in the context of the 80/20, or Pareto, principle, which separates problems into the significant few (those that deserve the most attention and hold promise for the greatest positive impact) and the trivial many (those which, even if solved, will not improve the problems in direct proportion to their numbers). The extraordinary concentration of QAT teams focused on two of the most numerous SQI failures is just one example of how Federal Express directs its quality improvement efforts based upon the Pareto principle. Even when root causes are found to be slightly, or even completely, outside of human control, Federal Express looks for alternative procedures and back-up systems to prevent or reduce service failures. For example, each night the company stations "hot spare" aircraft and flight crews at airports located strategically throughout its distribution system. These aircraft stand ready to be summoned on a moment's notice to compensate for regularly scheduled aircraft that are delayed by weather or mechanical failure. Even when a local sorting station has exhausted all possible options to trim the transit time from the airport to the sorting station, a

DISPLAY 4 ◆ QAT Case Studies

Hub Recycling

In 1989, when the Federal Express SuperHub sorting facility in Memphis began recycling aluminum cans to raise money for charity, a can recycler noted that the company might be missing other, potentially profitable, recycling opportunities.

Employees formed a QAT, the SuperHub Recycle Quality Action Team, including both management and hourly representatives. During the focus phase, the QAT identified several products with recycle or reuse value—including steel, batteries, paper, wood, plastic, oil, and tires—that the company was paying to have removed by refuse haulers.

In the analyze phase, the QAT identified the root causes of missed recycling opportunities as lack of awareness vis-à-vis the monetary value of such items and absence of a system for monitoring recyclable materials.

The team developed a quality action plan, which suggested performing a number of tasks:

- Draw up a comprehensive list of items with recycle, or second-use, value
- Establish collection points for recyclable materials within the SuperHub
- Create a manual system for tracking the monthly volume and monetary value of all recycled or reused materials
- Identify vendors to either purchase the materials or provide disposal services free in return for the right to resell or reuse materials
- Implement a recycling awareness communication program, which would, among other things, post notices on SuperHub bulletin boards, submit articles to the SuperHub newsletter, and produce segments on HTV (a regularly scheduled SuperHub news program on FXTV)

With approval from the vice president of hub operations, the QAT's plan was executed. For fiscal year 1990, the first year of the SuperHub recycling effort, the program returned more than $196,000 to the company's bottom line.

The QAT team has summarized its experience in a booklet that is now available to divisional quality facilitators and to the managing directors of other Federal Express facilities. Leaders of the QAT are advising others within the company who may be interested in pursuing similar recycling opportunities.

Better Back Safety

In January 1989, the Federal Express safety department's regularly published "Worst First" rankings of the most injury-prone work areas placed the SuperHub's input and nonconveyable area at the top of the list.

Employees in the area handle and sort large, awkward packages and hazardous-materials shipments. Back injuries were the major problem, with the work area averaging three lost-time back injuries per month.

A QAT was formed to focus on reducing the number of back injuries. Analysis of pertinent accident reports revealed that most back injuries resulted from lifting strain, and that employees who had been with the company less than one year were most susceptible. Of the thirty employees who had suffered back injuries during the studied period, twenty had been employed less than twelve months. The QAT identified a number of root causes: ineffective new-hire orientation, poor work habits and lifting techniques, and absence of a safety-training course designed specifically for this operational area.

The QAT developed an action plan that included:

- Refining general safety training programs to include specific back hazards posed by the input and non-conveyable area
- Creating a "new-hire checklist" to ensure comprehensive orientation of new hires
- Publishing a safety manual specifically targeted to input and nonconveyable work
- Implementing a seven-exercise "Stretch 'N' Flex" workout before each work shift
- Developing an employee tracking report for monitoring improvements

The company succeeded in getting the QAT's action plan in place by March 30, 1990. Over the next two months, there were no back injuries reported in the area.

Federal Express employee might strap himself into a seat in the cargo area of the truck and begin sorting packages while en route from the airport.

The 1-10-100 Rule

Roughly translated, the rule suggests that the longer a problem goes unidentified or unaddressed, the more expensive it is to fix. If a problem or mistake is identified and fixed immediately, it costs $1 to fix. If the problem is caught downstream, it might cost as much as $10 to correct. And if it reaches the customer, it would cost as much as $100—or worse, cost the company.

As COO Barksdale frequently points out to employees, "At least 15 percent of the cost of any product or service is spent on rework or repair. Federal Express spends an estimated $800 million annually to undo missorted packages, deal with delayed airplanes, take care of invoice adjustments, and resolve other errors. And that doesn't even include the lost customers our errors cost us."

Saturn's Blueprints for Success[11]

In the early 1960s, 7 out of every 10 cars sold were General Motors products, and over 30 other carmakers scrambled for the rest of the market. GM seemed to have a monopoly in the automobile industry and was even threatened with an antitrust lawsuit. GM considered splitting off the Chevrolet division, which by itself was still the largest car manufacturer worldwide. Of course, the split was never necessary because GM was soon relieved of its near-monopoly status in the automobile industry.

GM's market share really started to erode during the fuel crisis of the early 1970s when Japanese carmakers began importing smaller, more fuel-efficient cars. Thinking that conditions would return to normal when the energy crisis ended, GM tried to ride out the storm. Initially, GM was right. As fuel prices declined, its market share did rise slightly, but it quickly fell again. It seems that consumers found more than fuel efficiency in the Japanese imports; they also found quality. Even after U.S. automakers discovered they were up against serious competition, they reacted slowly. Perhaps because General Motors had never focused on the small-car market, it did not feel threatened. GM also had vast monetary reserves saved from its earlier success, which provided some financial security and desensitized managers to the need for immediate change.

Because market share continued to slip, top management at General Motors began to wonder if they could even compete in the small-car industry against the low-cost imports. Through benchmarking, GM learned that it had a lot of catching up to do. Alfred Warren, vice president of industrial relations, and Donald

---

[11]This case was written by Gregory Bounds and David Harrison. Reprinted with permission of The McGraw-Hill Companies from Gregory Bounds, *Cases in Quality* (Homewood, Il: Business One Irwin, 1996).

Ephlin, UAW vice president and director of the General Motors Department, began working on a new partnership that would give GM a competitive advantage. Trying to discover a better way of doing business, Warren and Ephlin established a committee of experts, including plant managers, superintendents, union committee personnel, production workers, skilled tradesmen, and other GM and UAW staff. The committee, known as the "Group of 99," showed the willingness of GM and the UAW to work together. The Group of 99 began a two month study of 49 GM plants and 60 benchmark companies all over the world. Collectively, they made over 170 contacts, traveled two million miles, and put in 50,000 hours of effort to discover how the best companies tick. Out of these efforts, Saturn was born.

On January 7, 1985, GM officially added its sixth nameplate and made Saturn a separate corporation. Saturn represented the first addition to the GM car group since 1918, when Chevrolet was added. General Motors was willing to invest a total of $5 billion in its new company, but it was not going to do so blindly. GM began studying new systems that would be required for competitive manufacturing, especially in the area that became known as People Systems. The blueprints for Saturn are contained in the "Memorandum of Agreement" jointly developed by GM and the UAW.

Saturn's mission is to "Market vehicles developed and manufactured in the United States that are world leaders in quality, cost, and customer satisfaction through the integration of people, technology, and business systems and to transfer knowledge, technology, and experience throughout General Motors." In support of their mission statement, Saturn developed a philosophy based on satisfying all of its stakeholders and a set of core values to help the company achieve its overall goals (see Displays 1 and 2). Below we discuss some of the key elements used to bring Saturn's philosophy and core values to life in its business strategy.

The Marketing of Saturn

All of Saturn's efforts are targeted toward providing customer enthusiasm. People at Saturn consider themselves and their company to be a complex system that, once fed by customer requirements, yields customer satisfaction (see Display 3). In its early stages, Saturn's biggest achievement had been the systems it had developed to give it the capability to provide customer satisfaction. Accordingly, Saturn's initial marketing efforts sold consumers on the company, not the car. The first advertisements never showed a vehicle. Instead, Saturn showed its workers, their families, and the Spring Hill, Tennessee, countryside. Saturn wanted to convey to the market that it had similar core values. With the curiosity of the American public piqued, Saturn began working on how to distribute and service its cars.

To develop a plan that used the latest in marketing innovation, Saturn sponsored a retailer council and invited dealers representing a variety of car manufacturers from all over the country. The dealers explained what had worked for them and what had not. The result was one of the most effective marketing strategies in the industry. Saturn has been able to spend considerably less on marketing than it had planned. When asked why Saturn refrained from more advertising, Training

DISPLAY 1 ◆ Saturn Values

We at Saturn are committed to being one of the
world's most successful car companies by adhering
to the following values:

Commitment to Customer Enthusiasm

We continually exceed the expectations of internal and
external customers for products and services that are
world leaders in cost, quality, and customer
satisfaction. Our customers know that we really care
about them.

Commitment to Excel

There is no place for mediocrity and halfhearted
efforts at SATURN. We accept responsibility,
accountability, and authority for overcoming
obstacles and reaching beyond the best. We choose
to excel in every aspect of our business, including
return on investment.

Teamwork

We are dedicated to singleness of purpose through the
effective involvement of members, suppliers, dealers,
neighbors, and all other stakeholders. A fundamental
tenet of our philosophy is the belief that effective
teams engage the talents of individual members
while encouraging team growth.

Trust and Respect for the Individual

We have nothing of greater value than our people! We
believe that demonstrating respect for the
uniqueness of every individual builds a team of
confident, creative members possessing a high
degree of initiative, self-respect, and self-discipline.

Continuous Improvement

We know that sustained success depends on our
ability to continually improve the quality, cost, and
timeliness of our products and services. We are
providing opportunity for personal, professional, and
organizational growth and innovation for all SATURN
stakeholders.

Director Gary High replied, "What good would extra demand do for us? We're already selling every car we can make!"

At the heart of the Saturn sales strategy is the Market Area Approach (MAA) outlined in Display 4. This approach is a form of area franchising, which grants each dealer exclusive rights to a given geographic area. With a protected franchise, dealers are assured that competition will come only from other manufacturers and not their own peers. In return for exclusive rights, Saturn dealerships enter a strict franchising agreement prohibiting sales of any cars not made by Saturn. All sales locations must also meet design standards that include everything from the sign with

DISPLAY 2 ◆ Saturn Philosophy

We, the SATURN Team, in concert with the UAW and General Motors, believe that meeting the needs of Customers, Saturn Members, Suppliers, Dealers, and Neighbors is fundamental to fulfilling our mission.

To meet our customer needs:

◆   Our products and services must be world leaders in value and satisfaction.

To meet our members' needs:

◆   We will create a sense of belonging in an environment of mutual trust, respect, and dignity.

◆   We believe that all people want to be involved in decisions that affect them, care about their jobs and each other, take pride in themselves and in their contributions, and want to share in the success of their efforts.

◆   We will develop the tools, training, and education for each member, recognizing individual skills and knowledge.

◆   We believe that creative, motivated, responsible team members who understand that change is critical to success are Saturn's most important asset.

To meet our suppliers' and dealers' needs:

◆   We will strive to create real partnerships with them.

◆   We will be open and fair in our dealings, reflecting trust, respect, and their importance to Saturn.

◆   We want dealers and suppliers to feel ownership in Saturn's mission and philosophy as their own.

To meet the needs of our neighbors, the communities in which we live and operate:

◆   We will be good citizens, protect the environment, and conserve natural resources.

◆   We will seek to cooperate with government at all levels and strive to be sensitive, open, and candid in all our public statements.

By continuously operating according to this philosophy, we will fulfill our mission.

the Saturn logo to the red canopy over the front door. Service sites are modeled after the service training center in Spring Hill, and every sales person and service technician must first go through the center's intensive training before they set foot on a Saturn facility. These high standards together with a "no hassle" sales policy has helped ensure growing customer demand for Saturn cars.

DISPLAY 3 ◆ Saturn Quality Network for Suppliers, Dealers, and Business Units

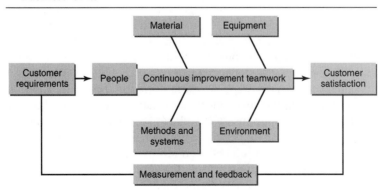

DISPLAY 4 ◆ Saturn's Market Area Approach

The Market Area Approach has many advantages over more traditional approaches:

Traditional Outlets	Market Area Approach
Assigned a single point	Larger defined geographic areas
Larger number of dealers within a market	Few dealers in a market
Combination of exclusive dealerships and dual dealerships	Exclusive, separate facilities, which are customer convenience oriented
Advertising dollars spent competing with dealers of the same brand	Encourages concentrated advertising dollars against Saturn competitors
Limited in establishing multiple facilities	Flexibility to expand facilities and locations
Limited opportunity to develop a strategic business plan	Market Area Plan (MAP) is jointly developed by the dealer and Saturn

Saturn makes sure that dealers know they are a part of the corporation by working together to set strategic goals for each site. The mission statement and philosophy hang not only on the walls of the manufacturing facility but in every dealership as well. Communication networks and newsletters help ensure that the owners always know what is going on at the plant. Saturn feels that dealer involvement is key to providing customer satisfaction. Saturn retailers are so excited about their product that their displays at auto shows are often staffed with volunteers from dealerships who want to promote the corporation.

The Employee Partnership

While the partnership between Saturn and its dealers illustrates the commitment to a new way of doing business, it pales in comparison to the partnership between Saturn management and the UAW. From the beginning, the two groups have been dedicated to building a constructive relationship. Since the usual distinction of salaried and hourly employees loses its meaning at Saturn (all employees are salaried), members are differentiated by those who are "represented" and those who are "nonrepresented." Management maintains an open-door policy that keeps them in touch with operational employees. During one training seminar, some employees argued that their suggestions for improvement would never be funded if management failed to listen to their ideas in the first place. Frustrated, the facilitator went to the office of the vice president of finance and brought him down to the classroom for a roundtable discussion on the issue. Such actions breed trust among union and management people.

One of the most dramatic examples of this trust is the Memorandum of Agreement, the union employment contract with Saturn. The standard contract between the UAW and GM is voluminous. It contains more information than either party can possibly hope to absorb. The Memo, in contrast, is a 26-page, pocket-size pamphlet that describes the relationship between represented employees and the corporation. While this document leaves many things undefined, it allows for greater flexibility. The only price for this flexibility is an increase in trust by both parties.

One way management has shown their trust in the operational employee is in the recruiting process. While Human Resources provides an initial screening to ensure applicants meet minimum requirements, the interviews and hiring decisions are made by those employees the new hire will be working with. Saturn wants to hire a competitive workforce that is intelligent, motivated, and willing to take risks. They are looking for team players who are proud to be autoworkers. Their recruiting campaign says, "GM was once the world's benchmark. If you'd like to do that again, come with us." Educational background is crucial to avoid remediation. The goal is at least a high school education in order to handle the rigorous training. Teams are made of 6 to 15 employees with established line responsibilities. If a new hire fails to perform to standards, the team who made the decision will have to bear the burden.

This responsibility on the operational level holds true for attendance as well. General Motors traditionally had full-time staff monitoring and calling absentees. Saturn considers this activity a non-value-added (or wasteful) activity. At Saturn, there are no time clocks at the plant; employees are simply expected to be at work. If someone misses, that is a loss to his or her team. But no team will put up with poor attendance for long.

When there is a conflict to be resolved or a decision to be made, teams make them based on consensus. Saturn defines consensus by saying that everyone responsible for the decision must be 70 percent comfortable and 100 percent committed to implementation. If someone on the team does not feel he or she meets these criteria, it is the employee's responsibility to explore alternative solutions and present them to the team or try to understand the root cause for the difference of opinion. By making decisions based on consensus rather than command and control, Saturn employees are more committed to seeing solutions placed into action.

To facilitate this decision-making process, Saturn's organizational structure is designed as a set of nested decision rings or councils. Any decision affecting only one team is made on the team level. If a decision impacts more than one team, like a change in work flow, then the team's counselor brings it to the work-unit level. As the impact grows, the decision is moved to higher councils through the WUMA (Work Unit Module Advisor), who acts as the equivalent of a general supervisor. A new supplier of parts may have to go as high as the Manufacturing Action Council for approval. Although a final decision is made on this level, the original concept can be suggested from any level. By avoiding the traditional hierarchical structure, Saturn makes it easier to push decision making responsibility to levels more appropriate to the action involved.

Because these decisions take time to resolve, Saturn requires that all teams meet at least one hour weekly on company time, and many teams meet after hours on their own. Every team is assigned a team center on the floor, which is equipped with small meeting rooms, china boards, and a personal computer for team use. Teams often meet between shifts so that the employees on both shifts can relate difficulties and suggest solutions for problems that occurred during their shift.

Because Saturn places greater responsibility on its operational employees, it also increases the potential reward. In addition to salaries, there is a reward system that in 1993 included up to $1,500 per quarter based on meeting quality and schedule goals. An additional incentive of $4,000 was based on profitability. In 1993 every employee received $1,000 the first month Saturn broke even, which occurred in April. If Saturn breaks even for the year they receive an additional $2,000, and if Saturn makes a profit, employees receive a percentage up to $1,000. In 1993, the total potential bonus was $10,000.

To balance the rewards it offers employees, Saturn also charges them 8 percent of the average base salary unless every employee spends at least 92 hours in training annually. This training can include honing of current skills or learning new ones. This intense training program is currently matched only by Motorola. Saturn considers itself a university with the unique characteristic that no one ever graduates. The only remaining questions, "What will you take next semester?"

In an effort to improve its working environment, Saturn initiated member-to-member interviews. Every employee, from the line workers to President Skip LeFauve, was interviewed and asked the same question: "When you came to Saturn you had certain expectations. How has Saturn met, exceeded, or fallen short of those expectations?" Responses to these interviews have been collected and organized for use as guidance in future improvement activities. To align goals within the corporation, Saturn is also in the process of sending its employees through a seminar called "Saturn: Yesterday, Today, and Tomorrow," which discusses where Saturn came from, what it is doing now, and where it hopes to be in five years' time.

All of these structural and human resource projects have given Saturn one of its competitive edges. Saturn calls it "People Systems," and it is not something easily seen on the factory floor. What is visible is a coordinated workforce that lends itself to continual improvement and cutting-edge technologies in operations. But this is just the foundation for the success of Project Saturn.

An Operational Advantage

Before Saturn could compete against imports, the company had to know what it was up against. In benchmarking studies Saturn purchases competitive vehicles and breaks them down to the smallest components. After breaking down the parts, Saturn measures total assembly operations, assembly time, number of parts, theoretical minimum member of parts, piece cost estimates, labor cost estimates, and total cost estimates. In one such study, Saturn was comparing its bumper to that of the Honda Civic. Although the Honda bumper included less than half the labor and parts of the Saturn, it might not be structurally better. But since Honda uses only half the fasteners, it gives Saturn a place to begin improving its own design.

Saturn uses a careful and structured process for solving any difficulties encountered on the line. The basic problem-solving process shown in Display 5 is used throughout Saturn. By following a "scientific method" and carefully documenting problems, teams ensure that they do not repeat the problem later. Employee training also includes financial management. Every team is responsible for its costs and value added. All teams submit budgets to the finance department and continually look for ways to reduce costs in their area.

DISPLAY 5 ◆ Problem-Solving Process for Teams

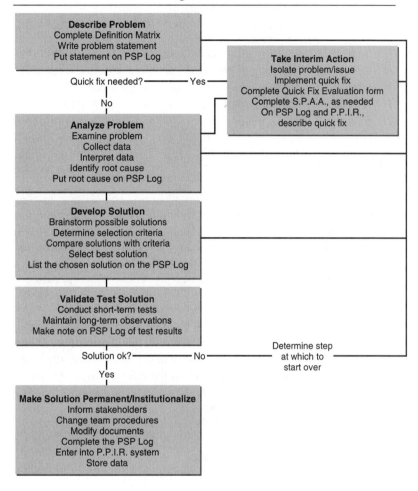

In an effort to empower employees, Saturn trained selected team members to serve as point personnel. These include auditors, educators, quality specialists, and financial managers, to name a few. Saturn management insists that their education will continue to benefit the teams they work with, but team cultures can change a great deal in three years. Other training includes honing skills that employees use on the job. Each team is responsible for 30 work-unit functions, such as finance, human resources production control, and materials management. Teams are allowed to distribute their tasks as they see fit as long as all tasks are accomplished. This allows for intensive cross-training and job rotation. At other GM divisions, when a guard on a machine broke, a millwright is called in to remove it, a tinsmith is called in to repair it, and a mechanical technician is called in to put the guard back on. Operators could do all of these operations with minimal training—as they do at Saturn.

Operators also have input in choosing supplies and capital equipment. (Some GM plants may or may not supply Saturn; they must earn Saturn's business just like any other supplier.) In addition to sourcing, employees give invaluable feedback to engineers enabling them to create designs that are easier to assemble and manufacture. Saturn provides at least 40 hours of process improvement training for everyone in the plant. For example, if experienced workers have difficulty with awkward assembly tasks, they make suggestions for redesigning either the parts or the assembly sequence. To find out just how hard it is to assemble a Saturn, engineers spent a week on the floor trying to assemble the parts they designed. By encouraging communication between operators and engineers, Saturn gets many suggestions for improvements. The resulting innovations save on labor, materials, and capital investment for Saturn as well as providing a more reliable product with fewer parts.

The entire Saturn production system is the largest "just-in-time" system in the United States. The plant is so integrated that if there is a glitch in body systems, the powertrain facility knows about it instantly. Integration is achieved through the processing of the product. Because there is relatively little work-in-process inventory, any problem impacts all the stations downline. This integration lends urgency to fix equipment and spurs better preventative maintenance of equipment.

Saturn encourages employees not only to fix obvious problems but to make improvements in the process. The Workplace Development Center (WDC), one of Saturn's 30 work-unit functions, was established to assist with these improvements. The WDC is an experimental lab for discovering improved work methods and making improvements in ergonomics. Workers are continually looking for ways to identify and eliminate waste. Anytime a team feels that it can improve the process, they send representatives to a three-week seminar on ergonomics, costs, and engineering. They then study the issue and propose solutions. Solutions are not automatically implemented but must be sold to the teams when the representative returns to the plant floor. Unless consensus is achieved, another representative is sent to continue looking for a solution.

Continuing the Journey

With cutting-edge operational technologies integrated with superior people systems, Saturn is striving to be the world leader in cost, quality, and customer satisfaction. While Saturn is very competitive in quality and customer satisfaction, it is still working to improve its cost position. Fortunately, Saturn has established the systems and structures that it will need to be a leader in the automobile industry. To realize this vision, Saturn plans to continually improve every aspect of its business.

◆ Discussion Questions

1. Describe the conditions that General Motors faced when deciding to launch Saturn.

2. How is Saturn's philosophy and strategy designed to cope with these conditions?

3. Describe how Saturn's culture encourages and supports continual improvement?

4. Characterize the relationship that Saturn's management and labor force have by listing and explaining the factors that support and the factors that might undermine its strategy for competing.

Index